Small Business

An Entrepreneur's Plan

Fifth Edition

J. D. Ryan, M.B.A.
Irvine Valley College

Robert J. Ray, Ph.D.
University of Washington

Gail P. Hiduke
Saddleback College, M.S.

The Dryden Press
Harcourt Brace College Publishers

Fort Worth Philadelphia San Diego New York Orlando Austin San Antonio
Toronto Montreal London Sydney Tokyo

Publisher	**George Provol**
Acquisitions Editor	**John Weimester**
Developmental Editor	**Rebecca Linnenburger**
Project Editor	**Claudia Gravier**
Art Director	**Burl Sloan**
Production Manager	**Darryl King**

ISBN: 0-03-022593-0

Library of Congress Catalog Card Number: 98-87087

Address for Orders
Harcourt Brace College Publishers, 6277 Sea Harbor Drive, Orlando, FL 32887-6777,
1-800-782-4479.

Address for Editorial Correspondence
Harcourt Brace College Publishers, 301 Commerce Street, Suite 3700, Fort Worth, TX 76102

Web site Address
http://www.hbcollege.com
www.dryden.com/mngment

Printed in the United States of America

9 0 1 2 3 4 5 6 7   066   9 8 7 6 5 4 3 2

Harcourt Brace College Publishers

The Dryden Press Series in Management

Preface

Introduction

When our publisher asked us to create a fifth edition of *Small Business: An Entrepreneur's Plan,* we clicked our modems and zoomed into cyberspace.

The Net was there, humming along, offering mountains of resources for small business. We found Websites on business plans, marketing tips for analyzing your competition and profiling your target customer, business brokers eager to help you buy a business, accounting programs like Quicken, to help you crunch the numbers, and electronic money trees and hamburger franchises in Asia. Early in our research, we became quite proficient in typing out the letters www, short for World Wide Web.

This book is your guide to small business enterprise. It saves you time by pinpointing precise targets. It offers tips on surfing the net for small business opportunities. It asks you to explore not only the needs of your Target Customer but your needs as well.

We have always emphasized opening your eyes to explore the world by reading incessantly and talking to everyone. The Net provides sources of information beyond your imagination.

As you surf the Net in search of your dream business, Action Steps throughout the text give definition and purpose to your quest. Because once you gather information about a specific small business, you must exit the web and return to the real world to test and verify the data.

Due to the changing nature of the internet, some of the sites featured in the text may not be active forever. Should you experience any trouble linking to a site referenced, consult the organization's home page or one of the search engines such as **www.yahoo.com** or **www.excite.com** to find what you are looking for.

Organization

Target the chapters that call to you.

- The Action Steps are paced out across sixteen chapters, from Chapter One, "Your Great Adventure," to Chapter Sixteen, "Faststart Business Plan."

- The first three chapters help you focus on yourself and your ideas. How to get ideas and how to test them in the marketplace before you plunk down money. If you are just exploring entrepreneurship, concentrate on these chapters and the accompanying Action Steps. You are not only designing your business but also your life.

- Chapters Four, Five, and Six help you locate the key to success in small business: Your Target Customer.

- Chapter Seven helps you find a location—on the street or at a crossroads in cyberspace.

- Chapter Eight plunges you into numbers—how much you will need to start up, how much to keep going—and Chapter Nine, "Shaking the Money Tree," helps you find the money.

- If you are a creative person trying to peddle a product, Chapter Ten—all about copyrights, trademarks, and patents—helps you keep control of what you invented.

- Chapter Eleven helps you build a winning team. Chapter Twelve guides you through taxes, insurance, and how to assess what kind of computer that you need to run your business.

- If you want to buy an ongoing business, Chapter Thirteen offers advice and counsel. If you want to join the Franchise Movement, read Chapter Fourteen first. There are franchisees around every corner in America, but not all of them are happy with their lot. If your goal is to be the Happy Franchisee, turn to page 274 now.

- The last two chapters offer you a choice: full blown plan or fast start business plan. All of the Action Steps have now led you to be able to complete a business plan. Chapter Fifteen follows the Software School as they develop their business plan. Chapter Sixteen is a "fast start" plan for a smaller business: one owner or a tight partnership, with few employees, where extra work is contracted out and the loss of investment will not sink your ship.

- Appendix A contains a beautiful business plan for Shelter Dynamics, a small manufacturing firm. Appendix B, "Nine Million Forms," contains forms to save you time: personal budget, limited liability company, personal finance, loan forms for the SBA, and such.

Key Features

Action Steps

Over 80 Action Steps take readers through every phase of an upstart, from the initial dream, developing marketing strategies, and finally how to implement the completed business plan.

Case Studies

Case studies full of strategies and real world applications provide readers with insights into entrepreneurial ventures. We have modified case studies for simplicity and clarity.

Business Plans

Featured business plans are Yes, We Do Windows, and Shelter Dynamics. These business plans cover service and manufacturing businesses.

Global Coverage

Global issues are integrated throughout the text providing insight and opportunities for students to explore.

Limited Liability Company Coverage

"Limited liability companies" are explained and compared to other business organizational structures.

Internet

Access to our internet site with hotlinks to statistics, marketing, finance, and legal information. Also, Web integration is seen throughout the text to support materials presented which allows students to reach the best sites on the net.

New to the Fifth Edition
Global Village

Throughout the text we have integrated global village boxes to encourage readers to explore global opportunities. Chapter 5's box, page 85, looks at how to explore international markets. Use the boxes to locate the incredible wealth of resources available to help expand your business globally.

Internet

As we conducted research for the fifth edition, we realized the Internet brought resources, previously only available at great cost, to the masses at no cost or very low cost. For example, Chapter 4, page 64, directs you to a manual from Find/SVP titled, *How to Get Your Products Into Supermarkets.*

Key Points from Another View

Key Points From Another View at the end of each chapter highlight and reinforce material in the chapter. In Chapter Four we focus on Profiling the Target Customer and the Key Points article on page 80 discusses the proliferation of magazines in our society aimed at very small target markets.

Incredible Resource

This box provides the reader with cutting edge information that they will value as an "incredible resource." For example, Chapter 10, page 194 directs you to resources for family businesses.

Videos

The accompanying video for the book highlights successful cosmetics firm Hard Candy and several other entrepreneurs providing insight into the entrepreneurial process-hectic, creative, problematic, and sometimes chaotic.

Website

Our Website, **www.dryden.com/management/ryan/** will lead you into the rich depths of cyberspace. Don't get lost!

Planning for Success

The reason we wrote this book was to help you write a business plan. The reason you write a business plan is to chart a course for your dream business. Writing a business plan sharpens your focus. When you sharpen your focus, you see better. Seeing better raises your confidence. In the big world of small business, as in life, confidence helps you keep going when the going gets tough. There is an adage in the business world: If you fail to plan, then you are planning to fail.

Before you write a business plan, you should study the form. From the outside, a business plan looks like a stack of paper. For the short plan, a thin stack; for the long plan, a thick stack bound together to look like a book.

However thick the stack, your plan will be a document with a beginning, middle and end. Do you open the plan with a spreadsheet? Of do you open with something jazzy, like a Target Customer Profile? Do you open with a letter to a banker asking for money? Do you open with an "Executive Summary?" What do you need with an executive summary if you are a one-person operation and you have no "executives?" Do you open your plan with a description of your dream location? A summary of hot services? A battle plan for one upping the competition?

There are some great plans in this book. There are more great plans floating out there in cyberspace. To access these plans, go to your search engine and type in "small business planning."

We hope you can open one of the three entrepreneurial doorways and find success along with the thousands of others who have followed the Action Steps. Good luck!

We have endeavored to provide current material but Internet sites will come and go and government programs will take new forms. Due to the dynamic nature of small business, we urge you to keep up to date by checking in with our website and its vast resources.

Because laws and tax issues are subject to change, you should consult with your counsel and advisors rather than relying only on the material contained in the text for legal and accounting advice. All forms have been provided as examples only and should not be used without benefit of counsel.

Instructor's Resource Materials

Instructor's Manual and Test Bank

Instructor's Manual includes teaching aids such as Learning Objectives, Lecture Outlines and Suggestions for Guest Speakers and Class Projects. The Test Bank is full of True/False, Multiple Choice, and Short Answer Questions.

Computerized Test Bank

Available in PC, Windows, and Macintosh compatible formats, the computerized version of the printed test bank enables instructor's to preview and edit test questions, as well as add their own. The test and answer keys can also be printed in "scrambled" formats.

Videos

Video segments including coverage of themes featured throughout the text. Provides an excellent supplement to classroom instruction.

Ackowledgements

We couldn't have written this book without a lot of help from a lot of people. The book is built on a foundation of people in the real world and the Action Steps are taken from real-life tactics in the marketplace.

A very special thank you to Josie Rietkerk, Founder and President of Caterina's, LLC, who improved each chapter with her current real world retailing experience. In the midst of opening her fourth store, she graciously offered to read and edit each chapter. Her insight was invaluable and will save readers thousands of dollars as they embark on their ventures.

We want to extend a thank you to the reviewers whose insightful comments helped to shape this edition:

William Allen
University of Alaska Fairbanks

Gary Apger
Mira Costa College

Ken Huggins
University of Colorado Denver

Herman Husbands
Grossmont College

Richard Leake
Luther College

Our thanks go to Eric Sandberg for his expertise in developing our Website, **www.dryden.com/mngment**.

We are grateful for the Dryden book team, John Weimeister, Senior Acquisitions Editor; Rebecca Linnenburger, Developmental Editor; Claudia Gravier, Project Editor; Darryl King, Production Manager; Burl Sloan and Scott Baker, Art Directors; Lise Johnson, Executive Marketing Strategist; and Craig Johnson, Executive Product Manager. They have helped shape this work into a book that we are proud of.

Last but not least we thank Barbara, Margo, and Kent for their support. In addition, a great big thank you must go to the boys, Casey and Troy, for their patience, ice waters, and love.

Joe Ryan
Robert Ray
Gail Hiduke

Brief Table of Contents

Table of Contents

Chapter 10   Legal Issues   187

Chapter 11   Building a Winning Team   215

Your Great Adventure

Exploring the Right Fit

Entrepreneurial Links

Books

No Experience Necessary: Young Entrepreneur Guide to Starting a Business, Jennifer Kushell, 1997.

The SOHO Desk Reference: A Practical A to Z Guide for the Entrepreneur, Peter Engel, editor, 1997.

Working Solo Sourcebook: Essential Resources for Independent Entrepreneurs, Terri Lonier, 1998.

Websites

www.americanexpress.com

www.quicken.com

www.smartbiz.com

Associations/Organizations

Young Entrepreneurs Network, www.idye.com, 617-867-4690

National Federation of Independent Businesses, www.nfibonline.com, 800-634-2669

National Association for the Self-Employed, www.nase.org, 800-232-6273

Publications

Inc., www.inc.com

Success, www.successmagazine.com

Entrepreneur Business Start-ups, www.entrepreneurmag.com

Additional Entrepreneurial Insights

E-Myth Revisited: Why Most Small Businesses Don't Work and What to Do About it, Michael Gerber, 1995.

Think and Grow Rich, Napoleon Hill, 1990 (reprinted)

Do What You Love, the Money Will Follow, Marsha Sinetar, 1989.

Learning Objectives

- Determine how you can fit in, survive, and prosper in business.
- Brainstorm a clear picture of success in small business.
- Identify successful and unsuccessful businesses in your community.
- Discover your personal strengths.
- Improve your information-gathering skills.
- Expand your knowledge of small business through interviewing small business owners.
- Understand your financial and family situation.
- Review the Three Doorways to Entrepreneurship.
- Start work on an Adventure Notebook.
- Design your own "entrepreneurial lifestyle."

Life is short, and you only go around once. So you want to make sure you're getting what you want, having fun, making money, and being the best person you can be.

How do you do that? Some people do it by going into business for themselves. If you are thinking about owning your own business, this book is written for you.

Try this line of thought: What do you want to be doing in the year 2005? In 2010? What's the best course of action for you right now? What might be the best business for you? What are your strengths? What do you want out of life? What are your dreams? This chapter will address these questions.

This is the age of the **entrepreneur.** According to the Small Business Administration (SBA), **www.sba.gov** there are almost 20 million small businesses out there. Each year, a million new businesses are started. If you are thinking about starting a small business, you are among the 7 million budding entrepreneurs currently dreaming the same dream. The Entrepreneurial Research Consortium's, **www.wm.edu/PSYC/erc.html,** statistics show one in three U.S. households have been involved in small business. Most of the new jobs in the private sector are created by firms with fewer than 20 employees. Yes, it's a great time for the entrepreneur. You could have the time of your life. Come along with us!

Building Your Road Map

This book, with its Action Steps, is your personal road map to success in small business. Beginning with Action Step 1, the book will guide you through the bustling marketplace—through trends, Target Customers, and promotion; through shopping malls, spreadsheets, and hushed gray bank buildings; through independent businesses that are for sale; and through franchise opportunities—all the way to your own new venture.

Along the way you will meet fascinating people, have fantastic adventures, and some fun. Further, by completing the action steps, you'll be drawing a customized road map for small business success, a complete **Business Plan** that clearly evaluates and illuminates your opportunity for entrepreneurial success.

Entrepreneur A visionary self-starter who loves the adventure of a new enterprise and is willing to risk his or her own money.

Business Plan A blueprint outlining finances and direction for a new start-up or expansion.

Figure 1.1

Entrepreneurial Roadmap

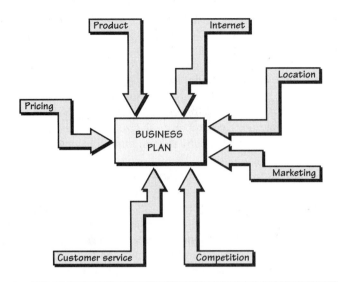

You will start your journey by taking a careful look at yourself and your skills. What kind of work pleases you? How secure is your present job? How long does it take you to get organized? What internal drive makes you believe that you are an entrepreneur? What do you value? What do you like to work with? Who do you like to work with?

Next, you'll step back and look at the marketplace. What's hot? What's cooling down? What's going to last? Where are the long lines forming? What are people buying? What distinguishes the up-and-comers from the down-and-outers?

You will brainstorm a business that will fit into an industry niche, toss around numbers to get a feel for how they turn into money, and keep having fun.

Then it will be time to profile your Target Customer, assess the competition, figure out some clever promotional strategies, and scout locations. By that time you will know where you're going and feel that you're in control of your own destiny.

By the time you reach Chapter 15, you will have gathered enough material to write a complete Business Plan for showcasing your business to the world—that is, to bankers, vendors, and lenders, venture capitalists, credit managers, key employees, your family, and your friends. Your finished plan will be a blueprint for your business. It will provide a walk-through of your industry, generate excitement in potential investors, demonstrate your competence as a thoughtful planner, and underline the reasons customers are going to clamor for your product or service. Your plan will also serve as a means of channeling your creative energies.

Let's think about that for a moment.

One reason you're reading this book is that you're creative. You like to build, to pull things together, to plant seeds and watch things grow, to develop projects, to produce. When your mind is racing, you probably come up with more ideas than you can process. That is when you need a plan to help keep your entrepreneurial energies on track while the creative steam rises. Perhaps you've always dreamed of working for yourself—being your own boss. Well, you can have that dream *if you are prepared.*

Internet Links

The links in this book hook you into the **Internet.** The Internet, accessed via a computer equipped with a modem that connects to the **World Wide Web** through a server (for example, America Online, Compuserve, or Earthlink) is your key to keeping up with what's happening in business and the world.

All of the links included in our text are listed on our home page at **www.dryden.com/management/ryan.** In addition, Internet hot links to business and general publications, statistics, associations, and other resources are available and continually updated through our home page. Throughout the text we will highlight useful sites. Remember these are only the tip of the iceberg. The Internet's resources are limited only by the amount of time you have available to surf the "Net."

If you're already computer literate, if you're online with a 56K flex modem or some other ethernet apparatus, keep surfing the Net. If you're new to computers and cyberspace, take a tour through the Net by accessing our home page **www. dryden.com/management/ryan** and clicking through Navigating the Net, Glossary of Internet Terms, Getting Online, Research Tools, and **Search Engines.**

As you read through this book and work through the Action Steps that lead you to a business plan, you can access a wealth of information, ask questions of experts, communicate with fellow entrepreneurs, and discover marketing and financial resources on the web. For example, if you had typed in the Internet address **www.sba.gov** previously cited, you would have reached the Small Business Administration's home page, which was still alive as this book went to press. If you type in an address and come up empty—Websites on the Internet come and go at warp speed—you could start your own search, using a "search engine" like Yahoo!, Web Crawler, or Excite. In the search slot, you could type "entrepreneur" or "small business planning" and access a world of information.

Internet (Net) Electronic window to the world.

World Wide Web (Web) Electronic storehouse of information available on the Internet.

Search engines Web content information sorter (software).

Figure 1.2

Window to the World

" ... R, S, T, U, V, W, W, W, DOT COM."

Web Link Starting Points

- **www.sba.gov**
- **www.entreworld.com**
- **www.brint.com**
- **www.americanexpress.com/smallbusiness**
- **www.quicken.com**
- **www.inc.com**
- **www.fastcompany.com**
- **www.nfibonline.com**
- **www.smartbiz.com**

We'll be linking to the Internet as we move through the phases of the book—personal assessment, trends, location, number-crunching, legal issues, and writing the plan. For example, if you'd like to review sample business plans, turn to the last two chapters and the appendices in this book; or, you could link to the Internet at **www.bizplans.com, www.bplans.com, www.money-hunter.com.** The World Wide Web offers numerous examples (some are free; some are for sale) of how to blueprint your business. This book shows you how to sharpen your vision so that you can write the business plan you need to achieve success in a fast-changing world. A sample business plan outline is shown in Figure 1.3. As you follow the action steps, you will be building your own personal business plan for your great adventure.

Knocking at the Entrepreneurial Doors

There are three doorways to small business ownership. Doorway I is buying an ongoing business: You search, locate a business that you like, and buy it. Sounds pretty easy, doesn't it? A business broker will make it sound even easier, so beware!

Doorway II is buying a franchise: You find a logo you like—one with national visibility—and buy it. In exchange for your money, the franchisor may (or may not) supply you with inventory, advice, training, buying power, shorter learning curve, and a product or service that is well-known in the marketplace. Sounds pretty easy, doesn't it? A slick franchisor will make it sound even easier.

Doorway III, our favorite, is starting a new business—a business that is compatible with your interests and skills, one that is backed up by careful research that demonstrates strong customer need. Entering the world of small business by any of these doorways demands a carefully designed Business Plan—words and numbers written out on paper that guide you through the gaps, competition, bureaucracies, products, and services. The Action Steps presented in this book will show you exactly how to write a Business Plan and how to have fun as an entrepreneur.

What about These Three Doorways?

Over two-thirds of all entrepreneurs enter the world of small business by buying an existing business or investing in a franchise operation. When these people have gained some experience and confidence, many of them decide to start a totally new business from scratch. Few entrepreneurs are happy with just one business. They start up; they sell; they start up again—and they become experts at writing Business Plans.

Figure 1.3

Business Plan Outline

SBA Business Plan Outline

Below is a sample outline for a Business Plan.
1. Cover sheet
2. Statement of purpose
3. Table of contents

I. The Business
   A. Description of business
   B. Marketing
   C. Competition
   D. Operating procedures
   E. Personnel
   F. Business insurance
   G. Financial data

II. Financial Data
   A. Loan application
   B. Capital equipment and supply list
   C. Balance sheet
   D. Break-even analysis
   E. Proforma income projections (profit & loss statements
      Three-year summary
      Detail by month, first year
      Detail by quarters, second and third years
      Assumptions upon which projections were based
   F. Proforma cash flow
      Follow guidelines for letter E.

III. Supporting Documents
   • Tax returns of principals for last three years
   • Personal financial statement (all banks have these forms)
   • In the case of a franchised business, a copy of franchise contract and all supporting documents provided by the franchisor
   • Copy of proposed lease or purchase agreement for building space
   • Copy of licenses and other legal documents
   • Copy of resumes of all principals
   • Copy of letters of intent from suppliers, etc

For more information, see **www.sba.gov/starting/indexbusplans.html.**

No matter which doorway you choose, you're going to need a Business Plan. If you buy an ongoing business you may inherit the seller's Business Plan. However, it's advisable to write one of your own. Ask the seller (again and again, if necessary) for the data you need for writing your own plan before you finalize the sale. That way—before you commit to purchase—you can check out those claims of huge potential profits and endless goodwill.

If you invest in a franchise, you'll be buying a Business Plan from the franchisor. But until you see it you won't know for certain if you'll need to prepare one of your own as well. If you don't understand the franchisor's plan, ask questions and, by all means, write your own. Writing a Business Plan is a lot cheaper than plunking down money on a franchise that may not be successful.

If you start your own business, a Business Plan is a must, an absolute must. That plan stands between you and failure.

The world is changing, and you must assess the changes and act accordingly. You want to survive. You want to have fun. You want your life to have meaning. You want substance and honesty and security and success. So, in order to decide which road to take, do some research and keep your eyes open.

As new technology opens, opportunities for entrepreneurs to compete, and personal financial security obtained by employment in large companies continues to wane, many people are recognizing that self-employment through one of the three doorways described is often the most secure and rewarding career option. This text is written to help you take control of your business life and prepare you to enter one of the three doors.

The Age of the Entrepreneur

If the business world is changing faster and faster—revving up like a high-speed motor—what do you do? If life is not what you imagined it would be when you were in high school, what do you do? If the big firm you targeted as your dream employer is busy downsizing, if the job you trained for is now obsolete, if the position you now have is spoiled by office politics—what do you do?

If you have a great idea for a product but your employer doesn't believe in it, what do you do? If you have found a great location for a small unique restaurant on your last vacation in Sun Valley, what do you do? If you saw a great product on your trip to Hungary and think it would sell well in Chicago, what do you do?

Get up to speed. Upgrade your computer. Surf the Web for opportunities. Figure out who you are and what you want from life. Think with your pencil while you figure out how much you're willing to pay for the "Good Life." How much time are you willing to spend? How much money? How much sweat? How much risk?

Getting Up to Speed Starts Now

Small companies (with fewer than 100 employees) employ more than half the workers in the United States. New start-ups create the new jobs. These jobs are created by an absolutely unique partnership—the marriage of money and hard work. The money comes from savings, friends, family, credit cards, second mortgages, bank loans, venture capitalists, and angels. The work comes from the driving force of the entrepreneur and from those who trust the entrepreneur. In the first decade of the twenty-first century, entrepreneurship should blossom and grow. The fields—biotechnology, software, short-run manufacturing, Web servers, telecommunication and others are ripe and ready for the harvest, so plant early. The millennium will certainly be the Age of the Entrepreneur.

Ready to Start?

First, you need to get organized. Action Step 1 will help you to do that. Some people believe that getting organized stifles creativity. Marci Reid was like that until she saw the value of using her **Adventure Notebook** in developing her new Internet travel business—Romantic Escapes.

Romantic Escapes—From Adventure Notebook to Internet Business

During her five years working as a travel agent for three different travel agencies, Marci kept a diary form of notebook, listing what seemed to be important elements of the travel business, her contacts, news and magazine articles, ideas, competitors' ads, and lots of business cards. Her Internet guru friend, Sandy Jones, was tired of working for other people and enthusiastically agreed to be her partner.

With knowledge of the travel business and the Internet, they developed a Net travel business. After reviewing her notes, Marci looked for a gap in the

> ## Action Step 1
>
> ### Adventure Notebook
>
> If you're a typical entrepreneur, you probably write 90 percent of your important data on the back of an envelope. That might have been okay in the past, but now that you're doing this for real, get an organizer and some type of container (a shoebox, a briefcase, a folder) in which to store your information. The best—and recommended way—to organize your data is to compile an **Adventure Notebook,** something with pockets, so that you can keep track of small items such as receipts, parking ticket stubs, and business cards. For some, utilizing their notebook computers or PDAs (personal digital assistant) may work best.
>
> Your **Adventure Notebook** should include:
>
> 1. a twelve-month calendar
> 2. an appointment calendar
> 3. a priority list of things you need to do
> 4. your name and phone number (on the front cover, in case you leave it someplace)
> 5. an idea list (continue to add items to this throughout your search)
> 6. a "new eyes" list for keeping track of successful and not-so-successful businesses you come across, plus notes about the reasons for their success or failure
> 7. a list of possible team members (Who impresses you and why? What are their key attributes?)
> 8. articles and statistics you gather that serve as supportive data for your business plan
> 9. a list of helpful Websites
> 10. a list of possible "taxi squad" members—experts who can serve as resource people when you needed them, such as a lawyer, a CPA, bankers, successful businesspeople, and so on
>
> *(continued on next page)*

Adventure Notebook Storage place for personal, valuable business information.

11. a list of potential customers.
12. a list of names and phone numbers of contacts for goods and services.

Your Adventure Notebook becomes the heart of your business plan.

Action Step 2

Why Do I Want to be an Entrepreneur?

In your Adventure Notebook make a list of all the reasons why you want to become an entrepreneur. Think about your personal, family, financial, professional, lifestyle; social, spiritual, and ego needs.

Now prioritize your list. Spend a few minutes reviewing how several businesses would fit into your prioritized list. What fits? What doesn't?

Review your current job situation. Are you happy? Are you excited about going to work each day? Is there something else you'd rather be doing? If money were no object, what would you do?

As you explore various businesses, continue to return to these lists and questions to focus on whether or not your selected business ideas will meet your entrepreneurial focus.

marketplace. She realized that many of her clients were looking for short breakaway escapes. Sandy suggested that they might possibly tap into the Internet focusing on utilizing Websites that offered weekend discounts on cars, hotels, and airfares. After extensive research, Marci and Sandy repackaged these deals into great weekend escapes. By adding extras such as dinners, flowers, and limousine service, they packaged affordable romantic weekend escapes.

Now they had to determine how to reach their market. They were fortunate in that Marci had retained most of her past clients' phone numbers and addresses. She and Sandy sent postcards announcing their new online Internet service and requested all to come online to give them their e-mail addresses. Surprisingly, 50 percent responded. Once online, they were asked to fill out detailed questionnaires about their travel desires for weekend escapes.

They now had the information they needed—the market and their desires. Every Wednesday at noon, Romantic Escapes posted their weekend escapes. Wednesday through Friday they were busy booking trips. Within six months, they were profitable. Customers quickly became repeat customers. Sales rapidly increased due to word of mouth and good publicity. Romance was in the air and money was in the bank for Marci and Sandy.

Why Do You Want to be an Entrepreneur?

For some, becoming an entrepreneur is a lifelong dream, for others it's buying a job. It's the excitement of an unlimited income or a way to pay the bills. It's the dream of never having a boss or the dream of being the boss. It's the desire to leave a legacy. It's the joy of producing the perfect product. It's the thrill of developing a new service. It's the desire to live out your dreams.

One of our students opened her retail store to keep an eye on her three teenagers. Seven years later she owns four stores and three franchise outlets. One of her teenagers (now 25) manages her stores.

Sam wanted to improve children's lives. He researched businesses that served children and located a Sylvan Learning Center franchise.

With a love of basketball and kids, Felix developed a summer basketball camp for kids age 8-12, using his local courts. The camp was successful and paid four years of tuition bills!

Figure 1.4

Mind map for Mystery Writer

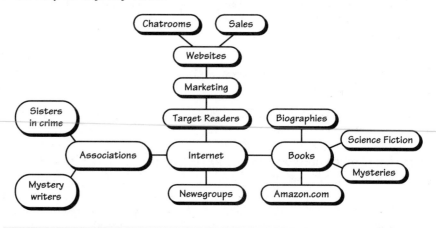

Complete Action Step 2 to discover your entrepreneurial motives. Your job situation can change quickly, your life situation may change, and/or your job and personal desires may change like Sally Honeycutt Binson.

Marketeer to Writer-Entrepreneur

When she turned 30, Sally Honeycutt Binson took a good look at her life. Sally lived in Charleston, South Carolina; had a good job as a marketing director of a restaurant chain; and earned a good salary. Her home—sunny with a view of the water—was wonderful. But Sally paid a price for the "good life" with endless meetings, squabbles with her boss (a second vice-president), and lots of air miles.

To plot her future in the twenty-first century, Sally drew some mind maps. When she put herself inside a bubble in the center of the page, she didn't get anywhere. When she added "Internet" inside a bubble she found a new career: freelance writer. Sally had a degree in English literature and read many books. As a savvy entrepreneur, Sally created a home office and began to write. Her first effort was rejected by agents and publishers. Sally then researched her local bookstore. She found large sections in romance, mystery, and science-fiction. Using her marketing knowledge, she took bookstore managers to lunch and asked: What was selling? What did readers want? What did editors want? Which books received the most promotion?

Armed with information about book sales and target readers, Sally enrolled in a writing course at her local community college. The instructor was a published author. With his guidance, Sally studied the mystery genre.

Before she began writing her second book, Sally checked out Websites for anything related to mystery. At **www.MysteryNet.com** she found a homepage for mystery: writing, selling reader's group, **webzines.** Sally joined two organizations: Mystery Writers of America and Sisters in Crime. A contact from Sisters in Crime connected Sally to several literary agents who might accept her as a client.

As she networked from one hot link to another, Sally discovered discussion groups, sometimes called **newsgroups,** which gave her information on the latest trends in mystery writing. Her favorite news group was Dorothy L, named for the famous British author, Dorothy L. Sayers.

A Book Is a Product

Because of her marketing background, Sally was able to visualize a book as a product for the marketplace. Before she developed her product, she engaged in some intensive R&D (research and development) by analyzing ten mystery novels.

Using the analytical techniques she learned in college, Sally discovered the secret of mystery writing: conceal and then reveal. Following her instructor's advice, the setting of her first mystery was a location Sally was familiar with: an island off the coast of South Carolina. Because she could relate easily to her own gender's thinking patterns, Sally's main characters were female: the sleuth, the victim, and the killer. The police bungle the investigation, leaving a niche for the sleuth.

Sally wrote on weekends and holidays and revised and edited on plane trips. In one year, Sally had a manuscript. Although her agent connections through Sisters in Crime didn't work out, Sally did find an agent on the Internet.

She mailed a plot outline and the first three chapters. The agent sold the book to a publisher. The publisher sold film rights to a film director and Sally consulted on the script. Her first mystery novel, *Murder on Drake Island,*

Webzines Magazines on the Web.

Newsgroups Group of individuals with similar interests on the Net.

► **Action Step 3**

Review Your Financial and Family Picture

Sit down with your family to discuss how opening your own business may affect the family's financial future. Complete the following financial worksheets, which can be found in Appendix B.

Personal Financial Statement
Budget

Utilize **www.quicken.com, www.cnnfn.com,** and **www.fidelity.com**

You will need these figures later to determine your financial needs and also to assess the financial contribution you will be able to make to your business.

After completing the above, ask yourself: Can I live on less? How much less? What can I cut from my budget? How long can I continue before feeling too deprived?

Talk with your family about the time and money sacrifices that may be involved in developing your new venture. A business is a living, breathing entity, and it takes time for the golden egg to hatch. Be prepared to wait a while.

► **Action Step 4**

Self-Assessment

• Complete the questionnaire in Table 1.1.
• If your entrepreneurial juices are flowing, surf the following:

www.sba.gov/BI/quiz.html
Quiz for Small Business Success

www.innonet.ck Are You the Entrepreneurial Type?

www.keirsey.com Myers-Briggs Personality Test

www.future.sri.com/vals/iVals.index.html Psychographic Profiling

Compile a list of:
• things you love to do.

(continued on next page)

became a best-seller and the movie's success gained her access to Hollywood.

When the royalty checks were enough to pay back her advance from the publisher, Sally tendered her resignation at the office. By then, her second book was underway: *Murder on Cannon Beach.*

What is Your Current Family and Financial Picture?

Action Step 3 will help you assess your current situation as you prepare for the future. Is your family dreaming the same dream? If so, that's great. If not, ask what they are willing to do to help. Family support is an essential element to achieve a successful entrepreneurial lifestyle.

Review your current financial picture. Complete the personal financial statements and the budget in Appendix B. Sit down with your family and review how you can reduce expenses. For many, short-term financial pain is worth long-term gain; for others it is not worth it! Before leaping into the new venture decide what you and your family are willing to sacrifice.

Believing in your dream opens your eyes to endless possibilities. Living at home for an extra year to save cash, working a part-time job to support your fledgling business, or moving to a less-expensive area of the country all become realistic options if one believes in his or her own dream.

What Does It Take to be an Entrepreneur?

To find out if you have what it takes to make it in small business, profile yourself as an entrepreneur in Action Step 4. You won't be a perfect fit because there is no such thing. You will, however, get much more out of this book if you mentally immerse yourself in a new and exciting venture.

Entrepreneurship isn't for everyone, and even if it is for you, you'll probably need some help along the way. Keep your mind open and your pencil sharp. The opportunities are unlimited.

Afar Bhide (Harvard School of Business) believes that there is no "ideal" entrepreneurial personality. "Successful founders can be gregarious or taciturn, analytical or intuitive, risk-adverse or thrill-seeking."

Entrepreneurial Success

Starting one's own business allows a person to design his or her own successful lifestyle. Action Step 5 asks you to design your "entrepreneurial lifestyle." Warren Bennis, author of *Organizing Genius,* developed a four-question test aimed at anyone seeking "success." The questions are:

1. Do you know the difference between what you want and what you're good at?
2. Do you know what drives you and what gives you satisfaction?
3. Do you know what your values and priorities are, what your organization's values and priorities are, and can you identify the differences between the two?
4. Having measured the differences between what you want and what you're able to do, between what drives you and what satisfies you, and between your values and those of your organization, are you able to overcome those differences?

Bennis concludes that the key to success is identifying those modules of talent—unique to you—and then finding the right arena in which to use them.

Success is a personal, subjective thing; whereas income and return on investments are measurable. Success wears many faces. You need to think about this as you start your adventure. The Success Checklist (see page 12) will help you. Add any other items that might signify success to you.

Defining Business Success

Action Step 6 is optional, but it's fun! Thinking about business success can be stimulating and enlightening. What makes a business successful? Unsuccessful? How do you measure success? How do your friends measure it?

You and your friends can merely speculate about which businesses are doing well financially. Only a detailed examination of each business's books would give the whole picture, but we still urge you to exercise your marketplace intuition. Personal observation is a good way to become more aware of what is happening

Table 1.1

25 Questions to Answer to See if You Have What it Takes to be an Entrepreneur

So you want to start a business on your own, be your own person, be an Entrepreneur! To find out more, answer the following 25 questions. If you really have what it takes, you should be able to answer each question, easily, with a "yes!"

1. When you've been disappointed, have you dealt with it and come back with a positive state of mind?
2. Do you like to be the center of attraction, sell yourself or the business you're in?
3. Is it easy for you to be organized?
4. Do you know how to take control of your life and be disciplined?
5. Are you a risk-taker?
6. Do you have a vivid imagination and know how to express your creative side?
7. Are you able to take what seems like a detriment and turn it into an opportunity?
8. Are you courageous and patient?
9. Is your family in a position to cope with the lack of freedom you will experience when you start your new business?
10. Do you know how to fight for what you believe in?
11. Do you like people?
12. Have you ever had any management experience?
13. Do you dread routine?
14. Are you reliable and self-confident?
15. Do you ignore the judgement of others when you really believe in someone or something?
16. Do you have a knack for influencing others?
17. Do others describe you as an enthusiastic person, full of life?
18. Do you like the idea of working alone most of the time?
19. Do you enjoy being on the telephone and talking to strangers?
20. Do you wake up early in the morning with a positive attitude?
21. Is your financial situation stable? (You should have enough money to get by for at least one year before you venture out on your own.)
22. Have you done your homework—studied all materials that cover the business you are going to start?
23. Do you know how to laugh at yourself?
24. Is it easy to control your temper with others?
25. Do you get bored easily?

If these are easy questions, you're a born Entrepreneur!

http://www.smartbiz.com

- skills you have acquired through the years.
- things you are good at.
- the times you were happiest in your life.

Review your lists and profiles. In Action Step 5, you will be putting together all your information. Add new items to the lists whenever they occur to you. Keep your lists current.

▶ Action Step 5

"Inc. Yourself"

Mind map your way to a picture of what you want you to become, your product—"YOURSELF." Mind mapping (also called clustering) is a sketch or a diagram using words inside of bubbles written almost at random and then connected by lines to form units (see Figure 1.4). There is no such thing as a wrong idea or a wrong direction.

So far you have looked at why you want to be an entrepreneur, what success means to you, and have reviewed your skills and accomplishments. It's now time for you to mind map the life you want.

Review your answers to Action Steps 2-4. Draw a small circle in the middle of a piece of paper. Write your name inside the circle. Close your eyes for a few minutes, and allow your imagination to take over. Think of yourself as a product. In 5-10 years, where and what do you want to be? What do you want your product to be? What do you want—personally, socially, spiritually, financially, family, friends, hobbies, lifestyle—and what are your material wants and needs? You can predict your future as well as anyone else; all you need to do is mesh information with your imagination and go for it!

If you "Inc. yourself," you'll be ready to explore the many business opportunities available. By meshing your personal desires with your business desires you are more likely to find success.

Success Checklist

Do you measure success in dollars? If so, how many $ _____ ?

Do you measure success in other ways?

- Being able to enjoy a certain lifestyle
- Dealing with friendly customers who appreciate the service
- Power
- Being able to live and work where you want
- Providing employment for others
- Being the best business in your area
- Time to enjoy your children and hobbies
- Participating in teamwork
- Building a legacy
- Early retirement
- Fame
- Making peoples' lives safer
- Helping others

_____

_____

_____

Action Step 6

Survey Your Friends About Successful Businesses

The next time you're at a party or with a group of your colleagues and there's a lull in the conversation, pass out paper and pencils and ask them to list three to five small businesses they perceive as successful. Then ask them to list the signs of those firms' success and the reasons for their success.

Group the negative thinkers together in a Devil's Advocate group and have them list unsuccessful businesses and point out the reasons why those firms are losing.

If you continue to assess businesses in your selected industry and other industries you will begin to recognize many factors that are constant throughout. Keep your eyes open at all times!

The Entrepreneur's Mind
www.benlore.com/index2.html

Log on to the Net and gain access to the minds of successful entrepreneurs. Bertucci's, Mecklermedia, Nantucket Nectars, and id Software have all been profiled recently. Reading about other people who are willing to risk their time and money for their dreams keeps entrepreneurial juices flowing.

The Entrepreneur's Mind (EM) is a Web resource that presents an array of real-life stories and advice on the many different facets of entrepreneurship and emerging businesses written by successful entrepreneurs and industry experts. Each EM article presents in-depth profiles of entrepreneurs telling how they grew their successful companies, as well as interviews with industry professionals discussing an aspect of start-up and growing new businesses.

Review "The Trade-Off Game" and "Key Strategies for Small Business" presented by Arthur Anderson. Global entrepreneurial ventures are also highlighted on this Website to encourage entrepreneurs to stretch outside U.S. borders.

Visit this Website on a regular basis for online entrepreneurial pep juice!

For more success stories, log on to: **www.microsoft.com/smallbiz/success/default.htm.**

to small firms in your community and your selected industry. For example, next time you dine out, try to estimate:

- the number of customers in the restaurant
- the total number of customers the restaurant serves each day.
- the average price per meal.

Then multiply the average per-meal price by the total number of daily customers. Perform your estimations on different days of the week and at different hours. Do this for other businesses you patronize as well. Soon you'll begin to get the "feel" for which businesses are losing and which are winning customers. If you observe small businesses with your "new eyes," success factors will begin to emerge.

The Ten Killer Factors

1. **Weak Personality:** The lack of sound psychological or emotional strength at the head of a company leads to failure in 50% of the cases. If a company founder cannot cope with the many challenges he must confront and if he has private problems as well, the collapse is predetermined.
2. **The Loner Syndrome:** Loners have a difficult life. Because they don't discuss their problems with colleagues or professionals, they lose that critical distance, the perspective, to their projects. They flounder with closed eyes into failure.
3. **Nebulous Business Ideas:** The loser doesn't know how to make his ideas work. He doesn't familiarize himself with the market and doesn't know his competition or his potential customers.
4. **No Plan:** If a clear concept is missing, one false decision follows another. When requested, a business plan is submitted to the bank, but it seldom has anything to do with reality. It is written just to be convincing.

5. **Too Little Financial Backing:** There are always young entrepreneurs who succeed without beginning capital. But then modesty is called for. Many founders use too much money too early for private purposes. Too little financial substance leads immediately to problems. A general rule of thumb has it that one-third of the balance or two-thirds of the fixed assets should come from one's own capital.

6. **Cash-flow Troubles:** Anyone without knowledge of business management and who fails to exercise cash-flow management is responsible for his own downfall. Many naively believe their customers will pay within 30 days. The opposite is true. If salaries and suppliers cannot be paid, then any attempt to save the sinking ship comes too late.

7. **No Marketing Strategy:** According to statistics, one-third of the young entrepreneurs disappear from the market because of insufficient marketing. An amateurish market approach undermines credibility. A lack of trust results in a lack of business.

8. **No Controlling:** Ignoring the need for a good evaluation system usually results in realizing too late that something has gone wrong, so it's virtually impossible to turn the situation around and correct it.

9. **The Wrong People:** Hiring the wrong people is the quickest way to lose a lot of money very fast.

10. **Underestimating the Competition:** Good ideas are not the perfect guarantee for getting a good hold in the market. The competition is not sleeping. It takes the offensive and tries to make up for opportunities it missed. New developments that are undertaken without first checking out the chances on the market simply cost a lot of money.

The Ten Success Factors

1. **Willingness to Succeed:** The successful entrepreneur spares no expense. He must be prepared to work 50 to 60 hours a week and give up his holidays. For that, he needs the support of his family.

2. **Self-Confidence:** Only those who believe in themselves will achieve their goals. That calls for optimism and trust in the future. A founder must take on challenges and confront constant changes and he should not be afraid of making mistakes.

3. **A Clear Business Idea:** The idea has to be right. The head of the company knows his strengths and weaknesses and his competition. He knows the reason for his success, whether it's because he has the better product, the better service, or the more intelligent sales and marketing approach.

4. **The Business Plan:** The business plan is the key to building up a company. This instrument, which is always being adapted to the latest developments, makes it possible to proceed with a systematic plan of action, to recognize problems in their early stages so the proper corrective measures can be taken in plenty of time.

5. **Exact Control of Finances:** A young entrepreneur doesn't have to be swimming in money. But success usually doesn't come as quickly as anticipated. That's why financial resources should be calculated somewhat generously. Anyone who understands something about business management and knows how to react quickly, has his finances and cash-flow under control. Any profits made are reinvested in the company.

6. **Targeted Marketing:** Only someone who has a clear concept about how to introduce his product or service onto the market will be able to succeed.

Action Step 7

Interview Self-Employed People

Interview at least three people who are self-employed. One should be in your own area of interest. If you are a potential competitor, you may need to travel 50 miles or more to find an interview subject and get real help.

Successful entrepreneurs love to tell the story of how they achieved success. Be up front about the type of information you need and why you want it. Then make appointments with them at their convenience.

Prepare for your interviews. Open-ended questions are best because they leave room for embellishment. Some suggestions are:

- What were your first steps?
- How did you arrange financing?
- If you had it to do all over again, would you do anything differently?
- How large a part does creativity play in your particular business?
- Are your rewards tangible? intangible?
- What was your best marketing technique?
- What proportion of gross sales do you spend on advertising?
- Did you hire more employees than you originally thought you'd need?
- What makes your business unique?
- Did you write a Business Plan?
- Are gross profits all you expected them to be?

Depending on how you relate to your subject, you might be able to think of these first interviewees as sources of marketplace experience. They may help when you begin to assemble your "taxi squad": your lawyer, accountant, banker, and so on.

It is helpful to take notes during interviews. If you use a cassette recorder, be sure to ask permission. Don't worry about evaluations at this stage. The information will assemble into patterns sooner than you think. Be sure to send a personal handwritten thank you . You will be amazed at how much help you receive from fellow entrepreneurs.

Income Statistics (Per Capita) for Selected Countries 1995

1.	Switzerland	$26,716
2.	United States	$20,698
3.	Canada	$16,121
4.	United Kingdom	$13,492
5.	Israel	$10,612
6.	Puerto Rico	$7,712
7.	Oman	$5,765
8.	Tunisia	$1,444
9.	China	$400
10.	Chad	$169

Seventy percent of the world's population receives 10 percent of the total world income. As you venture around the world as a potential global entrepreneur, you need to be aware of ... economic conditions that will preclude your selling high-ticket items in many countries. Although a huge market for basic products and services, clean water, electricity, communications, and infrastructure exists throughout the world, the global entrepreneur will view the above statistics as an opportunity not a threat to their business ventures. Half of the U.S. exporters employ less than 5 people, so explore and find the right opportunity for you.

SOURCE: **www.geocities.com/~combusem/WORLDGDP.HTM**

7. **A Step Ahead of the Competition:** Success must constantly be worked on. That includes a plan for research and development, so you don't lose your advantage on the market. Acting instead of reacting will give you the advantage.
8. **Management Support:** A young entrepreneur's power increases if he can fall back on the knowledge of an experienced entrepreneur. Possible advisers to call upon would be financiers or successful colleagues who are also entrepreneurs. This can also open doors for the company founder which might otherwise be closed to him.
9. **Cooperation:** No one is top in every field. Building up a network of cooperation often provides access to additional know-how that would otherwise cost a lot of money.
10. **Clear Company Structure:** A successful company has a clear structure. The employees are motivated and know exactly what their responsibilities are. The customers know who to contact.

SOURCE: **www.innonet.ch**

Attempt to develop a business's profit profile. In the course of your interview (see Action Step 7), try to ascertain key numbers, such as gross sales, cost of goods sold, rent, salaries (owner, management), how much is spent on marketing (advertising, commissions, promotions, and so on). You can estimate the other expenses and arrive at a range that will give you perspective when it comes time to work with your own numbers.

For example, let's assume a business with $500,000 in sales. The cost of goods sold (COGS) averages 53 percent; rent is $2000; total salaries are 15 percent of gross sales. The company spends 6 percent of their gross on marketing. These are the only numbers you acquired from the interview. Based on these numbers, you can estimate benefits, including FICA (social security) costs, at 20–30 percent of salaries; and other expenses (supplies, utilities, accounting, legal, auto, entertainment, and so on) at 8–12 percent. Combining what you have been given with your estimates yields the profit profile shown below.

On the high side, the profit profile is slightly better than 10 percent, or $51,000. On the low side, it's slightly below 5 percent, or $23,500. (That $23,500 may not be as low as it appears if the owner has already taken salary and auto and entertainment expenses.)

	High Side	Low Side
Sales	$500,000	$500,000
C of GS (53%)	−265,000	−265,000
Gross Profit	235,000	235,000
Less: Marketing (6%)	30,000	30,000
Salaries (15%)	75,000	75,000
FICA/Benefits	15,000	22,500
Rent ($2000/mo.)	24,000	24,000
Other Expenses	40,000	60,000
Net Profit	$ 51,000	$ 23,500

Interviewing Successful Entrepreneurs

Action Step 7 encourages you to interview entrepreneurs primarily within your selected industry—competitors, customers, distributors, suppliers, and wholesalers.

 *Summary*

According to Jim Collins, author of *Built to Last,* one should look at developing a business that looks at the intersection of three circles: (1) What you're good at, (2) What you stand for, and (3) What people will pay you for. You have answered the first two. In Chapter 2, you will be looking at your changing world for opportunities. In later chapters you will find the right target market, people who possess the dollars to purchase your product or service.

Think Points for Success

Remember:

- We are entrepreneurs. Work is our fun. We never sleep.
- Even though you may not be in business yet, you can intensify your focus by writing down your thoughts about the business you think you want to try. Stay flexible.
- Change is accelerating everywhere, and change is what provides you with opportunities to follow for your entrepreneurial venture.
- To find the doorway into your own business, gather data and keep asking questions.
- Get reckless on paper before you get reckless in the marketplace.
- Brainstorm.
- Draw mind maps.

- Be sure to confirm your venture with numbers and words before you enter the arena.
- Write a business plan.

Key Points from Another View

Top 15 Things I Learned in My First Year in Business

By Evan C. Williams from Edge Magazine online

1. I'm not as smart as I think I am.
2. If you don't pay close attention to the numbers, it's like you're running blind.
3. Taking the time and expense to do things right is always cheaper and quicker than doing things in a hurry NOW to buy some time in order to do things right LATER.
4. It's hard to be passionately committed to seven different projects at once—in fact, two is pushing.
5. There's a limit to the number of things I can do, and do well. Every time you decide to do something new, you have to decide to quit doing something else.
6. Focus. Focus. Focus.
7. I need to think very carefully about what I really want to do before committing to an ongoing, time-obligating project.
8. Make your expectations of those around you very clear; they can't read your mind.
9. Not everyone thinks as I do. (And that's good!)
10. Believe it or not, the rules of success also apply to me.
11. I am much more productive if I balance my life and take care of myself than I am if all I do is work 18 hours a day and eat junk food.
12. If I am floating around, unfocused, unproductive, un-energetic, and in general have a groggy, icky feeling, it is because I don't have a clearly defined worthwhile goal I am excited about. As long as I'm working toward a worthwhile goal, I feel great and accomplish lots.
13. A good way to not make any money is to try very hard to make money.
14. There is a great deal of difference between intellectually understanding something—even if you passionately agree with it—and knowing something. Some things it seems we just choose to learn for ourselves.
15. Knowing the laws of success, the road to riches, and the keys to the universe are not enough. The key lies in exercising the self-discipline to practice what you know.

SOURCE: **www.edgeonline.com**

Spotting Trends and Opportunities

Opening Your Eyes

2

Entrepreneurial Links

Books

Future Perfect, Stan Davis, 1997

Going Global: Four Entrepreneurs Map the New World Marketplace, William C. Taylor, Alan M. Webber, 1996.

Clicking: 17 Trends that Drive Your Business—And Your Life, Faith Popcorn and Lys Marigold, 1998.

Websites

www.ai.mit.edu (Artificial Intelligence Laboratory at MIT)

www.wfs.org (World Future Society)

www.roper.com (Consumer Research Information from Roper Starch)

Associations/Organizations

U.S. Chamber of Commerce, Small Business Institute, www.usccsbi.com

American Success Institute, www.success.org

The Entrepreneurship Institute, www.tei.net/tei

Publications

The Small Business Journal, www.tsbj.com

Fast Company, www.fastcompany.com

Futurist, www.wfs.org

Additional Entrepreneurial Insights

Only the Paranoid Survive, Andy Grove, 1996.

A Goal is a Dream with a Deadline, Leo Helzel, 1995.

What's Luck Got to Do with It? Twelve Entrepreneurs Reveal the Secrets Behind Their Success (Ernst & Young), Greg K. Ericksen editor, 1997.

Learning Objectives

- Train your eyes to read market forces that forecast future needs.
- Understand the "big picture" and its affect on trends and opportunities.
- Learn to become your own Futurist.
- . Understand the changing family structure and its impact on businesses.
- Gain an awareness of the splintering of the mass market and cultural changes.
- Research technological changes and their impact on your industry.
- Understand how to access the vast secondary resources available.
- Become excited about brainstorming techniques.
- Learn how to conduct "new eyes" research.
- To understand how to analyze the potential for small business success by applying the life-cycle yardstick to industries.

Opening Your Eyes and Mind

Where can you find a business idea that will really pay off? One that will make you rich? One that will make you famous? What are the best ventures to pursue today?

Only you can answer these questions because the best business for you is one that you will enjoy, and one that makes money. The best business for you uses those experiences, skills, and aptitudes that are unique to you. The Action Steps in this book are designed to help you discover what is unique about you: Who are you? What are your skills? What turns you on? What special knowledge do you have that distinguishes you from other people?

Look around, check out the new businesses in your town. Which new firms are operating in your selected industry? What new target markets are developing? What could you sell on the Internet? How can you meet the needs of the aging **baby boomers?** What about the **Y Generation?**

> **Six Leading Success Factors**
> **(for Firms in the Digital Revolution)**
>
> 1. **Responsiveness to Change:** How well does the company respond to market change?
> 2. **Market Opportunity:** How big is the potential market for the company's products?
> 3. **Marketing Expertise:** How good is the company at selling and marketing into the above opportunity?
> 4. **Human Capital:** How good are management, marketing sales, and support?
> 5. **Alliances and Partnerships:** How strong are its partners and its relationships?
> 6. **Prospects for Growth:** How fast is the company growing and can it continue to ramp up quickly?
>
> SOURCE: see *Forbes ASAP,* 2/98.

Baby boomers Persons born between 1946 and 1963.

Generation Y Individuals born between mid 70s and early 80s.

This chapter is designed to help you recognize opportunities in **market segments** so you can define the gaps in the marketplace. You want to be sure your business serves a need; that you will enter the marketplace from a position of strength. It's time to look at your changing world and selected industry to spot trends and opportunities. Be a trend-spotter and you can ride your way to a successful business. Don't forget to add blood, sweat, tears, energy, enthusiasm, money, and a good idea.

When we began working with entrepreneurs some 20 years ago, we handed out sage advice like "Just find a need and fill it." Now we say, "Examine the marketplace thoroughly for flaws and opportunities and use technology to keep track of your customer's needs continually." We also used to say, "If you're doing business now the same way you did three years ago, you're probably doing many things wrong." Now we say, "If you're doing business today the same way you did six months ago, you should think about a new strategic plan."

Use your marketplace radar to choose a growth segment of a growth industry; to ride the crest of the wave. Choosing the hot growth sector is usually the right way to begin before the trend turns down. Occasionally, however, the trend sours.

If you are already in a small business, or thinking about getting into one, make it easy on yourself by first identifying industries in the growth phase of their **life cycle.** The way to do that is to play "marketplace detective."

Look around you. When you focus in on a particular business, do you sense growth over the long term? Or is it involved with a fad that won't last? For your business, you want a growth industry that will generate new customers quickly; allowing you to build a customer base.

As a small business owner, one of the things you must have going for you is fast footwork, so you can adjust to change quickly. It's one of your best weapons in the marketplace. But you can benefit from fast footwork only if you operate from a position of knowledge: stay in touch with customers, and keep your ear tuned to the marketplace.

Look before you leap. Brainstorm with your family and friends, and interview your potential customers. Study the marketplace. Read industry journals. Use your **new eyes.** With trained eyes you'll be able to see the big picture.

It's a Dynamic World

- Today's computer chips are 10,000 times faster than chips of 25 years ago.
- Computers and telecommunications have created a global village.
- Software is being developed in 8-hour shifts in three countries: India, the United States, and Ireland.
- Industry deregulation has created incredible opportunities.
- Competition is everywhere and intense.

Environmental Variables

Changes occur in five major environmental variables:

1. Technology—biotechnology, computerization, miniaturization, Internet, telecommunications
2. Competition—deregulation, impact of "box stores," international
3. Social/cultural—immigration, single parents, religion, ethnic shifts
4. Legal/political—who is in power, tax laws, changing regulations
5. Economics—recessions, inflation, changing income levels, cost of housing, food prices

---

> ### Action Step 8
>
> #### Opening Your Mind to New Information
>
> Your community and workplaces are your marketing labs. It is time to open your mind to all the information around you. Time to head out!
>
> **First stop** (Large bookstore with lots of magazines) Select and read five distinctly different magazines that you have never read before. What did you learn? Did you read about a target market you didn't know existed? Next review the top 10 best-sellers: fiction, nonfiction, children's, trade, paperbacks. What does this tell you about your current world?
>
> **Second stop** (Music store) What's hot? What's not?
>
> **Third stop** (Local mall) What new stores are opening? Which department store has the best service? highest prices? best selection? Which food places are hot? Where are the longest lines?
>
> **Fourth stop** (Visit your favorite store) Compile a list of all the products and services that were not there two years ago (if you are visiting a computer store, shorten the time to six months). Can you guesstimate shelf velocity? What's hot?
>
> **Fifth stop** (TV time) Spend one hour watching CNN World Report. Make a list of the stories. Did any surprise you? Are there any opportunities?
>
> **Final stop** (Boot up) Surf the Web for at least an hour or two on topics you know nothing about.
>
> Your brain should be in high gear— or suffering from information overload!

Market segments Identifiable slices of market.

Life cycles Stages—from birth to death—of a product, business, service, industry, location, target market, and so on.

New eyes Observation with intuition.

Changes = Trends = Opportunities

Environ- mental Variables	Changes /Trends	Opportunities
Social/Cultural		
Competition		
Technology		
Legal/Political		
Economics		

Pick up the last six issues of *Time* or *Newsweek* (your local library should have copies), your notes from Action Step 8, and start reading. What is happening in the world? Fill in the chart with the areas that are changing within each environmental variable. If you are fortunate and have done your research, you will spot the changes before trends start to develop. Being at the forefront of trends has made business-savvy people rich. Remember when Web commerce began only a few short years ago? If you had spotted the change within this technology, hopped on it, and rode the trend to success, where would you be today?

Figure 2.1

Reeling in the Years

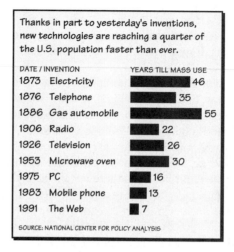

Thanks in part to yesterday's inventions, new technologies are reaching a quarter of the U.S. population faster than ever.

DATE / INVENTION		YEARS TILL MASS USE
1873	Electricity	46
1876	Telephone	35
1886	Gas automobile	55
1906	Radio	22
1926	Television	26
1953	Microwave oven	30
1975	PC	16
1983	Mobile phone	13
1991	The Web	7

SOURCE: NATIONAL CENTER FOR POLICY ANALYSIS

SOURCE: *Newsweek,* April 13, 1998.

Your goal is to constantly be aware of trends that develop due to changes within each of the above environmental variables. Each change within the environmental variables and subsequent trends affect how products are manufactured, marketed, and delivered to customers. Buy and read *Newsweek, Time,* industry journals, newspapers, and any other magazines and begin to learn how to spot the changes. Action Step 8 opened your mind to new information and now its time to start to evaluate the information and search for opportunities. Action Step 9 will help you to do this.

Changing Families

How does your world differ from the world your parents experienced? How will your children's world differ from yours? You can see how your world differs from your parents, but the new opportunities reside in how your children's world will differ.

The "Beaver Cleaver" family exists for very few today. The opportunities to serve the diverse family structures are vast: day care, afterschool care, recreation programs, shopping help, career college selection services. If you compiled a list of all the services June and Ward Cleaver provided to keep their household running, you would discover that all those services are still needed today, but service-oriented businesses are doing them, not June and Ward.

Who else is in need of these services? The elderly? single parents? disabled? chronically ill?

In 1997, 60 percent of our 5.5-trillion-dollar economy was spent on services. People are buying time. Do you see a need for a service? Do any of your friends or colleagues have the same need? Are people willing to pay for this service? Can you provide this service and get the word out? If you answered yes, go for it! In many instances, service-oriented businesses can be begin as home-based, with a low capital investment, few employees, and a great idea that fills a need.

People are marrying later, having fewer children and having them later; divorcing in greater numbers, remarrying and reformulating new families. Are there any opportunities here for you? Each change and trend in our society represents threats and opportunities to current businesses. If current businesses don't expand and change, new businesses will move in.

Can You Help Us? Please!
(The Family Today)

- **The workforce has changed dramatically.** Today's workforce is more racially and ethnically diverse (20 percent is non-white), older (the median age is nearly 40), and comprised of more women (48%) than it was 20 years ago. The study also found that higher proportions of workers have college degrees (31%) and hold managerial and professional jobs (34%).

- **The vast majority (85%) of workers have day-to-day family responsibilities at home.** Some 78 percent of married employees have spouses and partners who are also employed, compared to 66 percent in 1977. A full 46 percent of workers have children under 18 who live with them at least half-time. Nearly one in five employed parents is single, and surprisingly, 27 percent of single parents are men.

- **The roles of married men and women are changing.** Although employed married women spend more time on chores than employed married men do, this gap has narrowed substantially over the last 20 years. On workdays, men spend 2.1 hours on household chores (an increase of nearly one hour) compared to the 2.9 hours (a half-hour decline) women spend. Both men (1.6 hours per workday) and women (1.3 hours per workday) have less personal time.

- **When it comes to child care, two-thirds of all employed parents with pre-kindergarten children rely on partners and relatives as the primary source.** When one member of a dual-earner couple has to take time off to care for a child, 83 percent of employed mothers say they are more likely to take time off while 22 percent of fathers make this claim.

- **Today's jobs are more demanding than ever.** Employees today spend an average 44 hours per week working—six more than they are scheduled to work. Among employees who work at least 20 hours a week, the hours spent on the job each week has increased an average of 3.5 (from 43.6 to 47.1) since 1977. In addition, many workers say they have to work very fast (68%) and very hard (88%). One in three employees bring work home at least once a week, an increase of 10 percent over the last 20 years. The number of employees who would like to work fewer hours rose 17 percentage points over this time period.

- **Many workers experience stress and negative spillover from work.** Nearly one-fourth of all employees often or very often felt nervous or stressed; 13 percent often or very often had difficulty coping with the demands of everyday life; 26 percent often or very often felt emotionally drained by their work; 28 percent often or very often have not had the energy to do things with their families or others; and 36 percent often or very often felt used up at the end of the workday.

SOURCE: **http://www.familiesandworkinst.org/p1.html.**

Checkmate!

Chess had changed Sammy's life. He wanted to change others' lives too. At most local schools, chess isn't considered a trendy game. But Sammy knew he could make chess "cool." After graduating from college, he worked with local elementary schools volunteering his time to teach chess with four half-hour lessons. After providing incredibly fun lessons—bishops being conked

---

▶ **Action Step 10**

$1000 and a Working Car

How quickly can you think of a business to start with little capital and no employees? Place yourself in the position of having to make money in one week. You have to start a business and only have $1000. You have a working car or pickup truck, an apartment, and a phone. Remember, the business must be legal!

Start looking by asking friends what they need, driving through local neighborhoods, and reading. Find out what other people are accomplishing with what appears to be a small investment.

Compile a list of all the businesses you have discovered. Can you purchase products at a warehouse for resale? Could you tap a skill you already possess? Remember Felix's basketball skills in Chapter 1.

P.S. Apple Computer started with $1350

Dell Computer started with $1000
Nike started with $1000

P.P.S. Go for it! Remember, Walt Disney started in his garage!

on the head, three-foot-tall chesspieces, double chessboards, and lots of laughter, Sammy was ready to start afterschool chess classes at $5 per class per child. In some schools over 30 percent of the kids took his classes! Currently, several thousand children are involved in his programs.

Yes, Sammy was able to pull kids away from Nintendo, and parents were thrilled. They had been looking for an activity without a keyboard that would challenge their children's minds. Sammy was riding the trend of parents seeking alternatives to TV, computer games, and Nintendo.

Many of the moms and dads in the upscale community where Sammy lived were programmers and engineers, had played chess as children, but couldn't find the time to teach their own kids. Sammy came to the rescue. Friday night chess tournaments, traveling chess teams, and chess camps were born out of listening to his customers—parents and kids!

Boomer Explosion

Baby boomers, who have been a major economic and social force in our society for decades, are aging. As they approach their fifties, they are redefining aging and retirement. What products will they need? What do they want? Where will they buy them? How can you reach them?

Soon these boomers (29% of the population) will control over 75 percent of the nation's assets and 50 percent of its discretionary income. According to many sources, the boomers will not go gently into that good night. They will fight the aging process with every dollar they have. You can't look at past generations to predict the buying habits of this group. They are wealthier, more educated, have fewer children, and are in "new family" structures. Firms are going to the source—the boomers—and asking them what they want. Del Webb, a premier developer of retirement communities, recently completed a major research study of the boomers.

Scrutinize those boomers—from the tops of their heads to the bottoms of their feet. See if you can develop products or services to make some money. Brainstorm away! If you are twenty-something look at your folks; if you're forty-something look in the mirror. Be as creative and wild as you can! The following should help get you started:

- Hair—toupees, hair implants, wigs, great hats, special sunscreen for bald spots
- Eyes—eyedrops, cool magnifiers, trifocals, eye surgery
- Face—plastic surgery, skincreams, skin cancer checkups, facial exercise classes, facial massages, makeup

Every doctor, dentist, lawyer, accountant, travel agent, and/or financial planner is waiting in the wings for the boomers to break down their doors. Opportunities are enormous for those who want to capitalize on and meet the boomer's needs.

Modern Maturity, the largest distributed subscription magazine (distributed free to AARP members as part of their membership dues), is targeted at those over age 50, and may have one of the hottest Websites of the future: **www.aarp.org/mmaturity.** Legally and politically those over age 50 have always been a very strong political force. With the power of the Web, real social, political, and economic change is not only possible but also inevitable.

About Boomers

- In the U.S. between the end of World War II and 1964, 78 million baby boomers were born and now are part of the "Boomers" generation.

- Boomers are now entering middle age and changing the demographics of the total population. Four out of ten households are between ages 35 to 54 and the numbers of households ages 45 to 54 will increase 20 percent from 1995 to year 2000.

- As empty nesters, boomers have more money to spend as the median income bracket for boomers is $47,300 annually.

- The average household headed by boomer age 35 to 54 spends $12,000 annually for housing.

- The number of couples without children between the age of 45 and 60 will increase from 8 million in 1980 to 16 million in the year 2010.

- Every 7.5 seconds, a Boomer turns 50!

- Generation identified with Iron Curtain, Berlin Wall, Cold War, Sputnik, transistor radios, calculators, computers, Man on the Moon, hula hoop, "Leave It To Beaver," Mousketeers, Doo Wop, R & B, American Bandstand, Elvis, Little Richard, Chuck Berry, Motown, Beach Boys, Haight-Ashbury, Hippies, PEACE, VW Bug, LOVE, LSD, Woodstock, California Dreamin', hot tubs, TM, platform shoes, bell bottoms, mini skirts, hot pants, bikinis, tie dyed, flower power, communal, Nehru jackets, The Beatles, Rolling Stones, Chelsae, King's Road, Carnarby Street, Bohemians, The Mods, The Rockers, Liverpool, Twiggy, the fall of the Berlin Wall, PAN AM, and $5.00 a day in Europe.

SOURCE: **http://members.aol.com/boomersint/bindex.html.**

Where will boomers purchase products and services? Online sales are a possibility. Sales growth from online retailing is estimated to rise to $30 billion by 2005. To whom will the online products amd services be targeted and marketed?

Three menopausal women recognized a huge market of 50 million women entering menopause during the next 10 years. They developed "As We Change" (see Figure 2.2), a 32-page catalog of products to address the needs and concerns of this very large market.

Many firms such as Victoria's Secret, Sharper Image and Gateway, start with mail order and move to retailing as momentum builds for their products. Are retail stores in the future for As We Change? What about online retailing? Do you see any other avenues?

The Splintering of the Mass Market

Today's consumers are informed, individualistic, and demanding. Their buying habits are often difficult to isolate because they tend to buy at several levels of the market. For example, purchasing agents may buy copiers direct from Xerox, but the paper from Staples. High-fashion, high-income consumers may patronize upscale boutiques, but buy their household appliances at Wal-Mart.

For the consumer, three key factors have splintered the mass market:

1. A shrinking middle class—the wealthiest fifth of the populations' income has grown by 21 percent and the bottom 60 percent have stagnated or dipped according to U.S. Census data (see Figure 2.3). In 1996, 20 percent of all children in the United States were classified as poor—a family of four with an income below $16,036. Two distinct marketing strategies are developing to reach customers at both ends of the population: satellite phone services offering $3000 phones and $3-a-minute charges versus prepaid phone cards for those with no phone service.

Action Step 11

Spotting Trends in Your Selected Target Markets

Select a target market of your choice—**Generation Y,** Generation X, the over-80, frail, elderly, soccer kids. Search the net for statitistics and information. Start with census data at **www.census.gov** and continue on using search engines. Try **www.easidemographics.com, www.ends.com, www.awool.com/index.html.** Using your statistics, intuition, and knowledge of the target market work back through the baby boomer exercise or go through a day in the lives of your selected target market. What trends do they identify with? What products and services will your target market desire? How can you best meet their needs?

Next, review the list of products, ideas, and services the baby boomers identified with. Compile a similar list focused on your Target Customer.

As you continue through this book, you will learn how to refine your target market continually.

Figure 2.2

As We Change: Catalog Products

Get a better look.

Elegant sterling silver rimmed pendant doubles as a fashionable magnifier for those times when you need to see better quickly. Optical quality 1⅞" diameter glass magnifies 3 times and 6 times for super magnification. Sterling silver 24" chain with 3" drop, accented with onyx, freshwater pearls.

a. **Magnifier Necklace**

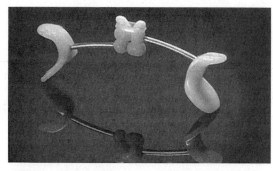

Tone and tighten your facial muscles.

Here's a completely natural way to noticeably improve facial skin tone and firmness. Facial Flex® Ultra provides a mini-workout for the muscles that support the skin of your mouth, cheeks and chin—areas that tend to sag over the years. Significant results in just 2 to 3 minutes twice daily over a 60-day period. Comes with instructional video and 2 strengths of replacement elastic bands.

h. **Facial Flex® Ultra**

SOURCE: As We Change Catalog.

Figure 2.3

The Rich Get Richer

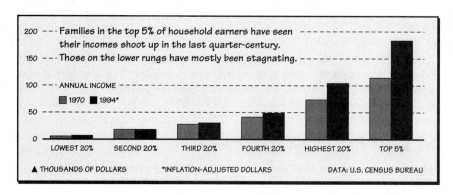

Families in the top 5% of household earners have seen their incomes shoot up in the last quarter-century.
Those on the lower rungs have mostly been stagnating.

ANNUAL INCOME
1970   1994*

LOWEST 20%   SECOND 20%   THIRD 20%   FOURTH 20%   HIGHEST 20%   TOP 5%

▲ THOUSANDS OF DOLLARS   *INFLATION-ADJUSTED DOLLARS   DATA: U.S. CENSUS BUREAU

SOURCE: *Business Week*, March 17, 1998.

2. The size of age and ethnic groups is shifting. Latinos will be the largest minority group by 2005 with 30 million people. The Latino market tends to be younger and more demographically centered than other market segments. Ethnic diversity is expanding rapidly. The greater Los Angeles area is already the most ethnically diverse in the world. TV stations are available in Spanish, English, Persian, and Vietnamese.

3. Living arrangements are changing and evolving: stepfamilies, dual-career families, single parents, grandparents raising grandchildren, grandparents living with children, children returning to the nest.

Figure 2.4

Changing Work-Age Population

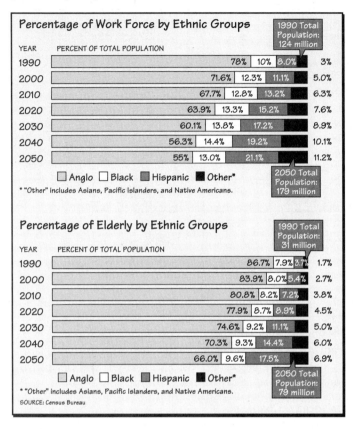

SOURCE: *Los Angeles Times.* March 25, 1998.

If you look with "new eyes" you can see additional major segments emerging, growing, and becoming more powerful: affluent 80-year-olds, Asians (5% of population), pre-teen consumers (see Figure 2.5), Silicon Valley millionaires, and so on. Take a few minutes to surf **www.mediafinder.com** and **www.srds.com.** Within minutes, you will discover hundreds of very narrow target markets reached by magazines. One of the latest, INTERRACE, addresses the concerns of interracial and multiracial couples, families, and singles. For the first time, the year 2000 census will collect multiracial data, which may open up other niche markets.

Today's technology allows us to define ever-smaller target markets. With the power of the Net and the right software, we can achieve one-to-one target marketing. If you order product B and 50 percent of customers who order product B also order product Z, product Z will pop up on your screen automatically. This is basically a salesperson in a box.

Cultural Changes

Information Overload!

The average person receives more information from their big-city Sunday newspaper than a Middle-Ages person received in their entire lifetime! Hence the need for Internet push technology. Human wants and needs of the American consumer are screaming: faster, pare it down, earn lots, save money, train me, quality over quantity, and give me excitement! **Generation X** does not take their tents to the mountains and veg out for the week. They take their mountain bikes,

Generation X Individuals born between the early 60s and the mid 70s.

Figure 2.5a

Pizza, Pepsi, and Power Rangers

Aggregate Spending in Millions of Dollars by Children Aged 4 to 12 on selected items, and per-child spending, 1997.

	aggregate spending	per-child spending
Food and beverages	$7,745	$220
Play items	6,471	184
Apparel	3,595	102
Movies/sports	1,989	56
Video arcades	1,326	38
Other	2,302	65
Total	$23,429	$665

Source: author's estimates and Census Bureau

The average U.S. child aged 4 to 12 personally spends more than $600 a year. Over half goes for food and toys.

SOURCE: *American Demographics,* April 1998, p. 40.

Figure 2.5b

Why Kids Are Hot

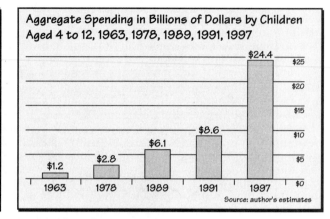

Aggregate Spending in Billions of Dollars by Children Aged 4 to 12, 1963, 1978, 1989, 1991, 1997

Kids' spending is growing fast, even though the population of children hasn't mushroomed.

SOURCE: *American Demographics,* April 1998, p. 38.

▶ **Action Step 12**

Have Some Fun with Identifying Problems

Form a focus group of your friends or colleagues and ask them about their wants and needs. Hopefully you will discover some gaps in the marketplace. Don't judge their answers; you're just seeking information and the more they provide the better. Ask them to respond to questions such as the following:

• What frustrates you most about your daily life? shopping? banking? dating? living? buying a car? grocery shopping? clothing shopping?

• What products or services do you need or want but can't find or get?

• What products or services would enhance your quality of life?

• How could you increase your productivity without working more hours?

If you are dealing with a nonconsumer product, change the questions to fit your market.

Make a list of the gaps that the group identifies. Then project the list out as far as you can into the marketplace and follow the wants, needs, and frustrations of your friends. Are

(continued on next page)

snowboards, and cross-country skis. No vegging out allowed! REI, a major outdoor retailer, is there to meet their needs.

Our private lives and work lives are converging. We spend less time at home and more time at work. Becoming more dependent on the workplace to provide us with parenting, financial-planning classes, travel services, company concierges, dry cleaning, child and adult day care, and so on.

**16 Major Societal Changes
(Roper Starch 1998)**

The Age of Autonomy

The Global Village

The PC Nation (50% of all US homes have PCs)

Better Quality/Decreasing Loyalty

The Search for Civility (the return of manners)

The Portable Workplace (Flextime/Flexplace)

It's the Love of Learning (Education + Curiousity = Success)

401Ks Forever (Taking financial responsibility)

Relationships Reconsidered

Comfort Rules (Friday casual is now everyday)

Driving a Hard Bargain (Price seekers and deal makers)

Pizza in Our Time (Take out food number one time saver tracked by Roper)

Self-Serve Advertising

Our Town (Incorporating small-town feel into suburban neighborhoods)

Green (& Don't forget it)

Angel on My Shoulder (Self-directed spiritual seeking)

Full Speed Ahead

The companies highlighted in this database have earned Entrepreneur's ranking as the fastest-growing franchises in the United States.

Rankings are based on straight growth in the number of franchises from 1996 to 1997 as verified in Entrepreneur's annual *Franchise 500®* listing. (Companies that tied are listed in alphabetical order.)

The following list is not intended to endorse any particular franchise but simply to provide a starting point for research. Perhaps after a careful investigation of these franchises, you may find a system that can put you on the fast track to success.

1. McDonald's
2. Burger King Corporation
3. Yogen Fruz Worldwide
4. 7-Eleven Convenience Stores
5. Jani-King
6. Subway
7. Baskin-Robbins USA Co.
8. Coverall Cleaning Concepts
9. Arby's Inc.
10. Taco Bell

SOURCE: **http://www.entrepreneurmag.com/franchise500/fast103_fran.hts**

Technology Revolution

The $20 microchip that runs a 1998 Nintendo 64 cost $1000 in 1993 and powered high-end servers. The computer has changed every facet of every life. We rarely reach a human being when we telephone a business. When frustrated, we look up their Website and e-mail our message. Computer-to-computer communication is now a way of life. Long handwritten letters seem to be a thing of the past. We use videophones, teleconferencing, and e mail new jokes to our best friends. What impact will technology have on your business? What opportunities are just waiting for you to exploit?

The Human Genome project is mapping out the 80,000 genes that make up human DNA. Possibilities for products and services are mind-boggling and will come at an incredible pace. Will there be genetic testing centers cropping up in every city? Will people go to one of these centers before getting married to have potential mates evaluated? Will these centers be franchised?

Embedded microchips are common in veterinary medicine giving veterinarians instant access to a pet's medical history. Will it be long before people also have embedded microchips? Can you discover any other new uses for embedded chips? What about in appliances? clothing? furniture? sports equipment? Keep up on technology news by watching technology-oriented programs on TV, surfing the Net, and reading *Forbes ASAP* special issues.

Artificial body parts and transplanted organs are an everyday occurrence. Will cancer, Parkinson's, Alzheimer's, and heart disease become a distant memory with the advances in biotechnology? If these diseases were cured, what could you do with the empty doctor's offices? medical buildings?

Surgeons provide online instructions in real-time to operating rooms throughout the world. When a patient's chest is open and a surgeon must cut in the exact spot, Dr. Melia from Syracuse is ready to assist—not only for his own patients in Syracuse but also to doctors and patients in places like Bolivia. Doctors monitor patients at home with products previously available only at a hospital. This saves untold hospital bed space and doctor visits. Do you know someone with a chronic illness? How could technology be of help to him or her?

New high-tech materials from the aerospace industry allow Flex-Foot of Aliso Viejo, California **(www.flexfoot.com)** to design and market innovative

any of what they mentioned national in scope? global?

Remember the women from the "As We Change" catalog. They not only discovered a 50-million-strong national market, but an international market as well. They listened to their friends!

Action Step 13

New Technologies

If you are a tech expert, share your insights with your class. Bring them up to speed! Technology affects every aspect of small business today—distribution, marketing, products, and so on. If you are not tech savvy, it's time to get up to speed!

1. Read one copy of Wired **(www.wired.com)** either online or in hard copy.
2. Surf the Net or visit the library and find five articles on new technologies. Can you discover any trends developing? future opportunities? Share your findings with your classmates. A technological breakthrough in one industry will often lead to a breakthrough in another industry.
3. Read several copies of *The Futurist, Science,* or high-tech magazines in your selected industry. List all the new, developing technologies. Can you spot any trends?

With the above information in hand, you will be better prepared to focus on the opportunities these changing technologies provide.

lower-limb prosthetic devices for amputees constructed out of 100 percent carbon fiber. New materials used creatively have allowed many new businesses to produce products for industry and consumers.

The list of *25 Cool Things* below proposes many incredible products that will revolutionize the way we live. People with disabilities have been greatly aided by technology, and the future holds even more promise.

Some people make a business of trend-watching. Nicholas Negroponte of the MIT Media Lab **(www.media.mit.ed),** author of *Being Digital;* Faith Popcorn, author of *Clicking;* Jennifer James, author of *Thinking in the Future Tense;* and Sherry Turkle, author of *Life on the Screen: Identity in the Age of the Internet* are leading trend-watchers. Faith Popcorn follows over 500 magazines and newspapers in order to predict trends. Jennifer James, an urban cultural anthropologist, studies language and symbol shifts with a keen eye on TV programs.

Find out who your "industry gurus" are and read everything they write. In addition to individual trend-watchers, major market research firms like Roper Starch, Nielsen, and Burke, provide extensive studies, many of which are available on the Net.

**25 Cool Things
(You Wish You Had. . . and Will)**

1. Smart ski
2. Powerful PDA
3. Injectable health monitor
4. All-Knowing appliance
5. Wearable computer
6. Surfing camera
7. Earthquake survivor detector
8. Personal shopper-on-a-card
9. Bionic ear-the deaf hear
10. Intelligent house
11. Thinking car
12. E-book
13. Dr. Toilet
14. Smart clothes
15. Common cold detector
16. Wise refrigerator
17. Bionic eye-the blind can see
18. Miracle implant
19. Drug screener
20. Label alert
21. Automative autopilot
22. Green-thumb chip-improve water utilization
23. Dick Tracy watch
24. Toxin tester
25. Digital spine

Presented to you by *Forbes ASAP,* which asked 30 analysts, engineers, and futurists where the embedded-chip revolution will take us in the next 5, 10, 20 years.

Information is Everywhere

Market research Collection and analysis of data pertinent to current or potential future of a product or service.

Market research, creativity, and intuition are needed to locate opportunities. Conducting research is easier with the advent of the greatest information source

Abbott Wool's Market Segment Resource Locator
www.awool.com

If you want to follow the demographic and economic trends of African Americans, teens, singles, Hispanics, Asian Americans, and those over age 50 this site provides a good start. While not a comprehensive list, the related links can start you on the never-ending Net search to your specific target market.

They have searched the Net for each category and provide a listing of advertising agencies, marketing and research services, media, and government and academic associations that are involved with each specific market.

Examples of some of the items on the teen link are:

- Thorne Creative Research: Qualitative Research
- Yankelovich Youth Monitor: Attitudes and Values Study
- Media: Empowered Young Women (female teens) Web magazine, Nomad, the Brat Journal (teens in military families), **www.WhatNext.com** (teens considering college).

ever—the Internet. Research data previously available only to large corporations with big R&D budgets is now available free to you—or, for a few dollars—Internet access to thousands of dollars of research can be yours. By keeping your eyes wide open your intuition and creativity will blossom.

Secondary Research

Researching industries and markets takes three forms—**secondary, primary,** and "new eyes" research. Secondary research should be your starting point. When you read what someone else has discovered and published, you're carrying out secondary research. Using the Internet and asking Yahoo! to search for census data, locating newspaper articles containing information you think will be helpful—both are forms of secondary research. For instant access to U.S. newspapers, use **www.contemporarybusiness.com/BusNewsN.htm.** For access to international papers, use **www.contemporarybusiness.com/BusNewsI.html.**

Get online and learn what's happening in the rest of the world: products you could import or export, service businesses that might do well in your community, new markets for you to reach.

Contact **trade associations** for industry, supplier, distributor, and customer information. Trade associations conduct research, publish trade journals, and offer books and courses. They also provide data to project how much money one can net in small business. Good research techniques here will save lots of footwork.

At the library begin with the *Encyclopedia of Business and Professional Associations.* Also ask people in the industry which associations they belong to and which magazines they read. Next, move on to the *Directory of Periodicals* or click on **www.mediafinder.com** to find magazines that reach your **target market** or are part of your industry. Use a search engine to locate various associations for your business. Many have online access to their research and periodicals.

Magazines develop **media kits** that provide statistics on their readership. This is one of the quickest ways to get a quick read on a marketplace. Reading magazines and media kits will show you competitive products, what interests your customers, and trends, as well as extensive **demographic** and **psychographic** information.

Secondary research Reading someone else's published (primary) research.

Primary research Interacting directly through interviews, observations, experimentation, questionnaires, and so on.

Trade associations Groups dedicated to the needs of a specific industry.

Target market Segment of market most likely to purchase the product or service.

Media kits Readership profiles, ad information, and market research developed by magazines for potential advertisers.

Demographics Quantifiable population data on race, age, education, income, gender, and so on.

Psychographics Descriptive features on lifestyles.

Figure 2.6

NAMM Home Page

International Music Products Association

5790 Armada Drive • Carlsbad, CA • 92008   760-438-8001 • Fax: 760-438-8257

What's New

Membership

Trade Shows

NAMM University

NAYMM

Research & Statistics

Industry Development

Government Affairs

AMC Home Page

Industry Calendar

Members Only Section

Members' Web Sites

About NAMM

SOURCE: **http://www.namm/com**

> **Action Step 14**

Start Your Industry Research

1. Use the *Encyclopedia of Business and Professional Associations* or the Net. Locate the name of a trade association your business would be part of and make note of the address and phone number. Contact the association and request information. Because you are a potential member, they should send you an enormous amount of information and provide membership details.
2. Use **www.mediafinder.com** or the *Directory of Periodicals* to locate (a) magazines or journals within your selected industry, (b) magazines or journals that reach your

(continued on next page)

Target Customers Persons who have the highest probability of buying a product or service.

Primary Research

After you have the basics about your industry, you are ready to conduct primary research, interacting with the world directly by talking to people—and perhaps interviewing them.

It is time to find out exactly what your potential customer wants. Don't make assumptions! Don't give him or her what you want to give them; *give them what they want.* Go out and ask questions:

- What do you wish your local music store would carry?
- How likely are you to use the Internet to purchase clothing?
- How much do you usually spend each month on fast-food meals?
- How would your ideal automobile dealer behave?
- What would you buy on the Net?

Vendors and suppliers are asked questions such as: What advertising works best in businesses like ours? What products are hot? What services are being offered? Small businessowners are asked: With whom do you bank? Where did you obtain your first financing? What percentage of sales do you spend on advertising? How do you encourage repeat customers?

"New Eyes" Research

"New eyes" research provides a variety of fresh ways to look at a business. Based on your knowledge, experience, and intuition, play detective. You might become a "mystery shopper" to check out your competition. You might sit in your car and snap pictures of a business you're thinking about buying; when **Target Customers** appear, photograph them so that you can profile them later.

Stand in a supermarket aisle and, trying not to look nosy, observe what's in people's shopping carts. For example:

hamburger + chips + ice cream + apples + *Family Circle* =
family with young active children

protein bars + pasta + Runner's World + GQ + chicken =
single man who is athletic, and clothes- and weight-conscious.

Doing this allows you to develop a demographic and psychographic profile of your Target Customer. Profiling will be covered thoroughly in later chapters, but to start training your observation faculties, have some fun and complete Action Step 15.

"New eyes" research is fun. Combined with books, magazines, trade journals, publications (the *Wall Street Journal,* for example) and talking to people, it will get you all the way to your Business Plan. And the Business Plan will either make you a success or show you that your idea isn't worth any more of your time. Better to waste time than money!

Train your mind. Remain open to new ideas, new information, new statistics, new people, and a changing world. Observe everything. Keep your ideas in your Adventure Notebook. The more ideas that pour in, the more likely you are to find the right fit for you and your target market. Chapter 3 will help you sort through the ideas.

The Big Picture

A Business Plan begins with the "big picture"—the industry overview. Industries go through life cycles. Product and services within industries also progress through the cycles—embryo, growth, maturity, and decline. Target markets also go through major changes. The industry overview helps you gain perspective on your **"niche"** and helps the reader (lender or investor) understand why you have chosen to pursue this segment of the market.

To be successful in small business you need to know what business you are really in, and where your business is placed on the life-cycle yardstick. Entrepreneurs tend to be in a big hurry. They want to push on, to get on with it, to throw open the doors to customers, and read the bottom line; and that's not all bad. But before you charge into the arena, step back and examine what's going on in your **industry segment.** Where are the lines? In what part of your community do you see "Going Out of Business" signs? Where are the start-ups? What's hot? What's cooling down? Which business segments will still be thriving three years from now? If you opened the doors of your new business today, how long would it be before your product or services were no longer valuable or wanted?

Let's back up and get the big picture. Before the Industrial Revolution, most people were self-employed. Farmers and sheepherders were risk-takers because they had to be; there were few other options. The family functioned as an entrepreneurial unit.

The growth of megacorporations should not be viewed as a threat to the small venture, but as an opportunity. First because most large corporations are dependent upon small business to produce support products and support services, second because bigger isn't always better, and many small businesses—even those whose markets are expanding rapidly—are barely noticed by large corporations. And therein lies the opportunity! If you're lucky, you'll hit on a high-tech idea and be bought out for millions by Bill Gates!

Target Customers, and (c) magazines or journals for your suppliers. Spend some time on the Net or in the library researching your list and delving deeper into the information.
3. After you have thoroughly done your industry research, select at least one magazine or journal from each of the categories and request a media kit. The media kits will provide you with an excellent start on your specific-category research. Complete this step before moving on, as you will need this information to complete the Action Steps in Chapters 3-5.

▶ **Action Step 15**

Decode the Secrets of the Shopping Cart

Use your "new eyes" to uncover the lifestyle of your customer by analyzing the contents of a supermarket shopping cart. Play detective the next time you're in a supermarket and make some deductions about lifestyles as you observe the behaviors of shoppers.

Give each subject a fantasy name, perhaps associated with a product (Susan Cereal, Steve Steak, and Eloise Sugar) so that you can remember your insights. What can you deduce about each shopper's lifestyle? What do their shoes say? their clothes? their jewelry? their hairstyle? their car? Put these deductions together with a demographic checklist (sex, age, income, occupation, socioeconomic level), and then decide how many of these shoppers are potential Target Customers for your business.

(continued on next page)

Niche A small, unique slice of an industry.

Industry segment Potential slice of industry market share.

Trained marketers look for a category of buyer known as a "heavy user." A heavy user of apples would eat 15-20 apples a week. A heavy user of soda would drink four a day. A heavy user of airlines—called a "frequent flyer"—flies 10-30 times a year. Who are the heavy users in your business?

So, look before you leap; **brainstorm** with your family, friends, and colleagues, and interview potential customers. They will tell you what they want and need. Study the marketplace with your "new eyes." Read! Read! Read!

Brainstorm Your Way into Small Business

Snowboard Express

Annie and Valarie loved to snowboard. For seven years, they went snowboarding every chance they could get—Mammoth, Vail, Tahoe, Snowbird. They kept looking for ways they could make a living snowboarding.

At school, Annie and Valarie discovered the technique of mind mapping—a method of note-taking using clusters and bubbles—to let information flow along its own course. They just knew they could mind map their way into the snowboarding business!

In the center of a large sheet of paper, they wrote "segments." In a bubble, next to "segments" they wrote "travel." Momentum built up. They wrote "beginners," "pros," "teens," "girls," and "parents." Then they wrote "clothes," "gloves," "pants," "sunglasses," "boots," and "shoes." Then they let their imaginations go even further and wrote "travel," "the West," "the East," "the Alps," "contests," "lessons," "trips," "fun," "exciting," "skateboarders," "transportation," "buses."

"This is great fun!" Annie said. "This smells like money and fun!" Valarie exclaimed.

The two friends kept on mapping until they had developed an idea for their business—Snowboard Express—roundtrip weekend bus transportation to the mountain ski resorts from five local pickup points surrounding Salt Lake City. Different resorts were selected each weekend.

Figure 2.7

Snowboard Express Mind Map

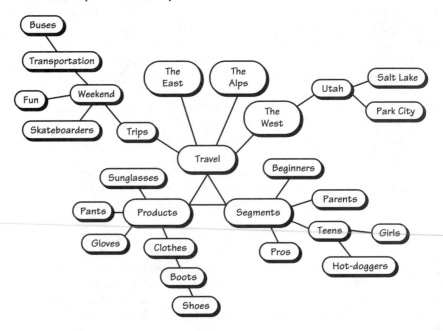

Two or three weeks after they began booking their trips they went back to their mind map and the word "clothes" jumped out at them. They went to one of the major manufacturer's and bought out their seconds and sold them all to their customers at 100 percent over cost within the next four weeks.

After they were in business for only two months, a few women asked if Valarie and Annie could provide weekday trips so they could have the mountains to themselves. A new market segment was uncovered! A gap was filled! They listened to their customers!

Sometime in April the riders were asking what Annie and Valarie were going to do for the summer, they responded by asking, "What are you doing this summer?" The answer they kept hearing was, "I'm going mountain-biking." Valarie and Annie were off to explore the regional mountain bike trails. Then they talked to their bus drivers to determine how they could transport all the bikes on the buses. With their answers in hand and market research completed, Mountain Bike Express was born.

Brainstorming Techniques

The point of the examples is to show what can result from a simple exchange of ideas. If you gather people around you with wit, spark, creativity, positive attitudes, knowledge, and good business sense, the result will almost always surprise you, and could lead to company growth, expanded profits, or perhaps the formation of a new industry. The possibilities are limitless, but the trick is to structure brainstorming sessions in a way that maximizes creativity. A few suggestions follow.

When gathering participants and planning your meeting:

1. Try to find imaginative people who can stretch their minds, and who can set their competitive instincts aside for a while.
2. Remember, in brainstorming sessions, there's a no-no on no's. You're not implementing yet. Skepticism will kill a session.
3. Find a neutral location. You don't want interruptions.
4. Encourage the members of the group to reinforce and believe in each other; challenge ideas.
5. Use helpful equipment. A cassette recorder, paper and pencil, and/or your laptop. If you haven't mind mapped before, look at *Use Both Sides of Your Brain* by Tony Buzan, or *Writing the Natural Way* by Gabriele Rico.
6. Pick a time that is convenient and unrushed (relaxed) for all who will be involved.
7. Find a site where you'll have no, or only very few, interruptions.
8. Invite 10-15 people (some will drop out and you should allow for the no-shows).
9. Schedule the starting time. Relax and serve some food, and begin after about a half-hour.
10. Allow time for self-introduction(s). Tell participants not to be modest. They're getting together with winners, and they want to come on like winners. Have them talk in terms of accomplishments, activities, and interests.

Tips:

- Have everyone arrive with a business idea.
- Before the close of the first meeting, select two or three hot ideas (cast a vote) and ask participants to prepare a one-page checklist summarizing and analyzing the ideas.

- Get together again within two weeks and brainstorm the hot ideas. Make it clear that the basic purpose is to get some energy rolling, not to form a huge partnership.

- The best brainstorming sessions occur when you come brain-to-brain with other creative, positive people. It helps remind you that you've still got it. Brain energy is real and you need to keep tapping it.

Life-Cycle Stages

Economically, socially, technically, and financially our world is changing at incredible speed. The world is at warp speed—a revolution. Product life cycles are measured in terms of months and years rather than decades and generations.

Internet coffeehouses in Africa with telecommunication satellites circling, China opening its doors, Russian capitalistic entrepreneurs, and the United States benefiting by providing services and products to all.

Review past Action Steps and make a list of all the trends and products you unearthed. Divide these into four groups according to the stage of their life cycle (see Figure 2.8). If a trend is just beginning, and is in its formative stage, label it Embryo. If it's exploding, label it Growth. If it's no longer growing and is beginning to wane, label it Mature. If it's beyond maturity and is feeling chilly, label it

Figure 2.8

Life Cycle

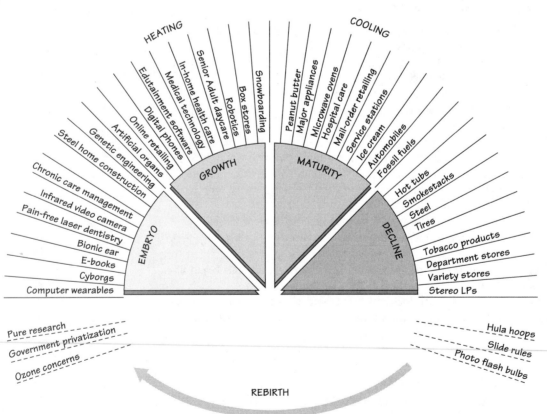

Decline. Think through these life-cycle stages often. Everything changes—products, needs, technology, neighborhoods. Complete Action Step 16.

Here can you find gaps in the life-cycle diagram? Constantly ask yourself where does your business idea and target market lie on the life cycle.

Market signals are everywhere—in the newspaper (classified ads, bankruptcy notices, display ads), in the queue lines at the theater, in the price slashing after Christmas, in discount coupons, rebates, closings, grand openings. With practice, you can follow a product or target market through its life cycle. Which items have you seen go through their life cycle from upscale out of sight to deep discounts? Looking at the life-cycle diagram, you can see that the auto industry as a whole is very mature. Nonetheless, some of its segments remain promising; for example, sport utility vehicles (SUVs), convertibles, and upscale imports—and the VW Beetle is back! In the suburbs you see Yuppie moms driving Volvo convertibles. Despite traffic jams, people are still driving, but the cars they drive reflect changing lifestyles.

You have looked at who you are and what you want. Become a trend-spotter. Now it is time to put the steps together and to generate the right opportunity for you.

▶ **Action Step 16**

Placing Trends on the Life Cycle

Throughout this chapter you have hopefully discovered many trends. Review Figure 2.8 and take the time to place the trends you have identified on the life cycle. How many did you find in the Embryo/Birth stage? in the Growth stage? in the Maturity stage? It's now time to move forward and to try to discover opportunities that are hopefully within the Embryo or Growth stage. If you are entering a Mature market, be ready to meet and beat the competition!

▶ Summary

Two tools will help you chart trends: looking around with "new eyes" (that is, playing marketplace detective), and applying the life-cycle yardstick to products, industries and so on. A life cycle has four phases: embryo, growth, maturity, and decline. Before you open the doors of your small business, you need to be aware of what phase your product is in.

Information on trends is all around you—on the freeways, in the headlines and classifieds, at government agencies, in the many trade associations. This information can give you the big picture, if you know how to seek it out.

For your business plan you will need to demonstrate your knowledge and understanding of the business opportunity you will pursue. Investors look for opportunities within growth segments of growth industries.

Think Points for Success

- The most valuable tool you can have for charting trends is using your "new eyes" research combined with extensive secondary and primary research.

- Keeping your eyes open, to not only your own selected industry, but also developments in other industries that may impact yours, will keep you one step ahead.

- The life-cycle yardstick helps you discover a growth industry, decide what business you're really in, and uncover promising gaps and segments.

- Trends don't usually develop overnight. The signs are out for all to read, months, and sometimes years, in advance.

- Try to latch onto a trend that will help you survive (in style) for the next 3-5 years.

- Keep your eyes posted for new trends at all times. Don't ever assume that because you have caught one trend, that another won't be down the road nipping at your heels.

- Once you know what segment you're in, you can focus your research.

- Save time and money by accessing valuable resources, such as associations and trade periodicals.

- Read everything you can, and talk to everyone you can. The opportunities will be endless.

- Trends are like customers. You can spot some by standing outside and others by staring through a window. Still others won't show up until you're in business, working and sweating away, wondering whether or not you'll make it.

- You're now a great trend-spotter, so it's time to analyze the opportunities you have unearthed.

Key Points from Another View

Better, Faster, Cheaper

Why Life in a Connected World Will Be Different

As transformations go, it is hard to imagine anything more thorough. The telephone industry, which only five years ago was an international club of big, rich corporate bureaucracies, has suddenly found itself swept up in the fastest innovation any business has ever experienced. That will turn traditional markets upside down, as wireless overhauls the fixed link, and data replace voice traffic as the staple of communications. It will burst through existing regulations, yet pose new regulatory dilemmas. And it will crowd the stage with new players; many of them too young to care about the conventions that have governed telecommunications for so long.

The two keys to the future are the plunge in costs—particularly for long-distance traffic—and the rise in capacity. Change may well seem disappointingly slow for the next five years, but in the early part of the new century the consequences will become startling and pervasive. Not only will the communications business itself be transformed, but also other industries that use communications will radically alter the way they work. The business of government will be revolutionized. New industries will spring up, some to run communications services, but far more to offer new services that are as unimaginable today as the spread of the Internet itself would have seemed ten years ago.

For the telephone industry, perhaps the biggest question is what the Internet will do to it. Probably, it will gradually assume the structure of the Internet, where the construction and management of the network is largely separate from the services sold over it. If that happens, the carriage of data will become a commodity business, like the carriage of electricity or freight. A few giant wholesales may buy their capacity from other specialists who finance and build cables, satellites, and other physical paraphernalia of communications.

At either end of the pipe, there will be markets for many smaller specialists. Some will offer business services, such as arranging for some live event to be connected around the world. Others will develop retail products, many of which may include unlimited communications in the purchase price. As Larry Levitan of Andersen Consulting puts it, just as PCs today are advertised as having "Intel inside," these products and services may be branded and sold as having "Telco inside."

If the Internet industry is any guide, this physical separation will be a wonderfully energizing force for telecoms. Mr. Conrades at GTE compares the "open and unregulated edge of chaos of the Internet" with the stable environment that the telecommunications industry has been used to. "The Internet is attracting more intellect and more capital than any economic phenomenon I'm aware of, and that includes the PC," he observes. At Columbia University, Mr. Noam takes

Why Go Global? Look at the Numbers!

World Population by Continents, 1995

	Number	Percent
Far East and Oceania	3,195,290,000	58.82
Africa	745,600,000	13.02
Western Europe	471,480,000	8.24
Eastern Europe	392,840,000	6.86
North America	388,020,000	6.78
Central and South America	382,620,000	6.68
Middle East	148,560,000	2.60
Total World	5,724,410,000	

Our world has grown from 3 billion to almost 6 billion in only 40 years! China and India currently comprise almost 40 percent of the world's population. Only one out of 20 people in the world live in the United States. Is it any wonder why all the huge multinational firms are heading off to the rest of the world? You can too!

Which products and services will those who live outside of the United States need? What resources are available? What cultural and financial obstacles must be overcome? Resources on the Net will be most helpful to you because they are constantly updated. Try the following sites to begin your international search:

www.tradeport.org (assists in searching international markets)

www.lowe.org (search for general international information)

www.gcc.net (in-depth information by country)

www.hg.org (excellent extensive checklist for global ventures and in-depth country information)

www.eyi.com/tdbaw.htm (Ernst & Young's Doing Business Around the World site)

Also look for state trade offices, local colleges with international programs, consulates, embassies, and international chamber of commerces.

the thought a stage further. "No large corporation in the world could match the pace of innovation among the little companies of the Internet."

Calling the 21st Century

Even more profound will be the changes the communications revolution will bring in other industries. An activity such as finding a high-rate certificate of deposit, which might take 25 minutes on the telephone, could take a minute or less using the Internet and some specialized search software (see Figure 2.09). The result should be that information technology, at long last, would visibly increase productivity.

It will also have a powerful affect on the way people do business. Companies and governments will be able to outsource many more activities because it will be easier for them to monitor delivery and quality. That will create many more niches for specialized firms.

For developing countries, the communications revolution should be mostly good news. The combination of wireless and the Internet creates an opportunity

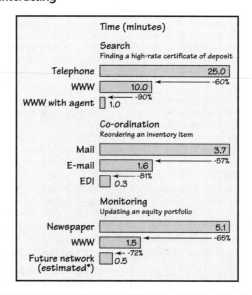

Figure 2.9

The Benefits of Interacting

*Intelligent agents, high speed access, and encryption.

SOURCE: McKinsey.

to leap several technological stages to bring them up to rich-world standards. A thought strikes Mr. Entwistle of Analysys, "Imagine what happens when the satellite telephone—or maybe just a simple mobile telephone—becomes an affordable tool for agricultural-produce trades, fishermen and lorry repairmen in developing countries. You will have an unparalleled turbo-charging effect."

Source: **www.economist.com/editorial/freeforall/21-9-97/tel9.html**

Opportunity Selection

Filtering Your Ideas

3

Entrepreneurial Links

Books

Honey, I Want to Start My Own Business, Azriela L. Jaffe, 1996.

Built to Last, Successful Habits of Visionary Companies, James C. Collins & Jerry I. Porras, 1997.

New Venture Creation, Entrepreneurship within the 21st Century, Jeffry Timmons, 1994.

Websites

www.workingsolo.com

http://sbinformation.miningco.com

www.entreworld.com

Associations/Organizations

American Home Business Association, www.homebusiness.com

Center for Entrepreneurial Studies, www.babson.edu/entrep/index.html

Small Business Advancement National Center, www.sbaer.uca.edu

Publications

Home Business

Nations Business

Black Enterprise

Additional Entrepreneurial Insights

Mary Kay Ash You Can Have It All: Lifetime Wisdom from America's Foremost Woman Entrepreneur, Mary Kay Ash, 1995.

Adventures of a Bystander (Trailblazers, Rediscovering the Pioneers of Business), Peter Drucker, 1998.

Sam Walton: Made in America: My Story, Sam Walton and John Huey, 1993.

Learning Objectives

- Mesh your personal and business objectives with one of the many opportunities in the marketplace.
- Understand that your business objectives provide a positive and unique thrust to your business.
- Narrow your industry research until viable gaps appear.
- Gain insight into using the life-cycle yardstick.
- Discover how problems can be turned into opportunities.
- Understand how to utilize SIC and the new North American Industrial Classification System (NAICS).
- Research your favorite industry using secondary data and the Net.
- Brainstorm creative solutions with mind mapping.
- Use a matrix grid for blending your objectives with your research findings to produce a portrait of a business.
- Define your business.

As you head for one of the doorways to small business, you may feel weighed down with information; that's part of life in the "Information Age." Hopefully, you may also be feeling exhilaration! Opportunities exist that were unheard of two years ago and, in some instances, two weeks ago. The speed of change is awesome. If you've done the research in Chapter 2, you are understandably experiencing information overload. Despite the fact that you're a creative, wound up, and ready-to-charge person, unless you live—vigorously—for 200 years, you'll never be able to follow up on all the changing trends you have discovered.

What you need is a "filtering" system, something like a winepress or a Moulie Mill (the kitchen machine that turns apples into applesauce) to get rid of peels (segments that aren't growing), stems (markets where barriers to entry are too high), and seeds (opportunities that don't mesh with your personal objectives). After completing the Action Steps in Chapter 3, you will have amassed valuable information and identified a well-defined business opportunity.

Welcome to Opportunity Selection

Conducting research will help you exploit gaps, that is, segments in the marketplace. Research shows you what new skills you need to develop. It aims the power of your mind at a particular segment of a small business. It opens up the world!

If you've been doing each Action Step as you read through this book, you're now ahead of the game. Here's a quick preview of the seven steps needed to achieve effective opportunity selection:

1. Keep personal and business objectives in mind throughout the filtering process
2. Learn more about your favorite industry

3. Identify three to five promising industry segments
4. Identify problems that need solutions through research
5. Brainstorm for solutions
6. Mesh possible solutions with your objectives
7. Concentrate on the most promising opportunity

At this point, you have just begun to plan. The marketplace lies open in all its excitement and confusion. The most important thing is not to lose your momentum. Momentum is related to confidence, and confidence helps you win.

Opportunity selection is like a huge funnel equipped with a series of idea filters (see Figure 3.1). You pour everything into this funnel: goals, personality,

Figure 3.1

Opportunity Selection Funnel

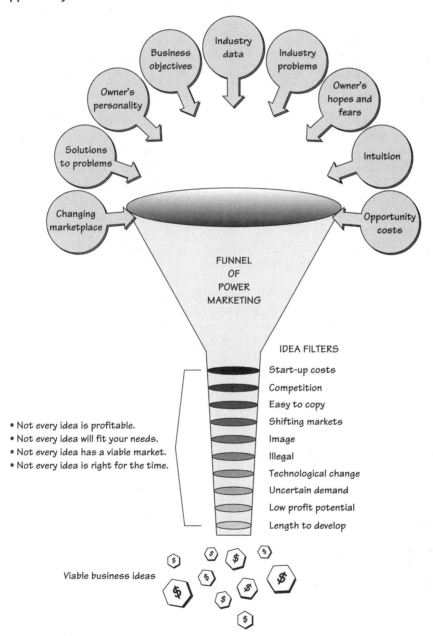

problems, hopes, fears, industry data and problems, research, intuition. And, after narrowing the choices, a viable business filters through to the bottom. Carrying out this process gives you the knowledge of where you're going. And knowledge is power.

International Freelancer

After Eric Duke graduated from law school, he freelanced as a lawyer while planning his wedding and year-long European and Asian honeymoon with his new wife, Christy who had just earned her accounting degree from the University of Minnesota. In planning the trip, Eric and Christy realized their true dream was to live overseas for several years. They figured now was the time to experience overseas living—no kids, no mortgage, no car payments!

They saw the opportunity selection funnel and began their search. On researching the overseas job market, Eric and Christy recognized that continuing to freelance might be the best choice. Eric spent a great deal of time on the Net and in the library researching opportunities. One day he came upon an article about a nearby conference for private investment abroad. Eric signed up and, for $250, was ready to begin his primary research.

At the conference he came into contact with 50 lawyers from around the world. Eric made the best use of every meeting and break by finding out each lawyer's interests and needs. By the end of the meeting he had set up three meetings for the following week. Eric accomplished two things: He had a handshake deal with a Greek lawyer, and a new idea for one of his current clients for an international office. His $250 was well spent!

Without the international research background information or his goals clearly in his mind, Eric would have not been able to respond to the opportunities. Although it may seem that some people fall into opportunities, most "lucky" people are fully prepared!

Before you begin your industry research, review Action Step 5, which asked you to "Inc. Yourself." Think back to what is important to you. Keep this picture in the front of your mind at all times. Stay focused on what you want your life and your business to become. As you begin to explore the vast opportunities within your selected industry, some will mesh better than others. Making your business work for you and your customers will bring you the most satisfaction. Hold your business objectives, personal skills, and strengths in the forefront as you begin to follow the unending research threads.

Industry Research

Searching for trends in Chapter 2, you probably found a half-dozen industries that sounded interesting. You will be brainstorming, mind mapping, funneling, and matrixing ideas and opportunities throughout this chapter. But it's time now to focus in on one industry in more depth and, by the end of the chapter, to define your main business idea. The industry that interests you most might be genetics, robotics, infotainment, food service, travel, education, publishing, **e-tailing,** construction, small manufacturing, or information services. Remember that it must be something that creates great interest and/or passion in you!

As you move to your favorite industry, collect information from your previous Action Steps. What were some of the problems? What were some ideas? Where can you take these ideas?

E-tailing Retailing on the Net.

Figure 3.2

Music USA

North American Music Merchants NAMM University

NAMM University currently offers 28 courses at various locations across the United States.

Sample Course Listing
- Hiring (and Keeping) Great Employees
- Get Wired! Computerizing Your Music Store
- Killer Promotions! Creating & Planning Retail Promotions
- Delivering Killer Service
- Managing Killer Service
- Building a Better Business—Assembly Required!
- Financial Management for Music Products Retailers
- Grow Your Business! Financial Management for Competitive Growth
- Get Organized! High Performance Time and Life Management

NAMM University's mission is to provide high quality professional developmental products and programs to the music products industry, providing performance-based, measurable results through flexible formats and effective instructive design, for both retail and commercial courses.

NAMM University's goal is to develop and enhance member's professional competitiveness, serving the strategic interests of both companies and employers by strengthening their competitive advantage in a changing industry environment.

For more information and/or a current listing, see **http://www.namm.com/namm_u/table_by_date.shtml**

While Chapter 2 focused on the broader picture—trends and problems, the focus of Chapter 3 is on the industry and opportunity you select. Chapter 4 asks you to profile your target market and Chapter 5 looks at **competition.**

What you're now looking for is an accurate picture of opportunities in your selected industry (see Figure 3.3). Conducting secondary and primary research does not eliminate risk but it does definitely reduce it. You need to learn what's breaking, what's cresting, and what's cooling down. You also need to know which potential industry changes are on the horizon. Action Step 14 asked you to start researching by finding at least one association and one periodical associated with a selected industry. Now it's time to explore your selected industry in great depth:

- What role is technology playing in the industry?
- Who are the key players?
- What are the trends?
- Are there barriers to entry? If so, what are they?
- What are the niches?
- Where are the gaps?
- What is the cost of **positioning** yourself?
- Are there distribution changes underway?
- Who are the leaders? What makes them successful?

Competition A contestant in the same arena who is fighting for the business; everyone is fighting for customer's dollars.

Positioning Where a firm or product lies in the buyer's mind.

▶ **Action Step 17**

Determine NAICS or SIC Codes

Find the NAICS or SIC codes for your:

- Industry segment (i.e., retail candy store)
- Suppliers
- Wholesalers
- Customers

Determine through your research the size of your market in dollars and/or volume.

Locate future sales projections for your industry. What is the growth rate? Are you in a **growth segment?**

- What is required to succeed?
- Can the market handle another player?
- Is the industry regulated?

Later, after you have gathered the data, you can use these and other emerging questions as idea filters for the Opportunity Selection Funnel. In addition, you are building background information and statistical data for your business plan. Remember, bankers and investors want to see back-up data; your research will provide facts and figures.

One of the reasons you were asked to look at the big picture in Chapter 2 was to be sure you kept your eyes open to technology and changes throughout the business world. For example, bookstore owners and **www.amazon.com** have to be looking over their shoulders at the new breakthrough with **e-books**—small computers that look and function much like a book. With an initial investment of about $500 for the computer, individuals can download books directly from the Net to their e-book computers, completely eliminating the need for traditional books, bookstores, and shipping costs. What will happen to textbook manufacturers? local bookstores? writers? graphic artists? paper manufacturers? Keep your eyes open!

The point is to find an industry segment where there is room for growth. Using the life-cycle yardstick sharpens a first look at any industry. While reading a newspaper you see a headline, CBS Tries To Shed Stodgy Image in Prime Time—But Can It Be Hip? and make three fast-reflex judgments: (1) the industry is entertainment, (2) the segment is network television, (3) the shows are in the mature phase and on their way to decline.

While driving down a street you see a shopping mall being renovated. You suspect that the face-lift is an attempt to move the mall from a mature or declining phase back to its initial growth phase.

In addition to growth, look for industry **breakthroughs.** What in your selected industry or segment is really humming? Early computers' memory banks filled large rooms and read data from punch cards. The first industry breakthrough was the printed circuit, the second was the microchip processor, the third was the Internet. And the fourth? What breakthroughs are now occurring in your selected industry? Does your business idea capitalize on these latest advances in technology and imagination?

Conducting Secondary Research for Your Selected Industry

Chapter 2 introduced secondary, primary, and "new eyes" research. You may have stumbled across a wonderful opportunity with your "new eyes" and now it's time to develop industry-specific knowledge. Is someone else already conducting a similar business? Is there a market? Are you in a **growth industry?** Will people pay for it? What do you need to know before leaping? The first place to start is with secondary research. If you are lucky, it will provide you with free excellent background information.

Research Using NAICS/SIC Codes

Almost all government statistics, business research, and tracking will utilize the new North American Industry Classification System (NAICS). NAICS will replace the U.S. Standard Industrial Classification (SIC) system. NAICS provides comparable statistics throughout businesses in North America. To locate your selected industry's NAICS code, refer to the government's NAICS manual or contact the NAICS Association at **www.2.viaweb.com/naics/**

E-book Hand-held computer that serves as electronic book.

Breakthrough A new way through, over, under, or around an obstacle.

Growth industry Annual sales increase well above average.

Growth segment An identifiable slice of an industry that is expanding more rapidly than the industry as a whole.

naicmanclait.html, or 435-755-6003. For some time both systems will be in use. NAICS is a numerical system that assigns a number to almost every identifiable industry. The structure of the new system is:

XX	Industry Sector (20 major sectors)
XXX	Industry Subsector
XXXX	Industry Group
XXXXX	Industry
XXXXXX	U.S., Canadian, or Mexican National specific industry

North American Industry Classification System

An example of this coding system follows.

31	Manufacturing
315	Apparel Manufacturing
3151	Apparel Knitting Mills
31511	Hosiery and Sock Mills
315111	Sheer Hosiery Mills
315119	Other Hosiery and Sock Mills
31519	Other Apparel Knitting Mills
315191	Outerwear Knitting Mills
315192	Underwear and Nightwear Knitting Mills
3152	Cut and Sew Apparel Manufacturing
31521	Cut and Sew Apparel Contractors
315211	Men's and Boy's Cut and Sew Apparel Contractors
315212	Women's and Girls' Cut and Sew Apparel Manufacturing
31522	Men's and Boys' Cut and Sew Apparel Manufacturers
315221	Men's and Boys' Cut and Sew Underwear and Nightwear Manufacturing
315222	Men's and Boy's Cut and Sew Suit, Coat and Overcoat Manufacturing
315223	Men's and Boy's Cut and Sew Shirt (except Work Shirt) Manufacturing
315224	Men's and Boy's Cut and Sew Trouser, Slack, and Jean Manufacturing
315225	Men's and Boy's Cut and Sew Work Clothing Manufacturing
315228	Men's and Boy's Cut and Sew Other Outerwear Manufacturing

NAICS and SIC codes help you to:

- discover what industry you're in for statistical purposes.
- define the boundaries of that industry.
- locate customers, suppliers, and competitors.
- reach out to other industries thoughtfully and systematically.
- track customer sales.

Once you have researched your NAICS or SIC codes you are ready to utilize all the resources available. Action Step 18 should be reviewed now and worked on throughout the chapter.

Libraries

The first research stop is the public or school library. Many large cities offer libraries focused on business with excellent technical expertise available—librarians love to help people find needles in a haystack. A librarian can be one of your best resources. Always ask questions.

Technical and very specialized journals may be available only through private corporate libraries. Use your local library's computer to generate a list of these. Also, certain trade groups and associations have specialized libraries. One student, researching the horse-racing industry, located a special library in Los Angeles. With one phone call and a plea—he was in! There are 1000 federal depository li-

---

▶ Action Step 18

Research Your Selected Industry Segment through Secondary Data

Which segment really attracts you? What magnetic pull can't you resist? To help you get started, recall what you discovered in Action Steps 8, 9, 11, 12, 13, and 15.

Keep your views wide-angled by looking at two or three segments that seem promising and interesting to YOU.

After you've decided on "your" segment, research in depth. It will help to organize your research if you categorize trends, target markets, competition, industry breakthroughs, and market share. But for now, while looking for opportunities, focus primarily on the segment and its changes, and be sure to file all extraneous data for upcoming Action Steps.

If you're working, alone, write an industry overview. If you're working with a team, there will be less confusion if each team member writes an overview, and later shares his or her perspective with the others.

This is a never-ending Action Step. Once you are in business you have to be as diligent in keeping up with the segment as you were in your initial research. Only now it's more important because your money is on the line!

Figure 3.3

NAMM University

North American Music Merchants Music USA

Music USA is NAMM's annual statistical review of the music products industry. It contains data on units shipped from manufacturers to retailers for 23 product categories and social and economic indicators affecting the industry. Music USA is available to both members ($15) and nonmembers ($45) of NAMM.

Features

- Industry Revenue at a Glance
- Segment Data
- Fretted Products
- Sound Reinforcement
- The Piano Market
- The Organ Market
- Microphones, Etc.
- Printed Music
- General Accessories
- The School Music Market
- Karaoke Products
- Portable Keyboards
- Electronic Music Products
- The Percussion Market
- The Music & Sound Industry Summary

- Import/Export Statistics
- Economic, Demographic, Education and other Industry Data
- Gallup Survey
- Salaries, Wages, & Benefits
- Music Retailing (Excerpts from NAMM's 1996 Cost of Doing Business Report)
- Profile of the American Music Dealer—Part VI
- NAMM Supported Research Projects and Initiatives
- SAT Scores and Arts Study

SOURCE: **http://www.namm.com/ rsrchdev/rsrchdev.shtml**

---

braries in the United States. Through them you can access a wealth of federal and international data at no cost.

Trade Associations

Your next research stop should be the trade associations within your selected industry. Detailed information about these associations is provided in the Directory of Associations. Select four or five that look the most promising and request information. Many of their products are available only to members, and membership fees for start-ups are usually low. Associations provide vast resources—you usually can't go wrong looking for data there.

As an example, the National Association of Music Merchants (NAMM) **www.namm.com** furnishes incredible resources for the music product industry. Want to learn about the Czech Republic's music marketplace? NAMM will sell you a report for $50, which is probably less than the cost of two international calls. Secondary information always provides you with a starting point. By first reading a report on the Czech marketplace, your primary research will be much easier. Your questions to those in the industry will now be more focused and productive. Secondary information sharpens intuition as well.

Globus & National Trade Data Bank (NTDB)
www.domino.stat-usa.gov/tradetest.nsf or your local federal depository library

For international market research, trade opportunities, individual country analysis, import-export statistics, and leads from defense, commerce and agricultural departments, this is the granddaddy of databases. The NTDB site sponsored by the U.S. Department of Commerce is available online at the above address or at your local federal depository library for free.

You will have access to daily trade updates as well access to individual country trade and business reports. The Commerce Department ranks the export prospects of 40+ countries. Rankings consider the size and projected growth, the market for U.S. exports and imports, and local and Third World competition. For example, one can enter the database and find out the top five export sectors for India or Turkey.

Music USA **(www.namm.com)** renders data on 23 product categories as well as general social and economic indicators. For $45 this information (see Figure 3.3) can be in your hands! This is information fortunately not used by many of your potential competitors. Get a leg up and know the industry upside down before you leap. Enter from strength!

For specific training opportunities, NAMM presents classes throughout the United States (see Figure 3.2) that get entrepreneurs up and running quickly and efficiently, saving time, money, sweat, and tears. If you can't attend classes, many associations offer start-up manuals. Some would-be entrepreneurs are cocky and won't take advice from others. Don't make this mistake! Developing expertise and experience takes time, energy, and money. Be open and willing to learn from others.

Trade Shows

Another way to research your selected industry is to attend trade shows—events where manufacturers and corporations in a common industry demonstrate their wares to potential customers. While there, snoop on your competition, pick up literature, talk to everyone you can, and soak it all in. Most trade shows are open only to firms within the industry. Ask your industry friends to take you as a guest or, if nothing else works, get business cards made and you may be able to get in. To locate trade shows for your industry click on **www.tsnn.com.** Search by industry, month, and/or city. Additionally, this Website locates where your potential competitors are exhibiting.

Additional Resources

Newspapers—Several trend-watchers monitor more than 6000 regional and daily newspapers. Study your local newspapers for business and other news. Scan papers throughout the United States to find out what is happening. For a bigger picture, read the *Wall Street Journal* or the *Christian Science Monitor.* Thousands of daily, weekly, national, and college papers are linked at **www.newslink.org.** If you are exploring a service business, research other towns' papers to see if someone is currently providing such a service, phone the owners, and ask questions! Remember, people love to talk about their "business baby."

Action Step 19

Net Research Assignment

Action Step 19 asks you to complete several industry-specific research assignments.

1. Research at least three associations in your industry. What services do they offer? What classes and publications do they offer? What research can they provide? What is the cost to join?
2. Click on **www.tsnn.com** to locate trade shows for your selected industry.
3. Using **www.newslink.org**, research your industry and customers. If you have a technical product you will need to research it through specific databases found in the library and online.
4. Prepare a list of all the better magazines and trade journals for your selected industry. Try to read at least four or five. This is time very well spent. If they are not available to you, locate someone in your desired line of business and ask if they will loan copies to you.
5. Go to **www.sba.gov.** What sources on the SBA site do you think will be most helpful?
6. Go to **www.census.gov** and explore census data.
7. Using *Standard and Poor's, Hoovers Online,* or *Dun and Bradstreet,* profile several of your competitors.
8. Locate a "virtual community" or newsgroups on the Net for your business.

Magazines—Reviewing magazines keeps one up to date. The ads tell you what's hot and where the money is flowing. Use **www.mediafinder.com** or **www.newslink.org.**

Trade Journals—These are a valuable resource once you have selected the industry you want to enter. Many journals are also available online.

Banks—Banks make money by "renting" or loaning money. Large corporate banks have staffs of economists, marketing experts, and so on, who research and write forecasts and reports of economic trends. Request copies of these reports.

Brokerage Firms—These service-oriented companies have staff analysts who survey specific industries. The analysts gather earnings statistics, attend corporate and stockholder meetings, read annual reports, and publish reports about individual companies and industry overviews. These data can help to predict the direction an industry is taking. Reports are available to clients of the firms, but are also sometimes available at libraries.

Planning Offices—Cities and counties employ planners to chart and plan future growth. Check the city and county offices' listings in the phone book to locate these offices. For the best service, however, you'll need to visit the office, make friends with the staff, and be pleasant and patient. Many counties use federal data to develop annual reports. If you are planning a retail establishment or a manufacturing facility, these visits are essential.

Reports from Colleges and Universities—State universities publish annual and semiannual reports on economic conditions in the state where they are established. You can probably get copies of these by writing to the university publications office. Reports are also published by private institutions of higher learning with special interests. A vast amount of technical research is conducted at universities throughout the world. Search directly on the Net and talk directly with cutting-edge leaders.

Real Estate Firms—Large commercial and industrial real estate firms have access to developers' site research. The more specific your request, the easier it will be for these firms to help you. Familiarize yourself with the dynamics of the area. Which firms are going into business? Which firms are relocating? Where is expansion occurring?

SBA—The Small Business Administration of the U.S. government has an excellent Website, **www.sba.gov.** This Website provides access to hundreds of resources: franchising, financing, start-up costs, federal and state programs, and so on.

U.S. Department of Commerce (www.doc.gov)—This department publishes an annual U.S. Industrial Outlook that forecasts growth rates for the coming year. Check your local chamber for additional information and support.

www.census.gov—This Website gives access to 100 current industrial reports on over 5000 manufactured products and is a treasurechest of data.

Bureau of Labor Statistics (**http://stats.bls.gov**)—Economic and employment statistics can be obtained in hard copy or downloaded from its Website.

www.marketingtools.com—Consumer trends and demographic changes are tracked on this Website.

www.brint.com—This is one of the most extensive general business sites on the Web. It searches the Net-for forums, books, articles, announcements, comprehensive indexes of magazines, journals, and publishers.

STAT-USA Internet
www.stat-usa.gov or your local federal depository library

STAT-USA Internet scours the government information vaults, assembles that information in one location, and delivers it via advanced computer technology. The information is available by subscription online for $150 a year. For free access to the information locate your local federal depository library at **www. access.gpo.gov/su_docs/dpos/adpos003.html.** This is compiled by the Economics and Statistics Administration within the Department of Commerce.

Historical and current economic and financial data are both available. This impressive collection of data is easy to use and provides excellent statistical back-up data for a business plan.

Consumer Price Index (CPI), housing, employment, manufacturing, economic policy and general economic indicators are available.

Websites—To locate industry information on the web begin searching under your selected industry and follow the never-ending thread. About 1,000 sites are added each day. Go to your competitors' Websites to get general industry information. In Chapter 5 we will delve deeper into researching competitors.

Standard & Poor's Industry Surveys—These provide an overall review of industry and major players and is available at your local library.

Company Directories on the Web—Hoover's covers 10,000 firms **www. hoovers.com;** Dun & Bradstreet (brief profiles are free), **www.dnb.com;** Thomas Register (manufacturers), **www.troam.com.**

Predicasts, Wall Street Journal Index, Find-SVP, Small Business Sourcebook, Encyclopedia of Business Information Sources—Excellent tools for information.

Locating Private Database Vendors

A number of private database service firms have emerged and many of them are frequent advertisers in *Marketing Tools* and *American Demographic Magazine.* Contact American Demographics, Inc. at 127 West State, Ithaca, New York 14850. Also, many metropolitan newspapers now sell special research studies at modest prices. Vendors specialize in niche markets, such as boomers, healthcare, teens, and Internet users. Others provide data for manufacturers, site selection, and locating foreign markets.

Market Statistics: Producers of the *Survey of Buying Power* and **www.sbponline.com** provides data for every United States city with a population over twenty-five hundred. The U.S. city edition includes lifestyles and market potential. Business characteristics, consumer expenditures, and five-year projections are also available. Contact Market Statistics, 355 Park Avenue South, New York, New York 10010-1789. 888 2SBP-WEB.

Business Geographic Magazine, **www.bg.geoplace.com,** focuses on business demographics and GIS (geographic information systems). Contact Business Graphics, c/o GIS World Inc., 400 N. College Ave. Suite 100, Fort Collins, CO 80524.

NDS (National Decision Systems), **www.natdecsys.com,** provides excellent demographic reports starting around fifty dollars. Contact NDS in San Diego, 800-866-6510.

Action Step 20

Brainstorming Solutions

Okay, here's where you need to get creative. Conduct primary research with everyone you meet. If your business idea is fairly well developed, you should be presenting it to people and asking them to brainstorm with you as to its fit in the marketplace.

You will generate better ideas and solutions now that you have completed your secondary research. Have fun at this stage as you continue to develop your ideas. Write down everyone's input. You may want to take a tape recorder.

- Which niches can you own?
- Which niches might be the most profitable?
- Which niches will be easiest to reach?
- What can you do to be unique?

Claritas, **www.claritas.com,** offers market assessments utilizing their PRIZM Profile Reports. Allows you to profile customers, competition, and markets. Contact Claritas, 53 Brown Road, Ithaca, NY 14850-1262. 800-234-5973.

American Business Information, Omaha, NE; Dun & Bradstreet, Murray Hill, NJ; Decision Systems Inc., Fairfax, VA; On Target Mapping, Pittsburgh, PA; CACI, Arlington, VA; and Wessex, Winnetka, IL are additional private database providers. Check the Web for additional vendors.

Searching the Web is an adventure because you never know what you will encounter. Many researchers and writers can be reached directly via the Web. University Websites lead you to researchers in your specific field, crucial for those involved in high-tech or manufacturing. First, visit home pages, if available. Your questions may be answered there. Additional links to sources may also aid you. If not, send an e-mail requesting information.

You may be lucky and find an online community such as **www.foodon-line.com**, a site that provides a virtual community and marketplace for professionals and vendors in the food equipment and ingredients industries. This Website saves enormous amounts of time in locating products, employees, proposals, regulations, and providing online chats to locate additional information. Jump on the Net and locate your **"virtual community,"** which will give you access to possibly thousands of experienced people. Start tossing out questions on the chatlines. What you basically will accomplish is access to free consultants.

Janet Shore had only three days to complete a restaurant proposal requiring California products. She jumped on the Net, completed the proposal, and won the contract. After awarding Janet the contract, the vendor asked how she was able to get the proposal together in three days. Hard work, diligence, past experience and THE NET!

If you are developing a product and need patent information, read Chapter 10 before going further.

Primary Research on Your Selected Research

After spending days or weeks researching your favorite industry, whittle down the opportunities to two or three by using the Opportunity Selection Funnel (see Figure 3.1). Use the questions on the funnel to help you.

Get off the Net and out of the library! Time to step out and talk directly with people involved in the industry: salespeople, developers, manufacturers, competitors, suppliers, and customers. You now have a strong knowledge base and a million questions. Ask away! Take notes. Now is the time to set your ego on the shelf. Listen to everything people say. Remember, your goal is to provide a service or product that your market needs and wants, not a product you want to give them!

Primary research can be conducted via phone, mail, and personal face-to-face interviews. Depending on your needs, time, and available money, select which research method is best for you. When conducting personal interviews, listen carefully, "read between the lines." Ask intelligent follow-up questions. Probe your potential customer's psyche. Action Step 20 helps you to define your opportunity further.

It's time to start sharing your business ideas with others. This is a scary time. Many entrepreneurs are afraid to share their idea for fear someone will steal it. It can happen. But if you don't share your idea, how can you turn it into a business? In Appendix B you will find a confidentiality agreement that may make you feel more comfortable.

Virtual community Online group of individuals within industry sector.

Industry Segmentation and Gap Analysis

Industry segmentation breaks down potential markets into as many "digestible" subsegments as possible, just as is done with NAICS codes. The more you learn about an industry, the further, you'll be able to go. This procedure helps you isolate opportunity gaps and see combinations of gaps that may constitute markets. Figure 3.4 illustrates a mind map that "explodes" one segment of the food industry. This is the kind of thinking we want you to do in Action Step 21. It's another brainstorming activity, so have fun with it.

Healthy Gourmet

Susan and John Johnson, founders of Healthy Gourmet, searched for gaps and opportunities by taking a look at a major, far-reaching trend—the meal replacement market. People want fresh, high-quality food but they don't want to cook! The "time bind" is fueling this market change.

Frozen dinners have been available since 1953 but these can't be compared to the freshly prepared, nutritionally balanced meals from Healthy Gourmet. How about grilled chicken with cous cous salad, peach dressing, and fresh fruit?

After coming home to face cooking one time too many, Susan realized that there had to be many other busy individuals hoping for a hot wonderful gourmet meal as they opened their front doors.

▶ **Action Step 21**

Mind Mapping Your Business

Narrow the Gaps; Watch Your Target Customer Emerge

Consider all the secondary and primary information you have gathered. Take out paper and pencil and start a mind map (see Figure 3.4). Review all the ideas you have researched. Sketch out your mind map focusing on the specific segment you have narrowed in on.

You need to stay with this segment until you know whether or not it will work for you.

Ideas come together as you place opportunities next to each other. You will be able to identify the most promising gap in your selected industry.

Figure 3.4

Healthy Gourmet Mind Map

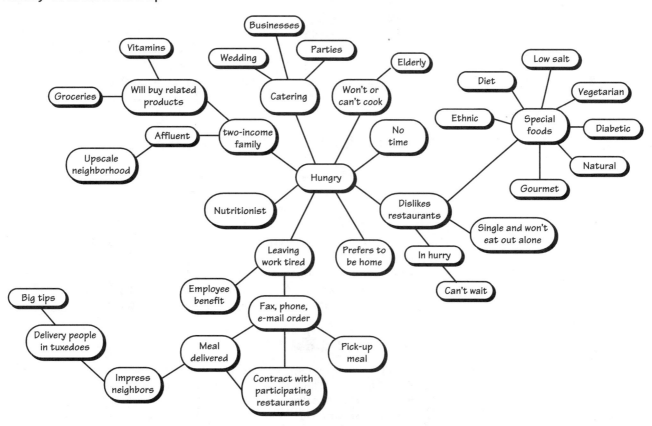

Researching their selected industry Susan and John recognized that no one was producing fresh, made-from-scratch, calorie-controlled gourmet meals that met the guidelines of the American Heart Association, the American Cancer Society, and the American Dietetic Association. Others merely produced frozen meals, diet replacement drinks, take-out food, and so on.

Quality meals that were convenient and nutritionally balanced represented a gap the Johnsons knew they could fill. With a 3000-square-foot kitchen, a varied menu of 1–21 meals per week, and delivery to one's door or at several pickup points twice a week, they had developed a product that met their customers' needs.

Healthy Gourmet located in the heart of a leading high-tech community whose demographics are "young" and "highly educated." Chapter 4 delves deeper into the Johnsons target market.

Two years after opening their doors they are grossing over $750,000 and have opened a second location in Los Angeles with plans for further expansion.

In business, one needs to segment markets and then differentiate products or services to meet their chosen target markets' needs. By requiring no minimum orders, Susan and John Johnson enabled busy people to access their product on their own terms without preset requirements.

Find gaps in the marketplace and exploit those gaps by developing products and services that fulfill the needs of the marketplace. Listen closely to your customers. They will lead you in the right direction.

Wrap your product around your target market through pricing, product development, marketing, advertising, and location. Many times, opportunities in the market exist not because there is a need for a new product or service, but because there are new target markets: a product can be delivered differently, priced lower, or offered in combination with another product or service.

When you write your Business Plan, explain why you have selected a particular industry segment (gap). If you have chosen a promising segment and have communicated your excitement about it, you'll have developed a "hook" for the banker or venture capitalist who will be reading your plan.

More Brainstorming for Possible Solutions

Brainstorming is a process used by many groups—think tanks, middle management, small businesses, and major corporations—to generate fresh ideas. The goal is to come up with lots of ideas, some that may seem far out or even erroneous, and then, as momentum grows, to see how concepts develop. The key to brainstorming is to reserve judgment initially so that creativity is not stifled.

What follows is a recap of a brainstorming session held by the Info Team, the founders of the Software School (see Chapter 15 for the final business plan), as they began to transform problems into business opportunities. As you read, consider not only the information you gather but also the process involved.

Software School

Before they began, three friends listed ideas for businesses that had come to them during the earlier steps of the opportunity selection process. One wanted to start a company to design computer games, and go into head-to-head competition with Nintendo. Another, a graphic artist, said he could certainly help with the artwork. "You're a writer," Robert Jericho said to Derek Campbell. "You could write the copy."

On a flipchart, Derek wrote "Design Computer Games."

"Here's another," Robert said. "Let's take over Microsoft!"

For a half-hour, they transferred their ideas—game design, leveraged buy-outs, software design, retailing, end-user training, and marketing—onto the flip chart. Robert, who was turning into a mad inventor, wanted to design a computer program that boiled down all election data into a single voter, who then made the decision on who became president.

Phil Carpenter suggested a takeover of all Chinese hardware manufacturers.

"Time for a break," Derek said.

When they came back from their break, Phil flipped to a clean sheet on the chart, and proceeded to draw a mind map. As Phil developed the mind map, five areas for a business emerged: hardware manufacture; software manufacture, including game design; retailing (both hardware and software); training, taking advantage of the speed of change in the industry, which left users in the dust; and marketing and promotion of software products.

Further refining of areas of the mind map brought training and marketing into the foreground, with the production of hardware and software receding into the background.

Excitement built up in the room as the ideas flowed, and soon all three friends were standing at the flipchart, adding their ideas and amendments to the mind map. As the brainstorming session wound down, they had identified two areas to explore.

The first area was computer training, taking up where software makers left off. They could start in one location and then do on-site training in businesses and corporations.

The second area was marketing and promotion. Robert, who had worked for Microsoft, knew there were many small companies, bootstrap operations run by dreamers whose basic skills did not include Target Customers, promotion, or building an image.

"You could consult," Phil said. "You love that."

"I'd love to do the promotions!" Robert said.

There was a silence.

"So," Derek said, "we've got two options that look pretty good. How do we decide?"

"How about a matrix," Derek said.

"A what?"

"It's a way of weighing what you really want. I learned about it from one of my inventor buddies. He called it an Opportunity Matrix."

"Let's try it," they said.

It's helpful to summarize after a brainstorming session so that you can identify the most useful ideas. Let's summarize what happened in this session:

1. Using the mind-mapping device, the team identified problems and possible solutions.
2. All ideas were good ideas.
3. The two ideas that looked best were computer training and software marketing and promotion.
4. Could they do both at once? Or, would one have to go on the back burner?

Matrix Analysis

Whereas some people like to use lists, mind maps, or opportunity funnels for arriving at conclusions, others prefer a more systematic numeric method. A **matrix grid** can provide a desired structure to serve as another type of filter. After you have brainstormed some possible solutions, you need to improve your focus on them and evaluate them. The matrix grid in Figure 3.5. helped Info Team do this.

At their next meeting, they rated each possible solution on the objectives, which they had designated earlier. On review the software school received the highest total of points from the group. The key people saw this as an area where their teamwork skills within a fast-growing industry could best be utilized. In addition, the cost to develop a school was relatively low compared to other choices. The opportunity gap seemed wider, there was little competition, and the barriers to entry (cost) were very low in comparison.

As trainers, they would have to:

Solve problems. Businesspeople have problems to solve and tasks to perform. Computers reduce the workload. All one needs is an open mind and the right software.

Provide clarity. Software documentation can be confusing. The school would devise a super-clear, streamlined, space-age teaching system.

Offer speed. Businesspeople are in a hurry—time is money. Could the school teach software in a week? a day? a half-day?

Build a psychological cushion. The founders would start a club. Once the students had taken a course, they'd be a software Club Member for life and entitled to take the course over again at no charge. In addition, the instructors would provide online assistance as needed for the first six months after they attended the class.

Figure 3.5

Opportunity Matrix Grid for Software School

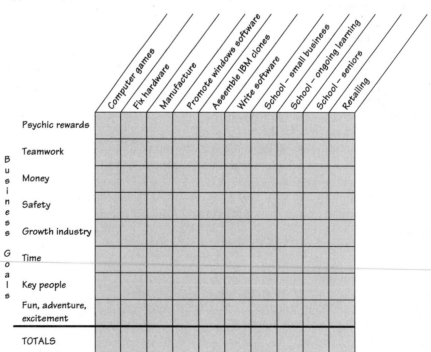

Matrix grid Screens through which ideas are passed in order to find solutions.

Psychological cushion A unique, untouchable rung on the ladder in your Target Customer's mind.

Charge reasonable fees. Research studies showed that businesspeople would pay $200 a day to learn software.

Be enjoyable. If clients are having fun learning, they'll relax and learn more. If they learn more, they'll spread the word about the school.

Now prepare a matrix grid to help you focus on the best course of action for your opportunity. Action Step 22 tells you how to do it.

Taking Stock

What have you learned about opportunity selection? Before you answer this, take a minute to rethink what you want to achieve with your small business. If you feel a little uneasy about how fast you've run the last couple of laps, perhaps it's because you haven't identified your industry or the right opportunity for you. If it doesn't feel like home, you should sense it now.

Have you whittled down the list from hundreds of trends to industry segments to the one opportunity that emerged through all your research? Does it feel like home? If so, you are ready to define your new business.

Define Your Business

Watch a painter at work at an easel. She works close to the canvas, layering the paint with brush and spatula. But at regular intervals, the painter steps back for a long view of the work. Up close, the artist can see only brushstrokes and colors, but from a few feet away, the entire painting can be seen. From a few more feet, the entire landscape being painted becomes apparent.

What business is the painter in?

Watch a carpenter framing a new house. He works close to the wood, nailing with quick strokes of his hammer. However, to get a view of the total house—the structure that will become someone's home—he must walk across the street. He has to step back, away from his detailed work, to see the shape of the whole.

What business is the carpenter in? Is he in the nail-driving business? the framing business? the home-building business? Or is he in the business of satisfying the age-old dream of home ownership?

Only by stepping back can you answer the question of what business you are in. This is a very important question.

The lesson here is to know what business you are in. You need to know who your customers are and what satisfies their internal and external needs. Mary Clark's experience illustrates the importance of understanding exactly what business one is really in.

Clark's Stables

Mary Clark, a 30-year-old software engineer, had always been more interested in riding her prize-winning quarter horses than in teaching school. When her grandmother died and left her $300,000, Mary made a down payment on a boarding stable and left the corporate world forever—or so she thought.

The boarding stable was rundown. It had stalls for 50 horses, but only 25 stalls were occupied. Mary did everything she could think of to make the place better for horses. She spent $57,000 rebuilding, painting, and grading and made Clark's Stables a very attractive place. She bought the highest quality of feed and gave the horses the best care money could buy.

When owners began to move their horses to other stables, Mary couldn't understand. She had not increased her fees, and she treated the horses like friends. In six months, only six customers remained. In nine months, she was behind on her mortgage payments. In her tenth month, Mary had to sell the stable.

Mary had made the simple mistake of thinking horses were her customers. Her real Target Customers were young girls between age 7 and 14 and their parents. Mary thought she was in the business of stabling horses. The business she should have seen she was in was providing girls a fun, social activity. Parents viewed the stables as a safe afterschool activity. The girls wanted recreation, training, and social activities. Mary's customers left because other stables provided parties, barbecues, and horse shows with lots of ribbons and trophies. Little girls wanted prizes, but Mary was more interested in satisfying her horses than the little girls.

What Business Are You Really In?

Now that you have defined a very specific industry segment it is time to define what you do. Naming anything is a game of words, and a small business is no exception. The following examples can help you define your business. If you're hesitant about defining at this early stage, remember what happened to Clark's Stable. When defining what business you are really in, ask yourself why people buy the product. People do not buy products or services; they buy what the product or service will do for them: enhance their lives; make life easier, safer, more fun, and so on. A founder of a major cosmetics firm always said the firm was in the business of "selling jars of hope." Use the following to help you to zero in on what business you're in.

If You're in . . .	Try Saying . . .
personal finance software	I'm in the peace of mind business.
small business teacher	I'm in the dream to reality business.
cosmetic plastic surgeon	I'm in the don't grow old business.
Porsche car sales	I'm in the ego gratification business.
gourmet cookware	I help people be Martha Stewart.
personal fitness trainer	I keep you young and buff.
coffeehouse	I provide a place to see and be seen.

Keep honing your definition of your business. Your **business definition** should be a work in progress as you further explore your target market and competition. Check your definition with your potential Target Customers, since they may perceive your business differently. You may have new stationary printed after you talk to them, but as business expenses go, that's a small price to pay to overcome customer confusion. Four of our favorite business definitions or mission statements are:

Peapod—"To fundamentally improve people's lives by bringing interactive grocery shopping to a broader consumer market. Amazing and delighting each of our customers."

Fast Company—"Fast Company is where best practice meets big ideas; new talent meets innovative tools; the emerging business community meets the emerging conversation about the future of business."

Deux Amis Needlepoint—"We believe there is nothing so beautiful as an exquisitely painted canvas: or the enjoyment, satisfaction and relaxation derived from fine handwork and stitching a lovely design with beautiful threads on fine canvas."

Chicken Soup—"We're selling stories that encircle the heart and penetrate the soul and cuddled up to make you feel better."

Business definition A clear picture of the enterprise.

Razzle-dazzle your consumer with the best business definition you can write in Action Step 23.

Being in business today is all about satisfying needs, and providing benefits. You find a need, you satisfy it, and then you translate the results into a benefit to your customer. This new era of knowledge-based/experienced-based marketing involves two key principles. First, all of a firm's efforts should be focused on satisfying the needs of a customer at a profit. Second, the name of the game is to create or develop your own pie; that is, to own the market as opposed to sharing it with competitors. You create and grow your market niche or segment by constantly changing your product or service as dictated by the customer. Marketing today emphasizes networking, creativity, associations, partnerships and requires:

1. Integrating customers' needs and desires and your strategies into the development of the product. Market needs drive the product.
2. Focusing your knowledge and experience on a specific and Targeted Customer segment, or niche. The idea is to own this niche. The old concept of sharing a market is obsolete for small business ventures.
3. Creating customer, supplier, and even competitor relationships that will sustain and grow your customer base. Cooperation is the key.

Marketing encompasses everything a business does to get products and services from the manufacturer to the customer so that the consumer is satisfied and the seller has met his or her objectives.

▶ Summary

You've found the industry that interests you. You've applied the life-cycle stick to learn what stage the industry is in and how long you've got to make your business go. If your skills don't exactly guarantee success, you're sure of at least three things: you know where to acquire the skills you need, you know how long it will take to get them, and you're having fun exploring the marketplace.

You have brainstormed your business objective and reviewed the interlocking concepts—life cycle, competition, and industry breakthrough. A business idea should be starting to mesh for you. Continue to explore the gaps in the marketplace.

Nobody wants to hear about a "me too" business. Stress your differentiation, your position—and translate features into market-hungry benefits. It is important to show how you have an edge over the competition. Try to think in terms of a "personal niche monopoly."

Think Points for Success

- Build your business around your likes and your strengths.
- Opportunity selection directs the power of your mind toward a particular industry segment.
- Spend time early on learning about the industry, its major players, and its trends.
- Utilize all secondary data available, so when you move out to conduct primary data research you will come from a position of knowledge and strength.
- Finding a gap and exploiting it is much easier and more successful than being a "me, too" competitor. If someone else owns the niche, find another, unless you are willing to hold on and fight the competition with deep pockets.

▶ **Action Step 23**

Define Your Business

1. Brainstorm what business you're really in. Let your mind play at this. Remember your customers' comments when you were probing their psyche.
2. Think of yourself riding up 50 floors in an express elevator. You have 30 seconds to explain to a stranger what your business is about. What will you say? Can you razzle-dazzle him or her so they will ask for more? Be sure you include the benefits and your target market.
3. Keep working and refining your "elevator speech" throughout the semester.

- Recognize that not all opportunities are equal.
- Acknowledge that not all opportunities can be profitable.
- Don't fall in love with a product or a market.
- There has to be a compelling reason for the customer to change.
- Dare to be different in your approach.
- Define your business. Razzle-dazzle in 50 words or less. Make them beg for more information.
- Research! Research! Research! And Never Stop!

Key Points from Another View

Benchmark: Encourage Wild Ideas

IDEO Product Development is the world's most celebrated design firm. Its ultimate creation is the process of creativity itself. For founder David Kelley and his colleagues, work is play, brainstorming is a science, and the most important rule is to break the rules.

Walk into the offices of IDEO Product Development and you quickly appreciate how many ways there are to describe new products. Computer screens display intricate designs embedded in software. Long rolls of butcher paper, spread out over conference tables, record doodles, scribbles, notes. Prototypes are everywhere and in every medium: cardboard, foam, wood, plastic.

Standing in the middle of things, admiring the creative chaos, is David M. Kelley, 45, IDEO's founder. Kelley describes IDEO as "a living laboratory of the workplace." The company "is in a state of perpetual experimentation," he says. "We're constantly trying new ideas in our projects, our work space, even our culture."

IDEO is arguably the world's most influential design firm. About 250 people work in a network of offices stretching from San Francisco to London to Tokyo. They create 90 new products a year, including some that have become familiar parts of our daily lives: Levolor blinds, Crest's Neat Squeeze toothpaste container, telephones and answering machines from AT&T. Others are icons of the digital age: cutting-edge laptop computers, virtual reality headgear, even automatic teller machines. But the firm's defining creation is the process of creativity itself. To understand how IDEO works, you have to see how it looks.

The company's main offices are spread over seven low-rise buildings in downtown Palo Alto, the heart of California's Silicon Valley. The people here (about 140 in all) work under tight deadlines and intense pressure. But you wouldn't know it from the feel of the place. Kelley is adamant that people can't be creative without heavy doses of freedom and fun. So there are no "bosses" or job titles at IDEO; all work is organized into project teams that form and disband in Chicago or Tokyo if they can find a colleague willing to switch.

"The most important thing I learned from big companies," Kelley says, "is that creativity gets stifled when everyone's got to follow the rules."

That same spirit infuses the offices, which display lots of funky touches and clever twists. Consider the small matter of bicycles. It seems nearly everyone at IDEO bikes to work, so "parking" is a problem. The solution? An intricate system of hangers and pulleys that allows people to wheel their bikes to their cubicles, raise them to the ceiling, and retrieve them as needed. It's a bicycle rack in the sky.

There's also the matter of noise. The firm's twenty-somethings like to play music while they work, which can drive the others crazy. So IDEO created a special area for the youngsters—dubbed the Spunk Space—complete with a DC-3 aircraft wing that pivots on a pole to serve as a room divider.

Of course, all this fun and freedom is in the service of something tangible; radical new ideas that become important new products. Kelley says the primary "engine for innovation" at IDEO is its distinct approach to brainstorming—the only part of company life where strict rules do apply.

Sessions are held in spaces dubbed (not-so-creatively) Brainstormer Rooms. There are three such rooms in Palo Alto, and they all have the same main features. Participants can draw almost anywhere: on whiteboard-covered walls, on conference tables covered with butcher paper. Multimedia tools—television, VCR, computer projector, video screen—allow for in-depth presentations or sensory stimulation. To help maintain the right spirit, IDEO's five principles of brainstorming are emblazoned on the walls: Stay focused on the topic. . . . Encourage wild ideas. . . . Defer judgement. . . . Build on the ideas of others. . . . One conversation at a time.

Project leaders call a brainstorm at the beginning of a new assignment or when they feel stumped. A typical session involves eight participants from a mix of disciplines: industrial design, engineering, human-factors analysis. Invitations go out over e-mail and attendance is voluntary, but no one takes brainstorming lightly.

These sessions generate a frenzy of activity. In fact, their very productivity creates a challenge: how to record all the ideas. So each Brainstormer Room has a clever device (sort of a hybrid camera-copier) that photographs every drawing on the whiteboards, every artifact on the walls. The project team selects the most promising ideas and moves quickly to develop them.

The key word is quickly. Kelley encourages his designers to model their ideas (usually from simple materials like foam or cardboard) within days of coming up with them. As an idea becomes more robust, it goes to the company's machine shop, where powerful computer-controlled machine tools generate prototypes from plastic or metal within hours of receiving software files from a designers computer. In creative work, Kelly believes, enlightened trial and error beats careful planning every time.

Indeed, one of the most popular slogans at IDEO is "fail often to succeed sooner." Which is why the company's designers store their diagrams, mockups and prototypes on large metal racks outfitted with wheels. When it's time to begin a new project, designers just grab an oversized roll of plastic wrap, seal their belongings, wheel them down the hall or across the street, and join their colleagues.

Can this formula for creativity work in other places? Some of the world's leading companies certainly think so. In a separate (and super-secret) building in Palo Alto, IDEO has opened a lab with Samsung, the Korean electronics conglomerate, where the two company's product developers can rub shoulders. In January, Steelcase, the office-furniture giant, made an equity investment in IDEO and named Kelley its vice president of technical discovery and innovation.

"Companies are coming to us and saying, 'How can you make us more innovative?" Kelley says. "They want us to help change their corporate culture to make it as creative as we are."

Tia O'Brien
SOURCE: *Fast Company*, April/May 1996, p. 83.

4

Profiling the Target Customer

Learning Objectives

- Draw a magic circle around your customer.
- Understand your key to survival in small business is the Target Customer.
- Learn how to use media kits to profile Target Customer.
- Identify primary and secondary Target Customers.
- Use interviewing, observation, and survey techniques to gain insight into your Target Customer.
- Understand Life Style Factors.
- Explore various profiling systems.
- Profiling the Internet Customer.
- Develop your customer profiling ability into a reflex.
- Picture your Target Customer by preparing a Target Customer Collage.

Chapters 4 and 5 go together. Your best strategy is to read both chapters quickly, grasping the heavy connection between competition (Chapter 5) and your Target Customer (Chapter 4). Then read the chapters again, taking notes, doing research, and completing the Action Steps for both chapters.

Your Target Customer is the lifeblood of your business—your resource base. You provide customers a product or a service, and they in return support your business by purchasing your product or service.

Competition occurs when someone else—some other entrepreneur or some other business—wants your resource base enough to wage war. This could be a price war: your competitor cuts the price of the same or competing product or service to steal away your Target Customers. This could be a quality war: the competitor has a superior product or better service. The war could be waged with a smear campaign: your product is not environmentally sound so the competition toots its horn about cleaning up the planet.

The best defense against competition is to know your Target Customer. Chapter 4 focuses on profiling your Target Customer through secondary, primary, and "new eyes" research.

Conducting ongoing market research:

- minimizes the risk of doing business
- uncovers opportunities
- identifies potential problems
- guides you to customers

Your prime concerns in Chapter 3 were: "Do I have a product or service that is in a growth segment of a growth market?" and "Are the business goals consistent with my own personal goals?" Hopefully, by now you have some pretty solid ideas as to what products are hot for you. Now it's time to establish whether or not there is a market for those products. If there is a market, are buyers willing to pay for it? Chapter 6 will focus on how to reach your Target Customers through marketing efforts.

The Power of Profiling

Your Target Customer is your key to survival in small business. Profiling draws a "magic" circle around your Target Customer. Placing the customer in the center of that circle transforms the whole arena into a target at which you can aim your product or service. Nothing happens without customers; every segment of your Business Plan must begin with a complete understanding of their wants and needs. Profiling is the instrument used to uncover the wants, needs, and behaviors of your customers. To generate this profile requires a combination of demographics—the statistical analysis; and psychographics—the firsthand intuitive insight into lifestyle, buying habits, patterns of consumption, attitudes, and so forth. In this chapter we'll focus on specific profiling techniques and sources to help you get a handle on that elusive customer.

It's often useful to ask prospects, "If you could make one wish, what could be improved?" If you talk to enough people, the gap you are aiming at will emerge and so will your Target Customers. Effective market research can help you target rich niches and avoid stagnant ones. For example, a plumber who was ready to leave his day job with a construction company asked his friends what would make them more likely to use his plumbing services. Their replies were almost universal: "Can you come during evening or weekend hours so I won't have to stay home from work?" In response, he called himself the "Midnight Plumber." He worked from 6-12 pm every day without charging overtime rates. He was an immediate success because he had profiled his customers and found a **market niche** with his positioning.

Two social workers found a niche by listening to their clients who were unable to visit their loved ones in prison. The clients had limited resources, no access to cars or to any public transportation that served the prison. Visits to husbands, wives, and children were therefore nearly impossible. The social workers believed, as did the families, that frequent contact was necessary for future rehabilitation of the prisoners and for keeping the family together.

On locating a used 15-passenger van, the social workers began "Family Express." They offered weekend roundtrips to the prison for $15 a passenger. Not only were they supplying a service, they were also providing a community for their riders, much in the same way that AOL's online chatrooms provide a community for its various targeted customer groups. Developing relationships beyond the product or service is essential in today's hotly competitive marketplace.

With over 1.7 million people in the U.S. prison and jail system today, the opportunity to serve family needs is vast. What other needs can you envision? How could you meet them?

A market segment profile identifies similarities among potential customers within a segment and explains the unique needs among the people and firms in differing segments.

Business-to-business profiling is unlike the segmentation of consumer markets. It is most effectively performed using geographic factors, customer-based segmentation, size of company, and end-user applications.

When profiling for a Target Customer, it is likely that several different prospective segments will be discovered. Further analysis will be required to focus on only the most worthy. These should then be separated by sales estimates, competitive factors, and the costs associated with reaching each segment.

Identifying the unfilled need (your niche) and clearly explaining the market potential for your concept can make or break a Business Plan. Before we get to profiling in depth, let's take a look at the different kinds of Target Customers (see page 63). We will focus on primary and secondary Target Customers. These are the only customers that you can see right now. However, once you open your business, a new customer may arrive on the scene, and you must always be ready to change so that you can take advantage of new market opportunities.

Market niche A small focused area of a market segment.

Three Kinds of Target Customers

Entrepreneurs we have known tell us you should be watching for at least three Target Customer (TC) groups.

1. **Primary.** This TC is perfect for your business and could be a heavy user.
2. **Secondary.** This one almost slips away before you can focus the camera. Sometimes your secondary TC will lead you to the third customer—who is invisible at first.
3. **Invisible.** This customer appears after you open the doors, after you have the courage to go ahead and start up.

What Can We Learn from Media Sources?

An easy way to understand the power of profiling is to analyze media sources that are aimed at different target markets. For example, what would you find if you contrasted information from three surfing magazines? Most, if not all, of the major media sources have conducted extensive research on the demographic and psychographic profiles of their Target Customer. In many cases, these profiles are available through media kits from the advertising departments of the media sources.

A media kit includes a copy of the magazine, reader profile, distribution figures, **rate card** (specifications for advertisements and costs), editorial calendar (monthly proposed content schedule), and an audited magazine circulation statement.

If your Target Customer were travel oriented, request media kit from travel-related magazines. The key here is to know which media sources your Target Customer reads, listens to, and watches. You can obtain in-depth profiles from these media companies because they compile this data for potential advertisers.

In this chapter, we will focus primarily on magazines. However, you can take advantage of almost any media—especially commercial ones—because of the useful information contained in ads. We could just as easily expand our discussion to include TV programs, radio stations, Internet sites and, to a lesser extent, books and movies.

We often walk past magazines without giving them a sideways glance. That's unfortunate because magazines hold the answer to many questions about customers. One way to view a magazine is as a glossy cover wrapped around pages of ads and editorial copy. With "new eyes," however, you can see that a mass-market magazine exists because it is a channel to the subconscious of a certain type of reader.

That knowledge is power! What can you learn about target markets, consumption patterns, and buying power from the advertisements in a magazine?

Put yourself in an analytical frame of mind. Begin by counting the ads. Then note the types of products that dominate the ads; these ads are probably aimed at the heavy users of those products. Next, study the models; they are fantasy images with which the Target Customer is expected to identify with, connect, and remember. The activities pictured in the ads enlarge the fantasy, and the words link it to real life. A good ad becomes a slice of life, a picture that beckons the customer inside toward the product.

We took an issue of *Surfing* and did a "new-eyes" analysis. After we looked at the articles and the advertisements, we completed a trial profile. We developed categories as we went along (one of the nice things about "new-eyes" research is that you can expand the model as you collect data). What we looked for was:

- total number of ads, half-page or larger
- ads aimed at heavy users (type of products that are advertised the most)

Rate card Magazine's advertising prices and details for ad placements.

Find/SVP Market Research Reports and Publications

Find/SVP, a worldwide research, advisory, and business intelligence firm, produces a wide range of very specific market and product research studies. Accessing their Website at **www.findsvp.com** or their report listings at your local library brings incredible secondary resources. Most reports can be purchased for hundreds to thousands of dollars, but short summaries of the reports can be accessed for free and provide a good deal of basic information about a market or product.

Example: A MarketLooks publication for Ultrasonic Flowmeters costs $200; but, a free two-page summary details the size of the market, the major players, trends, and industry structure.

In addition, we located an excellent resource for anyone dreaming of taking a product from their kitchen to the supermarket. Find/SVP publishes a hands-on manual titled, *How to Get Your Product Into Supermarkets,* for $29.95. The manual covers the following: shelf space, packaging, labeling, test marketing, food consultants and brokers, margins, advertising, and the top 100 supermarkets. If you plan on marketing a food product, a knowledge of the industry is essential.

SOURCE: **www.findsvp.com**

- large ads (two or more pages)
- demographics of models (estimated age, occupation, sex, and lifestyle)
- main activities depicted in ads
- content of magazine articles

Reviewing the Media Kit

The issue of *Surfing* we studied contained 160 pages, 90 of which were ads. These ads, mostly full page and two-page spreads, covered almost 60 percent of the magazine. There were four main categories: clothing, surfboards, sunglasses, and shoes.

The ads predominantly depict the surfer lifestyle. Professional surfers were showcased in several of the advertisements. The remaining models were primarily between age of 15 and 20, and are blond, surfer types. Text content and advertisements almost meld together.

After our initial profiling, we reviewed the following information supplied by *Surfing's* advertising department:

Sex	
Male	86%
Female	14%

Age	
Median	17.5
Average	20.5
Under 16	30%
16-20	32%
21-24	12%
25-30	11%
31-40	11%
41+	4%

Average household income

$57,135 (most live at home with parents, almost half in Hawaii and California—high-income states)

Average years surfing

6.7 years

Surf more than two days a week

76% (Southern California high schools have surf teams)

In or graduated from college

44%

Other sporting activities

Skateboarding	53%
Snowboarding	47%

Own or have access to a computer

88%

Have purchased surf-related items through the Internet

93%

The above reader profile (provided by *Surfing* magazine), the magazine's content, and what we know about our customer, we agree with *Surfing's* customer profile:

> They shun the pretension of the '80's for innovation and excellence, astutely seeking both value and "the latest." Upwardly mobile, educated or being educated, idealistic and stoked on their number-one passion—surfing—they are the first to try new maneuvers, new music, or new technologies they deem appropriate. Fashion and change leaders, they are the ones others turn to for advice.

The next step in profiling your Target Customer would be to compare the profiles of the readers of all the surfing magazines aimed at your target market to determine which best represents your customer, looking not only at demographics and psychographics but the spirit of the reader as well. One editor explained their target market as the "soul-surfer, one who lives to surf!"

Complete Action Step 24 to focus more clearly on your Target Customer.

Changing Profiles

In the past, we discussed segmenting the market like slicing a pie. Each business tried to aim their products at their slice. Slicing the pie was primarily based on demographic segmentation. As technology advanced and media outlets conducted extensive research on customers, we suggested to our readers that they try to aim for a single blueberry in a slice of blueberry pie. With the Internet and the explosion of relatively inexpensive independent target-market studies, we now suggest you aim for the seeds in the blueberry. If you add your intuition, demographics, psychographics, and extensive observation of your target market, you will accomplish **"one-to-one marketing"**: meeting the needs of the "seeds."

Seventy years ago there was usually only one grocer in town and he knew exactly what each of his customers wanted. He was in the business of one-to-one marketing. Today we have **www.peapod.com** conducting one-to-one marketing. The computer's brain is replacing the grocer's brain.

Even though society is becoming more fragmented, you should be able to focus more on the needs of your particular market segment. No longer only focus-

One-to-one marketing Meeting customer's needs on a very personal and individual basis.

Everything International
Lloyd C. Russow

Everything International provides links to a wide variety of international business, education, and research Internet sites. It is intended as an electronic library of resources for faculty, students, and practitioners in the field of international business. A brief explanation of each of the pages associated with the site can be found in the Everything International Site Information page.

This site is designed as a resource. It is assumed that people using this resource are on their way to another site, and for that reason, "bells and whistles" are kept to a minimum. The site will be maintained and updated regularly *(every hyperlink is verified for accuracy approximately every 10 days)*. New links will be added, those that no longer serve a purpose will be deleted. Sites added in the last 90 days are indicated by NEW!

Hyperlinks to public and private sources are listed; perceived usefulness being the only criteria used in selecting sites. Since my background is international marketing, and my interests lie with macroenvironmental secondary data, the lists reflect those biases to some degree. An attempt has been made to broaden the scope of recommended sites by including other functional areas.

When performing research, remember that *problem identification* and *interpretation of the data* are critical. The results are apt to be meaningless if either are performed inadequately. Be careful when using any data. Whether statistics come from the Internet, or any other resource, data is generally inaccurate to some degree.

For more information, visit **http://ib.philacol.edu/ib/russow.html.**

ing on age segmentation, you will now also look for lifestyle segments such as the difference between the purchases of 40-year-old first-time parents and the purchases of 40-year-old parents who just sent their youngest child off to college.

Market segmentation is easily understood if one looks at how various industries such as hotels, cars, tennis shoes, and pizza have aimed at specific niches. Your goal is to find a market that can be dominated easily and is more profitable than others.

Focus your efforts on your carefully selected blueberry seed!

Profiling in Action

Susan and John Johnson made a decision to locate their Healthy Gourmet business in Irvine, California. Let's review many of the secondary data resources available to the Johnsons to profile their consumer target market. Many of the sources are available both on the Net and in print form at libraries.

Healthy Gourmet actually serves the Tech Coast of Orange County primarily from San Clemente to Huntington Beach, a 60-mile stretch along the Pacific Coast. To narrow in on a specific area for illustration purposes, we are going to focus on their customers in the Newport Beach coastal area of Corona Del Mar (zip code 92625). Chapter 7 will discuss further issues in Healthy Gourmet's choice of physical location. Healthy Gourmet's initial research identified Orange County as a very good location, because it has high-income demographics. In addition, this location is centralized between Los Angeles and San Diego. With future expansion and growth, the Johnsons will be able to use the Orange County location as its main commissary kitchen, serving areas both to the North and to the South.

First we are going to focus on the demographics and psychographics of their Corona Del Mar customers.

First stop is U.S. Census data, **www.census.gov** (the last census figures available are for 1990). You can search the database by hundreds of different variables, from education, employment, family household size, income, race, sex, age groupings, and so on.

Your next stop is one of the easiest online databases to utilize, **www.easidemographics.com.** Searching a particular zip code produces a report on relevant variables based on 1990 census data (see page 68).

Utilizing National Decision System's (NDS), **www.natdecsys.com** online database allows you to search again by zip code. NDS profiles market segments into 50 Target Customer profiles focusing on lifestyle, retail, financial, and media. By searching for 92625, NDS produced profiles focusing on high-income earners, (35–65), active lifestyles, very comfortable, culturally and socially active, and couples and singles without small children.

Continuing on with the search for data brings one to SRI Consulting's VALS (Values and Lifestyles) Segment Profiles on the Web at **http://future.sri.com/vals/VALS/vals.index.html**. A quick check of the VALS segmentation diagram (see Figure 4.1) shows eight profiles of customer/buyers: Actualizers, Fulfilleds, Achievers, Experiencers, Believers, Strivers, Makers, and Strugglers. Read through each of the profiles.

Each of these segments defines adult consumers who have "different attitudes and exhibit distinctive behavior and decision-making patterns." Looking at the

Figure 4.1

The VALS™ Segment Profiles

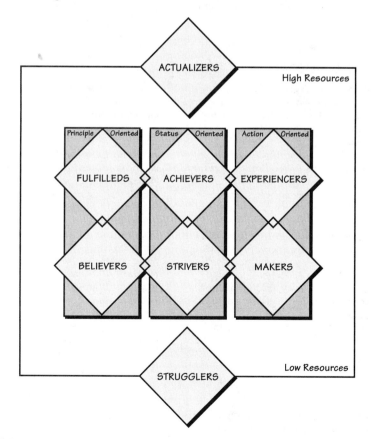

SOURCE: SRI Consulting

Summary Report & Analysis for Corona Del Mar

Zip Code: 92625
Post Office Name: CORONA DEL MAR
County Name: Orange, CA

State Name: CALIFORNIA
Metropolitan Area Name: Orange County, CA

Description	Value	EASI Score	EASI Rank (of 29291)	Description	Value	EASI Score	EASI Rank (of 9291)
Population	14,131	C	14635	Total White Collar Occupation	7,157	A	219*
Population Forecast (1/1/02):	14,936	B	8578	Total Blue Collar Occupation:	476	E	28896
Households:	6,629	A	892	EASI Total Crime Index:	158	B	8867
Total Household Income ($000)	877,464,445	A	60*	Annual Average Temperature:	64.3	A	4123
Median Household Income ($):	93,931	A	118*	Percent of Possible Sunshine:	75	A	1370
Average Household Income ($):	132,373	A	111*	Average Annual Percipitation:	12	E	27820
Median Age:	42.8	A	2285*	Average Annual Snowfall:	0	E	27495
White Population:	13,701	C	14078	EASI Weather Index (US Ave = 100):	199	A	597
Black Population:	17	D	18762	EASI Quality of Life Index (US Ave = 100):	199	A	412
Hispanic Population:	429	B	7301				
Asian, Pacific Islander Population:	365	A	3077				
Other Population:	48	D	17891				
Population Density:	816.8	A	5784*				

Footnotes:
EASI Rank: based on the concentration of the variable with a "1" being the highest rank and the number of areas in a geography being the lowest rank.
EASI Score: arranges the EASI Rank into a quintile frequency distribution ranging from "A" (the highest concentration group and top 20%) through "E" (the lowest concentration group and bottom 20%).
"(US Ave = 100)" indicates an index value that has a range of 0 (low) to 200 (high).
All data are copyrighted estimates of Easy Analytic Software, Inc.
All estimates are as of 1/1/97 unless otherwise stated.
SOURCE: **http://www.easidemographics.com**

National Decision Systems–MicroVision Segments For Corona Del Mar

Top Three MicroVision Segments In ZIP Code 92625

MicroVision Segment 8:
***Movers and Shakers* 52.41%**
Demographics: Very high income singles, age 25 to 54, with no children, one or two adults
Lifestyle: Recycle products, phone radio stations, do fund-raisers, participate in environmental causes and lift weights
Retail: Order flowers by wire, purchase greeting cards, soft contact lenses, laptop PC, Honda automobile and light beer
Financial: Have asset management account, VISA, accidental D&D, use financial planner, and has publicly held stock
Media: Read Money, Consumer Reports and Epicurean magazines; listen to album-oriented rock stations; and watches Seinfeld
Geography: Suburban areas such as Raleigh Durham, NC; Austin, TX; Madison, WI; and Gainesville, FL

MicroVision Segment 4:
***Mid-Life Success* 30.47%**
Demographics: Very high income married couples, age 50 to 54, with one or two children
Lifestyle: Go snow ski, collect coins, entertain at home, do aerobics, vote, read books, and contribute to PBS □
Retail: Buy imported beer, sport/utility vehicle, home gym system, use copy services, and buy items by phone and mail
Financial: Business owners, use ATM card to buy goods, have term-life insurance, IRA, and belong to limited partnerships
Media: Read Parade, Time, travel and Epicurean magazines; listen to adult contemporary and news stations; and watch Murphy Brown and Wimbledon
Geography: Suburbs along California coast, and Boston-Washington corridor

MicroVision Segment 14:
***Middle Years* 14.42%**
Demographics: Very high income married couples, age 40 to 69, many with no children
Lifestyle: Visit museums, belong to fraternal and civic clubs, collect coins, active in local issues, go on foreign trips
Retail: Buy costume jewelry, items from a flower shop, toys, compact pick-up, and furniture, heavy grocery store spender
Financial: Have asset management account, loan through a finance company, whole life, own a business and bank near work
Media: Read business, news, sports, travel and women's fashion magazines; list to soft contemporary and news/talk stations; and watch Baywatch, Nightline and Inside Edition
Geography: Suburban areas along the California Coast, Seattle and Reno

SOURCE: **http://www.natdecs.com**

neighboring types with similar characteristics will aid you in defining your primary and secondary target markets.

The Actualizer Profile, **future.sri.com/vals/VALS.segs.html,** seems like a close fit for Healthy Gourmet—"sophisticated, active, 'take-charge' people with

Figure 4.2

SRDS—Market Profiles

Los Angeles, CA- Orange County,CA

Demographics
Base Index US = 100

Total Adult Population	1,960,499		
Occupation	**Population**	**%**	**Index**
Administrative	333,285	17.0	133
Blue Collar	107,827	5.5	54
Clerical	148,998	7.6	88
Homemaker	237,220	12.1	88
Professional/Technical	570,505	29.1	115
Retired	268,588	13.7	74
Sales/Marketing	170,563	8.7	161
Self Employed	74,499	3.8	136
Student	52,933	2.7	113

Education (1990 Census)			
Elementary (0-8 years)	136,019	9.0	87
High School (1-3 years)	148,109	9.8	68
High School (4 years)	303,776	20.1	67
College (1-3 years)	503,270	33.3	134
College (4+ years)	420,147	27.8	137

Race/Ethnicity			
White	1,135,129	57.9	79
Black	33,328	1.7	14
Asian	243,102	12.4	365
Hispanic	541,098	27.6	263
American Indian	5,881	0.3	43
Other	1,960	0.1	100

Total Households	892,485		
Age of Head of Household	**Households**	**%**	**Index**
18-24 years old	46,409	5.2	98
25-34 years old	192,777	21.6	113
35-44 years old	215,981	24.2	108
45-54 years old	181,174	20.3	113
55-64 years old	106,206	11.9	95
65-74 years old	82,109	9.2	76
75 years and older	68,721	7.7	73
Median Age	**44.6 years**		

Sex/Marital Status			
Single Male	203,487	22.8	113
Single Female	207,949	23.3	96
Married	481,049	53.9	97

Children At Home			
At Least One Child	273,993	30.7	98
Child Age Under 2	44,624	5.0	116
Child Age 2-4	81,216	9.1	111
Child Age 5-7	71,399	8.0	99
Child Age 8-10	66,044	7.4	91
Child Age 11-12	45,517	5.1	88
Child Age 13-15	63,366	7.1	84
Child Age 16-18	58,904	6.6	86

Home Ownership			
Owner	537,276	60.2	92
Renter	355,209	39.8	114

Stage in Family Lifecycle	**Households**	**%**	**Index**
Single, 18-34, No Children	125,840	14.1	118
Single, 35-44, "	66,936	7.5	125
Single, 45-64, "	88,356	9.9	110
Single, 65+ "	63,366	7.1	78
Married, 18-34, "	49,087	5.5	120
Married, 35-44, "	33,914	3.8	115
Married, 45-64, "	116,916	13.1	96
Married, 65+ "	74,969	8.4	76
Single, Any Child at Home	67,829	7.6	92
Married, Child Age Under 13	131,195	14.7	111
Married, Child Age 13-18	75,861	8.5	87

Household Income			
Under $20,000	132,980	14.9	57
$20,000-$29,999	99,958	11.2	77
$30,000-$39,999	105,313	11.8	91
$40,000-$49,999	107,098	12.0	103
$50,000-$74,999	206,164	23.1	120
$75,000-$99,999	114,238	12.8	156
$100,000 and over	125,840	14.1	199
Median Income	**$50,022**		

Income Earners			
Married, One Income	205,272	23.0	89
Married, Two Incomes	274,885	30.8	103
Single	411,436	46.1	104

Dual Income Households			
Children Age Under 13 years	76,754	8.6	106
Children Age 13-18 years	49,979	5.6	82
No Children	148,153	16.6	111

Age By Income			
18-34, Income under $30,000	91,926	10.3	88
35-44, "	33,914	3.8	62
45-64, "	41,054	4.6	53
65+ "	66,936	7.5	52
18-34, Income $30,000-$49,999	63,366	7.1	109
35-44, "	50,872	5.7	93
45-64, "	58,012	6.5	87
65+ "	40,162	4.5	100
18-34, Income $50,000-$74,999	47,302	5.3	129
35-44, "	58,012	6.5	114
45-64, "	76,754	8.6	118
65+ "	23,205	2.6	124
18-34, Income $75,000 and over	36,592	4.1	186
35-44, "	73,184	8.2	178
45-64, "	111,561	12.5	181
65+ "	18,742	2.1	140

Credit Card Usage			
Travel/Entertainment	184,744	20.7	153
Bank Card	726,483	81.4	106
Gas/Department Store	326,650	36.6	114
No Credit Cards	103,528	11.6	71

Figure 4.2

SRDS—Market Profiles—cont'd

Lifestyles
Base Index US = 100

Los Angeles, CA- Orange County,CA

The Top Ten Lifestyles Ranked by Index

Snow Skiing Frequently	171	Wines	141
Foreign Travel	164	Real Estate Investments	141
Tennis Frequently	156	Running/Jogging	138
Use an Apple/Macintosh	151	Travel for Business	131
Frequent Flyer	150	Casino Gambling	131

Home Life	Households	%	Index
Avid Book Reading	320,402	35.9	97
Bible/Devotional Reading	141,013	15.8	83
Flower Gardening	261,498	29.3	86
Grandchildren	151,722	17.0	72
Home Furnishing/Decorating	193,669	21.7	97
House Plants	232,046	26.0	82
Own a Cat	222,229	24.9	95
Own a Dog	252,573	28.3	83
Shop by Catalog/Mail	227,584	25.5	86
Subscribe to Cable TV	570,298	63.9	98
Vegetable Gardening	129,410	14.5	64

Good Life			
Attend Cultural/Arts Events	162,432	18.2	116
Fashion Clothing	144,583	16.2	117
Fine Art/Antiques	109,776	12.3	111
Foreign Travel	209,734	23.5	164
Frequent Flyer	292,735	32.8	150
Gourmet Cooking/Fine Foods	194,562	21.8	121
Own a Vacation Home/Property	113,346	12.7	121
Travel for Business	239,186	26.8	131
Travel for Pleasure/Vacation	369,489	41.4	109
Travel in USA	341,822	38.3	105
Wines	170,465	19.1	141

Investing & Money			
Casino Gambling	156,185	17.5	131
Entering Sweepstakes	103,528	11.6	76
Moneymaking Opportunities	120,485	13.5	113
Real Estate Investments	83,001	9.3	141
Stock/Bond Investments	181,174	20.3	107

Great Outdoors			
Boating/Sailing	116,023	13.0	123
Camping/Hiking	221,336	24.8	102
Fishing Frequently	132,088	14.8	60
Hunting/Shooting	71,399	8.0	51
Motorcycles	70,506	7.9	104
Recreational Vehicles	82,109	9.2	106
Wildlife/Environmental	138,335	15.5	94

Sports, Fitness & Health	Households	%	Index
Bicycling Frequently	201,702	22.6	125
Dieting/Weight Control	182,067	20.4	91
Golf	199,024	22.3	112
Health/Natural Foods	170,465	19.1	114
Improving Your Health	229,369	25.7	109
Physical Fitness/Exercise	383,769	43.0	118
Running/Jogging	143,690	16.1	138
Snow Skiing Frequently	117,808	13.2	171
Tennis Frequently	82,109	9.2	156
Walking for Health	292,735	32.8	98
Watching Sports on TV	318,617	35.7	93

Hobbies & Interests			
Automotive Work	119,593	13.4	92
Buy Pre-Recorded Videos	157,077	17.6	95
Career-Oriented Activities	103,528	11.6	125
Coin/Stamp Collecting	55,334	6.2	91
Collectibles/Collections	96,388	10.8	86
Community/Civic Activities	62,474	7.0	77
Crafts	194,562	21.8	80
Current Affairs/Politics	160,647	18.0	108
Home Workshop	192,777	21.6	83
Military Veteran in Household	174,927	19.6	84
Needlework/Knitting	102,636	11.5	74
Our Nation's Heritage	41,947	4.7	94
Self-Improvement	193,669	21.7	118
Sewing	120,485	13.5	80
Supports Health Charities	141,905	15.9	83

High Tech Activities			
Electronics	117,808	13.2	114
Home Video Games	102,636	11.5	93
Listen to Records/Tapes/CDs	473,017	53.0	105
Own a CD Player	626,524	70.2	118
Photography	172,250	19.3	109
Science Fiction	85,679	9.6	107
Science/New Technology	99,958	11.2	123
Use a Personal Computer	498,007	55.8	131
Use an Apple/Macintosh	124,055	13.9	151
Use an IBM Compatible	420,360	47.1	126
VCR Recording	166,002	18.6	96

high self-esteem and abundant resources." The profile sharpens when you hot link to the Activities page where you find arts associations, dinner parties, cruises, foreign cars, and golf.

Actualizers

Various Other Actualizer-Related Products and Activities
These categories represent a sample of some consumer activities that involve Actualizers either markedly more (high index) or less (low index) than the population at large.

Category	Index	Category	Index	Category	Index
Membership in Arts Association	382	Cruise Ship Vacation in Past 3 Years	230	Have Wood Burning Stove/Heater	79
Visit Art Museum in Past Year	302	Swim 20+ Days in Past Year	218	Used 15+ Plastic Garbage Bags Past Mo.	69
Cross Country Skiing Past Year	291	Own Import/Foreign Car	202	Use Powder-Form Pain Relievers	61
Own Elect. Expresso/ Capuccino Maker	268	Bought Custom-Made Furniture Past Year	195	Use Cinnamon Flavor Toothpaste	58
Give Dinner Party 1/month or More	240	Own Hot Tub/Spa	189	Watch Professional Wrestling on TV	54
Foreign Travel in Past 3 Years	240	Play Golf	175	Own A Motorcycle w/ 300-649cc Engine	44
		Own Personal Computer at Home	175		
		Bought Sheet Music	168		

SOURCE: **VALS/Simmons; http://future.SRI.com/vals/actualizers.html**

Index numbers indicate the relative purchase of products and services by each VALS group. For example, an index of 100 means that the product is used by the segment on an average with the rest of the U.S. adult population. An index of 120 indicates that the segment's purchase of a product is 20% higher than the average of all segments. Indexes well under 100 indicate the group is relatively uninvolved with the category. Indexes over 120 indicate that the group is heavily involved with the product category.

Take the profile test yourself and ask several people who you see as your Target Customers to take the test as well. Always be careful to target your product to the needs of your customers and not your own needs.

SRDS also offers an insight into Healthy Gourmet's customer. Figure 4.2 includes SRDS's Lifestyle Market Profiles for Orange County. These profiles are available free in most libraries or through **www.srds.com**. The index figures are available for you to compare your target market to the overall marketplace as well as to contrast several different market areas. With 100 being the average throughout the United States, SRDS demonstrates that Orange County again is a high-income area with people traveling and participating in sports at a very high level.

The Johnsons describe their primary customer as follows:

- sophisticated
- knowledgeable and concerned about their health
- age 30 to 60
- baby boomers who are in excellent shape and interested in retaining their health
- professionals, entrepreneurs, and others who work long hours
- active physically with exercising a part of their lives
- highly educated
- expects the best
- purchases products to save time and energy and thus requires a high-level service and consistency

Healthy Gourmet also reaches two secondary markets—those over age 70 (many whose children purchase food for their parents) and dieters. Both have different needs and requests, and require a different marketing and sales effort.

Action Step 25

Initial Customer Profile

Based on what you know to date, profile your Target Customer using the following:

- **www.census.gov**
- **www.natdecsys.com**
- **www.easidemographics. com**
- **http://future.sri.com/vals/ valshome.html**
- SRDS Lifestyle Market Analyst (available in libraries).
- If you have a business-to-business customer:
- Access the customers' SIC codes or NAISC codes using the books available in the library or at various sites on the Net.

Use the following to begin to profile your customer:

- **www.abii.com**
- **www.hoovers.com**
- **www.dnb.com**
- **www.companiesonline.com**

Search the library and the Internet for directories that address your market.

How large is the market in terms of numbers of customers? In terms of potential sales? Who are the major players? List your top ten prospects.

Focus on your Target Customer throughout the remainder of the chapter. As you recognize variables to add, or questions to be asked, jot them down. Action Step 27 will entail further profiling.

After being in business for two years and keeping records diligently, Healthy Gourmet now knows exactly who their target market consists of. But for those just starting a business, utilizing the above resources gives a good headstart on defining Target Customers. By knowing your target market you can focus your promotional and marketing efforts.

Continue to refine your profile as you work through the remainder of the Action Steps. Before continuing, be sure to complete Action Step 25.

Profiling the Internet Customer with iVALS

Outside firms conduct extensive overall segmentation studies and are also capable of honing in on a very specific area such as Internet users. SRI Consulting, a world leader in psychographic consumer research, created iVALS to segment Internet users. At **http://future.sri.com/vals/iVALS.index.htm,** a questionnaire is available for you to profile yourself as an Internet user. They have separated the market into ten segments: wizards, pioneers, upstreamers, socialites, workers, surfers, mainstreamers, sociables, seekers, and immigrants. Each segment relates to the Internet in a different way. SRI's customers utilize the data to determine where to spend their advertising dollars; how to write, design, and create Websites; and to develop products that meet customer needs, wants, and desires.

Profiling Business-to-Business Customers

Business-to-business markets include a wide range of customers. You need to look at your customer based on demographics (size, geographic location), customer type, end-use application, and purchasing situation.

End-user profiling concentrates on how a product or service is used. Small firms can often thrive in specific niches because larger firms may ignore such markets. Example: Selling replacement parts for mobile homes.

Geographic profiling is used when customers are concentrated in a specific geographic area. Example: Furniture in North Carolina, film making in Hollywood, and biotechnology in San Diego. Such users have narrow and specific needs. If an industry leader is opening a plant in a different location, a new support business may do well because of less competition in the new area. If you were to follow the exodus of businesses to Las Vegas, you would be able to provide innumerable services to a growing industrial base.

Segmentation of business markets can include the following:

- NAISC or SIC codes
- sales revenue
- number of employees
- end-use application
- location
- purchasing method (i.e., bidding, low bid only, single sourcing)
- credit risk
- years in business
- type of ownership: public, private, federal or state government, non-profit organizations
- international versus U.S. sales
- ability to reach decision maker
- purchase decision: group or individual
- economic and technological trends affecting various industries
- competitive nature of particular segments
- barriers to entry in various segments

In addition to the variables above, personal traits of the individual buyers within each firm become important. Getting to know what hobbies, activities, and lifestyles the people you are selling to may be equally important as the listed variables.

For the reader profile information provided by Minority Business Entrepreneur (MBE), see Figure 4.3.

Primary Research Is Absolutely Necessary!

Secondary sources of demographic and psychographic information, especially media sources, may provide enough data to allow you to get a fairly accurate profile of your Target Customer. Chances are, though, that you'll need to test your profile against reality. Field interviews, surveys, and observation are three primary tools that will help you get a more accurate profile of your Target Customer.

Field Interviews

Sometimes people enter into small businesses because of personal circumstances rather than an initial grand desire. Often, they have to learn new skills and learn them fast. Fortunately, entrepreneurs tend to be bright, creative, and hard-working people. Julia Gonzales is a good example. When Julia discovered that she would have to work for herself, she quickly began to research her Target Customers.

Baby Store?

It was no secret that Julia Gonzales was distressed when her husband was transferred. She couldn't blame him for wanting the transfer; she would have wanted it, too. But Julia had had a terrific job as manager of a full-line baby furniture and bedding store, and to keep both job and husband she would have to commute over 150 miles, five days a week. Julia chose to relocate with her husband to a lovely town with affordable housing.

But she missed the store, and it was hard living on one salary when they had gotten used to two. She also missed the excitement of retailing and customer contact. When Julia started to look for work, she found that her reputation had preceded her. Storeowners knew of the store where she'd worked and were pretty sure that the only reason she wanted to work for them was to get a feel for the area so that she could open a store of her own and compete with them.

This gave Julia an idea. She hadn't considered doing that. So when she couldn't find work, Julia decided to go for it—to go ahead and compete with them. Their fear gave Julia confidence!

One thing Julia had learned on her way up from stock clerk to store manager was that it pays to know one's customer. So, in the mornings, after getting her children off to school, she'd drive to various baby stores, park her car a block away and, when customers came out of the store, strike up conversations with them, conducting **interviews.**

"Hi!" she'd say. "My name is Julia Gonzales and I'm doing market research in this area. I'm wondering if you might have a minute to answer a few questions about babies."

Her enthusiasm must have helped—she liked people and babies, and it showed. Being a mother helped her understand other mothers. She always dressed up a bit and carried a clipboard. Julia asked obvious questions like:

- What do you like about this store?
- How close is this store to your home?
- What things did you buy?

Interviews Planned conversations by phone, mail, face-to-face, or the Net with another person or group of persons for the purpose of eliciting specific information.

Figure 4.3

Minority Business Entrepreneur

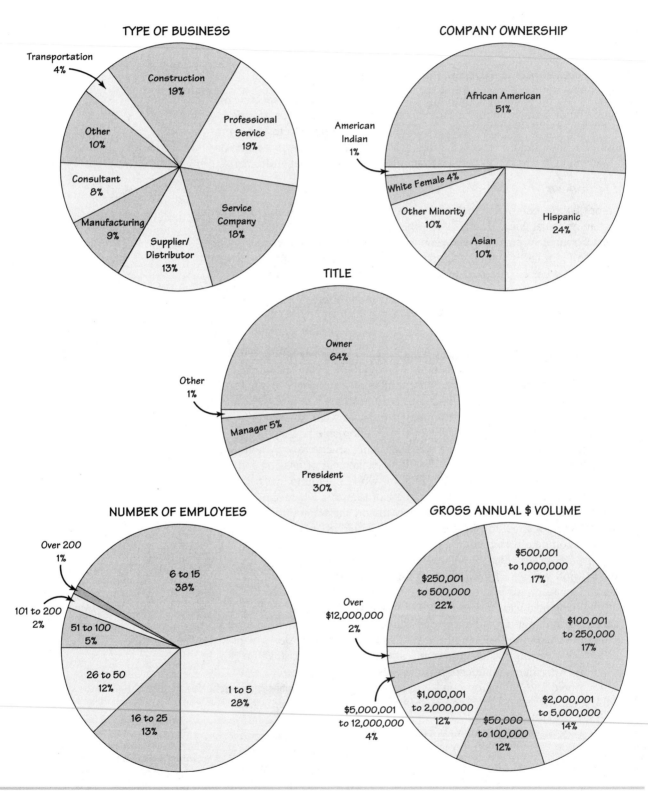

TYPE OF BUSINESS

- Transportation 4%
- Construction 19%
- Professional Service 19%
- Other 10%
- Consultant 8%
- Manufacturing 9%
- Supplier/Distributor 13%
- Service Company 18%

COMPANY OWNERSHIP

- African American 51%
- American Indian 1%
- White Female 4%
- Other Minority 10%
- Asian 10%
- Hispanic 24%

TITLE

- Owner 64%
- Other 1%
- Manager 5%
- President 30%

NUMBER OF EMPLOYEES

- Over 200 1%
- 101 to 200 2%
- 51 to 100 5%
- 26 to 50 12%
- 16 to 25 13%
- 6 to 15 38%
- 1 to 5 28%

GROSS ANNUAL $ VOLUME

- $500,001 to 1,000,000 17%
- $250,001 to 500,000 22%
- Over $12,000,000 2%
- $100,001 to 250,000 17%
- $5,000,001 to 12,000,000 4%
- $1,000,001 to 2,000,000 12%
- $50,000 to 100,000 12%
- $2,000,001 to 5,000,000 14%

SOURCE: Minority Business Entrepreneur, **http://www.mbemag.com**

- Was there anything you wanted you couldn't find?
- Were the people helpful and courteous?
- How frequently do you shop here?
- What other baby stores do you patronize?

Sometimes Julia parked in an alley, to research the delivery trucks. From past experience she could estimate the store's purchases.

Julia developed a separate list of questions for pregnant women:

- Have you had a baby shower?
- Which gifts did you like best?
- Which gifts seemed most useful?
- What things are you buying before your baby comes?
- What things are you waiting to buy?
- How are you going to decorate the baby's room?
- What do you really need the most?
- What services would be most helpful to you?

The research was time-consuming, but after 60 interviews Julia had a great deal of information to make some very sound decisions about her Target Customer. She also knew the weaknesses of her competition.

Observing Target Customers

In addition to interviewing, Julia was involved in **observing** her customers. This is the least expensive but one of the most effective forms of market research. You must put personal biases and intuition aside and truly listen and observe your Target Customer. Put away all you know about your product or service and Target Customer. Open your eyes and observe how your Target Customer truly behaves, not just what they tell you. Julia Gonzales was told by her Target Customers that they bought all their children's clothing at up-scale stores, but upon observation she recognized that over half of the kids were dressed in Target and K-Mart clothing. People often say one thing but do another. Also, people themselves don't always know why they make purchase decisions unless they spend some time thinking about their actions. They might not even recognize a need, but when presented with a new product or service based on your observations, it may be just what they wanted.

Private Phone Room Idea

Observation Pays Off

One supplier of a check-cashing service in a low-income Latino immigrant community also provided long-distance phone services. Each Saturday and Sunday large families—aunts, uncles, brothers, sisters—came to call their loved ones in Mexico, and Central and South America. The owner observed how difficult it was to have a private conversation in the open phone rooms and decided to partition off rooms to allow for private conversations. Additionally, he provided one large room where entire families could talk to their loved ones and celebrate birthdays with a song from all.

Observing Using "new eyes" to learn about Target Customers.

Use your curiosity as you observe and ask as many open-ended questions as possible.

► **Action Step 26**

Interview and Observe Prospective Target Customers

Now that you've profiled several Target Customers via computer search and media kit research, it's time for you to take a big step—time to move from the tidy world inside your head to the arena of the marketplace. It's time to rub elbows with the people who'll be buying your product or service.

You know where your Target Customer hangs out, his or her habits, income, sex, personality, and buying patterns. You can guess this customer's dreams and aspirations. Now you're going to check out these things directly by interviewing your potential Target Customers, through primary research and observation.

First, just observe your customer in the marketplace. Remember Julia Gonzales and the steps she took.

Make up questions in advance, most should be open-ended and call for more than just simple yes or no answers. Remember, the most important part of your research will be for you to keep an open mind!

Those of you who are Net savvy, may also choose to research by contacting news groups and posting questions; or read previous postings. The Net is an excellent choice because the Net community basically believes in the free flow of information.

When Julia Gonzales wrote down the answers her interviewees gave to her questions, she also made notes of the following information.

- makes and years of cars the women drove
- attitudes toward their children
- clothing worn
- types of strollers
- children's snacks
- hairstyles and grooming of the mothers
- spending on their own children versus gifts for others

In addition, Julia decided to go to the local playgrounds and snoop around. She borrowed her friend's two babies and off she went asking questions. Julia could not believe how much more open people were to her as a mother rather than professional interviewer.

Julia combined the information she gathered from **www.easidemographics.com,** *Standard Rates and Data Services Lifestyle Market Analyst* (available at the library), and VALS, with her observations, interviews, and secondary data. She was then able to focus in on her target market and make it the center of her dartboard.

Where can you spend some time observing your Target Customer?

In Chapter 5, when we research competition, we'll return to interviewing and observing. Here, we'll use another skill—surveying to get a more refined picture of a Target Customer.

Surveys

When Julia Gonzales and Patti Hale discovered that they were going to work for themselves, they quickly began to research their Target Customers. The methods they chose were observation, interviewing and surveying. You can do the same for your business. Action Step 26 will tell you how to do it. Read Action Step 26 and about how Patti Hale used the survey technique to get her well on her way to starting her own business.

Designing and Conducting a Survey

Patti was a supervisor at a local textile plant. She decided to leave the plant and turn her love of food and people into a business: a restaurant. For some time, Patti had been developing her business skills. She had taken several courses in restaurant and bar management. Next, Patti entered an evening small business course at a local college. In an attempt to get a handle on her Target Customer, Patti read many studies on the eating-out habits of people in the Southeast. But how did this translate to her local market? Although this secondary research was very revealing, Patti couldn't risk her future on someone else's research.

Patti decided to do her own survey. She studied survey design and got advice from her professor, who had experience in surveying. Joe's Joint was one of the most popular eating spots in town. Patti would often have a bite to eat there and got to know Joe, the owner, quite well.

She told Joe about her dream to open a small restaurant some day, and about how much she was learning in her small business course. Patti convinced Joe to let her do a survey of his customers. After all, the price was right. Patti would do the survey free of charge and would give Joe her results—a classic win-win proposition.

Patti spent the next few weeks designing her survey. How many customers should she survey? When should she do the survey? How should she conduct herself? There was so much to do. She launched a week-long written survey of Joe's customers. To Joe's surprise, customers wanted to fill out the questionnaire. To Patti's surprise, she overheard Joe explaining to someone that he thought it was about time he learned a bit more about what the customer wanted.

Make Customer Profiling a Reflex

We're trying to help you make customer profiling a reflex. Predicting the needs of every customer is almost impossible to accomplish with 100 percent accuracy. New previously **invisible customers** will emerge with needs that have not been anticipated. An alert entrepreneur will listen carefully to unexpected requests and be quick to respond to these opportunities. The following case provides a typical example.

Invisible Customers

Some people go into business for themselves because they can't work for someone else. Some are mavericks who don't like to take orders. Others are dreamers who love their own ideas. Still others, like Fred Bowers, have a physical handicap that makes them prefer self-employment over getting a job with a large firm.

Fred's experience illustrates that customers sometimes "come out of the woodwork."

Soccer City

Revealing "Invisible Customers"

Fred Bowers had planned to be a career Marine until he was injured in a fall from a training helicopter. He could still walk, painfully, but his military career was over. With a medical discharge in his pocket, Fred looked around for work but none was to be found.

"I'd always loved soccer," Fred said. "I'd been a pretty fair player, and my coaching experience had given me a good understanding of kids. I thought there might be a place for a soccer specialty shop in our community, but before I went for financing I spent several months checking it out."

Using the Internet, Fred found 30 sporting-goods shops in the area he was interested in. If he wanted, for about $5, he could access customer profiles on each of his potential competitors by conducting a search at American Yellow Pages, **http://ayp.infousa.com.**

When Fred began profiling his Target Customers, he came up with two easy targets:

- Primary target: boys, age 6 to 17 and their parents
- Secondary target: girls, age 6 to 17 and their parents

He also gathered the following information:

- Household income: $40,000–$60,000/year
- Level of education: Parents college educated
- Interests: Sports, video games, computers
- Cars: Chevy Cavaliers, vans, Ford Taurus

Then Fred segmented the youngsters into two groups: members of school teams, and members of American Youth Soccer Organization (AYSO) teams.

Because of Fred's knowledge of the game and helpful demeanor, his store prospered. Schools counted on him for an honest deal, and parents of

Invisible customers Surprise customers; usually a great find.

players counted on his advice for equipment. "I had thought I'd just be selling," Fred said. "What I was really doing was providing a service."

After being in business a year, a third market began to emerge. The customers in this third group were adults, mostly foreign-born, from such countries as Great Britain, Germany, Mexico, and Brazil. They had grown up playing soccer and loved the game. To them, it was a fiercely-fought national sport, and they still liked to play. These heretofore invisible customers would drive 50 to 75 miles to Fred's store for equipment they couldn't find elsewhere.

The next year, the local Boys and Girls Club started an indoor soccer league for 1200 kids. Fred offered to sponsor all of the team photos. Needless to say his business grew!

Fred now serviced AYSO in the fall, indoor soccer in the winter, and the adult leagues that played primarily in the spring and summer.

"If I hadn't opened up, I wouldn't have known about the adult players. Now they make up at least 30 percent of my business. One day they weren't there; the next day, they were. I like that. I like it a lot. It makes this whole adventure more interesting."

Healthy Gourmet's invisible customers proved to be the "diet junkies," described by the owners as, "People who want to lose weight rapidly with little effort. When the weight doesn't fall off in two to three weeks, they stop the program immediately."

Visualizing Your Target Customer

To this point, you have researched, surveyed, and observed your Target Customer. Now read about how Louie Chen from Seattle was able to visualize his customer.

Louie Chen and His Target Customer

Louie Chen was born in Seattle. He grew up playing baseball but switched to tennis. A good choice because he became a professional on the tennis circuit for three years.

Worn down by constant travel, Louie Chen left the pro tour and returned to Seattle and a comfortable life as a stockbroker. He was a member of the Chamber of Commerce and several organizations for Asian Americans. Because of his tennis, Louie did a lot of business at the Country Club. Louie was looking around for a new opportunity when he met Jiangli Chang, a recent immigrant to America.

Jiangli Chang, a middle-aged tennis player with a terrific backhand, was part of the Hong Kong exodus. His business consisted of importing objects of art from Japan, China, and Southeast Asia.

Jiangli expressed to Louie his difficulty in establishing a good banking relationship. Jiangli's problem started Louie Chen thinking. More and more Asians were coming to the Pacific Northwest. In the five years between 1990 and 1995, the Asian population in the Washington State had jumped 50 percent, from 215,000 to 323,000. With that kind of traffic flow, Louie Chen smelled opportunity.

Louie enrolled in an entrepreneurship course at the local community college. His instructor was Grace Rigby, a marketing specialist whose favorite tool was the Customer Profile.

"Profile your Target Customer. When you sleep, dream profiles. You'll have fun. You won't go wrong," said Grace Rigby.

With the help of Grace Rigby, Louie profiled his Target Customer. One of Grace's key teaching techniques was the Target Customer Collage.

"The Collage combines all your data and observations into a visual presentation," Grace said. "The idea is to clip pictures, statistics, phrases, advertisements from magazines that represent your Target Customer. Then paste them all together on a piece of cardboard or use your computer. Hang the collage on the wall near your desk. When you get stuck writing your Business Plan, check the collage. It should bring you right back into focus. At all times the collage pictures who your business is really all about."

Louie Chen's collage included the following pictures:

six Asian men and women in business suits

a jumbo jet

a private jet

the Bank of Hong Kong

an expensive leather briefcase

a laptop computer

a Palm Pilot

a cell phone

an Asian man in shirtsleeves

a hardhat studying blueprints at a construction site

an Asian man in golf gear teeing up at an expensive resort

Asian families traveling together

stock market tables

The collage kept Louie focused. Because he had an A+ credit history, Louie found financing to open his bank. He located in the International District adjacent to downtown Seattle. The name Louie chose was Shanghai American Bank of Credit (SABC).

Specializing in the Asian market, Louie hired greeters such as Maryann Wu, who was fluent in Mandarin Chinese and Korean, and spoke enough Japanese to get by. Maryann was studying Thai as well. She shook hands with customers and then directed them to the manager who spoke their language or was very familiar with their country of origin.

One day, while sitting at his desk, Louie saw an Asian male in his early fifties. He wore an expensive tailored suit, carried a briefcase, and looked just like one of the men in his original collage. Louie hurried out of his office and greeted the gentleman who subsequently deposited $1,000,000 in his new SABC account.

Louie never stopped focusing on his collage and had been adding to it during the past year in business. In fact, it was hanging in his office. But now he knew the person he wanted to celebrate with was Grace Rigby. Without Grace's insistence on focusing and refining his target market, he knew SABC would not have been a success.

The customer who entered Louie Chen's bank was probably an Actualizer on the VALS scale. An Actualizer is a person of high esteem who can take charge. Actualizers are attentive to their image in the world. Louie's Target Customer was a business leader with resources, with deep interests in music and art. Louie found out later that one reason the customer came to Seattle was to have access to the Seattle Art Museum. If you hot link from the VALS Internet page to the activity page, you'll see that visiting museums ranks high on the list.

It's now time for you to complete your own Target Customer Collage following the instructions in Action Step 27. Start to visualize your customer. Keep the picture of your Target Customer in the forefront as you move into evaluating your competition and promoting your product.

▶ *Summary*

Before you open your doors, you should profile your Target Customer at least five times. After your doors are open, continue to gather data through surveys, interviews, and observation, and to refine the profile monthly.

A profile combines demographic data (age, sex, income, education, residence, cultural roots, etc.) with psychographic insight (observations of lifestyle, buying habits, consumption patterns, attitudes, etc.). The magazines read by your Target Customers will reveal a fairly well drawn profile.

Questions you need to answer through profiling your Target Customer are:

1. Who are my Target Customers?
2. How can I best reach my Target Customers?
3. What need will my product or service fill? (For example, landscaping is not just mowing grass and trimming shrubs. Its major selling points are enhancing the appearance of property and providing its owner free time.)
4. Where and how can I communicate my message with a minimum of confusion?
5. What additional services does my Target Customer want?
6. What quality of service or product do my customers desire and are willing to pay for?
7. Who else is after my Target Customers?
8. Why do my Target Customers act the way they do?

Think Points for Success

- Psychographics is derived from psyche and graphos, Greek words for "life" or "soul" and for "written," respectively. Thus, psychographics is the charting of your customer's life, mind, soul, and/or spirit.

- Segmenting is discovering the piece of the pie you should focus in at. As you go deeper into your research, you will discover that perhaps you could reach the blueberries in the pie and, if you go further, you will reach the seeds—your true Target Customer.

- You can save a lot of steps by using market research that has been done by others.

- To discover your target market, use everything available: media kits, demographic studies, lifestyle segmentations, and census data.

- Use NAISC or SIC codes to begin your research for business-to-business customers.

- FOCUS! FOCUS! FOCUS on your Target Customer.

Key Points from Another View

Professor finds Life of Variety in Magazines

He has enough *Time* on his hands to be a real *Details* man. He's got *Allure,* and he's completely in *Vogue*—a real *Cosmopolitan* kind of guy. His *People* skills are formidable. He has a good sense of *Self,* has a *Spin* for everything and knows all about *Us.*

Got it yet? Samir Husni is a maestro of magazines, a potentate of periodicals who has parlayed his interest into a career of academics, consulting and just plain reading. And the University of Mississippi journalism professor's travels and page-turning have led him to a conclusion that counters a loudly spoken notion: that in a world of video and cyberspace, print is dying. In fact, it's thriving in many different ways—not in spite of new media, but because of it.

And Husni loves it all. *"Seventeen* has two different covers this month!" he enthuses, his arms full of reading material during a recent buying trip to Manhattan, Mecca of magazinedom.

For magazine lovers, the golden age is back. According to Husni, 5,200 consumer magazines were distributed nationally last year, up from just 2,500 in 1985. And the survival rate, he says, is a respectable four of 10.

He would know. His yearly book, "Samir Husni's Guide to New Consumer Magazines," is a must-read in the industry. He uses magazines as textbooks in his journalism classes. And his appetite sometimes costs $1,500 a month—only some of which Ole Miss will reimburse.

In his office in Oxford, Husni sits surrounded by hip-deep stacks of printed arcana, smiling broadly. In a back room, are thousands more; his wife, declaring that the magazine presence had reached critical mass in the Husni household, ordered all issues but the ones he's reading exiled to the campus.

"You could sit in here and read for months," marvels Charles Doudy, Hunsi's teaching assistant.

For Hunsi's collection takes *ad obscurum ad infinitum.* Consider the titles he has amassed: *Pool and Spa Living. Great Escapades of World War II. Naturally Nude. Gentleman Farms. Silicon India. Turkey Hunting. Golf Digest. Retirement Planner. Canoe Journal. Biblical Archaeology Review. Lotto World. American Cheerleader. Wine X,* a Gen-X wine magazine. *Leonardo DeCaprio Magazine. Atlanta Baby.* And scores of porn magazines with titles as risque as their pictures.

Then there's the trio of ferret magazines—*Ferret USA, American Ferret,* and yes, *Modern Ferret.*

"I guess that's as opposed to your traditional ferret," Husni says.

"When we reach this stage, when we have three magazines for ferret lovers, you know magazines are doing well," he says. "If I watch mud wrestling on ESPN and want to see more, I get a magazine. TV's fueling it all."

Newsstands today feature all manner of specialty magazines. Net sites—"Web 'zines"—are gathering readers online, then launching physical editions of their magazines. Individual television programs, from "Seinfeld" to "Star Trek," are spawning their own magazines.

One, "Mr. Food," is a cooking and recipe magazine based on the popular syndicated television gourmet. Introduced as a quarterly last year to ride a wave of viewership, it's circulation has already reached 400,000.

"We got such great response to viewers writing in for recipes, and they wanted more. It just seemed like a natural transition," says Howard Rosenthal, Mr. Food's publicist. "People are so loyal to TV, and you can only get so much time on TV. And people always want to know more."

Why is this happening? The Internet and cable television have driven a demand for more information on more obscure things. So, as niche marketing is carried further, magazines become "more human," Husni says.

While TV provides the viewership to feed the readership, the Internet—where niche marketing is far easier because distribution is cheap—is feeding a Balkanization of interests. And amateur 'zines, once almost guerrilla publications, are now entering the mainstream as desktop publishing becomes easier and the number of national distributors increases.

In short, everyone thinks *their* hobby-craft-obsession should have its own magazine.

Ted Anthony

SOURCE: The Orange County Register Business Monday, June 22, 1998, p. 18.

5

Reading the Competition

Entrepreneurial Links

Books

How to Drive Your Competition Crazy, Guy Kawasaki, 1996.

Up Against the Wal-Marts, How Your Business Can Compete in the Shadow of the Retail Giants, Dan Taylor and Jeanne Smalling Archer, 1996.

Competitive Advantage: Creating and Sustaining Superior Performance, Michael Porter, 1998.

Websites

www.demographics.com
www.bg.geoplace.com
www.zdnet.com/smallbusiness

Associations/Organizations

Society of Competitive Intelligence Professionals, www.scip.org
Air Force Resources (selling to the government), www.oakland.ecrc.org/resources2.html
National Retail Foundation, www.nrf.com

Publications

Forecast
Small Business Journal, www.tsbj.com
Minority Business Entrepreneur, www.mbemag.com

Additional Entrepreneurial Insights

Start-up: A Silicon Valley Adventure, Jerry Kaplan, 1994.
Faster Company, Patrick Kelly, 1998.
Nuts!: Southwest Airlines' Crazy Recipe for Business and Personal Success, Kevin and Jackie Freiberg, 1998.

Learning Objectives

- Define the competition in terms of size, growth, profitability, innovation, market leaders, market losers, and potential competitors.
- Discover your Target Customer's Touchpoints.
- Understand the value of positioning in relationship to competitors.
- Evaluate competitors using primary, secondary, and "new eyes" research.
- Develop skills as a marketplace detective.
- Use a competitor test matrix.
- Create uniqueness.
- Compete in a mature marketplace.
- Market product throughout.
- Prosper in a changing competitive marketplace.
- Become the best "snooper" you can.

Only a few years ago, the subject of competition conjured up warlike terms such as "beat the competition," "disarm your competitor," "take a piece of their market," and so on. This market-sharing mentality assumed that when one went into business he or she would take a piece of the action away from someone else. In a steady-state environment in which industries changed at a slow and predictable pace, the focus was on attacking the competition—after all, there was little change going on, and this strategy seemed to be the only way to drum up new business.

The knowledge-based economy, technology, and the new informed customer have changed the way business views competition. The new economy is about learning from and dancing with your competition. It's about creating your own market niche and continually changing and improving your product or service as the customer dictates. Today, competition is healthy (not easy), and it's there to help you change and respond to the market.

In the last few chapters, we've learned about trend-spotting, opportunity selection, and profiling Target Customers. We've tried to get you to focus your business toward growth industry segments and customer needs. This chapter explains how your perceived competition can help you further define your specific niche—and it all starts with the customer.

Debbee and Steve Pezman, founders of *Surfer's Journal*, a high-quality quarterly journal targeted to surfers over age 30, are guided by the following principle: "Identify your Target Customer and serve them with a plus that is hard to copy." As the Pezmans review new opportunities, they proceed only if they can answer "yes" to the following questions: "Is this a plus for our customer?" and "Is this something our competitors will find difficult to copy?"

As you read through the chapter, complete the Action Steps and develop your business idea, continually ask yourself these questions to keep you on track and your customer in focus.

Why the New Market Research?

Inc. asked Roger D. Blackwell to help make sense of the impact that accelerating product cycles has had on market research in his role as professor of marketing at Ohio Sate University and as an independent consultant to companies such as Victoria's Secret and J.C. Penny, Blackwell spends his time studying consumer behavior and the retail sector.

INC: Why is it more important than ever for companies to speed up their market research?

BLACKWELL: Fierce competition. There are too many companies chasing too few consumers, and the survivors are getting better and better at providing what consumers want. In the past, many companies faced competition from great, average, and bad companies. But the bad and the average are being eliminated rapidly, and we are left with only top-notch companies that are more likely to strive to have what the consumer wants. That puts pressure on all the surviving corporations, whatever their size, to conduct precise and speedy market research so they can offer products that match consumers' desires sooner than the competition.

Product cycles have shortened in part because new products and product improvements have come from countrywide chains. A good idea in one part of the country quickly rolls out across the landscape. Local companies no longer have the luxury of waiting years before their competitors come up with better ideas. Now new products that have been tested elsewhere— including in other countries—quickly become competitive with local products. Honda, for example, has cut conception-to-production time from years to a matter of months. Technological advances in product design and development also have greatly sped up the pace of new-product offerings.

INC: Does consumer opinion change more rapidly today?

BLACKWELL: For sure. Information now travels so quickly that consumers learn about new products and competitive improvements almost immediately. If Intel has a problem with a new chip, the information flies over the Internet in nanoseconds.

INC: Does information that flies around so quickly force the company owner to make faster decisions?

BLACKWELL: It increases the penalty for making wrong decisions. In the past, you might have corrected a problem long before very many people knew about it. But that era is history. Today there's real pressure to have dead-on market research. You've got to get it right because the whole world will know instantly if you've got it wrong. And they may never forgive you for a major mistake.

SOURCE: *Inc*, July, 1998.

Who Is Your Competition?

Think back to Chapter 2 when we talked about defining your business—not in terms of products—but in terms of benefits; not selling a book per se, but selling information, enjoyment, or pleasant memories. If your business was selling ice cream "old thinking" would ask you to list other ice-cream vendors and manufacturers. In the new school of thought, your competition is anyone who does or could provide the same benefit. If the benefit for your Target Customer is an afternoon treat, then your potential competitor is anyone who provides treats! Customers only have so many dollars and everyone wants those dollars. So your customer could stop and buy flowers, specialty coffee drinks, yogurt, sweet rolls, cookies, and so on. The other ice-cream store and yogurt stores in your area would be considered your primary competitors with the other businesses being your indirect competitors. Never underestimate the power of your indirect competitors.

The New Competitor Intelligence

by Leonard M. Fuld
www.fuld.com

Fuld explains how to locate vast amounts of data on your competitors and then discusses how to turn this data into useful analyzed information also known as "competitive intelligence."

Several of his book's chapters can be read online. We suggest you check out Chapter 6, which focuses on international competitor intelligence. Additionally, Fuld's Website provides excellent links to Asian, Canadian, European, and Latin American marketplace information.

Your competition is not necessarily who YOU think it is (although your views are important). Your customers define the competition in terms of those who can best satisfy their needs.

If you have truly listened to your customer as you completed the previous Action Steps, you may already be on your way to developing a profitable market niche.

Customer Touchpoints

As we have said before, people today are not just purchasing products or services, they are also buying what the products and services do for them. The customer's cry is "What's in it for me?" "How does it make my life better, easier, more effective, fun?" To get you started on evaluating your competition, first you need to recognize what is of value to your customer.

Ask them!

Gather together several of your potential Target Customers for a "group think" on your competitors. Walk together through the entire "experience" your customers encounter with your competition. We like to call this process "Evaluating Customer Touchpoints." Each touchpoint represents when the customer has contact with anything affiliated with your firm—from advertising, product, packaging, public relations, receptionists, salespeople, or the clean floor they walk on at your site. Making a list of all the touchpoints allows you to focus on areas where your competitors are weak. In addition, recognizing your competitors' strengths may indicate areas where you should not try to compete or where competition will be very intense. You want to not only make a list of these touchpoints but also to rank them in their importance to your Target Customer.

Where do openings exist? Can you successfully compete in those openings? What needs aren't being met? What area could you capitalize on? Where do you see yourself being strong? weak? What images are your competitors projecting? What image will you project?

Remember the Johnsons and the Healthy Gourmet from Chapter 4? Let's walk through the experience their customers encounter. (Many more steps could be added!)

- Receives advertisement in the mail
- What is the quality of the ad? Is it mailed first class? Is it addressed to the right person? How many mailings does the person receive before he or she responds?

▶ **Action Step 28**

Evaluating Customer "Touchpoints"

Investigate how your customers perceive the competition and what benefits are important to them. As you look for a niche in the marketplace, you must review your competitors' actions and products.

Work with a group of your potential Target Customers and walk through the "experience of purchasing your competitors' products." Make a very long list (at least 60-80 items) of each time the customer comes in contact with any facet of the competitors' business. Each facet makes up the entire product—the jewel.

Review the Healthy Gourmet example in the text before beginning the assignment.

After listing the touchpoints ask the Target Customers to select and rank the five most important.

You need to consider which facets are worth going head to head with, which are not worth dealing with, and which ones you can supersede your competition.

Keep your touchpoints handy, as you will return to them in Chapter 6.

Distinctive competency Area of greatest strength in the marketplace.

Competitor matrix A grid used to get a clear picture of competitors' strengths, weaknesses, and sales.

Positioning strategy Where you try to place a product in the customer's eye through pricing, promotion, product, and distribution.

- Responds to advertisement
- How quickly is the phone answered? Is the receptionist pleasant? How long does the customer wait on hold for a salesperson? Is the on-hold music appropriate? Is the salesperson knowledgeable and helpful? If the customer asks a question, how quickly does he or she receive a response? How well is the program explained in response to the customer's concerns?
- Places order
- Is the order form easy to fill out and understand? Is the form attractive? Is pricing clear? Are alternatives clearly spelled out?
- Customer receives order
- Was the correct order received at the right time and place? Is the meal attractively presented? Are heating directions clear? How does the meal taste?
- Customer calls to complain or change order
- How is a complaint call handled and the problem resolved?

To compete you need to stand out! Develop a **distinctive competency**. Own a niche. Success in business is not based merely on obtaining customers; success is achieved by retaining customers. So, as you seek out your competitors' strengths, look for those features that encourage customer loyalty. Remember to focus on the benefits your customers receive.

Discover the "customer touchpoints" in your business by completing Action Step 28. Later you will complete a **competitor matrix** to continue to evaluate your competitors.

Competition and Positioning

Basically, competition is a mind game played out in customers' minds where buying decisions are made. Inside customers' minds are many "ladders"—ladders for products, ladders for services, ladders for sports figures, TV programs, banks, and rental cars. To compete for a position at the top of one of these ladders, a business must first get a foothold and then wrestle with other businesses to improve its position.

It's that simple.

Looking at competition from this perspective helps you focus on the mind of the Target Customer. To explore this idea further, read the classic *Positioning: The Battle for the Mind* by Al Ries and Jack Trout.

The name of the competitive game is "change." It is the constant process of positioning your product or service to meet the changing needs of customers. You will use your **positioning strategy** to distinguish yourself from your competitors and create promotions that communicate that position to your Target Customers.

Complete Action Step 29 to help you get a foothold and improve your position on your customer's ladder.

How Can You Distinguish Yourself?

There are several different strategies for companies to look at as they research competitors and try to find an area where they can excel. In Key Points from Another View at the end of the chapter, Michael Treacy discusses the natural advantages small businesses have and how to capitalize on those advantages when meeting the Goliaths. He distinguishes three value disciplines:

1. Operational excellence such as Wal-Mart and Federal Express
2. Product leadership such as Intel
3. Customer intimacy such as Airborne Express and Nordstrom

No company can excel in all three, so focus on a value that differs from your major competitors. Reviewing your customer touchpoints, competitor information, and completion of a competitor matrix (at the end of the chapter) will help you focus further on your "distinctive competency" in the marketplace.

Scouting the Competition

Seek and Ye Shall Find

Now, let's really get an in-depth understanding of your competitors. When you understand your competitors, you'll be better able to visualize the position of your company in the grand arena of the marketplace. Action Step 30, which appears later in this chapter, will help you dig.

Remember, work from your strengths; strengths are built on knowledge. Knowing your competitors will increase your confidence. Then you can win.

Secondary Research

Before you begin your primary research, start with secondary data utilizing the library and the Net. In addition to the resources we have already introduced, the list of Resources (below) provides a great start on your researching. Many of these sources are also available on the Net.

Resources
Library References for Locating Information on Companies

Is the company publicly owned or is it privately owned/closely held?

1. *Directory of Companies Required to File Annual Reports with the SEC.*

Does the company have a parent company or subsidiaries?

1. *Directory of Corporate Affiliations.*
2. *International Directory of Corporate Affiliations.*
3. *America's Corporate Families.*

Do you need to know the company's type of business, executive officers, number of employees, annual sales?

1. *Standard & Poor's Register of Corporations.*
2. *Dun and Bradstreet's Million Dollar Directory.*
3. *Ward 's Business Directory of Largest U.S. Companies.*
4. *Career Guide: Dun's Employment Opportunities Directory.*
5. *Standard Directory of Advertisers.*

Do you need the company's corporate background and financial data?

1. *Standard & Poor's Corporate Records.*
2. *Moody's Manuals.*
3. *Walker's Manual of Western Corporations.*

Is the company newsworthy?

1. *Predicasts F&S Index.*
2. *Business Periodicals Index.*

Action Step 29

Scouting Competitors and Finding One's Position on the Competitive Ladder

Part A

Complete your secondary research on your Target Customers utilizing the text and other resources. Don't worry if your list of competitors gets too long. The more competitors you detect, the more you can learn.

Part B

Utilizing your touchpoints and past research, develop a competitor review sheet for each competitor. Go out on the streets and snoop away! Evaluate each competitor on each variable and rate them from 1-10. If you can't move inside without blowing your mystery shopper disguise, send in a friend with your checklist or do some cagey telephone shopping. You can elicit valuable information from a phone call survey that's prepared in advance. Interview everyone who will talk to you.

Is the company listed in a specialized directory?

1. *Thomas Register of American Manufacturers.*
2. *Best's Insurance Reports.*
3. *Standard Directory of Advertising Agencies.*
4. *U.S.A. Oil Industry Directory.*
5. *Who's Who in Electronics.*
6. *Fairchild's Financial Manual of Retail Stores.*
7. *World Aviation Directory.*
8. *Medical and Healthcare Marketplace Guide.*

How does the company rank in the industry?

1. Annual issues of *Fortune, Forbes, Business Week.*
2. *Dun's Business Rankings.*

SOURCE: Anatomy of a Business Plan, Linda Pinson

Utilizing Web sources can turn up a most helpful resource: the names and phone numbers of people involved in your industry, and those who may have conducted research in your area. You can also access fee-based services, as discussed in Chapter 3. Additional sources, such as the Science and Technical Information Network, provide incredibly detailed information. Private database vendors are invaluable to anyone in a technical field.

Remember when utilizing the Net, you can't believe everything you read. Act with caution before proceeding on information based solely on the Net. Track down the source. Information you pay for from the fee-based services may be more reliable.

12 Reliable Sources for Intelligence

Tracking the competition is no different from any other part of business life. The quality of your analysis can't exceed the reliability of your information. When it comes to finding reliable sources, nobody does it better than Helene Kassler (hkassler@fuld.com), 45, director of library and information services at Fuld & Company. That firm is the CIA of business intelligence—and she is its master operative. Her title is a cover for a fascinating job: unearthing information that no one else can find. With her help, *FAST COMPANY* assembled a list of reliable sites for you to use.

Web Site	What It Is	Helene's Hint
CEO Express **www.ceoexpress.com**	A fabulously comprehensive directory of links to major newspapers and trade magazines, custom news feeds, government agencies, and IPO alerts.	"My one-stop information shop. It has a truly remarkable collection of resources, and it's a great place to start a search."
Deja News **www.dejanews.com**	A Web-based search engine that monitors Usenet discussion forums. The site tracks more than 50,000 different newsgroups.	"Discussion groups aren't moderated, so many of the participants can be uninformed. It's up to you to validate what you find."
Northern Light **www.nlsearch.com**	A search engine on steroids. Its real treasure is its "special collection" of nearly 3,000 books, magazines, journals, news wires, and reviews.	"Northern Light gets rave reviews for being easy to use. It has a database of some really obscure publications."

**U.S. Industry and Trade Outlook—
Business Forecasts for 350 Industries**

Over 100 industry analysts in the Department of Commerce produce a
650-page annual outlook. Three hundred and fifty industries are analyzed
with both manufacturing and nonmanufacturing sectors included.
    Emerging trends, financial data, and review of economic and trade trends
are presented. The printed version is in your library and is also be available on
CD-ROM. To order contact 800 553-6847.

Web Site	What It Is	Helene's Hint
WhoWhere? **(Business and Investing)** **www.whowhere.com/ Business**	*The* place to start when you want to track down a person. WhoWhere? also lets you create a "Hotlist" of companies that it will watch for you.	"Great for alerting you to new information. You can have it send you an e-mail alert when one of your 'hot' companies submits a filing to the SEC."
Tierra Highlights2 & Web Whacker **www.tierra.com** **www.bluesquirrel.com**	These offline browsers monitor specific Web sites and alert you when information changes. Using them is like being on a perpetual stakeout.	"Basically, you get alerts about job postings and press releases right from a competitor's home page. Neat, huh?"
Corporate Information.com **www.corporateinforma-tion.com**	One of the few sites that offer in-depth information on companies outside the United States—an important feature in global economy.	"The other day, I clicked on 'United Kingdom' and discovered a bunch of really valuable sources. I recommend the site highly."
CareerPath.com & The Monster Board **www.careerpath.com** **www.monsterboard.com**	CareerPath.com posts classified ads from newspapers. The Monster Board lets companies post openings and job-seekers post resumes.	"I spend a fair amount of time on these sites—not because I'm looking for a job but because job openings can be a great source of intelligence."
IBM Patent Server **www.patents.ibm.com**	The ultimate resource for tracking technology. This site archives 2 million U.S. patent citations from the past 27 years.	"Patents offer a glimpse of the future, since a couple of years can go by from when a company gets a patent to when it markets a product."
CNBC/Dow Jones **(Business Video)** **www.cnbcdowjones.com**	Enough text—let's watch some tube! Live and archived audio, video, and multimedia clips for press conferences and corporate presentations.	"What a pleasure! You can see and hear analyst meetings and have access to information that you might not see in print for days—if ever."
Inquisit **www.inquisit.com**	The ultimate in alerts. Inquisit notifies you whenever there's news about companies, customers, markets or trends that you've asked it to track.	"Inquisit gives you same-day news that you might need days or weeks to get if you relied on just the industry trades."

SOURCE: *FAST COMPANY*, April/May, 1998.

Primary Research

If you've completed the customer touchpoints assignment, computer and library searches, it's time for you to become a "snoop" at your competitors. This is when your "new eyes" will come into full alert. If you are going to open a toy store, it's time to visit the toy stores within a 30-mile radius of your home. Take a notebook and write down information at each toy store. If it's easier for you, take a tape recorder and record your comments as you drive to the next store. Compile a list of customers' touchpoints and rank each store on a scale of 1-10. In addition, make a list of anything else you feel is vital for success in your selected industry and rank the stores accordingly. Actually pretend you are a customer at each store and walk through the total buying experience.

For each business make a Competitor Worksheet that includes all the important touchpoints, your criteria, and the following: competitor's business name, owner, address, phone, e-mail, fax, length of time in business, market share, Target Customers, image, pricing structure, advertising, marketing, customer service, strengths, and weaknesses. Take this part of your research seriously as you are discovering your niche in the marketplace by evaluating others.

Entrepreneurs frequently downplay their competitors. Do not underestimate the power of your competitors.

Manufacturing and Scientific Competition

The following areas may also need to be addressed in your competitor research, especially if you are in manufacturing or a scientific endeavor.

- manufacturing facilities
- distribution facilities
- patents
- financial strength
- profitability
- ability to acquire expansion capitalization
- cost of production
- employees (skilled sales force? incredibly great engineers? software designers beyond compare?)
- service reputation
- availability of spare parts
- repair costs

Additional Snooping

You may also want to conduct some snooping with suppliers. Fortunately or unfortunately they can and will provide a great insight to your competitors and the big picture. Beware of those suppliers who provide information they should not—they will provide the same information about you to your competitors in the future!

Attending trade shows and asking questions provides excellent market information. If you go with a friend or partner, split up so you can cover the entire show. Compare insights later.

No one knows an industry better than the salespeople who daily live in the trenches. The more of your competitors' salespeople you encounter the more you will learn.

Half the battle of succeeding is to understand the obstacles and to be on top of developments—to take advantage of all opportunities.

Never underestimate the loyalty, fickleness, and resistance to change of Target Customers. You must give them strong reasons to try your product and even stronger reasons to continue to utilize it.

The Competition's Life Cycle

Like everything else in life and business, competition has a four-stage life cycle: embryo, growth, maturity, and decline. In this chapter we will examine these stages and look at ways you can use them to meet and beat your competition. Briefly, we can describe the four stages of the competition life cycle as follows:

1. In the *embryonic* stage, the arena's empty. There's just you and your idea for a product or service and a tiny core market.
2. As your industry *grows,* competitors smell money and attempt to **penetrate the arena;** to take up positions they hope will turn to profit. Curious Target Customers come from all directions. You have visions of great success.
3. As the industry *matures,* competition gets fierce and you are forced to steal customers to survive. **Shelf velocity** slows. Production runs get longer. Prices begin to slide.
4. As the industry goes into *decline,* competition becomes desperate. Many businesses fail; weary competitors leave the arena, which is now silent except for the echoes of battle.

As discussed previously, competition life cycles have greatly changed over the past few years. For example, a few years ago, the embryonic stage for a computer software package might have lasted up to two or three years. The new economy has changed all that. Today, movement from one phase to another can occur at blinding speed.

It's not unheard of for a product to go through these four cycles in a matter of months. In the high-tech business, for example, a common rule of thumb is 3-6 months—that is, you've got six months from the birth of an idea to product penetration. After that time period, competitors have already entered the market, and the product begins to enter the declining phase.

What all this means is, to survive, you must constantly be in touch with the market and compete vigorously.

Where is your selected industry and segment on the competition life cycle? What does this mean to you if you're a start-up venture? What are the implications for your survival? When your industry enters maturity and decline, will you be ready with Plan B? Are you going to be a one-product wonder? The following information will help you get a feel for each stage.

Competition Life Cycle

The Embryonic Stage

The embryonic stage is marked by excitement, naive euphoria, thrust, clumsiness, a high failure rate, and much brainstorming. Pricing is high and experimental. Sales volume is low—because the market is very small and production and marketing costs are high. You need to locate your core customer and stress the benefits. Educating the customer may be necessary. Competition has not yet appeared. It's difficult to find distributors, and resellers demand huge gross margins. Profit is chancy and speculative. Shrewd entrepreneurs, however, can close their eyes and divine the presence of a core market. Keep trying! The writers of *Chicken Soup for the Soul* went to over 30 publishers before they found **the one,** which started their multi-million dollar empire.

Penetrate the arena Calculated thrust into the marketplace to secure market share.

Shelf velocity The speed at which a product moves from storage to shelf to customer.

The Growth Stage

Product innovation, strong product acceptance, the beginnings of brand loyalty, promotion by media sizzle, and ballpark pricing mark the growth stage. Distribution becomes all-important. Resellers who laughed during, the embryonic stage now clamor to distribute the product. Strong competitors, excited by the smell of money, enter the arena of the marketplace, as do new target customer groups. Profit percentages show signs of peaking. Brand loyalty begins as you try to establish your unique position. Media responses start to sizzle.

The Mature Stage

Peak customer numbers mark the mature stage. Design concentrates on product differentiation instead of product improvement. Competitors are going at it blindly now, running momentum even as shelf velocity slows. Production runs get longer so firms can take full advantage of capital equipment and experienced management. Resellers, sensing doom, cool on the product. Advertising investments increase, in step with competition. Some firms go out of business. Prices are on a swift slide down. Competition is very heavy. One needs to only enter this market if one has a very unique twist on the product or truly provides a better product. Also, can you realistically convey this message to the Target Customer?

The Decline Stage

The decline stage is marked by extreme depression in the marketplace. Competition becomes desperate. A few firms still hang on. R & D ceases. Promotion vanishes. Price wars continue. Opportunities emerge for entrepreneurs in service and repair. Diehards fight for what remains of the core market. Resellers cannot be found; they've moved on.

Competition and Positioning in a Mature Market

Sometimes it becomes clear to a lone entrepreneur or a big business think tank that making a **change in the arena** can spell opportunity in a mature market. Although we have encouraged you to aim for growth markets and growth industries, that is not always possible or desirable for an individual. But competing in a mature market takes even more creativity. The change may be very small—a slight change in some aspect of the product or service—but the effect on the market can be very large indeed. The world of business—large and small—is filled with stories of such breakthroughs, and the common thread of these stories is the discovery of an **area of vulnerability** in the existing product or service. Entrepreneurs love to hear these stories, and it's no wonder; the stories contain lessons and inspiration. That's why we include several here.

If you're in a mature industry, you're going to have to win customers away from competitors in order to survive. The name of the game is dictated first and foremost by your customers, and second by your competitors. Continually learn from your competitors and customers so that you can adjust your product or service to meet the needs and wants of the market. You can guide your business back into growth segments and thus create your own niche by using three major thrusts:

1. Beat the competition with superior service.
2. Create a new arena.
3. Create uniqueness by continually changing your product or service.

Change in the arena Transform a product or service by adding a benefit that has immediate customer appeal.

Area of vulnerability Competitor's soft underbelly or Achilles' Heel—a weakness ready for you to exploit.

Beat 'em with Superior Service

Tire Pro

Superior Service Reigns

James Grenchik was in the retail tire business. His father had passed away a few years back, and James was left with the opportunity to carry on the family business. With tires lasting longer, he became quite concerned. People (especially in the farming community, the mainstay of the family business over the past few years) weren't buying tires the way they used to. James tried price promotions and distress sales in an attempt to drive his competitors out of business. But these old techniques just didn't seem to work any more.

In fact, every time James looked around, there seemed to be a new competitor setting up shop in his market. Costco became a major competitor as well. James was getting discouraged and finally decided that this was no way to do business or, for that matter, to live. He had two choices—get out of business, or change. He knew before he went any further he needed to analyze his competitors so he developed a competitor matrix. (See Figure 5.1. In Action Step 30, you will complete a matrix for your business.)

After months of soul-searching, family discussions, networking, brainstorming, and reviewing his matrix, James finally decided to go for it:

1. He created a partnership with two key groups. First, he sold 25 percent of his business to a major tire manufacturer and retailer who he knew was the best in the market. His major competitor would now be his partner.
2. James sold 24 percent of his business to his key employees. They had been with him a long time, and he knew they were hungry to own a piece of his pie. Now his best employees were also his partners.
3. He created uniqueness by changing his product through service add-ons. These new services were the result of cooperative brainstorming by everyone in the firm. In addition, for three weeks each employee was to question each customer about additional services they might like to see Tire Pro offer. A few of the results are as follows:
   a. Tire Pro now offers an installment plan for farmers who need tires early in the growing season when they don't have much money coming in. This action also created a new arena—finance. Yes, the financial clout of his new manufacturing partner put Tire Pro in the finance business.
   b. All tire customers are given a free six-month rotation. At the same time they get a free report card on potential trouble spots. This new service strategy has changed their product, from just tires to "tires with a free rotation and inspection." Reminder postcards are mailed to each customer every six months.
   c. Tire Pro has another new customer service strategy. Customers who want a tire repaired can also get coffee, doughnuts, and the latest commodities report. A bulletin board for used farm equipment was installed in the waiting room which was now filled with farm, business, and kids magazines. Puzzles and coloring books were also added for the children. (One California car dealer now offers a putting green for its customers. Not the correct marketing tool for south Dakota farmers but just right for the Mercedes-driving entrepreneurs in Orange County, California!)

d. Everyone at Tire Pro now answers the phone with a first name and a pleasant hello—much easier now that they're making money again! The tire installers wear beepers and headsets so they can hear phone calls so distractions in the tire bays for both the employees and customers have been reduced greatly.
e. To encourage safe driving, Tire Pro now offers weekend driving classes for teenagers.

James and his new partners are now making money by providing the best products and services. But be aware that most of the above steps involve labor or marketing expenses, which must be recouped through increased profit and sales. His **core product** is tires; but James is also in repair and safety training—the rapidly growing service sector. Tire Pro is now getting ready to open its second outlet. Its market—financing, personnel, and competitive techniques—rescued Tire Pro from a declining sector and propelled it into a growth arena.

However, even if you start out in a growth market, there's one thing for sure. One day your market will enter a mature stage and eventually a declining one. You must adjust your product or service regularly to market changes. These, as we know, now can happen almost overnight.

Create a New Arena

Let's see how John George, owner of Home Office Havens, successfully changed the arena by developing a niche for himself in a very mature construction market.

Figure 5.1

Tire Pro Competitor Matrix

Potential competitor	Sales volume	Image/Advertising	Innovation	Location	Flexibility	Fullness of lines	Service rating	Personnel	Parking/Other services	Capital strength	Hours of service	Totals

Core product Item possessing perceived needs that best fits customers' needs.

Home Office Havens

Positioning Your Business

John George's family had been in the business of building new homes for 20 years. After a falling out with his family, John knew he wanted to remain in the same type of business but wanted to specialize and find a niche for himself.

Recently, many of his friends were purchasing computers and developing home offices. At parties, John's friends complained that their home-office situations were not ideal. There weren't enough electrical outlets, too much noise was entering the room from other rooms, and they needed more shelves and bookcases for their books and materials.

John kept listening and started scouting the area to see if anyone specialized in home offices. He found firms specializing in bathrooms, closets, kitchens, family rooms, and media rooms, but no one in the home office market.

He sat down with five of his friends and brainstormed about their needs and their willingness to invest in their home offices. After about five hours, the information indicated to John that his friends were willing to spend about $20,000 each to complete their home offices. John went into high gear, reading every home office magazine, contacting the Small Office Home Office Association, **www.sohoa.com,** and calling potential suppliers.

His best friend's sister, Samantha, became his first customer. Samantha agreed to show her remodeled office for three months to prospective customers in exchange for an extra desk.

To keep the competition at bay for a short time, John limited his advertising and built his first home-office projects through word of mouth. Once he was established, John developed his advertising and marketing with a beautiful professionally photographed portfolio of his projects. Since no other competitors had developed expertise in working within the home-office segment, John was a tough competitor. Knowing the benefits his customers desired gave him the edge when competitors came knocking. He owned the market! Upon realizing this, he contacted a franchise developer and, within two years, Home Office Havens became a successful franchisor.

Create Uniqueness by Continually Changing Your Product or Service

Change is the most predictable element of competition. Because of this, the entrepreneur needs to keep one eye on the market and the other eye on Plan B.

Ford Johnson has been in the mail order business for a dozen years now. He says it gives him a considerable freedom to be creative. Ford was trained as an electrical engineer, and spent 20 years in the aerospace industry before going into business for himself.

Always Ready with Plan B

Inventor Ford Johnson

Ford has developed and marketed more than 200 products—from a Mylar heat sheet (for pets) to Engine Coat (a motor lubricant using Teflon) to space monkeys (dried shrimp eggs that hatch when dropped into water). He's also developed a hundred strategies for handling his competitors. The best one is how he competes with himself. Here's the way it works:

Ford introduces a quality product into the marketplace. It retails for $12, which nets him a reasonable profit after overhead. Because he deals with

▶ **Action Step 30**

Construct a Competitor Matrix

The purpose of this Action Step is to rank your competitors and to visualize the positioning of each in the marketplace. Whenever you unearth some hard data, compare it with industry averages. Keep looking for those areas of vulnerability.

Now that you have a good picture of your major competitors and your Target Customers' desired benefits, you are ready to complete a competitor matrix.

List all of your major competitors on the vertical axis and all of the important benefits to your Target Customers and vital elements for operational success of your business in rank order on the horizontal axis.

Rank each competitor on a scale of 1 to 10 for each category (with 10 being the best). Total for each competitor by competitor. By the time you're finished you will have an overview of your competition and your opportunities.

Next, place and rank your new venture on the matrix and rate yourself. Note that the competitive marketplace is imperfect. Sometimes a few miles or a few hundred miles can make a significant difference in how competitive a business must be. If a mature marketplace is oversaturated, keep exploring other areas. You may find an underserved market that will welcome you instantly with warmth and healthy profit margins.

established mail order houses (they ship to thousands and thousands of customers), Ford knows someone out there will copy his idea and try to ace him by bringing out a lower-quality product for less money.

So, for the first couple of runs, Ford manufactures a quality product, using the best materials available. He charges full price for it, and waits for the phone to ring. When it does, he knows it's the buyer from the catalog house, telling him there's a competitor waiting in the wings with an **inferior product** that will retail for $6—half of what Ford's costs. So Ford has a cheaper one ready to roll.

"When do you need them, and how many can you handle?" Ford asks.

"Wait," the buyer says. "What kind of numbers are we looking at?"

"Mine will retail for $5.75," Ford says. "And I can have 10,000 on your loading dock by two weeks from tomorrow."

"You're kidding," the buyer says. (He's new on the block. Other buyers have watched Ford work before.)

"Can you move 20,000?" Ford asks.

"Ten for sure," the buyer says. "And if we need more I'll get back to you in two weeks."

"Over and out," Ford says. "It's great doing business with you."

You Can Do It!

We have provided you with a number of studies about entrepreneurs who worked with and learned from competitors and brought about big changes in the marketplace. It's altogether possible that we may someday be telling such a story about you. Yes, you too can do it. You just need to:

• Know what business you are in
• Know your Target Customers
• Know your competition
• Know the benefits of your product or service
• Develop strategies to capture and maintain your position
• Give rein to your creativity and your entrepreneurial spirit

Go for it! Surprise us! Surprise yourself! Action Step 30 will help you.

▶ *Summary*

Now that you have identified your Target Customers and evaluated your competition it's time to ask yourself. **"Am I offering my Target Customer a plus and is it hard to copy?"** Customers do not change their habits easily and businesses do not switch suppliers without extensive analysis. Unless you can offer something the other guys don't, you will struggle.

Competing on price alone is a very tough road. The big guy can almost always hold out longer than you and put you under quicker than you can ever expect.

Today, products and services cycle through the four life cycle stages rapidly. Being on top of your customers' needs and competitive changes in the marketplace is more important than ever. Use computer research, close contacts with customers and suppliers, and constant evaluation of your competitors to stay on top of the curve. Learn from your customers and competitors to help guide your business into a growth market. That's where the action is.

Inferior product Something that is lower in quality than what it's being compared to.

Think Points for Success

- Do it smarter
- Do it faster
- Do it with more style
- Provide more features
- Adjust your hours
- Provide more service
- Treat your Target Customers like family; consider their needs
- Be unique
- Change the arena through innovation
- Know your niche
- Keep your image in the prospect's mind
- Compete with yourself if necessary
- Disarm the competition by being better, faster, safer, and easier to use
- A new firm cannot win a price war
- Old habits are hard to break; give your Target Customer several reasons to switch over to you
- Develop your own personal monopoly
- Thrive don't just survive
- Talk to your Target Customer constantly and truly listen.

Key Points from Another View

Face to Face, by Michael Treacy

The first type of market leaders are focused on *operational excellence*. Those are the companies that, like Wal-Mart, are dedicated to providing low prices or, like Federal Express, concentrate on hassle-free service. The second kind of market leaders are companies that zero in on *product leadership*. They're companies like Intel and Nike that offer the best products in their markets and, through innovation, stay on top of product lines year after year. The third kind of companies that rise to the top star in what we call *customer intimacy*. Such companies promise to provide the best solution to whatever the customers' problems may be. They understand that the best product or the best price isn't the best value if the customer is unable to use the product effectively. Those companies *live* the customers' problems. Because of their close relationships, in fact, they are often the only ones in a position to recognize their customers' needs. Airborne Express and Nordstrom are good examples.

Does that mean that if your company focuses on customer intimacy, you can ignore operational efficiencies and product quality? Not by a long shot; you have to maintain a competitive threshold in the other two areas. But no company can succeed today by being all things to all people. Instead, the market leaders have organized themselves to achieve outstanding performance in only one area while remaining competitive in the other two.

SOURCE: *Inc.,* April, 1995.

6

Marketing Promotions Overview

Connecting with the Customer

Entrepreneurial Links

Books

Enterprise One to One, Don Peppers and Martha Rogers, Ph.D., 1997.
"301 Do-It-Yourself Marketing Ideas," Inc., *1997.*
Guerilla Marketing with Technology, Jay Conrad Levinson, 1997.

Websites

www.sbponline.com
www.gmarketing.com
http://advertising.utexas.edu

Associations/Organizations

National Association of Sales Professionals, www. nasp.com
International Customer Service Association, www.icsa.com
Customer Care Institute, www.customercare.com

Publications

Advertising Age, www.adage.com
Adweek, www.adweek.com
Guerilla Marketing Online Daily Bulletins, www.gmarketing.com

Additional Entrepreneurial Insights

The Discipline of Market Leaders, Michael Treacy and Fred
    Wiersema, 1997.
Best of Class: Building a Customer Service Organization, Ken Shelton,
    editor, 1998.
Send 'Em One White Sock and 66 Other Outrageously Simple (Yet Proven)
    Ideas for Building Your Business or Brand, Thomas L. Collins and
    Stann Rapp, 1998.

Learning Objectives

- Learn how to communicate with Target Customers using both conventional and creative promotional methods.
- Explore various promotional strategies.
- Promote your business through free ink/free air.
- Understand the value of sales reps and agents.
- Develop the best promotional mix for your business.
- Discover the importance of networking.
- View customer service as a key to promotion.
- Attach price tags to promotion ideas.
- Determine the dollar value of your customer.
- Understand the value of personal selling and sales strategies.

Promotion is the art and science of moving the image of your business to the forefront of a prospect's mind. Promotion comes from the Latin verb movere, which means, "to advance," "to move forward." It's an aggressive word, so learn to say it with a smile!

Now that you have visualized your customer with your Target Customer Collage and gained a sense of competition and market niches, it's time to plan a promotional strategy. Each business is unique, and you don't want to waste money on promotional schemes that won't work. For example, if your Target Customer is a college-educated, suburban female age 45 to 55, who earns over $100,000, owns three cars, rides horseback 10 hours a week, and reads Practical Horseman and Performance Horseman, your best chance of reaching her is with direct mail.

If, on the other hand, your Target Customers are male and female, age 18 to 25, with a high-school education, and incomes under $25,000, you'll achieve better results with some form of mass-market advertisement such as radio or television.

Developing a promotional plan requires four steps:

1. Determining your sales and marketing goals. (Increase sales by 10% this year.)
2. Developing strategies to achieve a goal. (Increase repeat business of best customers.)
3. Promoting a tactic that spells out a specific method for carrying out the strategy and having measurable objectives. (Mailer for special Christmas shopping night with a goal of selling $10,000 worth of merchandise during the evening.)
4. Enacting a program that details the specific promotional vehicle to be used. Programs should have budgets. (Gold embossed mailer sent to 300 best customers in November for special Christmas shopping night with free cookies, pastries, cider, and free gift-wrapping at a cost of $1000.)

Tie your promotional efforts into creating an overall image and presence consistent with your target market and business definition. Remember to stress customer benefits and your "distinctive competency."

Any promotion or **promotional mix** that advances the image of your business is worth considering. Survey some of the more common and traditional

Promotional mix All the elements that are blended to maximize communication with your Target Customers.

99

Opening Your Eyes to the North

Canada

Canada, as the United States largest trading partner, provides an easy entry into international trading. Travel is easy, language barriers are few, and a similar social and economic structure make Canada an excellent choice for your first international venture. With the North American Free Trade Agreement (NAFTA), opportunities are even wider.

Three great sources on the Net provide an excellent starting point:

- CanadaOne, **www.canadaone.com**, provides access to banks, business publications, chambers of commerce, media sources, legal issues, and much more.
- Statistics Canada, **www.statcan.ca**, is Canada's national source for Canadian data such as demographic, social, and economic, with many links to Canadian organizations and agencies.
- Doing Business in Canada, **www.dbic.com,** offers comprehensive information on how to trade with Canada.

means of promotion before you decide on your promotional strategy and be sure you remain open to all options. That's why we ask you to keep an open mind throughout this chapter, as you brainstorm for strategies, examine promotional campaigns, and come to understand the importance of planning ahead. You will then truly be able to make wise decisions on how to connect with the customer.

Critical to your campaign is what is appropriate for your Target Customer, what you can afford to spend (your budget), and your own prior experience. Most important, though, is what is *most likely* to give you "the biggest bang for your buck." Creativity, consistency, and repetition are the key elements to achieving a successful result.

Promotional Strategies

The Promotional Mix

The key to connecting with customers is to consider a wide variety of promotional strategies and then to choose the right one. Some of the potential elements of that mix are:

- paid media advertising
- point-of-purchase displays
- catalogs/catalog houses
- direct mail
- money-back guarantees
- free ink/free air
- personal selling
- trade shows
- industry literature
- working visibility
- specialty advertising/promotional products

- Web site and Internet advertising
- Web pages
- mailing lists
- sales reps
- networking
- exceptional customer service

The above allow one to pick and choose and combine various elements. You may use some at one time or with one product, and others at another time or with a different product or target market. For a closer look at each of these strategies, read on.

Potential Strategies

Paid Media Advertising

A surefire way to reach out is to advertise on radio and television, and in newspapers, magazines, and trade journals. Advertising tickles the Target Customer's mind. With a good ad, you can reach right into your Target Customer's mind and create the desire to buy from you.

If you are targeting consumers age 14 to 25, radio advertising is one of the best mediums. Contact your local radio stations for rate information. Creativity is essential in radio advertising. Figure 6.1 provides print advertising rate information from the Standard Rates and Data Services (SRDS) available in your library. Most entrepreneurs do not recognize the enormous cost for paid advertisements. We suggest you access the SRDS book, which covers radio and TV advertising as well.

Advertising has some obvious drawbacks: (1) it can be very expensive to create an effective ad, (2) you must spend even more money to ensure that the ad gets enough exposure, (3) **preferred placements** are reserved for the big spenders, and (4) costly repetition is essential for success.

Advice: Be sure that a large percentage of the listeners, viewers, and/or readers are in one of your Target Customer groups, otherwise your message will be wasted. Your practice with profiling in previous chapters should make you much wiser than the average entrepreneur.

Stock photographs are available for print ads. Look in the Business-to-Business Yellow Pages for stock photo studios. You describe what you want—for example, two Midwestern eighteen-year-olds on a date at the movies. They find the photo and, for a fee you are allowed to use it. Professional photographers supply these studios with hundreds of thousands of photos. Stock photo firms also ply their trade on the Net; or, CD-ROMs.

Stock TV commercials are available through firms that lease previously produced and successful local TV commercials. For a fee, you can lease the commercials for introduction into your local market—for example, a successful furniture commercial produced and aired in Spokane could have the firm's name replaced with your own and shown in Topeka. Be sure the commercial you select is aimed at the same Target Customers.

Contact your local cable TV stations to determine the cost of advertising. It may be surprisingly low. Many stations also sell production services, which will enable you to create your own original commercials.

Check with vendors. Ask for advertising copy, **co-op advertising** dollars, and help on layouts.

Ask for help, advice, and information from marketing departments of newspapers, radio and TV stations. Be sure to check out circulation figures and analyze the cost of various media. Newspapers often offer advertising in special supplements at reduced cost. The offer often includes free editorial copy.

Preferred placements The best locations within a publication, a store, or a business area; or the best time slots on TV or radio.

Co-op advertising A manufacturer's cosponsorship or contribution to a retailer's cost of advertising.

Figure 6.1
SRDS Information

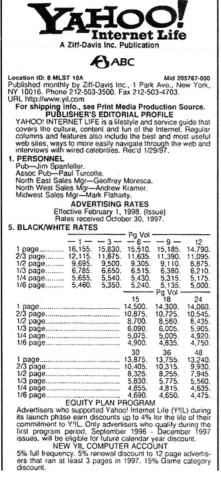

YAHOO! Internet Life
A Ziff-Davis Inc. Publication
(ABC)

Location ID: 8 MLST 10A — Mid 205767-000
Published monthly by Ziff-Davis Inc., 1 Park Ave., New York, NY 10016. Phone 212-503-3500. Fax 212-503-4703. URL http://www.yil.com
For shipping info., see Print Media Production Source.

PUBLISHER'S EDITORIAL PROFILE
YAHOO! INTERNET LIFE is a lifestyle and service guide that covers the culture, content and fun of the Internet. Regular columns and features also include the best and most useful web sites, ways to more easily navigate through the web and interviews with wired celebrities. Rec'd 1/29/97.

1. PERSONNEL
Pub—Jim Spanfeller.
Assoc Pub—Paul Turcotte.
North East Sales Mgr—Geoffrey Moresca.
North West Sales Mgr—Andrew Kramer.
Midwest Sales Mgr—Mark Flaharty.

ADVERTISING RATES
Effective February 1, 1998. (Issue)
Rates received October 30, 1997.

5. BLACK/WHITE RATES

Pg Vol	1	3	6	9	12
1 page	16,155	15,830	15,510	15,185	14,790
2/3 page	12,115	11,875	11,635	11,390	11,095
1/2 page	9,695	9,500	9,305	9,110	8,875
1/3 page	6,785	6,650	6,515	6,380	6,210
1/4 page	5,655	5,540	5,430	5,315	5,175
1/6 page	5,460	5,350	5,240	5,135	5,000

Pg Vol	15	18	24
1 page	14,500	14,300	14,060
2/3 page	10,875	10,725	10,545
1/2 page	8,700	8,580	8,435
1/3 page	6,090	6,005	5,905
1/4 page	5,075	5,005	4,920
1/6 page	4,900	4,835	4,750

Pg Vol	30	36	48
1 page	13,875	13,755	13,240
2/3 page	10,405	10,315	9,930
1/2 page	8,325	8,255	7,945
1/3 page	5,830	5,775	5,560
1/4 page	4,855	4,815	4,635
1/6 page	4,690	4,650	4,475

EQUITY PLAN PROGRAM
Advertisers who supported Yahoo! Internet Life (Y!IL) during its launch phase earn discounts up to 4% for the life of their commitment to Y!IL. Only advertisers who qualify during the first program period, September 1996 - December 1997 issues, will be eligible for future calendar year discount.

NEW Y!IL COMPUTER ACCOUNT
5% full frequency. 5% renewal discount to 12 page advertisers that ran at least 3 pages in 1997. 15% Game category discount.

6. COLOR RATES

2-Color:

Pg Vol	1	3	6	9	12
1 page	18,580	18,205	17,835	17,465	17,010
2/3 page	13,935	13,655	13,375	13,100	12,760
1/2 page	11,150	10,925	10,700	10,480	10,205
1/3 page	7,805	7,645	7,490	7,335	7,145
1/4 page	6,505	6,370	6,240	6,115	5,955
1/6 page	6,280	6,155	6,030	5,905	5,750

2-Color:

Pg Vol	15	18	24
1 page	16,675	16,445	16,170
2/3 page	12,505	12,335	12,130
1/2 page	10,005	9,865	9,700
1/3 page	7,005	6,905	6,790
1/4 page	5,835	5,755	5,660
1/6 page	5,635	5,560	5,465

Pg Vol	30	36	48
1 page	15,955	15,820	15,225
2/3 page	11,965	11,865	11,420
1/2 page	9,575	9,490	9,135
1/3 page	6,700	6,645	6,395
1/4 page	5,585	5,535	5,330
1/6 page	5,395	5,345	5,145

4-Color:

Pg Vol	1	3	6	9	12
1 page	21,000	20,580	20,160	19,740	19,230
2/3 page	15,750	15,435	15,120	14,805	14,425
1/2 page	12,600	12,350	12,095	11,845	11,540
1/3 page	8,820	8,645	8,465	8,290	8,075
1/4 page	7,350	7,205	7,055	6,910	6,730
1/6 page	7,100	6,955	6,815	6,670	6,500

4-Color:

Pg Vol	15	18	24
1 page	18,850	18,590	18,275
2/3 page	14,140	13,945	13,705
1/2 page	11,310	11,155	10,965
1/3 page	7,915	7,810	7,675
1/4 page	6,600	6,505	6,395
1/6 page	6,370	6,285	6,175

Pg Vol	30	36	48
1 page	18,040	17,880	17,215
2/3 page	13,530	13,410	12,910
1/2 page	10,825	10,730	10,330
1/3 page	7,575	7,510	7,230
1/4 page	6,315	6,260	6,025
1/6 page	6,100	6,045	5,820

7. COVERS
2nd cover gatefold, 4/C, extra 40%
4th cover gatefold, 4/C, extra 25%

8. INSERTS

	1 iss	3 iss	6 iss	12 iss
4-Color: BRC	6925	6715	6510	6025

9. BLEED
No charge.

10. SPECIAL POSITION
4/C, extra 15%

15. GENERAL REQUIREMENTS
Also see SRDS Print Media Production Source.
Printing Process: Offset Full Run.
Trim Size: 7-7/8 x 10-1/2; No./Cols. 3.
Binding Method: Perfect.
Colors Available: Black and white; Black and one color; 4-color process.
Covers: 4-color process.

NON-BLEED
AD PAGE DIMENSIONS
Sprd   15 x 10   1/2 h   7 x 4-3/4
1 pg   7 x 10   1/3 v 2-1/4 x 10
2/3 v 4-7/16 x 10

16. ISSUE AND CLOSING DATES
Published monthly.

Issue:	On sale	Closing (+)	(*)
Feb/98	1/13	12/2	12/5
Mar/98	2/17	1/6	1/9
Apr/98	3/17	2/3	2/6
May/98	4/14	3/3	3/6
Jun/98	5/12	3/31	4/3
Jul/98	6/9	4/28	5/1
Aug/98	7/14	6/2	6/5
Sep/98	8/11	6/30	7/3
Oct/98	9/15	8/4	8/7
Nov/98	10/13	9/1	9/4
Dec/98	11/10	9/29	10/2
Jan/99	12/15	11/3	11/6

(+) Space
(*) Material

18. CIRCULATION
Established 1995.
Summary data—for detail see Publisher's Statement.
A.B.C. 6-30-97 (6 mos. aver—Magazine Form)

Total Pd	(Subs)	(Single)	(Assoc)
275,796	204,929	70,867	

Average Non-Analyzed Non-Paid Circulation (not incl. above):
Total 55,928
TERRITORIAL DISTRIBUTION 3/97—280,660

N.Eng.	Mid.Atl.	E.N.Cen.	W.N.Cen.	S.Atl.	E.S.Cen.
16,508	35,844	37,733	16,780	47,450	12,114

W.S.Cen.	Mtn. St.	Pac St.	Canada	Foreign	Other
23,034	16,057	50,217	11,675	11,338	1,910

Publisher states: "Effective with February 1998 issue, rates based on a circulation average of 400,000."

ZD The Ziff-Davis Magazine Networks
A Ziff-Davis Publishing Co., Inc. Publication
Location ID: 8 MLST 10A — Mid 052228-000
One Park Avenue, New York, NY 10016.
See listing in Business Publication Advertising Source, in Domestic Publications section under classification No. 32C.

SOURCE: *SRDS Consumer Magazine*, p. 269.

Don't be afraid to **piggyback.** Let Madison Avenue build the market. Then use your promotional mix to tell the Target Customer to buy at your place.

Start small and test, test, test!

Consider classified ads in highly selected markets. Read publications on how to write an effective classified ad.

Check out Internet advertising opportunities; **www.wilsonweb.com** provides an excellent Web marketing information center with links to sources on Web branding, banner ads, design and pricing, Web demographics and more. Another useful Website is **www.e-land.com,** which provides information on Web advertising and building a Website.

Wizard of Ads

No cash for TV ads? Have we got a cream puff of a used commercial for you.

Eight years ago Randy Hecht was producing award-winning ads for J. Walter Thompson when he saw gold in commercial syndication: Why not buy the rights to successful local TV campaigns and lease them to smaller firms in different markets? Add a catchy voice-over and logo, and you've got a brand-new ad in the can.

Piggyback A technique that allows one to coordinate a local ad campaign with the hoopla generated by national advertising.

Small businesses benefit from the market research done by larger companies and are assured a quality presentation. Best of all, it's easy on the wallet. "Our clients will pay anywhere from $1,000 to $10,000 to use our ads, as opposed to paying $200,000 to make something from scratch," Hetch says. His company, AdvantEdge, has stockpiled more than 1,500 celluloid gems.

If a syndicated ad sounds right for you, contact a broker such as New York-based AdvantEdge (800-558-8237) or San Francisco-based AdExchange (800-243-2339), or call your local ad agency.

Aidan McNulty
SOURCE: *Success*, April, 1998.

Point-of-Purchase (P-O-P) Displays

These encourage impulse purchases of last-minute items like paperbacks, pantyhose, candy, magazines, and flowers. A sharp **P-O-P** must perform all of the selling tasks for you, serving as a tireless silent salesperson, always on duty. A good P-O-P can be used for customer education. If your product is difficult to use or the benefits unclear to the Target Customer, these silent salespeople can deliver your message. There are, however, problems with these displays: (1) you can't use them to sell large items because they crowd customers at the cash register, (2) merchants have limited floor space available and don't always want to use it for P-O-Ps, and (3) the display must sell itself as well as the product. A tacky P-O-P turns prospective customers off instead of on.

Advice: Do weekly evaluations of all P-O-Ps. Make certain your silent salespeople are doing their job. Consider hiring professional designers if this is your only distribution venue.

Catalogs

This sales tool is just right for isolated shoppers and shoppers in a hurry. Because we are so "time poor," even general items are now being purchased via catalogs. Customers can shop at their convenience and not have to worry about store hours, parking, or traffic. If you attempt to print your own catalogs, several problems can occur: (1) the costs associated with design, artwork, photography, and mailing can be very expensive—especially if you attempt a 4-color catalog; (2) your product may not show well in print; (3) the reader may not easily grasp the products' benefits; (4) it takes time and extensive resources to develop a successful mail order business. Catalogs can be considered as another kind of silent salesperson.

Catalog Houses

Catalog houses such as Lillian Vernon don't usually manufacture what they sell, so they are always looking for good products. Contact each of the major catalog houses you feel are aimed at your target market and ask for details about their product submission process. Products in catalogs are marked up (retailed) 3 to 5 times what the catalog houses pay (wholesale) for them. Determine first if you can make a profit in dealing with these houses based on the products and prices in their current catalogs. Look into QVC-type programs as well. Television shopping networks search for items that can sell in the tens of thousands. Their research is extensive and they know what will move.

Advice: There are now many online catalogs, which may also meet your needs. Let major catalog houses do your promotion, but make sure you can deliver if your product takes off. Ask for feedback from each catalog house you submit your **product description** to. If your product does not fit their needs, they may help you locate a better fit. Their feedback will be invaluable.

Direct Mail

This promotional tool lets you aim your brochures and flyers where they will do the most good. **Direct mail** is very important for small business because it

P-O-P A display that acts as a silent salesperson for a specific product.

Product description A list of features and benefits.

Direct mail Advertisement or sales pitch that is posted directly to Target Customers.

can go to the heart of your target market. Direct mail is also used extensively by business-to-business customers. Direct mail advertising is a science. If you are going to undertake writing the content for direct mail pieces, read the Direct Marketing Association's material before undertaking the effort. Per prospect reached, direct mail is very expensive. Check out the Website **www.dmworld.com** for an excellent library of information on direct mail advertising. If, after reading the material, you want to hire a professional direct mail expert, consider asking them to write your piece for a percentage of sales. If they believe strongly in your product, you may hit a goldmine with a terrific writer and achieve excellent results.

The success of direct mail depends on your ability to define the target market and develop an appropriate direct mail campaign. If the market is too fragmented for you to do this, direct mail is not for you.

Advice: Stay up nights if you have to, but define, refine, and refine again your Target Customer. If you aim wrong you have wasted all of your money! Develop customer lists. Check out mail list vendors in your Business-to-Business Yellow Pages. A vendor such as Polk will rent the right to mail to the names on a list of your choice one time and one time only. Mail list vendors work with you to select the proper mailing list or compilation of lists to meet your needs. Contact The Direct Marketing Association for further information at **www.the-dma.org** or *Direct Marketing World* at **www.dmworld.com.**

Money-Back Guarantees

If you haven't considered offering a guarantee as a form of promotion, consider it now! You can reach security-minded customers by emphasizing the no-risk features of your product. The problem is that you must back up your guarantee with time and money. Sally Jones purchased a kitchen remodeling business and found out that the former owners had treated several previous customers very badly. She decided to make good on their contracts and won not only their loyalty but the loyalty of everyone they told. It was a very expensive initial move but money was well spent.

Advice: Figure 5 percent into your pricing to cover returned goods. If the product is fragile or easily misused—and people have been known to misuse just about everything—build in a higher figure. Be sure all employees understand and honor guarantees.

Free Ink and Free Air

Reviews, features, interview shows, **press releases,** and newspaper columns cost nothing and are tremendously effective. **Free ink/free air** are an excellent promotional method because they establish your company in a believable way. Target Customers are likely to attach more credence to words that are not in the form of paid advertising. The obstacle here is getting a media person to believe your business is newsworthy.

Advice: Determine which media reaches your Target Customer and contact the writers and reporters who cover your type of business. Every business is newsworthy in some way. Dig until you find something—news, charity, controversy, photo opportunities, or humor. Call, write, or fax with your information. Make your press kit visual—send accompanying photos of your principals, your facility, and your product or service in use.

Personal Selling

It doesn't matter if you've never sold before; no one is a better salesperson than you. You are the business! If you listen carefully, your Target Customers will tell you how to sell your product or service to them. That's why a good salesperson is a creative listener, not a fast talker. Most customers like to talk with the owner of the business. Use that to your advantage. Unfortunately, **personal selling** is

Press release A news item written by a business about itself and sent to the media in an attempt to get cost-free advertising (free ink).

Free ink/free air Information about a business that is published or broadcast free of charge.

Personal selling Client service calls made by individual sales person or business owner.

expensive, especially if you have to pay others to do it, and it will boost your over-head unless you pay your salespeople on a commission-only basis. And if you try to do it all yourself, you may not have the time and energy for other things that only you can do. In the beginning, some entrepreneur's do not have many options. One inventor we know worked all night in his shop, took a nap, and then changed clothes for eight hours of selling on the road, only to return to his shop again at five to begin his design work. His firm is now valued at $20 million and customers still love to see him in the field. Building and maintaining relationships is essential for any small business.

Advice: Make everyone in your business a salesperson: delivery people, ware-house people, computer programmers, bookkeepers, and clerical workers. Never underestimate the importance of the person who is hired to answer the phone. Reinforce a positive attitude in all employees by reminding them that if nothing sells, they're out of a job; that your Target Customers need a lot of TLC.

Consider locating and hiring professional **sales reps** who will work on a per-centage-of-sales basis. Keep cheerleading. Reps need encouragement too. Be sure to never get so big that you can't personally go on some sales calls. If you loose touch with your customers, they may loose touch with you.

Trade Shows

These shows display your product or service in a highly intensive way. Trade shows develop a carnival and county-fair atmosphere. Your appearance at a trade show asserts your position in your selected industry. However, if the trade show is not local, you'll have transportation costs. Also, booths are expensive. Further, unless you're careful and study the layout, you could rent a space that is thin on **traffic**. If you haven't participated previously at a trade show, you may not be of-fered a choice location.

Advice: Share booth space with another small businessowner or with a com-plementary business. Combine functions by doing some market research while you're promoting. Study the trade show's floor plan and try to position yourself in a high-traffic area.

Industry Literature

Become a source of information in your industry by producing brochures, newsletters, handbooks, product documentation, annual reports, newspaper columns for the layperson, or even the "bible" for your industry. Become a rec-ognized expert in your field. We believe this is one of the best promotional de-vices around. If you're not handy with words that can be an obstacle, but it's not an insurmountable obstacle. Remember, expertise is admired and sought out by others. As you grow in expertise, you'll also grow in confidence and the ability to communicate with words.

Advice: Hire a writer. If you get your thoughts down on paper, you're two steps ahead of the talkers.

Working Visibility

Develop and maintain a presence. Make yourself stand out from your competi-tors. One pool-cleaning business required all pool cleaners to wear spotless white lab coats on their routes. In addition, the business paid for their cleaners' trucks to be washed each week. Because they looked professional, sales skyrocketed. Most service firms display their presence as they work—they put signs on everything: their business, their trucks and their worksites. Wherever they're busy, they let people know it. They make themselves visible. The drawback here is similar to one of the drawbacks with P-O-P displays. If the presence you maintain doesn't sell itself—if it is unattractive, or if it calls attention to an unsavory part of your business—you will lose rather than gain potential customers.

Sales reps Independent salespeople who sell a number of noncompeting products and services in a specific geo-graphic area on a commission-only basis.

Traffic The numbers of potential buyers who pass by, view, or stop at one's booth in a trade show; vehicles or pedes-trians that move past a business site in the course of a normal day.

Advice: Exploit your public activities with signs that tell people who you are. Review your displays frequently. Be sure the message is working. Walk around with a sandwich board—until someone stops you.

Specialty Advertising/Promotional Products

Specialty advertising, now known as promotional products, is a targeted, cost-efficient means of promoting a company's products or services. For the small business, this can be a very effective use of marketing dollars.

Promotional products break through communications clutter and leave a lasting impression. In addition to client marketing, many companies use promotional products for internal marketing to their employees, via recognition and employee motivation programs.

Promotional products keep a company's name or message in the front of a customer's mind. They can be used as a thank you, trade show traffic builder, goodwill builder, for customer or employee loyalty reward, or as a new product/service introduction tool.

The cost of promotional products ranges from pennies to several hundred dollars. When selecting an item, key considerations are: budget, quantity needed, time frame, the audience receiving it and, of course, the goal. What are you trying to achieve?

When used to build trade-show traffic, an item that involves the recipient can be effective at keeping a prospect at the booth, allowing time to be qualified or generate interest in your products. An example is a stress-testing card, which requires the user to place his or her thumb on a stress indicator patch for 10 seconds. After completing the test, the person often shows the result and asks the trade-show staffer to take it, allowing even more time to build a relationship.

Pre-show mailings also can be used to build traffic. An eyeglass case can be mailed with an invitation to stop by and pick up a free pair of sunglasses. Or a long-distance telephone card can be mailed, but activated only if the recipient brings it to the booth and perhaps fills out a short marketing questionnaire. Drawings for prizes and gifts can be used to develop a mailing list or ask market research questions.

Sound chip cards have proved an effective way to open doors or introduce new products and services. Available in many sounds, from a ringing phone to applause, these cards have impact and generate interest, helpful in reaching hard-to-reach prospects.

Continuity advertising programs can be developed where several gifts are sent over a period of time, often with a theme. A baseball theme campaign could include a stadium cushion, baseball, cap, pennant, ticket-shaped keychain, bat-shaped pen, cap-shaped paperclip dispenser, sound chip card that plays "Take Me Out to the Ball Game," and a package of peanuts.

SOURCE: Lesley Ronson, Lee Wayne Company, Powerful Promotional Merchandise, 630-752-0922.

Earlier we said that if you fail to plan, you're planning to fail. When it comes to promotion, if you fail to plan you're planning to keep your business a secret.

One way to avoid keeping your business a secret is to brainstorm an ideal **promotional campaign** with no holds barred and no worries about costs. Action Step 31 makes sure you consider all of your creative ideas before discarding them as unrealistic. Save the ideas you come up with in Action Step 31 because

Promotional campaign A sales program designed to sell a specific product or service or to establish an image, benefit, and/or point.

you will use them later. We hope you will apply ingenious and cost-effective solutions to your promotional needs.

As you'll see throughout Chapter 6, the entrepreneurs who succeed are the ones who have the best fix on their Target Customers. They are also the ones who understand the importance of market research and tracking their advertising expenses.

Winning Promotional Strategies

Choosing the right promotional strategy for your business may prove to be a big win. The examples show how several entrepreneurs discovered their winning strategies. While reading what these entrepreneurs have to say, you may discover your own winning strategy. Look for inspiration.

Earth to Air Travel, Inc.

Newsletter

Two years ago we missed the ironclad deadline for getting our ad in the Yellow Pages, so we tried to make up for that by placing fun-type ads in community newsletters within a 10-mile radius of our agency. The ads didn't cost much, and we hoped they would help to keep our visibility high. Our best response came from a mobile home park less than a mile away. It's a goldmine of steady-income retirees who dearly love to travel frequently. We offered monthly travel seminars at the mobile home park where we introduced new trips and our clients could share their travel experiences. For the cost of wonderful pastries and coffee, we are usually able to book four to six trips. An excellent return on our investment.

By studying community newsletters, we came up with our own format, and now send out our own monthly agency newsletter. On the front page of our newsletters, we picture our employees. The pictures help us connect, especially with first-time customers. They see our smiling faces, and most feel they know us when they walk through our door. We're already on the way to being friends.

The Software School

Direct Mail

When we started the Software School, we quickly discovered the major local newspaper covered the northern half of the county, while the entrepreneurial market we'd targeted lived in the southern half. The one way to reach the center of our target market was with a direct mail piece. Our strategy was to rent a list from a magazine whose readers matched our profile— in this case, Inc.—and then to send out our brochure.

The response was terrific. We generated enough business for a healthy start-up, and after that satisfied customers sold for us by talking up our one-day teaching system.

Direct mail allowed us to go right to the heart of our target market. When you're just starting out in a new venture, that kind of accuracy is worth every penny it costs.

Garment District Guide

Free Ink

When my partner and I got the idea for guiding shoppers through the Los Angeles garment district, we thought it would be so exciting we wouldn't have to do much except stop once a week to make bank deposits.

Were we ever wrong!

We ran a good-sized ad in our local paper. We filled a couple of buses, but then our market ran out because those customers didn't need a return trip to LA for shopping on the bus. We had some flyers printed up and covered every car in every parking lot in our community. Two thousand flyers and sore feet netted us half a bus.

Then a feature story appeared in the View section of the Los Angeles Times about a tour to Hollywood and Beverly Hills. On an impulse we called the reporter and told her about Garment Guide.

It worked.

On the next trip, the reporter came along, and brought a staff photographer. Two weeks later, our story was on the front page of the View section—a beautiful third of page—and customers began calling us! Our local papers followed a month or so later with features about the service, and after we got bigger, a TV reporter profiled us for one of the evening newsmagazines of television.

Now business is great. We haven't had to pay to advertise for 18 months. When times are slow, we increase our **networking** activities and try to book group trips. We also started targeting groups with special trips, such as the Back to School Bus, Santa Sleighs, Spring Fling, and Mother-Daughter Mother's Day Specials. With each trip being unique we get more free press. When people ask me what kind of promotion I believe in, I tell them free ink!

Mel's Toys

Customer Mailing Lists

The toy business is seasonal and with all the people coming through the door, I wanted to make sure I developed a solid customer base. So, for three weeks, I hired the most wonderful authentic Rent-a-Santa I could find and a professional photographer. Every child who came into my store was photographed and the parents filled out information cards with their child's name, age, toy preferences, and date of birth. As an added bonus, I made the negatives available to parents, many of whom ordered Christmas cards picturing their child talking to Santa.

At the end of three weeks, I had developed a fine customer list and one valuable piece of information—the birthday of over 500 children. Every time a birthday rolled around, I mailed a small inexpensive toy and a discount coupon.

As my mailing list grew, I came up with another idea.

I was at the cash register one day when I noticed five customers in a row who spent more than $75. I kept those checks and credit card slips separate, and at the end of the day I copied them and started a Big Spender list. Today, my Big Spender list has grown to several hundred customers, and I've developed a special mailer aimed just at them.

And to think it all began with a Rent-a-Santa!

Networking Communicating via person-to-person channels in an attempt to exchange information.

We hope you found inspiration by reading about these entrepreneurs who, through planning, perseverance, or luck found successful promotional strategies.

You may not need a Rent-a-Santa, but you do need a well-organized promotional campaign. Be sure to gather **customer files.** With good files, information becomes useful. Organized information is power.

Sales Reps as Connectors

Suppose you have a new product that has immediate sales potential across the country. How can you connect with the whole United States? Should you hire your younger brother to take care of it for you, or should you seek out a professional sales rep that acts like a commissioned sales agent?

An army of trained professional sales reps awaits your call. However, a rep is not a rep is not a rep; select your reps carefully. Exercise caution because the reputation of your sales reps will become your reputation.

The best way to find good reps is to interview potential buyers of your goods. Ask them to recommend reps who they consider the very best in their field and who they enjoy working with. When the same names surface several times, you will know who to start calling. In addition, contact the rep associations listed below.

Trade associations, shows, and journals also provide information on rep associations. Reps attend trade shows to discover new products to carry so if you have a booth actively try to reach reps at your show. Aggressive reps may contact you if you have a "hot product."

To determine the prevailing practices for commissions, territories, and termination agreements for your selected industry contact the associations listed below. Hire reps based on their knowledge of the industry, established customer base, and their ability to sell to your customers effectively and efficiently. Reps usually carry complementary lines.

Ask the reps:

- How many salespeople are in your firm?
- What is your background and experience?
- What geographic territories do you cover?
- What complementary lines do you represent?
- What ideas do you have for trade show presentations?
- Would you work with us on a regional rollout, while we prepare for national coverage?
- May I participate in sales meetings and help train the reps on my product line?
- What kind of reports on your sales calls can I expect?
- What kind of performance guarantees do you offer?

Provide all the encouragement and support to your reps that you can; never stop being a cheerleader. Insist on sales call reports that will keep you informed on what is going on in the field; pack your bags and make some calls with the reps. Write monthly sales letters and encourage feedback from both your reps and their customers. Feedback helps you to evaluate your product line and your reps.

Sales Rep Resources
Manufacturer Representative Associations

Manufacturers Agents National Association
www.MANAonline.org
23016 Mill Creek Road
Laguna Hills, CA 92654-3467
(949) 859-4040

Customer files Lists of persons or firms that have already made purchases.

North American Industrial Representative Association
www.nira.org
400 E. Randolph Street, Suite 500-6
Chicago, IL 60601-0820
(312) 240-0820

Electronics Representatives Association
www.era.org
444 N. Michigan Ave. Suite 1960
Chicago, IL 60611
800 776-7377

To locate sales representatives in foreign countries, call the embassy or consulate for each country and speak to a trade expert and request information on reps in your industry. The Department of Commerce also provides trade information.

Networking

Another source of promotional power is the technique of networking, which carries the image of your business to a support group of noncompetitive helpers. An expert on networking, Susan Linn, defines the term broadly: "Networking is utilizing your contacts to get what you want. Commonly, networking is used to refer to group situations in which business people can interact. It's a current buzzword for the age-old principle 'It's not what you know but who you know'."

Networking gives you confidence and allows you to pass on helpful information to people who aren't directly competing with you—as well as receive helpful information.

Networking for Success and Survival

When Rob and Gena D'Angelo decided to go into business, they looked around for more than a year. Gena had some training in graphics and Rob was good with numbers. They finally decided on a franchised mailbox operation. They paid a flat fee and agreed to pay the franchisor a percentage of their gross. The franchisor gave assistance and a well-developed Business Plan.

What they didn't tell Rob and Gena about was networking.

When one's in the mailbox business, giving good service is how to forge ahead. They knew they had to promote their image and tried everything— brochures, leaflets, flyers, and half-page display ads in the local newspapers. But the business didn't start rolling in until Gena joined her first network.

It was a sales lead club, and the membership varied: a real estate broker, an insurance agent, the president of a small bank, the owner of a coffee service, a printer, a sign manufacturer, the owner of a chain of service stations, a sporting goods storeowner, a travel agent, two small manufacturers, and a contractor. Breakfast meetings were held once a week. If a member didn't bring at least one sales lead for another club member, they had to put $5 into a kitty. Gena got more business from that club than from all other promotional efforts combined. So she joined another network club and used the contacts she made to build her own network.

Business has been good ever since. Rob and Gena opened a second mailbox shop last April, put in two new computers, a laser printer, and added an answering service. They continue to network their way to even more business, and are planning to open a third shop 10 miles south of their present location by this time next year.

Why You Should Network

You've probably been networking all your life. In school, you networked for information about teachers and courses. When you moved into a new community, you networked for information about doctors, dentists, car service, babysitters, and bargains—all the life-supporting details that make up existence. On the job, you networked your way to sales leads, brainstormed your way to better design, or got in a huddle with some fellow manager or coworkers to solve problems.

As a small business entrepreneur, you can network your way to a surprising number of new customer connections, which can spell success in big letters. Develop your network and build **core groups** of people within it. Because a network grows naturally from the loose association of people you already know, and because you are at the center of the net, it has to help you.

Networking Organizations

The bottom line for networking is—people do business with people they know and are most comfortable with. So get out there and meet people who can help you grow your business. When others spread the word about you, it is like having your own private unpaid sales force working for you! This doesn't just happen. Joining a networking organization is not enough. You must decide to become an active member of the organization. Take positions of leadership. Get to know everyone you can. Do things for others. Make networking a way of life. Be sure you have your paragraph from Action Step 23 down pat as you will have many chances to present it. Before you start to join organizations, ask yourself:

What is the purpose of this organization?

What type of people do I enjoy being with?

Do I want to make a political or social statement with this involvement?

Am I participating solely for business purposes?

Most organizations will allow you to attend at least one meeting free with no obligation to join. We suggest you attend as many organizational meetings as possible to determine which best fit your personal and business needs.

What kind of networking groups are out there?

Trade organizations that focus on a particular industry and where you will share primarily with your peers. An excellent place to make contacts to find suppliers, attorneys, accountants, and so on. Involvement at the local level can lead to positions at the national level, which will widen your exposure further.

Leads clubs such as the one Gena and Rob D'Angelo belonged to generally meet on a weekly basis for breakfast, lunch, or dinner to share leads. One national group is LeTip International, 4901 Morena Blvd., Suite 703, San Diego, CA 92117, **www.letip.org,** 800 538-4707.

Political clubs such as Democratic and Republican clubs provide excellent opportunities to expose your business widely.

Women's organizations such as American Association of University Women (AAUW), Women in Communications (WICI), National Association of Women Business Owners (NAWBO) focus on social, trades, or business efforts.

Chambers of commerce are excellent sources of local business contacts. One does not have to live or work in a city to join and participate in its Chamber of Commerce.

Local social and community groups offer the power of community participation to reach a local customer. Many realtors have found their local PTA efforts have paid off handsomely by increasing their client pool.

Core groups Clusters of influential, key individuals who share a common area of interest.

Score Free Assistance

Advice from the Start

A nonprofit association, SCORE was formed 34 years ago to provide education for entrepreneurs and to encourage small companies. Headquartered in Washington, D.C., it is sponsored by the U.S. Small Business Administration.

Through SCORE, more than 12,000 retired and active business owners and executives serve as volunteer counselors, offering advice on topics, such as writing a business plan, managing cash flow, and obtaining capital. There are 389 SCORE chapters and 450 additional branch locations around the country.

About 300,000 entrepreneurs received counseling or attended SCORE workshops last year.

Without her SCORE counselors, "I wouldn't be here," says business owner Lindsay H. Frucci of Elkins, N.H. "There's absolutely no way I could have accomplished what I have accomplished without them."

Frucci started No Pudge! Food, Inc., which makes fat-free brownie mixes, in 1995. Even before launching the company, she turned to the nearby SCORE chapter in Lebanon, N.H., for guidance.

She was assigned to two counselors, Robert Y. Fox of Hanover, N.H., who was a vice president and associate general counsel of General Foods, and Jason K. "Jay" Albert of Tetford Center, Vt., a former small-business owner and president of a specialty food company. They have worked with Frucci as a team, meeting with her in two-hour sessions about 50 times over nearly 3 1/2 years.

"They taught me everything from the ground up," says Frucci, 46, whose company, a home-based enterprise, brought in more than $250,000 last year, its second full year of business.

"The big thing we helped her accomplish was to get this business started without spending a great deal of money," says Fox. Instead of doing the manufacturing herself, for example, Frucci took her counselors' advice and found another company to make the mixes.

In addition, Fox and Albert guided her through getting a line of credit at the bank, doing a trademark search, registering her company name, setting up her corporate structure, finding distribution channels for her products, and helping her with all the other tasks associated with starting a business. "They both brought just volumes of knowledge, just amazing knowledge," says Frucci.

Here are some tips from business owners and SCORE staff members and counselors for getting the most out of SCORE:

Don't wait. Seek SCORE's help before you take steps that might become expensive mistakes. "We have too many people coming to us who have already signed leases and bought things," says Fox. "They shouldn't do that until they've got their business plans ready and their cash-flow projections lined up."

Now and then people are already in trouble when they go to SCORE. "We work hard to try to get them out of it, but sometimes that's not possible," says Fox, who has counseled about 70 business owners since joining SCORE six years ago.

Be choosy. If the first SCORE counselor assigned to you does not seem right for you or if you are uncomfortable with the person, ask to be assigned to someone else. "People need to go in and almost interview the counselor," says Frucci. "If they're hooked up with someone they're not comfortable with, they need to be free to say, 'Is there someone else within this SCORE office that you think might be suited to what it is I'm trying to do or that might have experience in the business I'm in?'"

Check out other SCORE programs. SCORE chapters offer modestly priced seminars and workshops on topics such as starting a business, developing a business plan, and protecting your invention. Such programs can help you frame questions for discussion with your counselor and make the counseling sessions more useful.

Take full advantage of the full counseling. You'll get more out of it, says Yancey, if you let SCORE become a mentor. He advises visiting your SCORE counselor regularly so the counselor can get to know your business well. One restaurant-owning couple have had nearly 90 sessions with their counselor, according to SCORE.

"If you're a counselee at SCORE, suck us dry," says Albert.

Look for teamwork. Many SCORE chapters emphasize team counseling so clients can receive the benefit of different types of expertise offered by different counselors.

If you think you need specific knowledge that your counselor lacks, you can request that someone with that knowledge be brought in to help.

At SCORE's Web sit, **www.score.org,** there's a new feature: the opportunity to get counseling via electronic mail from about 240 participating volunteers. In addition, the site answers questions about SCORE, provides profiles of successful SCORE clients, and find the SCORE locations nearest you. (You can also determine the nearest SCORE chapter by calling the national SCORE office at 1-800-634-0245).

Even though Lougheed has an MBA degree and has been a brand manager for major corporations, she says, "If you're starting a new business and you don't check out SCORE, it's just silly."

She emphasizes, however, that "this is someplace where people aren't just going to tell you what you want to hear." And that's good, she says, because if your business idea is not viable, it's better to find out up front.

For SCORE's Yancey, the bottom line is this: "We want to help people make better-quality business decisions."

SOURCE: Adapted from "Coaching the Women's Team," *Nakim's Business,* May 1998, pp. 70–72.

Visit many, join some, and heavily participate in a few, which will have the best payoff for you.

During the recession of the early nineties one marketing consultant, Nancy Hopp, continued to network in eight organizations. At one point, she was spending 20-30 hours donating her time to keep busy. As the recession wound down and the good times started to roll, her business skyrocketed. Her community contacts were back in business and so was she! Nancy has never advertised and has relied totally on word of mouth and community contacts for customers. Networking doesn't cost anything but time and can yield incredible results for those willing to develop relationships. Another low-cost promotional tool is customer service.

Exceptional Customer Service as Promotion

Exceptional customer service provides your firm with three vital ingredients for growth: relationships, reputation, and references. Building relationships early in a small business is essential. From strong relationships will come a good reputation and good references.

Take the time and effort early on to get to know everything you can about your Target Customers. The closer you are to customers the more likely you will be able to meet their needs. If you are passionate about your customers, you may be lucky enough to breed passionate customers who care about your success. Customers who want to continue doing business with you will tell you how to

► **Action Step 32**

Exceptional Service through Touchpoints

Pull out Action Step 28 on your customer touchpoints. Compile a list of each touchpoint. Now, brainstorm away and list how you could make each touchpoint a memorable point for your Target Customer. In building exceptional customer service, you can't just meet your customer's service needs; you have to exceed them!

- If you are sending a package, what could you include to brighten their day?
- If you are serving them a fast-food meal, what could you do to make it quicker?
- If you are sending architectural drawings for review, how could you help them to better understand the drawings?
- If you own a candy store, what extra could you give each time a customer came in the door?

Some things you come up with will not be possible due to time or money constraints, but those you can incorporate will be greatly appreciated by your customers and you'll be on your way to being an exceptional business.

Keep refining these touchpoints. As you travel to different businesses be sure to incorporate their strongest service advantages into your business.

improve. Listen to these passionate customers and encourage their participation in your business. Out in the community or in your selected industry, they will be your sales force. A sales force no money could buy!

Gaining a new customer costs fives times the cost of retaining a customer. Do *all* you can to retain your customers!

Remember, people are buying solutions to a problem and want an exceptional and memorable experience. Always be mindful of making the experience one they will want to share with friends and colleagues. You have studied your competitors and target markets extensively and should know what benefits and customer service level are not only desired but also expected. Exceptional customer service increases the bottom line. Complete Action Step 32 by returning to Action Step 28 on touchpoints and determining how you can make each touchpoint a memorable experience. You want your customers to shout your company name from the rooftops. Study premiere companies in customer service—Neiman Marcus, Nordstrom, Dell Computers. Implement the best of their service strategies into your business.

Talk About Service with a Smile

Irvine-based Claim Jumper did that and more when it mixed up the date of the wedding reception it was catering for Daniel McGirr and Leslie Kelly, says McGirr's grandfather, John Rau, president of David Industries in Orange. Wedding guests started showing up for the post-ceremony fun, but there was no caterer. Claim Jumper quickly corrected the error. Instead of sending the regular staff, though, top management handled the job, including Scott McIntosh, chief operating officer, who set up tables, served food and cleaned up. There was no charge for the catering, McIntosh said. And Claim Jumper also picked up the tab for the couple's Hawaiian honeymoon.

SOURCE: Orange County Register, July 8, 1998.

To be effective everyone in the organization must practice exceptional customer service. It has to be a way of doing business at all times. Employees must know their responsibilities:

- Proactively serve the customer. "How can I help you?"
- Power to act. "How can I solve the problem?"
- Provide information. Educate and communicate with customers. "No, we no longer sell Item B but let me show you Item C which we now carry and I will show you how it compares favorably."

When developing your customer service credo for your firm consider first what is most important to your customers and honor that variable first. You cannot be everything to everyone and have to be careful not to give away the store by offering more than you can provide profitably.

What Is Your Customer Worth?

Take a moment to determine how much your customer is worth. If you own a bookstore and your average customer purchases $25 of books a week, your customer is worth $1300 ($25 \times 52$) annually. If you plan on keeping that customer over the next 10 years, he or she now becomes a $13,000 customer.

Would you and your employees treat customers differently if you envisioned them with the figure $13,000 emblazoned on their forehead? The answer for most is a resounding yes! Taking it out further, what if that $13,000 customer brought in on average of three new customers to your store each year. Is that customer now a $52,000 customer?

The trick here is for everyone in your firm to truly realize the dollar value of each potential customer they serve. How can you get everyone to remember the $13,000/$52,000 figure? put it on the cash register? sales slips? order forms? paychecks? an employee contest for a new Mercedes based on the $52,000 figure?

Action Step 33 asks you to determine the dollar value of your customers and a creative way to make that figure memorable to all your employees.

You have reviewed the importance of networking, customer service, and an integrated promotional campaign. It's time to develop your ideas into a promotional strategy.

Attach Pricetags to Your Promotional Strategies

You are ready now to make decisions about your promotional mix. Look at the ideal promotional strategies you came up with in Action Step 31, pick the top four or five elements you can realistically do at this point, then determine the price of each. Action Step 34 walks you through this process.

Don't be discouraged if cost knocks out part of your ideal promotional mix. That's why we've filled Chapter 6 with so many inexpensive promotional ideas. And, in the meantime, you have used the powers of your imagination to brainstorm the best possible promotional effort for your business.

 Summary

Promotion is the art and science of moving the image of your business into the prospect's mind and keeping it there. Anything that will advance the image is a good tactic to consider. We recommend that you survey the whole range of promotional strategies available and then choose the promotional mix that will work best for your unique business and financial resources. Potential strategies include paid media advertising, free ink and free air, personal selling, trade shows, industry literature and exceptional customer service.

We also recommend that you seek creative solutions to the problem of small-business promoting. New businesses can take creative license and stretch the limits early on in getting their business off the ground. If you are not creative, hire people who are to help you stand out from the crowd.

A coordinated marketing plan focused on Target Customers is essential.

Think Points for Success

- Be unique with your promotions. Instead of Christmas cards, send Thanksgiving cards or April Fools' Day cards.
- Stand in your Target Customer's shoes. Think like your Target Customer. Find the need. Always refer back to your Target Customer Collage to keep the customer in the center.
- Maintain a presence.
- A world in transition means opportunities for entrepreneurs. Fast footwork can keep you in the game.
- To start your own mailing lists, give away something. In return, potential customers will give you their names.

Action Step 33

What is Your Customer Worth?

How Can You Remember It?

Review the discussion about the bookstore customer. Now it's time for you to determine the value of your customer.

Determine approximately how much he or she will spend in one year at your business. Take that number out for five or 10 years. Now that you have that dollar figure, design a way for you and your employees to remember that figure. Your firm is in business to make a profit and you can only make a profit if you have customers. Employees need to understand this concept and this exercise provides a memorable teaching tool.

Action Step 34

Attach a Pricetag to Each Item of Your Promotional Package

What will your customer connection cost? To get some idea, go back to Action Step 31, list the top four or five connections you want with your customers, then research what they cost.

Let's imagine that you have chosen the following promotional mix:

Magazine Ads. This choice assumes you know which magazines your Target Customers read. Good. Contact the display ad department of the magazines and request their media kit.

Direct Mail. Look up mail list brokers in the Yellow Pages under Direct Mail. Discuss the business you are in and which market you want to reach. Ask them for recommendations on appropriate mailing lists and strategy tips. Contact the magazines above and ask for their mailing list rental rates for the geographic areas you want to reach. Many magazines and direct mail houses rent their lists by ZIP code.

continued

Press Releases. Visit the marketing department of local newspapers for information on targeting its readers. Use this information to angle your release. Type the release double-spaced. Make sure you catch the reader's attention. Keep the message simple. Be sure to wield the five W's of journalism: who, what, where, when, why, and the noble H (how).

Personal Selling. If you cannot reach customers this way yourself, you will need to budget for someone who can. If you are planning on personally selling, locate networking opportunities and start building new contacts. Allocate a portion of your salary and expenses as a promotional cost. If you are going to use sales reps determine their cost to you.

Once you know the cost of each item of your promotional package, you can decide which you can afford. Remember to always consider "What is the message I want my Target Customer to receive?" and "How can I best reach my Target Customer effectively and cost efficiently?"

- Create excitement because excitement sells. Rent a Santa, a robot, a hot-air balloon.
- Remember to promote the benefits of your product or service.
- People buy experiences. Make them memorable! Make them want to come back for more. Make them want to send their friends and family.
- Keeping a customer is far cheaper than finding a new one. Make the customer happy. Solve problems. Ask the customer, "How can I solve the problem?"
- Make customer service a passion.
- Passionate customers become walking billboards! They care passionately and in their desire for you to succeed they will make you better.
- When you think you have it made, don't let your guard down—keep connecting with that customer! You will never be so big that you can afford to disconnect. Remember this and it will make you rich.
- Creativity! Creativity! Creativity!

Points from Another View

His Invention Is Anything But Old Hat

A machine-tool sales rep, Bret Atkins would be out on a work site pitching the product when a metallic voice would intone over the yard loudspeaker: "Yo, Bret. OSHA rules. Put on your hard hat."

Atkins would have to go grumbling back to the pickup to rummage through his safety bag for the ugly dome-shaped headgear. Worse, sometimes his fingers were grimy from handling machinery, and when he'd remove the immaculate white $100 straw cowboy hat he always wears, he'd get grease marks on the brim.

Finally, enough. He slammed into the kitchen after work one day and announced to his wife, Julie: "I'm gonna invent a cowboy hard hat."

Yeah right, she said. We all get these million-dollar ideas.

But for Atkins it was the beginning of an obsessive three-year journey that would take him through many failures and to the brink of bankruptcy before he produced the Western Outlaw, an OSHA-approved hard hat that looks exactly like a cowboy Stetson.

It's become the hottest item to hit industrial fashion since steel-toed boots.

Because of the Outlaw, Atkins was named inventor of the year at the 12th Annual Invention Convention held on the Queen Mary in Long Beach in April, beating out 400 competitors. And since start-up a year ago, his feisty little company has sold 150,000 cowboy hard hats, and has 1,000 distributors worldwide.

Although a construction worker can pick up an Outlaw for 30 bucks in an Orange County safety products store, out on the Louisiana oil rigs they go for $75, and in Saudi Arabia they bring $250 each to the customs-dodging roughneck who smuggles them in from the States a dozen at a time in a duffel, Julie Atkins says.

Chris Nielsen, owner of Bakersfield Glove & Safety, says the cowboy hard hat, which comes in six colors, including international orange, is the only excitement in what usually is a very boring business. "It's been our biggest topic of conversation."

But success for the 43-year-old Atkins was at the end of a long dusty trail.

On the very day he got the idea, he made a model for the Outlaw in his garage, modeling it after the straw Stetson he'd been wearing around Bakersfield since childhood.

The fiberglass model looked good. Exactly like a cowboy hat. But with any safety product, the crucial hurdle is approval by the Occupational Safety and

Health Administration. And to get that, the Outlaw would have to meet stringent demands of the American National Standards Institute.

Ten times his hat was tested by ANSI. Ten times it failed. Each test cost Atkins $8,000. All of his credit cards were maxed. To save money, Atkins began testing each new version at home before sending it on to the ANSI lab.

He'd get up on the garage roof and drop a large steel plumb bob through a pipe to see if he could bust the top of the Outlaw. He set the Outlaw on fire with a welding torch. He wrapped the hat in dry ice and stuck it in a freezer chest overnight to see if it would crack.

"At first I thought he'd just give up," his wife says. "But after each failure he'd just go back out again in the garage and start again."

Though skeptical at first, she admired his gumption and grew to share his vision, even when they were up to their eyeballs in debt.

Atkins had the same kind of patience and persistence he had employed in a younger day as a bow hunter of big game. He'd be shivering on a stand in a tree, but wouldn't quit. And then, the trophy buck would step into the clearing.

On the eleventh try, Atkins got the recipe right. The Outlaw passed ANSI with the highest rating, and won OSHA approval.

"At a trade fair in Atlanta an engineer said I obviously must have an advanced degree to figure this out. Obviously, I don't," says the laconic Atkins. "I didn't even go to college at all."

Atkins quit his job and began making the hats in a small workshop, at the rate of 15 a day.

"I'm not a great businessman," Atkins says, "I figured I could make a little bit selling them around Bakersfield."

Fate, however, had bigger plans. A friend of his wife's took a hat with her when she attended a physical therapy convention in New York. She was wearing it one morning when she was part of the crowd in front of the studios of NBC's "Today" show. Host Katie Couric came out to chat, took a liking to the Outlaw, and wore it on the air for 6 minutes. "It's an OSHA-approved Western hard hat," Couric said plainly to a nationwide audience.

"We didn't even have a regular office," Atkins says. "We didn't have our own phone. Orders were pouring in, and I had, maybe a dozen hats."

It was the once-in-a-lifetime knock, and Atkins was home. He quickly found a manufacturer, hired a staff of 10 to field the calls. He lined up distributors all over the United States. "The thing went right through the roof," he says.

His company just got an order from an Australian distributor for 10,000 hats. The Australian Cancer Society likes the hats because of the sun-shielding broad brim.

"In the West, the white and straw colors are the big sellers," he says. "In Texas and Louisiana the black is popular," Nobody likes the orange, but Atkins keeps a few in stock for road crews.

Friends have suggested that Atkins now broaden the line by inventing a Greg Norman-style golf hard had with a shark on it, but he isn't interested. Getting one ANSI approval was hard enough.

Besides, he doesn't golf.

SOURCE: Orange County Register, July 12, 1998.

7

Location, Location, Location

Entrepreneurial Links

Books

Webonomics: Nine Essential Principles for Growing Your Business on the World Wide Web, Evan I. Schwartz, 1998.

Location, Location, Location: How to Select the Best Site for Your Business, Luigi Salvaneschi, 1996.

Working From Home: Everything You Need to Know About Living and Working Under the Same Roof, Paul and Sarah Edwards, 1994.

Websites

www.claritas.com, Claritas

www.burke.com, Burke Research

www.cenus.gov, U.S. Census Bureau

Associations/Organizations

The GeoBusiness Association, www.gba.org

Society of Industrial and Office Realtors and the National Association of Industrial and Office Parks

National Association of Manufacturers, www.nam.org

Publications

Stores, www.stores.org

Home Business Magazine

Business Geographics & GIS World, www.geoplace.com

Additional Entrepreneurial Insights

Generation E Entrepreneur: The Do-It-Yourself Business Guide for Twenty-something and Other Non-Corporate Types, Joel Naftali, 1997.

How to Negotiate Real Estate Leases, 3rd Edition, Mark Warda, 1997.

Making Money With Your Computer at Home: The Inside Information You Need to Know to Select and Operate a Full-Time, Part-Time, or Add-On Business, Paul Edwards, Sarah Edwards, 1997.

Learning Objectives

- Explain a 100% location for your business.
- Understand the contribution of location to small business success.
- Recognize the uniqueness of your business location needs.
- Develop a checklist for evaluating potential sites.
- Use secondary and primary research to refine customer profile and select location.
- Consult commercial real estate brokers in your search for a location.
- Review major points in leasing agreements.
- Explore running your business from your home.
- Introduce locating on the Internet.
- Review small business incubators and enterprise zones.

One of the most important decisions an entrepreneur has to make is where to locate his or her business. The age-old axiom "location, location, location" has been touted as the three most important reasons for business success. To some extent, and especially in retail, this philosophy has a great deal of merit. For example, if you're planning to rent a location for a number of years, good site selection is critical, and most retail leases reflect this importance in their length and complexity; 30–50 pages is not unusual.

Chapter 7 will lead you through the processes of finding a good location for your business using primary and secondary research and, if necessary, negotiating a lease that will serve you well.

A cautionary note is in order, however. We want you to try and climb inside your customer's mind and answer the basic question, "According to the customer, what is the best location?" What you believe will be a good location is certainly relevant, but more important is what your Target Customer thinks is a good location. What happens, then, if you want to operate your business out of your home? First, congratulations! This is a growth market and you may just be on the right track. In this updated version of the cottage industry, more and more of us will be working out of the home. All kinds of services and products are now provided by home-based businesses. With the growth in the service- and knowledge-based industries, chances are that one day you will be operating some sort of business out of your home. In planning to set up your business at home, your location analysis is just as important as if you were to lease.

There are a number of critical location questions you're going to have to consider: Do local laws allow me to operate a home-based business? How do I balance my family and work life? Do I need a separate telephone line? In this chapter, we'll also encourage you to consider all the pros and cons of locating your business outside of the home and to establish your location strategy.

A new venue to consider for many will be the Internet. Can you sell your product or service online? Can you make a profit? How will people find you? Should you join one of the many online malls? Do you stand out from the many other businesses all vying for the same dollars?

The Importance of Location

What Is the Perfect Location?

The perfect location differs for every enterprise. If you're in the house-cleaning business, you can work out of a stationwagon equipped with a cellular telephone. If you're in the mail-order business, you can work out of a "cocoon" or a post office box. Action Step 35 asks you to brainstorm the perfect location for *your* business.

A good location can make everything easier for a new business. A highly visible building that's easy for your customers to reach will save you advertising dollars. Once you've been discovered and your customer base is well established, however, location is less important. Nonetheless, for a retailing firm, a good location is absolutely essential.

A Location Filter

Before you charge out to scout possible locations for your business, you need to decide what you really need. This checklist will help you zero in on that. Use a scale of 1 to 10 to rate the relative importance of each item on this list. When you finish scoring, go back and note the high numbers, anything, say, above 5. Then, after you've read the rest of the chapter, come back to this list if your priorities have changed.

Target Market

How far will your customers be willing to travel to get to you? Can your business travel/deliver to the customers (flowers, dry cleaning, plumbing, pizza, etc.)? If so, how far can you travel and still make a profit?

Transportation Lines

How much will your business depend on trucks, rail, buses, airports, shipping by water? If you're in manufacturing or distribution, you'll need to determine your major transportation channel. It's also a good idea to have a backup system. A good technique here is to make a diagram of the location and all the lines of transportation your business will use. (Common-carrier rate listings may help.)

Neighbor Mix

Who's next door? Who's down the street? Who's going to help pull your target customers to the area? Which nearby business pulls the most customers? If you're considering a shopping center, who's the anchor tenant (the big department store or supermarket that acts as a magnet for the center)?

Competition

Do you want competitors miles away or right next door? Think about this one. If you're in the restaurant business, it can help to be on "restaurant row." (A good example of a working "competitor cluster" is San Diego's well-known Miles of Cars; having Nissans, Dodges, Chevrolets, Toyotas, and others all in one area cuts down customer driving time and allows for easy comparison shopping.)

Security, Safety

How safe is the neighborhood? Is it as safe as a nursery at noon but an urban nightmare at midnight? Is there anything you can do to increase security?

Labor Pool

Who's working for you, and how far will they have to commute? Does your business require more help at certain peak periods of the year? How easy will it be

Neighbor mix The industrial/commercial makeup of nearby businesses

Labor pool Qualified people who are available for employment near one's business location

to find that kind of help? Will you need skilled labor? If so, where's the nearest pool of it? Is the site near a bus (train, subway)? Will you need technical people? How far will they travel? Don't overlook the potential of part-timers, teens, seniors, and homemakers.

Restrictions

What local rules (state, county, city, merchants' association, etc.) will affect your location? For example, what are the restrictions on signage? hours of business? parking? deed? zoning? covenants?

Services

What is included in the rent (police and fire protection, security, trash pickup, sewage, maintenance) and who pays for those services that are not?

Costs

The purchase price if you're buying; otherwise, the rent or lease costs. (We advise against buying property and starting a business at the same time, because it diverts your precious energies and capital that you need for the business.) Taxes, insurance, utilities, improvements, association dues, routine maintenance. You need to know who pays for what. Can you negotiate a few months' free rent?

Ownership

If you're still planning to buy property, who will you get to advise you on real estate? Consider a lease with an option to buy, but have the contract reviewed by a real estate attorney.

Past Tenants

What happened to the past tenants? What mistakes did they make, and how can you avoid those mistakes?

Accessibility to Customers

Will your target customers—lured by your terrific promotions—find you easily and then have a place to park when they get there? Consider highway access and potential obstacles that could make coming to your place of business inconvenient or unpleasant.

Space

If you need to expand, can you do it there, or will you have to move to a new site?

History of the Property

How long has the landlord owned this property? Is it likely to be sold while you're a tenant? If the property is sold, what will happen to your business? What will happen to your tax obligations? If the property goes on the market, do you want the first right to meet an offer?

Physical Visibility

Does your business need to be seen? If so, is this location easily visible? Can you make alterations to increase its visibility?

Life-Cycle Stage of the Area

Is the site in an area that's embryonic (vacant lots, open space, emptiness), growing (high-rises, new schools, lots of construction), mature (building conversions, cracked streets, sluggish traffic), or declining (vacant buildings, emptiness)? What will the area be like in five years? What effect would that have on your business? What do the municipal planners have in mind for the area? When will the highway department tear up the street?

Restrictions City/county laws governing business locations

Location life cycle The stages of a commercial/industrial area from birth to death

Image

Is the location consistent with your firm's image? How will nearby businesses affect your image? Is this an area where your customers would expect to find a business like yours? (Look for a place that reinforces your customers' perception of your business.)

Great Cities for Entrepreneurs

Annually *Entrepreneur Magazine* with Dun & Bradstreet select the top cities in the United States for entrepreneurs. They rate the cities in the five following areas:

1. government attitude toward business
2. business performance
3. economic growth
4. risk
5. affordability

**Entrepreneur Magazine
Best Cities for Small Business 1997**

TOP CITIES
Large Cities
1. Portland/Vancouver, OR/WA
2. St. Louis, MO/IL
3. Seattle/Bellevue/Everett, WA
4. Greensboro/Winston-Salem/High Point, NC
5. Charlotte/Gastonia, NC/Rock Hill, SC
6. Denver, CO
7. Minneapolis/St. Paul, MN/WI
8. Las Vegas, NV/AZ
9. Salt Lake City/Ogden, UT
10. Kansas City, MO/KS
11. Detroit, MI
12. Atlanta, GA
13. Milwaukee/Waukesha, WI
14. Ft. Worth/Arlington, TX
15. Nashville, TN

If you are not sure where to locate your business, every state and local economic development office throughout the United States will be more than happy to send you vast amounts of data on their area. Tax breaks, tax incentives, job training, reduced utilities, and infrastructure such as roads and utilities are just a few of the jewels counties and cities will dangle in front of you. Many low-income areas—including inner-city locations—are anxious to lure new enterprises and will offer incentives to employers willing to hire and train as few as 10 people.

To explore site selection further, read *Business Geographics,* a magazine that focuses on the use of geographical information systems (GIS). You can also visit their Website **www.geoplace.com.**

Where To Go for Location Information

Businesspeople tend to stay in a location for a while because it's expensive to pack up and move. Selection is a *very* important decision. You need to make sure you're in the heart of your target market. Where do you go for that information?

Figure 7.1

Census Breakdowns

The U.S. Census subdivides metropolitan areas into tracts, block groups, and blocks.

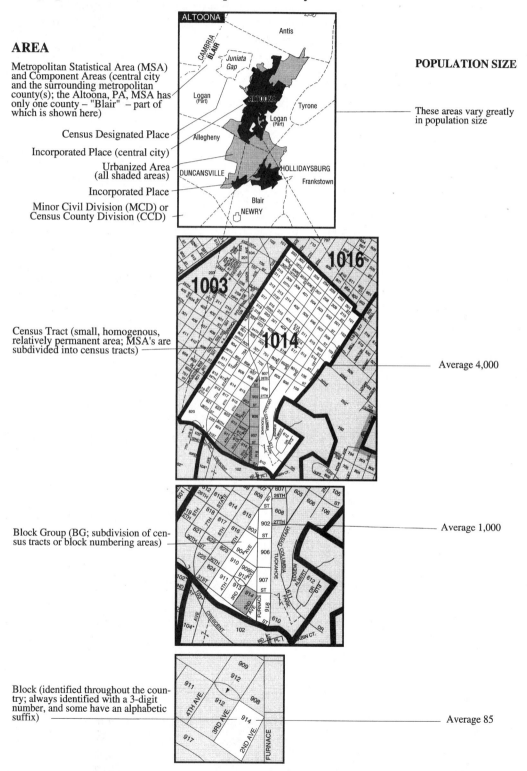

Geographic Subdivisions in a Metropolitan County

AREA

Metropolitan Statistical Area (MSA) and Component Areas (central city and the surrounding metropolitan county(s); the Altoona, PA, MSA has only one county – "Blair" – part of which is shown here)

Census Designated Place

Incorporated Place (central city)

Urbanized Area (all shaded areas)

Incorporated Place

Minor Civil Division (MCD) or Census County Division (CCD)

Census Tract (small, homogenous, relatively permanent area; MSA's are subdivided into census tracts)

Block Group (BG; subdivision of census tracts or block numbering areas)

Block (identified throughout the country; always identified with a 3-digit number, and some have an alphabetic suffix)

POPULATION SIZE

These areas vary greatly in population size

Average 4,000

Average 1,000

Average 85

SOURCE: The U.S. Census has several helpful services: www.census.gov, 301-457-4100 for customer service. Dept. of Commerce, P.O. Box 277943, Atlanta, GA 30384-7943 (for mail orders).

Previously, we discussed utilizing the Census Bureau, city and county data, and independent research firms such as Claritas, Equifax National Decision Systems, and Easy Analytic Software. In addition, we suggest you look to state and local economic development groups as well as utility services for location assistance. If you are involved in manufacturing your search should also include association information, Chamber of Commerce, Department of Commerce, and government assistance. You will also need to look into your competition, suppliers, and employee pool extensively.

Targeting by Census Tract

Every 10 years the government gathers together massive amounts of census data. The data from the 1990 U.S. Census is available online at **www.census.gov.** For updated information, the fee-based information services will provide data.

Census data is broken down from large areas such as state, to small areas such as city block. Figure 7.1 illustrates the geographic breakdown for Blair County, Pennsylvania. Locate your county–city tract and go to work.

For researching your retail or service location, you want data that gives you a picture of the lifestyles of your target customers: income, occupation, education, and housing. In addition to census data, fee-for-service and software programs combine census and various other research data to provide a much more thorough and updated evaluation of your potential customer.

Review the sample location worksheet, which highlights site selection factors and their weighting for an appliance repair business. Site location experts develop various worksheets and analyses of locations and demographics. If you are opening a business that is highly dependent on foot or car traffic, we suggest you hire an expert to assist you. At this time, review the worksheet and try to adapt the worksheet for your business location.

Sample Location Worksheet

Often a trade association will help you develop a scoring system that is helpful for a specific type of business location. Here is a 10-category worksheet that will allow a score to be developed for each prospective location for an appliance repair business.

Category	Conditions	Points
Traffic Flow	If two-thirds of the traffic is on the same side of the street as the location	+10
	If there is an even distribution of traffic	+7
	If two-thirds of the traffic is on the opposite side of the street	+5
Building	Free standing and close to road	+15
	Free standing away from road	+10
	Strip center with at least 5 stores	+5
	Strip center with more than 5 stores	−5
	Strip center with end cap location	+10
	Location within a mall	−10
Identification [Signage]	Signs visible for 300 feet	+12
	Signs visible for 150 feet	+6
	Flush mounted signs	+2
	No signage permitted	−10
Parking	5 or more spaces directly adjacent to store	+10
	3 to 4 spaces in front of store	+7
	All parking away from store front (no more than 50 feet)	+5
	Street parking in front of store	+1

	Street parking in front of store with parking meters	−2
	No parking within 50 feet of store and on street meters	−5
Vehicle Traffic	Under 5,000 cars (during business hours)	0
	5,000 to 7,500 cars (during business hours)	+5
	7,500 to 10,000 cars (during business hours)	+8
	10,000 to 15,000 cars (during business hours)	+10
	Over 15,000 cars (during business hours)	+15
Speed Limit	No stoplight or stop sign	+15
	Passing speed is under 25 mph	+10
	Passing speed is 25 mph to 35 mph	+7
	Passing speed is 35 mph to 45 mph	+5
	Passing speed is 45 mph to 50 mph	+2
	Passing speed is over 50 mph	0
Nearby Businesses	Near Wal-Mart, Kmart, Sears, department store	+15
	Near large appliance dealers	+10
	Near a strong business area	+5
	Near small and medium appliance dealers	+3
	Near bars, pawn shops, liquor stores	−10
Area Demographics	Single-family homes, 15 years or older, within 3 miles	+10
	Single-family homes, 10 years or older, within 3 miles	+5
	Apartment neighborhood	−5
Population of Trading Area	Over 25,000	+9
	15,000 to 25,000	+7
	5,000 to 15,000	+5
	Less than 5,000	0
Economic Conditions	Medium-high to upper income nearby	+5
	Medium income nearby	+4
	Low to medium income nearby	+3
Miscellaneous	Near well-known landmark	+5

Categories	Points	Categories	Points	Rating
Traffic flow	_____	Speed Limit	_____	90+ = Superior
Building	_____	Nearby Businesses	_____	80–89 = Excellent
Identification	_____	Area Demographics	_____	65–79 = Good
Parking	_____	Population	_____	60–65 = Marginal
Vehicle traffic	_____	Economic Conditions	_____	
Total	_____	Grand Total	_____	

A similar format could be used in a service business where customers generally bring in goods for repair or service. This type of summary should be placed in the appendix of your Business Plan.

Before You Sign a Lease

The property/owner's lawyer draws up a **lease** document. Although its language is very specific, the terms spelled out are *provisional;* that is, the terms are proposed as a starting point for negotiation. Nothing you see in the contract is cast in stone . . . unless you agree to it. Obviously, the terms proposed will favor the property/owner. Assume nothing when it comes to leases. Consider the proposed lease seriously. Discuss it with your own real estate attorney and with others who have experience with leases, and possibly some of the tenants if located in a center or multiuse building. Determine how best to begin the negotiation. The following information will guide you through this process.

Lease A legal contract for occupancy

International Small Business Consortium

Honored by Microsoft as a "Technology Success Story," the International Small Business Consortium (ISBC), **www.isbc.com**, provides support, information, and advice on international marketing, cyberspace law, and using the Internet for business. ISBC's goal is to help small businesses make international connections.

The Web site has several excellent moderated discussion groups. In addition, a database of international business opportunities and contacts is available for searching. ISBC focuses on international community building.

If you want to develop contacts and find a community of international business entrepreneurs, ISBC will meet your needs. ISBC reduces the barriers for new entrepreneurs and opens the doors to almost 6 billion customers.

Commercial Real Estate

Agents/Commercial Brokers

There is so much to know and analyze when making location decisions and an *experienced* commercial real estate agent can save you time and money. He or she can guide you through the maze of what is available and advise you on rents, prices, taxes, terms, financing, zoning, and public transportation.

Selecting the right broker can be as simple as asking for recommendations from friends or business people in your networking group. Another way would be to note the names of brokers posted at the sites you've been considering as possible locations. Newspaper commercial real estate ads are usually paid for by brokers. Their names and phone numbers appear in the ads. When you call to get information about a particular ad, you'll be connected to the listing agent. If you like what you hear about the property, but don't feel comfortable with that particular agent, don't be concerned. Any agent or broker can show you any listed property; he or she does not have to be the listing agent.

If an agent shows you property and then you choose not to use that agent to complete the transaction there may be problems.

Commercial brokers are paid primarily by the landlord or seller and earn their commissions only when a deal is final and money changes hands. Don't let yourself be rushed by these people, but bear in mind that they are probably the best sources of free market information available. Brokers affiliated with large commercial firms have extensive research departments at their disposal. You can save an agent a lot of time if you have already defined your needs. If you compare each site against your ideal location, you will probably have several workable alternatives. Typically, on-site leasing people have different objectives because they are employees of the developer. They want to fill the building. Most developers also cooperate with commercial brokers, so a broker can take you almost anywhere you want to go and, if asked, might help you negotiate more favorable terms.

If your business requires leasing or purchasing a site, complete Action Step 36.

Anticipate the Unexpected

Bette Lindsay has always had a soft spot for books, and when she finally chose a business, it was a bookstore in a shopping center. She had researched everything—trends, census data, newspapers, reports from real estate firms, suppliers—but she failed to anticipate an important potential pitfall, dependency on an **anchor tenant.**

Few small businesses are themselves "destination locations." They must count on anchor tenants to draw traffic. Bette made an assumption that the anchor tenant in her center would be there forever. This case study shows the importance of having Plan B ready.

> My husband and I researched the small business field for almost two years, and my heart kept bringing me back to books. I've read voraciously since I was 7 years old, and love a well-written story. So when a new shopping center was opening a mile from our home, I told my husband, "This is it."
>
> Everything looked perfect. They had a great anchor tenant coming in—a supermarket that would draw lots of traffic. The real estate agent we'd been working with during most of our search showed us the demographics of the area, which documented that we were smack in the middle of a well-educated market. According to statistics put out by the federal government, a book store needs a population of 27,000 people to support it. Our area had 62,000 people, and the closest bookstore was more than 5 miles away.
>
> Everything else looked good, too. We had lots of parking. The neighbors (three hardy pioneers like ourselves) were serious about their business and pleasant to work with.
>
> We wanted to be in for the Christmas season because December is the peak season for bookstores, so we set a target date of mid-October. The contractor was still working when we opened a month later.
>
> We started off with an autograph party and we ran some best-seller specials. And even though construction work from our anchor tenant blocked our access, we had a very good Christmas that year. We started the new year feeling very optimistic.
>
> One day in mid-January, construction work stopped on our anchor tenant's new building. The next day we read in the paper that the company had gone bankrupt.
>
> Well, the first thing I did was call the landlord. He was out of town, and his answering service referred me to a property management company. They said they knew nothing about what was happening and that all they do is collect the rent. January was slow. So was February and March. In April, two of our neighbors closed down. The construction debris was blocking customer access. It was a mess.
>
> In May, I finally succeeded in getting in touch with the owner and tried to **renegotiate the lease,** but his story was sadder than mine.
>
> Fourteen months after we moved in we finally got our anchor tenant. If I'd suspected it'd take anything like that long I could have built some provision for it into our lease. That expensive mistake does not bear repeating.

How to Rewrite a Lease

You live with a lease (and a landlord) for a long time. If you're successful in a retail business, your landlord may want a percentage of your gross sales receipts. If you're not successful or if problems develop, you're going to want several Plan Bs and a **location escape hatch.** For example, your lease should protect your interests:

    if the furnace or air-conditioning system breaks down

    if the parking lot needs sweeping or resurfacing

    if the anchor tenant goes under

    if the building is sold

    if half the other tenants move out

Anchor tenant A business firm in a commercial area that attracts customers

Renegotiate a lease Obtaining a new or modified contract for occupancy

Rewrite a lease Alter the wording of a lease to make it protect one's interests

Location escape hatch A way to cancel or modify a lease if the landlord fails to meet the specified terms

The possibility of such grief-producing eventualities needs to be dealt with in precise words and precise numbers in the lease.

Always negotiate free rent until the anchor tenant opens for business and make the lease itself contingent on the anchor's leasing and opening. Also, you will want an escape clause stating that if and when the anchor tenant leaves that you may leave also.

In your lease you also want to assure that if the building is sold you are protected; that other tenant's cannot disturb your business operations.

Read the lease slowly and carefully. When you see something you don't understand or don't like, draw a line through it. Feel free to rewrite the sentences if you need to. It's *your* lease, too, you see. *Always* hire a real estate lawyer to review and advise you before signing any lease. And make sure that the owner (or the leasing agent) indicates his or her agreement with your changes by initialing each one.

Here's a checklist to start you on your rewrite.

1. **Escape clause** If the building doesn't shape up or the area goes into eclipse, you will want to get out fast. Be specific. Write something like "If three or more vacancies occur in the center, tenant may terminate lease."
2. **Option to renew** Common leases today are for five years, unless you are a major player, like Pier I and then the lease might be 10 years. Options to renew are usually for two to five years. You should be planning for at least a five year run for retail. If you are too afraid to sign for five years, rethink your commitment.
3. **Right to transfer** Circumstances might force you to sublet. In the trade, this is called "assigning." Usually assigning requires landlord approval of the new tenant. Be sure the lease allows you to transfer your lease hassle-free if such circumstances arise.
4. **Cost-of-living cap** Most leases allow the property owner to increase rents in step with inflation according to the Consumer Price Index (CPI). To protect yourself, insist on a cost-of-living cap so that your base rate doesn't increase faster than your landlord's costs. Try for half of the amount if the CPI rises 10 percent; your rate will go up only 5 percent. It's fair because the owner's costs won't change much. Major tenants in your center will insist on a cap, so you should be able to negotiate one also. Proceed with confidence.
5. **Percentage lease** Percentage leases are common in larger retail centers. They specify that the tenant pays a base rate plus a percentage of the gross sales. **Example:** $3 per square foot per month plus 5 percent of gross sales over $500,000 per year. It is important that you do realistic sales projections because the natural break-even point before percentage rent kicks in is negotiable. The percentage rent is also negotiable.
6. **Floating rent scale** If you're a pioneer tenant of a shopping center, negotiate a payment scale based on occupancy. For example, you may specify that you'll pay 50 percent of your lease payment when the center is 50 percent occupied, 70 percent when it's 70 percent occupied, and 100 percent when it's full. You can't build traffic to the center all by yourself, and motivation is healthy for everyone, including landlords.
7. **Start-up buffer** There's a good chance you'll be on location fixing up, remodeling, and so on, long before you open your doors and make your first sale. Make your landlord aware of this problem and negotiate a long period of free rent. The argument: If your business is successful, the landlord, who's taking a percentage, will make more money. If your business doesn't do well or if it fails, the landlord will have to find a new tenant. You need breathing space. You've signed on for the long haul. By not squeezing you to death for cash, the landlord allows you to put more

Option to renew A guaranteed opportunity at the end of a lease to extend for another specific period of time

Cost-of-living cap An agreement that the rent from one year to another cannot be increased by more than the CPI for that period

Entrepreneurial Assistance for the Disabled

Entrepreneurs with a disability such as Jan Midori, who suffers from narcolepsy and runs a $20-million company that direct-markets art, can find assistance from the following sources:

Disabled Businesspersons Association
www.web-link.com/dba/dba.htm
SDSU-Interwork Institute
5850 Hardy Avenue, Suite 112
San Diego, 92182-5313

President's Committee on Employment of People with Disabilities
www.pcepd.gov

Many people have physical or mental disabilities that make working in a traditional setting difficult. For many disabled as well as for the able, developing a business allows people to gain control over their time and workplace.

For many disabled, insurance and possibly workmen's compensation benefits, tax issues, and health benefits are important variables and need to be discussed thoroughly with the appropriate parties involved.

money into inventory, equipment, service, atmosphere—the things that make a business go.

8. **Improvements** Unless you're a super fixer-upper, you don't want to lease a place with nothing more than a dirt floor and a capped-off cold-water pipe. Although in most retail sites, all you get is a plain vanilla shell with very few tenant improvements. If the economy is in a recession, tenant improvements will be easier to negotiate. Find space that does not require extensive and expensive remodeling if cash is tight. Do not go under before getting up!

9. **Use clauses** If you're running a camera store and part of your income derives from developing film, you don't want a Fotomat booth to move into your center. A video storeowner had a use clause that precluded any other video stores from the center. Unfortunately, the clause did not cover the empty pad, which soon became a Blockbuster store. Build use clauses into your lease to protect yourself. Use clauses must be worded *very carefully*. One owner of an ice cream and candy store had included the word *beverages* in her use clause, which the landlord approved. The landlord came back later to the owner and told her she could not sell smoothies or coffee. Fortunately, the owner showed the lease to the landlord and pointed out the word *beverages* and no more was said. Additionally, the store owner had inserted into the lease that she would not sell "soft-serve yogurt." When she began to sell hard-packed yogurt the landlord came calling. Again, she pulled out the lease. Wording your lease properly can mean the difference between success and failure.

10. **CAM (Common Area Maintenance)** Covers gardener, building repairs, trash, and so on. Know the CAM charges before leasing. CAM charges can vary greatly from $.20 to over $1 per square foot. Make sure your CAM charges are based on your square footage. If a portion of the center is empty, be sure the landlord pays the CAM charges for the empty square footage—not you!

Office/Business Location Alternatives

Alternative business locations are available depending on your needs and resources. If you have a business that requires employees to come to your site, your alternatives will be more limited. Find out if delivery services will deliver directly to your home or pick up at your home. They may be willing to deliver but only to the door and not inside your home. This may be a problem if you have large heavy deliveries or cannot leave packages outside.

Consider a "Just in Time" Location

Most cities have a wide selection of executive office suites available at modest prices. Services can include the part-time use of a corporate-style executive boardroom, a shared receptionist, phone service, mail receiving, photocopy equipment, fax, and a part-time or permanent office. Such situations may work well for consultants, sales representatives, architects, and owners of virtual companies.

Storefront mailbox services work well for some, but you may get a higher level of service for less money by simply renting a U.S. Post Office box. If a private mailbox service closes or moves you are suddenly out of an office.

Business Incubators

Incubators nurture young firms by helping them to survive and thrive during the sometimes-difficult start-up period. Over 450 incubators provide trained professional assistance in marketing, financing, and technical support. You will usually share office space, access to equipment, and storage or production areas. Generally your firm will remain in an incubator for one to three years.

Some incubators serve all types of clients: service businesses, light manufacturing, technology, and research. Other incubators specialize in specific areas such as biotechnology, software development, and retailing. To locate incubators throughout the United States, contact the National Business Incubation Association (NBIA) at **www.nbia.org**, 20 East Circle Drive, Suite 190, Athens, Ohio 45701-3751, 740-593-4331; fax: 740-593-1996.

Several incubator profiles follow.

Incubators—To Survive and Thrive

Pontotoc Area Vo-Tech School, Ada, OK

Pontotoc Area Vo-Tech's Business Development Center (BDC) is the ideal place to grow your own business if your plan is to enter the world of manufacturing products. In addition to plenty of space to begin your project and even more room to grow, the BDC offers assistance from the entire Business and Industry Services Team. Also available is consulting from industry specialists in areas of management, finance, marketing, and doing business with State and Federal Governments.

Technology Advancement Program, College Park, MD

The Technology Advancement Program (TAP), a program of the Engineering Research Center, is an "incubator" facility offering space and support services for early-stage companies engaged in developing technology-based products or services with commercial potential. Companies involved in the Program can adapt their research to market requirements while gaining business experience. They also benefit from the extensive facilities and services available from the University of Maryland, one of the country's largest public research and teaching institutions.

Rural Devel. Ctr. Business Enterprise Research Park, Univ. of Maryland, Princess Anne, Maryland

Located at the University of Maryland Eastern Shore, the RDC assists in public development projects that carry out approved economic development conversion strategies. The RDC assists community groups, non-profit organizations, local elected and appointed officials and private firms. We assist them to develop plans, loans, grants, projects and programs for community and county vitality on the nine-county Eastern Shore of Maryland. Emphasis is on public/private partnerships and regional approaches through which communities and businesses jointly prosper. The Center maintains a community-based approach to technical assistance development. It encourages and supports projects that address locally identified needs of rural people. The Center is sensitive to community diversity. The RDC is a professional community and regional economic development agency that is concerned with the causes and consequences of social, political, and economic changes in rural areas and the effective influence of rural people, businesses, and communities. Applied social and economic science dominates the research and technical assistance work of the Center.

Genesis Business Centers, Ltd., Minneapolis, Minnesota

The GENESIS program is designed with the high-tech entrepreneur in mind. If you are a founder, officer or director of a high-tech start-up company, you should learn about the benefits of getting your business started at a Genesis Business Center near you. We offer a program of rent combined with valuable professional services in exchange for a negotiated equity position in your company. GENESIS is looking for the best and the brightest of the new high-tech start-ups in Minnesota.

SOURCE: **www.nbia.org**

Home Office

Gloria Brookstone's home-based business began when her handbag was stolen in Venice, Italy where Gloria was traveling with her husband. They were crossing an arched bridge on their way to breakfast when two young men zoomed by on a motorbike. The tailpipes puffed blue smoke. Gloria felt a tug at her shoulder. She saw the teeth of the rider on the bike; saw her shoulder bag clutched in his fist, the strap swinging free. In his other hand was a pair of tin snips.

The ensuing paperwork stole the entire morning. A policeman interviewed Gloria and her husband. "Have you ever thought of a money belt?" the policeman asked. "So many purses are stolen here."

Gloria tried a money belt. It didn't feel right. She borrowed her husband's safari vest. It was handy, all those pockets, but it didn't look like Gloria. "I am not on safari," she said. "And this vest swallows me up. It's too big."

When she returned home to Indianapolis, she heard of other purse thefts. For her birthday, Gloria received a safari vest that fit. She wore the vest on their next trip. During her trip she had a dream about the perfect vest; one with gold buttons instead of a zipper. It had secret inside pockets to place money and valuables, and beautiful rich colors. It fit like a dream.

The dream vest haunted Gloria all the way home. When she got back to her real estate office, she contacted garmentmakers in Chicago and Knoxville. They were happy to take her money ($10,000 up front) and Gloria sat up nights designing her Women's Travel Vest.

The first vests (400 for $10,000) looked shabby and cheap. When Gloria complained, the garmentmaker said, "Business is business." Gloria threatened

► **Action Step 37**

Is a Home Business In Your Future?

Before starting a business at your home, answer the following questions and complete the exercises. What are the benefits? What are the negatives?

1. List reasons to work at home. Start with the obvious: low overhead, close to snacks, an easy commute, familiar surroundings. If you have children and want to be near them, working at home is one solution. Keep listing.
2. List the problems of working at home: How do you handle interruptions? How do you show that you are serious? How do you focus amidst clutter? If you have clients, where do they see you? What's the zoning situation in your neighborhood? Keep listing.
3. List solutions to the problems raised in #2, above. If you're being interrupted, you need to get tough. Set up a schedule and post a notice: "Mommy's working from 9–11. Lunch will be served at noon. If Mommy does not work, there's no lunch!"
4. Go technical. What will it cost you? Computer, scanner, modem, printer, answering machine, and so on. Use e mail to connect with your customers.
5. Where will your workspace be? garage? basement? bedroom? den? How can you keep it YOURS?
6. Check out your home insurance. What does it cover?
7. Check out health insurance if needed. Can you qualify? What will be the cost?

to sue, but the money was gone. Working with a large manufacturer taught her a lesson.

Brainstorming on paper, she discovered what she wanted to do. Down deep, Gloria was a dreamer and was tired of selling real estate. One thing she did not want to do was to finance her dream-venture by putting in overtime in the real estate market. What Gloria *did* want to do was work with cloth.

On her travels, she had gathered cloth from Butan, the Kashmir, China, Turkestan, Tadzhikistan, Kenya, and Madagascar. Instead of 400 vests for a faceless mass market, she would create one vest at a time envisioning a woman traveling the world wearing her vest.

Gloria used the Internet to locate the perfect seamstress–designer. She found an artists' newsgroup. Several women were interested. She used her scanner to scan designs. She sent the designs directly to the women via modem. Before giving up her precious and very expensive cloth, Gloria paid each woman to create a test vest. When the test vests were accepted, Gloria met with each seamstress before she handed over the cloth.

To market the vests, Gloria contacted friends who traveled extensively internationally. She invited each of them to bring two or three friends to her first trunk show in a hotel suite in downtown Indianapolis. Pastries and coffee were served and the women tried on the vests and discussed their travels. There were 50 vests, each unique, with special buttons, fabric, and pockets. Forty-five vests were sold for prices ranging $150–$500. Gloria also took several special orders.

Gloria sold her real estate business and started working from her home. The walls of her design room were covered with drawings, photos, and bits of cloth. She purchased a clothing design program for her computer. A techie friend helped her re-tool the program for vests. At work in her design room, she came up with a company name: QuestVest.

She used e-mail to communicate with her seamstresses. Two lived in Chicago, two in Indianapolis, and two in France. The seamstress in France had sold two vests to a customer in Versailles, outside Paris. The customer in Versailles opened her home for the first international trunk show for QuestVest.

Working at the computer gave Gloria a sore wrist. When she checked the Internet, she found a Website devoted to Repetitive Stress Injuries, **www.hoaa.com/HOCstress.htm,** which she quickly shared with her seamstresses. The exercises helped keep the women working happily.

Gloria discovered that "niches bring riches." Take a tip from Gloria Brookstone and follow your dream. If you always dreamed of working at home, complete Action Step 37.

Health insurance is a major problem for self-employed people working out of their homes. For insurance information and special group rates, contact the National Association for the Self-Employed, **www.nase.org,** and **800-232-6273.** In addition, chambers of commerce, trade associations, and business organizations offer group health insurance rates. Insurance is necessary in today's high-health-cost environment. If you cannot afford the initial policy quoted, look into high deductible health insurance. Check with your insurance agent on what is specifically covered by your homeowner's insurance. If you have customers coming to your home, your insurance may not cover any problems that occur. Chapter 12 contains additional information on insurance for home based businesses.

The following Internet Sites will answer most of your questions about working at home:

- Home Office Computing **www.smalloffice.com**

- Home Office Association of America **www.hoaa.com**
- American Home Business Association **www.homebusiness.com**

Internet Location

As retail sales and marketing sites continue to skyrocket on the Net, we suggest you visit many of the sites on the Net, which provide extensive help to those wishing to join the Net revolution. Enter "Web commerce" into the search engine and incredible amounts of help are just a click away. Due to the open nature of the Net more information is available here than from other sources.

Below are a few businesses that have taken advantage of the Net's offerings.

Here We Are; Come and Get It
By Christine Foster

One of the Internet's most unlikely success stories is a hole-in-the-wall tucked into Manhattan's Lower East Side. Ralph Berg sells bras and undergarments from the same dingy shop that his parents, both Holocaust survivors, bought 35 years ago. But whereas his parents' Orchard Corset Discount Center

Figure 7.2

Internet Location?

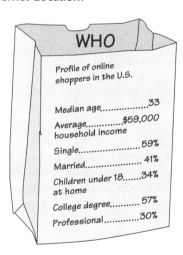

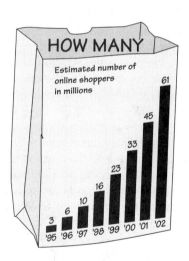

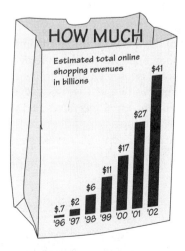

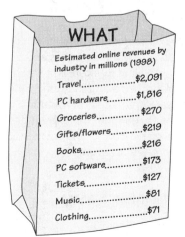

SOURCE: Time, July 20, 1998 p. 40–41.

catered to local residents, Berg markets to the world. The Internet has turned his tiny business into a global shopping site. Each week he ships hundreds of orders to customers as far away as Australia and South Africa.

The "E" in E-commerce no longer stands for "elusive." Small retailers are getting wired—gradually. Right now just 9% of businesses with under five employees have Web sites, according to New York-based Access Media International, but that's changing. Berg's business still does less than $1 million a year, but now does it all over the world and has a good chance at real growth.

Berg's speciality is the hard-to-please customer: bras from size 30 to 56, cup sizes A to I and girdles from size 24 to 54. If you can't find what you need at your local store, go online (**www.bway.net/orchard_bras/home.html**) from anywhere in the world. When women call him on the phone, Berg directs them to the site: "Do you have a computer? You can E-mail your order."

One drawback: the loss of personal contact. Berg's fitters have his mother's gift for being able to size up a customer on sight. They can't do that over the computer, but he can confer with women by phone before they place their orders. The Web has helped create a loyal following. A Florida woman sent Berg a postcard thanking him for selecting the right 46F bra. "I love you all," she wrote.

Rare-book dealers Charles Vilnis and Helen Kelly built their Web site (**www.rarebook.com**) in 1994, and have seen revenues rise 25%. Instead of 300 titles presented in bimonthly catalogs, Boston Book's Web site lists 16,000 books at a time. The site is updated at least twice a month.

Vilnis says the Internet is helping produce more rational pricing. He recently found six copies of a scarce mid-19th century Japanese travel book at prices ranging from $30 to $1,250. Pegging its true value at $400 to $900, depending on condition, he bought all but the most expensive. He figured that the price range was too broad and that he could easily sell the cheaper ones at prices closer to the more expensive examples.

Not many tourists make it to China Ranch in remote Tecopa, Calif., near Death Valley. Since 1995 Brian Brown and his wife, Bonnie, have been selling gifts, as well as shakes, cookies and bread from the date trees planted there in the 1920s by his great aunt.

But with the addition of a Web site (**www.chinaranch.com**) the Browns have attracted up to 300 additional visitors a year from Las Vegas and southern California and as far away as the East Coast and Canada. The Browns' revenues nearly doubled, to $96,000, between 1996 and 1997. This year they expect sales to climb another 25%.

SOURCE: *Forbes,* July 27, 1998, pp. 79–80.

Enterprise Zones

The government has designated certain areas of the United States, many in the inner city, as enterprise zones and economic zones. Special incentives are available to firms willing to locate in primarily economically depressed areas. In the recent tight labor market, many firms have discovered ready and eager employees in these areas. In addition to finding employees, the financial incentives and generally lower rents can be of great benefit to a start-up firm.

To gather further information, contact your local economic development office or **www.ezec.gov.**

A Success Story

We close this chapter with Charlene Webb's success story because it illustrates very well the things we've discussed. You could almost use this case study as a checklist for small business success.

"My partner and I were both in education, so carrying out a lot of research for our gourmet cookware store didn't seem unnatural. We hoped to open in October in order to capitalize on the holidays, so we spent our week of spring vacation talking to owners of gourmet cookware shops in the Los Angeles area—where it seems there's one on every corner.

"We spent five days and visited an average of 15 shops a day. The owners we talked to were helpful—since they knew our store would be 60 miles away.

"When spring vacation was over, we went back to our teaching jobs with our minds loaded with information and our hearts full of hope. Time pressures were heavy. If we were going to open in October, we knew we had to spend the summer on layout, image, and atmosphere. That meant we needed to find a good location very soon.

"Three days before the end of the school year we found a site—in a very safe and secure center near a convenient freeway off-ramp. Our nearest competition was 6 miles away, and a population study told us there were 55,000 people in the surrounding area to support us. It was perfect. All we had to do now was negotiate a lease we could live with.

"Perhaps it's because I was an English teacher, or because my dad's a lawyer, but whenever I came across a passage in the lease document I didn't like or didn't think was fair to us, I crossed it out. Several places I rewrote entire passages. When it was all over—after the landlord and I had discussed all my changes and we had both initialed the ones we agreed on—I had made four changes that really gave our business some flexibility and breathing space.

1. We got a 1-year lease with option to renew for the next 2. I knew if we were going to go under, it would be in the first year, and we certainly wouldn't want to have to continue paying a lease if our shop went under.
2. We got three months' free rent. I was very straightforward with the landlord on this. I said, "Look here, we can pay you three months' rent out of what cash we have left after fixing up the interior, or we can put that money into inventory that will help our start-up. I think it would be a benefit to both you and us if we put that money into inventory." The landlord agreed.
3. We got a 10 percent cost-of-living cap on the percentage the landlord can raise our rent each year. If I ever negotiate another lease, I'll go for 5 percent.
4. We refused to let the landlord or his representative look at our books."

Charlene and her partner's shop started off nicely, with a **grand opening** party for 200 friends and friends of friends. To bring in business, she started a cooking school.

Charlene has developed a customer list of 4,500 names, and remains visible in the community by being actively involved in music activities, the Chamber of Commerce, and the bank (she's now on the Board of Directors) and by writing a gossip column for the newspaper.

▶ Summary

Location decisions are one of the more difficult to make because, if you had to move, it would be very expensive. So, exercise caution! Research locations and target markets extensively. Legal advice is essential before signing leases or purchasing a building.

Explore the opportunities of home offices, Internet locations, and incubators. Staying in your office or garage can help you conserve cash for many years.

Before making decisions, reconsider your personal preferences, the availability of target customers, taxes, and available resources. Some short journeys will help you see how extremely important location is to retail businesses.

Grand opening A splashy celebration announcing one's entry into the market arena

First, walk up and down the main business street of your town. Walk it on different days (weekend, weekdays) and at different times of the day (midmorning, noon, afternoon, and evening rush hour). Take some notes on what you see happening.

Second, explore a local shopping center on weekends, weekdays, and different hours. Where is the action at these various times? Observe both vehicle and foot traffic, and what people are buying. Locate the dead traffic zones. A poor location can kill a new business. Location is probably the most important decision a retailer can make.

Think Points for Success

- The irony of the search for a retail or business start-up location is that you need the best site when you can least afford it.
- Take your time selecting a location. If you lose out on a hot site, keep looking. Don't give up. There are always more places to go.
- Do not desire a retail location where people have to turn into heavy traffic.
- Do not locate on a very busy street where traffic goes by too fast—potential customers will not see you and keep on going.
- Begin with a regional analysis that will allow you to compare neighborhoods.
- A site analysis should include everything that is unique to a specific building or space. Many successful centers have some dead traffic areas.
- Who are your neighbors? Are they attracting *your* type of customers or clients? What will happen if they move or go out of business?
- Know the terms and buzz words—net, gross, triple net, and so on—and be aware that they may mean slightly different things in each contract or lease agreement.
- Everything is negotiable: free rent, signage, improvement allowances, rates, maintenance. Don't be afraid to ask; $1 saved in rental expenses can be worth more than $10 in sales.
- Talk to former tenants; you may be amazed at what you learn.

Key Points From Another View

A Software Company Finds Greener Pastures in Cle Elum

Cle Elum has only one stoplight, and it's doubtful if the town needs even that. Just 90 minutes and one mountain pass east of Seattle, this former coalmining town, population 1,795, is in a different world: no traffic jams, no labor shortage, no economic boom.

It's just the place for Jeff Dantzler, CEO.

Six years ago, his software company, Comtronic Systems Inc., was in Federal Way—and feeling the squeeze. Microsoft was luring his employees away with stock options. Turnover was at 20 percent, and salaries were well above what competitors paid in Arizona and Texas.

Other things irked him. Every month, it seemed, he noticed another traffic signal between West Campus and Interstate 5. He saw graffiti, and didn't like what it meant. The rented space across the hall was filled by a therapist who specialized in sexual predators.

Dantzler began to think about getting out—far enough out that he wouldn't have to move again. "I wanted a place where I could definitely raise my kids in one spot," he says.

He chose Cle Elum because it is 90 minutes from Seattle and close enough to Sea-Tac Airport for that occasional flight out. And yet it is so far away in other respects.

Even today, when King County has a drum-tight unemployment rate of 3.1 percent, Kittitas County—where Cle Elum is located—is at 8.3 percent. The average annual pay in King County is $34,369; in Kittitas County it is $18,845. Much of that gap reflects seasonal farm work, but not all.

Many counties in Washington offer such enticements. Legions of legislators, officials and academics have been wondering why business has not responded, and how they might be inveigled to invest: Tax breaks? Training programs? Recruitment?

Cle Elum offered none of these things, but Dantzler found other berries to pick: lower costs for health, car and business liability insurance; lower sales and property taxes; and lower-priced land. Cle Elum also had fewer shopping opportunities, which meant regular trips to Seattle. It had no UPS pick-up service, but he was able to arrange it.

"I've always been one to totally check things out," Dantzler says. "We saved $4,400 a month. For that, you get a couple more employees, which is what we needed."

He had nine employees then. Most were renters, and eight moved. They took up every available place in town. Several have since bought land and built homes, as no one in Cle Elum is so bold as to build "on spec." Prices are lower. Says Dantzler, "People are still able to buy a house here on one income."

Dantzler bought seven acres of forested land just six minutes drive from the office. In the 1970s, he had grown up near more than 100 acres of forest—land that had since been developed. Now his kids could play in the woods like he did.

In town, he also bought a site for his company. No more renting and putting up with other people's tenants. His turnover fell by more than half. In high technology, he says, "we're the only game in town."

Dantzler, 35, has come a long way. He began the company out of high school to sell games for Radio Shack's first computer, the TRS-80. He sold more than 2,000 copies of such creations as "B-17 Flying Fortress" and "Raid on Entebbe" for $15 and $20 each. It was fun. But at that price, he figured, there wasn't enough of a future.

In the early 1980s he began offering business software. Comtronic now has three Windows products, one of which, Debtmaster, tracks deadbeat customers and sends out dunning letters for collection agencies. Comtronic has 3,000 customers and $2 million in annual sales.

Two years ago, he sold the company to Ontario Systems Corp. of Muncie, Ind., but remains chief executive. He wondered if being in Cle Elum would reduce his company's value; it didn't.

His employment has expanded to 25, of which only four were recruited locally. That bothers him. Comtronic has donated computers to Cle Elum's high school. Dantzler has taught a course there in programming, and hired two of his own students. His wife, Teri, is president of the parent association. But at school-levy time, computer education is a tough sell. It seems like a frill, and this is a community with no budget for fancies.

Kittitas County needs jobs. Some 500 people commute each day to jobs in booming King County. Dantzler will do his part; he expects his employment to be at 65 within two years.

If those people cannot be found in Kittitas County, Dantzler can always look west. "There's a lot of people on the West Side who would like to live here," he says. It may be a minority, but he says, "It gives me as big a labor pool as I'll ever need."

SOURCE: Seattle Times, April, 1998.

8

Numbers and Shoebox Accounting

Learning Objectives

- Learn how to keep score with numbers.
- Determine start-up costs.
- Discover ways to boot-strap your business.
- Develop sales projections.
- Determine seasonality scenario.
- Develop proforma profit and loss statements.
- Learn the importance of cash flow.
- Project monthly cash flow.
- Learn how to use industry financial ratios and benchmarks.
- Determine return on investment (ROI).

In this chapter, we urge you to move beyond your start-up plans and venture out into the uncertain future. It's time to set some numerical goals for your first year of operation. Running out of money in business is the end of the business. This chapter will show you how to avoid running out of money, develop your start-up costs, and prepare for capital searching.

Chart Your Business Future with Numbers

What will your start-up costs run? Which months will be strong in your particular business? weak? What will be your gross sales the first year? second? third? How much profit will you make? How much money will you lose? Can you project cash flow? bank loans? lines of credit? vendor credit? Can you add some people to the team who will bring in some cash? What will your cash picture look like when your start-up dollars are spread over a full year?

How fast will your business grow? How would rapid growth impact your cash picture? Have any of your life experiences prepared you for handling money in business? What steps should you take to be ready to handle your business's finances?

Your next step is to begin building a business budget. Generally, there are four things you need to consider before you plunge into the numbers of business management: start-up costs, Proforma income and cash flow statements, seasonality scenarios, and financial ratios. Each of these are discussed briefly below.

Start-up Costs

It's important to determine your costs before proceeding. For some businesses start-up costs will be minor; for others, major. A service business may be up and going with only $1000 in expenses whereas a retail store may incur over $200,000 in start-up expenses alone with manufacturing firms incurring costs of over $2 million. What can you buy used? lease versus buy? How can you conserve cash? Money saved in start-up can help cash flow later.

Sales Projections

Research and good guesstimates based on information gained from talking with competitors, associations, and suppliers will help determine your sales projections.

Resources for Women Entrepreneurs

Today, the growth of female entrepreneurs is twice the rate of men. And the growth of minority female entrepreneurs is even higher. We have included a few helpful organizations and Websites to get you started.

- American Women's Economic Development Corporation (AWED) provides telephone counseling and coaching to members nationwide.
  AWED
  (800) 222-2933
- National Association of Women Business Owners (NAWBO)
  www.nfwbo.org
  (301) 608-2590
- Office of Women's Business Ownership (Small Business Administration)
  (202) 205-6673
- Women Business Owners Corporation Network (links female suppliers and purchasing professionals)
  www.wboc.org
  (313) 458-7525
- Enterprising Women (online magazine)
  www.iepublishers.com/EW/Pages/ewmain.stm
- Small Business Administration (SBA) women's site (a complete listing of special programs and opportunities)
  www.sba.gov/womeninbusiness
- Women's Business Centers (sponsored primarily by the SBA)
  www.sba.gov/womensbusiness/websites.html

Proforma Income and Cash Flow Statements

Before you jump into a business, you need to figure out how much income and profit it will generate in a given period of time. You can pull together a first-year forecast by combining information on sales from businessowners and trade associations. Projections should be completed monthly for the first year and quarterly for the next three to five years.

For many businesses there is no time lag between delivering goods to receipt of payment. For others, a time lag of 15–60 days may exist. Find out what your selected industry standard is and develop your cash flow proforma accordingly. You will have to expend cash for labor, taxes, rent, utilities, inventory, and other expenses. If your business is to stay afloat in the interim, you're going to have to know where every dollar is going. You must make arrangements for help long before the money stops trickling in.

Unless you are an exception to the rule, you are not going to make lots of money your first year in business and, if you do get rich, it will happen slowly. A proforma income statement tells you when you should start making a profit—which has to happen before you can start getting rich.

Seasonality Scenarios

Most businesses experience peaks and valleys. What will be your best month? worst? Attempt to develop a seasonality scenario for the first year of your business.

Financial Ratios

Lenders will evaluate and compare your financial ratios to others in your selected industry. Their lending decisions are based on how you stack up. Ratios also provide a tool for maintaining your firm's finances.

Start-up Costs

When successful entrepreneurs are interviewed and asked what surprises they had not anticipated when they started, they can usually list quite a few. Almost always you hear it cost more and took longer than they had anticipated. We want you to get started in the planning process and make the best estimates so you are not caught off guard.

To help get you started, we have provided three worksheets which cover start-up concerns, necessary office supplies, and start-up costs. Each worksheet will need to be adjusted to fit your business operation. Review and complete as necessary.

Start-up Concerns Worksheet

Here's a checklist of some obvious start-up concerns. Add to this list as you think of things.

I. Taxi Squad (People who can help you)
   A. Lawyer
   B. Banker
   C. Accountant/bookkeeper
   D. Insurance agent
   E. Commercial real estate agent
   F. Mentor
   G. Consultant(s)
   H. Suppliers
   I. Chamber of Commerce
   J. SBA, SCORE
   K. Partners, board members

II. Organization
   A. Federal I.D. number
   B. DBA ("Doing business as" = fictitious business name)
   C. Partnership agreement
   D. Corporation
   E. Employees

III. Licenses, Permits
   A. Business license
   B. Resale permit
   C. Department of health
   D. Beer, wine, liquor
   E. Fire inspection permit
   F. Other

IV. Location
   A. Lease review (lawyer)
   B. First and last month's rent (Rent usually has to be paid while making improvements. Estimate time needed to do improvements.)
   C. Security deposit (last month's)
   D. Leasehold improvements
   E. Insurance
   F. Security system
   G. Utilities, deposits, estimated monthly costs
      1. Electric
      2. Gas
      3. Water
      4. Phone installation
   H. Other

V. Auto (Consider new, used, leased)
   A. Auto(s)
      1. New/used
      2. Lease/purchase
   B. Truck(s)
      1. New/used
      2. Lease/purchase
   C. Insurance
   D. Maintenance, repairs

VI. Equipment
   A. Office
   B. Retail space
   C. Warehouse
   D. Manufacturing area
   E. Kitchen
   F. Dining area
   G. Communication
   H. Other

VII. Fixtures
   A. Tables
   B. Chairs
   C. Desks
   D. File cabinets

Table 8.1

SBA Start-up Worksheet

Estimate how much cash you need

Estimated Monthly Expenses		Your Estimate of How Much Cash You Need to Start Your Business (See Column 3)	What To Put in Column 2 (These Figures are Typical for One Kind of Business. You Will Have to Decide How Many Months To Allow For in Your Business.)*
Item	**Your Estimate of Monthly Expenses Based on Sales of $_____ Per Year**		
	Column 1	Column 2	Column 3
Salary of owner-manager	$	$	2 times column 1
All other salaries and wages			3 times column 1
Rent			3 times column 1
Advertising			3 times column 1
Delivery expense			3 times column 1
Supplies			3 times column 1
Telephone and telegraph			3 times column 1
Other utilities			3 times column 1
Insurance			Payment required by insurance company
Taxes, including Social Security			4 times column 1
Interest			3 times column 1
Maintenance			3 times column 1
Legal and other professional fees			3 times column 1
Miscellaneous			3 times column 1
Starting Cost You Only Have to Pay Once			Leave column 2 blank
Fixtures and equipment			You can save a great deal by buying used equipment
Decorating and remodeling			Talk it over with a contractor
Installation of fixtures and equipment			Talk to suppliers from whom you buy these
Starting inventory			Suppliers will probably help you estimate this
Deposits with public utilities			Find out from utility companies
Legal and other professional fees			Lawyer, accountant, and so on
Licenses and permits			Find out from city offices what you have to have
Advertising and promotion for opening			Estimate what you'll use
Accounts receivable			What you need to buy more stock until credit customers pay
Cash			For unexpected expenses or losses, special purchases, etc.
Other			Make a separate list and enter total
Total Estimated Cash You Need to Start With		$	Add up all the numbers in column 2

*Contact associations and fellow entrepreneurs to determine costs.

SOURCE: **www.sba.gov**

E. Workbenches
F. Storage cabinets
G. Display cases
H. Lighting
I. Shelving/storage
J. Computers
K. Printers
VIII. Supplies
Business cards, pencils, pens, notepaper, tape, letterheads, dictionary, calendar, appointment book, coffee, tea, soft drinks, bottled water, and so on
IX. Inventory
What are the minimum/maximum average inventory requirements needed on hand in order to do business on your first day?
X. Advertising/Promotion
A. Signs
B. Business cards
C. Fliers/brochures

D. Displays
E. Ad layouts
F. Media (newspaper, radio, other) costs
G. Name tags
H. Other
XI. Banking
A. Checking account
1. Check charges
2. Interest on account
B. Savings/money market account
C. Credit
1. Credit cards
2. Personal lines of credit
3. Loans
4. Credit from suppliers/vendors
XII. Employees
A. Application/employment forms completed
B. Training program
C. Tax forms

Office Supplies Worksheet

Following is a list developed by the founders of a solar energy business (installation of hot water systems). They didn't need any start-up inventory as they would only order solar equipment after selling the system.

Equipment and Office Furniture
Desk chair
Two guest chairs
Lamp and table
Potted plant
Credenza
Secretary desk and chair
Locking file, two-drawer
File systems, folders
Computer/software/printer
Copier
Facsimile machine
Phone
Rolodex file
3 × 5 tickler file
In & out box (2)
Pager
Insurance

Business license
Air-postal-post-zone rates
Telephone directory
Supplies
Letterhead
Personal size pager
Envelopes/letterhead
Business cards
Second sheets for letterhead
Copy paper
Invoices/letterhead
Mail register
Organizer for mail
Printer toner/ink
Pencils, pens
Pencil holders
Tape
Stapler and staples

► **Action Step 38**

Attach Pricetags to Starting Your Business

Sit down at your desk and look around with new eyes.

A. List the items on your desk. Pencils, paper, telephone, typewriter, microcomputer, business cards, calendar, and so on. List the desk itself, the lamp, chair, bookcase, filing cabinet, coffee machine. Now go through the drawers, writing down every item you use to make your work run easier and smoother.

B. List your expenditures for things you cannot see, some of which you might take for granted. These include such things as insurance protection, rent, utilities, taxes, legal services, accounting services, and so on.

C. Beside each tangible item and each intangible expense, write down how much it will cost.

D. Discover all start-up costs and fill in SBA start-up sheet. Note that the SBA differentiates costs as either start-up expenses or operating expenses. This is an easy way to think about costs.

As you gather more information, you'll be able to refine the numbers on this sheet.

Staple remover
Rulers
Answering machine
Petty cash box
Postage meter (application for permit)
Postage scale
Coffee machine
Miscellaneous
Post office box
Instruction booklet
Tax deduction tables
Federal employer ID number
State employer ID number
Bank account
Checkbook
One-write checking/bookkeeping system
Utilities—telephone, water, gas, electricity
Hole punch (2/3 hole)
Scissors

Colored tabs
Erasers, paperclips
Telephone message pads
Minute book for corporation
Pocket appointment book
Desk appointment book
Dictionary
Reference book
Calendars
Long-distance call record
Clients and projects directory
Steno pads
Scratch paper
Coffee supplies
File folders and labels
Mileage log
Local area wall map
Local area map for truck

If you get into the habit of making lists, doing mind maps, writing everything down, you'll improve your chances of surviving in small business. Action Step 39 will help you anticipate potential surprises.

The American Booksellers Association (ABA) provides start-up expenses for a 2000-square-foot bookstore with 1800 square feet allocated for selling space. According to the ABA, inventory for a bookstore will depend on:

price point and ratio of hardcover to trade, paper to mass market
number of titles and number of copies per title
store layout

In addition to the above, one's financial resources will determine investment in inventory. The ABA estimates inventory at $25 to $100 per square foot of allocated selling space. Again, you need to do research and work with your professional association to determine appropriate start-up costs for your business.

In addition to outfitting your office, retail store, or manufacturing operation, there will be costs for computers, cash registers, professional organization dues and publications, deposits and fees for utilities, security deposits, advertising and promotion costs, grand opening expenses, and fees for professional help.

If you go over budget on your start-up costs your first year will be very difficult. This is the time to bootstrap. Think of every way you can save: buy used, borrow, barter, or beg. Conserve cash at all times. One entrepreneur we know, worth over $3 million, demands his staff check the local library before purchasing any books. Cash is king! Especially at the beginning, do not squander cash. Complete Action Step 38 using the SBA worksheet.

Summary of Bookstore Preopening Capital Needs

$90,000	Opening inventory (1800 sq. ft. × $50 per sq. ft.)
20,000	Leasehold improvements (2000 sq. ft. × $10) (based on space improvements *not* complete building of new facility)
40,000	Furniture and fixtures (2000 sq. ft. × $20)
15,000	Computerized cash registers and software
6,000	Professional consultants
4,000	Supplies
6,000	Deposits, registrations, fees, memberships
8,000	Preopening salaries
3,000	Training and conventions
10,000	Preopening advertising and promotion
202,000	Subtotal
23,000	Contingencies (10%)
$225,000	**Total Preopening Costs***

NOTE: Prior to consideration of anticipated first-year operating loss.

SOURCE: **www.bookweb.org/edu/676.html**

Manual on Bookselling: Practical Advice for the Bookstore Professional, 5th edition, 1996, edited by Kate Whouley with Linda Miller and Rosemary Hawkins, Tarrytown, NY: American Booksellers Association.

Paying the Piper When the Purse Is Thin

Small businesses are especially vulnerable at start-up time because that's when they're least able to afford surprises. If Ginny Henshaw had anticipated possible surprises, she'd have been better prepared for what happened to her.

The reason I decided to start a day-care center was because I really like kids. I talked it over with my family and they said they would help out if I got in over my head.

I think we planned things pretty well. We found a good location—smack in the middle of a neighborhood of young families with an average 2.3 children—and then spent weekends painting and fixing up. We worked hard, but it was fun, and it made us feel a part of something warm and cozy.

Well, about three weeks before our opening, we called the light and power people to ask them to turn on the lights. "Sure thing," they said. "Just send us a check for $700, and the lights will be on in a jiffy."

"What?" I asked. "Did you say $700?" We had around $800 in the kitty, but that was earmarked for emergencies.

"That's right. You're a new commercial customer with a good credit rating. That's the reason the figure's so low."

"You think $700 is low?" I asked, I was shocked.

"For your tonnage," they said, "it's right on the money."

"Tonnage? What tonnage?"

"Your air conditioner," they said. "You have a 5-ton unit on your roof. Figure you run it for a month, that's $310. The other $40 is for lights and gas."

"But we're not planning to run it!" I said. "The breeze here is terrific. We don't need the air conditioner."

"Sorry, ma'am. Our policy is pretty clear. As I said, sometimes we get three months' deposit, but for your business, we'll only require the two. Is there anything else I can help you with today?"

"No," I said. "Nothing."

Complete Action Step 39 as you explore possible start-up surprises.

Action Step 39

Preparing Your Checklist

Now that you've got your business well in mind, take a few minutes to brainstorm a list of surprises that could cost you money or time and thus threaten the survival of your business. Use our checklist to help you get started. Talk to businesspeople in your industry. Ask them to tell you how they handled unfortunate surprises. Once you select a site, ask the neighbors what has happened to them and how they're doing in this location. Talk to vendors, suppliers, customers, and insurance brokers. Ask. Probe.

When you finish your list, put a checkmark beside each item where you may incur costs. Determine the potential costs. How will you cover unforseen expenses? How much money should you put aside?

Bootstrapping

It's no secret that start-ups are expensive, and those first few months can be a make-or-break time for the entrepreneur. You want to make your dollars work efficiently. Here are some tips:

1. Find out who you have to pay right now.
2. Find out who can wait a while.
3. Keep asking what you're getting for your money.
4. Conserve cash.

How to Save Money

If you work the dollars you do have, you won't have to shake the money tree so hard. Here are some tips that could save you money. Read through the list. How many of these ideas have you thought of? How many are new to you?

1. Ask your customers for **cash deposits** when they place orders.
2. Persuade vendors to give you more **trade credit** or **dating** and more time to pay.
3. Lease your equipment.
4. Run a lean operation; do not waste anything.
5. Work out of your home if you can.
6. Get your landlord to make **on-site improvements** and finance the cost over the term of the lease.
7. Keep track of everything. Try to resell whatever waste or by-products you have in your business.
8. Take markdowns quickly on **dead goods.**
9. Use as little commercial space as you can.
10. If your customers do not visit your business facility, it does not have to be highly visible or attractive.
11. When you have to borrow money, shop around.
12. Make sure your **liquid cash** is earning interest.
13. Shop **nonbank lenders** like commercial credit firms.
14. Do not collateralize your loans unless you have no other alternative.
15. Survey your friends and relatives for loans. They might lend you money at rates higher than they would get in the money markets but lower than you would have to pay institutional lenders.

Getting Advice

There's a boatload of surprises awaiting every entrepreneur who enters the marketplace. We've talked about Plan B, formulating your strategy, checking and double-checking your market, and peering into the future to see what lies ahead. There's another angle to planning; it's called seeking advice.

Think for a moment about where you are right now on your road to the marketplace. You're halfway through this book. You've analyzed your skills and needs. You've probed your past and surveyed your friends. You've discovered what success means to you, and you've plotted trends and found your industry segment. You've profiled your target customer, studied the demographics, and developed a promotional campaign. You've examined the competition. You've used your new eyes to find a dynamite location. Now you need to find a **small business guru** and get some advice.

Where might you find a business guru? Well, what about your banker? Many people come to him or her for money—some of them carrying business plans, others not knowing a spreadsheet from a bed sheet. What about your accoun-

Cash deposits Funds paid in advance of delivery

Trade credit or dating A vendor's extension of the payment term into the near future

On-site improvements Modifications to real estate to accommodate the special needs of the business

Dead goods Merchandise no longer in demand

Liquid cash Funds that are immediately available, usually held in checking or other accounts

Nonbank lenders Institutional lenders other than banks

Small business guru A wise person on the sidelines who can help you with advice and counsel

The Ten Largest U.S. Import Markets

Country/Region	Value (billions of $)	Percent of World Trade
Canada	$156.5	20.3%
Japan	115.2	15.0
Mexico	73.0	9.5
China	51.5	6.7
Germany	38.9	5.1
Taiwan	29.9	3.9
United Kingdom	28.9	3.8
South Korea	22.7	3.0
Singapore	20.3	2.6
France	18.8	2.4
Subtotal	$555.5	72.3%
World	$770.6	

The Ten Largest U.S. Export Markets

Country/Region	Value (billions of $)	Percent of World Trade
Canada	$133.7	22.9%
Japan	67.5	11.6
Mexico	56.8	9.7
United Kingdom	30.9	5.3
South Korea	26.6	4.6
Germany	23.5	4.0
Taiwan	18.4	3.2
Singapore	16.7	2.9
Netherlands	16.6	2.8
France	14.4	2.5
Subtotal	$405.1	69.5%
World	$583.9	

SOURCE: Reported in the *New York Times*, 2 March 1997, 8.

tant? What about the real estate broker who helped you with your search for a location? What about your business insurance specialist?

You can use your network to find other people who may help you. Show them your list of potential surprises and ask for their advice. Ask them for their ideas about what other surprises might be in store for you. If one of these persons gives you wonderful advice, consider putting him or her on your board of directors.

Sales Projections

One of the most challenging and often the most difficult step in preparing financial statements is estimating sales for the first year of a new business. The thirteenth month becomes more manageable because you have a year of experience.

Marketing research is the key. The financial community wants to make sure that you spend a lot of time on your projections because it drives everything else.

You also want to minimize surprises—even "good surprises" can raise havoc with a well-thought-out plan—for example, you receive ten times the orders you expected and simply don't yet have the resources to deal with them.

You have already conducted an industry overview. You may have identified total sales internationally, nationally, statewide, and in your service area. Your task, after factoring industry and local growth, is to determine which part of the market you can reasonably expect to penetrate in the first, second, third, fourth, and fifth years. Annual issues of trade magazine, census data, suppliers, and major newspapers often have already performed your secondary research. For your Business Plan, attach any appropriate printed data to your market research section in the appendix to prove your numbers. Fine-tune these numbers by showing your own research and notes from industry experts that support your assumptions on projected sales. When you list your competitors, estimate their market share and the part of their market that you have targeted.

Projections are well-documented estimates. A third party's estimate will have more value than yours, so quote as many sources as you can to prove your numbers.

When projecting your sales, you may want to consider doing high, low, and medium sales projections. This will allow you to make plans for your expenses and revenues based on various scenarios. Continuing on with our bookstore example, the ABA has provided average first-year bookstore projections and the following advice: (see Table 8.2).

Table 8.2

ABA Bookstore

Proforma Profit & Loss Three Scenarios

	Low	Medium	High
Sales per square foot	$ 100	$ 125	$ 150
Sales Revenue	180,000	225,000	270,000
Less: Cost of Goods Sold*	108,000	135,000	162,000
Gross Margin	72,000	90,000	108,000
Less: Expenses			
Wages (1st year, 18%)	32,400	40,500	48,600
Rent ($14/square foot)	28,000	28,000	28,000
Advertising	3,600	4,500	5,400
Insurance	1,500	1,500	1,500
Postage	1,000	1,200	1,400
Conventions	1,000	1,000	1,000
Supplies	1,200	1,300	1,400
Telephone	1,200	1,300	1,400
Utilities	1,400	1,400	1,400
Taxes, Licenses, Fees	1,000	1,200	1,200
Depreciation	15,000	15,000	15,000
Payroll Taxes	2,500	3,200	3,850
Bank/Card Fees (1% of sales)	1,800	2,250	2,700
Professional Services	2,000	2,000	2,000
All Other Expenses	5,000	5,000	5,000
Total Expenses	$ 98,600	$109,350	$119,850
Net Profit or Loss	($ 26,600)	($ 19,350)	($ 11,850)

NOTE: Assuming 40% discount.

SOURCE: American Booksellers Association.

"It can be seen that even under the best sales projection, the first-year bookstore has an operating loss of $11,850; the loss with a medium sales projection would be $19,350; while under the worst scenario there is an anticipated loss of $26,600. In planning capital needs for a new bookstore, the anticipated operating losses during the first year should be taken into consideration. After a store has experienced an operating loss is not a good time to seek additional outside sources of capital, whether or not that loss is quite normal and anticipated. The bookstore owner must plan in advance how the capital depletion from the first year's operating loss will be covered. Cash-flow analysis gives a more accurate picture of what proportion of the first year's bottom-line loss must be replaced as working capital. For purposes of illustration, however, let us assume that the high sales projection's loss of $11,850 needs to be replaced. If this amount of capital is added to the preopening capital, the total amount of capital to be raised is:"

$$(\text{Preopening Capital}) + (\text{Year 1 Operating Loss}) = (\text{Total Capital})$$
$$\$225,000 + \$11,850 = \$236,850$$

Chapter 9 discusses how to raise capital. This scenario was taken from Book-Web: Education—Projecting Your Opening expenses and Start-Up Capital (August 1996) at **http://www.bookweb.org/edu/213.html**.

Seasonality Scenario

Determining our bookstore Know It All's inventory was fairly easy based on the information provided by the ABA. But now the owners of Know It All need to complete a seasonality scenario to determine monthly profit and loss and cash-flow projections. They talked with a local bookstore owner and he shared the following:

January (6.5%)

"January is an anticlimax to Christmas, but it's still busy because of gift certificates and exchanges. I run some good specials at the end of January, prior to taking yearly inventory. Even though sales are slowing down, I have to order new titles because publishers (our suppliers) are giving me advance notice on their spring lists."

February (4.5%) and March (5%)

"Very quiet. I take inventory, weed out stuff that didn't sell, send it back, and usually feel bad when I see the restocking fees. I meet publishers' reps who are out on the road pushing new titles. On March fifteenth, I have an Ides of March sale. Next year I'm planning a St. Patrick's Day tie-in."

April (5%)

"Still slow. We get a slight jump in sales after the tenth, mostly because spring vacations give some people time to read."

May (8%) and June (8%)

"Two holidays—Mother's Day and Father's Day—plus weddings and graduations give us our second-busiest season. Art books and gift editions do well, also encyclopedias and how-to's."

July (6%) and August (7%)

"We're not in a tourist area, and summers for us are slow. We sell mostly easy-to-read paperbacks and lots of Oprah Winfrey's book selections. Our minds, though, are on ordering books for Christmas."

September (9%)

"Back-to-school purchases. We're interviewing people for Christmas jobs and making last-minute purchases of gift items."

October (10%) and November (12%)

"The start of the busy season. Customers sense it, and we can feel the momentum. The rush is just around the corner. We usually hire more sales help at this time."

December (19%)

"The crush. Our computer does a great job of tracking sales. It's different every year, but with two years of great data gathering behind me, I am getting a feel for what really happens. And that helps us plan ahead for the next year."

Figure 8.1

Cash Flow

This simple cash-flow diagram shows the typical time lag between paper profits and the flow of real profits. Plan ahead for this lag.

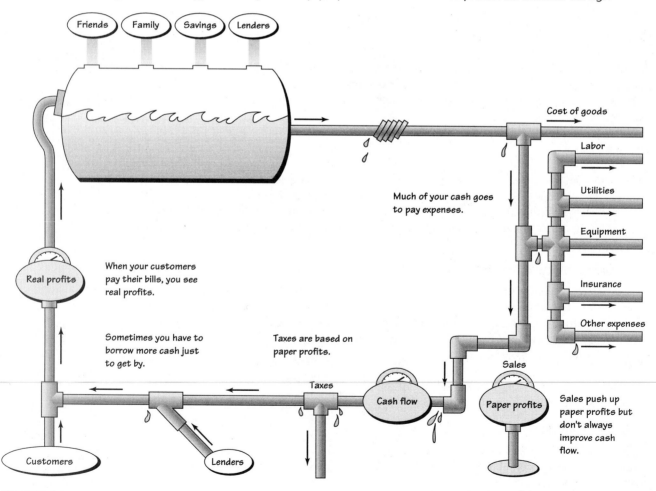

After the first year of business, seasonal sales forecasting will become easier. Keep very careful records that first year, so that you'll know how your own peaks and valleys correlate with the seasonality of your selected industry. Many businesses are seasonal, and you'll need to develop strong control systems to manage your financial resources. Start now to identify alternative sources of credit and find ways to collect cash from customers before all your products or services are delivered.

Proforma Monthly Income and Cash Flow Statements

Income statements track revenue and expenses but don't tell the whole story. (Even a documentary movie is shot from only one angle at a time.) It's nice to watch paper profits, but you must also be alert to what is happening to real cash. Figure 8.1 shows the typical pattern of cash flows.

Income statements tell you when you're going to make a profit on paper. A cash-flow projection tells (1) whether or not you can pay bills, and (2) when you'll need cash infusions to keep going. Both of these projections are essential to the survival of your business. Some SBA worksheets include both on one statement.

More than sales are involved in projections; you also need to project times of collection and other time lags so you can get a feel for the way cash will flow through your business. You need to discover all expense categories involved with your business to be able to make proper projections. Projecting your income is like projecting a moving picture of your business. If you're careful in how you prepare your numbers, that movie will be reasonably accurate.

Know It All's projections are based on ABA figures and local research. Advertising expenses are greater due to several very tough competitors. No salary or payroll expenses are included as Know It All will be managed by the owner who will not take a salary—"sweat equity." Please review how notes have been added to proformas to explain the figures. Be sure you do the same on your proformas.

Review Know It All's projected monthly proforma income statement (Table 8.3) and quarterly forecasts for the second through fifth years (Table 8.4). Action Step 40 leads you through a monthly proforma income statement.

Cash-flow projections are a tool used to help you control money. The lifeblood of any business is cash flow. Many businesses are profitable but fail because of cash-flow problems. Without completing proforma cash flows, entrepreneurs can truly underestimate their cash needs and fail early on.

Table 8.7 illustrates Know It All's proforma cash flow. Action Step 41 asks you to project your cash flow. Table 8.8 will help you to complete your proforma.

Review Know It All's proformas. What would you recommend to the entrepreneur? Could the owners increase sales dramatically to improve cash flow and income? Could they provide additional services to increase cash flow such as renting out the store in the evening for book or investment clubs? Could they sublet the premises for after-hours private speakers to conduct seminars? Could the owners run a special youth reading and arts program in the afternoon to bring in additional cash? To increase cash flow, look beyond the initial product or service and extend your facilities and products.

Are you willing to put in sweat equity? Are your projections realistic? What can you do to increase cash flow if necessary? Would you be able to forego

> ## Action Step 40

Complete a Proforma Profit and Loss Schedule

Write the scenario for a typical year in your business.

You can do part of the scenario with new eyes—just look around at obvious forces such as weather, heat, cold, time, and expense—and relate these to the life-cycle stage of your product, location, and competition. You will have to glean other information from other small businessowners and from trade associations.

When does your selected industry collect money? (Before the sale? during? after? long after?) When will you have to pay for your inventory? What is the shortest time lag you could see between the time you pay for inventory and the time you receive money (payment, hard dollars) for the sale of that inventory?

What is the *longest* time lag? When will you declare a time lag a bad debt?

If you are in manufacturing and have to alter, reshape, or rebuild raw materials into a product, what kind of time lag will there be?

Adapt Tables 8.5 and 8.6 for this action step. Generate your numbers for the year as follows:

1. Using data from trade associations and small businessowners, forecast your sales for the year.
2. Figure your cost of goods sold and subtract that figure from sales. This gives you your gross profit.
3. Add up all expenses and subtract them from gross profit. This gives you the net profit before taxes.
4. Subtract taxes. (Uncle Sam uses what we might call "old eyes." You will be taxed on paper profit, so you have to build in this figure.) The figure you arrive at is your net profit after taxes for the year.

Table 8.3

Know It All Proforma Profit & Loss (Monthly)

	July	Aug	Sept	Oct	Nov	Dec	Jan	Feb	Mar	Apr	May	June	Total
Sales	7,800	9,100	11,700	13,000	15,600	24,700	8,450	5,850	6,500	6,500	10,400	10,400	130,000
Cost of Goods Sold	5,070	5,915	7,605	8,450	10,140	16,055	5,495	3,800	4,225	4,225	6,760	6,760	8,450
Gross Profit	2,730	3,185	4,095	4,550	5,460	8,645	2,955	2,050	2,275	2,275	3,640	3,640	45,500
Expenses													
Rent		1,875	1,875	1,875	1,875	1,875	1,875	1,875	1,875	1,875	1,875	1,875	20,625
Utilities	200	200	200	200	200	200	200	200	200	200	200	200	2,400
Adv./PR/4%	310	365	470	520	625	990	340	235	260	260	415	415	5,205
Insurance	75	75	75	75	75	75	75	75	75	75	75	75	900
Supplies/1%	80	90	115	130	155	245	85	60	65	65	105	105	1,300
Misc./5%	390	455	585	650	780	1,235	425	295	325	325	520	520	6,505
Credit card fees	70	80	105	120	140	225	75	55	60	60	95	95	1,180
Loan interest													
Total Expenses	1,125	3,140	3,425	3,580	3,850	4,845	3,075	2,795	2,860	2,860	3,285	3,285	38,125
Net Profit/Loss	1,605	45	670	970	1,610	3,800	−120	−745	−585	−585	355	355	7,375

NOTE: Sales: the first-year forecast of $130,000 is based on industry information gathered by the owners. ($100 × 1300 sales space)

Cost of Goods Sold: Estimated at 65% of sales (includes all shipping)

Rent: 1.25 cents per square foot × 1500 square feet; no rent charged for the first month; the owners used the first month to get ready for their opening.

Utilities: Figures are estimates from the local utility company.

Advertising and Promotion: Estimated at 4% of sales based on information from other bookstore owners.

Insurance: $900 per year is the rate quoted by owners' insurance agent.

Supplies: Estimated at 1% of sales based on interviews.

Miscellaneous: Estimated at 5% of sales based on interviews; added a fudge factor to cover unexpected expenses.

Loan Interest: This represents interest on the line of credit at 1% per month of the unpaid balance.

Credit Card Fees: Projected on the basis of 30% of sales being credit-card sales; the credit card company charges 3%.

Table 8.4

Know It All Proforma Profit & Loss, 2nd-5th Years

	2nd Year					3rd Year	4th Year	5th Year
	1st Qtr	2nd Qtr	3rd Qtr	4th Qtr	Total	Total	Total	Total
Sales	34,320	63,960	24,960	32,760	156,000	201,175	210,800	237,200
Cost of Goods Sold	22,310	41,575	16,225	21,295	101,405	137,020	137,020	154,180
Gross Profit	12,010	22,385	8,735	11,465	54,595	64,155	73,780	83,020
Expenses								
Rent	5,905	5,905	5,905	5,910	23,625	24,805	26,045	27,350
Utilities	630	630	630	630	2,520	2,645	2,780	2,920
Adv./PR	1,375	2,545	1,000	1,310	6,230	7,330	8,430	9,490
Insurance	235	235	235	240	945	990	1,040	1,090
Supplies	345	640	250	330	1,565	1,835	2,110	2,370
Misc.	1,785	3,200	1,250	1,640	7,875	9,215	10,540	11,860
Credit card fees	310	575	225	295	1,405	1,650	1,900	2,135
Loan interest								
Total Expenses	10,585	13,730	9,495	10,355	44,165	48,470	52,845	57,215
Net Profit/Loss	1,425	8,655	−760	1,110	10,430	15,685	20,935	25,805

*2nd year: 20% growth

3rd year: 17.5% growth

4th year: 15% growth

5th year: 12.5% growth

Table 8.5a

Proforma Profit & Loss (Worksheet)

Income Chart (handwritten)

Write months here (handwritten)

($)	Month 1	Month 2	Month 3	Month 4	Month 5	Month 6	tot
Net Sales	~~2375.~~ 2500	~~543.75~~ 625	445.55 469	~~1143.80~~ 1172.51	1758.75 ~~1676.87~~	2198.44 ~~2088.52~~	
COST OF SALES:							
Goods/Materials *-cashflow*	625	156.25	117.25	293.14	439.69	549.61	
Production Exp *Service*	156.25	39.06	29.25	73.29	109.92	137.40	
Direct Labor	0						
Gross Profit A	781.25	195.31	146.50	366.43	549.61	687.01	
Expenses:	~~1212.95~~ 4718.75	~~388.44~~ 429.69	~~342.05~~ 322.50	~~841.37~~ 806.08	1209.14 ~~1212.50~~	1511.43 ~~1512.51~~	
GENERAL & ADMIN							
Payroll Expense	6400	6400	6400	6400	6400	6400	
Payroll Taxes	1600	1600	1600	1600	1600	1600	
Travel/Entertainment	400	400	400	400	400	400	
Rent/Util/Tel	1956	1956	1956	1956	1956	1956	
Ins/Legal/Acct	950	950	950	950	950	950	
Office & Supply	~~400~~ 200	~~400~~ 200	~~400~~ 200	200	200	200	
Equipment Exp	400	400	400	400	400	400	
Credit/Collect *Petty Cash*	200 –	200	200	200	200	200	
Maintenance	0	0	0	0	0	0	
Auto/Truck Exp	650	650	650	650	650	650	
Other	250	250	250	250	250	250	
SELLING EXPENSE	~~13006~~						
Payroll Expense							
Sales Commission							
Advertising							
Travel/Entertainment							
Auto Expenses							
Other							
OTHER EXPENSES							
Interest *- Ar ex per ce ×25%* *Divide by*	3.75	.94	.70	1.76	2.64	12.30	
Depreciation	~~520~~ 520	520	520	520	520	520	
Total Expenses =	~~13529.75~~ 15248.50	13956.65	13849.20	14333.84	14732.78		
OTHER INCOME	~~5.6~~ 15248.50	0	0	0	0	0	
Interest Income	0 (15248.50	0	0	0	0	0	
Other *subtot*	0 13529.75	13956.65	13849.20	14333.84	14737.78	15049.73	
PROFIT (LOSS) *-14467.25*	~~12748.5~~	-13761.34	-13702.70	-13967.41	-14188.17	-14362.72	
Income Taxes							
NET PROFIT/LOSS							

taking a salary for a few months if serious cash flow problems occur? When you have completed your projections, show the results to an expert. Ask him or her if they look accurate. It's better to know the truth now, while you're working on paper; paper truth is a lot easier on the pocketbook than reality.

Break-Even Analysis

Knowing a few key numbers can help to avoid painful surprises. If you know your costs (variable and fixed) and your gross sales, you can use a couple of break-even formulas that will tell when you will start making money. Break-even analysis is useful at start-up time, when you have completed your income and expense projections, and when you are considering launching a new product or service (see Figure 8.2).

Table 8.5b

Proforma Profit & Loss (Worksheet)

($)	Month 7	Month 8	Month 9	Month 10	Month 11	Month 12	First Year Totals
Net Sales							
COST OF SALES:							
Goods/Materials							
Production Exp							
Direct Labor							
Gross Profit							
Expenses:							
GENERAL & ADMIN							
Payroll Expense							
Payroll Taxes							
Travel/Entertainment							
Rent/Util/Tel							
Ins/Legal/Acct							
Office & Supply							
Equipment Exp							
Credit/Collect							
Maintenance							
Auto/Truck Exp							
Other							
SELLING EXPENSE							
Payroll Expense							
Sales Commission							
Advertising							
Travel/Entertainment							
Auto Expenses							
Other							
OTHER EXPENSES							
Interest							
Depreciation							
Total Expenses							
OTHER INCOME							
Interest Income							
Other							
PROFIT (LOSS)							
Income Taxes							
NET PROFIT/LOSS							

> ### ▶ Action Step 41
>
> #### Projecting Cash Flow
>
> If you don't have access to a computer and an electronic spreadsheet program, use the spreadsheet shown in Table 8.8 to project your cash flow across the first year of your business.
>
> 1. Write down the amount of cash you'll start the year with as the amount on hand (or in the bank) at the beginning of the first month.
>
> *continued on next page*

A small manufacturing company was completing a plan for its second year of operation. Its first-year sales were $177,000, and a sales breakdown for the last three months of their first year looked like this:

October	$24,000
November	29,000
December	15,000
	$68,000

The owners took a look at the numbers and called in a consultant to help. The consultant gathered information from sales reps, owners, and customers and then projected that sales for the second year would be a whopping $562,000. The owners reacted with disbelief.

"You're crazy," they said. "That's more than three times what we did last year."

The consultant smiled. "Didn't you tell me you were going to add three new products?"

Table 8.6

Proforma Profit & Loss Second Year/Summary (Worksheet)

($,000's)	Quarter 1	Quarter 2	Quarter 3	Quarter 4	Year Total
Net Sales					
COST OF SALES:					
Goods/Materials					
Production Exp					
Direct Labor					
Gross Profit					
Expenses:					
GENERAL & ADMIN					
Payroll Expense					
Payroll Taxes					
Travel/Entertainment					
Rent/Util/Tel					
Ins/Legal/Acct					
Office & Supply					
Equipment Exp					
Credit/Collect					
Maintenance					
Auto/Truck Exp					
Other					
SELLING EXPENSE					
Payroll Expense					
Sales Commission					
Advertising					
Travel/Entertainment					
Auto Expenses					
Other					
OTHER EXPENSES					
Interest					
Depreciation					
Total Expenses					
OTHER INCOME					
Interest Income					
Other					
PROFIT (LOSS)					
Income Taxes					
NET PROFIT/LOSS					

2. For each month, enter the amount of cash you'll receive from sales or accounts receivable.
3. Enter any loans in the month you receive the cash from the lender.
4. Total the above items to learn how much cash will be available each month.
5. List all disbursements (cash going out). Spread these out, too.
6. Subtract disbursements from cash available for each month. This gives you a monthly cash flow. Carry this figure forward (to point one for each succeeding month).

Now examine your work. Have you explored the quirks of seasonality? Have you discovered the minimum and maximum time lags between when you make a sale and when you get paid (in cash) for that sale? Does the picture look accurate? Have an expert check it for you.

Try the "what-if" test: If your cash flow picture looks good, introduce a couple of what-ifs. What surprise expenses could throw a monkey wrench into your new business?

"Yes."

"And new reps in March, June, and September?"

"Yes, but—"

"And what about those big promotions you've got planned?"

"Well, sure, we've planned some promotions, but that doesn't get us anywhere near three times last year."

"All right," the consultant said. "Can you do $275,000?"

The owners got into a huddle. Based on the fourth quarter, they were sure they could stay even, and four times $68,000 (the fourth-quarter sales) was $272,000. They knew they had to do better than last year.

"Sure, no problem. We can do $272,000."

"All right," said the consultant, rolling out his break-even chart. "I've just projected $562,000 in sales for the year. To break even, you only need $275,000."

"Hey," the owners said, "we're projecting $90,000 the first quarter."

Table 8.7

Proforma Cash Flow for Know It All

	July	Aug	Sept	Oct	Nov	Dec	Jan	Feb	Mar	Apr	May	June
Cash on hand	1,900	3,945	100	145	610	5,715	21,070	20,990	20,360	22,030	21,200	20,950
Sales	7,800	9,100	11,700	13,000	15,600	24,700	8,450	5,850	6,500	6,500	10,400	10,400
Less: Credit fees	−70	−80	−105	−120	−140	−225	−75	−55	−60	−60	−95	−95
Loan												
Total	9,360	12,965	12,965	13,025	16,070	30,190	29,445	26,785	26,800	28,470	31,505	31,255
Disbursements												
Book purchases	4,255	9,800	9,305	8,030	6,720	4,575	5,080	3,760	2,045	4,545	7,440	8,420
Rent		1,875	1,875	1,875	1,875	1,875	1,875	1,875	1,875	1,875	1,875	1,875
Utilities	200	200	200	200	200	200	200	200	200	200	200	200
Adv./PR/4%	310	365	470	520	625	990	340	235	260	260	415	415
Insurance	450											
Supplies/1%	80	90	115	130	155	245	85	60	65	65	105	105
Misc./5%	390	455	585	650	780	1,235	425	295	325	325	520	520
Interest				10								
Loan payment				1,000								
Total	5,685	12,865	12,550	12,415	10,355	9,120	8,455	6,425	4,770	7,270	10,555	11,535
Net Cash Flow	3,945	100	145	610	5,715	21,070	20,990	20,360	22,030	21,200	20,950	19,720

Table 8.8a

Proforma Cash Flow (Worksheet)

(handwritten: write in month here) *(handwritten: tot)*

($)	Month 1	Month 2	Month 3	Month 4	Month 5	Month 6
Cash Sources:						
FROM OPERATIONS	2500	625	464	1172.51	1758.75	2198.44
Cash Sales	2375	593.75	445.55	1113.88	1670.81	2088.52
A/R Collections	125	31.25	23.45	58.63	87.94	109.92
Other Cash Collections						
OTHER SOURCES						
Interest Income	0	0	0	0		
Loan from Bank	20834	20834	20834	20834	20834	20834
Investment						
Subtotal	23,334	21459	21303	22006.51	22592.75	23032.44
Cash Uses:						
TO OPERATIONS						
Accts Payable	0					
Goods/Materials	625	156.25	117.25	293.14	439.69	549.61
Services	156.25	39.06	29.25	73.29	109.92	137.40
Petty Cash	200.00	200.00	200.00	200.00	200.00	200.00
Payroll Expense	6400	6400	6400	6400	6400	6400
Sales Commission	0					
Travel/Entertainment	400	400	400	400	400	400
Rent/Util/Tel	1956	1956	1956	1956	1956	1956
Advertising	250	250	250	250	250	250
Auto/Truck Exp	650	650	650	650	650	650
Maintenance	0	0				
Equipment Exp	400 200	400 200	400	400	400	400
Ins/Legal/Acct	950	950	950	950	950	950
Miscellaneous	200	200				
OTHER USES						
Interest Exp	420.75	417.94	417.70	418.76	419.64	429.30
Dividends	420.75	417.9				
Loan Payoff	4167.					
Investor Payoff	0					
Reserve for Tax	1600					
Subtotal	15579					
Cash Incr/Decr	23334	21459	21303	22006.51	22562.75	23032.44
Beginning Bal	0	7759				
Ending Balance	7759					

(handwritten annotations at left:) 95, 5 ; 25%/608 total cost; 25%/608 ; 500 + 150 ; 300+ ; idleen

(handwritten at bottom:) A − B + C = D

Table 8.8b

Proforma Cash Flow (Worksheet)

($)	Month 7	Month 8	Month 9	Month 10	Month 11	Month 12	First Year Totals
Cash Sources:							
FROM OPERATIONS							
Cash Sales							
A/R Collections							
Other Cash Collections							
OTHER SOURCES							
Interest Income							
Loan from Bank							
Investment							
Subtotal							
Cash Uses:							
TO OPERATIONS							
Accts Payable							
Goods/Materials							
Services							
Petty Cash							
Payroll Expense							
Sales Commission							
Travel/Entertainment							
Rent/Util/Tel							
Advertising							
Auto/Truck Exp							
Maintenance							
Equipment Exp							
Ins/Legal/Acct							
Miscellaneous							
OTHER USES							
Interest Exp							
Dividends							
Loan Payoff							
Investor Payoff							
Reserve for Tax							
Subtotal							
Cash Incr/Decr							
Beginning Bal							
Ending Balance							

"I'm glad you're thinking my way," the consultant said. "Because if you don't believe you can reach a goal, you'll never get there." He paused, then said, "By the way, that $90,000 is three times what you did your first quarter last year!"

"Just tell us what to do," the owners said.

Based on a careful cash-flow analysis, the consultant determined that the company would need to borrow money. The owners knew their business—industry trends, product line, competitors, sales and promotion plans—but what banker would believe such growth? The key to getting the loan would be to convince the banker that the company could do better than break even. The consultant prepared a break-even chart on the $562,000 sales figure (see Figure 8.2). Note in the chart that after $280,000 in sales, the firm will have passed its break-even point and will be earning a profit.

The banker did grant the loan because he realized the company could pass the break-even point with room to spare. The key, as usual in business, was a combination of numbers and human confidence.

Table 8.8c

Proforma Cash Flow

| | Second Year | | | |
	Quarter 1	Quarter 2	Quarter 3	Quarter 4
Cash Sources:				
FROM OPERATIONS				
Cash Sales				
A/R Collections				
Other Cash Collections				
OTHER SOURCES				
Interest Income				
Loan from Bank				
Investment				
Subtotal				
Cash Uses:				
TO OPERATIONS				
Accts Payable				
Goods/Materials				
Services				
Petty Cash				
Payroll Expense				
Sales Commission				
Travel/Entertainment				
Rent/Util/Tel				
Advertising				
Auto/Truck Exp				
Maintenance				
Equipment Exp				
Ins/Legal/Acct				
Miscellaneous				
OTHER USES				
Interest Exp				
Dividends				
Loan Payoff				
Investor Payoff				
Reserve for Tax				
Subtotal				
Cash Incr/Decr				
Beginning Bal				
Ending Balance				

Shoebox Accounting: Leaving a Paper Trail

If you're the typical entrepreneur, you're not real big on details and you're very busy; nonetheless, you know it's important to keep good records. One solution for you is shoebox accounting—a simple procedure that will give your accountant or bookkeeper a chance to put together financial statements and prepare your tax returns. The point of this system is to leave a paper trail.

How to Implement the System

Open a business checking account—even if you are just doing business under your own name. Deposit all business income into this account, making a note in the

Figure 8.2

A simple break-even chart like this may be all it takes to convince your banker that a small loan now means big profits later.

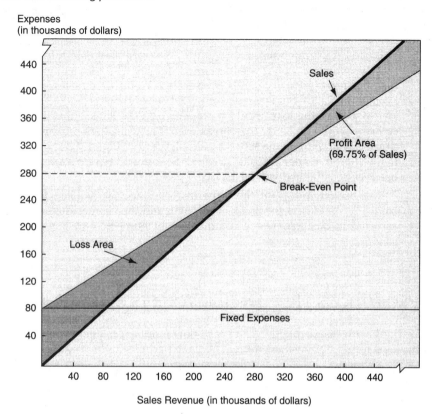

Projected sales:	$562,000
Projected fixed expenses:	$82,750
Projected variable expenses:	$392,000
Total sales needed to break even:	$\dfrac{\text{Fixed}}{\text{Expenses}} \div \left(1 - \dfrac{\text{Variable expenses}}{\text{Sales}}\right)$
	$\$83,000 \div \left(1 - \dfrac{\$392,000}{\$562,000}\right)$
	$\$83,000 \div (1 - .6975)$
	$\$83,000 \div .3025$
	$274,380
Break-even range:	$270,000 to $280,000

checkbook (or check register, or computerized check-writing program) as to the source of the deposit; for example, "Sat., 10/21, Swap Meet Sales." Write a check for each business expenditure, even if it's only $1. Enter what the check was for. Get a receipt and write the check number on the receipt. During the first few weeks, toss everything into a shoebox. When the shoebox begins to fill up, purchase an alphabetical file folder—one of those brown accordion jobs—and file all receipts there according to some system. (Ask your accountant or bookkeeper.)

If you must pay for items with cash, use a petty cash box or a bank bag. Get a receipt for every cash purchase also, and clip all the receipts for cash purchases together. When you have accumulated enough cash purchases—perhaps $10 to

$20—write yourself a check, being careful to record the check number on each cash receipt.

Together, the business checkbook and the file folder are the paper trail you leave for your accountant or bookkeeper—and the IRS. This trail could save your neck in an IRS audit. The system is a step up from the "pocket" system—that is, in one pocket and out the other—and only a stop-gap until you move into a one-write or computerized bookkeeping system.

Financial Ratios

Calculating a few simple ratios will help you analyze how your venture compares with other businesses in your selected industry. Lenders use ratios as measuring devices to determine the risks associated with lending.

To the entrepreneur, ratios are control tools for maintaining financial efficiencies.

Current Ratio

Does the business have enough money to meet current debt? Have you anticipated a safety margin for losses due to uncollectible funds owed to the business? Most start-up ventures are undercapitalized.

The current ratio is computed from the balance sheet. Divide current assets by current liabilities. If current assets are $200,000 and current liabilities are $100,000, you have a current ratio of 2.

Many lenders see this as a minimum, and like to see that you have at least twice as much invested as you owe. The current ratio is the most widely used method to determine the financial health of a business.

Liquidity Ratio

This ratio tells you if you have cash on hand or assets that can be converted into cash quickly to pay your debts. The more liquidity, the better. An untapped credit line will help beef up your liquidity.

Return on Investment (ROI)

ROI is the favorite tool of investors and venture capitalists. This ratio shows the return expressed as a percentage of their investment. Investors and entrepreneurs want the highest profit (return) for the least amount of money invested.

Most bankers use the ratio studies published by Robert Morris and Associates. Every lending officer has a current copy, as do most business libraries. This publication, considered the bible for statement analysis, covers over 200 types of businesses.

Also in your library and/or available at a nominal cost is *Dun & Bradstreet Business Information Systems*. This annual publication provides key ratios on over 100 businesses.

The U.S. Small Business Administration has reports for several industries.

Trade associations often provide the most comprehensive work on financial ratios. Some are a bit out of date, but most provide lots of specific, very valuable data.

Additional financial ratios are shown in Table 8.9.

Table 8.9a

Financial Ratios

Ratio Name	How to Calculate	What It Means in Dollars and Cents
Balance Sheet Ratios		
Current	$\dfrac{\text{Current Assets}}{\text{Current Liabilities}}$	Measures solvency: the number of dollars in current assets for every $1 in current liabilities
		Example: A current ratio of 1.76 means that for every $1 of current liabilities, the firm has $1.76 in current assets with which to pay it.
Quick	$\dfrac{\text{Cash + Accounts Receivable}}{\text{Current Liabilities}}$	Measures liquidity: the number of dollars in cash and accounts receivable for each $1 in current liabilities
		Example: A quick ratio of 1.14 means that for every $1 of current liabilities, the firm has $1.14 in cash and accounts receivable with which to pay it.
Cash	$\dfrac{\text{Cash}}{\text{Current Liabilities}}$	Measures liquidity more strictly: the number of dollars in cash for every $1 in current liabilities
		Example: A cash ratio of 0.17 means that for every $1 of current liabilities, the firm has $0.17 in cash with which to pay it.
Debt-to-worth	$\dfrac{\text{Total Liabilities}}{\text{Net Worth}}$	Measures financial risk: the number of dollars of debt owed for every $1 in net worth
		Example: A debt-to-worth ratio of 1.05 means that for every $1 of net worth the owners have invested, the firms owes $1.05 of debt to its creditors.
Income Statement Ratios		
Gross margin	$\dfrac{\text{Gross Margin}}{\text{Sales}}$	Measures profitability at the gross profit level: the number of dollars of gross margin produced for every $1 of sales
		Example: A gross margin ratio of 34.4% means that for every $1 of sales, the firm produces 34.4 cents of gross margin.
Net margin	$\dfrac{\text{Net Profit before Tax}}{\text{Sales}}$	Measures profitability at the net profit level: the number of dollars of net profit produced for every $1 of sales
		Example: A net margin ratio of 2.9% means that for every $1 of sales, the firm produces 2.9 cents of net margin.
Overall Efficiency Ratios		
Sales-to-assets	$\dfrac{\text{Sales}}{\text{Total Assets}}$	Measures the efficiency of total assets in generating sales: the number of dollars in sales produced for every $1 invested in total assets
		Example: A sales-to-assets ratio of 2.35 means that for every $1 dollar invested in total assets, the firm generates $2.35 in sales.
Return on assets	$\dfrac{\text{Net Profit before Tax}}{\text{Total Assets}}$	Measures the efficiency of total assets in generating net profit: the number of dollars in net profit produced for every $1 invested in total assets

continued

Table 8.9b

Financial Ratios (*continued*)

Ratio Name	How to Calculate	What It Means in Dollars and Cents
Return on assets —cont'd		*Example:* A return on assets ratio of 7.1% means that for every $1 invested in assets, the firm is generating 7.1 cents in net profit before tax.
Return on investment	$\dfrac{\text{Net Profit before Tax}}{\text{Net Worth}}$	Measures the efficiency of net worth in generating net profit: the number of dollars in net profit produced for every $1 invested in net worth *Example:* A return on investment ratio of 16.1% means that for every $1 invested in net worth, the firm is generating 16.1 cents in net profit before tax.

Specific Efficiency Ratios

Ratio Name	How to Calculate	What It Means in Dollars and Cents
Inventory turnover	$\dfrac{\text{Cost of Goods Sold}}{\text{Inventory}}$	Measures the rate at which inventory is being used on an annual basis *Example:* An inventory turnover ratio of 9.81 means that the average dollar volume of inventory is used up almost ten times during the fiscal year.
Inventory turn-days	$\dfrac{360}{\text{Inventory Turnover}}$	Converts the inventory turnover ratio into an average "days inventory on hand" figure *Example:* An inventory turn-days ratio of 37 means that the firm keeps an average of 37 days of inventory on hand throughout the year.
Accounts receivable turnover	$\dfrac{\text{Sales}}{\text{Accounts Receivable}}$	Measures the rate at which accounts receivable are being collected on an annual basis *Example:* An accounts receivable turnover ratio of 8.00 means that the average dollar volume of accounts receivable are collected eight times during the year.
Average collection period	$\dfrac{360}{\text{Accounts Receivable Turnover}}$	Converts the accounts receivable turnover ratio into the average number of days the firm must wait for its accounts receivable to be paid *Example:* An average collection period ratio of 45 means that it takes the firm 45 days on average to collect its receivables.
Accounts payable turnover	$\dfrac{\text{Cost of Goods Sold}}{\text{Accounts Payable}}$	Measures the rate at which accounts payable are being paid on an annual basis. *Example:* An accounts payable turnover ratio of 12.04 means that the average dollar volume of accounts payable are paid about 12 × a year.
Average payment period	$\dfrac{360}{\text{Accounts Payable Turnover}}$	Converts the accounts payable turnover ratio into the average number of days a firm takes to pay its accounts payable. *Example:* An accounts payable turnover ratio of 30 means that it takes the firm 30 days on average to pay its bills.

SOURCE: Kuratko, *Entrepreneurship*, 4/e pp. 280–282.

▶ *Summary*

Not surprisingly, many entrepreneurs find it difficult to project numbers for their businesses. There are several explanations for this:

They're action people who are in a hurry; they don't think they have time to sit down and think.

They're creative; their strengths are greater in the innovation area than in the justification area.

They tend to think in visual terms, rather than in terms of numbers or words.

They believe they can't fail.

Nonetheless, business is a numbers game, and despite the entrepreneur's feelings about numbers and projections, survival in the marketplace depends on having the right numbers in the right color of ink. Chapter 8 helps you get those kinds of numbers down on paper.

The point behind projecting numbers is to make the numbers as realistic as possible. You need to relate each projection to your specific business and to industry standards, and then to *document* them (tell where they came from) in your Business Plan. The case studies and examples in this chapter will help you make your projections believable to your banker as well as to yourself.

That is the key. Your numbers may seem reasonable to you, but you must make them seem reasonable to others as well. You make them believable by keeping them realistic and by documenting them properly.

What you don't need during the start-up phase is expensive surprises that knock you and your business for a loop. So, before you open your doors, you need to have anticipated as many potential unpleasant surprises as possible and have a plan of action for each one of them. For example, what will you do if . . .

your anchor tenant leaves?

your Yellow Pages ad stinks or you miss the deadline?

the customer that accounts for 75 percent of your business declares bankruptcy?

Expecting and *planning for* the unexpected can make the difference between life and death in business. Looking closely at your present assets and liabilities—by developing a personal financial statement—and calculating the opportunity costs of going into business for yourself will help you eliminate some surprises and may even cause you to question whether you're truly ready to take the plunge. Just remember two things: No one can anticipate everything, and it will probably cost more and take longer than your planning indicates.

Think Points For Success

- It's cheaper to make mistakes on a spreadsheet before you go into business.
- When you work out numbers for your Business Plan, hit the return-on-investment section with underlines.
- When you visit your banker to ask for money, make sure you know how much you're going to need for the long run.
- Projecting will help control the variables of your business—numbers, employees, promotion mix, product mix, and the peaks and valleys of seasonality.
- At the very *least,* leave a "shoebox" paper trail of your business dealings so that a professional accountant or bookkeeper can bail you out if you get into trouble.

- Cash flow is king!
- Walk away if it isn't going to work. There will always be new opportunities.

Key Points from Another View

The Money Trap: Preserving Cash Flow
by Jan Norman

STRATEGIES: Here's help with figuring out how much you need and how to get the most mileage out of what you have.

When you're out of cash, you're out of business.

That gem of business management is from Rick Lamprecht, partner of businessVISION, a Laguna Hills management-consulting company.

Businesses are always looking for cash. And for good reason.

Growth consumes cash to hire people, build inventories, cover the bases until clients pay. Decline consumes cash to cover operating costs that can't be cut fast enough.

The trick, Lamprecht says, is to figure out how much cash you need and to get the most mileage out of the cash you have. Here are fuel injectors to improve the cash mileage in your company.

1. **Look ahead.** businessVISION uses an interactive computer model in Lotus 1-2-3 software for cash-flow forecasting. Lamprecht says, "The issue is not how much cash will you need if things go right, but how much you need if things go wrong. And wrong they will go, because Murphy's Law is the rule of the entrepreneurial land." Don't look at your company's past financial performance. You must look at the effect such factors as product costs and human resources have on your cash.

2. **Profit is not cash.** "Profit is an accounting concept upon which you pay taxes," Lamprecht says. "You can be very profitable and still have no cash. It is cash that keeps the doors open."

3. **The most expensive cash is the cash you don't think you'll ever need.** Most entrepreneurs underestimate the time and money they will need to start and run their ventures. That's because they do a best-case scenario when planning, Lamprecht says. You can strike better deals with investors and lenders the first time you approach them, he says. If you must go back a second time for more money, your credibility as a manager will be damaged and the terms will be less favorable.

4. **Keep inventories lean.** Having too much unsold inventory on hand can cost a company in finance charges and warehouse space. Cash-flow forecasting can track those costs, Lamprecht says, so make adjustments if sales lag—or you'll run out of cash.

5. **Add employees with care.** Again, Lamprecht says, having too many employees can kill a company if sales lag. Grow conservatively, keeping costs variable.

Jan Norman

SOURCE: Orange County Register.

Shaking The Money Tree

9

Entrepreneurial Links

Books

How to Get a Small Business Loan, Second Edition, Bryan E. Milling, 1998.

Business Angels: Securing Start-up Financing, Patrick Coveney, 1998.

Entrepreneur Magazine Guide to Raising Money, Entrepreneur Magazine Series, 1997.

Websites

www.moneyhunter.com, MoneyHunter

http://FinanceHub.com/vc, FinanceHub.com

www.vfinance.com, Venture Capital Resource Library

Associations/Organizations

National Venture Capital Association, www.nvca.org/

Small Business Survival Committee, www.sbsc.org/

Foundation for Enterprise Development, www.fed.org

Publications

Bottom Line Business

Business Start-Ups

Wall Street Journal

Additional Entrepreneurial Insights

Direct Public Offerings, Drew Field, 1997.

Global Gold Panning for Profits in Foreign Markets, Ruth Stanat, 1998.

Money-Smart Secrets of the Self-Employed, Vol. 2, Linda Stern, 1997.

Learning Objectives

- Discover your risk tolerance.
- Determine your credit situation.
- Understand the Four C's of credit.
- Explore credit card usage for your business.
- Understand the inherent risks in borrowing from friends and family.
- Scour the lending arena for money to fund your new business.
- Review strategies for approaching bankers.
- Explore SBDC, SBA, state and local lending programs.
- Locate angels.
- Explore vendor financing.

Would it sound too easy if we told you to go out and simply shake a money tree to get financing for your business? Yes, of course. You know it will not be that easy. First you must become familiar with the world of money. Then you must learn to tell the forest from the trees. And then you must find the right branch. Once you've accomplished these things, you might be surprised how money turns up.

Looking for Money

Don Hawkins Case Study—Surgery Shunt

The Prototype

Don Hawkins started his work life as a model maker in a large medical manufacturing firm. Don had talent. His fellow workers both envied and admired him because, while they fussed around with trial and error, he got it right the first time.

Margo McKay, a product manager at Don's firm, often sought out Don when she needed help on a glitch that slowed production. One day, over a cup of coffee, Margo confided in Don.

"I've got this customer," Margo said. "He wants a special design."

"What's the gizmo?"

"A wound drainage device."

"Hmm. What size?"

"Five millimeters."

"Who's the customer?" Don asked.

"He's a surgeon. A friend of mine."

"If it's microsurgery," Don said. "I'm way behind."

"Are you interested?"

"Let me do some reading, see what I can come up with."

It took Don four days to comb through some literature on microsurgery. It took him three days to develop the prototype. A week after they had coffee, Don revealed the prototype to Margo. She was wild with joy. Because she understood a winner when she saw one, Margo revealed her plan: They would quit their jobs; they would put together a venture team; they would make millions.

The Team

In the next few weeks they recruited Bob Bernstein, a production supervisor, and Nancy Jones, the best salesperson in the company. Before they got too deep into dreams and celebrations, Margo warned the group they'd need cash. To get cash, they needed investors. To get investors, they needed a business plan.

Margo, who had put together several marketing plans, was weak on finance. Bob Bernstein, the production man, was weak on marketing and sales. Nancy understood people, but, as she admitted over a glass of wine: "I'm confessing. I need a videotape to tell me how to program my videocassette recorder."

To keep the weak spots to a minimum, and to maximize their strengths, all four members of the venture team enrolled in a college course titled "The Weekend Entrepreneur: Writing Your Business Plan." The system worked. Over the next 6 weekends, they cranked out a Business Plan. It was bullet proof. It gave them the confidence they needed.

Don, especially, was amazed at how much they already knew. But writing the plan helped them pull together their ideas. Getting organized on paper made them realize they would need $500,000 to make it through the first 12 months of their venture.

The Money

Each partner had to come up with $125,000, a quarter of the first-year's seed money. Margo McKay refinanced her house. Don tapped Uncle Marvin who was worth several million. Nancy got two investments of $62,500 each from a couple of go-getter doctors. Bob Bernstein borrowed from his credit union and cashed in two life insurance policies.

On a sunny day in June they said goodbye forever to the corporate womb. Their destination was a small warehouse. The rent was cheap; the security great. The microsurgery trade show was 62 days away. For a piece of the corporate pie, a shrewd attorney waived his fee for doing the patent work. With the "patent pending" in hand, production began on Don's prototype.

The trade show proved to be a goldmine. On opening day, their booth was swamped. News got around about their device. By the end of the first day, orders for the device exceeded their first-year sales forecast.

The best deal came from Surgery Unlimited, an old-line medical manufacturer, a small competitor of their former employer. The president of Surgery Unlimited offered them $750,000 for a two-year deal on exclusive distribution of the device.

Before she deposited the check for $750,000, Margo McKay interviewed bankers to find and establish a good working relationship.

The Niche

Encouraged by success, the partners explored the marketplace for more product possibilities. Bob Bernstein was put in charge of production, making the surgery shunt, and the other three partners became marketplace detectives. As they developed new products, they were careful not to operate in the same arena as their former employer.

Their niche was microsurgery.

In their third year, Don the inventor discovered the solution to a problem that had confounded two generations of optical surgeons. To get FDA approval would take two to three years. With such a long lag time between production and sales, developmental costs would hurt the firm, maybe even take it under.

Then their CPA introduced them to Dream Funds, Inc., a venture capital group in Minneapolis. This was Dream Funds deal: In return for 60 percent of the company's stock, Dream Funds would deposit $10 million to the company's bank account.

Two years later, with FDA approval, Don's invention took off. The numbers caught the eye of the second biggest firm in the medical products industry. The second biggest firm made an offer they couldn't refuse: $50 million in cash for their company of which they owned 40 percent.

Guess what?

They took the money.

Reflecting on his life since leaving that design job, Don Hawkins said: "We don't know whether we're out of work, or just into early retirement."

After paying off all debt, each partner came away with $4 million and change. Because of their positive experience in the big world of small business, they founded a new start-up—a venture capital firm. They named it The Honey Pot.

"Hey," said Margo. "Why not? We worked for a big company. All of us did that. Our big discovery was how much fun it was to do start-ups. With Honey Pot money, we can help start one a month. I can't believe I wasted all that time working for someone else."

Before Committing Money

Don and his colleagues put up their *own money first*. Committing your own nickel is essential for all entrepreneurs. Lenders and investors will make sure you have committed your own resources before they will commit theirs. Before committing your own nickel you need to take a few steps. Action Step 3 from Chapter 1 asked you to complete a budget and a personal financial statement. The Actions Steps in Chapter 8 asked you to determine your start-up costs and cash-flow requirements. You now know the amount you need to start and the amount you have to do it with. Now it's time to reconcile and determine how to fund the difference.

The vast majority of small businesses are self-financed in the start-up stage. We want you first to consider your risk tolerance, credit history, and availability of your own cash.

What Is Your Risk Tolerance?

How much are you willing to risk? $10,000? $20,000? $200,000? Are you willing to go deeply in debt for your venture? A sushi vendor worked for over seven years and spent millions of dollars before he hit on a successful way to flash freeze his product.

Are you willing to give up a successful career with benefits for the unknown? If you lose your house, will you be devastated or will you pick yourself back up and start again like a true entrepreneur? One fellow we know was a millionaire at age 22 and lost it; millionaire at age 28, and lost it! And millionaire again at 35!

Remember, you must also consider the risk tolerance level of the members of your family and any persons you partner with.

What Is Your Credit History?

Loan officers will look first at your credit report. If it doesn't pass, you are sunk at the bank! Take action to determine your credit history.

Credit Reporting Agencies—What Do They Know About You?

Credit reporting agencies keep track of all of your financial moves; the good, the bad, and the ugly. Bill paying, credit (requested and denied), payment of utility bills, and loans, liens and legal judgments. Information is retained for seven years and bankruptcies for 10 years.

If you have released financial statements, these may also appear as part of a credit report. Credit inquires from potential lenders will let others know where you might currently be seeking credit.

What might appear minor to you—one missed or late payment—may not appear minor to potential lenders.

Since most entrepreneurs will depend on their own credit history as they reach out for money, it is essential that your credit report be perfectly clean! Mistakes are very common. Spend less than $10 to check your credit report before moving forward. If there is a problem, go to the Web and research the steps you need to take to clear up problems as quickly as possible. Or call the credit reporting firm and talk directly with them.

A credit scoring system has been developed and you can request your score from the sources listed below. Future lending opportunities and interest rates may be based on your specific score, so take the time early on to complete your research.

To get a copy of your credit report:

Equifax Information Services Center
P.O. Box 105873
Atlanta, GA 30348
www.equifax.com

Experian
505 City Parkway West
Orange, CA 92683
800 682-7654
www.experian.com

Trans Union Corporation
Consumer Disclosure Center
P.O. Box 390
Springfield, PA 19064
www.transunion.com

What Is the Availability of Your Cash or Credit?

Looking at your personal financial statement from Action Step 3, how much money are you able to commit? Are you able to sell any of your assets? Take a second or a third mortgage on your house, or a home equity loan. Refinance your car? Sell your baseball card collection?

Reviewing your budget from Action Step 3, do you have any monthly income available to commit to the venture? How much do you need to live on each month? Are you willing to change your lifestyle? Are you willing to rent? share an apartment? live at home? Are you willing to go without healthcare and disability benefits? (If you have answered yes, please rethink!) Can you dine out less? Buy a cheaper car?

What sacrifices are you willing to make for your dream? Can you get a part-time job to help support your dream? Can you hang on to your present job and start your new venture part-time? Do you need to find a partner who has some cash? Can you start in your basement? living room? garage?

Find out how much unsecured credit you have. This will give you a general picture of how the financial world rates you at this time. Once taken, this step can help you determine if there are any untapped sources of funds for your start-up, or fallbacks and emergency sources for your business or personal expenses. Use Table 9.1 to determine your credit limits on charge accounts. Look at your last statement to discover available credit. You may need to call or write to several businesses for this information. When you've filled in the amounts for each of your credit accounts, add them up. Surprised? Few people are aware of how much credit they do have.

However, before you tell your boss what she can do with your job, there are a few things you might want to do. For example:

1. Get complete medical checkups for your entire family.
2. Check on the cost of continuing your health insurance.
3. Apply for additional credit cards. Set them aside to use only for business expenses when you start. Pay bills as they come due with a company check. Banks don't care who writes the check, as long as it clears. In addition, it will give you good documentation for your bookkeeper and the IRS. Plus, you will have some additional credit for your business.
4. Consider applying for a personal **line of credit.** Usually, depending on the **Four C's** of credit (your capital, character, capacity, and collateral), you can obtain anywhere from $5000 to $50,000 of unsecured credit at very attractive rates. If you have a personal line of credit, you are in a much more flexible position for your new business. If you need it to finance the new business, it's available. If not, it can be your security blanket, to be there for you if unexpected expenses should pop up and they will.

With regard to points #3 and #4, bankers are much more relaxed about extending credit to a "steady citizen"—a person with steady employment income. Also, you would be making arrangements for the money when you don't need it. Bankers tend to like lending money to people who don't really need it.

Don't quit your job until you've finished your business plan and checked with your banker. You need to have enough money to withstand setbacks. Don't be surprised when your business does not support you (right away) in the manner to which you've become accustomed or would like to be accustomed to!

Your Bottom Line

You are not risking your own capital and providing sweat equity for *just* an immediate paycheck or return. The future potential is what you are building. If you only consider the income from the first year or two, you will not be able to justify risking capital or putting in 12–14 hour days. You must look ahead three to five years. Money is a strong motivating factor; just thinking about it will help you keep your business on the success track. Here are additional thoughts to consider as you explore the bottom line for starting and building your business:

- **Income stream.** What can you count on from your business? How much salary? How much profit? What benefits? Company car? Insurance? Travel? Retirement fund?

- **Profit from sale of business.** What is the potential profit if the business is sold? What could you make if you took the company public via a stock offering? What will you leave to your children?

Line of credit An unsecured lending limit

Four Cs A classical series of questions lenders use to screen potential borrowers

Table 9.1

Your Current Untapped Financial Sources

Source	Amount/Limit
Department Stores	
Sears	
JC Penney	
Others	
Oil Companies	
Exxon	
Standard Oil	
Mobil	
Texaco	
Shell	
Others	
Bank Credit Cards	
American Express	
Diner's Club	
Visa	
MasterCard	
Discover Card	
Others	
Personal Lines of Credit	
Bank	
Savings & Loan	
Credit Union	
Others	
Home Equity	
Total Available Credit	

- **Life cycle.** How long will it take for your business to move from start-up to a profit position? Many businesses take two years, even three, to show a profit. What happens to your investment if you project it 5–10 years down the road?

- **The rule.** Your business should provide you with two sources of financial return: an income stream and growing equity. If you have income without equity, you're in trouble. If you have equity without income, you could starve to death.

Shaking the Most Fruitful Branches First

Shaking the money tree takes effort for most entrepreneurs. Many resources are available but they all come with strings attached. Type of company, control of the business, family and friends' emotions, your risk tolerance, and taxation issues all should play a part in determining which branches you should investigate. Sitting down with a knowledgeable small business accountant and/or attorney will give you great insight. While there are many funding opportunities available to entrepreneurs, over 70 percent of start-up capital comes from self-financing, friends and family. Banks provide less than 10 percent of start-up capital!

Self-Financing

Your Money and/or Your Credit

We have discussed several ways to tap into your financial resources. Many individuals can't tap retirement funds; home equity, stock or bond funds, and credit cards then come to the rescue. For many entrepreneurs, credit cards are the standard way of accessing capital to keep the doors open and the fires burning. Over 34 percent of entrepreneurs use credit cards routinely in their businesses.

Many large credit card companies, such as American Express, **www.americanexpress.com,** court small businessowners. Unfortunately, many of the small-business credit cards, which provide streamlined records, are available only to businesses with a two-year track record.

When selecting cards, consider the following:

- Payment dates. If you have several cards, with varying closing and payment dates, you may be able to creatively manage your cash flow by utilizing the cards in tandem as follows:

Card	Closing Date of Billing Cycle	When to Use		Time from Purchase to Payment
		Start	**Stop**	
Visa	4th of the month	5th	19th	Charge July 5th Pay Sept 3rd (60 days)
Discover	19th of the month	20th	4th	Charge July 20th Pay Sept. 18th (60 days)

- Annual Percentage Rate (APR). Check your newspaper or Bank Rate Monitor (**www.bankrate.com**) for the lowest current credit card rates. If you have a card and are paying too high of an APR, call the credit card company and request that they lower the rate. Yes, this can work!

- Consider annual fees.

- Check out maximum credit limits. Call your current credit card issuers and request an increase in your credit line. Many times all it takes is a phone call.

- Make sure any "extras" you get with the card are worth paying for.
- Compare grace periods. This is extremely important if you are using the card to manage cash flow.
- Late fees. *Never* incur late fees. In the past, credit card companies did not balk if you were up to 30 days late. Today, one day late may incur high late fees, show up on your credit report, and possibly increase your interest rate by 25 percent to 30 percent.

Judicious use of credit cards can be a lifesaver for many entrepreneurs. They help you track your expenses and help to build a financial history. But unless you realize that the credit card bills need to be paid on time and there are spending limits, you may find yourself over your head and your business underwater.

Credit Cards—Know the Risk

Using credit cards is a riskier-than-usual way to finance your company. You have the huge bill to face every month, instead of several smaller ones that can be juggled. Once you max out, you can't pay your bills any more. And the interest payments on carrying a balance can make a grown entrepreneur cry. Funding businesses with a credit card violates the consumer-cardholder agreement. Yet it's a standard practice for thousands of company owners.

For more information, visit **wysiwyg://mainbody.158/http://www.inc.com/incmagazine/archives/02980501.html**

Friends and Family

For many entrepreneurs, heading to Mom and Pop is the first branch to shake. If you plan on making it your first stop, think again! According to many experts, parents may be the largest single source of start-up capital in the United States but having a banking relationship with your parents is fraught with potential problems. Before continuing further, first ask yourself, "Is getting money for this venture worth loosing and damaging my relationship with my parents?" While at the moment, you may just be thinking about speeding ahead with your venture and all you can see is success, the reality is—you could fail. You might not be able to pay back your parents in a timely fashion—or ever!

Consider your parents' emotional tie to money. If your parents or grandparents are in their seventies and lived through the Depression, money means security. If you borrow money, they will never truly feel secure until you have completely paid it back. Also, if you take a trip to Paris and still owe them money, will they make you feel guilty? Will you feel guilty if you purchase a new car? Will you truly be secure in expanding your business if you are not secure in your lending relationship?

If you are borrowing money from friends or family, please be sure that the loss of that money will not impact the lenders' future or lifestyle. Borrowing Grandma's last $20,000 is not fair to Grandma.

It is much more responsible to remain at your job and save for another year before striking out on your own than to risk the capital of those you love. Money and relationships are never easy and with family they tend to be even more emotional and volatile. Long-running family issues come into play and brother–sister relationships may also be harmed. There are unseen and unknown issues for both parties. How will you deal with them? If your folks get sick, will you be able to pay back the loan? If your dad and mom want to be part of the business to oversee their investment, how will you feel? Do you want your parents only as lenders or will you consider taking them on as partners and investors?

If you are still willing to borrow from friends and family after reviewing potential problems, here are a few things you can do to alleviate some of the problems.

- Put everything in writing.
- Make it a business loan and not a personal loan. Have loan papers drawn up. State the amount, payments, time period of loan, interest rate, payment date, and late payment penalties.
- A provision in the loan should be included for repayment in case of emergencies. This will alleviate a lot of stress and concern for both parties.
- Discuss thoroughly with your lenders the company's goals. Make sure they understand that the loan will need to be for a certain length of time. If the business starts to be profitable, it will still require their cash infusion for working capital.
- Discuss your fears for potential problems and encourage your lenders to discuss their issues as well. Getting feelings out on the table early may stem future problems.

One family we know lends to all their children in a bank-like fashion. To purchase a home, one son might receive a $50,000 loan at 7 percent interest. Another son purchasing a franchise might receive a loan of $50,000 with a 9 percent interest rate. The youngest son, starting a high-tech business with two of his out-of-work and not-very-well-respected friends, will be required to pay 15 percent interest. All understand the MOM and DAD bank is only operating on the basic investment principal of risk versus return. If payments are late, a call goes out and payment is expected immediately. Just like a bank!

One son kept forgetting to pay on time. The MOM and DAD bank requested post-dated checks for the next six months to secure payments in a timely fashion. No comments about loans or the son's spending habits are made. Thirty-five years, no hurt feelings, and strong stable business and personal relationships remain.

It can be done! But it's hard work and takes exceptional people who have no axes to grind and a good relationship. Tread lightly and carefully. Friends and family cannot be bought or replaced.

Banks

Most new ventures begin with the entrepreneur's own capital. Funds may be borrowed if you have other sources of income and collateral—such as home equity, stocks, or bonds. Although banks are in the business of lending money, they also have a responsibility to their depositors. Thus bankers tend to choose the safest deals. They want to help businesses expand, but they have to be picky. Banks can help you in many areas, but they are neither investors nor venture capitalists, so don't expect them to take risks.

In a small local bank, the chief loan officer may be a part owner. You're hunting for a permanent relationship, not merely a place to park your money. Bear in mind that your business could outgrow a small bank and that some firms need support services (such as import-export assistance) that only a large bank can offer.

Few bankers are thrilled about lending money to start-ups. Nonetheless, bankers are people, so start seeking a banker who understands you, your selected industry, and your needs. Network your attorney, your tax person, the Chamber of Commerce, civic clubs, and people in your trade association for recommendations. Ask your accountant to accompany you on your introductory visit to the bank. Be prepared to spend a lot of time on this search.

Microlending programs, which generally refer to business loans under $100,000, are rapidly increasing. These small loans are giving new hope to entrepreneurs and banking relationships. According to SBA research, over 500 banks participated in microlending programs providing $17 billion in 1997.

Bankers' Expectations

In general, though, bankers seldom make start-up loans without home equity or stocks to secure the loan. When they do, they expect:

1. A very solid business plan with good projections and supporting data. Numbers are king! Bankers utilize the Annual Statement Studies published by Robert Morris Associates to determine operating ratios. Make sure you are in line.
2. Experience in managing a business.
3. Background in the industry.
4. Enough other assets for the borrower to live on while the business is growing.
5. Your personal financial commitment to be a major part of the financing.
6. Possibly a co-signer who guarantees your loan.
7. A second salary in the family.
8. Generally at least two to three years of successful operations. Unsecured bank lending is rare to start-ups without collateral.
9. Income statements that show that you are willing to take a reasonable salary or no salary in the beginning.
10. Detailed explanation of what you are going to do with the funds and how repayment will be made.
11. A compelling product or service with strong management.

Unsecured bank loans or lines of credit may not be available to an entrepreneur even after three to five years of successful business operations. Your personal assets and your business assets are therefore intertwined for a very long time.

Strategies

Bankers can lead you to money sources you had not considered and may be one gateway to the world of money. Seek your banker's advice on pulling your business plan together. If you get your banker's input, he or she will have a harder time refusing help later on.

Bring your banker into your **information loop** and involve him or her in your business idea. People lend money to people. Stop thinking about a banker as someone who will lend you an umbrella only on a sunny day. *You* would not lend money to a stranger, so make sure your banker knows exactly what you are up to.

Some strategies for dealing with bankers are as follows:

- Never ask directly for money; ask initially for *advice* and *information*. Ideally, a banker will *tell you* when it is the right time to seek money.

- A bank may seem like a formidable medieval fortress or a modern cathedral. Cut through this symbolism with new eyes. Make an appointment. It's important to schedule an appointment and not just to drop in. Dress conservatively. Ask lots of questions.

Information loop A network of people who need to be kept informed about your business

- Lure a banker to **your turf** if you have a retail or manufacturing operation. Say, "It's difficult to explain to you exactly what my shop is like. Why not come out for a look? We could have lunch. How's Thursday around noon?" On your own turf, you will be in a stronger position. You should feel more at ease, and communication will probably flow more easily for both parties.
- Keep in touch with your banker. Continue to position yourself on the ladder in your banker's mind.
- Comparison shop for money just as you would shop for any major purchase. The deals could surprise you. But like any major purchase, price is only one factor to consider.
- Negotiate for your line of credit or loan while you are still employed. A personal line of credit is often reviewed annually. You may have to prove that you are still a good credit risk after you are in your own business. If you keep up a good credit rating, however, the chances are good that you will be able to keep the personal lines of credit.

Keep a running list of questions to ask prospective bankers. The following questionnaire will help get you started.

Questions for Your Banker

What are your lending limits?

Who makes the decisions on loans?

What are your views on my industry?

What experience do you have in working with businesses like mine?

Could you recommend a highly qualified lawyer? Bookkeeper? Accountant? Computer consultant?

Are you interested in writing **equipment leases**?

What kind of terms do you give on **accounts receivable** financing?

Does your bank offer businesses Visa and MasterCard accounts?

What credit limit could I expect for my business credit cards?

What handling charge would I have to pay on credit card receipts?

What interest can I earn on my business checking account?

Do you have a merchants' or commercial window?

Do you have a night depository?

If you can't lend me money, can you direct me to people who might be interested in doing so?

Do you make **SBA-guaranteed loans**?

If I open up a business checking account here, what else can you do for me?

What will you be looking for in my business plan?

Would you describe the loan approval process?

Your turf One's place of business or the place one feels most comfortable

Equipment lease Long-term arrangement with a bank or leasing company for renting capital equipment

Accounts receivable What is owed to a firm

SBA-guaranteed loans Loans where up to 90% of borrowed funds are insured by the federal government

Make Your Banker a Member of Your Team

A helpful banker can be an entrepreneur's best friend and a member of his or her auxiliary management team or "taxi squad." Business growth demands money from external sources. The more successful you become, the more likely you will need a close bank relationship to help you finance prosperity. If you grow more than 25 percent a year, you'll need lots of financing help. Manufacturers get into trouble fast, but even service firms have to wait for their customers to make payments. Your creditors and employees will want their money when it's due them. So keep your banker in your information loop. Bankers are more willing to help if they understand your needs and know you are trying to anticipate your needs.

Now read about how Steve McWhorter handled his cash flow problems by helping a banker to understand the business he was in.

> Things went really well our first year. My third invention—a battery-operated fuel monitor for diesel turbos being made in Germany—was selling like hotcakes, and I'd found a great production manager to keep things going down on the line.
>
> Then cash flow troubles developed.
>
> It happened in February of our second year when a couple of the big car makers—customers that purchased at least half of our product—slowed down on their payments. Some payments were more than 90 days past due.
>
> I stay pretty much in the lab and the shop because that's the fun part of the business for me, so I didn't find out about the cash problems for almost three weeks. When I did find out, we invoiced the customers again. Still no money. The first week in March, I had trouble meeting the payroll. The second week I had to pay a couple of crucial supplier accounts. The third week, except for petty cash, the company was almost out of money.
>
> I gave my banker a call. We were on good terms, and I had four accounts at her bank. When I told her my problem, she simply asked me how much I needed and for how long. Instant line of credit. What a relief.
>
> Well, we got that squared away, and when things were rolling smoothly again, my banker sat down with me and the company books, and we worked out a strategy for bridging the gap between billing and customer payment.
>
> Those sessions really bored me, so I started looking around for someone to help out on the numbers. My banker helped here, too, with advice and recommendations about what kind of person would be best at keeping track of money.
>
> When I worked for someone else, I never thought of a banker at all. Since I've been in business, I've come to realize a banker can be a businessperson's best friend.

Action Step 42 will help you get started in developing your relationship with a banker.

If you have tapped out your own resources, investigated borrowing from friends and family, and made a few bank inquiries—and there is still not enough in the money pot, look to other sources.

SBA Programs

One of the first stops many people make is the Small Business Association with its myriad of lending programs. Extensive information on SBA programs can be accessed at **www.sba.gov/financing**. Current major SBA programs are as follows:

- The 7 (A) Program is the most flexible as it can provide financing for a variety of general purposes, such as to acquire or start a business, or to meet very specific financing needs such as contract or export financing.
- The Certified Development (or 504) program can finance a portion of a business's fixed asset acquisition with a fixed interest rate loan in combination with third-party financing and equity.
- The Microloan program provides loans under $25,000 to eligible businesses needing limited amounts of borrowed funds. The SBA provides its funds to a microlender who, in turn, makes the actual loan to the business.

> ▶ **Action Step 42**
>
> **Befriend A Banker**
>
> Money creates its own world. There are several doorways into that world. Your banker sits at the threshold of one of those doors.
>
> Start with a familiar place, the bank where you have your checking account. Make an appointment to talk to the chief officer (president, vice-president, or branch manager).
>
> Use the Questions for Bankers as a guide.
>
> If you are happy with your banker's answers, talk over the possibility of opening a business account for your business. If you have money tucked away in life insurance or a money market fund somewhere, ask about the bank's money market accounts.
>
> Check out checking and bank fees and compare.

- The Small Business Investment Companies (SBIC), are private lenders licensed by the SBA to provide equity capital to small businesses. The recipients may give up some ownership, but not necessarily control, in exchange for the funds. Offering both debt and equity financing, the SBICs expect to recoup their investment in five to seven years. Further information can be found at **www.sba.gov/inv**

- The Small Business Innovation Research (SBIR) program provides direct funding for development efforts. The SBIR offers ventures for an opportunity to develop innovative ideas that meet the research needs of the federal government while hopefully opening the door to future commercialization. For further information, contact the SBA for their publication *Proposal Preparation for Small Business Innovation Research.*

The SBA has two major categories of loans: guaranteed and direct. Banks and nonbank lenders make the guaranteed loans. The direct loans are made directly to businesspeople by the federal government. Direct loans are scarce.

The guarantee is between the SBA and the bank. If the business goes under, the government repays a majority portion of the loan. Real estate loans are a major component of the loan portfolio because they are collateralized and more secure than other loans. Banks lending in cooperation with the SBA like to see at least a 30 percent commitment of personal funds before they loan money. Your local SBA office will give you a list of the major SBA-guaranteed lenders in your area. It is a good idea to utilize one of these banks for their expertise and experience in dealing with government red tape.

The SBA's Standard Application Package below provides a list of requirements for the SBA's Standard Application Package. SBA Form 4 is included in the Appendix B as well as SBA Form 4L, which is required for loans under $100,000. Additional forms are available on the Web and at local SBA offices.

The SBA's Standard Application Package Includes:

For the Business

SBA Form 4	Application for Business Loan
SBA Form 4a	Schedule of Collateral
SBA Form 912	Statement of Personal History
SBA Form 1261	Statements Required by Law and Executive Orders
SBA Form 641	Request for Counseling
SBA Form 1624	Certification Regarding Debarment, Suspension, Ineligibility and Voluntary Exclusion—Lower Tier Covered Transactions (Lender Keeps)
Acceptable Form	Personal Financial Statement
Acceptable Form	Cash Flow Projection
Acceptable Form	Past Three Year Financial Statements
Acceptable Form	Financial Statements Current to Within 90 Days of Application
Start Up Applicants	Monthly Cash Flow Projection

For the Lender

SBA Form 4l	Lenders Application for Guaranty (with Attached Analysis)
SBA Form 159	Compensation for Service in Connection with Application and Loan

For more information, visit **http://www.sba.gov/gopher/Business-Develop...-Education-Training/Finance-Plan/fin34.txt**

SBA 1997 Statistics

- maintained a guaranteed-loan portfolio of more than $29 billion in loans to 200,000 small businesses that otherwise would not have had such access to capital

- backed over 49,400 loans totaling a record $10.9 billion to America's small businesses

- made a record 2,700 investments worth $2.37 billion through its venture capital program

- extended management and technical assistance to nearly 900,000 small businesses through its 12,400 Service Corps of Retired Executive volunteers and approximately 1,000 small business development center locations

- assumed a leadership role in the Administration's Welfare to Work Initiative by encouraging entrepreneurship and linking small businesses with potential employees

For more information, visit **http:www.sba.gov/advo/stats/answer.html**

Small Business Answer Card 1997

Small businesses . . .

- provide virtually all of the net new jobs
- represent 99.7% of all employers
- employ 53% of the private work force
- provide 47% of receipts (sales)
- provide 55% of innovations
- account for 35% of federal contract dollars
- account for 28% of jobs in high technology sectors
- account for 51% of private sector output

The Small Business Answer Card is published by the U.S. Small Business Administration, Office of Advocacy, Washington, DC 20416. For the SBA office nearest you, consult the U.S. Government listings in your telephone book or call the Small Business Answer Desk at 1-800-827-5722.

SOURCE: **http://www.sba.gov**

SBDCs

Federal funds are awarded to state universities and economic development agencies that establish Small Business Development Centers at universities, chambers of commerce, and community colleges. These centers provide assistance in marketing, finance, and management. In addition, some centers are very specialized and offer technology transfer and international trade programs. To access the SBDC sites in your area, click on **www.smallbiz.suny.edu/execsum.htm** SBDCs located in Florida are shown on page 180. These programs will not fund your venture, but will provide assistance and prepare you to seek funding.

The SBA also offers additional programs that target special groups such as women, minorities, veterans, and the disabled. In addition, many export financing programs are available.

**Minorities and Women Financial
and Technical Assistance Programs**

National Minority Supplier Development Council (NMSDC) (serves over
3,500 firms, who use minority suppliers for products and services)
212-944-2430

Minority Business Development Agency
(provides management and technical assistance)
202-482-5741

Business Consortium Fund
(bank network that loans to minority-owned firms certified by NMSDC)
212-243-7360

U.S. Hispanic Chamber of Commerce
202-842-1212

National Association of Black Women Entrepreneurs
810-559-9255

Florida SBDC Locations By City

Bartow	Boca Raton
Bonita Springs (Ft. Myers)	Dania
Daytona Beach	Ft. Lauderdale
Ft. Pierce	Ft. Walton Beach
Gainesville	Jacksonville
Melbourne	Miami
North Miami	Ocala
Orlando	Panama City
Pensacola	Sanford
Tallahassee	Tampa

FSBDC Specialized Programs

State Director's Office	Energy Conservation
Selling to the Government	INFO-BID Leads
Japan Trade Missions	Yucatan, Mexico Trade

SOURCE: **http://www.floridasbdc.com/info/city.html**

State Programs and Local Development Authorities

Contact you local SBA office for a copy of *The State and Small Business: A Directory of Programs and Activities*. Local development authorities are very helpful and interested in securing financing for growing businesses, and can be extremely flexible in their financing programs.

Angels

While Janice was sharing her business plan with her best friend Sally, Sally's mother popped in and said, "That sounds like a great idea. Tell me more." After a few hours, the "angel" loaned Janice $20,000 at 10 percent interest. The angel also offered to have dinner meetings once a week and provide business counseling. Her 30 years in various health-care management positions made her a great mentor for Janice's home healthcare agency.

Angels may just appear, but that's unlikely. You will need to search out potential investors. The first step is to tell all your friends and family about your business idea and ask them if they have any possible contacts for you. Within your own research you may come across potential investors. Always follow up on anyone who expresses an interest. Research shows that a business angel interested in your venture very often lives within 10 miles.

Angels come in many different sizes and types—from the small investor who just came into money to the professional angel investor who wants to help others follow their passion. Most angels like to invest in companies in industries where they have knowledge and experience. Hopefully, your angel will not only help the financial part of your business but will also offer their contacts and experience; in the end this aid may be far more important to your success than the money.

Specific industries and some communities offer angel networks. Some networks offer a matchmaking process for investors and entrepreneurs. Angel Capital Electronic Network (ACE-Net) sponsored by the SBA offers a way for people to find each other online. ACE-Net exists for businesses seeking $250,000 to $5 million in capital. Use the SBA site to access ACE-Net.

In some communities private or college sponsored investors' forums are offered, where individuals are given 10-15 minutes to present their idea to potential investors. Forums are a great place to sell your idea, receive feedback, and hopefully find financing. SBA research shows 250,000 angels providing over $20 billion annually to 300,000 new and expanding businesses each year. Your chance to find an angel may be better than you thought!

Vendor Financing

An often overlooked technique for reducing your capital requirement is to probe your vendors (major suppliers) for the best prices and terms available. Professional buyers and purchasing agents ask their vendors to fill out an information sheet that forces them to write down the terms and conditions of their sales plans. This is a good idea for you as well.

A small business must buy professionally, and a **vendor statement** will help you do just that. With this form, your vendors' verbal promises become written promises. How well you buy is as important as how well you sell because every dollar you save by "buying right" drops directly to the bottom line. To compete in your arena, you need the best terms and prices you can get. The statement will help you get the best.

Personalize your form by putting your business name at the top. Then list the information you need and provide blanks for the vendors to write on. This following list provides some of the basics:

1. vendor's name
2. vendor's address and phone number
3. sales rep's name (800 number)
4. business phone
5. amount of minimum purchase
6. quantity discounts? how much? what must you do to earn?
7. are dating or extended payment terms available?
8. advertising/promotion allowances
9. policies on returns for defective goods (who pays the freight?)
10. delivery times
11. assistance (technical, sales, etc.)

Vendor statement A personally designed form that allows one to negotiate with each vendor from a position of informed strength

International Resources Information

World FactBook A great resource for conducting background research on a country. Select a country and receive an extensive profile covering:

Geography: map, climate, natural resources, environmental concerns, land use, etc.

People: population, age structure, growth rate, life expectancy, ethnic divisions, languages, literacy, etc.

Government: type of government, legal system, governmental structure, political parties, etc.

Economy: summary of past and current economic status, GDP, inflation rate, profile of labor force, unemployment rate, major industries, agriculture, exports, etc.

Transportation: railways, highways, waterways, pipelines, airports, etc.

Communications: telephone, radio, television, etc.

Military: manpower, budget.

International Market Research Reports Provided by *Strategis,* a service of the Canadian government, this site is superb for gathering market information about industries, products or other aspects of a country's economy. After typing in your subject of interest and/or selecting a country and industry, you will receive a market research report. Although many of the reports are written in terms of economic relationships between Canada and the chosen country, a lot of general data may be obtained.

For example, when "Information Technologies and Telecommunications" for Germany was selected, ten documents were posted. One of them, "Germany—Computers and Peripherals," included the following information: trade analysis (country's population, level of computer literacy and spending on information technology according to specific categories of computer hardware and software) and German computer hardware and software manufacturers.

World Competitiveness Yearbook Executive Summary by Professor Stéphane Garelli at the University of Lausanne, Switzerland. An analysis of each major area or country in the world and its current competitive status, including relative strengths and weaknesses in the world market. If you want more details about the yearbook, such as the factors considered in preparing the analysis, or to review the competitiveness rankings for a country, visit the yearbook's homepage.

Big Emerging Markets Prepared by the International Trade Administration in the U.S. Department of Commerce, this site lists global markets with high potential for U.S. exporters, such as the Chinese Economic Area (China, Hong Kong and Taiwan) and India. You may also select a specific country or economic area for analysis and statistics in support of the country or area's market potential.

SOURCE: **www.dryden.com/mgment/**

12. product literature available
13. point-of-purchase material provided
14. support for grand opening (will supplier donate prize or other support?)
15. nearest other dealer handling this particular line
16. special services the sales rep can provide
17. vendor's signature, the date, and some kind of agreement that you will be notified of any changes

Remember, the information the vendor writes on this statement is the starting point for negotiations. You should be able to negotiate more favorable terms with some vendors because these people want your business. Revise your application form as you learn from experience how vendors can help you. If you are a new business, you will most likely be required to *personally* guarantee in writing payment of your purchase.

A Success Story

Rich Cameron was in marketing, working for a large firm, when he decided to go into business for himself. He attended seminars, interviewed owners, walked neighborhoods, and read trade journals for quite a while before opening his toy store.

The store opened in May, but Rich knew from doing industry research that he would have to start placing orders for the Christmas season right away. The problem was that although his store could hold $200,000 worth of toys, Rich only had $120,000 to use for inventory. He knew he would have to be well-stocked by Thanksgiving or miss out on the profitable holiday business.

The unwritten rule in a new business is that suppliers want you to pay cash up front—for everything. You are a new account, unproven in the grand arena of trade and commerce. They want to wait and see how well you do before they extend credit.

Rich found a way to get around this. He showed his Business Plan to his suppliers' credit managers.

What happened?

"They were amazed," Rich says. "They'd been dealing with toy store owners for years, and mine was the first Business Plan they'd seen from a toy storeowner. I showed them everything in black and white—industry trends, projections, marketing plan, management–team statistics, promotion strategy, everything—and when they had read it, they gave me extended dating terms."

The Business Plan didn't do all Rich's work for him. He also bought merchandise for his store very carefully and he developed his own personalized vendor statement to use when he spoke to sales reps.

"A vendor statement really helps," Rich says, "because the survival items are written down. It puts sales reps on the spot. If they want your business to succeed, they have to deal with the questions."

"I got some strong resistance when I brought out my vendor statement form. One guy spent 30 minutes on long distance, telling me why he wouldn't sign it. He wanted all cash up front for the first sale, 75 percent cash for the second, 50 percent for the third, and 30 percent of net after that. But using the statement, backed by my Business Plan, I was able to negotiate him into dating, which means I bought toys in early summer and didn't have to pay for them until December 10. Dating saved my business."

Rich smiles as he recalls those early days. "The interesting thing about negotiating is that it gets you in close enough so you can ask for other assistance. A lot of my advertising and promotion comes free through the vendors because they want my store to be a success. If I hadn't gone in to deal, they wouldn't have known I was going to be a major customer for the long run. And I couldn't have moved confidently without that vendor form."

If you're a new account, flash 'em your business plan. Then flash 'em your vendor form. Tell them you're going to be a very important customer very soon.

Now it's time to prepare your own vendor statement form. Action Step 43 will help you.

▶ **Action Step 43**

Designing a Vendor Statement Form

One of the best ways to save money is to get help from your vendor/supplier. To do that, you will need to create your own special form that specifies, in writing, the terms to be negotiated.

Be tough. Be firm. Be pleasant.

Personalize this form by putting the name of your business at the top. Prepare your list of needed information using the list of 17 suggestions we've given you.

The vendor form provides talking points. Most vendors hold something back; design your form to help you learn what those things are and get the best deal for your business.

When negotiating, use a lot of open-ended questions like "What else can you do for me?"

Remember, vendors will ask you for detailed information. Dating and credit may be very limited for new accounts.

Prepare to Meet Your Lenders

Know who your potential lenders are and why they should want to help you.

Part A. List potential lenders and investors. Begin with your family and friends and move on to business acquaintances and colleagues. Don't forget institutional lenders.

Part B. Now list some of the reasons why lenders should want to invest in your business. What inducements are you offering potential investors? If you're offering them a very small ROI, what are you offering that will offset that?

Think about the legal form of your business. Would you attract more investors if you incorporated?

Part C. Test your tactics by talking to a few friends. Tell them: "This is just a test, and I'd like your reactions to my new business venture." Watch their reactions, and make a list of the objections they give you—the reasons why they cannot loan money to you.

Using your list of friends' objections, write down your answers to those objections. Are there any you cannot answer? What does this mean for your business?

Venture Capital Firms

With venture capital firms we enter the world of high rollers and higher flyers. Unlike banks that lend money that is secured (usually by real estate), venture capitalists don't lend money; they buy a piece of the business. They gamble on the business's rapid growth, hoping to reap a 300- to 500-percent return on their investment within three to five years. The payoff for most venture capital firms occurs when the company interests enough investors in an initial public offering of common stock (IPO) or when the company they're invested in is purchased by another business. When the business "goes public," the venture capital people take out their money.

Venture capitalists vary but most prefer to enter the financial picture at the second stage of a firm's development—when the business has proven its potential and needs a large infusion of cash to support growth. Currently, they tend to prefer high-tech concepts in embryonic industries with high growth potential.

Venture capitalists come in lots of shapes. For example, there are family firms (Rockefeller), industrial firms (GE), banks, and other firms (insurance companies, finance companies). Some specific venture capitalist firms exist that target specific industries such as health care, biotechnology, Internet, software, and telecommunications.

There's an excellent list of names and addresses of venture capital firms in *Pratt's Guide to Venture Capital Sources* and the *Directory of Venture Capital,* available in most public libraries. Local newspapers sometimes compile names of local and regional venture capitalists. Utilize these sources to determine which firms are interested in your selected industry and to determine the firms' minimum and maximum investment levels.

For additional financing options, visit Idea Café's superb Financing Your Business Website, **www.ideacafe.com/getmoney/FINANCING.shtml**. The site also has several interesting self-exams that help you to explore your "financing psyche."

After reviewing all your options, it is time to test the waters with Action Step 44.

► *Summary*

Few start-up firms have access to venture capital markets, bank financing, vendor credit, or angels at the beginning. The majority of ventures start from the bottom up—bootstrapping their venture and using capital from friends and family. Keep excellent financial records. When investors come calling, you will be prepared with vital financial documents. Cultivate your banker while you are growing your business.

Be prepared to put in sweat equity for at least the first few years. Learn how to conserve capital, manage debt, and accounts receivables. If you are fulfilling your customers' needs and keeping your nose to the grindstone, your day will come.

Money creates its own world. It has its own customs, rituals, and rules. Before you start asking people for money for your business, research the world of money. Read *Money, Inc., Forbes, Fortune, Business Week* and the *Wall Street Journal.* Find someone who knows more about money than you do. Ask questions! Listen!

As you continue to work on your business plan, remember what lenders are looking for:

capacity to repay

character and commitment of borrower

strong idea with identifiable target market in a growing market

collateral

background and experience of management team

Think Points for Success

- Your banker can be a doorway to the world of money. Use that door.
- Conserving capital is essential in the beginning.
- Take as little capital out of your business as you can in the beginning.
- In dealing with bankers and vendors, use lots of open-ended questions like "What else can you do for me?"
- Become operational as fast as you can.
- Aim for break even and strong cash flow as soon as possible.

Key Points from Another View

Why Start-ups Fail

Entrepreneurs usually put the blame on lack of capital. But more often, the problem is how they use the capital they have.

You always hear that the vast majority of new businesses fail because they're undercapitalized. I don't buy that. It's true in maybe 50% of the cases—no more. I'll give you an example from the software company I do business with in California. Two of its employees left to start a competing business. They contacted me because I was a potential customer and they wanted me to help finance them. They had a plan of sorts, built around signing up 60% to 70% of their old employer's customers in the first year. I wasn't interested, but I kept in touch. I think in the end they raised about $200,000.

So what was the first thing they did? They rented a beautiful office suite and filled it with lavish furnishings. Understand, at least 90% of their prospective customers were outside California, so they were never going to see the company's offices. Soon I received a brochure the new company had done up. It was elegant, and so was the stationery. When I called the guys up, I said, "That sure is beautiful stationery you have, great logo." They said, "Oh yes, our PR people did it for us." I laughed. Then I got an invitation to their grand opening, a really extravagant party. Of course, almost none of their customers could attend it.

A couple of months later, I was at an industry meeting, and I ran into the old employer. He was very upset with these guys. I said, "Don't worry, Tim. They're going to fail." He said, "How can you be so sure?" I said, "Trust me." They were out of business within a year. I called them up and asked what had happened. They said they were undercapitalized. Baloney. They'd raised $200,000 and thrown $120,000 out the window.

That's a very common story. People who fail on their first venture always say they were undercapitalized, and I suppose they're right in the sense that their capital ran out. But it's *not* because they didn't have enough capital to start out with. It's because they didn't use their capital wisely.

So why does that happen? Part of the problem, I believe, has to do with optimism. When people go into business for the first time, they have wonderful, wonderful dreams. They think they're going to be successful in the first year and make a ton of money. They're wildly optimistic, and at the same time they're scared to death. They're thinking, "Oh, God, I'm never going to make it." Meanwhile, they're projecting 10 times more sales than they can possibly do.

It's weird, but those two things—fear and overoptimism—almost always go together. I guess people use optimism to overcome their fear. They do everything they can to bolster their confidence. They believe that they'll improve their chances if they just act the part. So they rent a fancy office in the most expensive part of town. Or they join an exclusive country club. Or they invest in a computer system they won't need for two years—if they're lucky. Or they do what I did— drive around in a brand-new Mercedes. When I later read about Sam Walton and his beat-up old pickup truck, it dawned on me that the truly successful entrepreneurs don't need those symbols of success.

I eventually realized that you can always tell when people are going into business fresh, without a plan, without knowing what they need to do to survive. All you have to do is check out their offices. Are there drapes on their windows? Did they upgrade the carpeting? Are the walls painted or papered? Did they rent more space than they need? Is the reception area too big for a company whose customers rarely come in? Those are all potential signs of trouble. When you see them, watch out—especially if people are asking you to give them credit.

Of course, if you happen to be one of those first-time entrepreneurs, I can only say this: Forget about image. Forget about making a splash. Forget about everything except getting your capital to last until you don't need it anymore. You don't have to give up your dreams. Dreams are important. Just wait until you can afford them.

• • •

Norm Brodsky is a veteran entrepreneur whose six businesses include a former Inc. 100 company, a three-time Inc. 500 company, and a start-up that he hopes will become eligible for the list in 1996. His column, Street Smarts, will appear every other month. Readers are encouraged to send him questions care of Inc.

SOURCE: *Inc.,* December 1995, page 27.

Legal Issues

10

Entrepreneurial Links

Books

The Small Business Legal Guide, Second Edition, Lynne Ann Frasier, Esq., 1998.

The Complete Book of Business & Legal Forms, Lynne Anne Frasier, 1998.

Great Idea! Now What? Howard Bronson and Peter Lange, 1995.

Websites

www.lectlaw.com

www.lawsource.com

www.hg.org

Associations/Organizations

Family Firm Institute, www.ffi.org/forums.html

IRS, www.irs.gov

U.S. Patent and Trademark Office, www.uspto.gov

Publications

Barron's

Family Business

IP-The Magazine of Law Policy for High Technology, www.ipmag.com

Additional Entrepreneurial Insights

Making Sibling Teams Work: The Next Generation, Arnonogg, Ward, Astrachan, Mendoza, 1997.

How to Register Your Own Trademark, Second Edition, Mark Warda, 1998.

How to Register Your Own Copyright, Second Edition, Mark Warda, 1998.

Learning Objectives

- Decide which legal form is best for your business.
- Explore the good, the bad, and the ugly of partnerships.
- Understand the importance of professional legal advice.
- Review the advantages of forming a Limited Liability Company.
- Recognize the importance of getting everything in writing.
- Understand legal escape routes.
- Protect your business with a buy-sell agreement.
- Review patent protection.
- Understand copyright laws.
- Take action to protect your trademark or service mark.

By now your "new eyes" should be pretty sharp. Use them to look ahead to your legal, insurance, and tax needs.

In your interviews of successful entrepreneurs, you've probably run across the four main legal forms for small business: sole proprietorship, partnership, corporation, and limited liability company. Which is the right form for you? It's common for a small business to start out as a sole proprietorship or a partnership and then to **incorporate** later. How will you exit a partnership? Is your insurance in place? Are you aware of taxes due? Are you ready?

It Pays to Look Ahead

Imagine that you are in a great business with a partner you trust and respect. When should you incorporate or sign a partnership agreement? Perhaps sooner than you think. That's what Phil Johnson would tell you now.

The power sailer was my idea. My partner, Steve Savitch, said it would break us, and I should have listened to him. Steve's an engineer and inventor. He's great with numbers and computers, but he doesn't know much about people, which is my department. We'd been friends for at least a dozen years and we'd been partners—Savitch and Johnson; Business Consultants—for the past three. This year we were going to each clear over $100,000.

Steve's tight with a nickel. I knew he'd sock his money away in a money market fund at a conservative rate. But I had this idea that we could buy a boat for the partnership, write off the down payment as an expense, and do our company image a world of good.

"Image, Steve," I said. "Image."

"Uh-oh," Steve said. "Here we go with the unmeasurable intangibles."

"It's not intangible when you think about those prospects coming from Chicago next week," I said. "A cruise to Sanibel Island should soften them up, don't you think?"

The first payment wasn't due for a month, and when Steve and I took the boat out with our wives, I tell you, I felt like a prince of the sea. We'd pulled off a smooth deal, and I patted myself on the back every time I thought about the **write-offs.**

Incorporate Form an artificial, immortal business entity

Write-offs Legitimate business deductions accepted by the IRS

Our boat, *Sunbiz*, boosted business, just like I'd thought it would. We closed the Chicago deal and were busy on a couple of other deals that looked promising. We made the first payment with no trouble, and when Steve **counter-signed** the check, he admitted he was beginning to like the boat.

For a couple of weeks, Steve took his laptop and slept on the *Sunbiz*. We took her out one weekend, with four prospects from St. Louis, and Steve seemed preoccupied. I closed the deal with them Sunday, 15 minutes before putting them on the plane for home. But when I called Steve's house to tell him the good news, his wife, Mary, told me he was still at the boat.

Monday, Steve didn't come to work until almost noon. He looked tired, but he handed me his projections and we got on with planning our strategy for the next couple of weeks.

"Anything wrong, partner?" I asked. "You seem a little far-off today."

"Sorry," Steve said. He was never one to admit to having problems. "My mind wandered a bit there. Where were we?"

On Thursday, Steve still didn't make it to work after missing Wednesday. I called his house. No answer. I thought of driving down to the dock to check the boat, but didn't. When I arrived at the dock with clients around 4:30 that afternoon, there was no *Sunbiz*. Someone on the next dock said Steve had taken off early that morning.

Then Joey, the guy who pumps gas, came up waving a gas bill for $800—one I'd thought Steve had paid. And the bad news didn't end there. The next day, a fellow who sells radar equipment called me with a $2000 bill.

I was in shock. There I stood, with two clients in deck shoes and shorts.

My cell phone rang. It was Mary, Steve's wife, wanting to know where Steve was.

Now my stomach was really hurting. My partner Steve was gone—no one knew where—and I was going to have to cover all his business debts, including the payments on the *Sunbiz*. Terrific.

The problem was that Steve and I had never seen the need for having anything in writing. We were both men of good faith. We had each pulled our weight in the business, and we had balanced each other's skills.

Now that Steve was gone, I felt lost, angry, and betrayed. For the first time in 22 years of business, I made an appointment to talk to a lawyer. He just shook his head.

"You should have come to me sooner, Phil," he said. "A lot sooner."

Last week when I was closing the place down and getting ready to go back to work for my old boss, I got a postcard from Steve, from Tahiti. "Sorry, Phil," it read. "Didn't mean to run out on you. It was the only way I could handle it. These things happen. Your partner, Steve."

Find and Use an Attorney from the Beginning!

A good small business attorney can help you to:

- create the right business structure for a partnership or a corporation—a structure that gives the protection and flexibility you'll need.

- review advertising and marketing materials to assure no laws are violated.

- organize your human resources department to keep you outside the courtroom, hiring and firing of employees is problematic to say the least—improper handling of even one employee may cause you to loose your business.

- research and protect you in regards to **product liability.**

Countersigning A situation in which two or more signatures are required before action can occur

Product liability legal exposure if customer becomes ill, sustains injury, or property damage

continued on page 192

Action Step 45

Entertain a Lawyer

Network your business contacts for the names of three to five attorneys with experience in forming small business corporations and partnerships. Concentrate on those who have worked in your industry.

Check them out on the phone and then take the most promising candidates to lunch.

The first thing you're looking for is someone you can get along with. Then look for experience in the world of small business. A hot trial lawyer may have a lot of charisma, but you want a nuts-and-bolts small business specialist who can save you time, pain, and money.

Trademark a word, phrase, logo, design or anything used to identify goods or services and differentiates from competitors

Copyright protects the expression of an idea

Patent right to make, sell, offer for sale, use, or import an invention

Bankruptcy legal and financial process if a debtor's financial obligations are greater than his or her assets

Exit strategy A plan to disengage from business at a future point in time.

Buy/Sell agreement an advance contractual agreement that determines how a business is to valued if one or more partners buy out another

Taxi squad Human resources outside one's business that can be called on as needed

Retainer fee an agreement to secure the services of an attorney for a fixed fee for a given period of time or for a specific legal problem

- review all contracts and agreements before you sign.
- protect you through proper use and development of **trademarks, copyrights,** and **patents.**
- handle collection and possible **bankruptcy** problems.
- help you plan your **exit strategy.**
- write partnership agreements and **buy–sell agreements.**

Network your contacts for a lawyer with experience in your selected industry. This is not the time to save money by using your niece who just passed the bar exam. Large law firms may be very advantageous for rapidly growing technology firms. These firms have access to many specialists who can provide answers quickly. Intellectual property, biotechnology, and manufacturing all have very specific legal issues where expertise is vital for initial and continued success.

One of the most important roles an attorney plays is to provide you entrée to his or her contacts throughout an industry as well as bankers, investors, and accountants. No amount of money can buy you such access.

You need to have a good lawyer, accountant, banker, and insurance agent on your **taxi squad.** Their support and expertise can keep you on track, out of jail, and protected from seen and unforeseen circumstances.

Develop an attorney–client relationship before an employee or customer sues you or your partner leaves for Tahiti. Preventive legal fees are far less costly than clean-up fees if one is sued.

After you have networked to find a lawyer you believe to be right for you, make an appointment with him or her. You are looking for someone who you are comfortable with and someone who understands the needs of your business. Many attorneys will not charge for an initial half-hour meeting.

Be sure to prepare for your meeting. If you're organized, you will be able to gather a great deal of information in a short time. Complete Action Step 45.

Understanding How Lawyers Charge and Operate

Lawyers charge by the hour for services they render or work on a **retainer fee.** Or you may have access to a prepaid legal plan where you get a variety of services for a flat annual fee. Legal fees range from $100 to more than $400 an hour. Specialized attorneys such as patent or copyright experts may have higher hourly charges.

Get the most out of each appointment with your lawyer by doing basic research yourself using the library or Internet. Be thoroughly organized for each meeting, with your questions ready. This will cut down the time you would be charged.

Legal Forms of Business

You can start doing business as a sole proprietorship with a minimum of hassle. You might need only a city license, a resale license, and perhaps a DBA (fictitious name) statement (see Figure 10.1). It is also advisable to obtain an employer's identification number (EIN) from the federal government (see Appendix B).

The legal paperwork for a partnership is sometimes as simple if all agree on basic concepts. You can form a partnership with a handshake and dissolve it without one if you're lucky. If you decide a partnership is right for you, get a lawyer to prepare a partnership agreement to protect you against trouble. Less than 10 percent of the small businesses in the United States are partnerships.

A limited liability company (LLC) may be ideal for closely held firms. It offers limited personal liability protection to all owners (termed members) and is treated

Figure 10.1

Fictitious Business Name Statement (Sample)

A MAIL CERTIFIED COPIES TO:	**B** PUBLISH IN NEWSPAPER:
NAME _____ ADDRESS _____ _____ ☐ First Filing ☐ Renewal Filing Current Registration No. _____	COUNTY CLERK'S FILING STAMP

FICTITIOUS BUSINESS NAME STATEMENT
THE FOLLOWING PERSON(S) IS (ARE) DOING BUSINESS AS:

1. * — Fictitious Business Name(s)

2. ** — Street Address, City & State of Principal place of Business in California — Zip Code

3. ***

Full name of Registrant (if corporation – show state of incorporation)

Residence Address	City	State	Zip Code

Full name of Registrant (if corporation – show state of incorporation)

Residence Address	City	State	Zip Code

Full name of Registrant (if corporation – show state of incorporation)

Residence Address	City	State	Zip Code

Full name of Registrant (if corporation – show state of incorporation)

Residence Address	City	State	Zip Code

4. **** — This Business is conducted by: (CHECK ONE ONLY)

( ) an individual   ( ) a general partnership   ( ) joint venture   ( ) a business trust
( ) co-partners   ( ) husband and wife   ( ) a corporation   ( ) a limited partnership
( ) an unincorporated association other than a partnership   ( ) LLC

5. ***** — The registrant commenced to transact business under the fictitious business name or names listed above on _____

6A.
Signed _____
Typed or Printed _____

6B. If Registrant a corporation sign below:
Corporation Name _____
Signature & Title _____
Type or Print
Officer's Name & Title _____

This statement was filed with the County Clerk of _____ County on date indicated by file stamp above.

NOTICE

THIS FICTITIOUS NAME STATEMENT EXPIRES ON DECEMBER 31, 19____, A NEW FICTITIOUS BUSINESS NAME STATEMENT MUST BE FILED PRIOR TO DECEMBER 31, 19____.

I HEREBY CERTIFY THAT THIS COPY IS A CORRECT COPY OF THE ORIGINAL STATEMENT ON FILE IN MY OFFICE.

_____
COUNTY CLERK

BY _____ DEPUTY

File No. _____

During your meeting, find out about fees and costs. Compare the cost, for example, of having your lawyer draw up a complex partnership buy-out agreement with the cost of setting up a corporation. This section of this book lists some questions to start you off in your discussions with your prospective attorney.

A good lawyer will offer perspectives that will be helpful in the formation of your business. You may have to look a while, and it may cost you some dollars up front, but there's no substitute for good legal help.

like a partnership or **Subchapter S corporation** on the members' individual tax returns. This avoids the double taxation of income and is usually less costly to form (an operating agreement (see Figure 10.2a and 10.2b) must be filed with the state).

Forming a corporation takes the most paperwork but gives you more flexibility, as well as a shield that may protect you in case your business harms someone.

If you are forming or currently operating a business with your spouse, the following may provide some insight for you. For a detailed review of the correct structure of a family business venture read the "Key Points from Another View" article at the end of the chapter. The Incredible Resource box for this chapter (page 194) provides you with resources for family businesses.

For Couples Working Together, Setting Ground Rules is a Must

You married your beloved **for better or for worse,** in sickness and in health, for richer or for poorer.

But **for profit or for loss?** If you're in business together, that's about the size of it.

Take David and Sharon Nevins, for instance.

David Nevins credits much of Owings Mills-based **Nevins and Associates'** success to his wife. Sharon Nevins joined the 10-year-old public relations, marketing, advertising and customer service firm two years ago and **started the company's advertising division.**

But David Nevins, whose firm had capitalized local billings of $6 million last year, admits the partnership—the business one—**isn't necessarily a "forever" thing.** "It's advantageous now, but we have no long-term plans," he says.

That's not because the two don't work well together. They do, and it's because **they've established certain rules that they follow,** he says.

Having **individual lines of authority** is essential for a successful business partnership, say family business experts.

"You need a **clear definition of responsibility,**" says **William Ross Adams,** president of Baltimore's Baker-Meekins Co., financial advisers to owners of family and private businesses.

That advice is **echoed by Harsha Desai,** professor of management and director of the Loyola Center for Closely-Held Firms at Loyola College.

"A couple **has to have different areas of expertise,** so you don't run into each other's area," Desai says. "One of you has to be a boss. You can take turns—one is boss for six months, then the other one is—but **someone has to defer to someone else.** One person has to have the final decision-making responsibility."

Leaving Some Room

One tip Nevins offers other married business partners is to **give each other space—literally.**

"Sharon has an office down the hall. Other than the times we meet with a client together, she runs her division and **we don't see that much of each other.** If we were in the same room or meeting together all the time, that would be too much of a good thing," he says.

Another policy both Nevins and Susana V. Ptak, co-owner of Gascoyne Laboratories Inc., recommend is **leaving work at the office.**

Ptak, who co-owns the Baltimore environmental testing lab with husband Francis, agrees: "Two things have helped us not to kill each other," she says, laughing. "One is that **we don't do the same thing** (Francis is a chemist and handles the analytic end of the company; Susana takes care of the business side), and the other is that **we don't talk business at home.** In the car, yes, but once we're actually at home, we just talk family stuff.

Subchapter S legal entity which may provide positive tax treatment for small business

"Don't confuse your business with your family," Ptak continues. "If you do, you'll go berserk."

Handling Conflict

To make the business work, a couple must **recognize that the company has specific needs,** says Patrick O. Ring, Baker-Meekins' managing director. "Make a plan, examine your goals, and build in some mechanism to achieve those goals and to resolve conflicts."

The overriding issue to be addressed is, "**What makes sense for the business?** How is the business going to grow? In which direction is it going to grow? How can you make it grow?" Ring adds.

"You need to explicitly talk about such issues," says Desai. "**You can't wait until a crisis occurs** to make a decision."

In times of conflict, **keep the argument between yourselves.** "Don't put the employee, or the business itself, in the middle," Adams advises.

"It's important to **be fair to your workers,**" agrees Susana Ptak, whose lab has 61 employees. "Be careful that your employees see you and your spouse as a united front."

Of course, **not all partnerships work out as successfully** as the Nevins' and the Ptaks'.

Sometimes couples get divorces, just as sometimes business partnerships fail. That's an eventuality couples should be prepared for, says Adams.

He recommends that spouses **make an agreement at the beginning** that one partner can buy out the other in case of divorce. Without an agreement, you could spend time and money in litigation.

"Life's too short to **spend all that energy on disputes,**" he says.

While arguments are bound to crop up, whether in a marriage or a business partnership, **they don't have to destroy either relationship.**

"Money breeds all sorts of snarling snakes," Adams says, "but you can work out your problems. **It just requires discipline and a willingness** not to let a disagreement destroy a marriage—or a business."

SOURCE: **http://NMQ.com**   *—Carol Sorgen*

Which Form of Business Is Best for You?

Only you, your lawyer, your business advisor, and your accountant will know for sure what form is best for you and your particular situation. You and your taxi squad should consider the following before making the determination.

- international exposure
- tax implications
- liability issues
- litigiousness of customers, employees, and businesses in your state
- plans for business growth
- exit strategy
- family structure and involvement in the business
- relationship with potential partners

Spend time and money consulting with your taxi squad to determine what is best for you early on because there are many pitfalls. Let your taxi squad help you avoid major errors.

The legal form of your business is just that—a form, a shape. To your customers, the particular form you choose may not be obvious; but to you, the

**Family Businesses
Who Can Help?**

American Academy of Matrimonial Lawyers
150 N. Michigan Ave. Suite 2040
Chicago, IL 60601
312-263-6477
fax, 312-263-7682
www.aaml.org

Lists member attorneys and provides consumer-oriented articles on aspects of divorce. To order *A Divorce Manual: A Client Handbook* (item 5953-0; $10), call 800-422-6595.

California Family Business Institute
4055 E. Thousand Oak Blvd.,
West Lake Village, CA 91362
800-952-2324
www.cfbi.com

A multidisciplinary consulting team provides comprehensive services for family business owners, advising on succession, family conflicts that affect business strategies, designing exit strategies, and advanced estate planning.

Family Business Roundtable
727 E. Bethany Home Rd. Suite 125
Phoenix, AZ 85014
602-285-1207
fax, 602-285-0663
www.fbrinc.com

A group of family business consultants offers coaching, strategic planning, and divorce mediation.

Genus Resources
161 Highland Ave.
Needham, MA 02194
781-444-9200
www.nmq.com/genus

Clinicians and business people consult large, family-controlled companies on resolving issues or dissolving the business.

Institute for Certified Divorce Planners
2724 Winding Trail Place
Boulder, CO 80304
800-875-1760
fax, 303-444-9209
www.webwise.com/divorce

Certifies financial professionals in the intricacies of pre- and postdivorce discovery, negotiation, and financial planning. Provides referrals to Institute-trained financial planners around the country.

Internet Legal Resource Guide
www.ilrg.com

A searchable directory of lawyers and their areas of expertise.   —J.C.

SOURCE: *Working Woman,* March 1998, p. 69.

right shape is absolutely essential. You want your business to be rock-solid, stable, and protected—and you want to be able to change its form if the first choice doesn't work.

Beyond the mental images we have of these forms of ownership, there are business realities—and various amounts of paperwork—which you should know about. Table 10.1 summarizes the differences.

Sole Proprietorships

Most small businesses start as sole proprietorships. If you start a business on your own—without partners—you are a sole proprietor unless you form an LLC or corporation. If this form is your choice, the paperwork will be relatively easy. Check with your local city offices to determine which licenses will be needed. If you are a service business, you may be required to purchase a license to do business

Table 10.1

S Corp., C Corp., or No Corp., Choice of Business Entities—A Comparison

Applicable Factor	Sole Proprietor	Partnership	Limited Liability Company*	S Corporation	C Corporation
Formation					
Method	None	Partnership agreement	Articles of Organization filed in state recognizing LLCs	Articles of Incorporation	Articles of Incorporation
Owner Eligibility					
Number of Owners	One	Two or more for limited partnership; one or more general and one or more limited for general partnership	No limit	35	No limit
Type of Owners	Individual	No limitation	No limitation	Individuals and certain trusts	No limitation
Affiliate Limits	No limitation	No limitation	No limitation	No subsidiaries	No limitation
Capital Structure	No stock	No limitations (multiple classes)	No limitation	Only one class of stock	No limitations (multiple classes permitted)
Liability	Unlimited	General partners jointly and severally liable. Limited partners are generally limited to capital contributions.	Limited to member's capital contribution	Limited to shareholder's contributions	Limited to shareholder's capital contributions
Operational Phase					
Tax Year	Calender year	Generally calendar year	Generally calendar year	Generally calendar year	Generally any year permitted (limit for personal service corporation)
Tax on Income	Individual level	Owner level	Member level	Owner level	Corporate level
Allocation of Income/Deductions	N/A	Permitted if substantial economic effect	Permitted if substantial economic effect	Not permitted (except through debt/equity structure)	Not permitted (except through multiple equity structure)
Character of Income/Deductions	Flow-through to individual	Flow-through to partners	Flow-through to members	Flow-through to shareholders	No flow-through to shareholders

NOTE: *Some states (New York, for example) use the term LLP—Limited Liability Partnership, which has some to liability protection.

in each city that you operate. In some cities, inspectors visit work sites to assure that all businesses are in compliance. Fines are much more expensive than licenses.

If you are conducting a business in a name other than your own the Uniform Commercial Code requires that you publish notice in your community newspaper to notify customers and creditors who is the owner of the business. Corporations are usually exempt. Contact your newspaper for the forms and send a check usually for less than $100. A sample of a Doing Business As/Fictitious Business Name Statement is on page 191.

You will also need to discuss tax requirements with your accountant and insurance matters with an insurance representative before you begin.

Partnerships

A partnership, as lots of people find out too late, is only an accounting entity. It does not shield one from trouble. It won't make your business immortal or continuous, and it's taxed at the same rate as you.

A partnership is made up of at least two parties. There can be more—six, ten, a baker's dozen—but the more partners a business has, the trickier the decisions. Think of a ship with a dozen captains. Who makes the decisions?

In a limited partnership—composed of two or more limited partners and one general partner—the general partner assumes both managerial duties and the downside risk. A limited partner's liability is limited to the *amount* of his or her original investment as long as he or she has had no role in management decisions. *Do not proceed without legal advice.*

You can form a partnership with a handshake, and dissolve it without one. We do not advise you to proceed with *any* partnership without benefit of an attorney's counsel. One plus about a partnership is that it allows the financial and moral support of a teammate.

A partnership is somewhat of a paradox. In a legal sense the partnership doesn't do much for you, but as many partners admit, there are sound psychological reasons for some for going into business with someone else.

What are some of those reasons? Let's say you've analyzed your personal skills, and realize you need balance in a couple of critical areas. For example, you may be an engineer who can come up with 20 original ideas a day but couldn't sell ice in Florida in the summer. Or perhaps you don't have much money so you need a partner who can supply your new business with capital. Or maybe you get along with people and love to sell and need to team up with an inventor/producer who can supply you with products to sell. Many successful business-owners could never have started a business without a partner.

Before committing to a partnership, realize that friendship alone will not resolve business problems. All involved partners need to decide what exactly each brings to the table and then decide if what is brought is worth the complications of a partnership. There will be many unspoken fears and needs of all involved parties. Keeping the lines of communication open is essential for survival.

Business counselors do a rip-roaring business trying to work out the problems of warring partners. To reduce problems do your research before starting a partnership and continually talk to keep the partnership going. You must trust your partner(s) and have confidence in their decisions.

Partnership Agreement Questions for Discussion

- **Management and control.** Who will make the final decision? In one partnership, the owners take turns each year trading off being the President and final decisionmaker.

- **Financial contributions.** It is necessary to determine not only initial contributions but also possible future contributions. An initial 50-50 partnership may turn into a 75-25 partnership if capital needs arise. How will you deal with this change?
- **Time contributions.** How much time will each partner commit? Are these contributions considered equal? If you commit 20 hours and the other partner(s) 40, will profit distribution reflect this variance?
- **Demise of the partnership.** If the partnership is to be dissolved, how will the ending be dealt with?
- **New partners.** Can new partners be added? If so, what will the process be to include new partners?
- **Participation of family members as employees and input into the business.** See Key Points for Another View.

Review the sample partnership agreement that follows and remember to consult your attorney before signing any agreement. On the surface, partnerships make a lot of sense. Two or more entrepreneurs face the unknown together and pool their skills. They can raise more capital than one person could alone. But forming a *good* partnership is more difficult than forming a good marriage.

Sample Partnership Agreement

(NAME), and (NAME), the below signed hereby enter into this Partnership Agreement on behalf of themselves, their heirs, successors and assigns, and set forth following terms and conditions as constituting the Partnership Agreement in its entirety:

1. The partnership shall go by the following name: (NAME).
2. The partnership's principle place of business shall be (DESCRIBE).
3. The first day that the partnership shall begin business is: (DATE) and it will continue until the partners agree to terminate it or until forced to cease its operations by law.
4. The partnership's operations shall be primarily in the following field or area: (DESCRIBE)
5. The partnership shall be capitalized as follows: For each $ (AMOUNT) (dollars) each partner shall receive (#) shares with contribution being made as follows:

   Partner A contributes $ (AMOUNT). and shall receive (#) shares, the same being (#)% of the total shares available.

   Partner B contributes $ (AMOUNT). and shall receive (#) shares, the same being (#)% of the total shares available.

6. Losses and gains on contributed capital and other property shall be assigned as follows: (DESCRIBE)

   The IRS's general allocation rule shall apply, and gains and losses shall be allocated according to the % of total capital contributed by each partner as set out in paragraph #5 above.

7. Profits and losses shall be allocated according to the same percentage allocation set forth in paragraph 6. above.
8. Salary, if any, for the services rendered shall be determined by unanimous approval of the partners.
9. Control and management of the partnership shall be split equally amongst the partners.

10. Each partner shall maintain both an individual drawing account and an individual capital account. Into the capital account shall be placed that partner's initial capitalization and any increases thereto. The drawing accounts shall be used for withdrawal of amounts, the size of which is limited to $ (AMOUNT) on any one day.

11. Adequate accounting records shall be made and maintained. Any partner or his/her agent, may review any and all accounting or other records at anytime.

12. The partners designate the following as the Partnership's business and checking accounts into which all the funds of the Partnership shall be placed and maintained: (DESCRIBE)

13. Accounting records and books shall be kept on a (select one) 1. cash basis 2. accrual basis and the fiscal year shall begin on the (#) day of (MONTH) and shall end (#) day of (MONTH).

14. At the close of the fiscal year there shall be an annual audit conducted by the following accounting firm: (DESCRIBE)

15. The partnership shall dissolve upon the retirement, death or incapacity of any partner unless the remaining partner elects the option of buying out that partner's share. If so elected, the partnership shall be valued by submission to arbitration with GAMA, Inc., according to reasonable accounting and valuation principles, and as set forth in paragraph #17 below. The finding of the arbitrator as to the value of the partnership shall be final and binding upon the partners, their heirs, successors, and assigns. Upon the issuance of this finding, the remaining partner shall have (TIME) to buy out the previous partner's share. Should more than one remaining partner desire to buy this share, the share shall be split evenly between the same.

16. Upon termination or dissolution of the Partnership, the Partnership will be promptly liquidated, with all debts being paid first, prior to any distribution of the remaining funds. Distribution shall be made according to the percentage of ownership as set out in paragraph #5 above.

17. Any controversy or claim arising out of or relating to this Agreement, or the breach thereof, shall be settled by arbitration in accordance with the Commercial Arbitration Rules of the American Arbitration Association, and judgement upon the award rendered by the arbitrator(s) may be entered in any court having jurisdiction thereof.

So agreed, this (#) day of (MONTH), 19 _____ .

_____
(NAME)

_____
(NAME)

Brought to you by—THE 'LECTRIC LAW LIBRARY™
The Net's Finest Legal Resource For Legal Pros & Laypeople Alike.
WWW: **http://www.lectlaw.com—e-mail: staff@lectlaw.com**

This information is from the 'Lectric Law Library Website at
http://www.lectlaw.com

Limited Liability Company

Most states have recently allowed a Limited Liability Company (LLC) to be an acceptable form of business. This entity does not limit the number of investors,

Figure 10.2(a)

Limited Liability Company Articles of Organization

State of California
Bill Jones
Secretary of State

LLC-1

LIMITED LIABILITY COMPANY
ARTICLES OF ORGANIZATION

IMPORTANT - Read the instructions before completing the form.
This document is presented for filing pursuant to Section 17050 of the California Corporations Code.

1. Limited liability company name:
   (End the name with LLC, L.L.C., Limited Liability Company or Ltd. Liability Co.)

2. Latest date (month/day/year) on which the limited liability company is to dissolve.

3. The purpose of the limited liability company is to engage in any lawful act or activity for which a limited liability company may be organized under the Beverly-Killea Limited Liability Company Act.

4. Enter the name of initial agent for service of process and check the appropriate provision below:

   _____, which is

   [ ] an individual residing in California.

   [ ] a corporation which has filed a certificate pursuant to Section 1505 of the California Corporations Code.
       Skip Item 5 and proceed to Item 6.

5. If the initial agent for service of process is an individual, enter a business or residential street address in California:

   Street address:

   City: State: California   Zip Code:

6. The limited liability company will be managed by: **(check one)**

   [ ] one manager   [ ] more than one manager   [ ] limited liability company members

7. If other matters are to be included in the Articles of Organization attach one or more separate pages.
   Number of pages attached, if any: ☐

Describe type of business of the Limited Liability Company.

Declaration: It is hereby declared that I am the person who executed this instrument, which execution is my act and deed.

For Secretary of State Use

File No. _____

_____
Signature of organizer

_____
Type or print name of organizer

Date: _____ , 19 _____

SEC/STATE (REV. 2/98)   FORM LLC-1 -- FILING FEE: $70

Figure 10.2(b)

Limited Liability Company Articles of Organization

INSTRUCTIONS FOR COMPLETING THE ARTICLES OF ORGANIZATION (LLC-1)

All references are to the California Corporations Code unless otherwise indicated.
Type or legibly print in black ink.

DO NOT ALTER THIS FORM

Item 1.   Enter the name of the limited liability company which must end with the words "LLC", "L.L.C." or "Limited Liability Company". The words "Limited" and "Company" may be abbreviated to "Ltd." and "Co." Section 17051(a)(1). The name of the limited liability company may not contain the words "bank", "insurance company", "insurer", "trust", "trustee", "incorporated", "inc.", "corporation", or "corp." Section 17052(d).

Professional limited liability companies are prohibited from forming or registering in California.

Item 2.   Enter the latest date (month/day/year) on which the limited liability company is to dissolve. Section 17051(a)(2).

Item 3.   The articles of organization must contain the following statement of purpose which is preprinted on the form and may not be altered: "The purpose of the limited liability company is to engage in any lawful act or activity for which a limited liability company may be organized under the Beverly-Killea Limited Liability Company Act". Section 17051(a)(3). If the provisions limiting or restricting the business of the limited liability company are desired refer to Item 7 for instructions on attaching additional pages.

Item 4.   Enter the name and address of the initial agent for service of process. Check the appropriate provision indicating whether the initial agent is an individual residing in California or a corporation which has filed a certificate pursuant to Section 1505 of the California Corporations Code. Section 17051(a)(5).

Item 5.   Enter a business or residential street address in California, box numbers and "in care of" (c/o) are not acceptable.

Item 6.   Check the appropriate provision indicating whether the limited liability company is to be managed by one manager, more than one manager, or the limited liability company members. Section 17051(a)(6).

Item 7.   The articles of organization may contain additional provisions including, but not limited to, provisions limiting or restricting the business in which the limited liability company may engage, powers that the limited liability company may exercise, admission of members, events that will cause a dissolution, or limitations on the authority of managers or members to bind the limited liability company. Such matters must be submitted on single-sided, standard white paper. Number and identify each page as an attachment to the articles of organization. Enter the number of pages attached to the form, if any, in Item 7. Section 17051(c).

Briefly describe the general type of business that constitutes the principal business activity of the limited liability company. Note restrictions in the rendering of professional services by Limited Liability Companies. Professional services are defined in California Corporations Code 13401(a) as: "any type of professional services that may be lawfully rendered only pursuant to a license, certification, or registration authorized by the Business and Professions Code or the Chiropractic Act."

Declaration: The articles of organization must be executed with an original signature. Facsimiles and photocopies of the articles of organization are not acceptable for the purpose of filing with the Secretary of State. The person executing the articles of organization need not be a member or manager of the limited liability company. Section 17051(a).

• The fee for filing the articles of organization with the Secretary of State is seventy dollars ($70). Section 17701(b).

• Return the acknowledgment of filing to:

    Name: _____
    Firm/Company: _____
    Address: _____
    City: _____
    State: _____ Zip Code: _____

• Send the executed document and filing fee to:

    Office of the Secretary of State
    Limited Liability Company Unit
    P.O. Box 944228
    Sacramento, CA 94244-2280

allows profits to be distributed in a manner other than investors' capital contribution, and limits liability. It is expected that LLCs will be the entity of choice for closely held businesses in the near future. LLCs are designed to provide the tax flexibility and ownership of partnerships with the limited liability features of corporations.

The operating agreement sets out the company's membership and operational rules. In addition, the agreement states how members' profits and losses are shared.

LLCs provide the flow-through tax treatment that has been available to partnerships and subchapter S corporations. The required documentation, known as "articles of association," is less detailed than articles of incorporation and is usually less costly. See Figure 10.2 for an example of an application for registration of the articles of organization.

The articles of organization contain an "operating agreement" that resembles a partnership agreement. LLC members may manage the business themselves or delegate such authority to active managers.

Most state statutes require that identifying information such "Limited Liability Company" or "LLC" appear in the name of the company to notify others as to the limited liability enjoyed by the organization. The IRS has ruled that such organizations will be taxed at the individual rate. Be careful! If an LLC is not properly structured, it will be taxed as a corporation.

LLCs generally will not be appropriate for existing corporations or businesses that have or want to raise capital through the public or venture capital markets. If you are considering converting to an LLC, be aware there may be significant tax consequences. It is vital that you consult competent tax, legal, and accounting advisors.

A few states have LLPs (Limited Liability Partnerships), which contain liability exceptions for certain professional service firms (doctors, architects, engineers, etc.). Check the laws in your state.

Corporations

There are at least six good reasons for incorporating. In general, we think most owners of small businesses fail to incorporate because they don't see the signals their businesses are giving. Ask yourself is there any chance your employees, customers, or suppliers might sue you? The truth is that for almost all firms a great deal of risk exists, therefore incorporating should be seriously considered.

Employees driving your vehicles, customers being harmed in some way by a product or service (in ways you would never believe or consider), customers or employees slipping and falling, are just a few of the potential litigious situations that can occur. The text following lists reasons why you should consider incorporating.

1. ***You Limit Your Liability.*** A corporation may act like a shield between you and the world. If your business fails, your creditors can't come after your house, your condo, your Porsche Boxster, your first-born, or your hard-won collectibles—provided you've done it right. And that is the key. To keep your corporate shield up, make sure you: (a) hold scheduled board of directors meetings, (b) keep up the minute's book, and (c) act as if you are an employee of the corporation.

    The fact is almost all entrepreneurs use most of their personal assets as collateral and thus the limited liability provided by a corporation may only limit your risk of personal financial loss.

    Ask your attorney how to reduce personal liability issues within your firm's operations. Safety precautions, disclaimers on products, having your employees covered by very high liability policies on their own cars, and proper hiring and firing methods are just a few ways to reduce your risks.

2. **To Change Your Tax Picture.** Consult the current IRS schedule and ask a CPA for advice.

3. **To Upgrade Your Image.** What does the word *corporation* mean to you? IBM? Intel? TWA? GM?

 Let's look at that word. It comes from the Latin *corpus,* which means, "body." To *incorporate* means to make or form or shape into a body. Looked at from that angle, *incorporating* starts to sound creative. As a corporation, you may enjoy more prestige, attract better employees, and have more clout in the world.

4. **To Have the Opportunity to Channel Some Heavy Expenses.** Medical and insurance premiums as well as FICA payments become business expenses.

5. **To Guarantee Continuity.** If one owner goes to Australia, dies, or becomes ill, the corporation keeps on chugging. That's because you've gone through a lot of red tape and planning to set it up that way.

6. **To Offer Internal Incentives.** When you want to reward special employees or retain your best employees, you can offer stock or a promotion (for example, a vice-presidency) in addition to (or in place of) pay raises. Becoming a corporate officer carries its own special excitement, and this gives you flexibility.

Subchapter S Corporations

In addition to the standard C corporations, there are subchapter S corporations, which are semicorporate bodies, that limit an owner's liability while still allowing a pass-through of business losses to the personal income statements of the owners, founders, and others. Subchapter S refers to the section of the 1958 IRS code that describes the way the corporation will be taxed.

The number of stockholders is limited to 35, and corporate income (or loss) is allowed to be passed directly to the stockholders. There is no corporate tax. The IRS has specific time requirements for filing, and some states do not recognize the tax aspects of the Subchapter S category. Check out these things for your state. Your attorney can help you. In a subchapter S corporation, you cannot have any corporate stockholders, partnership(s) stockholders, and trusts as investors. Thus most S corporations lose their S status when venture capital firms invest.

You will be required to supply each of your stockholders with an "K-1" tax report by April 15 of each year. You must follow a calendar tax year with few exceptions. You can drop your S corporation status if you find there are tax advantages to being a regular corporation, but timing is important.

Protect Yourself

If you don't use a good lawyer to help structure your business, you probably won't have a plan to handle **contingencies,** and unforeseen events can take you by surprise. If Paul Webber had used his imagination to look ahead, his story might have turned out differently.

A Partner's Unforeseen Death

Paul Webber was a software game developer when he met Gerry Dominic. Gerry was a likable woman with experience in designing game software and a dynamite salesperson. They got together and formed "Gamestar."

Contingencies Steps taken to protect one against unforeseen future events

Their first year was okay—they netted over $40,000 apiece—and their second year was looking even better.

By May of their second year, their projections told them they could make $100,000 each before the end of the summer. They thought it felt great to have cash, and to celebrate, they went out to dinner.

Gerry passed out and was pronounced dead by the paramedics. At 32 years old, Gerry Dominic was dead of a heart attack. Two weeks after the funeral, Paul was on the phone with a customer when Gerry's widower, John, walked in. John had just inherited Gerry's half of the business.

Paul didn't like John being his partner but there was nothing he could do. He knew he would have to break his back to teach him the business. Game software was fast track and competitive—it changed before you could take a breath—and John would have to learn an awful lot in a short time.

Paul was a good guy, so he tried. The first week, he was extra tired because he was handling his own customers while also spending long hours trying to teach John the business. The second week, two of Paul's customers kept on hold defected to a competitor. Paul heard about it through the grapevine. The third week, the company almost ran out of cash, and Paul had to dump in $5,000 from his personal account to keep suppliers happy.

Another problem was that John wasn't learning the business. He was getting in Paul's hair, and was spending money. John wasn't able to hold up his end, and there was no improvement in sight.

Paul hung on for a couple more weeks. Then he did the only thing he could do for his own survival: He took what customers he had left and rented an office six blocks away and tried to keep going. He figured he had paid his dues to Gerry. He hoped Gerry understood.

Buy–Sell Agreements

Many small businessowners ignore the need for buy–sell agreements, or having a will drawn up. They keep putting if off. A buy–sell agreement would have solved Paul's problems after Gerry's death.

When forming your partnership, one of the major contingencies to consider is the **dissolution of the partnership.** Partnerships can end due to death, illness, divorce, lack of interest, financial or philosophical differences, or desire for a change in lifestyle. Protect your business, yourself, and your loved ones.

These agreements are often funded by a key man life insurance policy on the owners, so that if one dies, the business or other owners can collect the life insurance policy's proceeds and use those funds to buy out the deceased's interest in the business. Otherwise, surviving family members might find it very difficult to sell the interest in the business they inherit, except at a give-away price.

For dissolving the partnership under other circumstances, your buy–sell agreement should include who will evaluate the business and how payment will be made by the remaining partners and over what time period. As your business grows and changes, you will want to reevaluate your agreement.

When partners split up, and most eventually do, a buy–sell agreement keeps the dissolution out of court. Think of it as a prenuptial agreement.

The few thousand dollars you may spend in legal fees to draw up a buy–sell agreement and the key man insurance premiums are probably two of the best investments you and your partners will ever make.

Protect Your Intangible Assets

Copyrights, patents, and trademarks are important elements of your business. Without protecting them, you may (1) lose your business, (2) your ideas may be

Dissolution of a partnership The separation of partners, an eventuality that needs to be prepared for with intricate planning and much thought

stolen, and/or (3) your products may be copied. The following material on patents, trademarks, and copyrights is published by permission from the copyright holder: Knobbe, Martens, Olson, and Bear. Because Intellectual Property laws are subject to change, you should consult with your Intellectual Property counsel rather than relying on this material for legal advice.

Ten Things You Should Know to Protect Your Inventions

1. What Is a Patent?

A patent is a right granted to inventors by the government to exclude others from making, selling, offering for sale, using or importing an invention. The U.S. Government has issued over 5,000,000 patents during the past 200 years. These patents cover many types of inventions and discoveries, including machines, compositions of matter, methods, computer software, plants, microorganisms and designs. Three types of patents are available in the United States. The first, called a utility patent, covers inventions and discoveries, which are defined in the claims of the patent. A utility patent expires 20 years from the day a regular patent application is filed for the invention. In addition to the claims, a utility patent must include a written description of the invention and drawings, where applicable. A second type of patent, a design patent, gives the patent owner the right to exclude others from the nonfunctional, ornamental designs shown and claimed in the patent. This type of patent expires 14 years from the date it issues. The third type of patent is a plant patent, which gives the patent owner the right to exclude others from asexually reproducing a patented plant, or from selling or using an asexually reproduced patented plant. Plants that are sexually reproduced, i.e. through seeds, can be protected under separate, non-patent protection available under the Plant Variety Protection Act.

2. What Is the Test for Getting a Patent?

To obtain a utility patent, the invention defined in the patent claims must be new and nonobvious to a person of ordinary skill in the field of the invention. Many patents are for combinations of previously existing parts combined in a new, nonobvious ways to achieve improved results. A design patent requires a new, nonfunctional, ornamental design which is nonobvious to an ordinary designer in the field of the invention. In all cases, the initial evaluation and patentability decision will be made by an Examiner at the United States Patent and Trademark Office. Only the first and original inventor(s) may obtain a valid patent. Thus, you cannot obtain a patent in the U.S. for an invention you saw overseas because you are not the first or the original inventor. Similarly, someone who sees your invention cannot obtain a valid patent on it because that person is not the first or original inventor. But someone else could improve your invention, and patent the improvement. It typically takes about one year from filing the U.S. application before the Examiner sends the initial evaluation of patentability, although the process can be expedited with additional effort and cost.

3. What Is a Patentability Search?

When a U.S. patent application is filed, the Patent Office will conduct a search of the patents on file in the U.S. Patent and Trademark Office in Washington, D.C., as well as a smaller selection of foreign patents and non-patent references. Inventors can have a similar patentability search conducted in order to better evaluate the cost and probability of obtaining patent protection for their invention. Evaluating patentability search results is complex, requiring not only an understanding of the pertinent technology but also of patent law. The U.S. Patent Office tests and authorizes persons with appropriate technical backgrounds to file and prosecute patent matters before the Patent Office. You should consider contacting a registered patent attorney authorized to practice before the U.S. Patent and Trademark Office to assist with your evaluation.

4. What Is a Patent Notice?

A product or accompanying literature is typically marked with a patent notice such as "Patent 5,000,000" or "Pat. No. 5,000,000" when the product, or the method used to produce the product, is patented. Marking the patent number gives notice of the patent rights to potential infringers. The term: "Patent Pending" means a patent has been applied for, but has not yet issued.

5. When Must I Apply for a Patent?

An application for a patent must be filed in the United States within one year of the first date that the invention is (1) disclosed in a printed publication, (2) publicly used, or (3) offered for sale. In most foreign countries a patent must be filed before any public disclosure is made anywhere in the world. The rules for determining when an invention is publicly disclosed, used, or offered for sale are complex, and you should seek the advice of a patent attorney, if you have a question in this regard. By treaty with most, but not all, foreign countries, if a U.S. application is filed before any public disclosure is made, a foreign patent application may be filed up to one year after the U.S. filing date. Thus, if a U.S. patent application is filed before any public disclosure of the invention, the option to pursue foreign patent rights in many foreign countries is preserved for one year. Filing a U.S. patent application after a public disclosure, however, usually prevents filing in most foreign countries.

Recent amendments to the patent laws created a "provisional patent application" that enables an informal and less expensive filing to preserve patent rights for 12 months. It also extends the term of the patent one year. The provisional application is not examined and lapses after 12 months. Accordingly, a regular patent application must be filed within those 12 months in order to claim the benefit of the provisional application's filing date and to have the patent claims examined and issued.

6. What Is a World-Wide Patent?

There is no single, world-wide patent. Each country has different laws. Thus, a patent covers only the country or countries issuing the patent. For example, a U.S. patent can prevent an infringing product which is made overseas from being sold in the U.S., but will not prevent it from being sold in a foreign country. There are several international treaties which enable much of the patent prosecution to be consolidated for many countries, provided there was no public disclosure before the U.S. application was filed. Ultimately, however, the patent application must be translated and filed in each country where a patent is sought. The Patent Cooperation Treaty allows the additional cost of translating and filing in each foreign country to be delayed for up to 33 months from the U.S. filing date. During this 33 month period, it is often possible to test the market for the product and better judge the potential benefits of pursuing foreign patent protection.

7. Does a Patent Guarantee My Right to Sell My Product?

A patent gives its owner the right to exclude others from practicing the patented invention for the duration of the patent. It does not give the owner the right to make the patented invention. It is thus possible to have an improved and patented product that infringes a prior patent. For example, one person obtains a patent for a chair. Later, a second person obtains a patent for a rocking chair. The first person could stop the second person from selling rocking chairs because they incorporate the original chair and, thus, infringe the first person's patent.

8. What Is an Infringement Study?

An infringement study determines whether an unexpired patent has claims that might encompass a product or method which is being made, used or sold without authorization by the patent owner. If it is determined that a product or method may infringe someone else's patent, the design may be altered to avoid infringement, or a license may be negotiated with the patent owner.

Infringement studies require an ability to understand and apply the pertinent technology to the applicable patent law.

You should consider contacting an experienced patent attorney for such infringement studies. If a defendant is found guilty of willfully infringing another's U.S. patent, the court can treble the damage award and require the payment of the patent owner's attorneys' fees. Thus, questions of patent infringement should not be taken lightly.

9. Are Patents Worth the Costs?

For many years, courts often held patents invalid or not infringed, making it difficult to enforce patents. That changed dramatically with the creation of a single Court of Appeals which now decides the appeals from all patent cases throughout the United States. Patent law is now applied much more uniformly. A presumption of patent validity is being upheld, fewer patents are invalidated, and more patents are found infringed. Patents can be a significant source of income. Texas Instruments Inc. is reported as having received $600 million dollars in patent royalties over a four-year period.

Polaroid's lawsuit against Eastman Kodak shut down Kodak's entire instant-camera facility, and the damages awarded were nearly a billion dollars. The bottom line is that patents are now easier to enforce.

While that is good for patent owners, it also means that those accused of patent infringement must take prompt steps to minimize their exposure.

10. Where Can I Get More Information on Patents?

Additional information on patents may be obtained from the U.S., Patent and Trademark Office, Washington, D.C., 20231. Patents from 1970s on are accessible over the Internet from the U.S. Patent Office and from IBM. Patent Depository Libraries containing the text of many of the over 5,000,000 issued U.S. patents are available in major libraries.

Ten Things You Should Know to Protect Your Artwork, Ads, Writings and Software

1. What Is a Copyright?

Copyright exists in any original "expression" of an idea that is fixed in any physical medium such as paper, electronic tapes or floppy discs. Copyrights cover such diverse things as art, songs, technical and architectural drawings, books, computer programs and advertisements. Copyright protects only the expression, not the idea itself; it does not protect facts, short phrases or slogans.

2. What Protection Does a Copyright Give?

Copyright protection encompasses a bundle of exclusive rights which include: (1) the right to reproduce the work; (2) the right to make derivative works; (3) the right to distribute copies by sale, lease or rental; (4) the right to publicly perform certain works such as plays or audiovisual works; and (5) the right to publicly display certain works such as pictorial or sculptural works.

These rights may be licensed or transferred together or separately. For example, an author may grant a book company the rights to reproduce a book, may grant a movie studio the rights to make a movie derived from the book, and may grant foreign distribution rights to other companies.

3. How Long Does a Copyright Last?

U.S. Copyright protection for works created after January 1, 1978, will last for the life of the author plus 50 years after his death. If the work was created for an employer by an employee within the scope of his or her employment, the copyright protection will last for 75 years from the date of first publication, or 100 years from the date of creation, whichever is shorter.

If a U.S. work was created before January 1, 1978, and the copyright was not forfeited so as to place the work in the public domain, then the copyright can last for a total of 75 years, provided that any necessary renewals are made in a timely manner. Determining precisely when the term of the copyright ends, and who owns any renewal rights, are complex matters for which legal advice should be sought.

4. Can I Copyright Factual Information?

Compilations of factual data, like names or part numbers, may be copyrightable, but the protection is limited to such things as the selection and arrangement of the information. Facts by themselves cannot be protected by copyright, even if considerable time and expense went into compiling the facts. In appropriate cases, trade secret protection may be available for the factual information.

5. If I Change 10%, Can I Use Copyrighted Works?

If the portion taken is the heart of the copyrighted work, or from a widely recognized portion of the work, then infringement can exist even though less than 10% of the copyrighted work is taken. The test for copyright infringement is whether the accused work is copied from, and "substantially similar" to, the copyrighted work. Thus, there is no "rule" or fixed amount with respect to the portion of a work which one must change in order to avoid infringement.

6. Must Copyrights Be Registered?

Under current law, a copyright need not be registered until a U.S. citizen wants to file a lawsuit against an infringer. Registration, however, offers the copyright holder some significant advantages. For example, if a work is registered before an infringement commences, then the infringer may be liable for statutory damages up to $100,000 for each copyright that is infringed, and may also have to pay the attorneys fees incurred by the copyright owner in the lawsuit.

7. Do I Need a Copyright Notice?

For U.S. works first published after March 1, 1989, a copyright notice is not necessary to maintain copyright rights. But using a copyright notice makes it difficult for other people to claim that they are "innocent" infringers who were misled by the absence of a copyright notice.

For U.S. works first published between 1978 and 1989, the omission of copyright notice from published works could result in the loss of copyright rights unless certain steps were taken in a timely manner. For U.S. works first published before 1978, omission of copyright notice from published works usually resulted in the loss of any copyright protection.

A copyright notice consists of the copyright symbol c, the year a work is first published and the name of the copyright owner, e.g., © 1996 Knobbe, Martens, Olson & Bear, LLP. If a sound recording is copyrighted, use R along with the first publication date and owner. If the copyrighted material is revised, add the year of the revision to the copyright notice. It is also advisable to add "All Rights Reserved."

8. Do I Own Copyrights I Pay Others to Create?

You probably do not own the copyright in material you pay independent contractors to prepare, unless you have a written agreement transferring the ownership of any copyrights.

While a business usually owns the copyrights in works created by full time employees within the scope of their employment, the business has only limited rights to use copyrightable works created by independent contractors. Ownership of works created by employees, but not in their normal course of employment, varies with the facts of each case.

Ownership issues are often complex. An attorney should be consulted on such issues.

9. Do Foreign Countries Protect Copyrights?

The United States has long been a member of the Universal Copyright Convention through which copyright protection may be obtained in many foreign countries. In 1988, the United States joined the Berne Convention through which copyright protection may be obtained in the vast majority of foreign countries.

Obtaining and enforcing copyrights in foreign countries requires complying with the laws and treaties of each individual country. An attorney knowledgeable in copyright law should be consulted about any specific needs.

10. Where Can I Get More Information on Copyrights?

Information on copyright registrations may be obtained from the Register of Copyrights, Library of Congress, in Washington, D.C.

Ten Things You Should Know to Protect Your Product and Business Names

1. What is a Trademark?

A trademark is usually a brand name for a product. However , it can be a word, phrase, logo, design, or virtually anything which is used to identify its owner's product and distinguish it from competitors' products. CHEVROLET ®, "Ford has a better idea," and the logo ⮑ are trademarks.

A trademark represents the goodwill and reputation of a product and its source. Its owner has the right to prevent others from trading on that goodwill by using the same or a similar products in a way that is likely to cause confusion as to the source, origin or sponsorship of the products.

A service mark is just like a trademark, except it is used to identify and distinguish services rather than products. SEARS ® is a service mark for retail store services.

The terms trademark or "mark" are often used interchangeably to refer to either a trademark or service mark.

2. How Should a Mark Be Used?

If used incorrectly the rights to a mark may be lost, allowing anyone to use the mark. For example, these rights can be lost if the mark becomes the generic name for the product. Because competitors need to use generic words to describe their products, no one can own trademark rights to generic terms. Kerosene, cornflakes, and nylon were once trademarks, but are now generic names.

To prevent loss of trademark or service mark rights, the generic name for the product should appear after the mark, and the mark should appear visually different from the surrounding text. Use different type size, type style, color, or quotation marks for the trademark or service mark, as in **KODAK** ® cameras, AST ® computers, or "Carl's Jr. ®" restaurant services. You may also use an asterisk (*) after a mark where the asterisk refers to a footnote explaining the ownership of a mark.

Marks should be used only as proper adjectives, and never as nouns or verbs.

Referring to a XEROX ® brand copier is fine, but it is improper to say you "bought a XEROX" or that you want to "XEROX a paper."

If a mark is registered with the U.S. Patent and Trademark Office, then the federal registration symbol ® should be used next to the mark, such as **AST** ®. If the mark is not federally registered, the letters TM may be used to indicate a trademark, or SM to indicate a service mark.

3. What Is a Trade Name?

A trade name is the name of a business. Unlike trademarks, a trade name can be used as a noun, and is not required to be followed by generic terms.

It is permissible to use all or a portion of a trade name as a trademark or service mark. While "XEROX Corporation" is a trade name, **XEROX** ® is a trademark when used on copying machines, and may be a service mark when properly used with a copy machine rental, repair and maintenance services.

4. Does My Incorporation or Fictitious Business Name Statement Give Me the Right to Use My Name?

Most businesses form a corporation or file a Fictitious Business Name statement. Neither the Certificate of Incorporation nor the Fictitious Business Name statement gives a business the right to use in commerce a trade name which is likely to cause confusion with a trade name, trademark, or service mark that was previously used by someone else in the same area of trade.

The state or county agencies which issue the Certificates of Incorporation and Fictitious Business Name statements do not perform searches sufficient to ensure that your use would not infringe another's prior rights.

A court's determination of trademark infringement will override any Fictitious Business Name statement or any Certificate of Incorporation. Further, the legal test which the courts apply to determine the right to use trade name, trademarks or service marks does not require that the names or products be identical: it requires only enough similarity to cause a <u>likelihood</u> of confusion. Thus, neither of these filings means that you have the right to use your name in the advertising, promotion, or sale of goods or services.

5. Must Trademarks Be Registered?

There is no requirement to register your mark, but there are many advantages to doing so. A federally registered mark is presumed to be a valid mark and the registrant is presumed to have the exclusive right to use the trademark throughout the United States on the goods or services listed in the registration. After five years the registration may become incontestable, which significantly limits the grounds on which competitors can attach the registration. A registered mark will also be revealed in searches conducted by other businesses in their effort to avoid selecting marks which may conflict with those of others. Finally, only federally-registered trademarks or service marks may use the ® symbol in the U.S.

An application for a federal registration may be filed before a mark is ever actually used in commerce, provided that the applicant has a good faith intent to use the mark. Marks may also be registered in one or more of the 50 states, with the advantages of a state registration varying according to the laws of each state. A registration with the California Trademark Unit is usually obtained faster, cheaper, and with less difficulty than a federal registration. It also allows its owner to sue infringers under several California statutes which offer advantages not available under federal law. You must actually use a mark before applying for a California State trademark registration.

6. What Is a Trademark Search?

There are a number of professional search services which may be used to help insure that your mark or trade name does not conflict with the existing rights of another business. The goal of such searches is to avoid spending time, effort and money promoting a product name or business name only to have to change it at a later date because it conflicts with someone else's rights.

These searches are typically performed through attorneys because the search report is evaluated to determine whether there is an actual or potential conflict with another name or mark, and this evaluation depends upon the consideration of numerous legal factors and case-law decisions.

7. Is My Product's Shape or Packaging Protectable?

The non-functional features of a product's shape or packaging (its "trade dress") are being protected with ever-increasing frequency. The appearance of a "C" clamp, of Ruger's 22 caliber pistol, a fingernail polish bottle, and the red border and format of **TIME** ® magazine, have all been protected against look-alike competitive products. To help achieve this type of protection, non-functional and distinctive product features or packaging should be selected, and then promoted through "image advertising" so that customers recognize the product shape or packaging and associate it with a single source.

8. Can I Register My Trade Dress?

If your trade dress is non-functional, and is either inherently distinctive or has acquired customer recognition from sufficient promotion of the

International Intellectual Property Laws

Legal details are a concern to a growing number of U.S. exporters because of the increasing technological and informational content of our products. Before going abroad, you should be familiar with the appropriate patent, trademark, copyright, and licensing laws of the country. Use the Internet for your initial search and then work directly with international intellectual property attorneys. There are a number of ways of protecting your product in a foreign market, and each has its merits according to circumstance.

Patent laws vary from country to country and a few do not have patent laws. Keeping your trade secrets to yourself often works well overseas, except that others may be able to copy your product on the open market. For an entrepreneur, selling patent rights or granting licenses is often the best way to operate in a foreign market.

protectable features, it may be registered as a trademark. For example, the shape of the **WEBER** ® barbecue grill and the clear tip of a **SHAKESPEARE** ® fishing rod have been registered with the U.S. Patent and Trademark Office.

9. What about Protection in Foreign Countries?

Trademark owners who have not registered their marks in foreign countries may find that the mark has been appropriated by a third party who was the first to register in that country as the true owner of the mark, even if it is a pirate who saw the mark in the U.S. and appropriated it. This pirate may even be a trusted foreign distributor of the trademarked product.

Foreign pirates may be able to prevent the original U.S. owner of the mark from using it in one or more foreign countries. In some cases it may be possible to recover the mark, but the U.S. owner may face expensive litigation or exorbitant demands from the pirate.

Generally, if a U.S. product is sold overseas, care must be taken to ensure the U.S. federal registration symbol "®" is not used unless the mark is registered in the foreign country where the mark is used.

Some countries have both civil and criminal penalties for using the ® symbol with a mark not registered in that country. Improper use of the ® symbol may also make the mark unenforceable in some countries.

10. Where May I Get Information on Protecting Product & Business Names?

Information on trademarks may be obtained from the Trademark Unit of your Secretary of State's Office. Information on federal registrations may be obtained from the U.S. Patent and Trademark Office in Washington, D.C.

The assistance of an attorney experienced in trademark matters can help avoid problems before they arise.

SOURCE: Knobbe, Martens, Olson, and Bear.

▶ *Summary*

It is important that every entrepreneur be familiar with basic legal concepts, as well as with some of the special problems that can arise in particular areas of his or her business. Determining your legal form of business should be undertaken with the advice of your attorney, accountant, and business advisor. As you grow and change, you will need to continually reassess your decision.

Partnerships can be a rocky road. Evaluate your need for a partner and do not enter into a partnership without legal assistance.

Protecting yourself through copyrights, trademarks, and patents requires the assistance of intellectual property attorneys. You will be able to do a great deal of initial research utilizing data on the Internet. Due to the significance of these issues and the many nuances and complications, do not skimp on finding the best advice.

Think Points for Success

- We only remember what we want to. Get *everything* in writing.
- If your business is small and you like it that way, keep it simple—like your hobby.
- Most growth businesses need outside infusions of cash. Your business structure may hinder or enhance your ability to reach out for money.
- Don't pay Uncle Sam more than you have to and make sure you pay what is due. Have your accountant structure your business according to your needs.
- When you create corporate stock in your by-laws, think about creating at least ten times more than you intend to sell at start-up.
- Even if you incorporate, a banker may still want a personal guarantee for loans. And this guarantee may be in place for years to come.
- The increase of lawsuits should encourage most businesses to at least consider incorporating or establishing a limited liability company.

Key Points from Another View

Which Business Form Is Best for Your Family Business?
by Paul and Sarah Edwards

If you're working with your spouse or a family member, you might be wondering if you should go through the trouble and expense of forming a partnership or a corporation. The answer to this question depends on your own needs, the tax implications, and the laws in the state where you live. Here are the issues you may want to consider.

Your Own Needs

If your business started as a sole proprietorship and your spouse or a family member has decided to join your already ongoing concern, the easiest solution may be to simply hire your relative as an employee. Any salary you pay may be deductible as a business expense to you. In fact, hiring your children can prove to be a tax bonus, since their salaries are a deductible business expense to you while their earnings will in most cases be taxed at a lower rate than your own.

When hiring an employee, however, you will need to comply with many federal and state regulations on employees. This means two things:

1. If your business is home based and your city has a zoning code forbidding employees to work in your home, you could run into a problem if the employee is a family member other than your spouse or children.
2. When you become an employer, you must maintain payroll records and file and pay many tax items. For more information about payroll taxes, try Handling Your Payroll, or from the IRS website, visit Alternative Methods for Figuring Withholding.

All this record keeping can be a headache for some people, and if that's the case for you, it might be easier to have your spouse or family member work on a volunteer basis—without pay.

In some cases, however, the better choice is to make your spouse or family member a co-owner (partner) in your business, complete with a written partnership agreement. A partnership agreement and the Uniform Partnership Act provide both you and your relative with some form of protection in the event of a disagreement or dispute that might eventually force you to divide up the business.

Of course, if you've decided to form a C corporation, S corporation, or LLC, you won't have any choice about how you handle your spouse or family members who co-own the company with you. In using these forms of business, you still need to file papers with your state listing them as directors or officers of the company.

Tax Implications

There are specific tax implications to be aware of when a partnership or corporation is owned by members of the same family. For example, if you try to include your child as a partner in your family partnership with the intention of transferring a portion of the partnership income to him or her (thereby reducing all the partners' shares of income and hence their taxes), the current income tax laws dealing with children and earned income make this option less worthwhile. Such an outright transfer of partnership income to a child may arouse IRS scrutiny.

However, hiring your child is feasible and has some advantages as long as you pay him or her a "reasonable" wage for actual work done. In this way, your child's wages are deductible business expenses to your partnership, and the child's earnings will likely be taxed at a lower rate than your own. In addition, if your child becomes an employee in your business, he or she is entitled to open an IRA and put up to $2,000 in earned income per year toward his or her retirement. However, no business deduction is allowed to the partnership or a partner for any contribution you make toward your child's IRA.

There are also ways of setting up a limited partnership or LLC in such a way that your children, by working for the family business over a number of years, increase their percentage ownership by means of nontaxable "gifts" each year from parents, who continue to receive a steady stream of income until they formally retire from the business. The documents necessary to create such entities must comply strictly with the estate-planning provisions of the Internal Revenue Code and can be quite complex; usually you will need the assistance of a tax attorney who specializes in "succession planning" for small businesses.

Be aware that there are many special IRS regulations affecting family members who are owners/employees of a C or S corporation. These regulations are intended to prevent families from shifting expenses among family members to create losses (through making sales of corporate assets to one another at a so-called loss, or from taking a loan from their corporation at "special low" rates for example). In short, if you are choosing to start a C or S corporation that includes your spouse or other family members, be sure to see an accountant so you can properly plan how to best divide the ownership of the company.

Your State Laws

Spouses have a legal interest in the business matters of their mates. This is especially true in the "community property states" of Arizona, California, Idaho, Nevada, New Mexico, Texas, Washington, and Wisconsin, where each spouse automatically owns one-half of all community property. This is also true in those common-law states in which divorce proceedings require an equitable division of property. In some states, personal agreements between spouses as to how they will divide their interests in a family business upon divorce or separation are not enforceable, and the family court is required to divide the business ownership based on the state's rules of equitable distribution. This does not preclude you from writing a partnership agreement with your spouse to use as the basis for your working relationship, however, if you desire. In fact, we think it can be a good idea.

Paul and Sarah Edwards have written eight books and hundreds of articles covering a range of home-office an self-employment issues. They have also produced and broadcast their show "Working From Home" on the Business News Network since 1988. You can learn more about Paul and Sarah by visiting their Website **paulandsarah.com.** This tip came from their book: *Teaming Up: The Small Business Guide to Collaborating.*

SOURCE: **www.quicken.com**

Building A Winning Team

Entrepreneurial Links

Books

Smart Hiring, Second Edition, Robert W. Wendover, 1998.
Leader of the Future, Peter Drucker, 1997.
Team-Building Kit, Harrington, Mackin, 1993.

Websites

www.nolo.com
www.wageweb.com
www.cnnfn.com/smbusiness

Associations/Organization

Information Technology Training Association, www.itta.org
Internal Revenue Services, www.irs.gov
National Association of Professional Employer Organizations,
www.napeo.org

Publications

Executive Excellence
Training & Development Magazine
Technical Training Magazine

Additional Entrepreneurial Insights

Managing People is Like Herding Cats, Warren Bennis, 1997
21st Century Leadership, Dialogues with 100 Top Leaders, Lynee Joy
McFarland, Larry E. Senn, and John R. Childress, 1998.
*301 Great Management Ideas from America's Most Innovative Small
Companies,* Bradford W. Ketchum, Tom Peters, and Leslie
Brokaw, 1995.

Learning Objectives

- Accept that you can't do everything well.
- Understand the importance of balance to the survival of your business.
- Explore new ways of putting together a team including the virtual organization.
- Look back and see if there's anyone who could work with you in this venture.
- Write a profile of the founding team.
- Review utilizing independent contractors and part-time employees.
- Learn about employee leasing.
- Explore hiring practices and setting salaries.
- Locate a mentor to help guide you.
- Use a personality profile system to identify who you are and the types of people you need for balance.

Building a winning team can be one of the most enjoyable tasks you face. To do this, you must first look at yourself objectively, and then build a team that will fulfill business, psychological, and financial needs. That's what the successful entrepreneur does. Chapter 11 will show you various ways to build a winning team.

You will want to build a team composed of people who have a common purpose and specific goals. In a small venture, it is important to share the rewards of success with your team players. As you grow, consider stock ownership for your employees. In good economic times, stock ownership can be a key to keeping your best and brightest. As the leader of your company, you must represent and live by the mission you have set forth for your firm.

It is fun being an entrepreneur. You're on your own, doing your own thing, running your own show. And one of the toughest things you have to admit is that you can't perform all business tasks with the same success. Once you know where you need help, today's options to find assistance are vast.

We touch on how to build a team and stress the importance of internal understanding for a stronger team. Balance, proportion, the right materials, and the structural forces of personality—all are equally important in building a winning team.

The Founding Team

Your business plan reader will be most impressed by a founding team with industry-related experience and complementary skills as well as a record of achievement. Investors want you to learn on *your* dime and time not theirs. They will be evaluating your background in depth. You will need to prove to investors that your team has the experience, ability, and pedigree to ensure success. Information about the founding team is the most-read section of any business plan.

The following management team examples are not full-blown résumés, but brief bios that demonstrate that the founder or founders understand what they are doing. Vendors, bankers, investors, and teammates want to know about the founders.

Manufacturing Examples

Bill Jones and Lee Gray have spent over 11 years in the fitness business, Bill as a product designer and Lee as a sales representative. Bill developed and patented the Velopedical, an exercise bicycle that burns energy faster than a Stair Climber, and has sold over 10,000 units. Lee has been in the top 10 percent of the sales force of Acme Exercise Equipment for the past four years and has been personally responsible for over $8 million in sales.

Bill has hired Lee to be Vice President of Sales. A recently retired manufacturing manager of Sport Tech, Ed Riggs, has been hired to serve as the Vice President of Manufacturing. Ed has an Operations Management degree from Purdue University and has managed a light assembly operation for more than 20 years. He also teaches quality management classes part-time.

Jan Wilkes, a retired CPA with manufacturing experience, has agreed to serve as CFO on a part-time basis.

Service Example

Dorothy Foltz served as Executive Chef of the Carlton Hotel, has won many awards, and is well-known in the community.

Ms. Foltz trained in Paris at the Culinary Institute and is certified as a Master Chef. She will supervise the kitchen. Ms. Foltz owns a majority interest in the limited liability company.

Leslie Perk was, until December, a training manager for the French Connection restaurant chain. Ms. Perk will act as general manager under the direction of Ms. Foltz.

Pat Watter is the minority investor. Ms. Watter intends to retain her position as Food and Beverage Manager of Crooked Stick Country Club, but will be available as needed to monitor inventory and accounting activities.

Internet Example

Nancy Hipp (a graphic artist) of Indianapolis, Indiana, will develop the Internet site for a children's bookstore.

Cindy Barn, who recently retired from a management job in New York, will serve as the fulfillment manager for all Internet orders. She will continue living in New York.

Three former teachers—Pat Tran in Arizona, Casey Duke in Florida, and Troy High in Iowa—will answer all customer inquiries and review all new books.

No matter how you begin your business, at some point in time you will find yourself needing the assistance of others. The above examples illustrate solutions found to round out a team. As you look to fulfill your business needs, remember to find other people who will balance your skills and personality.

In one firm, the owner, Sam, had poor customer-relation skills; he scared off all but the heartiest customers and employees. His brother was one of those employees and realized that the business was headed for disaster. Taking a chance, he approached Sam. They agreed—the front office and customers should be off limits for Sam. Several months later the business was back on track and the employees were relieved and much happier.

Do what you do best and hire the rest!

Now let's discuss various ways to get the help you need to grow your business.

World Trade Institute's School of International Trade and Commerce

Through Pace University's online education program, **www.paceonline.edu**, the World Trade Institute offers an array of courses for exporters and importers. Below is a list of their offerings:

- Introduction to World Trade
- Import Regulations and Documentation
- Customs Entry Preparation Workshop
- Customs Law Issues for Importers
- Export/Import Letters of Credit
- Customhouse Brokers License Preparation
- Importing Techniques
- Import Transportation Management
- Import Techniques

These courses allow one to gather a thorough knowledge of importing and exporting techniques. If you are not prepared to take courses, we suggest you mine Internet sites and the myriad of books that cover international business. As we have discussed previously, the federal government and many state offices can provide you with detailed information and leads.

The Virtual Organization

The virtual organization has become a buzzword. It is often called a virtual company or virtual corporation.

A virtual organization can allow the little guy to compete with the larger firm without sacrificing scale, speed, or agility. It is much like forming an all-star team to exploit a market opportunity.

Let's back up and examine how the old motion picture studios used to work. They owned real estate, studios, equipment, performers, and a lot of other fixed assets with which they cranked out movies both good and bad. Most of the old giants have gone the way of the dinosaurs.

In their place are project teams of highly creative people hired "just in time to make a great picture" who then disband until the next opportunity presents itself. They rent everything they need and are never left with any overhead between projects.

An advertising agency may consist of a single person who presents the client with an idea. Once the idea is approved, the single person assembles graphic designers, copywriters, photographers, models, performers, and media experts to produce the package. The virtual ad agency has no overhead but can bring together the best talent to provide the client with a high-quality campaign at less cost.

A general contractor pulls together a team of subcontractors who can be trusted to build a high-quality building. If the job goes well, there will be other opportunities for this team of specialists.

Suppose you have an idea for a new widget. You develop a prototype, demonstrate it at a trade show, and take orders. Why build a factory or hire workers? You can find other partners who can do almost anything. The big firms call this *outsourcing*. By using SIC codes and industry sources, you can almost always find assemblers, packagers, box makers, food mixers, toolmakers, public warehouses, sales agents, and whatever else, just as you need them.

At another level, consider as partners firms with special capabilities that will share your risk in bringing a product or service to market. These partners are often called *strategic partners*. A team that includes retailers or end users may solve your marketing problems.

A sales agent who represents paper mills gathers specifications from retail stores in order to supply private-label napkins, toilet paper, and allied paper products to be packaged with the retailer's name. The price is negotiated with the supplier, and the agent pockets a commission.

A local printer discovered that her sales ability exceeded her ability to produce. She redefined herself as a "Printer's Broker" and used her knowledge to select from a wide variety of printers available for the most appropriate product. She sold her own small shop to an employee and increased her income several times over by providing assistance to customers who knew little about printing. Her virtual organization had just-in-time access to over 1000 experienced printers.

With continued corporate downsizing comes mushrooming opportunities to alert "virtual organization" entrepreneurs. The benefits include:

- having access to the skills and experience of proven experts in their field.
- paying only for services needed.
- obtaining variable production quantities.
- gaining higher reliability.
- achieving better quality and consistency.
- having lower internal developmental costs.
- getting a customer who is pre-sold.
- maintaining flexibility to instantly address new market opportunities.

The virtual organization needs to be customer-driven and opportunity-focused. There must be agreement and a shared vision among all the participants.

Partners and opportunities must be selected with care. Performance standards are critical. The virtual organization might exist for weeks or years—and then, when the opportunity has been fully exploited, be prepared to disband quickly. Action Step 46 will help you explore the virtual organization alternative.

Although it is wise to build a web of complementary business associations to assure the success of the virtual company, the day may come when you need an employee—or several.

Many people misunderstand the rules on independent contractors. If you tell the worker when to start and stop work, and if you supply the tools or office equipment, you have an employee. On the other hand, if the work assignment is task-driven, if the worker sets his or her own hours, if you pay by the job and not by the hour, and if most of the work takes place away from your office using the workers resources, then you may have an independent contractor relationship. Most real estate agents working on commission qualify as independent contractors.

You can save a lot of money if your workers are independent contractors—no Social Security, Medicare, worker's compensation insurance, health care insurance, retirement benefits, paid holidays, vacations, sick days, and so on. Most employers can find workers who will work without mandated benefits—but sooner or later they will get hurt, apply for unemployment, or attempt to collect Social Security benefits. When they do, the government will come back to the employer with high fines and penalties. Review Independent Contractor rules with a CPA because the IRS rules are rigid.

Be aware that state laws may differ from federal rules.

Make sure your independent contractors carry their own insurance, if they don't have their own liability coverage you'll be responsible under *your* worker's

Action Step 46

Consider a Virtual Organization

Make a list of people or firms who might assist your efforts on an as-needed basis. To keep your overhead to an absolute minimum, ask and shop around, and look for those people who share your vision. Compile your list using a pencil so you make adjustments as you continue to learn.

▶ **Action Step 47**

Brainstorm Your Ideal Team

What do you need to win at the game of small business? Money, of course. And energy, tremendous energy. (You've got that or you wouldn't have read this far.) You also need footwork, a terrific idea, intensity, the ability to concentrate, a sense of industry and thrift, and the curiosity of a Sherlock Holmes.

And you need people. People to support your effort. People to balance your skills. People to take up the slack. People to help you with tasks you find distasteful or don't understand.

So analyze yourself first. What do you like? What are you good at? What do you hate? What does your business need that you cannot provide yourself? Who can fill that need for you?

Get started on building your ideal team.

After you've taken the time to do some research into your own personality (your strengths and weaknesses), you'll begin to get the feel for what kind of help you need in your venture. Is there anyone out there who can balance some of your skills?

Now that you have the idea of balance firmly in mind, network your vendors and your competitors for potential team members. Whenever you meet someone new, keep asking yourself: "How would this person work out in my new business?"

List people or firms that could become part of a virtual organization, and independent contractors or strategic partners.

Keep looking for your future team with new eyes.

compensation. If a window washer being paid cash in your store falls through your windows, guess who pays!

Easy Answer to Independent Contractor/Employee Question

The 14-point test to differentiate between employees and independent contractors no longer is needed. IRS now issues a one-page document titled "Independent Contractor of Employee" with three so-called safe harbor requirements, all of which must be met. They are: the employee treats certain workers as independent contractors because that's how it's done in the industry where the company operates, the contractor does not perform the same tasks as regular employees; and the employer faithfully files Form 1099-MISC reporting compensation earned by an independent contractor whenever in excess of $600 a year. Employees prefer the independent contractor classification because then they do not have to withhold income taxes or pay workers' comp premiums, unemployment taxes and Social Security and Medicare taxes.

SOURCE: Giftware News, 1998.

For further hints on hiring entrepreneurial employees, check out the Key Points article at the end of this chapter.

Action Step 47 uses the idea of balance to scout potential team members. If you're able to imagine how each candidate will work in your new venture, you'll be well on your way to building a winning team.

Building a dream . . . working 60–80 hours . . . spending more time together than with your family . . . the reality of a new venture team working together. How do you keep the employer–employee relationship? It is one of the toughest parts of the job for many an entrepreneur. To understand the potential pitfalls and to explore ways to avoid problems review the following advice.

Boss vs. Buddy

It's human nature to want people to like you, but separating the roles of boss and buddy can help head off management headaches.

That doesn't mean you need to chuck compassion when you become a manager. Warmth and openness are valuable elements of an effective working relationship. Nor do you need to adopt an aloof attitude that says, "I'm above all the grunt work that I hired you to do." New companies especially are finding that nonhierarchical structures where managers and employees work together can be productive and morale-boosting.

"Those issues are separate from treating people differently based on how well you get along with them," contends Susan Stites, a human resources consultant with Management Allegories, Madison, Wisconsin.

The two foremost risks of befriending employees are the potential conflict of interest (and discomfort level) in giving friends job performance feedback, and the perception of unfairness.

The latter pitfall surfaces regularly when a work group plans after-hour outings or social gatherings around activities some employees aren't interested in or can't join in. For instance, some employees may have family commitments that limit their spare time.

Thus a good rule of thumb is to plan social activities that everyone enjoys at a time when everyone can attend.

Another issue is the interplay of personalities in the workplace. Effective managers need to get along with people with varied approaches to life and work. Stites cites the example of companies that suffer when the presidents "hire themselves." They end up with a staff that supports their strengths—and magnifies their weaknesses.

"A manager needs to be a role model in accepting diversity in work and thinking styles and in capitalizing on that diversity," she suggests. Building on everyone's strengths is a foolproof recipe for success and for turning personality differences into complementary assets.

To learn more about personalities in the workplace, Stites suggests that managers look into seminars on personality profiling by Myers-Briggs, Social Styles and DISC. They can be expensive, but are well worth the money, even for managers in small companies, she says.

Good books include "Personal Styles and Affective Performance" (based on the Social Styles program) by David W. Merrill and Roger H. Reid and "People Smart" (based on the DISC program) by Tony Alessandra and Michael J. O'Connor.

"Coach" or "mentor" may be a better title than "friend" to strive for when you become a boss. "There's been a lot of recent emphasis on those terms," Stites adds, "but I think good business leaders—even back in the '20s when everything was autocratic—have always been good mentors."

Your business experience may be a valuable guide for new owners. Get or give advice in the Workshop Forum.

SOURCE: **www.nfibonline.com**

The First Employees

When to hire your first employee is a question often asked. You may require people immediately, but many small firms do well using part-time or temporary workers until the owners have a strong feel for what needs to be done and who is best suited to do the job.

If the first worker needs to provide a high level of technical skill and/or is a person who can take your organization to the next level, you may need to provide an extra carrot, such as profit sharing or stock options. A lot of talented workers prefer the entrepreneurial adventure to big business bureaucracy and will work for less if they share your vision and passion for entrepreneuring.

As you continue to add people, you must understand that competence is not the only criteria to consider. You are assembling a venture team that wants to see growth and prosperity as much as you do. It is impossible to grow and expand until you have people who are not only capable but also motivated to ensure success.

The quest for new employees begins with a written job description. You may not find a perfect fit so don't fence yourself in with too many specifications. Define the duties to be performed and the skills needed to perform them. A small business cannot afford a misfit or an unproductive person. If one person in a four-person organization doesn't work, you have lost 25 percent of your efficiency. Hiring and keeping good people is a critical factor in a firm's success.

If experience is not critical, consider vocational, trade, and professional schools. Local colleges and high schools have placement offices. There are many programs offered through social agencies that might subsidize the training of workers.

Be prepared: you *will* have employee turnover in the beginning. Either they will quit or you will decide to terminate their employment. Suggestion for restaurants and retail—over hire for opening.

Stay Out of Court

Review Table 11.1 and Ask the Right Questions on page 223 before conducting any interviews.

Table 11.1

Legal & Illegal Pre-Employment Inquiries

Copyright © Nolo Press, 1998
http://www.nolo.com

The chart below outlines the type of information you can ask for in applications and during job interviews as specified in federal laws. The chart may also be sufficient for complying with the laws of your state, but double check with your state's civil rights department to be sure.

Subject	Lawful Pre-employment Inquiries	Unlawful Pre-employment Inquiries
Name	Applicant's full name. Have you ever worked for this company under a different name? Is any additional information relative to a different name necessary to check work record? If yes, explain.	Original name of an applicant whose name has been changed by court order or otherwise. Is any additional information relative to a different name necessary to check work record? Applicant's maiden name.
Address or Duration of Residence	How long have you been a resident of this state or city?	
Birthplace		Birthplace of applicant. Birthplace of applicant's parents, spouse or other close relatives. Requirements that applicant submit birth certificate, naturalization or baptismal record.
Age	Are you 18 years old or older? This question may be asked only for the purpose of determining whether applicants are of legal age for employment.	
Religion or Creed		Inquiry into an applicant's religious denomination, religious affiliations, church, parish, pastor or religious holidays observed.
Race or Color		Complexion or color of skin.
Photograph		Any requirement for a photograph prior to hire.
Height		Inquiry regarding applicant's height.
Weight		Inquiry regarding applicant's weight.
Marital Status	Is your spouse employed by this employer?	Requirement that an applicant provide any information regarding marital status or children. Are you single or married? Do you have any children? Is your spouse employed? What is your spouse's name?
Gender		Mr., Miss or Mrs. or an inquiry regarding gender. Inquiry as to the ability to reproduce or advocacy of any form of birth control. Requirement that women be given pelvic examinations.
Disability		Inquiries regarding an individual's physical or mental condition which are not directly related to the requirements of a specific job and which are used as a factor in making employment decisions in a way which is contrary to the provisions or purposes of the Civil Rights Act.
Citizenship	Are you a citizen of the United States? If not a citizen of the United States, does applicant intend to become a citizen of the United States? If you are not a United States citizen, have you the legal right to remain permanently in the United States? Do you intend to remain permanently in the United States?	Questions below are unlawful unless asked as part of the federal I-9 process. Of what country are you a citizen? Whether an applicant is naturalized or a native-born citizen; the date when the applicant acquired citizenship. Requirement that an applicant produce naturalization papers or first papers.

Table 11.1

Legal & Illegal Pre-Employment Inquiries—cont'd

Subject	Lawful Pre-employment Inquiries	Unlawful Pre-employment Inquiries
Citizenship—cont'd	To avoid discrimination based on national origin, the questions above should be asked after the individual has been hired even if it is related to the federal I-9 process.	Whether applicant's parents or spouse are naturalized or native-born citizens of the United States: the date when such parent or spouse acquired citizenship.
National Origin	Inquiry into language applicant speaks and writes fluently.	
Education	Inquiry into the academic, vocational or professional education of an applicant and public and private schools attended.	Inquiry into applicant's lineage; ancestry; national origin; descent; parentage or nationality. Nationality of applicant's parents or spouse. Inquiry into how applicant acquired ability to read, write or speak a foreign language.
Experience	Inquiry into work experience. Inquiry into countries applicant has visited.	
Arrests	Have you ever been convicted of a crime? Are there any felony charges pending against you?	Inquiry regarding arrests which did not result in conviction. (Except for law enforcement agencies.)
Relatives	Names of applicant's relatives already employed by this company.	Address of any relative of applicant, other than address (within the United States) of applicant's father and mother, husband or wife and minor dependent children.
Notice in Case of Emergency	Name and address of nearest relative to be notified in case of accident or emergency.	Name and address of person to be notified in case of accident or emergency.
Organizations	Inquiry into the organizations of which an applicant is a member, excluding organizations the name or character of which indicates the race, color, religion, national origin, or ancestry of its members.	List all clubs, societies and lodges to which you belong.

Nolo Press: **www.nolo.com**

Ask the Right Questions

The trick is to use open-ended questions to get the applicant talking. Develop your own list of questions that are appropriate to the position you want to fill. Affirmative action laws make it important to ask each applicant the exact same questions. You might consider similar questions on an application form for screening purposes. The following questions will help get you started.

1. How did you prepare for this meeting?
2. What are some of the obstacles you have overcome?
3. Can you work independently without close supervision?
4. What gives you satisfaction in a job?
5. What do you like and dislike about this kind of work?
6. What have been your most pleasant work experiences?
7. Have you ever organized an event?
8. What did you like or dislike about your last job?
9. How well do you handle change and uncertainty?
10. Are you a team player?
11. How do you evaluate yourself?

A Team of Part-Timers

Charlene Webb has built a winning team of part-time employees.

After Charlene Webb sold her gourmet cookware shop, she opened a women's specialty store. The shop is small—about 2000 square feet—and is located in a neighborhood in an upscale community center of about 40,000 people.

Charlene discovered that her ideal employees were local women who were active in community life and who prefered to work only one day a week. Monday's help is a golfer whose country-club friends come in to visit and buy from her on her day of work. Tuesday the tennis player is on, and her friends have followed her to the store. Wednesday is the yacht club member; Thursday, a leader of hospital volunteers; Friday, a well-known club woman; and Saturday, an attorney's wife. All of them are friendly women who know a lot about fashion and have a lot of energy. They never tire from the routine.

Charlene, who writes a society column (as free PR) in the community newspaper, has positioned herself as a social force, and many women have come to view her shop as *the one* to buy from for formal events at the country club and the nearby Ritz Carlton Hotel.

Her part-time workers are not only an effective marketing tool; they also serve as local fashion consultants. They help Charlene make wise purchasing decisions and are valuable members of her team.

What Do Employees Really Cost?

If you plan on hiring individuals on an employee basis, consider *all* the costs associated with hiring, training, and retaining an employee.

- Ad placements (very expensive)
- Recruiting and hiring
- Salary
- Employment taxes—Social Security, Unemployment and Medicare
- Worker's Compensation Insurance
- Benefits—health, retirement, dental, vacation, sick leave
- Space, furniture, equipment
- Additional management time
- Any additional perks you might offer—child care, car allowance, etc.
- Training

It is estimated that each employee will cost you 130–200% of their salary. Employees in an entrepreneurial venture need to pull *more* than their own weight. Select wisely. If you find an excellent employee, encourage him or her to send their friends. For many companies, finding "friends of employees" is their main recruiting avenue.

For salary comparison information on the Internet click on the following two sources:

Recruitment Extra!
http://recruitmentextra.com/salarysurveys.html
Wage Web
www.wageweb.com

Maintaining Compliance

Ignorance is not an acceptable defense if you are charged with breaking labor laws. Check with all government agencies to be sure you do not overlook any legal requirements. The penalties for failure to comply may be very stiff. Many firms have lost their businesses for failure to comply.

Contact the following federal organizations to learn about your legal responsibilities:

- Occupational Safety and Health Administration (OSHA) **www.osha.gov**
- Equal Employment Opportunity Commission (EEOC), **www.eeoc.gov/smallbus.html**
- Department of Labor, **www.dol.gov**
- Internal Revenue Service (IRS), **www.irs.gov**
- U.S. Department of Justice, Americans with Disabilities, **800-514-0301, www.usdoj.gov/crt/ada**
- Immigration and Naturalization Service, **www.ins.usdoj.gov/employer/index.html**

In addition to the above federal offices, you will need to contact your state offices for further employment law information. Review the short description of selected employment statutes most applicable to new ventures below.

Also, check to see that all employees can legally work in the United States and have them fill out an Employment and Eligibility Verification Form (I-9 in Appendix B).

Know requirements for complying with the American with Disabilities Act before you complete your tenant improvements for your new office or retail complex. Be aware of all overtime laws and laws pertaining to employment of anyone under 18. Post a copy of the labor laws conspicuously—where they can be read by everyone. If you have even *one* non-English-speaking employee, also post the laws in that employee's language.

U.S. Department of Labor Statutes

The U.S. Department of Labor administers and enforces more than 180 federal laws. These mandates and the regulations that implement them cover many workplace activities for about ten million employers and 125 million workers.

Following is a brief description of the principal statutes most commonly applicable to businesses. *The intent is to acquaint you with the major labor laws and not to offer a detailed exposition of laws and regulations enforced by the Department of Labor. For the fuller requirements of these statutes, see information sources at www.dol.gov*

Wages and Hours

The Fair Labor Standards Act prescribes standards for wages and overtime pay, which affect most private and public employment. The act is administered by the Wage and Hour Division of the Employment Standards Administration. It requires employers to pay covered employees the federal minimum wage and overtime of one-and-one-half-times the regular wage. It prohibits certain types of work in an employee's home. It restricts the hours that children under 16 can work and forbids their employment in certain jobs deemed too dangerous. Wage and Hour Division also enforces the workplace provisions of the *Immigration and Nationality Act* that apply to aliens authorized to work in the U.S.

Workplace Safety and Health

The *Occupational Safety And Health Act* (OSH) is administered by the Occupational Safety and Health Administration (OSHA). Safety and health conditions in most private industries are regulated by OSHA or OSHA-approved state systems. Employers must identify and eliminate unhealthful or hazardous conditions; employees must comply with all rules and regulations that apply to their own workplace conduct. Covered employers are required to maintain safe and healthful work environments in keeping with requirements of the law. Effective OSHA safety and health regulations supersede others originally issued under these other laws: the *Walsh-Healey Act,* the *Services Contract Act,* the *Contract Work Hours and Safety Standards Act,* the *Arts and Humanities Act* and the *Longshore and Harbor Workers' Compensation Act.*

Pensions and Welfare Benefits

The *Employee Retirement Income Security Act (ERISA)* regulates employers who offer pension or welfare benefit plans for their employees. It preempts many similar state laws and is administered by the Pension and Welfare Benefits Administration (PWBA). Under the statute, employers must fund an insurance system to protect certain kinds of retirement benefits, with premium payments to the federal government's *Pension Benefit Guaranty Corp.* Pension plans must meet a wide range of fiduciary, disclosure and reporting requirements. Employee welfare plans must meet similar requirements. PWBA also administers reporting requirements for continuation of health-care provisions, required under the *Comprehensive Omnibus Budget Reconciliation Act of 1985 (COBRA).*

Unions and Their Members

The *Labor-Management Reporting and Disclosure Act* (also known as the *Landrum-Griffin Act*) deals with the relationship between a union and its members. It safeguards union funds, requires reports on certain financial transactions and administrative practices of union officials, labor consultants, etc. The act is administered by the Office of Labor-Management Standards which is part of the Employment Standards Administration.

IRS! YES the IRS!

For information to keep you in line with IRS regulations contact:

   800-829-3676 for publications

   800-829-1040 to talk with a Taxpayer Education Coordinator

   www.irs.gov for downloading of many IRS publications

For most ventures the following publications will be of interest:

- Form SS-4—Application for Employer Identification Number (see Appendix B.)
- Publication 334—Tax Guide for Small Business (for individuals who use Schedule C or C-EZ)
- Publication 560—Retirement Plans for Small Business
- Publication 587—Business Use of Your Home
- Publication 509—Tax Calendars
- Publication 583—Starting a Business and Keeping Records

Additional statutes and information at **www.dol.gov/dol/opa/public/ aboutdol/lawsprog.htm**

In addition to complying with labor laws, you must also comply with all tax laws. See Chapter 12 for a brief review of employee taxes. We suggest you hire a payroll services company to complete your payroll and to keep you in compliance with all tax laws.

Employee Leasing

Consider employee leasing as a way to reduce administrative costs, paperwork hassles, legal issues, and costly benefits. Not unlike leasing physical property, in this instance you will be leasing people (employees) whose leasing organization handles payroll and most if not all the human resources functions.

The leasing firm will help you stay in compliance with the myriad of federal, state, and local employment laws. California and federal labor codes run more than 460 pages! Keeping in compliance is a full-time job.

For your own protection, we suggest you use only a firm that has a strong track record and a sound financial background. Many new ventures are unable to offer employees health insurance benefits and retirement programs and thus lose out on top employees. Due to economies of scale, large leasing firms are able to provide these benefits to your "leased employees." The National Association of Professional Employer Organizations, **www.napeo.org,** phone: 703-836-0466, can provide further information on employee leasing.

Employee leasing may appear to cost more initially but allows for additional benefits as follows:

- Background screening checks completed by leasing organization
- If you don't like the employee you can send him or her back thereby eliminating termination issues
- Reduce turnover
- Nearly eliminates costs of hiring (ads, interviewing time, reference checks, turnover, etc.)

Find a Mentor

If you're starting up a business for the first time, there's a good chance you need a mentor—a person who can give you advice and encouragement. Perhaps you have a mentor already. If not, how can you find such help? First, network with your friends, coworkers, and business associates. Tell them what you're looking for—that is, a successful businessowner with a good track record. The perfect mentor would be one with experience in your particular segment. Second, join the chamber of commerce and one or more civic clubs. Third, keep your new eyes peeled for a mentor appearing on the horizon. If your community has a chapter of Service Corps of Retired Executives (SCORE), contact them to see if you can find a match.

Once you've located some candidates, develop a set of questions and arrange a meeting. You want to pick the brains of all the candidates. Here are some things to consider when selecting a mentor:

Do you feel comfortable with this person?

Can you trust him or her?

Is he or she easy to communicate with?

Does he or she have experience and contacts that can help your new business?

▶ **Action Step 48**

Tap Your People Resources by Brainstorming with Your Team

Before you sign a lease, go into the hole for $50,000 of equipment, hire a lot of people, or spend $2000 for a six-line telephone service, get your new team together and brainstorm the organization and objectives of your new business. A chalkboard is a handy tool here, so that everyone can follow the track of the session. One way to begin is to ask every member of your team to write down what they believe would be good objectives for the business.

You've found some good people, and that's taken hard work. Make that work pay off by tapping your human resources. Brainstorming will get you going. You'll be surprised at what develops.

▶ **Action Step 49**

Who's in Charge? Tell It in Your Business Plan

Investors or vendors are often more interested in the founders than in the business plan itself. Experience in the same type of business and former businesses are powerful positive components of the plan. You will need to focus on past responsibility and authority. Present balance and diversity of your founding team.

Several paragraphs in the business plan may be sufficient for each key founder. If experience is lacking, discuss consultants or committed strategic partners who can balance the management team and contribute experience and special skills. You may also want to include an organizational chart in your business plan.

Write short, strong bios for each member of your team. Full résumés will need to be completed later for the appendix of your business plan.

Once you've made your choice and the person has agreed to help you, keep in close contact. See the person at least once a month, and use phone calls or e-mail to smooth out rough spots. Your mentor may be able to help you establish banking connections and vendor-supplier relationships. A good mentor can be invaluable for checking your leases and contracts.

Here's a story that illustrates the kinds of assistance mentors can provide.

Dick Knox T-shirts, Inc. is the proud owner of a seven-year-old, $3 million company, Dick started selling from his garage and moved to a warehouse facility. He had the energy but not the knowledge to start up a small business, so he kept his eyes open for a mentor.

Enter Bob Redman. Bob's clothing firm had just been purchased by a *Fortune/1000* company. When Dick approached him with the mentor offer, he jumped at it. He loved being associated with a start-up, and the day he left his president's chair he was ready to step into his own business—a five-person clothing firm. [Mentoring works both ways, you see. Dick gave Bob a new angle on a tired life; Bob gave Dick almost a million dollars in sales leads.]

Dick's second mentor was Mickey McCarthy, a wild and crazy entrepreneur who had sold his last venture for $40 million. Mickey was tired. Starting businesses took energy and he was ready to retire to a cabin in the mountains. Before he packed his bags, however, he agreed to be a mentor to Dick.

A month later, Dick was having cash-flow problems. He was meeting payroll but had not taken a salary himself for three months. The cupboard was bare, and Dick had lost 8 pounds.

Over the next couple of months, Mickey worked with Dick on a complete business plan/bank package with projections for the next five years. These projections in hand, Dick met with Mickey's banker. Three weeks later, he had a credit line of $500,000 and the provision that he could expand it to $750,000 when he needed it.

With mentors like Bob and Mickey, how could Dick lose?

Getting Help

If you are an entrepreneur, you like to move fast. You want quick answers and quick action. You've studied the marketplace. You've found your market niche. You didn't think you'd need much of a team, but now you're growing so quickly that you have to do some team building. You're an entrepreneur, so you want to move fast building this team. To do so, you need a key to human behavior. You want people who can help you, not harm you, because every person counts in small business. A test—called an assessment instrument in the training field—might help you locate the key that unlocks the door that leads to the room where your team awaits.

We would like to point out that the search for the key to human behavior is not a recent phenomenon. In the earliest civilizations, astrologers and star-gazers tried to explain human behavior based on the four elements: earth, air, fire, and water. In the fourth century B.C., Hippocrates, who gave us the Hippocratic Oath, kept the four-part framework developed by the astrologers but changed the labels: choleric, phlegmatic, sanguine, and melancholic.

The four-part grid continued into the Middle Ages, where physicians treated patients based on which of the Four Humours—blood, phlegm, choler, and black bile—dominated the bloodstream.

As this century comes to a close, we find other behavioralists renaming the quadrants again, calling them driver, expressive, amiable, and analytical. Or, controller, organizer, analyzer, and persuader.

Our advice is to leave name-calling to the experts and to get help building your team. If you are an entrepreneur, there's a good chance you are either a

Dominant Driver–Controller or an Expressive Inducer–Persuader. In either case, you're busy leading and charging, so you need help with details and organization. Find a simple test. Take it yourself. Use it to build your team. Check with your attorney to be sure that the test is legal as a screening or evaluation device. It might slow you down before you hurtle into a skid.

Think of these sources for help:

1. The counseling-testing center of your local community college.
2. The Internet under "Training" or check out site from **www.dryden.com/ mngment.**

Now it's your turn. Action Steps 48 and 49 are to be completed once you have built your team. It's your chance to brainstorm for ways to win. Make the most of all the creative human resources you've just brought on board! We think these Action Steps are a great way to end this chapter on team building and to start your new business.

Summary

An entrepreneur's venture team often goes beyond bankers, lawyers, and accountants. A single-person entrepreneur may never need to hire an employee to grow and prosper. Many of today's successful firms use strategic partners and customer alliances for almost everything.

But if you grow beyond current capacity, and need to hire employees, hire wisely, train carefully, and encourage greatly. Remember, very few employees will ever have the "fire in their belly" for your business as you do. If you expect them to believe in your dream as much as you do, you may be very disappointed. Remember this is "your baby" and unless you are willing to share the financial successes, your employees are not likely to share the same dream.

Consider the costs of hiring an employee full time. Review your options of hiring part-timers, independent contractors, and employee leasing. Build the best team you can under the current constraints.

You have the right and responsibility to build a culture for your firm and its employees. What kind of environment do you want to provide for your employees? strict and by the law? easy-going and free-flowing? open door? Jeans and t-shirts? three-piece suits? employees who can rise from inside the firm? hiring from outside? offering the best benefits around? child-friendly policies? hiring cheap? Friday bashes?

You wanted your own business. Now build the environment you want to work in!

Think Points for Success

- People tend to "hire themselves." How many more "like you" can the business take?
- A winning team is lurking in your network.
- Look to your competitors and vendors for team members.
- Your company is *people.*
- Balance the people on your team.
- Have each team member write objectives for his or her responsibilities within the business. Set up your own internal management by objectives system.
- You can't grow until you have the right people.
- How much of your team can be built of part-timers and moonlighters?

- Consider a virtual organization.
- Consider independent contractors.
- Consider employee leasing.
- Find a mentor.

Key Points From Another View

Seven Characteristics of Highly Effective Entrepreneurial Employees

Fast growing, entrepreneurial organizations need employees who regularly demonstrate entrepreneurial characteristics and work habits. Management of entrepreneurial companies must work diligently to recognize, identify and attract this type of employee during the recruitment process to assure a steady stream of the people with the "Right Stuff" to fuel growth of the venture.

Employees come in all shapes and sizes with all sorts of different skills and quirks. Their outlook and approach has been tempered by past experiences, good or bad. In the relatively short period of time which you have to do hiring, you have to cut through the prospective employee's resume and verbal statements and figure out if he or she has the "Right Stuff." This is really important because just as "a bad apple will spoil the barrel", an employee with the "Wrong Stuff" will drag your whole effort down. It would be one thing if a Wrong Stuff employee simply didn't contribute, but it is worse than that—he usually sucks up scarce management time, creates diversions for Right Stuff employees—you get the picture.

So what are the characteristics of highly effective "Right Stuff" entrepreneurial employees? Here are a few to keep in mind as you interview potential new hires, you probably can think of others.

Ability to Deal With Risk. An entrepreneur has to operate effectively in an environment filled with risk. The Right Stuff employee can deal with risk and uncertainty. He is able to make progress toward goals and is able to make decisions when lacking one or several critical resources or data.

Results Oriented. The Right Stuff employee is results oriented, she takes ownership to get the task done. She is a "can do" person who demonstrates common sense in her decision and actions and is able to cut through and resolve problems which divert others. Her business judgment is sound and becomes stronger with each experience, decision, or recommendation. While supervisors and managers may disagree with her ultimate recommendation, they usually agree that the alternatives she presents are reasonable for the situation at hand.

Energy. The Right Stuff employee has high levels of enthusiasm and energy; he consistently generates output that is higher than could be reasonably expected. He is fully committed to the organization, its goals and overall success. Not only does he desire to make a contribution to results, he needs to see the results of his contributions quickly, not measured in years! He will seek out an organization that solicits and acts upon his ideas, gives credit where credit is due and points out errors and poor decisions quickly and clearly. He performs effectively with limited supervision and is able to self-motivate and set priorities with minimal guidance.

Growth Potential. The Right Stuff employee's reach exceeds her grasp today. Today's Right Stuff employee is often next year's supervisor and a department manager soon thereafter. She is willing to accept much higher levels of responsibility than is the norm for her position, title, experience level or salary. She acts as a strong role model, trains and coaches others, and soon begins to assume supervisory responsibilities, again much earlier than would be expected in a normal corporate environment.

Team Player. The Right Stuff employee is a true team player, she recognizes how her role contributes to the overall effort and success of the organization. She accepts accountability and ownership for her area of responsibility and expects others on the team to do the same. She also recognizes the roles and contributions of others and applauds their efforts sincerely.

Multitasking Ability. The Right Stuff employee is flexible to accept new duties, assignments and responsibilities. He can perform more than one role until the incremental duties and functions assumed can be assigned to co-workers in newly defined roles. He is also willing to dig in and do grunt work tasks which eventually will be performed by lower-level employees.

Improvement Oriented. The Right Stuff employee is more than willing to challenge in a constructive way existing procedures and systems; to her the status quo is temporary. She suggests changes and improvements frequently and encourages others to do so also.

Right Stuff employees are easier to manage in some ways but require a higher level of management involvement in others. Ordinary (average) employees will not produce extraordinary results over time; Right Stuff employees will generally produce extraordinary results consistently over time. Unfortunately, unless properly motivated, managed and rewarded, Right Stuff employees could perform at lower levels and only produce ordinary results. So what makes a Right Stuff manager?

First of all, the Right Stuff manager must herself have the characteristics of the Right Stuff employee. Beyond that she must have the basic skill set of sound business judgment, practical hands-on experience, general management skills and common sense. She must be committed to and contribute to the organization's vision and mission and must convey this commitment in multiple ways: written, verbal and by actions. She needs an awareness, understanding and interest in the technology trends that affect the venture and its customers.

Externally, the Right Stuff manager must be able to identify and build creative strategic relationships, especially for partnering opportunities in areas of limited resources. Internally, he must effectively produce and manage change as the organization evolves, gaining enthusiastic support for change and improvements from the Right Stuff employees in the ranks.

So when you interview each new employee or manager, look beyond the mere facts of the resume and ask yourself is this a "Right Stuff" person? You are most likely interviewing the person because of the résumé. Now is the time to put the résumé aside and focus on the "Right Questions."

SOURCE: **http://web.mit.edu**

12

Entrepreneurial Toolkit

Entrepreneurial Links

Books

The New York Public Library Business Desk Reference Essential Information for Every Office–At Your Fingertips, New York Public Library, 1997.

World Factbook, http://www.odci.gov/cia/publications/factbook/index.html, published yearly.

Secrets of Self-Employment, Surviving and Thriving on the Ups and Downs of Being Your Own Boss, Sarah and Paul Edwards, 1996.

Websites

www.iii.org, Insurance Information Institute

www.vusme.org, Virtual University for Small and Medium-Sized Enterprises

www.zdnet.com/smallbusiness/, ZD Net Small Business Advisor

Associations/Organizations

Research Institute for Small and Emerging Businesses (RISE), www.riseb.org/

U.S. Chamber of Commerce, www.uschamber.org/

American Success Institute, www.success.org

Publications

Upside, www.upside.com

Wired, www.wired.com

Home Office Computing

Additional Entrepreneurial Insights

aol.com, How Steve Case Beat Bill Gates, Nailed the Netheads and Made Millions in the War for the Web, Karen Swisher, 1998.

How to Win Friends and Influence People, Dale Carnegie, 1994 (reprint).

In the Company of Giants: Candid Conversations with the Visionaries of the Digital World, Rama Dev Jager and Rafael Ortiz, 1998.

Learning Objectives

- Learn how to keep current on technology.
- Identify tasks in your business that can be done better with the aid of a computer.
- Use Cyberspace to your advantage.
- Explore your need for a Web site.
- Learn about key office appliances and communication systems.
- Recognize the strength of computer retailing and manufacturing systems.
- Understand the importance of protecting your assets through insurance.
- Explore insurance needs for your specific business.
- Recognize the need to file all tax forms in a timely matter.
- Understand the importance of tax planning not just tax filing.

This chapter will help you investigate the technological tools you need for operating and controlling your new and growing business. In addition, we have included tax information to keep the IRS at bay and insurance information to protect your business and keep the lawyers away.

Technology Checklist

What follows is a technology checklist (as of this writing) for the budding entrepreneur. It begins with equipment (hardware) and includes data-processing programs (software) and leads you into the wonderful world of cyberspace. This checklist is designed to help you plan. If you check off every item, you can skip ahead. If you are not familiar with all the equipment and software, time to hit the computer stores and ask questions, hit the Net and research away, and contact entrepreneurs and discuss their software and hardware use.

Checklist for Small Business Technology

_____ Computer

_____ Monitor (color and size of screen are important)

_____ Extended Keyboard

_____ Printer (laser)

_____ Zip drive (backup)

_____ Speakers and sound card

_____ Video card

_____ CD-ROM drive

_____ Memory (32K or better)

_____ Surge protection panel

_____ Fax

_____ Scanner

_____ Video camera

> ## Action Step 50
>
> ### Tech Needs
>
> 1. Make a wish list of all the goodies you want from cyberspace and your computer:
>
> **Part A**
> Write down all the things you want from cyberspace: e-mail, information, sample business plans, market research, plot maps for site locations, target customer profiles, your own Website:
>
> **Part B**
> Write down all the non-cyberspace things you require of your computer: letters, memos, reports, spreadsheets, inventory control, invoicing customers, check writing, graphic design, customer lists, organizational charts, Power Point presentations, writing biz plan.
>
> 2. Find a guide.
>
> Things change quickly in electronics and telecommunications. The modem you bought a year ago is a tortoise compared to the supersonic modems of today. To find the best set up for the best price, get some help before you plunk down your plastic or sign that lease agreement. To find a guide, begin with someone you know who understands computers. Network to find a guide who understands how to purchase technology products cost effectively. Entertain him or her (breakfast, lunch, dinner) and pick their brain. Talk with others in your same line of business to discover what works best for them. Learn from their mistakes. Contact your professional association to determine if they use special software programs or offer advice.
>
> Order and accept delivery of your system. Hook up. Log on. Congratulations. And welcome to cyberspace.

_____ Video conferencing
_____ Word-processing program
_____ Spreadsheet program
_____ Graphics package
_____ Database labels, inventory
_____ Accounting program
_____ Modem
_____ Separate phone line
_____ Networking software
_____ Software to build Web pages

If you do not currently have a system it is time for you to complete Action Step 50. If you do have a system, consider what additional needs you might have as you begin your business.

Product reviews are everywhere on the Net. Keep current on technology in business by reading *Fortune, Forbes,* and *Inc.'s* special technology issues. Each of these issues highlights firms integrating technology into their business.

The microcomputer seems to have been created especially for the entrepreneur. The right micro, with the right software, can make all the difference in the world in your small business. In fact, we believe computers have been one of the major factors in the growth of entrepreneurial ventures. It can become an electronic extension of your mind and personality. It will take orders, handle details, send items to the printer while you're doing something else, file, cross-check files, probe future profit and cash flow, printout payroll checks, keep track of competitors, and put you in touch with business information that will help you survive.

Your computer is amazing. It sits on a table, or a desk, or your lap. It doesn't cost an arm and a leg. It can handle any repetitious detail in your business and thus leave your hands and head free for entrepreneurial creativity. It will perform many tasks: accounting; word-processing; mailing lists; customer, patient, client, student files; flyers; inventory control; newsletters; memos; and so on. A good start-up computer, including basic software, excellent printer, and modem can be purchased for approximately $1000-$2000. You should also look into leasing options because computer technology moves so rapidly. Some lease agreements offer trade-up options.

The mark of a successful entrepreneur is fast footwork. You succeed not because your advertising budget can compete with the hefty purses of Madison Avenue, but because you can spot an opportunity and get tooled up to deliver faster than the big guys. And with the right technology at hand, you can be even quicker.

Purchase your computer set up with an 18–24 month time frame in mind and be sure the brand you buy can be serviced and repaired locally. Your job is to shop for solutions to problems in your business. Today's software offers solutions to mundane problems as well as providing creative tools. Continually explore new software and technology. A $50 software package may put you on the path to producing a monthly newsletter that will reach your 200 best customers in the privacy of their home. Provide customers with useful information and a coupon for their next visit to your store.

Educate yourself. Keep taking computer classes. Read constantly. Copy your competitors' technology usage. Knowledge will keep you on the leading edge. Also, keep comfortable at your keyboard by following the exercises on page 235.

ISO in Brief

ISO (International Organization for Standardization) develops International Standards over almost the entire range of technology. Its membership comprises the national standards institutes of some 130 countries.

ISO is a non-governmental organization and the standards it develops are voluntary. However, a certain percentage of its standards—mainly those concerned with health, safety, or environmental aspects—has been adopted in some countries as part of their regulatory framework.

ISO standards are market-driven. They are developed by international consensus among experts drawn from the industrial, technical or business sectors which have expressed the need for a particular standard. These may be joined by experts from government, regulatory authorities, testing bodies, academia, consumer groups or other organizations with relevant knowledge, or which have expressed a direct interest in the standard under development.

Although ISO standards are voluntary, the fact that they are developed in response to market demand, and are based on consensus among the interested parties, ensures widespread use of the standards.

International Standards are increasingly important to business. They are essential to global communication, technology transfer and international trade.

To increase your competitiveness in the international market, learn more about ISO standards at **www.iso.ch**

SOURCE: **www.iso.ch**

Quains Top 10 Computer Exercises from Fast Company

How to make hours in front of the computer easier, more comfortable and safer.

1. **Get up and walk around!** Take a 1-minute break from the computer every 30 minutes, and a 5-minute break every couple of hours. Go to the water cooler and catch up on office gossip.
2. **Learn the keyboard commands.** Try to remember commands such as "Ctrl A" to mark text. Avoiding the mouse will preserve your wrist and forearm.
3. **Don't cradle the phone with your neck.** If you're right-handed, put the phone on the left side of the desk so you hold the handset with your left hand and take notes with your right.
4. **Keep the screen clean.** Dusting it off once a week will relieve eye strain.
5. **If it hurts, don't do it.** Pay attention to your body. If your wrist aches, print out so you can get away from the computer.
6. **Have your eyes examined regularly.** Slaving over a hot CRT only exacerbates improperly corrected vision.
7. **Change your gear.** From time to time, switch to different keyboards and pointing devices. The more variety you put into your computer work the better.
8. **Be kind to your mouse.** By using a light grip, you won't tense the muscles and tendons in your arm.
9. **Keep warm.** Colder muscles and tendons appear to be more susceptible to repetitive stress injuries (RSI).

10. **Is it just your office?** Repetitive activities such as playing a musical instrument can cause RSI. You might have to make some changes outside of work.

For more information, visit **http://www.fastcompany.com**

SOURCE: First appeared in *Fast Company*, issue 10, page 192.

Phone System

Your phone or phone system can be the most important communication tool in your business. This is not the place to skimp on quality. Your phone should link with answering machines, fax machines, fax-modems, pagers, and cell phones. When contemplating a cellular connection—competition is fierce and new technology is always on the way—shop prices and services. Most local phone companies provide a sophisticated voice mail system at a modest cost. If your customers need immediate access to you, get a pager. Pagers are always useful if your home or business can't accommodate "one more line" without incurring a major expense.

Figure 12.1

Caterina's Daily Report

Caterina's
Daily Report

Day: Thursday
Date: 7/16/98

Yogurt	$506.12	Employee Discount	
Ice Cream		Coupons	-$5.00
Candy / Chocolates	$177.28	Gift Cert. Redeemed	
Bakery	$1.49	Sales Tax	$35.11
Bulk Bins	$93.06		
Beverages	$26.00		
Non Food Items	$444.05		
Fancy Foods			
Packaging / Wrap	$9.00		
Shipping Fees			
Gift Certificates Sold			

Gross Sales	$1257.00	Net	$1287.11
Last Years Gross (+/-):	$752.99	Last Years Net (+/-):	$819.66

Hourly

1:00 AM		1:00 PM	$165.80
2:00 AM		2:00 PM	$25.44
3:00 AM		3:00 PM	$133.28
4:00 AM		4:00 PM	$83.79
5:00 AM		5:00 PM	$72.32
6:00 AM		6:00 PM	$222.28
7:00 AM		7:00 PM	$14.46
8:00 AM		8:00 PM	$140.61
9:00 AM		9:00 PM	$103.91
10:00 AM		10:00 PM	$110.06
11:00 AM	$3.45	11:00 PM	$130.95
12:00 PM	$58.98	12:00 AM	

CUSTOMER

Time	Count
1:00 AM	
2:00 AM	
3:00 AM	
4:00 AM	
5:00 AM	
6:00 AM	
7:00 AM	
8:00 AM	
9:00 AM	
10:00 AM	
11:00 AM	2
12:00 PM	11
1:00 PM	17
2:00 PM	7
3:00 PM	22
4:00 PM	20
5:00 PM	12
6:00 PM	16
7:00 PM	6
8:00 PM	13
9:00 PM	20
10:00 PM	27
11:00 PM	5
12:00 AM	

Retailing Computer System

The cash registers of old have turned into computerized magicians (see Figure 12.1). The magic computer can tell you:

- what is sold
- who sold it
- hourly sales total
- sales per each employee
- when employees open cash drawer
- bar code scans to prevent misentering product data
- coupon usage
- sales by category (bulk candy, ice cream, espresso drinks, etc.)

In addition, a retail computer system will calculate and track:

- sales per man hour (SPMH)
- labor percentage
- average closed sales
- when employees clock in and out
- inventory
- daily, monthly, yearly sales and comparison data from previous sales periods as well

One entrepreneur installed video cameras in each of her four stores to deter shoplifting and keep an eye on her employees. The cameras are hooked up via a modem line and computer and send digitized images to her main home office.

In addition to retailing systems, software is of great advantage to manufacturing firms.

Control Manufacturing Through Technology

The kind of control once available to only the tiniest sliver of manufacturers through MRP packages is now available to all—or at least 399,000 of the 400,000 manufacturers in the United States, most with annual revenues of $5 million to $50 million. This affordable technology lets small manufacturers get a grip on their businesses rather than just their production lines. Specifically, it permits so-called make-to-order manufacturing—that is, making products when, and only when, customers want them. That, in turn, eliminates the costly trio of long lead times, huge inventories, and bad bets on products that turn out to be dogs.

In short, today's technology forces small manufacturers to adapt to what they might have preferred to sweep under the rug: the idea that running their businesses means getting a grip on scheduling, inventory control, production and capacity planning, purchasing, distribution and receiving—any myriad of other tasks—as well as the making of the product itself. It means taking total control.

Tips for Taking Control

With that in mind, here are four tips for capitalizing on a development that is to manufacturing what the automobile is to the hand-carved stone wheel.

1. If you're one of those small manufacturers who thinks technology means a computer in the bookkeeper's office—and you'd be surprised

at how many do—realize that you need to educate yourself about technological developments. You might even need to overcome a deep-seated fear of technology.

2. If you have the latest computer-controlled turret lathe or milling machine, understand that in today's manufacturing environment, that isn't enough. Your goal is to take control of your business, not just your production line.

3. Get the right technology. While all manufacturers require materials, labor, and capital to get the job done, each company is different. Each requires a unique solution. Take the time to talk with various vendors, and examine several packages, to select the one that's best for you.

4. Learn how to make optimal use of the technology by working side by side with your vendor. Then, teach your people to make optimal use of the technology by helping them have a close working relationship with the vendor.

Total control through technology spurs a geometric addition to the bottom line. It creates believers out of skeptics. That, to us, is the sweetest music.

SOURCE: **http://www.EntreWorld.org**

The Mistress of Mystery

Alma and Chantal met in a newsgroup (Bulletin Board with Focus) that was devoted to mystery writing. Alma was a published author of British-type "cozies" (a mystery modeled on the classical work of Agatha Christie) with five books in print and one halfway through the computer. Through the Internet, Alma had made connections across America and across the ocean. Though her fans were loyal and consistent, book sales kept slipping.

Chantal was a poet with a marketing background and a keen interest in what was happening to the arts (including writing) in the Cyberspace Age. She taught writing at a community college in a suburb of St. Louis. When Chantal discovered that her job was two miles from Alma's house, they made a date for lunch.

After the waitress had cleared away the dishes, Chantal (who had always wanted to write novels) asked questions about Alma's work. Finally, Chantal asked Alma what she thought of the "noir" novels (Raymond Chandler, Dashiell Hammett, James M. Cain) from the thirties and forties.

Alma didn't, much like the idea of "noir" fiction—actual violence onstage made her quite nervous—but she was the soul of politeness, so she listened to Chantal's idea: What if they collaborated to design a mystery that combined the Christie-esque setting and locked-room atmosphere with the classic "noir" novel—its darkness, its irony, its penchant for action?

Alma said she would sleep on it.

The idea of the new novel (her publisher called Alma's writing a "product") kept Alma awake many nights. Because her books hadn't been selling well lately, her publisher kept asking for fresh material. But Alma felt really afraid of this new idea.

A week later Chantal handed Alma a present—a how-to for writing mystery books using only the weekend time.

Putting her doubts aside, Alma worked up a mystery with her new friend, Chantal. The working title was "Mystery of Michiana Shores." The setting for their book was in Michiana Shores on Lake Michigan an hour's drive from downtown Chicago. Both sleuth and drowning victim were female. The victim was a young woman of 26. To this setting, they added a rock concert, ambitious politicians, a shortsighted policeman, and a wealthy man with a castle-like house built on the lake.

Chantal was organized, linear; a person who took things step by step. Alma, by contrast, wrote from intuition; in wild bursts of insight. Chantal learned early in their partnership to stimulate Alma who would then flash out several pages of writing. In less than a year, the book was finished. But before they submitted the book to Alma's publisher in New York, Chantal designed a Website.

The Website began as an information source: table of contents, quotes from the book, bios of both authors, brief stories about the art of collaboration, and a cleverly designed mystery quiz.

Alma's author friends sent her e-mail questions about the quiz. When Alma didn't know the answers, she researched until she found them. Alma's answers were so clever, so witty, that the Website was deluged with e mail. Alma became "The Mistress of Mystery" and Chantal charged $10 per answer. By the time their novel was published, Alma's Answer Room had 50,000 subscribers—a ready market for new fiction.

They sold the book online, with direct hookups from their Website to booksellers like Amazon.com, Barnes and Noble, and Powell's.

The Answer Room was a place where writers could connect to other writers. Where they could chat about writing, publishers, agents, writing conferences, revising, editing, and problems like writer's block. As the Answer Room grew, people got to know Alma and Chantal.

Knowing the authors made them curious about the book.

The first printing sold out.

Could a Website help your business? Work through Action Step 51 and find out.

Insurance

Managing Risk

What type of insurance should I carry? How much coverage should I have? Can I forego insurance? First consider:

- the size of any potential loss.
- the probability of loss.
- the resources available to meet a loss should it occur.
- the probability of lawsuits (some industries and businesses are heavily targeted).

Can you eliminate all risks? Can you reduce some risks? You *must* assume some risk.

How do you decide whether a particular risk should be transferred to an insurance company or personally assumed? Figure the maximum potential loss that might result. If the loss would force your company into bankruptcy or cause serious financial damage, *don't assume the risk!*

Losses that occur with predictable frequency are such shoplifting and bad debts. These can usually be absorbed by the business and are often budgeted as part of the normal costs of doing business; the cost of the loss is incorporated into the price. Where probability of loss is high, a more effective method of controlling the loss is to adopt appropriate precautionary measures and purchase better-than-adequate insurance. The key to purchasing insurance (and all risk management) is: *Do not risk more than you can afford to lose.*

Insurance Planning

First consider all of the insurable risks faced by your business. In general, the following risks can be covered by insurance:

- Personal injury to employees and the general public. Some retail stores have become targets for slip and fall claims. Certain businesses have inherently higher personal injury claims and you need to protect accordingly.

- Employment practices such as hiring, firing, sexual discrimination, libel, and so on.

- Loss to the business caused by the death or disability of key employees or the owner—an essential coverage needed to protect your business

- Loss or damage of property—including merchandise, supplies, fixtures, and building.

- Loss of income resulting from interruption of business caused by damage to the firm's operating assets (storms, natural disasters, electrical blackouts).

A standard fire insurance policy pays the policyholder only for those losses directly due to fire. Make sure when dealing with your insurance agent that you understand your policy thoroughly. Other indirect losses, known as consequential losses, may be even more important to your company's welfare. You can protect yourself against these losses by obtaining business-interruption insurance. Consequential losses include the following:

- Extra expenses of obtaining temporary quarters.

- Loss of rental income on buildings damaged or destroyed by fire, if you are a landlord.

- Loss of use of a facility.

- Continuing expenses after a fire—salaries, rents paid in advance, interest obligations, and so on.

Do not fail to provide safe equipment and working conditions, hire competent fellow employees, or warn employees of any existing danger. In every state, an employer must insure against potential workers' compensation claims. However, employee coverage and the extent of the employer's liability varies from state to state. The cost of workers' compensation varies greatly by occupation and risk involved. Worker's compensation can cost up to thirty-five cents on every dollar you pay your employees. Ask your insurance company if they have any loss-prevention services. If your employees speak several different languages, you need to make sure *everyone* understands the safety rules. Chapter 11 covers this in fuller depth.

General liability covers any kind of nonemployee bodily injury except that caused by automobiles and professional malpractice. In some cases, this coverage may even extend to trespassers. As a businessowner, you may also be liable for bodily injuries to customers, pedestrians, delivery people, and other outsiders—even in instances where you have exercised "reasonable care." In highly litigious states, you will need to carry exceptionally high liability coverage to protect your business.

Vehicles are a source of liability. Under the "doctrine of agency" a business can be liable for injuries and property damage caused by employees operating their own or someone else's vehicle while on company business. The company may have some protection under the employee's own liability policy, but the limits are probably inadequate. When it is customary or convenient for employees to use their own vehicle while on company business (e.g., salespeople on the road or covering a route), you should purchase nonownership liability insurance.

The best form of general liability insurance for the small business consists of a comprehensive general liability policy combined with a comprehensive auto liability policy and a standard workers' compensation policy.

One retail store recently discovered that the merchandise she transported in her van from store to store was not covered while she was in transit. An additional rider needed to be added to her policy to provide insurance protection. Sitting down and going through various scenarios with your insurance agent is one of the best ways to make sure you are protecting *all* areas of your business. Consider an umbrella policy, which provides an additional layer of protection.

Types of Coverage

You can purchase insurance to cover almost any risk. Businessowners most commonly protect themselves with the following types of coverage.

1. **Fire and general property insurance**—protects against fire loss, vandalism, hail, and wind damage.
2. **Consequential loss insurance**—covers loss of earnings or extra expenses when business is interrupted due to fire or other catastrophe (see also item 4 below).
3. **Public liability insurance**—covers injury to the public, such as customer or pedestrian injury claims.
4. **Business-interruption insurance**—covers in case when the business is unable to continue.
5. **Crime insurance**—protects against losses due to burglary, robbery, and so forth. Fidelity bonds provide coverage from employee theft.
6. **Malpractice insurance**—covers against claims from clients who suffer damages as a result of services you perform.
7. **Errors and omissions insurance**—covers against claims from customers who suffer injury or loss because of errors you made, things you should have done but failed to do, or warnings you failed to supply.
8. **Employment practices liability insurance (EPLI)**—covers against claims from employees for employment practices: sexual harassment, wrongful discharge, discrimination, breach of contract, libel, and so on.
9. **Key man insurance**—covers the life, death, dismemberment, or physical disability of owner(s) or key employee(s).
10. **Product liability insurance**—covers injury to the public, such as customer use or misuse of product.
11. **Disability insurance**—covers owner employees against disability and usually allows for payments to be continued during rehabilitation. Disability for an owner is a much greater risk than death and few owners insure themselves adequately.
12. **Life and health insurance for employees.**
13. **Workers' Compensation insurance**—protects employees if they are injured while on the job.
14. **Extra equipment insurance**—covers specialized equipment not covered in standard policies.
15. **Directors' and Officers' liability insurance**—if company stock is held by outside investors, directors and officers, should be protected.

According to the Insurance Information Institute, **www.iii.org**, 212-669-9250, about 40 percent of small businessowners are estimated to carry no insurance at all due to cash concerns. If you cannot afford minimal insurance coverage, rethink your business plan and delay starting your business until you *can* afford *adequate* coverage. One mishap or incident can destroy everything you have worked for. Do not let this happen to you. Complete Action Step 52 using the Insurance Planning Worksheet (page 242) to discover your insurance needs and costs.

▶ **Action Step 52**

Protect Your Venture

Network your way to a business insurance salesperson. Discuss your business plan with him or her and complete the insurance worksheet on page 242. Discover the cost of insuring your business for the first year. If you are a home-based business. Review the information on pages 242–243 and discuss with your agent/broker.

Insurance Planning Worksheet

Insurance Types	Required		Annual Cost ($)
	Yes	**No**	
1. Personal liability	☐	☐	
2. General and public liability	☐	☐	
3. Product liability	☐	☐	
4. Errors and omissions liability	☐	☐	
5. Malpractice liability	☐	☐	
6. Key man insurance	☐	☐	
7. Directors and Officers	☐	☐	
8. Term life	☐	☐	
9. Health	☐	☐	
10. Workers Compensation	☐	☐	
11. Crime Insurance	☐	☐	
12. Vehicle	☐	☐	
13. Business interruption	☐	☐	
14. Extra equipment	☐	☐	
15. Consequential loss	☐	☐	
16. EPLI	☐	☐	
17. Fire and theft	☐	☐	
18. Business loan	☐	☐	
19. Bonds (fidelity, surety)	☐	☐	
20. Other	☐	☐	
Total Annual Cost			

Special note for home-based businesses: A homeowners' policy alone may be inadequate for your special needs. Consider purchasing specialized home-based business insurance.

Home-Based Business Insurance
from Insurance Information Institute

If you're working at home—STOP—and review your insurance coverage. Your homeowners insurance probably doesn't cover your business. A typical home-owners policy provides only $2500 coverage for business equipment, which is usually not enough to cover all of the business property. You also need coverage for liability and business interruption.

To insure your business, you have three choices—endorsements to the homeowners policy, an in-home business policy or a small businessowners' package policy.

1—Endorsements

Depending on the type of business you operate, you may be able to add an endorsement to your existing homeowners policy. For as little as $14 a year, you can double your standard homeowners policy limits for business equipment from $2,500 to $5,000.

Some companies have begun offering endorsements that include property and limited business liability coverage. Endorsements are typically only available for businesses that generate $250,000 or less in annual receipts. They are available in most states.

2—In-Home Business Policy

The insurance industry has responded to the growing number of home-based businesses by creating in-home business insurance policies. For about $200 per year you can insure your business property for $10,000. General liability coverage is also included in the policy. A business owner can purchase anywhere from $300,000 to $1 million worth of liability coverage. The cost of the liability coverage will depend on the amount purchased.

If your business is unable to operate because of damage to your house, your in-home business policy will cover lost income and ongoing expenses such as payroll for up to one year. The policy also provides limited coverage for loss of valuable papers and records, accounts receivable, off-site business property and use of equipment.

In some cases, the companies that offer these policies require that you purchase your homeowners and auto policies from them.

3—Businessowners Package Policy (BOP)

Created specifically for small businesses, this policy is an excellent solution if your home-based business operates in more than one location or manufactures products outside the workplace. A BOP, like the in-home business policy, covers business property and equipment, loss of income and extra expenses, and liability. However, these coverages are on a much broader scale than the in-home business policy.

Automobile Coverage

If you are using your automobile for business activities—transporting supplies or products or visiting customers—you need to make certain that your automobile insurance will protect you from accidents which may occur while on business.

In order to get insurance coverage that will not overlap with your homeowners policy or leave any exposures, you should consult with an insurance professional with experience in this field. To find an expert, contact your home insurer, other professionals with similar businesses, or other home business owners.

SOURCE: **http://www.iii.org**

The Taxman Cometh!

What are the laws? What forms do I have to fill out? If I get audited, how can I protect myself? These are just a few of the questions the IRS's Publication 334 Tax Guide for Small Business can answer. See the Incredible Resource box (in Chapter 11) for further IRS publications. Table 12.1 lists the most common tax forms businesses are required by law to file.

Schedule C and Schedule C-EZ for sole proprietors are provided in the Appendix B.

A tough tax for many sole proprietors to absorb is the self-employment tax. As of 1998, the tax is 15.3 percent of the first $68,400 of income and 2.9 percent on anything above that amount. Use Schedule SE in the Appendix B to calculate your tax.

In addition to federal taxes, you will also be responsible for state, county, and local taxes. State and federal rules do not always mesh. Be careful to understand both systems. An *experienced* CPA who specializes in your selected industry will be able to keep you on track with what is acceptable practice to the IRS.

The best thing you can do for your business is to keep excellent records of *all* transactions. Recently one of our colleagues was audited and the audit took one day instead of the usual three—excellent recordkeeping. The IRS and your accountant can tell you exactly what is required.

Table 12.1

Which Forms Must I File?

If You Are a:	You May Be Liable for:	Use Form:
Sole proprietor	Income tax	1040 and Schedule C[1] or C-EZ (Schedule F for farm business[1])
	Self-employment tax	1040 and Schedule SE
	Estimated tax	1040-ES
	Employment taxes:	
	• Social security and Medicare taxes and income tax withholding	943 for farm employees 941 for all others
	• Federal unemployment (FUTA) tax	940 or 940-EZ
	• Depositing employment taxes	8109[2]
	Excise taxes	See *Excise Taxes*
Partnership	Annual return of income	1065
	Employment taxes	Same as sole proprietor
	Excise taxes	See *Excise Taxes*
Partner in a partnership (individual)	Income tax	1040 and Schedule E[3]
	Self-employment tax	1040 and Schedule SE
	Estimated tax	1040-ES
Corporation or S corporation	Income tax	1120 or 1120-A (corporation) 1120S (S corporation)
	Estimated tax	1120-W (corporation only) and 8109[2]
	Employment taxes	Same as sole proprietor
S corporation shareholder	Income tax	1040 and Schedule E[3]
	Estimated tax	1040-ES

[1] File a separate schedule for each business.

[2] Do not use if you deposit taxes electronically.

[3] Various other schedules may be needed.

SOURCE: Starting in Business & Keeping Records, Publication 583, IRS, Washington, D.C., 1998.

Your CPA can be of most assistance to you in *tax planning*. Tax preparation is sometimes too late! Keep your accountant abreast of any major business change. *Make your accountant part of your team.*

You will be responsible for corporate or personal income taxes, employment taxes, sales taxes, and property taxes. If you have employees, you will need to file an Application for Employer Identification Number, Form SS-4 (found in Appendix B). On filing this form you will receive an Employer Identification Number (EIN). Keeping up with employee taxes and laws is a headache for most employers. Use a payroll service. Some employers pay their employees cash in an illegal attempt to save on taxes and worker's comp. If an employee gets injured the deception will be found and fines assessed are very heavy. In addition, if an angry employee calls the IRS, the IRS will call you! Another scenario is when a competitor turns you in to the IRS for suspected tax evasion. Tax laws and regulations are a burden but they are *not* to be avoided or taken lightly at any time.

 **Global Legal Information Network**

The Global Legal Information Network (GLIN) maintains and provides a database of laws, regulations, and other complementary legal sources. The documents included in the database are contributed by the governments of the member nations from the original official texts which are deposited, by agreement of the members, in a server initially at the Library of Congress of the United States of America. The basic elements of this database are: (1) full texts of the documents in the official language of the country of origin, (2) summaries or abstracts in English, and (3) thesauri in English and in as many official languages as are represented in the database. The summaries or abstracts are linked electronically to the corresponding full texts. Currently, information can be searched in English using the instructions appearing on the screen.

SOURCE: **http://lcweb2.loc.gov**

Sales Taxes

For sales tax and resale numbers, contact your State Board of Equalization. Do not forget to remit your collected sales tax! Many small businessowners attempt to avoid reporting sales taxes for cash transactions. The IRS has many ways to determine your true sales figures. They look at the number of disposable cups you purchased and used to determine how much coffee you sold, or review your electric and water bills to estimate how many loads your laundromat washed and dried. Fines are considerable. Once audited the chance to be audited again increases. Realize that everyone is audited some time or other.

If you are starting up, don't overestimate projected sales. If projections are high, you will be required to post a higher bond to get a resale number/permit.

▶ Summary

Computers help you run your business profitably. Insurance protects you. Taxes keep the country rolling!

Think of computer acquisition as a three-step process—define your tasks and problems, purchase software to do the job, buy or lease hardware to run the software. Choose a system that can be expanded or updated. Keep taking computer courses and keep reading.

Discover your insurance needs early on and pay to protect your business and personal investment. Work with an experienced agent in your selected industry who is qualified as a business insurance broker.

Work with your accountant (CPA) and payroll service to be sure you are complying with *all* federal, state, and local tax laws. Tax planning is an important element in the financial success of your business. Your accountant not only will keep you in compliance with the laws but can also help you look toward the future as well.

Think Points for Success

- A computer can be an extension of your creative, entrepreneurial personality.
- The hardware for your computer system should be relatively easy to select—if you work from problem to solution to software. Software needs determine hardware needs—check suggested equipment requirements of software manufacturers.
- You've got to compute to compete.
- Protect your investment with insurance.
- Find and hire an expert tax accountant and/or consultant.
- Pay taxes on time.
- Keep impeccable records. They will help you survive an audit.
- Keep personal and business funds separate.

Key Points from Another View

Quain's Top Ten E-mail Hints

1. Beware the forward feature. Remember that any e-mail you send can be forwarded to anyone with an e-mail account. If you want to keep your musings private, don't go public with e-mail. Consider yourself warned!
2. Double-check the "To" field. It's happened many times: someone writes an e-mail that's critical of someone else and inadvertently puts that person's name in the "To" field. Don't let it happen to you.
3. Avoid mass mailings. If you can't decide where the message really needs to go, your recipients may decide for you. (Think "trash.")
4. Don't reply if you don't have to. And when appropriate, tell recipients that you don't need a reply. It will save everyone a lot of time.
5. If you get flamed, don't respond through e-mail. Pick up the phone and call the sender. Your voice conveys far more nuance than e-mail, so you'll be less likely to get into an argument that both of you will regret later on.
6. When replying, keep original subject headings. They make it easy to follow a discussion—even if you think that your headings are wittier.
7. Don't look at e-mail when you're doing something else. If people are in your office, give them your full attention. That way you won't need to reread messages.
8. Ban company-wide e-mails. Messages about bikes for sale and puppies that need a home just clog up the system and distract people from their work. Be brutal and ban them from your company.
9. Don't let messages linger in your inbox. Once you've read a message, file it or delete it so you don't waste time reviewing it later on.
10. Everybody's overloaded, so make a high-priority e-mail stand out. Use the colored priority-check option, or add colored fonts when possible. But don't overdo it.

SOURCE: **http://www.fastcompany.com**
December 1997

By John R. Quain
(FastCompany)

13

Buying a Business

Entrepreneurial Links

Books

A Basic Guide for Buying and Selling a Company, Wilbur M. Yegge Ph.D., 1996.

Valuing a Business: The Analysis and Appraisal of Closely Held Companies, Shannon P. Pratt, et al., 1995.

The Small Business Valuation Book, Lawrence Tuller, 1998.

Websites

www.enterprise.org/enet/, EntrepreNet

www.slu.edu/eweb, eWeb

www.bizbuysell.com, BizBuySell.

Associations/Organizations

Institute of Business Appraisers

Appraisal Foundation

American Society of Appraisers

Publications

The Growth Company Guide to Investors, Deal Structures, and Legal Strategies Practical Advice for Growing Companies and Private Company Investors, Clinton Richardson, online book, www.once.com/gcg/

Industry Week Growing Companies, www.iwgc.com

Small Business Computing and Communications

Additional Entrepreneurial Insights

Beyond Entrepreneurship: Turning Your Business into an Enduring Great Company, James C. Collins and William C. Lazier, 1995.

Honey, I Want to Start My Own Business, A Planning Guide for Couples, Azriela L. Jaffe, 1997.

To Build the Life You Want, Create the Work You Love: The Spiritual Dimension of Entrepreneuring, Marsha Sinetar, 1996.

Learning Objectives

- Understand how a business broker operates.
- Explore the advantages and disadvantages of buying a business.
- Learn how to protect yourself from a dishonest seller.
- Understand the role attorneys, brokers, appraisers, and accountants play in purchasing a business.
- Locate businesses for sale.
- Learn how to use an earn-out to save cash at the beginning.
- Evaluate a business from the outside.
- Explore inside a business to determine if the numbers are accurate.
- Assess the market value of a business for sale.
- Evaluate good will.

In this chapter, you'll learn some ways to evaluate businesses that are for sale. Although we focus on ongoing, independent operations, many of the tactics are the same for evaluating franchise opportunities. We'll discuss franchising more specifically in Chapter 14.

When you buy an ongoing business, you're buying an income stream. You may also be buying inventory, a location, goodwill, and an agreement that the seller will not compete with you. When you buy a franchise, you're primarily buying the right to use a name. In addition, you may also be buying a training program, a Business Plan, advertising assistance, lease negotiation assistance, and purchasing advantages.

As you begin your search for a franchise or business to purchase, make sure that you do not fall in love with a "deal" but fall in love with a business that hopefully will fulfill your needs and desires. Return back to the beginning Action Steps in Chapter One, where you explored your interests, strengths, weaknesses, and "Your Inc. Plan." You will be expending a great deal of your time, energy, and emotion so choose wisely based on intuition and factual information. Trust your instincts. Investigate the deal thoroughly and completely. Make sure you stress the importance of finding the "right opportunity" first and the "right price" second.

Spend time searching for an opportunity that feels right. Will this be something you will enjoy doing day in and day out? Can you visualize yourself at work each day and improving the business? Are the customers the type of people you want to interact with on a daily basis? Does this look like fun?

You need to be very careful as you explore business opportunities to make sure the business will be able to show a profit and a return on your investment. If you purchase an ongoing business, someone else has already taken the risk and high cost of starting a business from scratch. Your goal is not to pay too much for their risk-taking.

One entrepreneur we know loved the idea of buying businesses. She improved each business and tried to resell within twelve months. Some entrepreneurs become "serial entrepreneurs" purchasing and improving businesses and then selling for a profit. Some people enjoy the start-up phase but do not enjoy

Global Dos and Don'ts

According to global-business expert Ruth Stanat, some general rules of thumb can smooth the executive ride. For example, check visa requirements at least two weeks in advance of a trip. For spur-of-the-moment trips, check with airlines and travel agents, who can often expedite visas in 24 hours. Make copies of passports and plane tickets, in case they get lost or stolen. Try to take evening flights, and stack a lot of meetings for the first day of the trip. "You want to stay on that country's time zone to maximize every minute of the trip," Stanat says. Some region-by-region tips:

Carefully research each country, and get to know its customs. "In Thailand," Stanat says, "it is an honor to take the last bite of food during a meal, but in China, you are supposed to leave food on your plate at the end of a meal. You don't want to ruin a business deal in China because you've cleaned your plate." **Don't underestimate the traffic problems.** In Bangkok or Hong Kong, for example, allow at least an hour for travel between appointments. **Avoid travel in the summer.** "In June or July in Singapore, it can be 110°F."

Learn at least the basics of Spanish or Portuguese. If you're not fluent, have someone with you who is. "Having a grasp on the language is crucial in these countries," Stanat says. **Patience is a virtue.** "Don't arrive with all of your facts and figures out, expecting to get right down to business. Latin Americans will first want to build a relationship with you. Until they trust you, they're not going to do business with you." **Allow for late meals.** "Americans want to eat early and go to bed by 9. That doesn't happen in Latin America. Dinner begins at 9."

Expect to be entertained. In Eastern Europe in particular, where business relations with Westerners are still relatively new, Stanat says, **thoroughly research your clients.** "With the demise of communism, a lot of these firms try to make themselves appear more highly skilled and financially better off than they are. Once you are doing business with them, you don't want to find out that they really don't have the skills and the financial backing." **And try to stay in at least a four-star hotel for access to fax machines and good phone lines.**

The workweek is Sunday to Wednesday in Muslim culture. (Thursdays and Fridays and typically all of Saturday are holy days). There is **no alcohol consumption.** Westerners should use only their right hand—even when writing—and **avoid crossing their legs** (Muslims consider the left hand unclean, and are prohibited from showing the bottom of their feet). **Taboos are particularly hard on women.** "If their skirt is too short, they can have their legs whipped in Saudi Arabia. Women should wear a dark pantsuit and always keep their arms and legs covered.

SOURCE: From *TIME,* MAY 25, 1998, vol. 151, no. 20.

the management phase of operating a business. Determine which type of entrepreneur you are before making the leap.

You should explore businesses for sale whether you're serious about buying or not. By now, you're far enough along on your quest to sense the atmosphere of the marketplace. Talking to sellers is just one more step in your education in entrepreneurship.

So have fun, but leave your checkbook at home.

Explore Buying a Business

- Terms
- Fixtures and equipment
- Training
- Customers (goodwill)
- Suppliers
- Distributors
- Location
- Employees
- Technology
- Licenses and permits

Why Buy an Ongoing Business?

The overwhelming reason for buying an ongoing business is money, primarily the income stream. If you do your research and strike a good deal, you can start making money the day you take over an ongoing business. Since most start-ups must plug along for months (even years) before showing a profit, it's smart to consider this doorway to business ownership. Other advantages of buying an existing business may include the following.

1. If you find a "hungry seller," you should be able to negotiate good terms. You might get into the business for very little up-front cash, and might also negotiate seller financing.
2. Fixtures and equipment will be negotiable. Be sure the equipment is in good working condition and has been well maintained. Ask to see service records.
3. Training and support may be available through the seller and can sometimes be negotiated. If the seller is financing, he or she will have a stake in your success. Many banks like to see some seller financing because they believe it secures the seller's interest and thus the bank's interest.
4. An established customer base should be in place. You will need to determine how loyal the customers are and whether there is good- or ill-will. If the customer base is not strong or loyal, consider this in your price negotiations.
5. Relationships with suppliers and distributors are in place. Make sure you spend time talking to the suppliers and distributors to determine the status of the relationship. They should provide great insight.
6. The location may be excellent and not easily duplicated. Determine if the lease can be reassigned to you. The owner of the building may have other goals for the location.
7. Employees may possess specialized knowledge that you covet. In high-technology industries, purchasing businesses for brainpower is common practice. You will have no guarantee, though, that the employees and their expertise will remain—you must also consider the possibility that key employees may leave and compete.
8. Existing licenses and permits may be difficult to replicate. Check with your attorney and/or licensing agencies to determine availability and process to transfer licenses and permits before proceeding with the purchase.
9. The uncertainties of a start-up business are reduced.

10. You will be able to see actual financial data and tax-reporting forms. Investigate! Investigate! Investigate! Assume they may have two sets of books and ask to see both.
11. An inside look into the business operation will determine if utilizing advanced technology could increase operational effectiveness and thus profits.

How to Buy and How Not to Buy

Smart buyers scrutinize everything about a business with a microscope, Geiger counter, computer analysis, clipboard, and sage advice from business gurus. They do not plunge into a business for emotional reasons. For example, you may have eaten lunch around the corner at Millie's Cafeteria with your pals for years, and when the place goes up for sale, nostalgia may make you want to write out a check for it on the spot. That would be a wrong reason to buy. *Don't* buy a business that way.

In purchasing an ongoing business, you will need to utilize the expertise of experienced **business opportunity brokers,** accountants, small business attorneys, and business appraisers. As when searching for all professionals, use your eyes and ears to search out the best. Pay for their expertise! Business appraisers can be reached through the Institute of Business Appraisers, **www.instbusapp.org,** P.O. Box 1447, Boynton Beach, FL 33425, 561-732-3202, Fax: 561-732-4304.

You can also contact business brokers through FranNet or VR Business Brokers, the largest business brokerage firm. Business brokers have helped hundreds of individuals find their dreams and meet their financial goals. Business broker's expertise can be very helpful in your search.

Locate an attorney with expertise in business sale transactions as well as an accountant who understands thoroughly the tax implications involved in the transfer of a business. A good accountant may be able to turn up some interesting loopholes that will benefit both buyer and seller.

Every business in the country is for sale sometime. Deals are like planes. If you miss one, another one will be along soon.

Good buys are always available to the informed and careful buyer, but they may be difficult to discover. Seeking the right business to buy is much like an employment search: the best deals are seldom advertised. In contrast, the worst business opportunities are advertised widely, usually in the classified sections of newspapers. When you see several ads for a particular type of business, you know where the unhappy businesspeople are.

Running your own ad can be a good idea, however. A man ran the following ad in the business section (not the classifieds) of a large-circulation Midwestern newspaper:

> Sold out at 30. I'm tired of retirement and ready to start again. Want to buy business with over 1 million dollars in annual sales. Write me at Box XXXX. H.G.

H.G. received more than 100 replies and says that reading the proposals was one of the most educational and entertaining experiences he's ever had.

Getting the Word Out

Once you're ready to look for a business to buy, you'll need to learn what's for sale. These tips will help you do that:

1. Spread the word that you are a potential buyer.
2. Contact everyone you can in your chosen industry—manufacturers, resellers, agents, dealers, trade associations, and so on; let them know you are looking.

Business-opportunity broker A real estate broker who specializes in representing people who want to sell businesses

► **Action Step 53**

Preparing a Letter of Inquiry

Write a form letter of inquiry and send it to three to five firms that you may be interested in buying. Keep it open-ended; let them make the disclosures.

It's best to learn of businesses for sale by networking, but you can find some of the most eager sellers by their advertising in the newspaper classified section.

Leave your checkbook right where it is for now. This action step will cost you practically nothing. The goal is to learn what's out there and how sellers talk about their businesses.

3. Ask your network of bankers, attorneys, CPAs, and community leaders to help you in your search.
4. Advertise your needs in trade journals.
5. Send letters of inquiry to potential sellers (see Action Step 53).
6. Knock on doors.
7. Check with business opportunity brokers.
8. Talk with firms that deal in mergers and acquisitions.
9. Don't allow yourself to be rushed; time is your ally, and the deals will get better.
10. Check out businesses you would like to operate and buy. Ask the owners if they would consider selling.
11. Look for owners who want to retire or sell for other reasons such as partnership disagreements, illness, boredom, or divorce.
12. Look for businesses that aren't doing well but where you believe your expertise and energy would improve the business. Make sure the business is not in a shrinking marketplace.
13. Check out businesses with a great product but possibly bad marketing or location. Would a new location or a great marketing campaign help the business take off? If it is a manufactured product, could reducing the costs of production by moving the facility reduce costs enough to make the business profitable?

Action Step 53 will help you get the word out. It should be quite interesting to read the letters you receive in response to your form letter.

Investigate the Business from the Outside

Once you've found a business that looks promising, check it out by playing marketplace detective. This section suggests some techniques that will make you feel like a superspy. After checking it out from the outside, you'll be ready to move inside, to check the books, and talk to the owners in an attempt to learn the real reasons they are selling. But the first step is to get your telescope and your telephoto camera and gather as much information as you can from the exterior. Unfortunately, Ben and Sally Raymundo didn't do this, and learned about fraud the hard way.

A Horror Story from the Suburbs

Ben and Sally Raymundo bought a women's sportswear store in a thriving community about two miles from a regional shopping mall. They learned too late that the seller had a more profitable store in another part of the county and that she had used that store's records to misrepresent the store they bought. Here are the particulars:

1. The seller moved the cash registers from the higher-volume store to the store she wanted to sell so that the store's sales were greatly inflated.
2. The price was fixed at inventory plus $10,000 for goodwill. This seemed a bargain for a store whose cash register records showed it was grossing $500,000 per year at a 40 percent average gross margin.
3. Ben and Sally paid full wholesale value ($100,000) for goods that had been shipped there from the other store. The goods were already shopworn and out of date and eventually had to be marked down to less than $20,000.

4. Ben and Sally assumed the remainder of an iron-clad lease at $6000 per month, and the landlord made them sign a personal guarantee that pledged their home as security on the lease.
5. The location proved to be a dead foot-traffic location in a marginally successful center.

Fortunately, Ben had kept his regular job. Sally worked at selling off the unwanted inventory and replaced it with more salable stock. They spent another $30,000 for advertising during the 12 months they stayed in business. It was another year before the landlord found a new tenant and Ben and Sally could get out of the lease.

Learn from Others' Mistakes

What could Ben and Sally have done to avoid this fiasco? Many things. They could have asked the mall merchants how well the shopping center was doing. They could have spent some time observing the store and the shopping mall before they committed. They could have insisted that Sally be allowed to work in the store prior to or during the escrow period, with a clause that would have allowed them to bail out.

Ben and Sally were honest, hardworking people who took the seller at face value. That was a huge mistake. A talk with suppliers might have uncovered the seller's fraud. They are now suing, and the CPA and attorney they have hired could have helped them before they purchased the business. It's only going to get more expensive for them, and their chance of recovery is slim.

Some sellers don't count the value of their own time as a cost of doing business. This makes the firm show an inflated return on investment (ROI). Let's say such a firm earns $100,000 per year and has an inventory of $200,000. This could be a bad buy if the seller, his spouse, and their two children work a total of 200 hours per week and if a $200,000 investment could earn 10 percent or more per year in high-yield bonds.

Look at each deal from the viewpoint of what it would cost to hire a competent manager and help at market wage rates. In this case, let's suppose you had to pay $40,000 a year for a manager, $30,000 a year for an assistant, and $30,000 a year for two hourly employees. You would have spent $100,000 and lost the opportunity to earn another $20,000 on your investment. Yes, this would be a "no-brainer," but a lot of businesses are bought with even less going for them.

It's time now to go out and investigate a business on your own. Remember what you've learned from Ben and Sally's bad experience, and take along your new eyes and your camera. You'll be surprised how much there is to see. Action Step 54 tells you how to do it.

Know When You Need Outside Help

We've already discussed the need for a team of small business gurus to help you realize your dream of small business ownership. When you evaluate a small business for purchase, however, you may need a special kind of outside help. If you have any lingering doubts about the business you are researching, you may need the perspective of someone who is more objective than one of your team players. If you're not the Sherlock Holmes type yourself, hire someone who is. Your dream may be shattered by this kind of investigation, but you'll save money in the long run.

Georgia Webster had some doubts about the business she and her husband were considering. See what you can learn from the Webster's experiences.

▶ **Action Step 54**

Study a Business from the Outside

Let's say you've got your eye on a business you think is a real money machine. What can you do to find out more about it without tipping your hand and driving up the asking price?

1. Make sure the business fits into the framework of your industry overview. You want a business that's in the sunrise phase, not the sunset phase, of the life cycle.
2. Diagram the area. What's the location and how does the area fit into the city/county planning for the future? What is the life-cycle stage of the community? Where is the traffic flow? Is there good access? How far will your target customers have to walk? Is parking adequate? Is the parking lot a drop-off point for car poolers? What is the employee pool of the area?
3. For retail, take some photographs of the exterior. Analyze them carefully. Is the building in good repair? What are the customers wearing? driving? and buying? What can you deduce about their lifestyle? Take photographs on different days and at different times of day.
4. Ask around. Interview the neighbors and the customers. What do the neighbors know about the business? Will the neighbors help draw target customers to your business? Be up front with the seller's customers, since they may soon be your customers. What do they like about the store? Is the service good? What changes would they recommend? What services or products would they like to see added? Where else do they go for similar products or services?
5. Check out future competition. Do you want to be close to competitors (like Restaurant Row, Mile of Cars, and other such successful

continued on next page

business areas), or do you want to be miles away? Could a competitor move in next door the day after you move in?

Studying the business from the outside will tell you if you should go inside and probe more deeply. Adjust the steps if necessary to apply to manufacturing or service businesses.

Saved by a Bulldozer

I'd worked for a large ad agency in New York for 12 years before I gave it up and moved west, to the Bay Area. I couldn't believe it—no snow, no grey-black winter slush, no icicles in April—and I soon became a sports freak, to make up for all the years I'd spent indoors, I guess. I took up tennis, then racquetball, then biking, then volleyball, then hiking.

I met Fred on the tennis court. It was love at first sight, for both of us, and we were married six months later. Fred is really creative, and he'd always wanted to have a business of his own. Since we both loved sports, we decided to look around for a sporting goods store to buy.

We found the perfect store by networking with our sportsminded friends. It was called The Sports Factory, and it was located a block from a complex of tennis courts, three blocks from a new racquetball club, and a quarter-mile from a park where volleyball tournaments are held every other month.

A friend of ours who's an accountant checked over the books. He said they looked perfect. "Great P and L," he said, "and accounting ratios you wouldn't believe for this business. If you get the right terms, you could clear 50 Gs every quarter, and *that's* only the beginning. This guy doesn't even advertise."

We learned that the owner wanted to sell the store because he was tired of it—the long hours, being tied down, and so on. He'd been doing that for a dozen years and he wanted to start enjoying life.

I asked around—networking again—and located a community college professor who knows a lot about small business. His name is Harry Henkel, and he's written a book about going into small business. I called him, and he listened very patiently when I told him our story. Then we made an appointment to talk some more. After 15 minutes he told me he'd be glad to check things out for us for a small fee. I told him to go ahead, but I didn't tell Fred about it.

Two days later, my marketplace detective called and said he had some news.

"Oh?" I said. "So soon?"

"Yes. Do you remember seeing a bulldozer working across the street from The Sports Factory?"

"No, I don't. *What* bulldozer?"

"It started grading last week. Right across the street."

"We were just there Sunday," I told him, "and we didn't notice anything like that."

"Well," he said, "I talked to the driver on his lunch break. It seems a developer is putting in a seven-store complex, and one of the stores is going to be a discount sporting goods store." He paused.

"Oh, no," I said. "Are you sure?"

He explained that the store going in was part of a monster chain. I could see that we would have a hard time competing with them. I asked him if the owner knew, and if maybe that's why he's so "tired."

"Yes," Harry said, "I double-checked at the city planning office, where building permits are issued." And he paused again.

This marketplace detective work cost us $475, but it saved us thousands of dollars and years of heartache. Armed with what we learned through that experience, we examined almost a hundred businesses before we found the right one for us. It pays to investigate.

Georgia and Fred Webster came very close to buying the wrong business. The outsider's perspective helped them avoid making a very terrible mistake. Now it's time to get some inside perspectives.

Investigate the Business from the Inside

Once you've learned all you can from the outside, it's time to cross the threshold for a look at the interior. This is an important, time-consuming process, and it's an important milestone in your quest.

There are two ways to get inside the business: either contact the owner yourself, or you get assistance from a business-opportunity broker. We recommend that you use a broker because brokers have access to a lot of listings. You can locate these brokers in the Yellow Pages under *Real Estate* or *Business Brokers* and in the newspaper classifieds.

Call some brokers to learn if they have any listings in your area of interest. If so, check out the ones that appear interesting. Be prepared for disappointment. You will probably look at a great many businesses before you find anything close to your requirements. Nevertheless, you will learn a lot from the experience.

Dealing with Brokers

Business-opportunity brokers are active in most communities and play an important role in matching up sellers with buyers. Their level of competency ranges from specialists who know as much about fast-food franchises as McDonald's, to part-timers who know so little about business that they will only waste your time. A good broker can save you time and be very helpful in playing a third-party role in negotiations.

A broker has a **fiduciary** responsibility to represent the seller and is not paid unless he or she sells something. Typically, the broker's commission is around 10%, but it's less on bigger deals; and everything is open to negotiation. You may prefer a buyer's broker whose first responsibility is to you—but the seller will still pay the commission.

Some sellers list with brokers because they do not want it generally known (to their customers, employees, competitors) that they want to sell their business. Most sellers who list with brokers, however, do so out of desperation because they've already tried to sell their business to everyone they know. Probably nine out of ten fall into this category.

Spending time with a skilled broker can be a fascinating educational experience. If you want a particular type of business and are able to examine a half-dozen that are on the market, you will probably end up with a better grasp of the business than the owners. Network your business contacts to locate a competent broker. Ask brokers for referrals from their former clients. Quiz their business knowledge. (Can they explain a cash-flow forecast, an **earn-out,** the bulk sales law?) And as we've said so many times before, leave your checkbook at home. Don't let anyone rush you.

The following provides an example of broker listings.

Sample of Business Brokers Listings
SUNBELT®
Business Brokers of Sarasota
February/March '98 Hot Sheet

Professional
1. Medical Testing Clinics 14 centers in 3 states equipped with the latest technology. '97 revenue of $2.3MM. Ready for next level!
2. Optician Practice Lab on premises. Sales for '97 were substantially higher than '96. Full services available. Asking $175K.

Fiduciary Primary obligation is owed to the person who is paying (the seller)

Earn out The seller agrees to accept (a portion of) his payment for the business from the business's future earnings

Manufacturing

1. Clothing Manufacturer Makes America's most popular sportswear! Sales of over $6MM. Some RE included. $1.070 MM down.
2. Metal Fabricator One-man business working in all metals. Custom work incl. fences, frames, signs, etc. Asking $100K; 50K dn.
3. Sign Manufacturer Creates custom designs; quality craftsmanship. Large user of redwood. Experienced staff. Over $700K in sales.
4. Wood Products Manufacturing Business will do $700K in first year of operation. Great owners benefit. Asking $380K.

Construction

1. Clean-Up and Removal Contractor Use 2 dump trucks and a big bobcat to clean up construction & remodeling. Asking $100K dn.
2. Environmental Wastewater Requires engineering background and financial qualifications. Very profitable! Asking $1.1MM.

SOURCE: **http://www.sarasotaonline.com**

How to Look at the Inside of a Business

Once you have gotten your foot in the door and established yourself as a potential buyer, you will be able to study the inner workings of the business. Take full advantage of this opportunity.

Study the Financial History

What you need to learn from the financial history is where the money comes from and where it goes. Ask to see all financial records, for at least five years back if they're available, and take your time studying them. Hire an accountant to review the records. Your aim in buying an ongoing business is to step into an income stream. The financial records give a picture of that stream.

Before reviewing financial documents, most sellers and brokers will screen and qualify you as a potential buyer. They want to make sure only buyers with financial ability to purchase are shown company financial data. You will be required to present your personal financial data to the seller or broker. In addition, signing a nondisclosure agreement assures the seller that you will not talk to employees, suppliers, or customers until an appropriate agreed upon time. You will also be required not to disclose any information about the business to others except your advisors (who also must not disclose anything).

You may also be requested to sign a nonpiracy agreement, which prevents you from pirating the business's system, products, or ideas.

Look at the history of cash flow, profit and loss, and accounts, receivable. If the seller has a stack of accounts receivable a foot high, remember that:

after three months, the value of a current accounts dollar will have shrunk to 90 cents;

after six months, it will be worth 50 cents;

after a year, it will be worth 30 cents.

Review every receipt you can find. If a tavern owner tells you he sells 600 hamburgers per week, ask to see the receipts from the suppliers. If none is offered, ask permission to contact the suppliers for records of shipment. Make him prove to you what he has bought from suppliers. You can then accurately measure sales. If the seller won't cooperate, run—don't walk—away; he's hiding something. You can use this technique with any firm that is buying and marking up material or merchandise.

Evaluate closely any personal expenses that are being charged to the business. (Your CPA will help you determine a course of action that will keep you out of trouble.) This allows you to get a clearer picture of the firm's true profits.

It's also a good idea to look at canceled checks, income tax returns (probably for the last five years), and the amount of salary the seller has been paying him- or herself. If your seller was stingy with his or her own salary, decide whether you could live on that amount.

Many cash business will be very difficult to evaluate. As owners many times skim cash off the top and do not report it to the IRS.

If the seller brags that he doesn't pay his taxes, ask yourself, "can you trust him?" If he's willing to lie to the IRS, who can put him in jail, he will more than likely be willing to lie to you.

Make sure the owner has not been paying his employees in cash. If he is, employee costs will be underestimated. Explore if family members are working in the business and not getting paid. If so, projected employee costs will need to be revised. Many owners also underestimate the number of hours they work. If you will be hiring a manager to run the business, you may need to hire a full time manager and an assistant to cover the number of hours the owner has been willing to devote to the business.

The following provides a list of items you need to review with the owner, your accountant, lawyer, and business broker before finalizing your purchase of any business. Following the steps we have outlined in Chapter 13 may take you several weeks or months. Do not skip any steps in your haste to get on with the show of starting your own business.

Tip: You can use the seller's accounts receivable as a point for negotiation, but don't take over the job of collecting them.

Due Diligence—Items for Review

Accounting Services Contract

Accounts Payable Records

Accounts Receivable Records

Advertising Agreements with Media Companies

Asset List incl: maintenance records, warranties, invoices, title, encumbrances, operating instr.

Bank Account Statements incl: deposit receipts, & checking account stmts with canceled checks

Contributions and Dues records

Corporate Minutes Book

IRS Tax Returns, Personal property Taxes, Municipal, Employment, Unemployment

Credit Card Company agreements

Customer Agreements (wholesale)

Employment Contracts

Equipment Lease Agreements

Equipment Operating Manuals

Equipment Suppliers List

Financial Statements for 19____ through present

General Ledger

Insurance Policies including: property, liability, medical, business interruption

Inventory List—invoices

Leasehold Agreements

Licenses and Fees

List of Employees

Loan Agreements

Maintenance Records/Receipts and Agreements

Non-Compete Agreements

Payroll records

Personnel Policies including: vacation, sick leave, maternity, commission

Recipes

Records of litigation outstanding notice of litigation pending

Sales Receipts for last 12 months and/or 2 tapes

Sales Receipts on sales of capital assets

Stock Certificates

Supplier Agreements and Contracts

Travel & Entertainment Details

Utility bills including telephone

Compare What Your Money Could Do Elsewhere

How much money would you be putting into the business? How long would it take you to make it back? Have you figured in your time?

Let's say you would need to put $100,000 into this business, and that the business will give you a 33.3 percent return, which is full payback in three years. Are there other investments you could make that would yield the same amount on your $100,000?

If you will be working in the business, you need to add in the cost of your time; that's $30,000 per year (your present salary) over the three-year period, or $90,000 (assuming no raises). In three years, the business would need to return $190,000 after expenses and taxes in order to cover the risks involved with your $100,000 investment and to compensate you for the loss of $30,000 in annual salary.

Evaluate the Tangible Assets

If the numbers look good, move on to assess the value of everything you can touch, specifically the real estate, the equipment and fixtures, and the inventory.

1. **Real Estate** Get an outside professional appraisal of the building and the land.
2. **Equipment and Fixtures** Remember, this stuff is used. You can get a good idea of current market values by asking equipment dealers and reading the want ads. Scour your area for the best deals because you don't want to tie up too much capital in equipment that's outmoded or about to come apart. Suppliers have lots of leads on used equipment, so check with them. If you're not an expert in the equipment field, get help from someone who is.
3. **Inventory** Count the inventory yourself, and make sure the boxes are packed with what you think they are. Make certain you specify the exact contents of shelves and cabinets in the purchase agreement. Don't get careless and write in something vague like "All shelves are to be filled"; specify what goes on the shelves.

Inventory Items carried in stock

Tangible assets Things that can be seen and touched

Once you've made your count, contact suppliers to learn the current prices.

Where to Find Federal Contract Opportunities

The federal government buys just about anything a small business can offer. Its unending need for goods and services covers everything from catering to trash hauling to computer equipment and training to plumbing supplies.

The challenge is finding out what's on Uncle Sam's shopping list so you can decide whether it's worth your company's time and effort to pursue this market. The good news is the government makes this information readily accessible through a wide range of outlets, many of which are free. Here are some of the most common methods to learn about opportunities to bid on government contracts:

- Read *Commerce Business Daily*
- Register with Pro-Net
- Introduce yourself to your customers
- Use your local Procurement Technical Assistance Center
- Attend procurement seminars
- Don't overlook subcontracting and supplier opportunities.
- Consider using VANs

Read *Commerce Business Daily* (CBD)

The CBD is published Monday through Friday by the Department of Commerce and is the most common method of advertising contracting opportunities for purchases over $25,000. You can subscribe to the CBD by calling the Government Printing Office at 202-512-1800 and paying the $324 annual subscription fee. Or, you can get the CBD for free and in a more timely fashion by accessing it on the web at **http://cbdnet.access.gpo.gov.** Be aware that the CBD reflects only a fraction of the government's total needs, so read it faithfully, but make it only one part of your government marketing strategy.

Register with Pro-Net

Help procurement agents find you by registering with this free online database. Pro-Net is the largest small business database in the world. It is operated by the U.S. Small Business Administration, and is designed to be a one-stop-procurement shop for government purchases. You can use it as a marketing tool by profiling your business on it. Government contracting officers use it as a search engine when they're interested in making a purchase. For more on how to register with Pro-Net call the SBA at 800-827-5722.

Introduce yourself to your customers

Federal government purchases under $25,000 are made directly by the end users in each agency—so get to know the people at each agency who might be interested in your product. Send brochures and letters introducing yourself, and follow up with a phone call to make an appointment. Like any of your customers, government purchasers prefer doing business with people they know and trust. Remember that selling to the government still means selling yourself and your business to people.

Use your local Procurement Technical Assistance Center

These centers (sometimes called PTACs or programs) are another free resource designed to assist local businesses in marketing and selling to federal and local governments. There are about 60 PTACs located around the country. Call 409-886-0125 or 703-767-1650 for the one nearest you.

continued on next page

Attend procurement seminars

Various federal agencies offer briefings, conferences, and seminars to teach interested firms about doing business with government. In addition to learning how to engage in the process, you are likely also to find out about specific procurement opportunities. As an added bonus, you'll have an opportunity to network and make important contacts with procurement officers. Get in touch with individual government agencies, your nearest PTAC, or your local SBA office to find out about upcoming events.

Don't overlook subcontracting and supplier opportunities

Market your business to prime contractors, emphasizing your interest in becoming a subcontractor or supplier. The SBA publishes the Subcontracting Directory, which lists several prime contractors for multiple agencies. The GSA publishes the GSA Subcontracting Directory twice a year and the Department of Defense annually publishes Subcontracting Opportunities with DoD. In addition, many agencies publish procurement forecasts that can help identify future subcontracting opportunities, giving your business lead time to prepare a proposal.

Consider using VANs

Value Added Networks are private companies that gather and sort government procurement opportunities and match them with individual businesses. Some VANs are better than others, so ask each for references and samples of the types of opportunities they might pair you with before you sign up and pay for the service. Some VANs are certified by the government for electronic commerce using electronic data interchange (EDI). This certification does not guarantee the quality of the information they provide. Call the Electronic Commerce Resource Center at 800-231-2772 to get information about your nearest VANs.

If you find merchandise that is damaged, out of date, out of style, soiled, worn, or not ready to sell as is, don't pay full price for it. *Negotiate.* This is sacrifice merchandise and it should have a sacrifice pricetag.

Make sure closing is based on satisfactory inspection of all building, inventory, fixtures and equipment.

Talk to Insiders

There's no substitute for inside information. Every detective takes it seriously.

Suppliers Will suppliers agree to keep supplying you? Are there past difficulties between seller and supplier that you would inherit as the new owner? Remember, you're dependent on your suppliers.

Employees Identify the key employees early, and talk to the credit manager. In small business, success can rest on the shoulders of one or two persons, and you don't want them to walk out the day you sign the papers and present the seller with a fat check.

Competitors Identify the major competitors and interview them to learn what goes on from their perspective. Expect some bias, but watch for a pattern to develop. (Chapter 5 tells how to identify the competitors; refer to that discussion if you need to.)

Get a Noncompetition Covenant

Once you buy a business, you don't want the seller to set up the same kind of business across the street. Customers are hard to come by, and you don't want to pay for them and have them spirited away by a cagey seller. So get an agreement, in writing, that the seller will not set up in competition with you—or work for a competitor, or help a friend or relative set up a competitive business—for the next five years. You may need a lawyer to help you.

Whether you get a lawyer or do it yourself, be sure to specify the exact amount you're paying for the noncompetition covenant. That way, the IRS will allow you to deduct it against ordinary income over the life of the covenant Appendix B provide further discussion and a sample non-compete agreement.

Analyze the Seller's Motives

People have all kinds of reasons for selling their businesses. Some of these reasons favor the buyer, and others favor the seller. Here are some reasons for selling that can favor the buyer:

1. retirement
2. too busy to manage—seller has other investments
3. divorce, family problems
4. disgruntled partners
5. expanded too fast—out of cash
6. poor management
7. burned out, lost interest
8. ill health
9. change in lifestyle
10. wants new challenge

Buyer beware of the following:

1. local economy in a decline
2. specific industry declining
3. intense competition
4. high insurance costs
5. increasing litigation
6. skyrocketing rents
7. technological obsolescence
8. problems with suppliers
9. high-crime-rate location
10. lease not being renewed
11. location in a decline

Examine the Asking Price

Many sellers view selling their firms as they would view selling their homes; that is, they are emotionally attached to the business and therefore overvalue its worth. Pride also plays a role: they might want to tell their friends that they started from scratch and sold out for a million. If you run into irrational and emotional obstacles, walk away or try to find a professional who can intervene and bring together all parties.

Business valuations can be determined by valuators trained by the National Association of Certified Valuation Analysts (NACVA), **www.nacva.com,** 801-486-0600. The following information from NACVA details why you might want to utilize the services of a business valuation analyst.

Business Valuation Analyst

Preparing an accurate assessment of value for any business, enterprise or intangible asset requires in-depth specialized knowledge. Valuation professionals have this special skill. Valuation professionals from the National Association of Certified Valuation Analysts (NACVA) have practical experience as Certified Public Accountants (CPAs), practice in business evaluation or performing evaluations while working for the government. Their experience in accounting, tax, auditing, finance, insurance, economics and investments combined with NACVA's training in valuation theory, practical application, and litigation support prepares them to provide you a comprehensive analysis and competent valuation.

Numbers, facts, figures, balance sheets and financial statements by themselves are not accurate measures of the true fair market value of your assets. There is much more to the process of determining value. Different approaches and methods of valuation analysis should be reviewed and selectively matched to the business being valued—your business. Determining the most appropriate methodology—along with various analyses, sophisticated mathematical calculations, ratios, industry comparisons, economic and market analyses, business risk assessments—is needed for a competent valuation of your business.

SOURCE: **http://www.nacva.com**

In addition, we have discussed utilizing expertise from your business broker and trained business appraisers. The Institute of Business Appraisers also should be contacted to find a qualified appraiser. Table 13.1 illustrates one firm, BIZCOMPS, use of data to determine the valuation and selling prices of electronic manufacturers sold throughout the United States which appear in their database. Reach BIZCOMPS at **www.bizcomps.com** or 619-457-0366 to determine comps for your area and selected industry. Reports are less than $100.

Some industries have rule-of-thumb pricing. For example, a retail firm might be priced at three times its earnings or four times cash flow. One of the most important formulas for you to consider is the return on your investment (ROI) minus the value of your management time.

$$\text{ROI} - (\text{hours spent} \times \text{value of your time per hour})$$

If you can earn 16 percent without sweating on high-grade bonds, you should earn at least a 30 percent return on a business that will make you sweat.

You should be willing to pay a higher price for a firm with above-average-growth potential than one that is declining. In fact, you should not buy a declining business unless you believe you can purchase it cheaply and turn it around or dispose of its assets at a profit.

When evaluating the business for sale reconsider the list of reasons to purchase a firm presented above and the following:

- Terms—interest rate, down payment, length of note
- Operating profit
- Buyer's income
- Lease, location, equipment, competition, and customer base
- Return on investment
- Employees
- Growth potential
- Potential tax advantages

The buyer determines the true selling price of a business. During tight economic times, prices decrease; with a good economy prices rise. Be sure to purchase a business that meets your income needs. If you pay too much, there may not be enough left to pay yourself an adequate salary. If this happens, you will sour on the business early on and may not put in the effort needed for success.

Tax issues, as follow, should be considered in the buy—sell agreement.

Table 13.1

BIZCOMPS for Electronic Manufacturers

SIC #	Bus Type	Asking PR(000) w/Inv.	Ann Sales (000)	SDCF (000)	Sale Date	Sale PR(000) w/Inv.	% Down	Terms	Sale/ Sales	Sale/ SDCF	Inv. Amt	FF&E (000)	Rent/ Sales	Area
3625	Mfg-Electronics	480	320	157	12/31/96	380	100%	N/A	1.19	2.4	0	148	N/A	Mid-West
3625	Mfg-Electronics	2000	4,886	618	2/28/96	1800	33%	7 Yrs @ 9%	0.37	2.9	250	400	3%	Texas
3661	Telephone Interconnect	275	945	0	8/31/97	287	28%	6 Yrs @ 9%	0.30	#ERRC	62	21	1.7%	Maine
3671	Mfg-Security Systems	1200	1,500	300	9/30/93	1300	38%	5 Yrs @ 7%	0.87	4.3	200	139	5%	Austin, TX
3672	Mfg-Electronics	400	1,945	96	4/30/96	400	100%	N/A	0.21	4.2	95	86	1.4%	Utah
3672	Mfg-Circuit Boards	425	1,364	45	4/23/95	275	100%	N/A	0.20	6.1	128	65	2.8%	Michigan
3672	Mfg-PC Circuit Boards	1650	2,370	391	6/30/94	1340	22%	10 Yrs @ 10.5%	0.57	3.4	104	312	2%	Ventura County, CA
3672	Mfg-Electro Assembly	500	1,000	306	1/31/93	276	100%	N/A	0.28	0.9	40	150	4.5%	Dallas, TX
3672	Mfg-Electr Circuit Boards	435	300	60	6/30/89	320	56%	5 Yrs @ 10%	1.07	5.3	70	450	14%	San Diego, CA
3674	Mfg-Custom Electronics	3400	3,200	633	11/15/96	3650	27.4%	6 Yrs @ 10%	1.14	5.8	445	720	1.3%	Midwest

All Electronics Manufacturers In Data Base Sold
For An Average of 93.2% of Asking Price.

Average Sale Price Divided By Gross Sales = .62
(ie: Sale Price Was 62% of Gross Sales)

Median = .57

Average Sale Price Divided By In SDCF = 3.7
(ie: Sale Price Was 3.7 Times SDCF)

Median = 4.2

SOURCE: **www.bizcomps**
SIC = Small Business Industry Classification Number
BUS TYPE = Best Description of Subject Business
ASK PRICE = Asking Price (000's) (Does not include inventory)
ANN GROSS = Annual Gross Sales (Normally Net of State Sales Tax)
SDCF = Seller's Discretionary Cash Flow (Net Profit Before Taxes AND ANY COMPENSATION TO OWNER
plus Amortization, Depreciation, Other Non-cash Expense and Non-Business Related Expense. (SDCF As-
sumes One Working Owner)
SALE DATE = Actual Date of Sale
SALE PRICE = Actual Sale Price (in 000's) (Inventory has been deducted if it was in Sale Price)

% DOWN = Down payment as a Percent of Sale Price
TERMS = Terms of New or Assumed Encumbrance
SALE/SALES = Sale Price Divided by Gross Sales
SALE/SDCF = Sale Price Divided by Seller's Cash Flow
INV = Inventory At The Time of Sale. (in 000's) (Inventory is not included in Sale Price)
RENT/SALES = Rent as a Percent of Sales
FF&E = Estimate of Value of Furniture, Fixtures & Equipment
AREA = Region of Geographical Location of Business

Tax Considerations

A major consideration in structuring a business transaction is the tax consequences to both the buyer and the seller. Like other terms of the agreement, the structure that is best for the buyer from a tax standpoint may not be optimal for the seller, or vice versa. Unlike some other elements of the negotiation, however, taxes provide opportunities for the buyer and seller to work together to improve the economics of the total transaction.

From a tax standpoint, the best strategy is to minimize the total taxes paid on the transaction, taking into account both the seller's taxes and the taxes that the buyer will ultimately pay. By minimizing the combined taxes, value is added to the transaction. The buyer and seller can then negotiate how they will share that added value.

The following discussion deals only with federal taxes. However, state and local tax considerations can also play major roles in structuring a transaction and should be carefully analyzed as well.

The Buyer's Issues

The buyer will want to structure the sale to reduce the after-tax cost of acquiring the business. Consequently, a primary concern will be the allocation of the acquisition cost. The buyer will want this cost to be allocable to assets that can be expensed or depreciated quickly for tax purposes. The business may also have net operating loss (NOL) or tax credit carryforwards that the purchaser may want to preserve for future use.

To the extent that the transaction can be structured to allocate the acquisition cost favorably or to preserve carryovers or minimize the restrictions on their future use, the buyer may be in a position to pay more for the business.

The Seller's Issues

The seller will want to structure the sale so that the taxes on the gain from the sale are minimized. A related concern is the timing of the taxable gain. If the seller provides financing by accepting payments in installments or by accepting the purchaser's stock, the seller will want the transaction structured so that the tax to be paid on the gain is delayed until the receipt of the installment payments or the sale of the stock received.

A second related issue is the character of the gain (i.e., capital gain versus ordinary income). The tax rate on capital gains is less than the tax rate on ordinary income, making characterization as a capital gain desirable.

SOURCE: **www.dtonline.com**

Negotiate the Value of Goodwill

If the firm has a strong customer base with deeply ingrained purchasing habits, this has value. It takes a while for any start-up to build a client base, and the wait for profitability can be costly.

Some firms have built up a great deal of **ill will**—customers who have vowed never to trade with them again. A large proportion of the businesses on the market have this problem. If the amount of ill will is great, the business will have little value; it may be that *any* price would be too high.

A smart seller will ask you to pay something for goodwill. Thus you'll need to play detective and find out *how much* **goodwill** there is and *where* it is. For example, consider the seller who has extended credit loosely. Customers are responding, but there's no cash in the bank. If you were to continue that policy and keep granting easy credit, you could be in the red in a couple of months. Or maybe the seller is one of those very special people who is loved by everyone

Goodwill An invisible commodity used by sellers to increase the asking price for a business often its worth the price

Ill will All the negative feelings about a business; the opposite of goodwill

and will take the goodwill with him or her—like a halo—when he or she walks out the door.

So negotiate.

Let's say the asking price for the business you'd like to buy is $100,000 and that its tangible assets (equipment, inventory, and so on) are worth $50,000. In other words, the seller is trying to charge you $50,000 for goodwill. Before you negotiate, do the following:

1. Compare the goodwill you're being asked to buy to the goodwill of a similar business on the market.
2. Figure out how long it would take you to pay that amount. Remember, goodwill is intangible; you'll be unhappy if it takes you years to pay for it. Even the most cheerful goodwill comes out of profit.
3. Estimate how much you could make if you invested that $50,000 in T-bills.

This gives you a context in which to judge the seller's assessment of the value of goodwill, and you can use the hard data you have generated to negotiate a realistic—and no doubt, more favorable—price.

Learn If Bulk Sales Escrow Is Needed

You need to know if any inventory you would buy is tied up by creditors. If it is, the instrument you'll use to cut those strings is a bulk sales transfer, a process that will transfer the goods from the seller to you through a qualified third party. In most states, bulk sales transfer is specified under a series of regulations known as the Uniform Commercial Code.

If there are no claims by creditors, the transfer of inventory should go smoothly. If there are claims, you'll want to be protected by law. Either consult an attorney who has experience in making bulk sales transfers, or get an **escrow company** to act as the neutral party in the transfer. The quickest way to find an escrow company is to look in the Yellow Pages under *escrow*. A *better* way is to ask your banker or CPA to recommend one. Try to find one that specializes in **bulk sales escrows**.

(*Escrow* comes from *escroe*, Old French for "parchment," "deed," or "scroll." The distant Indo-European root is *skeru-*, which means "to cut"—and you'll need an expert to help you cut off creditors who have strings attached. For a look at the jungle of documents you can encounter in buying a business, read *A Basic Guide for Buying and Selling a Company* by Wilbur M. Yegge, Ph.D.

An Earn-Out Success Story

Sam Wilson had held several key executive positions in large manufacturing firms after receiving his MBA in the 1950s. His last position was as president of a medium-size U.S. firm with branch offices throughout the Free World. Sam got squeezed out when a large conglomerate purchased the firm and moved the headquarters to London.

After doing some freelance management consulting, Sam arranged to purchase an executive search firm that specialized in finding engineering talent in the aerospace industry. Buying the business seemed like a good idea to Sam because the business had been profitable for more than 20 years. The key personnel agreed to stay with the firm. It had loyal customers, a solid reputation, and Sam knew it would take him years to build a similar business from scratch, even though he understood the business.

He purchased the business for no cash down and agreed to pay off the entire purchase price from the earnings over the next five years. [This is called an **earn out**.] The seller was an older man who had known of Sam's reputation as a winner. Sam was one of the few prospective buyers who

Escrow company A neutral third party that holds deposits and deeds until all agreed-upon conditions are met

Bulk sales escrow An examination process intended to protect buyers from unknown liabilities

Earn out The seller agrees to accept (a portion of) his payment for the business from the business's future earnings

► **Action Step 55**

Study a Business Inside Out

Looking at a business from the inside enables you to determine its real worth and to see what it would be like to own it. Make an appointment—or have a business-opportunity broker arrange it—to take a serious inside look at the business you think you want to buy. Before you go, review everything we've explained in this section and write down a list of things you hope to learn while you're there. Don't allow anyone to rush you. Leave the checkbook at home; this fun is free.

were willing to pay full price for the business and seemed qualified to continue the growth of the firm. The business did prosper, but its growth was somewhat limited to what could be achieved while keeping a watchful eye on cash flow. Sam had to pay the salaries long before he received payment from clients.

Sam worked in the firm one to two days a week, and monitored activities by daily reports. He had plenty of time to run another business, but it would have to be a type of business whose cash flow is "front-loaded," rather than "back-loaded" like the search firm. Front-loaded businesses are those whose customers pay cash up front before the product or service is delivered. They include such businesses as hotels, bed and breakfast inns, bridal shops, custom printers, magazine publishers, and so on.

Sam chose to purchase a travel agency. He found a medium-size firm that had five excellent travel agents but was only slightly profitable. He purchased it for a low six-digit figure on a no-money-down, earn-out basis.

The travel agency cash flow was positive, and Sam saw some opportunities to make the firm more profitable. Observing that many travel agencies are run by "hobbyists" who know little about marketing and management, he refocused the agency efforts on exotic cruises and upscale vacation adventures. The agency was located in a very affluent area, and yet none of the competitors were specializing like this. He also knew that volume is the key to profit; some of the large chain agencies were earning 17 percent commissions on trips that paid small firms only 10 percent. Sam is now in the process of purchasing four more good agencies on an earn-out basis so that he can take advantage of the larger commissions.

Buying a business on an earn-out basis is an option only if the seller has great confidence in the buyer's skills and knowledge of the business. Thus the burden of convincing the seller to agree to such terms is on the buyer. It's necessary to show the seller that the business will continue to show a profit.

Sam Wilson developed a detailed business plan that demonstrated to the sellers that he was an expert—and his track record and references backed him up.

The Decision to Buy

Too many people purchase businesses emotionally. They buy a business as if it were a home, a car, or a suit. They are drawn to businesses that they think will enhance their image—that will impress their friends and relatives. Physically attractive businesses are often the worst investments because "image-conscious" buyers have bid the price up to an unreasonable figure. The "ugly" business or the "invisible" business often provides the best return on time and investment.

Many people view buying a business as buying a *job;* they look at it as providing them with "employment." (Sam's experience demonstrates that this is a narrow view.) Such people lack the experience to make a good choice, and often invest their life savings in ventures that demand 70–100 hours per week to run and pay them less than their 40-hour-week jobs did.

Does the thought of walking into someone's business for the purpose of "snooping" around, looking at the books, and asking the owner probing questions fill you with anxiety and make you nervous? It shouldn't. Sellers expect prospective buyers to do those things, and you are seriously looking for a business to buy. What's more, you are now *prepared* to investigate a business close up—and to enjoy it. You are ready for Action Step 55.

Even if you think you're ready to make your decision, do it—but not yet. Read the checklist below first. It reminds you of important details you might have overlooked. Even if you *know* you've found your dream business, complete this checklist before you sign the papers.

Final Checklist

_____ How long do you plan to own this business?

_____ How do you plan to exit this business?

_____ How old is this business? Can you sketch its history?

_____ Is this business in the embryonic stage? the growth stage? the mature stage? the decline stage?

_____ Has your accountant reviewed the books and made a sales projection for you?

_____ How long will it take for this business to show a *complete* recovery on your investment?

_____ What reasons does the owner give for selling?

_____ Will the owner let you see bank deposit records? (If not, why not?)

_____ Have you calculated utility costs for the first 3–5 years?

_____ What does a review of tax records tell you?

_____ How complete is the insurance coverage?

_____ How old are receivables? (Remember, age decreases their value.)

_____ What is the seller paying him or herself? Is it low? high?

_____ Are there any unpaid employees?

_____ Have you interviewed your prospective landlord?

_____ What happens when a new tenant takes over the lease?

_____ Have you made spot checks on the currency of the customer list?

_____ Who are the top 20 customers? top 50?

_____ Is the seller locked into 1–3 major customers who control the business?

_____ Are you buying inventory? If so, how much is the seller asking?

_____ Have you checked the value of the inventory with vendors?

_____ Have you checked the value of the equipment against the price of used equipment from another source?

_____ Who does your seller owe money to?

_____ Has your attorney checked for liens on the seller's equipment?

_____ Do maintenance contracts exist on the equipment you're buying?

_____ Has your attorney or escrow company gone through bulk sales escrow? Is there any pending litigation?

_____ Have you made certain that:

    _____ you're getting all brand names, logos, trademarks, and so on, you need?

    _____ the seller has signed a noncompete covenant?

    _____ the key lines of supply will stay intact when you take over?

Probe the Depths of Ill Will

How many products have you vowed never to use again? How many places of business have you vowed never to patronize again? Why?

Make a list of the products and services you won't buy or use again. Next to each item, write the reason. Does it make you sick? Does it offend your sensibilities? Was the service awful?

After you've completed your list, ask your friends what their negative feelings about particular businesses are. Take notes.

Study the two lists you've made. What are the common components of ill will? How long does ill will last? Is there a remedy for it, or is a business plagued by ill will cursed forever?

Turn your attention to the business you want to buy. You need to learn as much as you can about the ill will that exists toward that business.

Have fun with this step, but take it seriously—and think about the nature of ill will when your seller starts asking you to pay for goodwill.

_____ the key employees will stay?

_____ the seller isn't leaving because of stiff competition?

_____ you aren't paying for goodwill but taking delivery on ill will?

_____ you're getting the best terms possible?

_____ you're buying an income stream?

_____ all utility bills have been paid?

Prepare for Negotiations

Let's say you know you're ready to buy. You've raised the money, and the numbers say you can't lose, so you're ready to start negotiating. (If you're an experienced entrepreneur, you already know how to negotiate. If not read *Getting to Yes: Negotiating Agreement Without Giving In* by Roger Fisher and William Ury.)

We suggest two things about negotiations. First, when it comes time to talk meaningful numbers, the most important area to concentrate on is *terms*—not asking price. Favorable terms will give you the cash flow you need to survive the first year and then move from survival into success. Unfavorable terms can torpedo your chances for success, even when the total asking price is well below market value.

Second, when the seller brings up the subject of goodwill, be ready for it. Goodwill is a "slippery" commodity; it can make the asking price soar. It's only natural for the seller to attempt to get as much as possible for goodwill. Because you know this ahead of time, you can do your homework and go in primed to deal. Action Step 56 will help you do your homework. When the seller starts talking about goodwill, you can flip the coin over and discuss ill will—which hangs on longer, like a cloud over the business.

Only you can negotiate out a high price for goodwill, the intangible commodity. You're going to be on your own. Action Step 56 will help you. Go for it!

Protect Yourself

Evaluate each business opportunity by the criteria we present in this chapter. When you find one you think is personally and financially right for you, start negotiating. Your goal is the lowest possible *price* with the best possible *terms*. Start low; you can then negotiate up if necessary.

When asked to put down a deposit, handle it this way:

Deposit the money in an escrow account, and

Include a stipulation in your offer that says the offer is *subject to your inspection and approval* of all financial records and all aspects of the business.

Doing this gives you an escape hatch so that you can get your deposit back—and back out of the deal—if things aren't what they should have been.

One of the best things you can do to protect yourself is to work within the business for a few weeks with the option to back out if you have a change of heart. Sondra Butra fell in love with a retail photography business. Her husband suggested she work in the business for free for several weeks to determine if they should explore the business further. She discussed the arrangement with the seller. While reluctant at first, he gave in to Sondra.

After three weeks, Sondra knew working with fussy children, crabby parents, and stressed-out brides and grooms brought her little joy. This was not the business for her! She continued on her search and recently purchased an established Sylvan Learning franchise after working there free for four weeks.

Working in a business allows one to see the daily routine, the employee interaction and atmosphere, and potential issues one may be faced with. The cost is zero and the return incredible! If at all possible, try before you buy.

Expect Some Pleasant Surprises

Well, you've come a long way and you've worked hard on your research. You may be wondering if the digging was worth it. Only you can answer that. There *are* bargains to be found out there—businesses like Woolett's Hardware. For hunter–buyers with vision and persistence, beautiful opportunities are waiting behind ugly facades.

I heard about Woolett's being up for sale more than a year ago. I'd just opened up my second store at the time—it's also in the hardware line—and it took me just about a year—April to April—to streamline the paperwork. Thanks to an incredible retail computer system and a good manager, my sanity remained intact.

Woolett's had been on the market a year and a half or so. One look from the street, and I could see why.

The store was a mess. The building was pre–World War II, and so was the paint. Out front, the sign was sagging. The parking lot needed lots of work; there were potholes six-inches deep. The entryway was littered with scraps of paper, and the front door was boarded up.

Inside, things weren't much better. The floor needed a good sweeping. The merchandise was covered with dust. And all around there was this feeling of mildew, age, and disuse. It was dark—like a *cave*. It was tough finding a salesperson, and when you did, you couldn't get much help. Yet there were customers all over the place.

After you've been in business a while, you develop a sort of sixth sense about things. And the minute I stepped into the store, I knew there was something special about it—something hidden, something the eye couldn't see right off. I knew I had to dig deeper.

A visit to the listing real estate broker didn't help much. "Make us an offer," he said. "We just dropped the price yesterday. To $400,000."

"What do the numbers look like?" I asked.

He dug into a slim manila folder. "Last year," he said, "they grossed just under $800,000. The net was around $100,000."

"What about inventory?" I asked. "What about loans and **liens** and accounts receivable? When can I interview the manager? And why is the owner selling?"

"Are you just asking that," he said, "or is this for real?"

"This is for my son," I said. "He's new to the business, and we don't want a lot of surprises."

"Like I said, make us an offer."

"Let me check the books," I said.

I deposited $500 with an escrow company, making sure I got my usual escape clause—a deposit receipt saying my offer for the business is contingent upon my inspection of all assets and my approval of all financial records. Doing this has saved me tons of heartburn over the years.

The minute they got wind of a buyer, the manager and two of the employees up and quit. The back office was a mess, and it took me three days of searching to find something that would tell me I was on the right track. I found

Lien A legal obligation filed against a piece of property

a supply of rolled steel. It was on the books at $12,000, but I knew it was worth $40,000. I took that as a buy signal.

The next day, I made an offer—$12,000 down, with the balance to be paid out of profits over the next five years. The owner accepted, and we cleared escrow in 60 days.

The first thing we did was clean the place up. We surfaced the parking lot with asphalt, added a coat of paint, fixed the door, added lighting.

Business picked up right away. My son, newly married, was settling down and learning the business. He seemed to have managerial talents.

Then we found another set of records that had been hidden away in a safe. They showed us that the Woolett Corporation owned a bank account containing $30,000 and five acres of land, mostly along the road leading to town, right in the path of future growth! We had bought the *whole corporation.*

The first year we did just over a million dollars in sales. And there was every indication that we would do better from then on.

People who come into the store now hardly recognize the place. We've spent some more money on new lighting fixtures and we've added a large kitchen section. And in the summer we're staying open until eight.

▶ Summary

There are two good reasons to explore businesses for sale: You'll learn a lot by exploring the marketplace, and you might find a gem like Woolett's Hardware—a business that will make money right from the start.

If the seller is "hungry," you may be able to obtain terrific terms. For example, let's say you find a business for sale with an asking price of a $300,000. Its net profit last year was $50,000. You and the seller agree on

$20,000 down

a no-interest loan of $280,000

payments of 20 percent of net profits each year until the loan is paid off

Your loan payment would be 20 percent or $50,000 a year. You would have a profit of $40,000 left each year. After 10 years, you would have paid the owner upwards of $100,000, and your profit would have been a minimum of $400,000 if sales and profit did not even increase (hope that doesn't happen). With such good terms, you wouldn't need to think about paying off the loan for a long, long time.

Trained and experienced lawyers, accountants, and bankers are necessary for you to complete a business purchase transaction. Sellers are tied emotionally to their business and you are tied emotionally to your dream. You need impartial third parties to keep the sale on a rational basis.

Accountants will be able to evaluate financial statements to determine where the owners are hiding money, bad debt, employee theft, and a zillion other problems, which you might never discover.

Keep your checkbook at home as you initially explore. Make sure once you have entered into any negotiations that you sign nothing without your lawyer's review. Work in the business if at all possible before signing a final purchase agreement.

Buy a business that fits your personal and financial needs.

Think Points for Success

- Stick to what you know.

- Do not buy a business you know nothing about.

- If your seller looks absolutely honest, check him or her out anyway. Private detectives can run a thorough background check for very little money. A wise investment!
- Worry less about price; work harder on terms.
- Most good businesses are sold behind the scenes, before they reach the open market.
- Make sure you're there when the physical inventory takes place. Look in those boxes yourself.
- Get everything in writing. Be specific. Don't sign anything without understanding every word and your lawyer's OK.
- Always go through bulk sales escrow.
- Buying a corporation is tricky. Have an experienced corporate attorney assist you.
- Be ready to hold your own through the negotiation process but do not nit pick. Look at the whole picture.
- Income stream is vital. Be sure it is there and that your interest payments will not take it all away from you.

Key Points from Another View

By: VR Business Brokers

Over the years, VR Business Brokers has negotiated or supervised the sale of tens of thousands of businesses and seen some savvy negotiating styles. We've also seen the same negotiating mistakes over and over, leading to the same results—blown deals, disgruntled parties, money left on the table, and serious disputes.

Here are a dozen ways to **RUIN** a deal (and suggestions on how to save it):

1. **Concentrate on disagreements.** It's tempting to go straight to the problems in the deal. This creates a deadlock, and no reason to continue. Start with, and emphasize, the points of agreement, no matter how small. This gives the other side hope that compromise is possible on the big issues.
2. **Hide the flaws.** A seller should make sure serious flaws are disclosed **before** the first offer. A buyer's motivation to buy peaks at the time of the offer, and goes down from there. Disclosing serious flaws after an offer is made is not only unethical, but it is poor negotiating strategy.
3. **Ignore the marketplace.** Everyone wants to buy low and sell high. The fact is, almost all buyers who insist on paying less than market for a business never buy a business (or they fall for a "pig in a poke"). And, sellers who overprice their business end up owning it forever.
   Statistics prove my point. I analyzed my firm's 400 sales. I found that sellers who offered their business within 15 percent of our estimate of market value, ended up selling within 2 percent of average market value. Pretty close! Now for the eye opener: Sellers who offered their business for more than 40 percent over market value, ended up selling for an average of **26 percent below market!** By asking too much, they got less than they could have.
4. **Take unreasonable positions.** Unreasonable positions create distrust, and distrust ruins deals. I believe the major reason sellers suffer so much when they overprice their business is that it makes the buyer wonder what's wrong with the business. Buyers that make lowball offers usually don't get a business, but they do get the seller's bad feelings.

5. **Unrealistic objectives (Buyers).** Many buyers want the perfect business: no risk, high profits, no competition, and of course a bargain price. It doesn't exist! I believe a more realistic objective is to find an interesting business with prospects for growth, with disclosure of important facts from the seller, and a fair price.

6. **Unrealistic objectives (Sellers).** Many sellers want to retire or buy another business with the proceeds of a sale. They need all cash, a quick sale, no income taxes and the highest possible price. Unfortunately, this choice isn't available. The real choice is between selling for market value, or over pricing the business and not selling at all.

7. **Nickel and diming.** Some people can't quit when they're ahead. Dragging out the negotiations with multiple counteroffers decreases the chance of ever reaching an amicable agreement.

8. **Don't listen.** Most of us assume the other side wants to take away that which is most important to us. Listening carefully to the other side's position often allows you to solve their problem at very low cost to you.

9. **Negotiate against yourself.** Good negotiators will ask you to do better before they respond to your last position. Don't fall for it!

10. **Delay.** Time is the enemy of every deal. We all have second thoughts about committing ourselves. As time goes by, the more likely we think we made a mistake.

11. **Don't make friends.** People want to do business with people they like. Cultivating the other side and listening to their needs will often get you a better price and certainly an easier deal. Making enemies will often get you lack of cooperation and possibly a lawsuit!

12. **Don't put it in writing.** This is the most avoidable, yet most frequent negotiating mistake made. Whether through honest misunderstanding or worse, the deal you thought you had will change if it's not in writing (and signed).

SOURCE: **http://www.vrbusinessbrokers.com**

Buying a Franchise

14

Entrepreneurial Links

Books

Directory of Franchising Organizations: 1998/1999 Edition, Robert Ungerleider.

Franchising 101: The Complete Guide to Evaluating, Buying and Growing Your Franchised Business, Ann Dugan (Editor), Association of Small Business Development Centers, 1998.

Franchise Bible: How to Buy a Franchise or Franchise Your Own Business, Erwin J. Keupa and Vickie Reierson, 1995.

Websites

www.betheboss.com, Be the Boss

www.franchise.org, International Franchise Association

www.bison1.com, Business International Sales & Opportunity Network

Associations/Organizations

American Association of Franchisees, http://infonews.com/franchise/afa

American Association of Franchisees & Dealers, www.aafd.org, (619) 209-3775

Federal Trade Commission, www.ftc.gov

Publications

Franchise Opportunities Guide
Franchising World
Franchise Handbook Europe

Additional Entrepreneurial Insights

Franchising Organizations, Jeffrey Bradach, 1998.

The 1998 Franchise Annual: The Original Franchise Directory and Handbook, Lori Marsh (Editor), Ted Dixon (Editor), and J. Rittenhouse, 1998.

Bond's Franchise Guide 1998 (11th Ed), Robert E. Bond (Editor), Minjia Qiu (Editor), and Jeffrey Bond, 1998.

Learning Objectives

- Learn how your daily life is influenced by the franchise system.
- Explore franchising as an alternative doorway.
- Gain an overview of how the franchise system works.
- Develop techniques for examining franchises.
- Evaluate the pros and cons of being a franchisee.
- Understand risk-reward factors in "ground floor" opportunities.
- Learn why a franchise may not be for you and why some people should consider *only* franchises.
- Understand what you need to look for in the Uniform Franchise Offering Circular (UFOC).
- Recognize the advantages of owning multiple franchises.
- Understand why the true entrepreneur is always the franchisor.

Your walk-through of opportunities in small business is almost finished. Decision time approaches. If you've followed the Action Steps, you've spent several months gathering data and talking to people in small business. You have spent some time exploring businesses that are up for sale and talking to sellers. If you wanted to write a business plan now, you could sit down and do it. Before you do that, however, there is one other doorway to explore, the doorway to a franchised business.

Doing Biz with a Franchise

Did you have a Big Mac hamburger this week? Did you scarf down an Egg McMuffin on your way to work? Did your kids lead you to Burger King or Taco Bell? On your way from Tacoma to Taos, did you stop at a Perkins for pancakes? When you bought your last piece of real estate, did you happen to check out properties with Prudential?

When was your last trip to a 7-Eleven store? What do you think of the ads for Sir Speedy, the instant printer? If you wanted a business of your own, but do not feel strong enough to strike out on your own, would you check out a Play It Again sports equipment franchise or an educational franchise called Primrose School?

If you had some money from an early retirement buyout package, would you plunk down $1.5 million for a By rider System used auto franchise? Would you search the marketplace for a Boston Chicken outlet that still had some legs? Or would you opt for a clever business like Takeout Taxi—delivering gourmet meals to upscale diners at home?

Whether or not you personally patronize franchises—burgers, real estate, printing, tax preparation, equipment rental, travel agent, soft drinks or used cars—the franchising game is big.

According to estimates from the International Franchising Association (IFA), there are 2000 franchisors in the country and approximately 600,000 franchisees.

Surfing the Net for Franchise Information

Before you decide to buy a franchise, surf the Net.

Surfing the Net for Franchising Basics

The Internet has a ton of material on franchising. If you go to your favorite search engine (Yahoo, Excite, Alta Vista, etc.) and type in the word *franchise,* the first thing you'll access are names like "Brasileiro na Internet," "UFRAD–Turkish Franchising Association," and "OFFERTA–Slovenia–biancheria intima in franchising."

If you type in "buying a franchise," you'll narrow down the options to stuff you can use to locate and evaluate a franchise. The steps that follow walk you through some Websites that can save you time.

1. **FAQs.** Start with answers to Frequently Asked Questions, a Web staple, at **www.afww.com.** Questions include: What kind of franchise should you buy? Is financing available? What's a UFOC? Who provides the location? Do you need professional help?

2. **Terminology.** If you're new to franchising, you would be smart to acquire some of its specialized vocabulary. Check out the glossary of terms at **www.franchisearchitects.com.** The glossary begins with "Advertising Co-op" and ends with "Waiver." One of the key terms you'll need to know is "UFOC"–a disclosure document provided by the franchisor to the prospective franchisee. If you reach this step in your dream search–receiving a UFOC–consult an attorney who specializes in franchising.

3. **Searching Yourself.** The Internet bristles with tools to help you know yourself better. Tools for the franchisee come in two forms: admonitions (do this, do this, don't do that) and questions on a test (Can you work long hours and not whine? Are you averse to aggressive sales techniques?).

    There's a peachy franchising test, "Are You an Entrepreneur?" at our Website **www.dryden.com/mngment.** Click your way and take the test.

    If you're averse to tests and prefer admonitions (study hard; don't rush in; peer deeply into the marketplace), go to the U.S. Government Gopher Website at **www.sba.gov/gopher,** where you will find a workable definition of franchising: ". . . a legal and commercial relationship between the owner of a trademark, service mark, trade name or advertising symbol and an individual or group seeking the right to use that identification in a business."

4. **Franchising with Smarts.** A must read for any incipient franchisee is an *Inc. Magazine* piece (Nov. 1, 1995) called "The Smartest Franchisees in America," written by Jay Finnegan. This online essay at **www.inc.com/incmagazine/archives/** explores the survival tactics of savvy entrepreneurs who come to franchising with money, experience, and education.

    For example, to increase his used car sales, a savvy franchisee for J.D. Byrider Systems launched his own brand of Road Show. First, the cars were repaired and warranted. Then they were transported to an outlying town too small to support a major car dealer, where some 60 vehicles were parked in a large lot (arrangements made with Wal-Mart, etc.), next to a country band performing on a flatbed truck. A Road Show cost the franchisee $5000 and unit sales doubled.

    This essay, with its excellent examples, demonstrates what can be done with smart marketing.

    On this same *Inc. Magazine* Web page, you'll find links to other articles on franchising: management, customer feedback, research, scoping out the future, and so on.

5. **Searching the World.** For a super-positive view of franchising in the world, check out the Website for the IFA (short for the International Franchising Association) at **www.franchise.org.** At this writing, you can join the IFA for 30 days by typing in your name and e-mail address. The IFA offers multitudes of services to members.

Action Step 57

Web Search

Take a couple of hours to check out some of the e-links listed. As with any Web search, you'd be smart to set a timer—the Internet eats time—and to make a checklist of what you're after:

FAQs—do you need more than one set of frequently asked questions?

Glossary—Print out the glossary of franchising terms instead of trying to commit the whole thing to memory in a single gulp. Take along a page to study over coffee or while you're waiting for the bus.

Hot Franchise for Sale—Use the Internet to start your comparison shopping. For example, if you're handy in the kitchen and leaning toward a food franchise, compare a Perkins (each unit has its own in-house bakery) to a Bagel House.

Tips to Make You Smarter—Keep a list of the good ideas gleaned from reading about franchises. The owner of Takeout Taxi, a gourmet food delivery service, cranked a lot of money and design effort into their menus.

Legal Beefs—The Internet is such a happy place of sizzling super-hype, you might not find much information about which unhappy franchisee is suing which corporate franchisor. But file this image away—the Unhappy Franchisee Stung by Shrewd Franchisor—and bring up the question when you do field interviews. See Action Step 59

Franchising Chapters Online

Check out three chapters online from the *Franchise Bible,* Erwin Keup, Oasis Press, 1997. **www.smartbiz.com/sbs/cats/franch.htm** will lead you to:

- Checklist of Information to Secure from a Franchisor
- Learning about Franchise Documents
- State Franchise Information

6. **A Mouse Click Away, Opportunities Abound.** How about those opportunities you encountered by typing in *franchise* in your search engine slot? If they gave you an edgy feeling, go to **www1.shore.net**—a Website run by Franchise Services Associates that lists interesting franchises: Bagel House & Deli (breakfast and lunch eatery), Compu-Fun (computer education for kids and adults), Corporate Cafe (office complex cafeteria), Java's Brewin (watch out, Starbuck's), and Jim's Greenery (interior landscape service).

    Also at this Website: questions for the entrepreneur.

    If you haven't run across the Website for *Entrepreneur Magazine,* it's time to access **www.entrepreneurmag.com** and a Website for all seasons. If you don't bypass all the interesting stuff and go directly to the Franchising Channel, you'll stay here for weeks. When you hit the mouse for specific sightings in the Franchise Channel—like "Low-Investment 150" and "International 200"—make sure you set your alarm clock so you can get out.

7. **Litigious Gloom.** The wonderful world of franchising is not all rosy sunsets and profits made easy. A dour U.S. government Website at **www.ftc.gov** leads you to case summaries involving franchisors and creative business developers who landed in court for attempting to flim-flam opportunities that either: (a) did not exist, or (b) were misrepresented by these creative folk. Franchising is a very litigious business. Lawyers get real rich over the problems. People who buy franchises have to do things *exactly* the way things are laid out for them. They can't deviate from the system. When people try to deviate from the system they often end up in court.

Franchise agreements are airtight and *always* favor the franchisor.

If your dream franchise appears on this list, bypass that opportunity and continue your search.

The franchise industry is enormous. If you were to buy or rent a car tomorrow morning, put gas in it, and then drive it to a fast-food restaurant for lunch, you might be supporting a franchise at every stop.

Why Buy a Franchise?

The overwhelming reason for buying a franchise is to benefit from name recognition. Consumers grow to trust brand-name products and services. Look at the places where you do business. Do you drink Coca-Cola? The Coca-Cola headquarters are in Atlanta, but the beverage is bottled by regional franchisees. Do you buy gas at a Mobil, Texaco, Exxon, or Shell? They're franchises, too. If you buy milk at 7-Eleven, buy hamburgers at Burger King or use a Century 21 Realtor, you're into the franchise system. Franchised products and services are predictable and reliable. Many consumers go out of their way to do business with franchisors. This customer loyalty is worth paying for.

What the Franchisee Gets

Let's examine what you can get when you pay money to a **franchisor** for a **franchise**—that is, when you become a **franchisee.** A franchise can provide:

1. Brand-name recognition. If you ask the right questions and pick the right franchise, the marketing boost you get from the name of your franchise might be worth what it will cost you.
2. Support. Corporate support services can include help with selecting a site, employee training, inventory control, vendor connections, a corporate-produced business plan, and more.
3. Training. The franchisor will teach you the business (two days to four weeks), and training is continuous.
4. Money. Lenders prefer to lend to new franchisees over new start-ups. (Franchisor may also provide financing.)
5. Planning. You are buying a proven business plan.
6. Bargains. You may share in economies of scale in purchasing goods, services, and promotion.
7. Psychological hand-holding and field visits from the franchisor (support varies greatly).
8. Assistance in layout and design.
9. Location and leasing assistance.
10. Reduced odds of failure.
11. Pretested products and promotion.
12. The opportunity to buy another franchise in your area. Area franchises can lead to riches.
13. Assistance of a store-opening specialist. This person can help get you off to a running start.

What the Franchisor Gets

Franchisors earn money in several ways:

1. They collect a franchise fee for the rights to use their name and system. This ranges from $3000 for a small service firm to over $200,000 for a well-established name such as that of a hotel, auto dealership, or major restaurant.
2. They collect a **royalty fee,** which ranges from 2 percent to 15 percent of gross sales.
3. They may make a profit on items they sell to franchisees.

In addition, franchisees commonly pay franchisors advertising and promotion fees. These generally range from 2 percent to 5 percent of a franchise's gross sales.

Some of the fees may be open to negotiation—especially with a new franchisor. For example, it might be possible to delay the royalty fee for six months or until the franchise is profitable. It's always a good idea to ask for concessions.

Investigating Franchise Opportunities

As you can see from Table 14.1, franchising is a major force in the U.S. economy. You can learn a lot about small business by investigating franchises. We recommend that you talk with franchisors and franchisees to get a feel for the world of franchising. Also, talk to franchisees who have left the system. Their phone numbers are in the UFOC. The following discusses how to evaluate the earnings potential figures presented in the UFOC.

> **Action Step 58**

Franchise Information Packet

Using the insights gained from searching out franchises on the Internet, magazines, or franchise directory your next step is to request information from selected franchisors.

At this point, you're the prospective buyer. You have the funds, the drive, and the will to succeed. The franchisor has a product to sell. The product will be represented by the franchise information packet.

Write and request some of these packets.

Take time to study and compare: Subway to Blimpie's, Ace Hardware to True Value . . .

Addresses are on the Web. Type in your franchise choice at the search engine site. Then mouse click your way to "corporate." When you have examined the packets, write a page or two summarizing what you have learned. Focus on the need, the uniqueness, and the advantages of the franchise format.

Advantages should include economies of scale in advertising and bulk buying and the established "goodwill" of the name, proven track record, and reputation of franchisor.

Franchisor A firm that sells the right to do business under its name to another for a fee, but continues to control the business

Franchise Authorization granted by a manufacturer or distributor to sell its products/services

Franchisee An individual who, for a fee, is licensed to operate a business under the franchisor's rules and directives

Royalty fee Ongoing obligation to pay a franchisor a percentage of gross sales; may or may not include advertising fee

Action Step 59

Investigate the Franchise System

Franchises are everywhere...

To learn more about the system, interview people on both sides of a franchise agreement.

Part A—Franchisors. Leave your checkbook at home and interview at least three franchisors. Here are some questions to start you off:

What's included in the franchise fee?

What's the duration of the agreement?

How can the agreement be bought back?

What are the royalty fees and other assessments?

What level of training and service could I expect?

Is the territory well defined?

What are the minimum volume requirements?

How much help could I expect with advertising and promotion?

Part B—Franchisees. Now interview several franchisees. Ask them the same questions. A handy reference is the *Franchise Opportunities Handbook* published by the U.S. Department of Commerce.

Global Village   **A Franchise Overseas?**

Let's say you like to travel. You speak three languages—one of them is French—and your friends say you could pass for a Parisian in Nice in August. You'd like to spend some time overseas, so you think of running a business instead of working for someone else. If you latch on to a business that's already up and running, your chances for success look better.

You've seen the news on TV about McDonald's in Red Square, so you think "How about a franchise?" You think Paris, but then you locate the home page for *Entrepreneur Magazine* at **www.entrepreneurmag.com** and click the International 200 box under the Franchise Channel and a new idea floats into view.

China

The Great Wall

Genghis Khan

Tianamen Square

A teeming market of 1.2 billion.

Before you scale that formidable wall, you can read all about franchising in China on the Internet. The key essay from the Franchise Channel, "Spotlight On . . . China," leads the eager entrepreneur through the basics of small business—the same basics that form the journey of this book—location, target customer, legal hurdles, and finding good help.

Before you buy a franchise in China, or Paris, or Tibet, check out *Entrepreneur International Magazine* online.

Earnings Potential—Evaluate in Depth

You may want to know how much money you can make if you invest in a particular franchise system. Be careful. Earnings projections can be misleading. Insist upon written substantiation for any earnings projections or suggestions about your potential income or sales.

Franchisors are not required to make earnings claims, but if they do, the FTC's Franchise Rule requires franchisors to have a reasonable basis for these claims and to provide you with a document that substantiates them. This substantiation includes the bases and assumptions upon which these claims are made. Make sure you get and review the earnings claims document. Consider the following in reviewing any earnings claims.

Sample Size. A franchisor may claim that franchisees in its system earned, for example, $50,000 last year. This claim may be deceptive, however, if only a few franchisees earned that income and it does not represent the typical earnings of franchisees. Ask how many franchisees were included in the number.

Average Incomes. A franchisor may claim that the franchisees in its system earn an average income of, for example, $75,000 a year. Average figures like this tell you very little about how each individual franchisee performs. Remember, a few, very successful franchisees can inflate the average. An average figure may make the overall franchise system look more successful than it actually is.

Gross Sales. Some franchisors provide figures for the gross sales revenues of their franchisees. These figures, however, do not tell you anything about the franchisees' actual costs or profits. An outlet with a high gross sales revenue on paper actually may be losing money because of high overhead, rent, and other expenses.

Net Profits. Franchisors often do not have data on net profits of their franchisees. If you do receive net profit statements, ask whether they provide in-

Table 14.1

Number of Establishments and Sales by Kind of Franchised Business, 1980-1990

Kind of Franchised Business	Number of Establishments (1,000)						Sales (billions of dollars)					
	1980	1985	1987	1988	1989[1]	1990[1]	1980	1985	1987	1988	1989[1]	1990[1]
All franchising, total	442.4	455.2	479.1	480.8	498.8	533.0	336.2	543.0	599.4	648.1	678.8	716.4
Auto and truck dealers[2]	29.4	27.5	27.6	27.8	27.6	27.6	143.9	282.6	319.7	345.1	353.6	362.3
Percent	6.6	6.0	5.8	5.8	5.5	5.2	42.8	52.0	53.3	53.2	52.1	50.6
Restaurants (all types)	60.0	73.9	83.3	90.3	94.3	102.1	27.9	47.7	56.8	64.3	69.1	76.5
Percent	13.6	16.2	17.4	18.8	18.9	19.2	8.3	8.8	9.5	9.9	10.2	10.7
Gasoline service stations[2]	158.5	124.6	115.9	113.2	112.0	111.7	94.5	100.8	89.2	101.9	108.5	115.1
Percent	35.8	27.4	24.2	23.5	22.1	20.9	28.1	18.6	14.9	15.7	16.0	16.1
Retailing (nonfood)	35.2	45.1	47.9	46.2	49.2	54.1	10.5	20.6	25.4	23.3	26.0	28.6
Percent	8.0	9.9	10.0	9.6	9.7	10.2	3.1	3.8	4.2	3.6	3.8	4.0
Auto, truck rental services	7.3	11.2	10.0	9.5	9.9	10.6	3.1	5.7	6.5	6.6	7.0	7.6
Automotive products and services[3]	40.2	36.5	39.3	34.7	35.8	38.6	7.1	10.7	12.3	11.4	12.2	13.6
Business aids and services	40.7	49.8	56.7	55.6	59.8	67.3	6.7	12.0	14.7	15.7	17.1	19.5
Employment services	4.4	4.8	6.1	6.5	6.6	7.4	1.6	2.7	3.7	4.7	5.0	5.8
Tax preparation services	9.2	8.1	8.5	8.3	8.2	8.5	0.3	0.4	0.5	0.6	0.7	0.7
Accounting, credit, collection, and general	2.4	2.1	2.0	1.7	1.7	1.9	0.1	0.2	0.2	0.2	0.2	0.2
Real estate[4]	17.3	13.9	15.2	15.3	16.0	17.0	3.6	4.6	5.6	5.9	6.2	6.8
Printing and copying	2.8	4.5	5.6	5.9	6.5	7.4	0.4	0.9	1.2	1.5	1.6	1.9
Other	4.8	16.4	19.4	17.9	20.8	25.1	0.8	3.1	3.5	3.0	3.4	4.1
Construction, home improvement, maintenance, and cleaning	14.3	17.5	21.7	22.0	24.7	28.3	1.5	4.1	5.2	5.3	6.0	6.8
Convenience stores	15.6	15.1	16.3	17.2	17.3	17.5	7.8	10.8	12.3	13.9	14.1	14.4
Educational products and services	3.2	8.2	9.6	11.6	11.9	13.3	0.3	0.8	1.0	1.7	1.9	2.3
Equipment rental services	2.2	2.5	2.8	3.0	3.0	3.4	0.4	0.7	0.7	0.7	0.7	0.8
Food retailing[5]	15.5	18.7	20.5	21.6	23.0	25.4	7.4	10.1	11.1	10.2	10.9	11.9
Hotels and motels[6]	6.4	7.5	9.3	9.3	10.1	11.1	9.5	14.8	17.7	19.7	21.3	23.9
Laundry, dry cleaning services	3.4	2.3	2.2	2.3	2.5	2.6	0.3	0.3	0.3	0.3	0.3	0.3
Recreation, entertainment, travel	4.6	7.8	8.2	8.8	9.5	10.3	0.5	2.3	4.0	3.5	4.1	4.7
Soft drink bottlers[2][7]	1.9	1.4	1.1	0.9	0.8	0.8	14.4	18.3	20.9	22.7	24.2	25.8
Miscellaneous	3.6	5.5	6.8	6.9	7.3	8.4	0.4	0.9	1.5	1.7	1.9	2.2

SOURCE: *Statistical Abstract of the United States,* 111th ed. (Washington, D.C.: U.S. Department of Commerce, 1991), p. 778; based on data in International Trade Association, *Franchising in the Economy, 1986-88* (Dept. of Commerce, 1988) and, beginning 1988, *Franchising in the Economy, 1988-1990* (Washington, D.C.: Intl. Franchise Assoc. Foundation; and New York: Horwath Intl., 1990).

[1]Estimated by respondents. [2]Estimated by source on basis of Bureau of the Census and trade association dates. [3]Includes some establishments with significant sales of nonautomotive products such as household appliances, garden supplies, etc. [4]Gross commissions [5]Excludes convenience stores. [6]Includes campgrounds. [7]Includes soft drinks, fruit drinks and ades, syrups, flavoring agents and bases. Excludes independent private label and contract-filler bottling companies, which accounted for 22 percent of the value of shipments of the total industry in recent years.

formation about company-owned outlets. Company-owned outlets might have lower costs because they can buy equipment, inventory, and other items in larger quantities, or may own, rather than lease their property.

Geographic Relevance. Earnings may vary in different parts of the country. An ice cream store franchise in a southern state, such as Florida, may expect to earn more income than a similar franchise in a northern state, such as Minnesota. If you hear that a franchisee earned a particular income, ask where that franchisee is located.

Franchisee's Background. Keep in mind that franchisees have varying levels of skills and educational backgrounds. Franchisees with advanced technical or business backgrounds can succeed in instances where more typical franchisees cannot. The success of some franchisees is no guarantee that you will be equally successful.

SOURCE: **http://www.ftc.gov/bcp/conline/pubs/invest/buyfran.htm**

It may be that you would not be comfortable operating by the rules and regulations set down by franchisors—many entrepreneur-types are not. Nonetheless, it makes good sense to check out franchise opportunities (especially those in your selected industry) because it will give you a better picture of the marketplace. Action Step 59 will get you started on this.

Franchise Problems

Some notable pitfalls plague franchising in general:

1. Competition is becoming intense among competitive franchisors. Franchisors of fast-food outlets, quick-printing shops, and specialty retailers often oversaturate markets. This causes many failures.
2. Many of the training programs are poor or nonexistent.
3. Multilevel distributorships and pyramid sales schemes may only benefit the promoters.
4. The best opportunities are seldom offered to outsiders.

Beware of "ground-floor" franchise opportunities; it's pretty risky to be an early franchisee. A franchisor offering such an "opportunity" would be experimenting with *your money*. You want to buy a recognized brand name, a proven business plan, excellent field support, and experience that demonstrates the particular franchise will work in your location.

Voluntary chains—such as True Value and Ace hardware stores—are often a more desirable option. Members of voluntary chains remain independent and pay no royalty or franchise fee. Look for more such organizations in the near future.

A Franchising Success Story

Susan Moore and her husband were lucky when it came time to investigate franchises; they had a source of inside information right in the family. They were also lucky because the franchisor they chose provided excellent support. Note that **corporate** support was more important than name-brand recognition to Susan and her husband.

Three years ago, my husband had to travel a lot in his job and I was working very hard for a large company. While we were both drawing good salaries, we felt we had what it took to succeed in small business. We decided to go the franchising route.

We were both interested in the printing industry, and we chose a medium-sized national chain that seemed to have a franchise package we could live with. We did have some inside information on this particular franchisor. My brother had been with them for three years, in the Pacific Northwest area, and he was making a good living.

While we were interested in the quick-print industry, we weren't experts, so the two weeks of training was incredibly valuable. In addition, the people from corporate helped us with site selection, market analysis, negotiating the lease, and the layout and design of our shop. There are so many details to think of when you're starting a business; it's very helpful to have experts take over some of the tasks.

Another good feature of this franchise is that corporate will allow you to finance up to 80 percent of your start-up costs. This particular franchise can run as high as $200,000 up front, so that helped us.

We opened a second shop last January, and both stores are doing nicely. We print stationery, business cards, fliers, invitations—and we're developing a reputation for being on time in an industry known for being perpetually late.

Voluntary chain Organization (consortium) formed by individual wholesalers and/or retailers to gain purchasing power and other economies of scale

Corporate The franchisor

A good way to learn a lot about franchising in a short time is to attend a franchise exposition. You can learn when and where they are to be held in your area by watching for announcements in major newspapers.

As you look for a good franchise opportunity, bear in mind that the best opportunity may lie with a young franchise that has proven its concept, has 20 to 30 winners, and is looking for growth in an area with which you are familiar.

Evaluating a Franchise

Evaluating a franchise opportunity is much like evaluating any other business that's up for sale, but because of the nature of franchisors, you need to ask some additional questions. For example:

How long has this franchise been in business?

Who are the officers? What is their track record?

How many franchise outlets are currently operational?

How well does this franchise compete with similar franchises?

Where is this franchise in its life cycle?

What will this franchise do for me?

In Chapter 12 we presented a checklist to use in evaluating an ongoing business you are considering buying. That checklist applies to franchises as well. To supplement it, we're giving you a checklist prepared specifically for evaluating franchise opportunities (see Table 14.2). The questions will help you generate a profile of the franchise and make a wise decision.

Typically, current franchisees are offered new locations before they are offered to outsiders. Rarely is a new player offered a sure thing. New players are offered those that have already been passed over. Read about Myron Bailey's introduction to franchising.

Three Wins, One Loss

By the time Myron was 29 years old he'd made a lot of money in the stock market, but he felt he was too young to retire. After making several attempts to purchase one of the better-known fast-food franchises and waiting almost a year, he was offered a location in another state.

The store had been open for three years and not yet turned a profit. Other franchise owners had already turned down the opportunity to take over the operation. Myron liked what he saw and made an offer. The unsuccessful franchisee welcomed his offer as a graceful exit, and the franchisor could hardly wait to see if a new franchisee could turn the loser around.

Myron is a "people person" and a strong manager. His employees followed his enthusiastic leadership, and new customers came in droves. In less than a year the store became very profitable, and the franchisor offered Myron three new locations, all of which he accepted.

Myron's touch was magic; two of the three new stores also became very successful. But try as he would, he couldn't make money on the third one. After three more years, Myron decided that too much of his time was being drained by the one loser. He called the franchisor and asked them to assist him in selling it. They found several prospective buyers and chose the one they thought was the best operator. He wasn't able to turn it around either. Myron now devotes all his time to working with his winners.

Action Step 60

Visit a Franchise Exposition

Most major cities have at least one franchise show a year. Attend one and visit with the exhibitors. Learn what you can from their sales presentations.

Collect their literature and select one that seems worth a second look. Compose a brief summary of your findings and present to your colleagues. Have your colleagues evaluate the franchise along with you.

Remember, it's usually the small and new franchisors that exhibit at the shows, and their salespeople work on commission. Don't allow yourself to be pursued; you are there to observe and evaluate. You are probably not yet ready to buy.

Table 14.2

Franchise Evaluation Checklist

General

1. Is the product or service: yes   no
   a. considered reputable?   _____   _____
   b. part of a growing market?   _____   _____
   c. needed in your area?   _____   _____
   d. of interest to you?   _____   _____
   e. safe,   _____   _____
      protected,   _____   _____
      covered by guarantee?   _____   _____
2. Is the franchise:
   a. local?   _____   _____
      regional?   _____   _____
      national?   _____   _____
      international?   _____   _____
   b. full-time?   _____   _____
      part-time?   _____   _____
      possible full-time in the future? _____ _____
3. Existing franchises
   a. Date the company was founded _____
      Date the first franchise was awarded _____
   b. Number of franchises currently in operation or under construction _____
   c. References _____
      Franchise 1: owner _____
                   address _____
                   telephone _____ date started _____
      Franchise 2: owner _____
                   address _____
                   telephone _____ date started _____
      Franchise 3: owner _____
                   address _____
                   telephone _____ date started _____
      Franchise 4: owner _____
                   address _____
                   telephone _____ date started _____
   d. Additional franchises planned for the next twelve months
4. Failed franchises
   a. How many franchises have failed? _____
      How many in the last two years? _____
   b. Why have they failed? _____
      Franchisor reasons: _____
      Better Business Bureau reasons: _____
      Franchisee reasons: _____
5. Franchise in local market area
   a. Has a franchise ever been awarded in this area? _____
   b. If so, and if it is still in operation:
      owner _____
      address _____
      telephone _____ date started _____
   c. If so, and if it is no longer in operation: _____
      person involved _____
      address _____
      date started _____ date ended _____
      reasons for failure _____
   d. How many inquiries have there been for the franchise from the area in the past 6 months? _____
6. What product or service will be added to the franchise package
   a. within 12 months? _____
   b. within 2 years? _____
   c. within 2 to 5 years? _____

7. Competition
   a. What is the competition? _____
8. Are all franchises independently owned?
   a. Of the total outlets, _____ are franchised, and _____ are company-owned.
   b. If some outlets are company owned did they start out this way, _____ or were they purchased from a franchisee? _____
   c. Date of most recent company acquisition _____
9. Franchise operations
   a. What facilities are required, and do I lease or build?

	build	lease
office	_____	_____
building	_____	_____
manufacturing facility	_____	_____
warehouse	_____	_____
_____	_____	_____
_____	_____	_____

   b. Getting started—Who is responsible for:

	franchisor	franchisee
feasibility study?	_____	_____
design?	_____	_____
construction?	_____	_____
furnishings and equipment?	_____	_____
financing?	_____	_____
employee training?	_____	_____
lease negotiation?	_____	_____

Franchise Company

1. The company
   a. Name and address of the parent company, if different from the franchise company:
      name _____
      address _____
   b. Is the parent company public, or private? _____
   c. If the company is public, where is the stock traded?
      New York Stock Exchange   _____
      American Stock Exchange   _____
      over-the-counter   _____
2. Forecast of income and expenses can only be presented in UFOC. The franchisee should not give you any other estimates.
3. What is the best legal structure for my company?
      proprietorship   _____
      partnership   _____
      corporation   _____
      limited liability company _____
4. The franchise contract
   a. Is there a written contract? _____ (Get a copy for lawyer and accountant to review.)
   b. Does it specify

	yes	no
franchise fee?	_____	_____
termination?	_____	_____
selling and renewal?	_____	_____
advertising and promotion?	_____	_____
patent and liability protection?	_____	_____
home office services?	_____	_____
commissions and royalties?	_____	_____
training?	_____	_____
financing?	_____	_____
territory?	_____	_____
exclusivity?	_____	_____

For additional review questions, see www.ftc.gov/bcp/conline/pubs/invest/buyfran.htm

Reasons for Not Buying a Franchise

Many entrepreneurs have decided against buying franchises. Here are some of the reasons they have given:

1. I know the business as well as they do.
2. My name is as well-known as theirs.
3. Why pay a franchise fee?
4. Why pay a royalty fee and advertising fee?
5. My individuality would have been stifled.
6. I don't want others to tell me how to run my business.
7. I didn't want a ground-floor opportunity where I'd be the guinea pig.
8. I'd have been committed for the rest of my life.
9. There were restrictions on selling out.
10. If I didn't do as I was told, I would lose my franchise.
11. The specified hours of business did not suit my location.
12. The franchisor's promotions and products did not fit my customers' needs or tastes.
13. They offered no territory protection.
14. I would not be in control of my business.

If you can develop a winning formula, you can become a franchisor yourself. Many entrepreneurs have done this. This is another reason to learn all you can about franchising now.

A Final Word about Franchises

If you're really interested in making money as a franchisee, do some research on owning more than one by becoming an area franchisee. If you go to the Burger King home page and click on the burger, you can locate Gamma III, a family-owned franchise in the Chicago area who owns (at this writing) 13 Burger Kings.

Interviewing key people at a multiple franchise operation could save you lots of time and money. And maybe even some heartache.

Selling franchises is a numbers game. You, the potential franchisee, are a "lead." You will be told what you want to hear.

If you have few business skills, or perhaps little business experience, then your chances of succeeding are far greater as a franchisee. A franchisor with a well-developed business plan will keep you on track. Ask to see that business plan.

The key here is gut feeling. If you should decide to buy a franchise and then feel like an employee of the franchisor, strike out on your own. Develop your own plan, and go for it. Look at franchising as an option—an example to learn from—and then blend that knowledge into a unique business that explores the gaps exposed in Chapter 3, "Power Marketing."

If you're not ready to be on your own yet, franchising may be the way for you to start.

▶ *Summary*

There are two good reasons to consider buying a franchise: (1) If the brand name is respected, you'll already be positioned in the marketplace. (2) If the franchisor is sharp, you'll inherit a business plan that works. Examine the franchise's appeal with consumers carefully; you want to get a marketing boost from the name. Depending on the franchise, you may also get other services for your money (for example, help on site selection and interior layout, and vendor connections), but the main thing you're buying is brand-name recognition.

▶ Action Step 61

Writing About a Dream Franchise

A franchise costs money.

The franchisee (that's you) pays money to the franchisor (a corporate entity like Coke, Perkins, Century 21, or Sir Speedy) for the right to a specific niche in the marketplace. In the case of Sir Speedy, the niche is fast printing. In the case of Century 21, the niche is real estate.

Because the corporate franchisor wants you to succeed, to make more money for the corporate entity, a lot of stuff comes bundled with the niche: a big-time logo, a business plan, a thick disclosure document, and so on.

After you have perused some information packets from various franchisors, take up your pen and write a couple of paragraphs. What do you like? What do you dislike? Do you need more information? Is this the franchise for you? Is there a number you can call for more information?

Include a single paragraph description, then detail initial license fee, royalties, other fees, all other capital costs, training, location, accounting and reporting requirements, training, terms, duration, renewability, and termination conditions. Use one to two pages.

Don't be afraid to share your feelings with yourself: "I love this franchise because . . ." or "This franchise packet gives me the shakes because . . ."

The franchisor cannot promise anything and earnings claims are not legal unless in the Uniform Franchise Offering Circular.

Just as if you were investigating an ongoing, independent business, study the opportunity thoroughly. Examine the financial history, and compare what you'd make if you bought the business to what you'd make if you invested the same money elsewhere.

Buying a franchise does not assure success. The ultimate responsibility for success or failure of the business is the franchisees. You are purchasing a name brand and a system to follow. Follow it carefully.

Think Points for Success

- Avoid ground-floor opportunities. "Grow with us" can mean *caveat emptor* ("Let the buyer beware").
- Talk to franchisees, especially ones who have left the system. Franchises who have left the fold are listed in the UFOC. Current franchisees sometimes get a "finders fee."
- Remember you are purchasing a "job" and *have* to do it their way not your way.
- The franchisor gets a percentage of gross sales for advertising and royalty fees whether or not the franchisee is profitable.
- Do you really need the security blanket of a franchise?
- Read the proposed agreements carefully. They are airtight, favor the franchisor, and are usually non-negotiable.
- Would you be comfortable relinquishing your independence?
- If you like to break rules, be creative, stretch things to the limit, don't buy a franchise because you will very likely end up in court.

Key Points from Another View

Buying a Franchise? Investigate before it's too Late

The best system for the franchisee is one in which the franchisor looks to the same source as you for profits: the ongoing royalties from your sales.

Evaluating a Franchise

The following steps will help you choose the right franchise for you:

I. Assess Yourself
A. The first year, you will work harder than you've ever worked in your life. Are you ready for that?
B. You need to put pride of ownership and the rewards of personal achievement first.
C. Making a financial success of a business is key, but money alone is not.

II. Research the Industry
A. It is far easier to evaluate a franchise if you are already familiar with the industry it represents.
B. Many people do look outside their field of experience for a franchise; in that case, it pays to investigate the industry very carefully before you examine the particular franchise.

III. Research the Company
A. The franchisor is required by law to give the prospective franchisee detailed information about the company through the Uniform Franchise Offering Circular (UFOC).

    B. Not only should you read this information yourself, but you should also have a lawyer specializing in franchising look it over.

IV. Visit the Corporate Staff

Most franchisees agree about the importance of making a personal visit to a potential franchisor.

V. Talk to Franchisees

Not only should you talk to and visit other franchisees and former franchisees, but you should also find out how satisfied their customers are.

VI. Check Out the Territory

    A. Most franchisees assume that their franchise comes with a guarantee of exclusivity within a certain territory, but unless exclusivity is specified, assume the worst.

    B. Check not only the territory, but also the demographics. Make sure the demographics match the franchisor's Target Customer profile.

VII. Negotiate

You should feel free to negotiate points in the contract that confuse or disturb you, but don't expect to be able to rewrite the franchise agreement.

VIII. Have Realistic Financial Goals

Have a realistic sense of what will happen, and beware of salespeople.

IX. Guarantee Long-term Security

There are, alas, no guarantees. All you can do is choose a franchisor that is concerned about the welfare of its franchisees.

Sometimes there's a good living to be made franchising for those who choose wisely and work hard.

Do your homework before, not after, you sign the franchise document.

SOURCE: From: Geraldine M. Strozier, "Buying A Franchise? Investigate Before It's Too Late—It's Not So Elementary, Watson," *Entrepreneur*, January 1990, 69–73.

Pulling the Plan Together

Entrepreneurial Links

Books

Business Plans for Dummies, Paul Tiffany and Steven D. Petersen, 1997.

How to Really Start Your Own Business, David E. Gumpert, 1994.

The Complete Idiot's Guide to Starting Your Own Business, Ed Paulson and Marcia Layton, 1998.

Websites

www.business.gov

www.businessfinance.com

www.smallbusinesscenter.com

Associations/Organization

American Society of Women Entrepreneurs
http://women.aswe.org/ASWE

Association of Collegiate Entrepreneurs

Young Entrepreneur's Organization

Publications

Asian Enterprise

Writing an Effective Business Plan-Deloitte & Touche

Small Business Government Publications,
http://www.pueblo.gsa.gov/smbuss.htm

Additional Entrepreneurial Insights

Republic of Tea: The Story of the Creation of a Business, As Told Through the Personal Letters of Its Founders, Mel Ziegler, Bill Rosenzweig, and Patricia Ziegler, 1994.

Black Entrepreneurs in America: Stories of Struggle and Success, Michael D. Woodard, 1997.

Burn Rate: How I Survived the Gold Rush Years on the Internet, Michael Wolff, 1998.

Learning Objectives

- Pull all the information together into one coherent unit, which becomes a portable showcase for your business.
- Understand the importance of YOU completing the Business Plan.
- Review the advantages and disadvantages of Business Plan software.
- Understand the significance and importance of a sample Business Plan to see how one group of entrepreneurs defined and showcased their business.
- Words can talk but numbers show it can be done.
- Review the Notes section for the financials.
- Recognize the importance of providing all backup data for your readers.
- Match or surpass the sample Business Plan in power and effectiveness.
- Complete a Pert chart to organize the work ahead.
- Put your finished Business Plan to work.

You may be closer to completing your business plan than you think. *If* you have completed the Action Steps in the preceding chapters, you *already* have the major components of your plan. Through the past chapters you have researched your Target Customer, found gaps in the market, defined your business, developed marketing and promotional ideas, and completed basic financials. As you develop your business plan using the Action Steps you've compiled, you may recognize areas that need further attention and research. Chapter 15 provides you with the structure to put your facts, figures, ideas, dreams, and intuition into a workable plan.

Your business plan could be one of the most important documents you have ever pulled together. If you need to get started with your business immediately, consider using the Fast-Start Business Plan in Chapter 16. If your business is less complex and has low capital needs, this may be the alternative for you. With your completed business plan in writing, you've got something to show to the people who are important to your business: banker, lenders, relatives, venture capitalists, vendors, suppliers, key employees, friends, the SBA, and others. The plan is portable and you can make as many copies as needed to show to people who can help you succeed. You can either mail it to contacts across the country or post on the various Internet sites that link investors with entrepreneurs.

Planning is hard work. You will stay up nights over this, maybe lose some sleep, but in the end you will have saved time. Just as a pilot would not consider a long flight without a plan, neither should you consider a business venture without a business plan.

Your plan should become a working, breathing, living document for your business dreams. Share your plan with others; they may have ideas, insights, and recommendations. Review these and revise your plan if necessary. Business plan reviewers sometimes ask for further details or back-up data that, when added to your plan, will make your plan stronger and more effective. Sometimes we become so close to our business plans we omit important and relevant details and/or information.

Internet Assistance for Writing Your Business Plan

Log on to **www.dryden.com/mngment** to connect to the following resources:

Business Plan Outline by the Small Business Administration. Very detailed outline and template for preparing a business plan. Helpful directions and tips are provided for completing each section of the plan.

Business Plan Template Shorter template than the one from the Small Business Administration for preparing your business plan.

BPlans.com Browse through a variety of complete business plans.

Business Resource Center's Sample Business Plans:
Acme Consulting: "consulting company specializing in marketing of high technology products in international markets."

American Management Technology: "sells computers, software, and service to local small businesses."

BizPlanIt Separate guidelines for each section of the business plan, including common mistakes to avoid.

The Role of the Business Plan This article covers the reasons why a business plan is important and three key elements of it. One of those elements is a discussion of why the proposed business venture offers "an economically viable product or service with attractive markets." Two other resources, Benefits of a Written Plan, from the Business Owner's Toolkit, and Plan Your Business, from the Small Business Administration, outline the benefits of preparing a business plan.

Ten Key Questions for Your Business Plan For example, "Is Your Product (Service) and Business Mission Clear and Simple?" or "Who Is Your Customer?" Each question has elaboration points to help answer it.

SOURCE: www.dryden.com/mngment.

How to Start Writing Your Business Plan

Before you begin, gather in one place all your completed Action Steps and back-up data. Outline your plan, fill in the information from your Action Steps, refine, ask a knowledgeable person to review your plan, refine further, and prepare to present the plan to potential investors.

If you're a creative thinker, chances are your thought processes don't always follow a linear sequence. That's great—it will help you as an entrepreneur! Nonetheless, the Action Steps in Chapter 15 do follow a linear sequence; the sequence of the parts of a completed business plan. This is a matter of convenience—you get to see an example of each part as it would appear in the finished product. Bear in mind, however, that we don't expect you to sequentially write each part.

The best way to begin writing a business plan is to start with the material with which you feel most comfortable. For example, if you really enjoyed interviewing target customers, you might begin with "The Market and the Target Customers."

In Chapter 15, the Action Steps will serve as a checklist for keeping track of which parts of the plan you have written. For example, in practice you would probably write the cover letter last, although that is the first Action Step we present. Think of the writing of this first cover letter as a valuable exercise. After completing Chapter 15 and your business plan, rewrite your cover letter. The more cover letters you write, the easier it becomes to write them effectively.

To jump-start your writing skills, review the business plans for "Yes, We Do Windows" (Chapter 16) and "Shelter Dynamics" (Appendix A). In addition, you can log on to **www.dryden.com/mngment** and access a wide variety of business plans online. A great deal of assistance and advice on the referenced sites can help you write a winning business plan.

Three-Part Structure: Words, Numbers, and Appendixes

Your business plan tells the world what kind of business you are in. For ease of handling, divide your plan into two sections, and provide the needed documentation in appendixes at the end.

In Section I use *words* to briefly introduce your strategies for marketing and management. Try to "hook" your reader with the excitement of creating a business, assessing the competition, designing a marketing plan, targeting customers, finding the right location, and building a team—all those human things that most people can relate to, even if they're not in business.

In Section II present *numbers:* Pro forma income statements, cash flows, and balance sheets. This section is aimed primarily at bankers, credit managers, venture capitalists, vendors, SBICs, and/or commercial credit lenders. At the same time, you must also make it accessible to the casual reader who searches for the bottom line.

Support the Sections I and II with *appendixes.* This is where you place: résumés, maps, diagrams, photographs, tables, reprints from industry journals, letters from customers, letters from vendors, credit reports, personal financial statements, bids from contractors, and other documentation that demonstrates the viability of your plan.

Note that in most cases, material in the appendixes comes from existing sources. You are not stating anything new here; you are merely supporting what you have already said.

Appendixes vary according to type of business; *for that reason sample appendixes are not included in this book.*

If you follow and complete the Action Steps in this and past chapters, you'll have all the components you need to make a winning business plan in hand.

Business Plan Software

Software can help you write your business plan. You can download an excellent free business plan template at **www.moneyhunter.com**. Check out the SBA site as well for assistance.

Additionally, the following business plan software programs (at this writing) may help you:

- BizPlan Builder, from Jian, **www.bplans.com**
- Business Plan Pro, Inc., **www.inc.com/products**
- Automate Your Business Plan, from Out of Your Mind. . . . and Into the Marketplace, 714-544-0248.

The above software automatically merges text with financial tables and charts. If you utilize business plan template software, be sure to personalize your plan. Each software program needs to be adjusted to fit one's particular business venture.

Outside Assistance in Writing a Business Plan

Many people ask, "Should I hire a pro to write my business plan?" Our response is always; "*You* are the pro!" If you do not want to put the time and effort into writing your own business plan, it is doubtful that you will have the energy and drive to develop a business.

With the vast amount of resources available—books, Internet, and software— you have enough help to get you well on your way to developing a complete business plan. We do suggest on finishing your initial plan that you look for several businessowners and possible investors to review it. Take their comments to heart and rework your plan where necessary.

Hiring a business consultant to refine your plan is acceptable but do not allow him or her to dream your dream! If you do not have total input into your plan, you may embarrass yourself by not being able to explain the details of your plan to investors and bankers.

Reminders

Completing a business plan helps reduce the risk of failure. No plan can guarantee success or eliminate failure, but a well-researched plan will help acknowledge issues, anticipate problems, and determine resources.

The plan should be easy to read with each number and figure well documented. Use bullets, graphs, and appendixes to support the plan's strongest points. Be sure to ascertain that there are no misspelled words, and that the plan is well written. If you are not comfortable with your writing skills, hire an editor to review your plan.

Focus on the potential opportunities the business provides for investors. Be sure to tie together—with a clear consistent message—all elements of the plan.

The plan should consist of about 20–40 pages with additional pages of appendixes. Make the plan easy for your reader to write notes on and include how the reader can reach you—fax, e mail, address, phone, pager, and so on.

Chapter 15 illustrates the steps involved in completing a business plan along with providing you samples of each step for The Software School. The Software School has been in operation for six months and has been self-financed by the owners who are now seeking to expand and need additional outside financing. Read each area and The Software School's example before completing the Action Steps.

Cover Letter

To aim your plan so that it will achieve the most good, use a cover letter. Each time you send the plan to someone, write a special cover letter addressed to that specific reader and his or her interests. The cover letter introduces the excitement of your plan, and tells the person specifically why you have chosen to send it to him or her.

Read the sample cover letter for The Software School.

47 Turbo Drive Ste. 108-9
Santa Ana, CA
Campbell@net.com
949 555-5555

Mariners Bank
Ms. Nancy Hopp, Vice-President Lending
1400 Market Circle
Santa Ana, CA

Dear Ms. Hopp,

I have been meaning to write a formal thank you for the immense help you provided on revising and updating the business plan for the Software

School. Your input was helpful in the marketing area and invaluable on the financial section. Everyone here at The Software School appreciates the care you took reading over earlier business plan drafts.

We are now in the market for a loan of $60,000 to be used for capital expenditures. The location we have in Santa Ana is built out but will require additional phone lines, electrical outlets, and appropriate lighting to enable us to provide another classroom. We would appreciate any guidance you can give us concerning sources of capital available through your bank and/or additional avenues.

Each of the founders has put in $50,000 to launch the software school.

We are planning to repay loans out of profits over the next three years. For more information, please refer to the financial section.

Again, thank you very much for your help and advice. We couldn't have done it without you.

Cordially,

Derek Campbell
Chief Executive Officer

Let's summarize what's good about our sample cover letter. We can see that:

1. The writer is making use of a previous contact.
2. The writer tells the reader—the manager of a bank—that he is in the market for a loan. He does not put her on the spot by asking for money.
3. Instead, he asks for advice on where to find sources of capital.
4. The writer struck the right tone. (To do that, he rewrote the letter several times.)

You can do as well or better—and it's worth the effort! As you draft your cover letter, remember that the reader will pass judgment on your business plan (and on your business ability) on the basis of the letter. Do you want your small business to look bright? attractive? welcoming? Your cover letter needs to give the same impression. A good cover letter will make its readers want to become involved in your venture. Action Step 62 will help you write your cover letter.

Elements of a Business Plan

The Table of Contents

Our sample table of contents provides a quick overview of a finished business plan. In practice, the table of contents is prepared last.

The Software School Table of Contents

Executive Summary

- I. Description of the Business
  - A. The Service We Provide
  - B. Industry Overview and Target Customers
  - C. The Competition
  - D. Marketing Strategy
  - E. Our Facility
  - F. Management and Personnel
- II. Financial Section
  - G. Pro Forma Income Statement
  - H. Pro Forma Cash Flow

> ► **Action Step 62**
>
> **Write a Cover Letter for Your Plan**
>
> Address your letter to a specific person who can help your business. Be brief; aim for about 200 words.
>
> State the reason you are sending the plan. If you are asking for money, tell the person what you want it for, how much you need, and how you will repay the loan. Several well-written paragraphs should be all you need to do this.
>
> Your purpose in writing the cover letter is to open the door gently and prepare the way for further negotiations. The cover letter is bait on your hook.
>
> If you are putting money into the business, or if you have already contributed, indicate how much.
>
> The tone you are after in this opening move is confident and slightly formal. You want to appear neat, bright, organized, and in control of your venture.
>
> Refer to The Software School's sample letter.

▶ **Action Step 63**

Write an Executive Summary

Imagine you had two minutes to explain your business venture to a complete stranger.... This gives you an idea of what information you need to put into writing for your executive summary.

Practice explaining your venture to friends and strangers, limiting yourself to two minutes. Ask them to raise questions, and use their questions to guide you as you revise and hone, your presentation.

When you are satisfied with your oral summary, write it down and type it up. It should not exceed three typed pages. (The Software School's executive summary that serves as our example was less than one single-spaced page.) This may constitute a very small portion of your business plan, but it could be the most important part of it.

Rewrite your executive summary again after completing your business plan.

I. Balance Sheets
III. Appendixes*
   A. Market Research
   B. Quotes from Hardware and Software Suppliers
   C. Personal Résumés
   D. Personal Financial Statements
   E. Personal Credit Reports
   F. Letters of Reference
   G. Bids from Contractors
   H. Floor plan for Turbo Drive Location?
   I. Map with Competitors' Locations
   J. Census data
   K. Quarterly Income Statements for next 3 years
   L. Break-even Analysis

*The need for specific appendixes varies greatly from business plan to business plan. For that reason, we have not included sample appendixes. As you draft your plan, you will see items requiring further documentation to substantiate your business strategies; the most logical place for this kind of documentation is in appendixes.

Executive Summary

The executive summary serves as an introduction to the business plan. Its function is similar to that of a preface in a book. It is written to (1) acquaint the reader with the subject matter of the material that follows, (2) direct the reader's attention to whatever strengths the author (entrepreneur) wants to emphasize, and (3) make the reader want to turn the pages and read, read, read. Because the executive summary overviews the entire business plan, it must be written last. After the plan is completed, condense the information in two to three pages. Pay special attention to the *business description, current position and/or future outlook, management, uniqueness* and, if funds are being sought, *funds sought, how they will be used, when they will be repaid,* and *how they will be repaid.* This summary appears right after the table of contents (and confidentiality statement, if used).

As a preview to your plan, the executive summary should excite, entice, and bring the reader into the plan. A well-written executive summary captures the reader's attention and makes him or her eager to explore further. Because many readers never go further than the executive summary, it's important to expend a great deal of effort to make your executive summary an excellent selling tool.

As you write your executive summary, remember that lenders prefer "hard," numerical data and facts. Therefore, such phrases as "30 percent return on the original investment" and "secured training agreements from three retail computer stores in the area" make the following example *a strong* executive summary. The words help to paint a picture of good management and solid growth for The Software School.

You, too, can write an effective executive summary. Action Step 63 will help you decide which facts and numbers portray you and your business venture as credible and promising and then to summarize them in writing.

After you have completed your business plan, return and revise your executive summary.

Executive Summary

The Software School is a user-friendly, state-of-the-art software and Internet training center. We are tapping into the growing need for quick, one-day Internet and software training. Our market area is growing as new industries and businesses continue to hire new employees and expand their operations. In addition, Orange County is one of the largest markets for entrepreneurs and we will market our training to them extensively. The Software School's sophisticated electronic classroom provides "hands-on" education that teaches computer users how to use new software programs and make the most of the Internet.

We are currently operating with one classroom and hope to add an additional classroom within the next six months. This expansion will allow us to attain sales of $400,000 by the end of fiscal year 1999. At that time, our pretax profits will have reached almost $40,000, representing a 26-percent return on our original $150,000 investment.

According to our research, our target customers appear to have insatiable appetites for software application knowledge and Internet training. The Software School anticipates an annual sales growth rate of 30 percent over the next three years. We have secured training agreements for more than 200 employees from 15 of our current business users.

Our competitors continue to train in the traditional classroom style and currently show no sign of copying our unique instructional approach. At this point, none of our competitors are offering Internet-specific training or focusing on small businessowners, and we hope to capitalize on these gaps in the market. By offering Internet training for medical personnel, educators, and legal personnel we will corner a niche in the marketplace.

Management, led by Derek Campbell demonstrates how to offer superior training at competitive prices. Our plans for the future include developing additional profit centers by providing on-site counseling and training for firms throughout Southern California. Research and customer surveys indicate that we have just begun to satisfy the ever-increasing need for software education.

Phil Carpenter focuses on sales and marketing and Derek Campbell is the lead teacher and curriculum developer. Robert Jericho manages the technical aspects of keeping the hardware and software up to date and online. All three are involved in teaching courses.

We are seeking funding of $60,000 to cover remodeling costs to provide an additional classroom. In addition, funds will be used for additional site license fees, furniture and equipment costs. The appendix has a listing of contractor, computer, and furniture estimates. We have been looking at purchasing refurbished classroom furniture at a potential cost savings of $15,000 to $20,000.

Bank loans will be paid back from the operating profits of the business over the next three years.

Section I

Description of the Business

Marketing, Location and Management

How well do you know your business? You need to prove it with words and numbers. By the time your reader finishes reading your business plan, you should have an ally on your side. To give you examples to follow, we reprint key sections from the Business Plan for The Software School, a business that is seeking financing for remodeling and equipment expenses. Regardless of whether your business is ongoing or just starting up, the goals of Section I and II are the same: to demonstrate that you know your business and are a winner.

► **Action Step 64**

Describe Your Product or Service

Excite your reader about your business. Excitement is contagious. If you can get your reader going, there's a good chance you'll be offered money. Investors love hot ideas.

If this is a start-up, explain your product or service fully. What makes it unique? What industry is it in? Where does the industry fit in the big picture?

Mention numbers wherever you can. Percentages and dollar amounts are more meaningful than words like *lots* and *many*.

If this is an ongoing business, your records of sales, costs, and profit and loss will substantiate your need for money.

Keep the words going and the keyboard smoking. You need to convince the reader to keep reading.

The Service We Provide

Review how the Software School tackled this part. The Software School will get its funding because the writer of the plan proves that his business is a winning concern. The writer has:

let the facts speak for themselves.

supported all claims with numbers.

avoided hard-sell tactics.

refused to puff the product.

The writer does a terrific selling job without at all appearing to be selling. Now it's your turn. Complete Action Step 64.

The Service We Provide

The Software School, a California Limited Liability Company, is a software and Internet training facility located in Santa Ana, between John Wayne Airport and a high-density executive business complex and manufacturing area.

We train individuals on computer software from the top ten list of best-selling software. Because of their power these programs are complex. To enable users to get the maximum value out of the software—training is desirable.

As Internet usage skyrockets, we believe offering specialized Internet courses will provide our firm with the greatest area of growth in the future.

Students are drawn to our teaching method because it gives them hands-on experience and because it's fast. Working people are busy, and a student can upgrade a given software skill by 80 percent in 8 hours. Slow learners are guaranteed a second try, and a third, at no cost.

Most of our courses can be completed in one day or two evenings. In contrast, the average college course (which emphasizes concepts, rather than hands-on) takes 12 to 18 weeks. Our price is $99 for most one-day courses, which is about 25 percent lower than our competitors' offerings.

The Software School achieves space-age learning speed with a sophisticated electronic teaching system adapted from flight-simulation techniques used by airlines for training pilots.

As a service business, we sell seats as well as skills and information. We constantly survey our current customers as to the additional classes they would like to see offered.

We are open five days a week from 8 AM to 10 PM and Saturdays from 9 AM to 5 PM. This allows us to offer one-day, eight-hour courses as well as short three-hour evening courses thus maximizing the use of our facility. Local community colleges cannot meet the demand for weekend courses.

The Software School is in the business of increasing business productivity by providing the following:

• Effective and efficient Internet searching techniques

• Sales force automation software training

• Manufacturing software training

• Inventory control software training

• Assistance with writing a business plan utilizing the most popular software programs

• Database, word processing, accounting and presentation software training

• Web page and Web store design

Telcom Upstart Rings Up Win in Mexico (07/31/98)

A tiny San Diego telecommunication company has landed one of the most lucrative phone licenses in the world, a license that will place it head-to-head with giants like AT&T, MCI, and Sprint for a share of the long-distance phone market in Mexico.

Presto Telecommunications won the license in July, according to the *San Diego Union-Tribune*. The newspaper reports the 35-person company plans to invest $150 million into building a fiber-optic network that it hopes will enable it to capture 2 percent of Mexico's $5 billion long-distance phone market.

Presto's investment in Mexico pales in comparison to the size of those made by its rivals. Avantel, MCI's Mexican partner, has sunk $900 million into its presence, and Alestra, AT&T's Mexican affiliate, has spent $450 million on the country, according to the *Union-Tribune*.

SOURCE: www.inc.com

> ## Action Step 65
>
> ### Describe the Market and the Target Customers
>
> Bring all your marketing research into this section and wow your reader with a picture of your target customers just sitting there waiting for your product or service.
>
> Use data from secondary sources to give credibility to the picture you are painting.

The demand for our classes will increase dramatically when we sign training contracts with the leading Orange County computer stores. As a sales promotional tool we plan to offer free training to several salespeople from each of the major stores. The salespeople in turn will likely refer their customers to us for training. Computer retailers quickly have learned they can sell upgraded systems if they can provide or offer software training.

They are in the business of selling systems and we are in the training business.

Our equipment is top quality. Our staff combines excellent training skills with attention to people and their needs. We have launched a solid start-up in a heated growth industry, and plan to continue our growth and success.

Industry Overview and Target Customers

Knowledge is power, especially in the Information Age. The Software School—an information business—capitalized on expert knowledge to define the marketplace. In the same way, if your research is sound, it will show up in your writing.

Use your industry research from the Action Steps in Chapters 2 and 3 to give your reader an overview of the industry. The reader needs to know the size of the market, trends in the marketplace, how the industry is segmented, where the industry is headed, and what specific part of the market you are aiming your product toward. In addition, briefly discuss technological advances that are changing the industry and how you will capitalize on these changes.

Prove to your reader that you understand the market and are meeting a customer need. Discuss market segmentation. Define your target customers in great detail. Provide research data to back up your assumptions on demographics, psychographics, market size, and buying patterns. Return to your Action Steps from Chapter 4 to assist you in describing your target customers.

The reader should have a clear idea as to how your product or service will be positioned to capture a unique position in the marketplace. An in-depth explanation should be provided in the competition section of your business plan.

Action Step 65 gives you a chance to show that you know the industry and your target customers. Review what the business plan for The Software School says about its industry and target customers. Be sure to use secondary sources (like documents, tables, and quotes) to lend this section credibility.

Industry Overview and Target Customers

Industry Overview

Today's powerful computers and software are fueling a constant need for upgrading and training on new or updated versions of popular and new software programs. Many managers with little computer experience need to learn programs quickly and expect to be productive within a short period of time.

With the sales flurry of hardware and emphasis on space-age speed, some people are being left behind because they don't know how to fully utilize the software. A computer can be your best friend, but only if you learn how to maximize its capabilities. This makes training people to use computers a booming industry, and The Software School is on the leading edge of a major growth segment.

Target Customers

Geographically, our target area encompass Long Beach, La Habra, and Brea on the north; San Clemente on the south; Huntington and Newport Beaches on the west; and Orange, Fullerton, and Mission Viejo on the east. Realistically, most of our customers come from a 10-mile radius of our location. We are looking ahead to possible future expansion throughout Southern California over the next five years.

Orange County's population is expected to grow an additional 10 percent over the next five years. Local industry is expanding rapidly and firms are willing to expend capital to provide training for their employees.

Within this highly concentrated population area, our target customers are (1) firms with less than 50 employees whose employees require training, and (2) individuals who will pay to upgrade their technical skills.

The majority of our target customers are in the service sector. Our service area has a high concentration of technology, biotechnology, health care, and food businesses with annual sales up to $5 million. Target customers are age 25 to 50, college educated, with incomes of $40,000-$150,000. They live or work within a 10-15 mile radius of The Software School. Our research indicates that 50 percent of our target customers will be women and 90 percent have a computer in their own home; most have Internet access.

We track all sales and marketing efforts to refine our target customer profile and focus marketing efforts on the strongest and most profitable markets.

The Competition

Obviously, if you know who your competitors are and how they fail to meet market needs, you are well on your way to strategic competition. You need to persuade your reader how great your competitive tactics are. Reread Chapter 5 and review your Action Steps.

If your competitive strength derives from patents, copyrights, or trademarks, include information about them in this area. Provide copies of any patents or copyrights received or pending in the Appendix.

How tough do your competitors look? As you read The Software School's assessment of its competition, note that the writer takes a cool, objective look at the competition. He does not belittle them, and certainly does not underestimate them.

The Software School's plan leaves no doubt that management is exploiting a market gap that is ignored by the competition: training adults how to use the Internet and popular software programs.

This is more than a matter of writing skill. Early on, the entrepreneurs who founded The Software School did the right research so they could make decisions ahead of time—just as you were asked to do in the earlier chapters.

How will you handle your competition? Your readers will expect you to provide an honest appraisal of each of your major competitors.

Now you are ready to complete Action Step 66.

The Competition

While there is considerable computer training available in Orange County, we hope to capitalize on the need for business software and Internet training, which our competitors are not currently providing. On reviewing our competitors, we discovered the major players in the industry have developed specific niches in the marketplace. A brief review of our four major competitors follows:

- **Trayhart Schools.** Our oldest, most entrenched competitor. Three locations in Orange County: Brea, Garden Grove, and South Coast Plaza area. Trayhart conducts primarily 6-hour classes on database and word-processing software. Their primary target market consists of upgrading secretarial skills for local employers. Classes are offered only during the day, Monday through Friday. Average two day courses cost $250. Trayhart's South Coast Plaza location will be a major competitor if they decide to expand their class offerings.
- **Big Micro Instruction.** Excellent classroom facilities located in El Toro, with easy freeway access. All instruction is free if you purchase your hardware from Big Micro; otherwise, courses generally cost around $120 for 6–8-hour classes. The instructors try hard, but Big Micro is really in the business of pushing hardware. No Internet courses are offered. The classes are aimed at the novice user and classes tend to have users as young as age 14.
- **Your Micro and You (YMAY).** Developed by professional educators, their local facility in Irvine is five miles from our site. The atmosphere of YMAY is excellent. They offer a normal range of classes and one course in using the computer in a small business, each two day course costs about $275. Their market seems to be divided between adults with a casual interest in computers and children age 10 to 15.
- **Max Software Training.** A professional high-tech facility aimed at providing Microsoft, Oracle, and Novell training and certification specializes in meeting the needs of retraining people to become advanced software technicians. Max has done it right by offering week-long and month-long courses.

Our business is geared to offering $99 courses and to get people up and running in a very short time period. Most of our competitors' class offerings take two days in contrast to our one-day training offerings.

Marketing Strategy

Now it is time to describe your marketing strategy. Need a reminder? Look back at your work from Chapter 6.

The marketing strategy example from The Software School's business plan demonstrates a carefully reasoned approach, and describes conscious marketing policies that will help this small business be competitive. If you were to read a

> ### Action Step 66
>
> #### Describe Your Major Competitors
>
> Briefly profile the businesses that compete with you directly. Try to be objective as you assess their operations.
>
> What are their strengths? weaknesses? What can you learn from them?
>
> After you've described your competitors, indicate how you're going to ace them out of the picture.

business plan in which the writer does not demonstrate this care and deliberation, how much faith would you have in the writer's business abilities?

Note that The Software School uses a three-pronged approach to reaching the public. This business understands the importance of finding a good promotional mix.

The entrepreneurs who own The Software School will stay on top of the changing market picture by:

- looking to radio and TV exposure.
- logging calls and gathering information on callers and students to maintain a base of up-to-date information on their target market.
- tracking how they gain their largest accounts and planning to intensify their efforts in those areas.

In your business plan, include the distribution channels, selling methods, and use of public relations. If your firm has plans to sell products or services internationally discuss those plans in this section. Present a list of potential customers/clients and sales forecasts. Action Step 67 will help you refine your marketing strategy. Note that your marketing strategy must continue to focus on the target customers.

Marketing Strategy

We use a wide range of strategies to let our customers know about our class offerings including mass-media advertising, special promotions, personal selling, and networking. We are in the productivity and information business, and toward that end we are presently developing an Internet site that will provide a community for Orange County's budding entrepreneurs.

Networking

Each owner belongs to two professional trade organizations focusing on small businessowners within a 10-mile radius. In addition, each owner has joined a local chamber of commerce organization to network. All three owners serve as guest speakers to civic and educational organizations. A discount program will be designed for entrepreneurs in venture-training programs.

Mass-Media Advertising

The Software School will initially place advertisements in the *Orange County Business Journal* and Chamber of Commerce newsletters as soon as the second classroom is available. As we grow we plan to expand our advertising to cable news shows, radio, and specific Internet sites.

Personal Selling

Fortunately, our owners have experience and talent in the area of personal selling. Each owner spends 5–10 hours per week calling on potential clients. In addition, phone selling is an important aspect of our business. Converting phone queries into sales is a major goal of each and every person answering the phone. Logging all calls and making sure they are followed up on in a timely matter is essential for our success.

Creative Promotions/Free Ink

Phil Carpenter is very active in Junior Achievement (JA) and will be offering one scholarship to each JA chapter.

A monthly newsletter will highlight success stories of our customers and introduce new classes and products for entrepreneurs. Training programs are being developed for local stores such as Staples and Office Max to offer at a discount to their business customers.

Geographical Factors and Site Selection

The next part of your business plan concerns location, site selection, and physical facilities. You may want to review your work from Chapter 7 now.

If you are planning a retail establishment, this area is critical and should include extensive research data to back up your site-selection decision. Discuss the accessibility and visibility of the site as well as the demographics and psychographics of the surrounding population. Download from the many online databases graphics showing roads, competition, and potential customers for support data in the Appendix.

For a retail business to be located in a shopping center or strip center, discuss the retail market mix and how it will help draw customers into your store. Drawings of the actual facility and store layout may help your reader visualize the store as well.

If you are planning a manufacturing firm, facility layout and equipment will need to be discussed. Read how The Software School shows off its location to advantage.

You need to paint an attractive picture of your business site and, at the same time, keep your reader interested by inspiring confidence in your choice. Location takes a tremendous amount of analyses. The Software School writer gives himself a subtle pat on the back by describing the lease arrangements and by identifying the need for a second classroom. If the reader needs more, he or she is referred to the Appendix. This is smart writing.

Your plan will become very real when you showcase your physical facility. Complete Action Step 68.

Our Facility

The Software School has secured a five-year lease at 47 Turbo Drive, Santa Ana, California. The facility is all on the ground floor and occupies 1500 square feet. The area, which is zoned for business use, is near a hotbed of high technology and entrepreneurial activity. Within a four-mile radius of the facility, there are two computer superstores, five other computer sellers, one computer furniture store, Staples, and Office Max.

During our lease negotiations, we persuaded the landlord to make extensive improvements to the interior, and to spread the cost out over the three-year term of the lease. The decor—blue carpet, white walls, and gray furniture—gives the effect of a solid, logical, somewhat plush business environment in which our target customers will be comfortable and learn fast.

The building is divided into four areas: a reception and lounge area (200 square feet), a director's office (100 square feet), a classroom (600 square feet), and a storage area (600 square feet).

The principals envision the storage area as a future second classroom (see diagram in the Appendix).

Management

Management will make or break a small business. You are a member of the management team, and you want this business plan to inspire confidence in your

---

> ### Action Step 68
>
> #### Show Off Your Location
>
> The great thing about a location is that it's so *tangible*. A potential lender can visit your site and get a feel for what's going on.
>
> Bankers often visit a client's business site. That's good news for you because now the banker is on your turf.
>
> Clean up the place before your banker arrives.
>
> In this section, you want to persuade potential lenders to visit your site. Describe what goes on there. Use photographs, diagrams, and illustrations to make it feel almost like home.

▶ **Action Step 69**

Introduce Your Management Team and Personnel

Almost every study you read on small business failure places the blame on management. Use this section to highlight the *positive* qualities of your management team.

Focus on quality first—their experience, accomplishments, education, training, flexibility, imagination, tenacity. Be sure you weave in experience that relates to your particular business.

Remember—dreamers make terrific master-builders, but they make lousy managers. Your banker knows this, and potential investors will sense it. A great team can help you raise money.

The key to a great team is balance. Describe the kinds of people you will need as employees and how they fit into your plan.

What skills will they need? How much will you have to pay them? Will there be a training period? If so, how long? What fringe benefits will you offer? How will you handle overtime?

If you haven't yet written job descriptions, do that now. Job descriptions will help avoid potential problems with the people who work for you.

team. Writing this section will help you focus more closely on your management team members. If you need a refresher, review your work from Chapter 11. Many plan reviewers read the management section first. They want to have confidence not only in the business idea but also in the team who will take the concept to reality.

Now is the time to discuss the legal form of business you have chosen as well. Any agreements or legal papers can be included in the Appendix.

Read about how The Software School introduced its management team. This team shows balance, diversity, experience (some interesting track records), the will to succeed and, above all, a love of adventure. Robert Jericho was a flight instructor and former Microsoft employee. Derek Campbell had computer teaching experience, and Phil Carpenter had experience in opening several small businesses. Now they are using space-age industrial training techniques in the computer classroom. Pilots must plan and take responsibility—good experience for running their own show.

Balance is important, too; this shows up in the short résumés. Longer and more detailed résumés should be included in the Appendix.

Jericho is the technician who handles systems management. Campbell is the lead teacher, and Carpenter handles sales and marketing. All have good people skills. Who do you suppose is the idea man?

The Software School was wise to include short résumés of the directors. In this case, the background of the directors enhances the balance of the team. All have admirable depth in their business careers, sharing a combined 45 years of experience in the corporate world. Carpenter very wisely uses his directors to assist him in the sales function.

The listing of the legal counsel, accounting firm, insurance broker, and advertising agency also adds to the impression of solid business practices. These people are sometimes referred to as the "taxi-squad," but in a business plan, the language is more formal.

Nothing is more important than the people who will make your business successful. Present their pedigrees, and focus on their track records and accomplishments as you complete Action Step 69.

Personnel

For a start-up business, you are peering into the future with confidence—doing informal job analyses for key employees who will help you to succeed. For an ongoing business, you need to list your present employees and anticipate your future personnel needs. If you currently employ five people but want to indicate growth, try projecting how many jobs you will be creating in the next three years.

When you start thinking about tasks and people to do them, review your work in Chapter 11. Preparing this part of your plan is important because it gives you one more chance to analyze job functions before your begin interviewing, hiring, and paying benefits—all of which are expensive.

Note that The Software School gives a very brief rundown of the personnel situation. In describing their lean operation, the entrepreneurs who run The Software School keep their job descriptions lean as well. They show good sense when they express a commitment to hold down operating costs. Their decision reflects business discipline and foresight. If you were a potential investor in this business, wouldn't you appreciate some tight pursestrings and sweat equity?

Every person on your team is important. Action Step 69 will help you to describe the kinds of people you will need and how you will help them to become productive.

Management and Personnel

Owners

Derek Campbell was born in Shaker Heights, Ohio, in 1954. He earned his BS degree in Industrial Engineering at Purdue University. After graduation, he spent five years in the Marine Corps, where he was a flight instructor, a check pilot, and a maintenance officer. While in the service, Mr. Campbell completed an MS in Marketing.

Following military service, Mr. Campbell was employed as a pilot for United Airlines. He is currently the owner and CEO of EuroSource, a software importing company.

Robert Jericho was born in Dallas, Texas, in 1965. He has a BS degree in Information Science from the University of Oklahoma. After graduation, he served six years in the Marine Corps, where he was a flight instructor, flight operations officer, and schedules officer.

Following military service, Mr. Jericho completed Microsoft and Novell certification training and has worked in several high-tech start-up firms over the past seven years.

Phil Carpenter was born in Duluth, Minnesota, in 1963. He graduated from Purdue University with a BS in Management and a minor in Operations Management. Mr. Carpenter then worked for one of the big-six accounting firms for five years before returning to Purdue for his MS in Management. His research projects during his Master's program focused on small business ventures. Mr. Carpenter is currently Professor of Business at Huntington Beach Community College, a general partner in two businesses, and a small business consultant. He has written and lectured widely in the area of small business.

Directors

Cheryl Hughes Smith was born in Corpus Christi, Texas. She has an MBA from Harvard and a law degree from the University of Texas at Austin. Ms. Smith is a partner in Smith, Jones, and Schultz, an Orange County law firm. She is the author of numerous articles in the field of corporate planning and taxes.

Dan Masters was born in Palo Alto, California in 1934. His degrees (BA, MBA) are from Stanford, where he specialized in Marketing and Finance. Mr. Masters served his Army duty in Korea, where he worked on the United Nations Korean Civil Assistance Program, a long-term plan for making Korea economically independent.

Following his military service, Mr. Masters worked for Eastman Kodak and then for Sylvania (senior account sales executive, sales manager) for a total of 25 years.

Mr. Masters is currently Associate Professor of Business at San Juan Capistrano Institute of Business Science. He is active in several small businesses, lectures widely, and has published numerous articles in the field of small business.

Other Available Resources

The Software School has retained the legal firm of Farney and Shields and the accounting firm of Hancock and Associates; The insurance broker is Sharon Mandel of Fireman's Fund; the advertising agency is Friend and Associates.

Personnel

For the first three months of the year, the owners will be operating the business with one full-time receptionist/bookkeeper. In month four an additional person will be hired to assist with registration and the phones. Most of the classes will be taught by one of the three owners. Additional instructors will be hired on a contract basis. We need to run a lean operation and the owners are willing to put in sweat equity.

Section II

Financial Section

Good Numbers

The financial section is the heart of your business plan. It is aimed at lenders—bankers, credit managers, venture capitalists, vendors, SBICs, commercial credit lenders—people who think and dream in numbers. Lenders are professional skeptics by trade; they will not be swayed by the enthusiasm of your writing in Section I. Your job, therefore, is to make your numbers do the talking. This is easier than you may believe.

In Chapter 8 you projected cash flow and income. You have tested your numbers on real lenders in the real world. If you have not already done so, you need to organize your numbers into three standard instruments:

1. Pro forma income statements
2. Pro forma cash flow statements
3. Balance sheet

Examples from The Software School will serve as models for you; adapt them to suit your business type.

The idea is to know where every nickel is going. You need to show when you will make a profit and appear neat, orderly, in control, and conservative. You will know you have succeeded when a skeptical lender looks up from your business plan and says, "You know, these numbers look good."

Good Notes

One way to spot a professional lender is to hand over your business plan and watch to see which sections he or she reads first. Most lenders first study the notes that accompany income and cash-flow projections. Knowing this allows you to be forewarned. Use these notes to tell potential lenders how you generated your numbers (for example, "Advertising is projected at 5 percent of sales") and to explain specific entries (for example, "Leased Equipment—monthly lease costs on IBM microcomputers"). Make these notes easy to read, with headings that start your readers off in the upper-left-hand corner and march them down the page, step by step, to the bottom line. Some projections use tiny footnotes, on the same page. We recommend *large* notes on a separate page with a heading "Notes." Notes are important, so they should be big.

Creating your business plan takes a lot of time. It is only natural for you to hope that lenders will read it, become enthusiastic, and ask questions. The notes to your plan can help you accomplish that, even if you have not as yet started up and the numbers are projections into the future.

If your business has been ongoing for some time, a detailed financial history should be included. For those seeking funding, the financials will be very significant. You need to describe which type of funding you are seeking and specific details on how that funding will be used and repaid. Completing your financial statements requires business finance and accounting knowledge.

Pro Forma Income Statement

Your next task is to put together your Pro forma income statement (also called a "profit and loss" statement). With the information you have gathered so far, it should not be too difficult. In fact, it will be enjoyable if the numbers look good. If they don't, reconsider before you commit.

Review The Software School's pro forma income statement and the careful documentation of each item. For instance, if a lender wanted to know how the figures for commissions were generated, Note 6 explains that they are estimated as 10 percent of sales.

Action Step 70 will help you project your own monthly profits and losses for 12 months. You should also include a pro forma income statement for the next three to five years for your business. The Software School's pro forma income statement will help you in developing your income statement.

Notes for Pro Forma Income Statement

1. **Instruction.** Based on 2.5% occupancy growth per month, starting at 35% (235 students) and growing to 60%. Students pay $99 per course.
2. **Books.** Revenue from books sold averages approximately 1% of instructional sales, rounded to bring total sales to an even $100 figure.
3. **Classroom Materials.** Per student.
4. **Instruction Personnel.** Contract teachers.
5. **Books.** Cost of books is 70% of selling price.
6. **Commissions.** Average 10% of instructional sales are split between owners.
7. **Advertising.** Projected at 5% of sales.
8. **Credit Cards.** Approximately 50% of sales are paid with credit cards. The cost is 2.5% of the sale.
9. **Salaries.** Start with 1 full-time employee. Add one part-time person beginning the 10th month.
10. **Payroll Taxes.** The company's share of employee taxes averages 7% of commissions and salaries.
11. **Leased Equipment.** Monthly lease costs on microcomputers.
12. **Licenses and Fees.**
13. **Accounting.** Average accounting and bookkeeping costs for the area and size of the business.
14. **Rent.** Based on 3-year lease.
15. **Office Supplies.** Estimated at 0.25% of sales.
16. **Subscriptions.** Estimated costs for magazines and newspapers.
17. **Repair and Maintenance.** Projected to be 1% of sales.
18. **Insurance.** Based on current insurance contract for next 12 months, payable every 6 months.
19. **Telephone.** Figured at 1.5% of sales.
20. **Utilities.** Figured at 2% of sales.
21. **Depreciation.** Schedule established by accounting firm.
22. **Interest.** Loan at 13% with $5,000 payments due every 6 months until paid off.
23. **Miscellaneous.** Figured at 3% of sales.
24. **Reserve for Taxes.** State and federal taxes estimated at 20% of net profit.

Pro Forma Cash Flow

Next, focus your attention on the projected cash flow—the lifeblood of your business. By projecting cash flow figures across the year, you get a month-by-month picture of how healthy your business will be.

Table 15.1

Pro Forma Income Statement/Software School

	7th Month	8th Month	9th Month	10th Month	11th Month	12th Month	13th Month	14th Month	15th Month	16th Month	17th Month	18th Month	Total
SALES													
Instruction (1)	$23,285	$24,950	$26,630	$28,215	$29,900	$31,580	$33,265	$34,945	$37,915	$39,600	$42,770	$42,770	$395,825
Books (2)	215	250	270	285	300	320	335	355	435	500	530	530	4,325
TOTAL SALES	$23,500	$25,200	$26,900	$28,500	$30,200	$31,900	$33,600	$35,300	$38,550	$40,100	$43,300	$43,300	$400,150
Cost of Instruction													
Clssrm. Matrls. (3)	$1,765	$1,890	$2,020	$2,140	$2,265	$2,395	$2,520	$2,650	$2,875	$3,000	$3,240	$3,240	$30,000
Instruction Personnel (4)	2,500	2,500	2,600	2,600	2,700	2,700	2,800	2,800	2,900	2,900	3,000	3,000	33,000
Books (5)	150	175	190	200	210	225	235	250	305	350	370	370	3,030
TOTAL COST/MATRLS/INST/BOOKS	4,415	4,565	4,810	4,940	5,175	5,320	5,555	5,700	6,080	6,250	6,610	6,610	66,030
GROSS PROFIT	$19,085	$20,635	$22,090	$23,560	$25,025	$26,580	$28,045	$29,600	$32,270	$33,850	$36,690	$36,690	$334,120
EXPENSES													
SALES:													
Commissions (6)	$2,330	$2,495	$2,665	$2,820	$2,990	$3,160	$3,325	$3,495	$3,790	$3,960	$4,275	$4,275	$39,580
Advertising (7)	1,175	1,250	1,335	1,410	1,495	1,580	1,660	1,750	1,895	1,980	2,135	2,135	19,800
Credit Cards (8)	295	315	335	355	380	400	420	440	480	500	540	540	5,000
ADMINISTRATIVE:													
Salaries (9)	3,300	3,300	3,300	4,500	4,500	4,500	4,500	4,500	4,500	4,500	4,500	4,500	50,400
Payroll Taxes (10)	570	580	600	695	715	725	745	755	785	795	825	825	8,615
Leased Equip. (11)	1,270	1,270	1,270	1,270	1,270	1,270	1,270	1,270	1,270	1,270	1,270	1,270	15,240
Licenses/fees (12)	2,300	2,495	2,665	2,820	2,990	3,160	3,325	3,495	3,790	3,960	4,275	4,275	39,580
Accounting (13)	500	500	500	500	500	500	500	500	500	500	500	500	6,000
Rent (14)	3,890	3,890	3,890	3,890	3,890	3,890	3,890	3,890	3,890	3,890	3,890	3,890	46,680
Office Supplies (15)	60	65	65	70	75	80	85	90	95	100	110	110	1,005
Dues/Subscript. (16)	20	20	20	20	20	20	200	20	20	20	20	20	420
Repair/Maint. (17)	235	250	265	285	300	320	335	385	385	395	435	435	3,995
Insurance (18)	80	80	80	80	80	80	80	80	80	80	80	80	960
Telephone (19)	355	380	405	430	455	480	505	530	575	600	650	650	6,015
Utilities (20)	470	505	540	570	605	640	670	705	765	800	865	865	8,000
Depreciation (21)	1,170	1,170	1,170	1,335	1,335	1,335	1,335	1,335	1,335	1,335	1,335	1,335	15,525
Interest (22)				650	650	650	650	650	650	595	595	595	5,685
Miscellaneous (23)	705	755	805	855	905	955	1,010	1,060	1,150	1,205	1,300	1,300	12,005
TOTAL EXPENSES	$18,755	$19,320	$19,910	$22,555	$23,155	$23,745	$24,505	$24,920	$25,955	$26,485	$27,600	$27,600	$284,505
NET PROFIT	$330	$1,315	$2,180	$1,005	$1,870	$2,835	$3,540	$4,680	$6,315	$7,365	$9,090	$9,090	$49,615
Reserve for taxes (24)	65	265	435	200	375	565	710	935	1,265	1,475	1,820	1,820	9,930
NET PROFIT AFTER TAXES	$265	$1,050	$1,745	$805	$1,495	$2,270	$2,830	$3,745	$5,050	$5,890	$7,270	$7,270	$39,685

We have shown only one-year's Pro forma cash flow and income statements for The Software School. For the actual business plan, projections should be performed quarterly for the next two years and in some cases four years.

The Software School's cash-flow projection demonstrates how the loan infusion will be used. Remember to read the notes that accompany and explain the pro forma cash flow.

If you compare the pro forma income statement to the cash flow projection, you will see that some items are treated differently in the figures. For example, expenses in the pro forma income statement are divided into monthly installments, whereas the same expenses in the cash-flow projections are shown as bulk payments when due.

Now, look at insurance expenses. In the income statement, we find a total expense of $960 shown as twelve monthly debits of $80 each. The same expense in the cash flow is shown as two payments of $480 each, falling due in the seventh and thirteenth months. Profits do not pay the bills and the payroll; cash flow does! Potential lenders look at cash flow first, so successfully completing Action Step 71 can make or break you.

Notes for Pro Forma Cash Flow

1. Beginning of the Month. Cash available as the month begins.
2. Sales. Includes all sales paid by cash, check, or credit card at the time the class is taken. Does not include accounts receivable.
3. Credit Card Expense. Fees of 2.5% paid to credit card companies. Approximately 50% of customers use charge cards.
4. Loans. Loan for new course development and equipment.
5. Total Cash Available. Sum of all money available during the month.
6. Books. Books for sale are ordered and paid for one month in advance of projected sale.
7. Instructional Materials. Covers course materials purchased from license.
8. Salaries. Net salaries paid employees approximately 80% of gross salaries paid.
9. Payroll Taxes. Total of amount withheld from employees, plus Income Statement payroll tax item.
10. Advertising. Established as 30-day accounts with all media companies.
11. Leased Equipment. Lease payments are due the first of each month.
12. Licenses and Fees. License fees are due the 15th of the following month.
13. Legal and Accounting. Due 30 days after bill is received.
14. Rent. Due the first of each month.
15. Office Supplies. Paid at time of purchase.
16. Insurance. Paid every 6 months in advance.
17. Telephone and Utilities. Paid within 30 days of receipt of bill.
18. Interest. Interest only , paid each month.
19. Loan Payback. $5,000 loan payment due every 6 months.
20. Miscellaneous. Paid in month expense occurs.
21. Income Tax Reserve. Paid into a special tax account at the bank.
22. Total Disbursements. Total cash expended during the month.
23. Net Cash before Capital Investment. Cash balance before capital investment payments.
24. Capital Equipment. Purchase of additional equipment.
25. Additional License fees.
26. Contractor fees based on estimates.
27. Monthly Cash Flow. Cash balance after all payments at the end of the month.

Action Step 71

Project Your Cash Flow

Get used to keeping records of cash flow. Once a month is not too often to do it. If you prepared a cash flow projection for your business in Chapter 8, bring those numbers forward. If you skipped that step, do it now. Here's how it's done:

1. Write down all the cash you will have for one year.
2. Add net profit.
3. Add any loans.
4. Figure your total cash needs for the year.
5. Spread these numbers out across the year. You may have a lot of cash at the start of the year; you want to make sure you have enough to get all the way through.
6. Now list all disbursements. Spread these out, too.
7. Now examine the figures. Is there any time during the year when you will run short of cash? It's better to know the truth now, while you're still working on paper.
8. If your cash picture looks good, drop in a couple of what-ifs. (Let's say you've budgeted $300 for utilities, and the air conditioner breaks down. It will cost $200 to repair it, and the lease says it is your expense. Or let's say you see an opportunity for additional work, but you would have to hire someone to handle it for you. Can your cash flow handle such surprises?)

Table 15.2

Pro Forma Cash Flow/Software School

	7th Month	8th Month	9th Month	10th Month	11th Month	12th Month	13th Month	14th Month	15th Month	16th Month	17th Month	18th Month	Total
CASH-RECEIPTS													
Beginning of Month (1)	$3,970	$7,365	$6,015	$51,575	$47,060	$35,275	$31,840	$28,645	$27,900	$33,115	$43,895	$47,800	$364,455
Sales (2)	23,500	25,200	26,900	28,500	30,200	31,900	33,600	35,300	38,350	40,100	43,300	43,300	400,150
Less: Credit Card Expense (3)	(295)	(315)	(335)	(355)	(380)	(400)	(420)	(440)	(480)	(500)	(540)	(540)	(5,000)
Loan (4)			60,000										60,000
TOTAL SALES	$27,175	$32,250	$92,580	$79,720	$76,880	$66,775	$65,020	$63,505	$65,770	$72,715	$86,655	$90,560	$819,605
DISBURSEMENTS													
Books (6)	$175	$190	$200	$210	$225	$235	$250	$305	$350	$370	$370	$385	$3,265
Inst./Materials (7)		6,000			7,500			9,000			9,000		31,500
Salaries: (8)													
Instruction	2,000	2,000	2,040	2,080	2,120	2,160	2,200	2,240	2,280	2,320	2,360	2,360	26,160
Administration	2,640	2,640	2,640	3,120	3,600	3,600	3,600	3,600	3,600	3,600	3,600	3,600	39,840
Commissions	1,730	1,865	1,995	2,130	2,255	2,390	2,530	2,660	2,795	3,030	3,170	3,420	29,970
Payroll Taxes (9)	2,045	2,195	2,250	2,435	2,690	2,755	2,805	2,870	2,925	3,025	3,075	3,170	32,240
Advertising (10)	1,080	1,175	1,250	1,335	1,410	1,495	1,580	1,660	1,750	1,895	1,980	2,135	18,745
Leased Equip (11)	1,270	1,270	1,270	1,270	1,270	1,270	1,270	1,270	1,270	1,270	1,270	1,270	15,240
Licenses/fees (12)	2,160	2,330	2,495	2,665	2,820	2,990	3,160	3,325	3,495	3,790	3,960	4,275	35,305
Accounting (13)	500	500	500	500	500	500	500	500	500	500	500	500	6,000
Rent (14)	3,890	3,890	3,890	3,890	3,890	3,890	3,890	3,890	3,890	3,890	3,890	3,890	46,680
Office Supplies (15)	60	65	65	70	75	80	85	90	95	100	110	110	1,005
Dues/Subscript.	20	20	20	20	20	20	200	20	20	20	20	20	420
Repair/Maint.	235	250	265	285	300	320	335	355	385	395	435	435	3,995
Insurance (16)	480						480						960
Telephone (17)	325	355	380	405	430	455	480	505	530	575	600	650	5,690
Utilities	430	470	505	540	570	605	640	670	705	765	800	865	7,565
Interest (18)				650	650	650	650	650	650	595	595	595	5,685
Loan Payback (19)									5,000				5,000
Miscellaneous (20)	705	755	805	855	905	955	1,010	1,060	1,150	1,205	1,300	1,300	12,005
Inc. Tax Reserve (21)	65	265	435	200	375	565	710	935	1,265	1,475	1,820	1,820	9,930
TOTAL DISBURSEMENTS (22)	$19,810	$26,235	$21,005	$22,660	$31,605	$24,935	$26,375	$35,605	$32,655	$28,820	$38,855	$30,800	$339,360
Net Cash before Capital Invest. (23)	$7,365	$6,015	$71,575	$57,060	$45,275	$41,840	$38,645	$27,900	$33,115	$43,895	$47,800	$59,760	$480,245
Furniture/equipment (24)			10,000										10,000
License (25)			10,000										10,000
Contractor fees (26)				10,000	10,000	10,000	10,000						40,000
Monthly Cash Flow (27)	$7,365	$6,015	$51,575	$47,060	$35,275	$31,840	$28,645	$27,900	$33,115	$43,895	$47,800	$59,760	$420,245

Table 15.3

The Software School's Balance Sheet

	ACTUAL Sept. 30, 1998 (After first 6 months)	PROJECTED Sept. 30, 1999 (After first 18 months)
Current Assets		
Cash	$3,970	$59,670
Books/Materials	2,500	4,495
Total Current Assets	$6,470	$64,165
Fixed Assets		
Leasehold Improve	91,000	131,000
Furniture	15,100	20,100
Equipment	40,600	45,600
Total Fixed Assets	$146,700	$196,700
Other Assets		
License	25,000	35,000
TOTAL ASSETS	$178,170	$295,865
Debt and Equity		
Current Debt		
Accounts Payable	7,060	9,545
Accured Wages	2,500	7,500
Loan Payment		1,800
Total Current Debt	$9,560	$18,845
Long Term Debt		
Bank Loan	0	58,600
TOTAL DEBT	$9,560	$77,445
Equity:		
Owners Net Worth	168,610	218,420
TOTAL DEBT & EQUITY	$178,170	$295,865

Projected Balance Sheet

Professional lenders look at your balance sheet (also called a "statement of financial position") to analyze the state of your finances at a given point in time. They are looking at things like liquidity (how easily your assets can be converted into cash) and capital structure (what sources of financing have been used, how much was borrowed, and so on). Professional lenders use such factors to evaluate your ability to manage your business.

The Software School's projected balance sheet position at the end of its first 18 months of operations (see Table 15.3) shows a net worth of $218,420. Let's talk for a minute about return on equity (ROE) a bottom-line figure that shows how much is earned on the total dollars invested in a business. You have this kind of information up front if you invest money in bonds. The interest tells you your ROE. You compute ROE for a business by dividing the net profit by owner's equity. For The Software School, the profit after taxes is $39,685. Divide that by the owner's equity of $218,420:

$$\$39,685/\$218,420 = 18.17\%$$

Could you get a 18.17% percent from a savings account or a bond fund? It is not a bad ROE.

The Software School did not provide notes to its balance sheets because in their case no notes were needed. In conjunction with the income statement and cash-flow projections, all the entries in the balance sheet will make sense to professional readers. Under some circumstances, you would want to note unusual features of a balance sheet for an actual fiscal year, but in most cases—and in most projections—this won't be necessary. Complete Action Step 72 to help you prepare and include a balance sheet in your business plan.

Epilogue

Act on What You Know

Well, do you feel like you are ready? You are. You have thoroughly researched your product or service, your market and target customers, your competition, marketing strategy, and location. You have discovered how to prepare for surprises you cannot afford; how to handle numbers; how to pursue financing; when and why you should incorporate; how to build a winning team; and whether you should buy, franchise, or start on your own. And you have written it all up in a beautiful showcase: your winning business plan.

Before you take off running, we want to give you one more tool we believe every entrepreneur should have—a tool to help you put your business plan to work. It is called PERT—Program Evaluation and Review Technique—and is often used to establish schedules for large projects. PERT was pioneered in military research and development as an aid for identifying activities and their optimal sequence, and then monitoring progress. The aerospace industry, the construction industry, and other big businesses that must plan complicated projects use PERT charts, and so can you.

A PERT chart (see Table 15.4) is just the thing if you feel overwhelmed by the tasks of starting up and don't know where to begin. If you are a person who sometimes tries to do everything at once, PERT will help you focus your energy on the right job at the right time. A sample PERT chart is provided. Yours will need to be bigger and more detailed. You can use days, weeks, or months to plot the tasks ahead.

Table 15.4

Sample PERT Chart

	Week					
Task	**1**	**2**	**3**	**4**	**5**	**6**
Befriend banker	X	X	X	X	X	X
Order letterhead		X				
Select site	X					
Get fictional name statement	X					
Bulk mail permit			X			
Ad agency	X					
Lunch, lawyer			X			
Appointment, accountant				X		
Vendor statement					X	
Utilities deposits					X	
Review promotional material					X	
Survey phone system			X	X	X	
Order phone system						X
Open house						X

Action Step 73 is the last Action Step for Chapter 15. It is the end, yes, but also the beginning. All our best wishes go with you as you embark on your great adventure. We hope that this book and its Action Steps have convinced you that you can achieve success—whatever it means to *you*—and have *fun* at the same time. Good luck! Work smart, and enjoy your adventure!

▶ Summary

It has been a long haul, and you are now ready to create your business plan—a portable showcase for your business. When you visit vendors, bankers, and potential lenders you can take along a copy of your business plan to speak for you, to demonstrate to all that you have a blueprint for success.

Begin writing by starting with the material you feel most comfortable with. Once you have completed one portion of the plan, the other parts will fall into place more easily. Fortunately, your work in earlier chapters has prepared you for each section.

Make sure your business plan has answered the following questions:

- What is your mission?
- How are you going to market your product and/or service?
- Who is going to purchase your product or service?
- How will you reach your target customers?
- What makes your firm unique?
- How will you support the financial needs of your growing firm?

After you have completed the plan. Rewrite your executive summary highlighting the most relevant information and data for your readers. Personalize each cover letter. Go for it!

Think Points for Success

- The executive summary should read like ad copy. Hone it until it is tight and convincing.
- Section I should generate enthusiasm for your business.
- Section II should substantiate the enthusiasm with numbers.
- Be sure to use footnotes sufficient to explain the numbers in your financial statements.
- Do not inflate numbers to impress.
- Use your business plan as a road map to success.
- Your business plan is a working, living document.

Key Points from Another View

Pearls of Wisdom from Leo Helzel*

1. Set your goal and go for it.
2. Be tireless and persevere.
3. Focus on niche markets.
4. Be decisive and implement decisions quickly.

▶ Action Step 73

Constructing a PERT Chart

Rehearsal is over. Now it's time to step onto the stage and get the drama under way. One way to shift from planning into action is to develop your own personal PERT chart. A PERT chart will serve as a script for you. It also will tell you and the other members of your team how long certain jobs should take.

List the tasks you need to accomplish—befriending a banker, filing a fictitious name statement, taking a lawyer to lunch, ordering business letterhead, selecting a site, contacting vendors, and so on—and set your deadlines.

As you already know, a successful package is made up of many, many details. If you take the details one at a time, you'll get there without being overwhelmed. The sample PERT chart in Table 15.4 can guide you.

5. Listen and be responsive to customers, suppliers, employees, and investors.
6. Maintain CFN-cash flow now.
7. Innovate.
8. Minimize layers of management.
9. Maximize profits by keeping costs low and productivity high.
10. Believe in yourself.

SOURCE: **www.moneyhunter.com**

Note: *Leo Helzel is the author of *A Goal Is a Dream with a Deadline*. New York: McGraw-Hill, 1995.

Fast-Start
Business Plan

Entrepreneurial Links

Books

Launching Your Home-Based Business: How to Successfully Plan, Finance, and Grow Your Venture, David H. Bangs and Andi Axman, 1997.

Your First Business Plan, Third Edition, Joseph Covello and Brian Hazelgren, 1998.

Finding Your Perfect Work: The New Career Guide to Making a Living, Creating a Life, Paul Edwards and Sarah Edwards, 1996.

Websites

www.homebusiness.com, American Home Business Association
www.wahm.com, Work at Home Moms
www.ideacafe.com, Idea Café: The Small Business Channel

Associations/Organizations

Corporation for Enterprise Development, 202-408-9788
Independent Business Alliance, www.ibaonline.com
National Association of Entrepreneurs, www.nae.org

Publications

Money
Success
Working Woman

Additional Entrepreneurial Insights

Been There, Done That: 16 Secrets of Success for Entrepreneurs, Angi M. Wong, 1997.

The American Dream: How Latinos Can Achieve Success in Business and in Life, Lionel Sosa, 1998.

The E-Myth Revisited: Why Most Small Businesses Don't Work and What to Do About, Michael E. Gerber, 1995

Learning Objectives

- Admit that you are in a hurry.
- Acknowledge you are starting with funds you can afford to lose.
- Launch a start-up without the help of bankers.
- Hop on a hot opportunity in the marketplace.
- Start small while you explore the possibilities of growing larger.
- Work with numbers so that you can keep going when the going gets tough.
- Review "Yes, We Do Windows" Business Plan.
- Develop your own Fast-Start Business Plan.
- Continue to plan as you work in your new business.
- Make money now!

Maybe you're in a hurry. If so, we have some help. But first you need to make sure the Fast-Start Plan is the right start for you. In this chapter, we help you thought to your big decision, your business description, your start-up costs, and your final pass. We also provide a model business plan.

The Big Decision

If you're going it alone, with money you can afford to lose ($1000; $5000; $10,000; $50,000), and if the loss of that money won't jeopardize your loved ones and make wolves howl at your door, use the Fast-Start Plan.

If other people are involved—investors, bankers, advisors, company officers—then return to Chapter 15 and write a comprehensive plan.

The comprehensive plan gives you a blueprint to follow month by month through the first year. It tracks your business through seasonal ups and downs. It allows for contingencies.

The Fast-Start Plan lets you get going now. It's great if you've been in business before and know the footwork of entrepreneurship. With the Fast-Start Plan, you're using the business as a probe into the marketplace. You can start quickly because you have an instinct for beating out the competition. You have a market sense. You have a good feel of the business you are starting.

The Fast-Start Plan is quicker to write. Marketing, pricing, and advertising employ a low-key approach. As you gain experience, you fold that experience into a rolling projection. You can write a Fast-Start Plan in several weeks. The full Business Plan, because of extensive data gathering and passing through many hands, takes three to six months. Gather up all the information from your past action steps. For assistance use one of the online business plan templates discussed in Chapter 15 or develop the Fast-Start Plan on your own. Read through the "Yes, We Do Windows" Business Plan at the end of the chapter before you start writing your Fast-Start Plan.

Quick Checklist

Here's a quick checklist for implementing the Fast-Start Plan:

1. Can you afford to lose your dollar investment? How much money can you afford to lose at the slots in Reno or Las Vegas or Atlantic City? Can you lose $100? $500? $1,000? $5,000? more? What's your deductible on your car insurance? your boat? your major medical? Write down the amount you can afford to lose. If you have excess money to speculate with, then the Fast-Start Plan is for you.

2. How easy is it to enter this business? Is it easy to talk to other owners? Are role models in great abundance? Do the prospective customers have a clear understanding of the goods and services provided? Examples of businesses with wide doors: window washing, auto detailing, landscape maintenance, vacation pet-sitting, house-sitting.

3. Can you start this business on a part-time basis? Starting part-time lessens your risk. You have a chance to prove the business. You see how much you really like it. You keep a running tally of customer responses. You keep your other job and the income it provides.

4. How tough is it to gather needed data to formulate a Fast-Start Business Plan? In breaking new ground, be careful. In a venture like this, the market is not clearly defined. There are very few competitors. Pricing is not clear. You must make certain you've got a market out there.

5. Can you start using only your own funds? Bill Gates, the founder of Microsoft, could use the Fast-Start Plan for a business start-up costing millions. A single parent of two with rent and a car loan to pay can afford much less. Be honest with yourself. Be honest with your family.

Structuring Your Plan

Use these questions to structure your Fast-Start Plan:

How do you describe your business?

What business are you really in?

Who is your competition and how are they doing?

What is your pricing strategy?

Who is your target customer?

Why should target customers buy from you?

How will you advertise?

What are your start-up costs?

What are your sales goals for the first three months?

What are your operating expenses for the first three months?

If you crash and burn, what can you salvage for cash?

What have you forgotten?

Business Description

It's night. The family's gone to bed. The house is quiet. The pets are snoozing.

It's time to sit back in your favorite chair, time to relax, time to dream about your new business. So dream a while and then write down your dream:

> You step out of your van. It's a handsome vehicle, spotless, white, and gleaming. On the side, in red letters, is your sign: MY CARPET CLEANERS—QUALITY AND SERVICE—A NUMBER-ONE JOB. Your company phone number is lettered underneath. You are all in white: white jumpsuit, white shoes. The starched look

Test Your Export Quotient

Test Your E.Q. (Export Quotient)	Yes	No
1. Are you entrepreneurial?	☐	☐
2. Do you have a reliable service-oriented character?	☐	☐
3. Are you a natural networker, building and maintaining relationships?	☐	☐
4. Do you see yourself as highly organized and research oriented?	☐	☐
5. Have you a sense of "mission" . . . ?	☐	☐
6. Do you possess good communication skills?	☐	☐
7. Is a sales, marketing, or distribution background featured in your résumé?	☐	☐
8. Do you excel in finance and business-related subjects?	☐	☐
9. Do you pride yourself in your strong negotiating skills?	☐	☐
10. Are you experienced in handling complex documentation?	☐	☐
11. Are you an avid follower of global politics?	☐	☐
12. Do you have the ability to speak and write more than one language?	☐	☐
13. Are you sensitive to different cultures?		
14. Do you consider yourself able to adopt ideas easily, even under pressure?	☐	☐
15. Are you well-traveled or curious about other cultures?	☐	☐

Total (award 1 point for every "yes"):

Evaluating Your Score

1–6   Although you have acquired some skills related to exporting, you need further assessment to find out if you are suited to this field.

7–10   You show a keen interest in the subject. However, you should consider increasing your knowledge, language, and technical trading skills training.

11–15   You have a high rating in the critical factors that make companies and individuals successful in the exciting field of global trade.

SOURCE: Forum for International Trade Training, Global Entrepreneurship Skills, Module I, p. 206.

look gives you the image of the best carpet cleaner in town. You catch your reflection in the mirror. The jumpsuit makes you look taller. The company logo stitched on your breast pocket makes you proud.

The house of your prospect is large: three stories, well-kept lawn, a three-car garage, a curved driveway. The walkway leading to the front door is paved. The doorway is large enough to drive a truck through. Out back, you can hear the happy shrieks of children as they splash in the pool.

Cut to the job. You're in a big room with wall-to-wall carpet. Your machine sucks up the dirt. The customer enters, walking on a dropcloth you laid down for your equipment. Pointing to a transparent tube attached to your super-steam vacuum, you show the customer the dirt coming out of her carpet. The carpet sparkles in the sunlight as you go after those drapes. The customer, overwhelmed with such service, hands you the biggest check you've ever seen.

This check is 4-feet long and 2-feet high. The customer smiles. You read the amount—fantastic money for a fantastic job—and dance your way out of the house and down the walkway to your van.

Great Dream Equals Great Business

A business dream separates your business from everyone else who's out there trying to clean carpets.

You're clean and you're in the cleaning business. You're proud of being in business. You care. The customer, owner of expensive things, cares that you care. We like to do business with people who care about what they're doing. Such people take pride in a job well done.

By being spotless when you enter this home, you show the customer respect. Your equipment is spotless. You're not dragging someone else's dirt into this place. The dropcloth is a nice touch.

You look like a carpet cleaner. You act like a carpet cleaner. Your dream gives you a jump start. Now you add in details.

What products and/or services will you offer? Will you limit yourself to carpets? Will you also clean chairs and drapes? Will you specialize in homes? offices? Will you provide a simple service? Will you also sell spot remover, touch-up cleaners, other extras?

What Business Are You Really In?

Are you selling clean carpets? a better-looking home or office? better health? Are you helping the customer preserve an investment?

To help you get a handle on this, let's profile two different businesses in the same industry.

Business A is a family restaurant. It's open 24 hours. There's nothing on the menu over $9.95. The menu for children is extensive. On each table is a digital clock and a sign that says you eat free if your meal is not on the table within 10 minutes of being ordered. The clock invites the customer to set it, and invites the waiter to beat it.

Business B is a restaurant with limited hours. Weekdays it's open from 11 A.M. to 2 P.M. and from 5 P.M. to 10 P.M. Weekends it's open from 5 P.M. until midnight. Each table features large, comfortable chairs. The lighting is soft. The china is fine, the silverware first-cabin. The waiters wear tuxes and their manners are impeccable, right on the edge of snooty. The wine list contains fine vintages from Europe and California. If you can stump the bartender by requesting a drink she cannot mix, your drink is served free by the maitre d'hôtel. The cheapest entree on the menu is $25. (This restaurant rounds off prices.)

Both A and B are in the food-service business. You can find both in the restaurant section in the Yellow Pages. But are they both in the same business?

For your answer, look at the customers.

Customers go to Business A for fast service. Their desire is to feed the whole family without going broke. They don't want a long travel time, so Business A is close to home. The food is good. Not wonderful, not divine, but good.

Customers go to Business B for excellent food and superior service. They go to relax, to enjoy a perfect moment over a rare vintage. They may be driven by fantasy or romance or escape. They may go just to watch the staff perform. That's entertainment.

What business is A in? What business is B in?

Business A is in the family-feeding business. Business B is in the entertainment business. A provides nourishment at affordable prices. B provides more than food—B provides a dining experience.

If you were the manager of Business A, you would do these things:

purchase good food in quantity

get it at the lowest price

▶ **Action Step 74**

What Business Are You Really In?

This is a tough question.

Start by interviewing customers of your competitors. Why do they buy what they buy? Why do they shop there instead of somewhere else? What are they after? What are they trying to satisfy? What itch does this business scratch?

Stimulate your thinking by analogy. What, for example, do you get when you have your car washed? It costs you anywhere from $5 to $50 and for what? A clean car? A savings in time? Pride of ownership? A car your customers will ride in? Or maybe it's maintenance: Do you live near the beach, where the salt air eats your chrome?

Where do you buy clothes? Why? Where do you buy gas? Why? Who cleans your carpet? Why?

Probe your own buying habits. Probe the buying habits of your friends. Keep an open mind. Gather data. All this will lead you to discover what business you're really in.

control waste in the kitchen

develop a fast and efficient delivery system

turn those tables

If you were the manager of Business B, you would do these things:

train all employees to fit the upscale image and offer exceptional service

provide upscale interior

select high quality meats, unusual food, specialty produce

employ a professional bartender who knows the latest mixes and can smile

Take a couple of steps back, look at your business from the viewpoint of the customer. Then plan your course of action. To begin complete Action Step 74.

Who Are Your Competitors?

This is a good time to try out your new eyes. How much can you learn from your competitors? How do you find them?

If you're hunting for retailers or restaurant owners, hop in your car and drive around. But how do you find a home-based word-processing business? How do you find a home-based cleaning service? How do you find a mobile auto detailer?

You know this: In order to stay in business, a business must communicate with potential customers, so tune in your entrepreneurial radar. Check Yellow Pages; area newspapers; look for business cards in copy services, in service stations, in local food stores, on kiosks.

Once you find your competitors, take a closer look. Were they easy to find? How visible was their advertising? As you study their advertising strategy, what kind of a customer profile can you draw? Are they spending a lot on their advertising? Are they working on a shoestring?

What can you tell from their pricing? Are prices firm? Are they negotiable? Are they high? low? competitive? What kind of customer will go for these prices? Who will get shut out? Do your competitors understand the marketplace? Is their pricing structure positioned properly?

Are your competitors zeroed in on a specific target customer, or are they using the shotgun approach? Just for practice, profile the target customer of your competitors.

Which of your competitors are successful? Can you tell why? Which are just hanging in there? Why? If a business has been operating for some time, there's a good chance the owner's doing something right. What is it? Nose around. What customer benefits do they offer: fast service? quality work? free delivery and pick up? low prices?

Even the most successful business overlooks something. Find out what they missed. Did they overlook a market segment? Did they get sloppy with their advertising? Is their range of services actually limited? Is their inventory sparse? Thousands of businesses have been built on the weaknesses of competition.

Take the time to chat with the customers of your competitors. Are they satisfied? If not, why not? How do they see the competition? What image does the competition project? How do customers feel about price? quality? timeliness?

Take the time to chat with competitors outside your area. Is there a gap no one has thought to close? Complete Action Step 75.

How Much Should You Charge?

Pricing is key. Don't be misled by thinking you can whisk customers away from established competitors by charging less for the same thing. It didn't work for now-bankrupt department stores. It won't work for you.

Young Entrepreneur's Network
www.yenetwork.com

The Network publishes *Visions,* an online magazine, and provides resources for young entrepreneurs. The Website is building a community for young entrepreneurs to Network throughout the United States.

For an additional membership fee you will have access to online advisors for finance, marketing, franchising, public relations, and so on. Jennifer Kushell, the founder of the Network, has written an inspirational resource manual for young entrepreneur's, *No Experience Necessary: Young Entrepreneur's Guide to Starting a Business,* 1997.

Find out what is important to the customers. It's probably time or dependability or quality or convenience. Then learn to see the value of your product or service through your customers' eyes.

For example, when you eat lunch at a fast-food restaurant, you buy French fries, coffee, tea, a soft drink. You pay one dollar or more for each of these items. The cost to the seller is a dime or a quarter. Within limits, these items are not price-sensitive. The question is: What is the customer's perception of value? Develop your pricing strategy with Action Step 76.

When you shop, train yourself to make price comparisons:

a. Pricing Newspapers at the Newsstand:	
Wall Street Journal	1.25
USA Today	.75
local paper	.25
b. Coffee:	
at local doughnut shop	1.00
at a luxury hotel	3.50
c. Car Wash:	
high school students' Saturday special	5.00
do-it-yourself	4.00
you watch them	5–50
d. Transportation:	
Ford	22,000
Mercedes	60,000
Lamborghini	275,000
e. Education:	
a year at Stanford	30,000
a year at state college	12,000

Profile Your Target Customer

Who will receive the biggest benefit from your business? Who can pay the price? Who can you target? Where do they live? What's their income range? What do they need? What work do they do? Are they married? single? divorced? retired?

To profile your customers, become a marketplace detective. To practice, study the customers that buy from your competitors.

Do women outnumber men? What's the average age? What cars do they drive: make? year? price range? How are the customers dressed? How expensive are their shoes? If you can get inside, check out methods of payment. Do they use cash? checks? credit? How expensive are the items they're buying?

Practice trains your new eyes to consider the person as a prospect.

Action Step 75

What Do Your Competitors Look Like?

Are they winners? losers? Why?

What things are they doing right? doing wrong?

How many competitors do you have? What customer groups are they serving? Who are they overlooking? Where do they advertise? Where do they promote? What do you think of their location? What market area do they cover?

If you owned a competitor's business, what would you change?

What can you learn from studying your competitors?

After you have opened your business, do some more marketplace detecting as you study your competitors. You'll learn more because you'll know more. A veteran entrepreneur knows what to look for.

Action Step 76

What Is Your Pricing Strategy?

What does your target customer see as good value?

What is most important to your target customer: convenience? quality? on-time delivery? image? price?

What stage of the product/service life cycle are you in? How many competitors do you have? How nearby are they?

If price is the main decision factor, try to add something a little extra. What's unique about your product? Is it unique enough so that you can charge a little extra?

Describe Your Target Customer and Develop Your Advertising and Sales Program

A. Who is your primary Target Customer? Complete a profile: sex, age, income, occupation, residence, vehicle(s)—anything that gives you a picture of needs and wants. What do they read? watch? listen to?

When you have profiled your primary customer, do the same thing for secondary customers.

How large is your main market area? Will you sell in one section of town? the whole town? the country? the state? the region? If you're driving around to service accounts, how far will you have to drive?

B. How will you let potential customers know that you are open for business? How will you let them discover the benefits of buying from you?

Start with a budget. How much money can you spend on promotion? Once you know what you can afford select advertising that matches your budget.

As part of your plan, set up an evaluation procedure. You want to know how well each promotion works.

How Do You Make that Customer Connection?

Before you spend a bundle on a TV ad, or three months knocking on doors of houses along Golf Course Drive, take some time to put together a message.

What image do you want to project? How do you want the marketplace to receive your product or service? What position do you want to assume among your competitors? What are the key benefits your business will offer customers? How soon do you want to start? How many autos can you detail—or homes can you clean—in one day?

Once you answer these questions, design your business card. Use a logo that offers an insight into your business. If you're starting a word-processing business, use something along the lines of "On Time Quality Service." If you're thinking of house cleaning: "Only Sparkle—Not a Speck of Dust." Always carry lots of business cards. They're inexpensive memory seeds, handy reminders, and often your most cost-effective advertising.

Once your business cards are done, research ways of reaching customers. Do they gather at church? at school? at football games? at Little League? What do they read? watch? listen to? Could you reach them best through the Yellow Pages? radio? billboards? What can you afford? Match that amount with the most effective communications channel.

Stay visible. If your target customers gather in groups, try to reach them there. Attend their meetings. Get on their list of speakers. Give a demonstration. Hand out business cards. Offer a freebie.

If you must find your customers one at a time, spend a few hours each day knocking on doors. Telephone prospects. Work your mailing list. If you use mail contacts, be sure you do phone follow-ups.

Join the local chamber of commerce. If you're lucky, your chamber will run a short piece about you, the newcomer, in their newsletter. Stay visible at chamber meetings. Don't get pushy with your business cards, but have them handy.

While you're connecting with customers, don't overlook organizations that might act as your sales force. For example, let's say you've found a school where the parents' group is trying to raise funds to support an athletic endeavor. Put together a flyer for students to take home. In return for each sale from the flyer, your business will donate 10 percent to 25 percent to the fund-raising group. Consider the donation a part of your promotional budget. Develop an advertising plan using Action Step 77.

What Are Your Start-up Costs?

At your local office supply store, make these purchases: a mileage log, an expense journal, and a folder to hold receipts. You can deduct mileage and expenses related to your business start-up.

List everything that you need to get started. Don't worry if the list would cost a bundle. You're brainstorming at this point. The key here is not to overlook anything. A visit to your competitors will add ideas to your list. An interview with an owner will trigger new items. When you're chatting with businesspeople, ask questions: What kind of computer register do you use? What kind of bookkeeping system do you have? What's the cost of start-up inventory? When your list is fat, add pricetags.

When you start purchasing, check the large discount stores. Also investigate mail-order houses, especially for personal computers. If one company in your area can supply most of your needs, try to make a package deal and develop a long-term relationship.

On equipment items, save by buying used. Used equipment might be scratched or dented, but you stand to save 50 percent to 90 percent. Check the newspaper classifieds under "Equipment for Sale" or "Office Furniture." Talk with potential suppliers—they usually know someone who's going out of business. You can find good deals from an owner who's folding.

You should also consider leasing your equipment. Leasing costs more in the long run, less when you're getting started. As your business grows, and your leases expire, you can decide whether to replace by buying new or used. Leasing provides you a lot of up-front flexibility.

Divide your start-up list into two columns. Column 1 contains items that are absolutely necessary. Column 2 contains "nice-to-haves."

Check Column 1. Is there anything you can borrow from home? parents? friends? Scrape to the bottom of the barrel here. Your goal is to cut costs so you'll have cash to run the business. Complete Action Step 78.

Charting Your Sales Goals for the First Three Months

How much would you like to sell the first month? the second? the third? How much can you afford to sell? What is a realistic target for your new business?

Sales goals provide the information you need to forecast your variable expenses—those expenses forced to change in relation to sales volume. If you are selling a product, sales goals will allow you to estimate the cost of goods sold.

Sales goals provide the driving force for you and your team. They help you focus on your target for the month. When the month is finished, compare how you did with your initial sales goals. Did you make it? If not, why not? Did you exceed your goal by 25 percent? Why? What worked well? What didn't? As you evaluate, decide how to improve next month, and how to keep improving.

To chart a reasonable sales goal, focus on three factors:

1. **The weight of your marketing program.** Do you plan a wide-area campaign? Will you start by calling on friends and neighbors, counting on them to spread the word slowly? How much energy are you putting into this? Will you start full-time? Will you keep your job? If you're in school, will you stay enrolled?

2. **The experience of entrepreneurs in businesses like yours who operate in a noncompeting area.** How much effort does Entrepreneur A have to put out to make a $100 sale in his or her area?

3. **The capacity you have to deliver the product or service.** What do you need to make this venture go? If it costs you $500 for materials to build one computer cabinet and you only have $500 worth of capital, then you will be limited to building one cabinet at a time. You have to get paid before you can build a second cabinet.

Or let's say you're starting a part-time business detailing autos. Detailing one auto takes three hours. In addition, driving, collection and scheduling takes approximately one hour per car. Your maximum sales activity per week will be based on the number of hours you can devote to your business after you put in your hours at your full-time job. If you can devote 24 hours a week, then your sales would be 24 hours, divided by time, multiplied by your charge. Let's try that:

24 divided by 4 = 6 autos per week
Your charge per auto is $120.
6 times $120 = $720 per week.

Make a list of your friends and relatives. Find out how many of them have their autos detailed. Add the repeat factor: How often do they want detailing: once a month? once every quarter? once a year? When your list is finished you have 24 prospects. You have a realistic shot at eighteen of those prospects. For your business, that's enough for a start-up.

> ▶ **Action Step 78**
>
> ### What Will It Cost to Open Your Doors?
>
> List your expenses—equipment, rentals, inventory—everything you'll need to start your business. Start your list with business cards. End with the key for the front door. What comes in between?
>
> When you have listed all the items, give each one an estimated cost. On equipment, buy used. If you can't buy used, try leasing. On inventory, negotiate with each supplier to see if you can get credit terms right from the start. If you can't get credit, find out how you can qualify.
>
> When the list is complete—items and costs—go through it with a marker, deleting items you can do without for a month or so. You are trying to keep your up-front cash outlay to a minimum.

▶ **Action Step 79**

Setting Realistic Goals

How much will you sell in your first month? How much will you spend?

Your goal in this Action Step is to set realistic goals. To do that, you need to know your maximum capacity. For example, how many houses with an area of 1500 to 2000 square feet can you clean in one day? one week? one month? This will give you the top sales figure you could reach. That's your ideal.

Fixed expenses don't change with sales volume. List those first. Then list the variable expenses.

For fixed expenses, check with people who can give you answers: public utility companies (water, gas, electricity, phone, natural gas); leasing agent for rental rates; insurance agent for estimated insurance costs.

For variable expenses—those that change with sales volume—figure out how far they go up relative to some fixed unit of change; for example, $100 of sales per house cleaned. If you can establish a percentage relationship between sales and each individual variable expense, then it will be easy to fill in your projections each month.

As a wise entrepreneur, you know that your first few jobs will take longer than later ones. You're new. You're learning the business. You want to make sure you do a super job. You have four prospects who want monthly detailing. You have six who want it quarterly. Start with these ten prospects and lay out a chart. (See Table 16.1).

Assumptions Using

1. Assume that the first and second months contain four weeks and the third month has five weeks.
2. Assume sign-ups of four monthly detailing prospects from your list of 24. Add one new monthly prospect out of every six new customers from the "Need to Find" group.
3. Assume a sign-up of six quarterly customers from your list of 24 prospects. Add one new quarterly customer out of every six new customers from the "Need to Find" group.
4. Assume a sign-up of eight one-time prospects from your list of 24 prospects.
5. Action: Must find new customers from the remaining six prospects on the 24 names list. Other sources are referrals, sales calls, and advertising.
6. We only plan for the first three months. The fourth month is easy to start building from monthly and quarterly customers.

Expense Forecast

List everything you'll need to pay for on a regular basis to operate your business, for example, phone, supplies, truck, advertising/promotion. Next, list everything you can think of under each heading. Here's a partial example:

Supplies	Truck
rags	gas
soap	oil/maintenance
wax	insurance
cleaner	car signs
Q-tips	promotion

Now consider each specific item. Which ones can you tie to the detailing job? For example, for each auto detailing job, you use two packages of rags, one-half can of wax, one-quarter can of cleaner, 10 Q-tips; $2 for gas, and so on.

Add these expenses to your first sales forecast. Also add expense items that don't change. See Table 16.2.

Assumptions for Table 16.2

1. Phone monthly basic rate, plus pager.
2. $20 per month, plus $1 per job.
3. $50 per month toward oil change, tires, and vehicle maintenance.
4. $2400 a year, $200/mo., expense paid quarterly.
5. Estimated at $20 per job.
6. Yellow Page ad at $70 a month, plus $50 a month for four line ad in weekly paper, and $100 for flyers and business cards each month.
7. Set aside: Plan for surprise expenses.
8. Profit before depreciation (a noncash expense). In time, you should get an estimate from your accountant for depreciation.

Table 16.1

Pro Forma Sales—Auto Detailing

	1	**2**	**3**	**4**	**5**	**6**	**7**	**8**	**9**
1									
2	First Sales Forecast								
3									
4		1st Month		2nd Month		3rd Month		4th Month	
5	Monthly Detailing (2)	480	(4)	480	(4)	600	(5)	720	(6)
6	Quarterly Detailing (3)	360	(3)	360	(3)	0		360	(3)
7	Rest of 18 Prospects (4)	360	(3)	600	(5)	0			
8	Need to Find (5)			720	(6)	3000	(25)		
9	Sales	1200		2160		3600			
10									
11									
12									

See Assumptions.

Table 16.2

Pro Forma Income Statement—Auto Detailing

	1	**2**	**3**	**4**	**5**	**6**	**7**
1	First Income Statement Forecast						
2							
3		1st Month	2nd Month	3rd Month			
4	Sales						
5	Monthly	480	480	600			
6	Quarterly	360	360				
7	Original Prospects	360	600				
8	Need to Find		720	3000			
9							
10	Sales Total	1200	2160	3600			
11							
12	Expenses:						
13	Phone (1)	60	60	60			
14	Gasoline (2)	60	76	100			
15	Oil/Maint (3)	50	50	50			
16	Insurance (4)	200	200	200			
17	Supplies (5)	200	360	600			
18	Ad/Promotion (6)	220	220	220			
19	Depreciation (7)						
20	Miscellaneous (7)	150	150	150			
21							
22	Expense Total	940	1116	1380			
23	Profit	260	1044	2220			
24							
25							

See Assumptions, page 320.

"Things to Do" List

Now that your plan is complete, act on it. Your first step is to compile a list of things that need doing. You need this list for at least three reasons:

1. It gives you easy steps to follow.
2. It keeps you on target.
3. It gives you a sense of getting there at last.

Following is a sample "things to do" list from a catering service started by Doris and Mike in a mid-sized city on the east coast.

List of Necessities Before Opening Day—Catering Service

1. Talk with experienced caterers.
2. Prepare Fast-Start Plan.
3. Stay organized.
4. Choose a business name.
5. File for fictitious business name.
6. Make arrangements to use pizza or other food-service kitchen.
7. Determine what area to service.
8. Have business phone installed. Purchase answering machine or voicemail.
9. Set up business checking account. Check out several banks. Fees and services vary.
10. Locate suppliers: refrigeration, cooking, baking, utensils, cash register, tables, chairs, other.
11. Check city and county business license regulations.
12. Get federal ID number—needed by all employers.
13. Get an insurance agent.
14. Hire employees: full-time? part-time? how many? Make sure to get all information: Social Security number, correct name and address, phone, citizenship. Develop application form. Have each employee fill out a W-4.
15. Complete advertising before the opening so people will know opening date.
16. Join a discount price warehouse.
17. Choose food suppliers.
18. Support business contracts:
    a. rental tents, equipment
    b. florists
    c. entertainment
    d. service staff
    e. other bakeries, specialty suppliers, ice carvers, props, lighting, and so on.
19. Business cards should be ordered and ready to hand out.
20. Preprinted billing statements for customers who do not pay upon receipt. Preferably get money up front.
21. Record all income and expenses daily in a ledger.
22. Find a bookkeeper to prepare financial statements. Check out computerized accounting systems.
23. Get an attorney.
24. Network with friends, relatives, other caterers.
25. Join chamber of commerce. Good place to meet potential customers.
26. Do projected profit and loss statement for three months.
27. Contact Health Department.
28. Contact Yellow Pages.
29. Order signs for vehicles.

▶ *Summary*

The Fast-Start Plan is *not* a substitute for preparing a full-fledged plan. Use the Fast-Start for a specific venture that is easy to start, carrying minimal risk. Also use it for a business that's breaking new ground, where there is little data available.

The key to any business, and to any business plan, is how well you understand the needs of your target customer. Find an itch that isn't being scratched and you can ace your competitors.

Write your own Fast-Start Plan. Keep it handy. Refer to it often. Use it to keep your business on track in those early months of operation. When you've been in business for three months, use your Fast-Start Plan as a launching pad for your next nine months of operation. For your second year, write a full-fledged business plan.

Think Points for Success

- Your Business Plan—Fast-Start or full-fledged—is your pathway to success.

- Looking at your competition helps you see your target customer. Seeing your target customer clearly helps you position your business strategically in the marketplace.

- Building a plan builds confidence. Confidence breeds excitement. If you don't feel excited and confident about your business, bail out now.

- Once you get started heading around the track, don't forget to keep your new eyes on the marketplace.

Key Points from Another View

Ten Commandments from Sam Walton

1. Commit to your business
2. Share your profits
3. Motivate your partners
4. Communicate all that you know
5. Appreciate what your associates do
6. Celebrate your success
7. Listen to everyone in your company
8. Exceed your customer's expectations
9. Control your expenses better than competitors
10. Swim upstream and avoid conventional wisdom

SOURCE: Guerilla Marketing Communiquee **www.gmarketing.com**

Model Fast-Start Business Plan

Yes, We Do Windows

1. Definition of your business
2. What business am I really in?
3. Competition
4. Pricing
5. Target customer
6. Ad/sales program
7. Start-up costs
8. Sales goals/expenses/first three months
9. "To do" list

1. ***Definition of the Business.*** I have been a window washer for three years. For two years I worked for Windowlite Ltd., a large organization with over 250 satellites across three states. For the next year, I worked for a local operator who owned a truck and three squeegees. I feel that I know the business from both ends.

My plan—and the subject of this plan—is to do window- and house-cleaning.

> Window cleaning: I will clean windows; screens, and window casings.
>
> House-cleaning: I will vacuum, dust, polish/wax, mop. I will do bathrooms, mirrors, kitchens, range tops, ovens.

A customer may contract for one or more services. House-cleaning will be offered on a once-a-week or once-every-two-weeks basis. Window-cleaning will be offered monthly, quarterly, twice a year, or as needed.

2. ***What business am I really in?*** Determine the answer by identifying customer benefits:

> **Pride of ownership**—a home is a person's most expensive investment. Keeping it clean makes the customer proud.
>
> **Time-saving**—homeowners work hard to pay for their investment; many homes today are supported by double incomes; few homeowners have the time to do their own cleaning.
>
> **Preserving the value of the investment**—dirt and grime damage the home. Cleaning on a regular basis enhances and preserves the value of the home.
>
> **Comfortable, healthy living area**—a clean home is a healthier home. Who wants to live with dirt?

The business I am really in: "providing a clean and healthy environment while at the same time preserving the value of an investment and deepening pride of ownership."

3. ***Competition*** At this writing there are 77 window cleaning services and 102 housecleaning services listed in my metropolitan area Yellow Pages.

Taking the time to make phone calls to these competitors made me feel even better about my idea for a business. Their phone skills need retooling. The clerks who answered were impolite. They didn't seem interested in the prospect of making money. Out of 59 businesses polled, a hefty 68 percent charged for an on-site estimate.

The phone bids were vague. When pressed, the people who answered the phone said they would have to call me back. Very few did call back.

I can see two "musts" for the business. (a) My bids must be firm and (b) my phone skills must be customer-oriented. If I can't answer the phone, I must find a phone person who can fulfill these two musts. The image we're presenting here is "We aim to please. We're interested in servicing your home."

One question I asked was: "Will the same person be in my home each visit?" A mere 6 percent said yes. The other respondents were vague. That indicated a problem in scheduling.

Measuring the competition has given my start-up a real advantage. Since I'll be doing all the work myself, I can gather customer data as I work. As I expand, I shall match employees to homeowners. A home is a private place. It's a place where one goes to escape from the day. You don't want it invaded by different strangers every week. My plan is to expand only when I find the right employees.

4. **Pricing** My strategy is to price my services just slightly higher than the current competitors' rates. Every three months, to stay current, I will survey the competition.

Basic Rates for Housecleaning

Checksheet Items Only	
Square Feet	*Price*
	1st Cleaning
1,000	$ 50
1,000–1,500	75
1,500–2,000	100
2,000+	100 + $25 per 1000 sq. ft.
	Weekly Cleaning
1,000	$ 35
1,000–1,500	55
1,500–2,000	75
2,000+	75 + $30 per 1000 sq. ft.
	Bi-monthly
1,000	$ 45
1,000–1,500	70
1,500–2,000	90
2,000+	90 + $30 per 1,000 sq. ft.

Window Washing	
One-Story House	
Up to 15 windows	$ 25
Each additional 5 windows	10
Two-Story House	
Up to 25 windows	$ 60
Each additional 5 windows	10

5. **Target Customer** I can classify three types of target customers for my business:

Customer A—family dwelling. A married couple with one or more children. The household income is $80,000 or more. Two vehicles. Both parents work. Reason for the service: Spare time is at a premium for child-care, recreation, and entertainment. Parents cannot spare the time to do windows or other cleaning.

Customer B—single-person condo. A single or divorced person living alone, usually in an apartment or waterside condo. Age range from 28 to 40. The income here runs from $45,000 to $75,000. Time is at a premium. Customers are seldom at home on nights or weekends.

Customer C—high roller. Customer C is distinguished by incomes in the six-figure range. Home values start at $400,000 and move up the scale to $2.0 million. Customer C has high standards, wants a spotless home. Has zero desire to perform menial tasks. As long as the work is excellent and they feel they're not getting ripped off, price is no object.

6. Ad/Sales Program

1. I will maintain an image of high visibility. My truck is washed daily. The color is white. If there is mud on the tires after a job, the mud is washed off before the next job. I wear a white jumpsuit that bears the company logo. My employees will wear similar jumpsuits. Footgear is white sneakers; They're easy on the feet and look professional, almost a sporty image.

2. My business cards are white with blue lettering. On the reverse side is a list of my services. I make it a habit to get a business card whenever I hand one out. Data from these cards is entered into a computer. Names are added to a master list.

3. Flyers will be placed door to door in target neighborhoods. I plan to do one neighborhood of 100 to 200 homes, and then evaluate the response. I ask questions of each person who calls about the flyer: What did he or she like? What was missing? From this marketing survey, I'll redesign the flyer before approaching a second neighborhood.

I make a habit of leaving flyers and business cards at all day-care centers in the area. In exchange for each customer I gain, I donate to a fund for schoolbooks or toys.

7. Start-up Costs

Insurance	700
Truck (used white)	8000*
Ladder rack (custom-made)	550
Ladders	612
Supplies—windows	400
Supplies—housecleaning	1000
Signs for new truck	295
Advertising	500
Answering machine	75
Phone and pager installation	200
P.O. box per month—first and last month	40
Chamber of commerce	300
Fictitious business name	85
Business license	155
Used desk and chair	375
Desk calendar	6
Date book, home	65
Date book, truck	15
Rolodex, supplies, file system	50
Bank account	125
Total Estimated Start-up Expenses	13,548*

*I should be able to buy this for $1000 down and $250 to $275 per month for 36 months. Thus, start-up cash may be as low as $6548.

8. Sales Goals and Expenses, First Three Months My plan is to work six days per week. Until I gain experience, I can work a maximum of three jobs per day. As a carrot for customers, I will do windows at half price with the first housecleaning. I will devote two full weeks to marketing my new business. On the schedule at present, I have four weekly customers and two bi-monthly scheduled for the third week. When not on the job, I plan a strong marketing effort, so that I can add one customer per week until I'm up to 18 customers, my maximum for the week. At that time, I will evaluate my ability to add additional customers and/or hire a part-time employee. (See Table 16.3).

"Things to Do" List

File for fictitious business name

Design business logo, cards, and flyer

Order phone installation

Purchase phone

Lease pager

Set up bank account

(continued on page 328)

Table 16.3

Pro Forma Income Statement—Yes, We Do Windows

	1	2	3	4	5	6	7
1	Sales Goals and Expenses						
2							
3		1st Month	2nd Month	3rd Month			
4							
5	Sales (1)	1087.50	2580	3500			
6							
7	Expenses:						
8	Gas (2)	80	80	100			
9	Maintenance (3)	100	100	100			
10	Insurance (4)	200	200	200			
11	Phone (5)	75	75	75			
12	Advertising (6)	105	105	105			
13	Supplies (7)	65	155	175			
14	Truck Loan Interest	250	250	250			
15	Credit Card (8)	300	300	300			
16	Expense Total	1175	1265	1305			
17	Profit	(87.50)	1315	2195			

Notes for Table 16.3

1. Average customer will own a one-story house of 2000 square feet with 15 windows. Month 1 = four weeks. Month 2 = four weeks. Month 3 = five weeks. Every other new customer bi-monthly. All window-washing contracts on a quarterly basis. First two weeks marketing and second two cleaning.

2. Gas, $20 per week.

3. Maintenance—mainly a reserve for tires, repairs, oil changes, $25 per week.

4. Auto insurance and bonding, $1,500 per year.

5. Basic phone, pager, post office box.

6. Approximately 400 flyers per month comes to $55, plus $50 for distribution.

7. Approximately $5 per job.

8. Credit card payment for start-up expenses.

Order business cards

Set up post office box

Locate source of supplies

Purchase supplies

Purchase truck

Order signs for truck

Purchase answering machine

Buy ladder rack for truck

Buy ladders

Join chamber of commerce

Purchase desk, chair, and office supplies

Business Plan for Shelter Dynamics Inc.*

January 5, 1999

By Alexxe Fritz

---

*Note: For additional sample business plans and assistance in writing your business plan see:

www.moneyhunter.com (Download a sample business plan template)

www.bplans.com (Browse through sample business plans)

www.sba.gov

Business Plan: Shelter Dynamics Inc.

Table of Contents

Confidentiality Statement

The information, data, and drawings embodied in this business plan are strictly confidential and are supplied on the understanding that they will be held confidentially and not disclosed to third parties without the prior written consent of Shelter Dynamics Inc. (see Appendix B for confidentiality agreement).

Memorandum of Risk

This business plan represents management's best current estimate of the future potential of the business. It must be recognized that no business is free of major risks and few business plans are free of errors of omission or commission. Therefore, investors should be aware that this business has inherent risks that must be fully evaluated and discussed with management and experts fully capable of interpreting the information prior to any investment.

Executive Summary

Company Name:	Shelter Dynamics Inc.
Contact:	Alexxe Fritz, President
Address:	1600 Smithy Road, Suite 100
	City of Commerce, CA 90078
Telephone:	(213) 555-1100

Business Description

The company develops, manufactures, and markets survival, shelter, and camping equipment for severe service use. The high-performance survival equipment market is a small, but fast-growing segment of the outdoor shelter market. The company has been in operation for three years primarily selling to government and defense agencies. It operates as a subchapter S corporation, registered in the State of California.

Current Position and Future Outlook

The company has become well established as one of the leading suppliers of survival equipment to the government. This industry is experiencing major growth due a rapid improvement in available materials and increased testing and specifications, caused by a spate of accidents. The company is in the best position to take advantage of this opportunity by using new technology coupled with a marketing thrust into the oil and mineral exploration markets. The success of the company has been founded on the expertise, knowledge, and prominence of the two founding partners. The goals of the company are to increase sales to $3 million over the next four-year period, increase net profit to 10% of sales, and become the market leader in this industry (government and industrial markets). We will achieve this by using new technology and expanded manufacturing and marketing operations to penetrate the oil/mineral exploration market and the consumer market.

Management and Ownership

Alexxe Fritz, President and 45% owner, has over 14 years experience in the chemical/textile business. Her prior management expertise included the development and marketing of new textiles, fibers, and composite materials at the ABC Chemical Company. She has a BS in Chemistry and MBA in marketing from Purdue. John B. Jones, CEO with 45% ownership, has operated two wholesale businesses in the marketing of composite materials to industry and government. He has a BA in economics from UCLA. Other managers include Bill Jones, Director of Marketing; Jane Jones, Manufacturing Manager; Bill Smith, Accounting Manager.

Product Uniqueness

The protective clothing, insulated shelters, and associated survival gear owe their uniqueness to a combination of ultra lightweight, fire resistance, insulating capability, and resistance to rough and abusive environments. They are marketed under the trade name "Lite-XX-Rite." The ability to pass all recent industry tests has given the company a substantial competitive edge and has set the company apart. The company is the "sole source" specified at one of the largest oil companies. Two types of competitors exist: small specialist companies, and divisions of major apparel manufacturers. None currently are able to meet these new standards.

Funds Sought and Usage

The company is seeking $550,000 in exchange for 35% of the common stock of the company: $300,000 will be used to purchase adjacent land for manufacturing expansion, new machinery, and new test equipment; $250,000 will be used to hire a new marketing/sales force and increase advertising and promotion.

Going Public

The company is forecast to go public in 2002. The 2002 estimated company value (using a 10 times pre-tax earnings formula) is as follows:

Median case (below)	$1.6 million
Low case	$1.2 million
High case	$3.0 million

Financial Summary

Summary Income Statement

	Actual		($ 000s)	Estimates		
	1997	1998	1999	2000	2001	2002
Net Sales	235	707	1,458	1,748	2,260	2,681
Cost of Goods Sold	129	358	633	702	893	1,046
Gross Profit	106	349	825	1,046	1,367	1,635
S.G. & A. Expense	185	371	848	974	1,239	1,449
Other Expense	27	19	17	(11)	(8)	(9)
Other Income	0	0	0	0	0	0
Net Income	(106)	(41)	(40)	47	96	155
Income (After Tax)	(106)	(41)	(40)	47	96	109

Objectives

1. Become the market and technology leader in the development and supply of lightweight, fire-retardant, high-performance survival equipment for severe service markets.
2. Increase sales to $3 million in the next four-year period.
3. Increase net profit from the current deficit to over 10% of sales.

Strategies

1. Continue to fund research and development (R&D) to utilize the latest fiber and composite technology, maintaining our technology lead.
2. Seek out and secure sole source specifications for our products.
3. Develop a strong sales and marketing capability for penetrating the oil/mineral exploration market and the small business, retail, and consumer market.
4. Increase both the scope and size of the manufacturing facility.
5. Increase the scope and size of distribution activities.
6. Maintain close liaison with the major developers of specialty fibers and composite materials.
7. Maintain the excellent relationships already established in the government and defense department.

Business Description, Status, and Outlook

Shelter Dynamics Inc. develops, manufacturers, and markets survival, shelter, and camping equipment for severe service use. It has operated for three years, primarily selling to government and defense agencies. The company has become well established and is known for its innovative use of new materials. The protective apparel and shelter market for severe service use is recognized as a high growth market due to changes in the technology and response to a series of accidents.

The business has recently reached a profitable status on a monthly basis. The current year will show a loss in total; however, the final two months have been profitable. We anticipate the next quarter will record a profit, with the remaining three quarters of the year showing a loss due to investment in a concentrated sales and promotion effort. The overall outlook is strong. Management is stable and the financial picture is improving.

The facilities consist of a 10,000-square-foot production facility/warehouse with an attached 2000-square-foot office building with technical facilities. They were constructed 18 years ago and are in good condition. The location is close to a major freeway, in an industrial park.

Management Team

The strength the company's management team has its source in the two partners who started the company.

Alexxe Fritz (47), President and 45% owner, has management experience in the chemical/textile business for over 14 years. Her prior expertise at the ABC Chemical Company included management of several divisions, developing and marketing new textiles, fibers, and composite materials. She has a BS in Chemistry and an MBA in marketing from Purdue.

John B. Jones (43), CEO and 45% owner, has operated two wholesale businesses in the marketing of composite materials to industry and government. He has a BA in economics from UCLA.

The new Director of Marketing is Bill Jones, who was northern zone manager for the ABC Manufacturing Company, which manufacturers and markets composite materials to industry. He will receive an equity position in the company (approximately 10%) after completing one year of service.

The team is complemented by Jane Jones, who heads up the manufacturing and supply functions; and Bill Smith, who is accounting manager. Both Jane and Bill have been with the company since its inception. Each own 5% of the common stock.

Product or Service

The Unfilled Need

Survival equipment has been in use since the great explorers of the early twentieth century. In the past 20 years there have been great advances in the technology, primarily through the use of synthetic lightweight materials, were born out of the space program and the needs of the defense department. Both partners recognized this change and the need for new materials when they were in their prior corporate positions. The gap developing in the marketplace became evident due to a rapid improvement in available materials and tightening of specifications caused by a spate of accidents.

Product Uniqueness

The two product lines marketed by the company are:

Survival apparel
Survival shelters

Survival apparel is developed from a number of ligthweight, fire resistant synthetic fabrics and insulating materials. The shelters are developed from the above materials together with composite materials. The incorporation of permanent fire retardant characteristics has been patented and gives the company a clear differentiation to competition. Competitive products are usually treated to make them fire retardant. This process makes them lose their soft feel and their fire retardance when washed. Our process does not affect the feel of the product or the permanence of the fire retardance. Several of our products are now sole source-specified with several oil companies.

Pricing and Value

The company's pricing policies are based on perceived and measured value rather than cost. Recent surveys show that we are seen as the innovative leader in the industry. We have priced our products at the upper end of the industry scale. This gives us higher margins than our competitors. Gross profit margins are targeted in the range of 45% to 60%, dependent upon the volume of the bid and the position of our product in the specification. We will continue this policy and expect our competitors to raise prices as the cost of materials and test procedures rises.

Trademarks, Copyrights, Licensing, and Patents

Patent applications have been filed in the U.S., U.K., Common Market, Japan, and Canada. Counsel advises that we stand an excellent probability of being issued patents to cover and protect this new technology. The trademark Lite-XX-Rite has been registered in the same countries. We are in the discussion phase with two overseas companies to license the technology. They have asked for confidentiality at this time. Our financial statements do not include royalty payment projections.

Market Assumptions

Market Overview and Size

Survival equipment has been in use since the great explorers of the early twentieth century. In the past 20 years there has been significant change in both technology and usage. This has occurred due to the availability of new lightweight materials and the development of resources and defensive establishments in hostile environments.

The total sales of outdoor protective apparel in the United States in 1997 was over $10 billion, growing at an annual rate of 6% a year. In Canada it was $2 billion, growing at 8% a year. The U.S. and Canadian insulated outdoor shelter and survival market is estimated at $35 million, growing at 10%/year (statistics provided by trade association).

Market Segments

The outdoor protective apparel market is dominated by the sale of rainwear, overcoats, skiwear, and insulated jackets. The lightweight survival apparel is a small segment of this market. Insulated outdoor survival shelters make up a very small but fast-growing portion of the outdoor camping and survival market. The total U.S. market is broken down as follows:

	Sales $ Millions	Growth Rate (%)
Consumer rainwear	3,500	5
Overcoats/jackets	3,900	6
Skiwear	745	8
Survival apparel	32	17
Consumer camping equipment	2,090	5
Survival shelters	25	22

The end user breakdown for the survival markets is as follows (combining the U.S. and Canadian markets):

Government	($ Millions)		
	Industry	Individuals	Survival
Apparel	18	8	6
Shelters	12	7	6

The sales are concentrated geographically (combining the U.S. and Canadian markets) as follows:

N.E. U.S.	42%
N.C. U.S.	20%
Canada	33%
Other	5%

The industrial sector is projected to maintain the highest growth rate (18%/year) for the next three-year period due to upgrading of current equipment and the increase in exploration activity of the oil and mineral companies. The upgrading has been fueled by the recent spate of tragic accidents, leading the insurance companies to require greater focus on safety issues. The government sector is projected to grow at 10%/year due to some upgrading of equipment (SOURCE: Jones Consulting Inc.).

Customer Profile

Three categories of customers are targeted:

- Federal government (U.S. and Canadian)
- Oil, gas, and mineral companies
- Independent retailers to small companies and individuals

Federal government business is usually a "specification and bid" activity. We enjoy a number of contracts that are individually negotiated due to the uniqueness of the products and the uses.

The oil/gas and mineral exploration companies are readily identifiable, with engineering, testing, safety, and procurement departments in central locations. These central operations are being contacted and targeted for sales and technical calls.

The independent retailers have been more difficult to identify and target. We plan to increase efforts by hiring marketing specialists.

Competition

There are two types of competitor in this market:

- Small, specialized manufacturers
- Divisions of major apparel manufacturers

The ranking of the major competitors is as follows:

Rank	Company
1	Survive! (Milwaukee)
2	Outdoor Shelter Enterprises (N.Y.)
3	Protection Clothing (Boston)
4	Shelter Dynamics (Commerce)
5	Johnson Survival (Seattle)

The top two companies are divisions of major manufacturers. Their strength comes from marketing and distribution muscle. They have not updated their technology due to a lack of focus. This has been caused by a high turnover of management. The recent shift in technology has caught them unaware. They are still trying to market older technology to a market that is looking for something new. The smaller companies (Protection Clothing, Johnson Survival, etc.) have kept up with the technologies but have put little effort into marketing or distribution. These two sets of competitors have left a middle-ground gap that we plan to fill. The opportunity can be grasped by the development of strong marketing and distribution channels for the new technology. The financial condition of the smaller companies has recently improved.

Market Share

The company did not exist before 1997. It has grown since then to become the number four supplier of survival equipment behind Survive!, Outdoor Shelter Enterprises, and Protection Clothing. We estimate that we have secured an 11% market share. Estimated shares are:

Rank	Company	% Share
1	Survive! (Milwaukee)	19
2	Outdoor Shelter Enterprises (N.Y.)	16
3	Protection Clothing (Boston)	14
4	Shelter Dynamics (Commerce)	11
5	Johnson Survival (Seattle)	8

Geographical Market Factors

The primary market for our products are those areas that have continuously cold temperatures or a combination of moisture and lower temperatures. These are the northern United States and Canada. At this time we have shelved plans to sell to Europe, we will however continue our discussions with several interested licensees.

Barriers to Market Entry

This type of business has become increasingly difficult to enter primarily due to the rapid change in the technology and the testing and specification requirements of both the government and industrial companies.

Marketing Strategies

The target markets and objectives are:

- Increase penetration of the oil/mineral exploration market
- Enter the small business/consumer/retail market
- Maintain our position in the government/defense industry

The marketplace gap caused by the rapid improvement in available materials and increased specification testing presents us with a critical window of opportunity. The company will use the new technology to develop products that meet or exceed the most stringent of the specifications.

The company will develop and implement a promotional package that sells the features and benefits specific to the industries' needs.

The sales strategies will be tailored to the individual markets:

Oil/mineral exploration market: Focus on key accounts and appoint a dedicated sales/marketing team capable of fully determining their needs and selling to them.

Small business/consumer/retail market: Determine the scope of the market and appoint a retail marketing manager to develop a plan of action.

Government market: Maintain our contacts and current sales team and posture.

Product delivery will be improved through new warehousing procedures and stocking policies.

Technical service staffing will be increased to provide a faster response time to customer inquiries.

Customer service will become a new department that includes order entry.

Operational Plans

Sales Forecasts

The plan for 1999 is to reach $1.458 million in sales and a gross profit margin of $825,000. This will be achieved by increasing our penetration of the oil/mineral exploration market, increasing the marketing efforts to the small business/retail industry, and by maintaining our ties to the federal agencies. The forecasted sales by market for 1999 are:

Market	Sales ($000s)	Gross Profit (%)
Government related	1,079	51
Oil/Mineral	292	60
Retail and other	87	44
Total	1,458	57

Services

Survival apparel will incorporate a number of lightweight, fire resistant synthetic fabrics and insulating materials. The shelters will also indicate composite materials. The incorporation of permanent fire-retardant characteristics has been patented and gives the company a clear differentiation to competition. Several of our products are now sole source-specified with several oil companies. The product sales plan is:

	Product Line ($000s)		
	Shelters	**Apparel**	**Totals**
1998 Actual			
Government related	409	220	629
Oil/Mineral	35	21	56
Other	14	8	22
Total	458	249	707
1999 Estimated			
Government related	701	778	1,079
Oil/Mineral	175	117	292
Other	57	30	87
Total	933	925	1,458

A list of new product opportunities will be completed by June 1999.

Advertising and Promotions

Promotional plans include:

Place four-color/full-page space advertisements in critical issues of the following two trade magazines: *Defense Monthly* (March, April, May 1999) and *Oil/Mineral Exploration Monthly* (April, July, Sept., Oct., Nov. 1999).

Develop a four-color/four-page industry brochure for the oil/mineral exploration market by May 1999.

Change the technical datasheets over to two-color/two-page in September 1999.

Selling Methods

The oil/mineral exploration market will be penetrated through the following selling activities:

1. Develop the list of key accounts in February 1999.
2. Through telemarketing and personal calls qualify and rank the accounts for coverage (March–April 1999).
3. Establish a sales team for penetrating the oil/mineral exploration market:

   - Hire a sales representative by April 1999 for oil/mineral markets
   - Hire a sales representative based in the N.E. United States to call on major accounts (June 1999)
   - Refine the target list of oil and gas and mineral companies for sales activities (June 1999)
   - Develop the detailed sales forecast (August 1999)
   - Work with technical researchers to ensure the specification testing is performed in a timely manner

The small business/retail market will be penetrated through the following sales activities:

1. Establish the consumer market's true needs and feedback information to the design group (January to July 1999)
2. Hire a retail consultant to develop a marketing plan (February 2000)
3. Hire retail marketing manager in March 2000

The dedicated selling effort to the government agencies will be continued unchanged during 1999.

Service and Delivery

The customer service capability will be improved through the hiring of a second order-entry clerk and the installation of new software in March 1999.

Collections will be improved through the subscription to an online reporting system in June 1999.

Raw Materials and Supplies

Production capacity will be doubled in February 2000 by:

Completing the purchase of adjoining land in June 1999

Completing the design of the new facility in April 1999

Purchasing and installing the new manufacturing equipment by October 1999

Purchasing agreements will be negotiated with the two raw material suppliers in May 1999.

Two new warehouses in the Northeast and Midwest will be located and contracted by June 1999.

Hire the second shift supervisor in November 1999.

Facility Plans

The facilities consist of 10,000-square-foot production facility/warehouse with an attached 2000-square-foot office building and technical facilities. They were constructed 18 years ago and are in good condition. The location is close to a major freeway, in an industrial park.

The company plans to purchase the adjoining land to the south of the current facility in June 1999. The two-acre site will house the new manufacturing facility together with the fire test facility. Tentative plans submitted to the city planning department have been approved. The current office/showroom will not be affected by this expansion. Parking will be improved by this expansion. The company does not anticipate delays in receiving the necessary government approvals for manufacturing or firetesting on this site.

Design, Technical, and Engineering Plans

A full-time technical manager will be hired in May 1999 to manage all internal and contracted-out design and technical work.

The new fireproof (Class A) protective product will be developed by June 1999.

Close continuing contacts will be maintained with the oil company testing labs to ensure we secure timely and accurate testing (ongoing).

Close liaison will be maintained with the major fabric and chemical/composite innovative companies.

A new lab technician will be hired in August 1999 to take over all internal testing and quality control work.

State-of-the-art fire testing equipment will be purchased and installed in October 1999.

Administration Plans

Management is seeking capital to expand the production facilities and the marketing activities. Both partners are projected to remain actively involved in the day-to-day running of the business for at least the next five-year period. The company will switch from being a subchapter S corporation to a regular California corporation in 1999.

Employment and Personnel Plans

The current full-time employees:

Current full-time employees:

Two general partners, accounting clerk, one laboratory technician, and two production line employees.

Projected new hires for 1999:

Sales representative for oil/mineral exploration markets

Sales representative for Northeast

Two production line hourly employees

Wage and salary increases are projected to average 6% in 1999. Recent audits by the federal government show we are in compliance with EEOC vendor requirements.

All training is conducted in-house. Sales personnel are part of a separate incentive plan based on individual profitability contributed.

Critical Issues

The major competitors are pressuring the government and industry to lower their testing standards. If this is unchallenged, our competitive advantage will be reduced. We are taking steps to show that the standards can be passed using current technology. It is our belief that the standards will remain unchanged.

Financial Plans

Assumptions, Definitions, and Notes

The following financial information assumes equity financing of $550,000 in May 1999 from an outside investment company.

The sales data were developed by the two partners. In 1998 sales were 89% government related. In 1999 this will drop to 74% as the industrial sales continue to expand. In 2000 the industrial sales are forecast to occupy over 40% of our sales revenues.

FY1999 will show a loss primarily due to heavy investment in sales and promotional activities associated with the penetration of the industrial market.

Pricing is expected to increase significantly above inflation due to a change in product mix and tightening specifications. Gross profit margins are forecast to increase slightly during the planning period.

The costing information was developed from internally generated data with assistance from our retained accounting firm. Cost of goods sold is based on past manufacturing costs. Operating expenses were developed through a detailed Pro forma budgeting process. The income statement is accrual accounting based.

Salary increases will be held to an average of 6%/year through the planning period. Inflation is projected to remain below 6% throughout the planning period.

Three scenarios have been developed:

Scenario 1. This is the plan or most likely projection

Scenario 2. This is the low projection. It assumes that the penetration of the industrial market is slower than forecast. Sales are only 90% of the most likely case (plan); cost of goods sold would also be 90% of plan. Expenses would be trimmed 5%.

Scenario 3. This is the high scenario where our penetration of the industrial market is greater than forecast and is complemented by faster penetration of the consumer market. Sales and cost of goods sold are 10% over plan. Expenses would rise only 4%.

Summary of Income Statement

Scenario 1. This is the "median" or most likely case (plan).

	Actual		($000s)	Estimates		
	1997	**1998**	**1999**	**2000**	**2001**	**2002**
Net Sales	235	707	1,458	1,748	2,260	2,681
Cost of Goods Sold	129	358	633	702	893	1,046
Gross Profit	106	349	825	1,046	1,367	1,635
S.G. & A. Expense	185	371	848	974	1,239	1,449
Other Expense	27	19	17	(11)	(8)	(9)
Other Income	0	0	0	0	0	0
Net Income	(106)	(41)	(40)	47	96	155
Income (after Tax)	(106)	(41)	(40)	42	70	109

Scenario 2. This is the low projection.

	Actual		($000s)	Estimates		
	1997	**1998**	**1999**	**2000**	**2001**	**2002**
Net Sales	235	707	1,312	1,573	2,034	2,413
Cost of Goods Sold	129	358	570	632	805	941
Gross Profit	106	349	742	941	1,229	1,472
S.G. & A. Expense	185	371	806	925	1,179	1,379
Other Expense	27	19	17	(11)	(8)	(9)
Other Income	0	0	0	0	0	0
Net Income	(106)	(41)	(81)	27	58	102
Income (after Tax)	(106)	(41)	(81)	27	44	69

Scenario 3. The best case scenario.

	Actual		($000s)	Estimates		
	1997	**1998**	**1999**	**2000**	**2001**	**2002**
Net Sales	235	707	1,604	1,923	2,486	2,949
Cost of Goods Sold	129	358	696	772	983	1,151
Gross Profit	106	349	908	1,151	1,503	1,798
S.G. & A. Expense	185	371	882	1,013	1,291	1,510
Other Expense	27	19	17	(11)	(8)	(9)
Other Income	0	0	0	0	0	0
Net Income	(106)	(41)	9	149	220	297
Income (after Tax)	(106)	(41)	9	121	170	201

The following pages show detailed Pro forma Cash Flow, Pro forma Income Statements, and Projected Balance Sheets. For brevity, only the median scenario (1) is shown. Information is available on all three scenarios by request.

Pro Forma Monthly Cash Flow, 1999

Estimates 1999 ($000s)

	Actual 1998	Month 1	Month 2	Month 3	Month 4	Month 5	Month 6	Month 7	Month 8	Month 9	Month 10	Month 11	Month 12
Cash Sources:													
FROM OPERATIONS													
Cash Sales	32	4	4	4	4	4	5	5	5	6	7	5	5
A/R Collections	664	100	98	104	115	117	116	120	119	118	117	122	125
Other Cash Coll	2	1	2	2	2	1	1	1	1	2	2	1	1
OTHER SOURCES													
Interest Income	2		1		1		4	2	1	1	1	1	1
Loan from Bank	20			10									
Investment	10					550							
Subtotal	*730*	*105*	*105*	*120*	*122*	*672*	*126*	*128*	*126*	*127*	*127*	*129*	*132*
CASH USES:													
TO OPERATIONS													
Accts Payable													
Goods/Mater'ls	255	36	37	42	40	40	41	40	38	40	40	41	41
Services	43	7	7	7	7	7	7	7	7	7	7	7	7
Petty Cash	3	1	1	1	1	1	1	1	1	1	2	2	2
Payroll Expense	349	40	44	47	48	48	48	48	48	48	48	48	48
Sales Commiss'n													
Travel/Entert	27	4	4	6	6	7	8	6	6	6	5	5	5
Rent/Util/Tel	14	3	3	5	5	5	7	7	7	7	7	7	7
Advertising	4	1	1	1	1	1	10	5	2	30	30	30	2
Auto/Truck Exp	3	3	3	4	4	6	5	5	5	5	5	5	5
Maintenance		4	1	1	2	2	1	1	1	1	2	1	1
Equipment Exp	8	1			1	1	300	1	1				
Ins/Legal/Acct	9	1	1	2	1	1	5	2	2	2	2	2	2
Miscellaneous		2											
OTHER USES													
Interest Exp	21	1	1	1	1	1	1						
Dividends													
Loan Payoff			100										100
Investor Payoff													
Reserve for Tax													
Subtotal	*742*	*98*	*103*	*117*	*117*	*220*	*434*	*122*	*117*	*147*	*148*	*149*	*221*
Cash Incr/Decr	*(12)*	*7*	*2*	*3*	*5*	*452*	*(308)*	*6*	*9*	*(20)*	*(21)*	*(20)*	*(89)*
Beginning Bal	*44*	*32*	*39*	*41*	*44*	*49*	*501*	*193*	*199*	*208*	*188*	*167*	*147*
Ending Balance	*32*	*39*	*41*	*44*	*49*	*501*	*193*	*199*	*208*	*188*	*167*	*147*	*58*

Pro Forma Monthly Cash Flow, 2000

Estimates 2000 ($000s)

	Month 1	Month 2	Month 3	Month 4	Month 5	Month 6	Month 7	Month 8	Month 9	Month 10	Month 11	Month 12
Cash Sources:												
FROM OPERATIONS												
Cash Sales	5	5	6	6	6	7	7	7	7	9	7	7
A/R Collections	129	130	129	133	143	140	135	132	135	139	145	143
Other Cash Coll	1	2	2	2	1	1	1	1	2	2	1	1
OTHER SOURCES												
Interest Income		1		1		2	2	1	1	1	1	1
Loan from Bank												
Investment												
Subtotal	*135*	*138*	*137*	*142*	*150*	*150*	*145*	*141*	*145*	*151*	*154*	*152*
Cash Uses:												
TO OPERATIONS												
Accts Payable												
Goods/Mater'ls	42	43	42	45	46	47	45	44	45	45	47	45
Services	8	7	7	9	8	8	7	7	8	8	9	8
Petty Cash	1	1	1	2	2	1	1	1	2	2	2	2
Payroll Expense	49	51	51	52	52	53	54	54	54	54	54	54
Sales Commiss'n												
Travel/Entert	5	6	6	7	7	8	7	7	7	8	7	6
Rent/Util/Tel	8	8	8	8	8	8	8	8	8	8	8	8
Advertising	3	5	5	3	3	3	5	2	4	3	4	2
Auto/Truck Exp	5	5	5	5	6	6	6	6	6	6	6	6
Maintenance	2	2	2	2	2	1	2	1	2	2	2	2
Equipment Exp	1			1	1	1	2	1	1	2	1	2
Ins/Legal/Acct	3	3	3	3	3	3	3	3	3	3	3	3
Miscellaneous												
OTHER USES												
Interest Exp												
Dividends												
Loan Payoff												
Investor Payoff												
Reserve for Tax					4	4	2	1	2	2	3	4
Subtotal	*125*	*131*	*130*	*137*	*138*	*143*	*140*	*134*	*140*	*141*	*146*	*142*
Cash Incr/Decr	*10*	*7*	*7*	*5*	*12*	*7*	*5*	*7*	*5*	*10*	*8*	*10*
Beginning Bal	*58*	*68*	*75*	*82*	*87*	*99*	*106*	*111*	*118*	*123*	*133*	*141*
Ending Balance	*68*	*75*	*82*	*87*	*99*	*106*	*111*	*118*	*123*	*133*	*141*	*151*

Pro Forma Quarterly Cash Flow, 2001 and 2002

($000s)

	2001				2002			
	Quart. 1	Quart. 2	Quart. 3	Quart. 4	Quart. 1	Quart. 2	Quart. 3	Quart. 4
Cash Sources:								
FROM OPERATIONS								
Cash Sales	24	25	26	27	28	29	30	31
A/R Collections	490	509	530	551	573	596	620	645
Other Cash Coll	5	5	6	6	6	6	6	7
OTHER SOURCES:								
Interest Income	2	2	2	2	2	3	2	2
Loan from Bank								
Investment								
Subtotal	*521*	*541*	*564*	*586*	*609*	*634*	*658*	*685*
Cash Uses:								
TO OPERATIONS								
Accts Payable								
Goods/Mater'ls	154	159	165	171	177	183	189	196
Services	28	29	30	31	32	33	35	36
Petty Cash	5	6	6	6	6	6	7	7
Payroll Expense	190	196	203	210	218	225	233	241
Sales Commiss'n								
Travel/Entert	24	25	26	27	28	29	30	31
Rent/Util/Tel	29	30	31	32	33	34	35	37
Advertising	13	13	13	14	14	15	15	16
Auto/Truck Exp	20	21	22	23	23	24	25	26
Maintenance	6	6	6	6	7	7	7	7
Equipment Exp	2	2	3	3	3	3	3	3
Ins/Legal/Acct	12	12	12	12	12	13	13	14
Miscellaneous								
OTHER USES								
Interest Exp								
Dividends		100				150		
Loan Payoff								
Investor Payoff								
Reserve for Tax	8	10	13	15	16	17	17	18
Subtotal	*491*	*609*	*530*	*550*	*569*	*739*	*609*	*632*
Cash Incr/Decr	*30*	*(68)*	*34*	*36*	*40*	*(105)*	*49*	*53*
Beginning Bal	*159*	*181*	*113*	*147*	*183*	*223*	*118*	*167*
Ending Balance	*181*	*113*	*147*	*183*	*223*	*118*	*167*	*220*

Pro Forma Income Statement

1999 ($000s)

	Actual 1998	Month 1	Month 2	Month 3	Month 4	Month 5	Month 6	Month 7	Month 8	Month 9	Month 10	Month 11	Month 12	Year Total
Net Sales	707	102	104	120	118	121	127	126	126	126	128	130	130	1458
COST OF SALES:														
Goods/Materials	255	36	37	42	40	40	41	40	38	40	40	41	40	475
Production Exp	44	6	6	6	7	6	7	6	7	7	6	6	6	75
Direct Labor	59	6	7	7	7	7	7	7	7	7	7	7	7	83
GROSS PROFIT	349	54	54	65	64	68	72	73	74	73	75	76	77	825
EXPENSES:														
GENERAL & ADMIN														
Payroll Expense	221	20	21	23	23	23	23	23	23	23	23	23	23	271
Payroll Taxes	53	4	4	5	5	5	5	5	5	5	5	5	5	58
Travel/Entert	21	2	2	3	3	4	5	3	3	3	3	3	3	37
Rent/Util/Tel	14	3	3	5	5	6	6	6	6	6	6	6	6	64
Ins/Legal/Acct	9	1	1	2	1	1	5	2	2	2	2	2	2	23
Office & Supply	8	1	1	2	2	2	2	2	2	2	2	2	2	22
Equipment Exp	8	1			1		1	1	1	1	1	1	1	9
Credit/Collect	5			1	1		1	1		1	1	1	1	10
Maintenance	3		1	1		2	1	1	1	1	2		1	14
Auto/Truck Exp	2	1	1	1	1	2	1	1	1	1	1	1	1	13
Other	1	1	1											2
SELLING EXPENSE														
Payroll Expense	16	9	11	12	12	12	12	12	12	12	12	12	12	139
Sales Commiss'n														
Advertising	3	1	1	1	1	1	10	5	2	30	30	30	1	113
Travel/Entert	6	2	2	3	3	3	3	3	3	3	2	2	2	31
Auto Expenses	1	2	2	3	3	4	4	4	4	4	4	4	4	42
Other														
OTHER EXPENSES														
Interest	21	1	1	1	1	1	1							6
Depreciation							3	3	3	3	3	3	3	24
Total Expenses	392	42	52	62	64	70	83	72	69	97	97	96	67	878
Other Income														
Interest Income	2		1		1		4	2	1	1	1	1	1	13
Other														
Profit (Loss)	(41)	5	3	3	1	(2)	(7)	3	6	(23)	(21)	(19)	11	(40)
Income Taxes														
Net Profit/Loss	(41)	5	3	3	1	(2)	(7)	3	6	(23)	(21)	(19)	11	(40)

Pro Forma Income Statement

2000 ($000s)

	Month 1	Month 2	Month 3	Month 4	Month 5	Month 6	Month 7	Month 8	Month 9	Month 10	Month 11	Month 12	Year Total
Net Sales	*139*	*139*	*140*	*141*	*150*	*151*	*148*	*141*	*144*	*149*	*154*	*152*	*1748*
COST OF SALES:													
Goods/Materials	42	43	42	45	46	47	45	44	45	45	47	45	536
Production Exp	6	6	6	6	6	6	7	7	7	7	7	7	78
Direct Labor	7	7	7	7	7	7	7	7	8	8	8	8	88
GROSS PROFIT	84	83	85	83	91	91	89	83	84	89	92	92	1046
EXPENSES:													
GENERAL & ADMIN													
Payroll Expense	24	25	25	25	25	25	25	25	25	25	25	25	299
Payroll Taxes	5	6	6	6	6	6	6	6	6	6	6	6	71
Travel/Entert	3	3	3	3	3	3	3	3	2	2	3	3	34
Rent/Util/Tel	6	6	6	6	6	6	6	6	6	6	6	6	72
Ins/Legal/Acct	3	3	3	3	3	3	3	3	3	3	3	3	36
Office & Supply	2	2	2	2	2	2	2	2	2	2	2	2	24
Equipment Exp	1	1	1	1	1	1	1	1	1	1	1	1	10
Credit/Collect	1	1	1	1	1	1	1	1	1	1	1	1	12
Maintenance	1	1	1		1	1		1	1	1	1	1	9
Auto/Truck Exp	2	2	2	2	2	2	2	2	2	2	2	2	24
Other													
SELLING EXPENSE													
Payroll Expense	20	20	20	21	21	22	23	23	23	23	23	23	262
Sales Commiss'n													
Advertising	3	5	5	3	3	3	5	2	2	3	4	2	40
Travel/Entert	3	3	3	4	4	4	4	4	4	5	4	3	45
Auto Expenses	3	3	3	3	3	3	3	3	3	3	3	3	36
Other													
OTHER EXPENSES													
interest													
Depreciation	3	3	3	3	3	3	3	3	3	3	3	3	36
Total Expenses	*80*	*83*	*83*	*83*	*84*	*84*	*87*	*85*	*84*	*86*	*87*	*84*	*1010*
Other Income													
Interest Income		1	1	1		2	2	1	1	1	1	1	11
Other													
Profit (Loss)	*4*	*1*	*2*	*1*	*7*	*9*	*4*	*(1)*	*1*	*4*	*6*	*9*	*47*
Income Taxes						*2*	*1*				*1*	*1*	*5*
Net Profit/Loss	*4*	*1*	*2*	*1*	*7*	*7*	*3*	*(1)*	*1*	*4*	*5*	*8*	*42*

Pro Forma Quarterly Income Statement

($000s)

	2001					2002				
	Quart. 1	Quart. 2	Quart. 3	Quart. 4	Year Total	Quart. 1	Quart. 2	Quart. 3	Quart. 4	Year Total
Net Sales	524	551	578	607	2260	631	657	683	710	2681
COST OF SALES:										
Goods/Materials	161	167	174	181	683	188	196	203	212	799
Production Exp	23	24	25	26	98	27	28	30	31	116
Direct Labor	26	27	29	30	112	31	32	33	35	131
GROSS PROFIT	314	333	350	370	1367	385	401	417	432	1635
EXPENSES:										
GENERAL & ADMIN										
Payroll Expense	90	93	97	101	381	105	109	113	118	445
Payroll Taxes	21	22	23	24	90	25	26	27	28	106
Travel/Entert	10	11	11	11	43	12	12	13	13	50
Rent/Util/Tel	22	22	23	24	91	25	26	27	28	106
Ins/Legal/Acct	11	11	12	12	46	13	13	14	14	54
Office & Supply	7	7	8	8	30	8	9	9	9	35
Equipment Exp	3	3	3	3	12	4	4	4	4	16
Credit/Collect	4	4	4	4	16	4	4	5	5	18
Maintenance	3	3	3	3	12	3	3	3	4	13
Auto/Truck Exp	7	7	8	8	30	8	9	9	9	35
Other										
SELLING EXPENSE										
Payroll Expense	79	82	85	88	334	92	96	99	103	390
Sales Commiss'n										
Advertising	12	12	13	13	50	14	15	15	16	60
Travel/Entert	14	14	15	15	58	16	16	17	18	67
Auto Expenses	11	11	12	12	46	13	13	14	14	54
Other										
OTHER EXPENSES										
Interest										
Depreciation	10	10	10	10	40	10	10	10	10	40
Total Expenses	304	312	327	336	1279	352	365	379	393	1489
Other Income										
Interest Income	2	2	2	2	8	2	3	2	2	9
Other										
Profit (Loss)	12	23	25	36	96	35	39	40	41	155
Income Taxes	3	6	7	10	27	10	12	12	12	46
Net Profit/Loss	9	17	18	26	70	25	27	28	29	109

Actual and Projected Balance Sheet

	Actual	**($000) Projected**			
	1998	**1999**	**2000**	**2001**	**2002**
Assets					
Current:					
Cash	16	30	38	47	63
Accounts Receivable	73	150	188	235	314
Inventory	78	171	213	266	356
All Other Current	4	7	9	11	15
Fixed/Plant and Equipment	25	325	305	291	291
Intangible/Goodwill	1	2	2	2	2
Less Accumul Depreciation	(2)	(21)	(36)	(72)	(108)
Other Non Curr (& Prepaid)	12	14	18	24	27
TOTAL ASSETS	207	678	737	804	960
Liabilities and Net Worth					
Current:					
Short-Term Notes Payable	*26*	*33*	*41*	*51*	*68*
Long-Term Debt Due	*8*	*9*	*5*	*5*	*5*
Accounts Payable	*35*	*75*	*94*	*118*	*158*
Accrued Interest	*5*	*11*	*13*	*16*	*19*
Income Taxes Payable	*6*	*16*	*20*	*23*	*31*
Long Term Debt	*104*	*10*	*10*	*10*	*13*
Deferred Taxes	*8*	*10*	*13*	*17*	*22*
All Other Non Current	*0*	*0*	*0*	*0*	*0*
Net Worth/Equity	*15*	*514*	*541*	*564*	*644*
TOTAL LIABILITIES/ NET WORTH	*207*	*678*	*737*	*804*	*960*

See Appendix for additional data.

Forms, Forms, Forms

1. Personal Budget
2. Personal Financial Statement
3. Employment Eligibility Verification (Form I-9)
4. Self-Employment Tax-Schedule SE
5. Application for Employer Identification Number-SS-4
6. Confidentiality/Non-Compete Agreement
   a. Explanation
   b. Agreement
7. Net Profit from Business-Schedule C-EZ
8. Profit or Loss from Business-Schedule C
9. Application for Business Loan (Up to $100,000)-SBA FORM 4-L
10. Application for Business Loan-SBA Form 4

PERSONAL BUDGET

	AMOUNT
Food	
At home	_____
Away from home	_____
Housing	
Rent or Mortgage Payments	_____
Property taxes	_____
Maintenance	_____
Insurance	
Life	_____
Health	_____
Car	_____
House	_____
Other	_____
Credit Card Payments	_____
Loan Payments	_____
Clothing	_____
Transportation	
Loan/Lease Payment	_____
Gas/Oil	_____
Maintenance	_____
Licenses	_____
Public transportation	_____
Child Care	_____
Health Care	
Insurance	_____
Medical Services	_____
Dentist	_____
Drugs/Supplies	_____
Entertainment	
Weekend/Dates	_____
Hobbies	_____
Other	_____
Personal Care	_____
Education	_____
Charitable Contributions	_____
Utilities	
Phone	_____
Electricity	_____
Gas	_____
Cable	_____
Water/garbage	_____
Spending money	_____
Miscellaneous	_____
Children's allowances	_____
Gifts	_____
Vacations	_____
Retirement Contributions	_____
Savings	_____
Taxes	
Social Security	_____
Federal	_____
State and local	_____
Other	_____
TOTAL	_____

PERSONAL FINANCIAL STATEMENT

U.S. SMALL BUSINESS ADMINISTRATION

As of _____ , 19 _____

Complete this form for: (1) each proprietor, or (2) each limited partner who owns 20% or more interest and each general partner, or (3) each stockholder owning 20% or more of voting stock, or (4) any person or entity providing a guaranty on the loan.

Name	Business Phone
Residence Address	Residence Phone
City, State, & Zip Code	
Business Name of Applicant/Borrower	

ASSETS	(Omit Cents)	LIABILITIES	(Omit Cents)
Cash on hands & in Banks	$	Accounts Payable	$
Savings Accounts	$	Notes Payable to Banks and Others	$
IRA or Other Retirement Account	$	(Describe in Section 2)	
Accounts & Notes Receivable	$	Installment Account (Auto)	$
Life Insurance-Cash Surrender Value Only	$	Mo. Payments $	
(Complete Section 8)		Installment Account (Other)	$
Stocks and Bonds	$	Mo. Payments $	
(Describe in Section 3)		Loan on Life Insurance	$
Real Estate	$	Mortgages on Real Estate	$
(Describe in Section 4)		(Describe in Section 4)	
Automobile-Present Value	$	Unpaid Taxes	$
Other Personal Property	$	(Describe in Section 6)	
(Describe in Section 5)		Other Liabilities	$
Other Assets	$	(Describe in Section 7)	
(Describe in Section 5)		Total Liabilities	$
		Net Worth	$
Total	$	**Total**	$

Section 1. Source of Income		Contingent Liabilities	
Salary	$	As Endorser or Co-Maker	$
Net Investment Income	$	Legal Claims & Judgments	$
Real Estate Income	$	Provision for Federal Income Tax	$
Other Income (Describe below)*	$	Other Special Debt	$

Description of Other Income in Section 1.

*Alimony or child support payments need not be disclosed in "Other Income" unless it is desired to have such payments counted toward total income.

(Use attachments if necessary. Each attachment must be identified as a part of this statement and signed.)

Name and Address of Noteholder(s)	Original Balance	Current Balance	Payment Amount	Frequency (monthly, etc.)	How Secured or Endorsed Type of Collateral

SBA Form 413 (2-94) Use 5-91 Edition until stock is exhausted. Ref: SOP 50-10 and 50-30   (tumble)

This form was electronically produced by Elite Federal Forms, Inc.

Section 3.

Number of Shares	Name of Securities	Cost	Market Value Quotation/Exchange	Date of Quotation/Exchange	Total Value

Section 4. (List each parcel separately. Use attachment if necessary. Each attachment must be identified as a part of this statement and signed.)

	Property A	Property B	Property C
Type of Property			
Address			
Date Purchased			
Original Cost			
Present Market Value			
Name & Address of Mortgage Holder			
Mortgage Account Number			
Mortgage Balance			
Amount of Payment per Month/Year			
Status of Mortgage			

Section 5. (Describe, and if any is pledged as security, state name and address of lien holder, amount of lien, terms of payment and if delinquent, describe delinquency)

Section 6.   Unpaid Taxes.   (Describe in detail, as to type, to whom payable, when due, amount, and to what property, if any, a tax lien attaches.)

Section 7.   Other Liabilities.   (Describe in detail.)

Section 8.   Life Insurance Held.   (Give face amount and cash surrender value of policies - name of insurance company and beneficiaries)

I authorize SBA/Lender to make inquiries as necessary to verify the accuracy of the statements made and to determine my creditworthiness. I certify the above and the statements contained in the attachments are true and accurate as of the stated date(s). These statements are made for the purpose of either obtaining a loan or guaranteeing a loan. I understand FALSE statements may result in forfeiture of benefits and possible prosecution by the U.S. Attorney General (Reference 18 U.S.C. 1001).

Signature:	Date:	Social Security Number:

Signature:	Date:	Social Security Number:

PLEASE NOTE: The estimated average burden hours for the completion of this form is 1.5 hours per response. If you have questions or comments concerning this estimate or any other aspect of this information, please contact Chief, Administrative Branch, U.S. Small Business Administration, Washington, D.C. 20416, and Clearance Officer, Paper Reduction Project (3245-0188), Office of Management and Budget, Washington, D.C. 20503.

EMPLOYMENT ELIGIBILITY VERIFICATION (Form I-9)

1 **EMPLOYEE INFORMATION AND VERIFICATION:** (To be completed and signed by employee.)

Name: (Print or Type) Last	First	Middle	Birth Name
Address: Street Name and Number	City	State	ZIP Code

Date of Birth (Month/Day/Year)	Social Security Number

I attest, under penalty of perjury, that I am (check a box):

☐ 1. A citizen or national of the United States.

☐ 2. An alien lawfully admitted for permanent residence (Alien Number A _____).

☐ 3. An alien authorized by the Immigration and Naturalization Service to work in the United States (Alien Number A _____ ,
or Admission Number _____ , expiration of employment authorization, if any _____) .

I attest, under penalty of perjury, the documents that I have presented as evidence of identity and employment eligibility are genuine and relate to me. I am aware tha
federal law provides for imprisonment and/or fine for any false statements or use of false documents in connection with this certificate.

Signature	Date (Month/Day/Year)

PREPARER/TRANSLATOR CERTIFICATION (To be completed if prepared by person other than the employee). I attest, under penalty of
perjury, that the above was prepared by me at the request of the named individual and is based on all information of which I have any knowledge.

Signature	Name (Print or Type)		
Address (Street Name and Number)	City	State	Zip Code

2 **EMPLOYER REVIEW AND VERIFICATION:** (To be completed and signed by employer.)

Instructions:

Examine one document from List A and check the appropriate box. *OR* examine one document from List B *and* one from List C and check the appropriate boxes
Provide the *Document Identification Number* and *Expiration Date* for the document checked.

List A Documents that Establish Identity and Employment Eligibility	List B Documents that Establish Identity	and	List C Documents that Establish Employment Eligibility
☐ 1. United States Passport ☐ 2. Certificate of United States Citizenship ☐ 3. Certificate of Naturalization ☐ 4. Unexpired foreign passport with attached Employment Authorization ☐ 5. Alien Registration Card with photograph	☐ 1. A State-issued driver's license or a State-issued I.D. card with a photograph, or information, including name, sex, date of birth, height, weight, and color of eyes. (Specify State)_____ ☐ 2. U.S. Military Card ☐ 3. Other (Specify document and issuing authority) _____	**and**	☐ 1. Original Social Security Number Card (other than a card stating it is not valid for employment) ☐ 2. A birth certificate issued by State, county, or municipal authority bearing a seal or other certification ☐ 3. Unexpired INS Employment Authorization Specify form #_____
Document Identification #_____	*Document Identification* #_____		*Document Identification* #_____
Expiration Date (if any) _____	*Expiration Date (if any)* _____		*Expiration Date (if any)* _____

CERTIFICATION: I attest, under penalty of perjury, that I have examined the documents presented by the above individual, that they appear to be genuine and to
relate to the individual named, and that the individual, to the best of my knowledge, is eligible to work in the United States.

Signature	Name (Print or Type)	Title
Employer Name	Address	Date

SCHEDULE SE (Form 1040)	Self-Employment Tax	OMB No. 1545-0074
Department of the Treasury Internal Revenue Service (99)	▶ See Instructions for Schedule SE (Form 1040). ▶ Attach to Form 1040.	1997 Attachment Sequence No. **17**

Name of person with **self-employment** income (as shown on Form 1040)	Social security number of person with **self-employment** income ▶

Who Must File Schedule SE

You must file Schedule SE if:

- You had net earnings from self-employment from **other than** church employee income (line 4 of Short Schedule SE or line 4c of Long Schedule SE) of $400 or more, **OR**
- You had church employee income of $108.28 or more. Income from services you performed as a minister or a member of a religious order **is not** church employee income. See page SE-1.

Note: *Even if you had a loss or a small amount of income from self-employment, it may be to your benefit to file Schedule SE and use either "optional method" in Part II of Long Schedule SE. See page SE-3.*

Exception. If your only self-employment income was from earnings as a minister, member of a religious order, or Christian Science practitioner **and** you filed Form 4361 and received IRS approval not to be taxed on those earnings, **do not** file Schedule SE. Instead, write "Exempt–Form 4361" on Form 1040, line 47.

May I Use Short Schedule SE or MUST I Use Long Schedule SE?

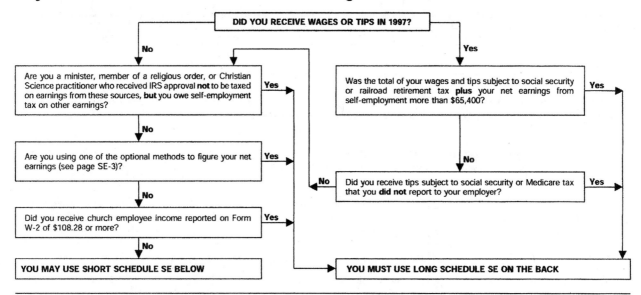

Section A—Short Schedule SE. Caution: *Read above to see if you can use Short Schedule SE.*

1	Net farm profit or (loss) from Schedule F, line 36, and farm partnerships, Schedule K-1 (Form 1065), line 15a	**1**	
2	Net profit or (loss) from Schedule C, line 31; Schedule C-EZ, line 3; and Schedule K-1 (Form 1065), line 15a (other than farming). Ministers and members of religious orders, see page SE-1 for amounts to report on this line. See page SE-2 for other income to report	**2**	
3	Combine lines 1 and 2	**3**	
4	**Net earnings from self-employment.** Multiply line 3 by 92.35% (.9235). If less than $400, **do not** file this schedule; you do not owe self-employment tax . . . . ▶	**4**	
5	**Self-employment tax.** If the amount on line 4 is: • $65,400 or less, multiply line 4 by 15.3% (.153). Enter the result here and on **Form 1040, line 47.** • More than $65,400, multiply line 4 by 2.9% (.029). Then, add $8,109.60 to the result. Enter the total here and on **Form 1040, line 47.**	**5**	
6	**Deduction for one-half of self-employment tax.** Multiply line 5 by 50% (.5). Enter the result here and on **Form 1040, line 26**	**6**	

For Paperwork Reduction Act Notice, see Form 1040 instructions.	Cat. No. 11358Z	Schedule SE (Form 1040) 1997

Schedule SE (Form 1040) 1997 | Attachment Sequence No. **17** | Page **2**

Name of person with **self-employment** income (as shown on Form 1040)	Social security number of person with **self-employment** income ▶	

Section B—Long Schedule SE

Part I Self-Employment Tax

Note: *If your only income subject to self-employment tax is* **church employee income,** *skip lines 1 through 4b. Enter -0- on line 4c and go to line 5a. Income from services you performed as a minister or a member of a religious order* **is not** *church employee income. See page SE-1.*

A If you are a minister, member of a religious order, or Christian Science practitioner **and** you filed Form 4361, but you had $400 or more of **other** net earnings from self-employment, check here and continue with Part I. . . . . . ▶ ☐

1	Net farm profit or (loss) from Schedule F, line 36, and farm partnerships, Schedule K-1 (Form 1065), line 15a. **Note:** *Skip this line if you use the farm optional method. See page SE-3* . .	**1**	
2	Net profit or (loss) from Schedule C, line 31; Schedule C-EZ, line 3; and Schedule K-1 (Form 1065), line 15a (other than farming). Ministers and members of religious orders, see page SE-1 for amounts to report on this line. See page SE-2 for other income to report. **Note:** *Skip this line if you use the nonfarm optional method. See page SE-3.*	**2**	
3	Combine lines 1 and 2	**3**	
4a	If line 3 is more than zero, multiply line 3 by 92.35% (.9235). Otherwise, enter amount from line 3	**4a**	
b	If you elected one or both of the optional methods, enter the total of lines 15 and 17 here . .	**4b**	
c	Combine lines 4a and 4b. If less than $400, **do not** file this schedule; you do not owe self-employment tax. **Exception.** If less than $400 and you had **church employee income,** enter -0- and continue ▶	**4c**	
5a	Enter your **church employee income** from Form W-2. **Caution:** *See page SE-1 for definition of church employee income* **5a**		
b	Multiply line 5a by 92.35% (.9235). If less than $100, enter -0-	**5b**	
6	**Net earnings from self-employment.** Add lines 4c and 5b	**6**	
7	Maximum amount of combined wages and self-employment earnings subject to social security tax or the 6.2% portion of the 7.65% railroad retirement (tier 1) tax for 1997	**7**	65,400 00
8a	Total social security wages and tips (total of boxes 3 and 7 on Form(s) W-2) and railroad retirement (tier 1) compensation **8a**		
b	Unreported tips subject to social security tax (from Form 4137, line 9) **8b**		
c	Add lines 8a and 8b	**8c**	
9	Subtract line 8c from line 7. If zero or less, enter -0- here and on line 10 and go to line 11 . ▶	**9**	
10	Multiply the **smaller** of line 6 or line 9 by 12.4% (.124)	**10**	
11	Multiply line 6 by 2.9% (.029).	**11**	
12	**Self-employment tax.** Add lines 10 and 11. Enter here and on **Form 1040, line 47**	**12**	
13	**Deduction for one-half of self-employment tax.** Multiply line 12 by 50% (.5). Enter the result here and on **Form 1040, line 26** **13**		

Part II Optional Methods To Figure Net Earnings (See page SE-3.)

	Farm Optional Method. You may use this method **only** if:		
	● Your gross farm income[1] was not more than $2,400, **or**		
	● Your gross farm income[1] was more than $2,400 and your net farm profits[2] were less than $1,733.		
14	Maximum income for optional methods	**14**	1,600 00
15	Enter the **smaller** of: two-thirds (⅔) of gross farm income[1] (not less than zero) or $1,600. Also, include this amount on line 4b above	**15**	
	Nonfarm Optional Method. You may use this method **only** if:		
	● Your net nonfarm profits[3] were less than $1,733 and also less than 72.189% of your gross nonfarm income,[4] **and**		
	● You had net earnings from self-employment of at least $400 in 2 of the prior 3 years.		
	Caution: *You may use this method no more than five times.*		
16	Subtract line 15 from line 14	**16**	
17	Enter the **smaller** of: two-thirds (⅔) of gross nonfarm income[4] (not less than zero) or the amount on line 16. Also, include this amount on line 4b above	**17**	

[1]From Schedule F, line 11, and Schedule K-1 (Form 1065), line 15b.
[2]From Schedule F, line 36, and Schedule K-1 (Form 1065), line 15a.
[3]From Schedule C, line 31; Schedule C-EZ, line 3; and Schedule K-1 (Form 1065), line 15a.
[4]From Schedule C, line 7; Schedule C-EZ, line 1; and Schedule K-1 (Form 1065), line 15c.

Form **SS-4**

(Rev. February 1998)

Department of the Treasury
Internal Revenue Service

Application for Employer Identification Number

(For use by employers, corporations, partnerships, trusts, estates, churches, government agencies, certain individuals, and others. See instructions.)

▶ **Keep a copy for your records.**

EIN

OMB No. 1545-0003

Please type or print clearly.

1 Name of applicant (legal name) (see instructions)

2 Trade name of business (if different from name on line 1)

3 Executor, trustee, "care of" name

4a Mailing address (street address) (room, apt., or suite no.)

5a Business address (if different from address on lines 4a and 4b)

4b City, state, and ZIP code

5b City, state, and ZIP code

6 County and state where principal business is located

7 Name of principal officer, general partner, grantor, owner, or trustor—SSN or ITIN may be required (see instructions) ▶

8a Type of entity (Check only one box.) (see instructions)

Caution: *If applicant is a limited liability company, see the instructions for line 8a.*

☐ Sole proprietor (SSN) _____
☐ Partnership   ☐ Personal service corp.
☐ REMIC   ☐ National Guard
☐ State/local government ☐ Farmers' cooperative
☐ Church or church-controlled organization
☐ Other nonprofit organization (specify) ▶ _____
☐ Other (specify) ▶

☐ Estate (SSN of decedent) _____
☐ Plan administrator (SSN) _____
☐ Other corporation (specify) ▶ _____
☐ Trust
☐ Federal government/military
(enter GEN if applicable) _____

8b If a corporation, name the state or foreign country (if applicable) where incorporated | State | Foreign country

9 Reason for applying (Check only one box.) (see instructions)
☐ Started new business (specify type) ▶_____
☐ Hired employees (Check the box and see line 12.)
☐ Created a pension plan (specify type) ▶
☐ Banking purpose (specify purpose) ▶ _____
☐ Changed type of organization (specify new type) ▶ _____
☐ Purchased going business
☐ Created a trust (specify type) ▶ _____
☐ Other (specify) ▶

10 Date business started or acquired (month, day, year) (see instructions)

11 Closing month of accounting year (see instructions)

12 First date wages or annuities were paid or will be paid (month, day, year). Note: If applicant is a withholding agent, enter date income will first be paid to nonresident alien. (month, day, year) . . . . ▶

13 Highest number of employees expected in the next 12 months. **Note:** *If the applicant does not expect to have any employees during the period, enter -0-. (see instructions)* . . . . ▶ | Nonagricultural | Agricultural | Household

14 Principal activity (see instructions) ▶

15 Is the principal business activity manufacturing? . . . . ☐ Yes ☐ No
If "Yes," principal product and raw material used ▶

16 To whom are most of the products or services sold? Please check one box.   ☐ Business (wholesale)
☐ Public (retail)   ☐ Other (specify) ▶   ☐ N/A

17a Has the applicant ever applied for an employer identification number for this or any other business? . . . . ☐ Yes ☐ No
Note: *If "Yes," please complete lines 17b and 17c.*

17b If you checked "Yes" on line 17a, give applicant's legal name and trade name shown on prior application, if different from line 1 or 2 above.
Legal name ▶   Trade name ▶

17c Approximate date when and city and state where the application was filed. Enter previous employer identification number if known.
Approximate date when filed (mo., day, year) | City and state where filed | Previous EIN

Under penalties of perjury, I declare that I have examined this application, and to the best of my knowledge and belief, it is true, correct, and complete. | Business telephone number (include area code)
| Fax telephone number (include area code)

Name and title (Please type or print clearly.) ▶

Signature ▶   Date ▶

Note: *Do not write below this line. For official use only.*

Please leave blank ▶ | Geo. | Ind. | Class | Size | Reason for applying

For Paperwork Reduction Act Notice, see page 4.   Cat. No. 16055N   Form **SS-4** (Rev. 2-98)

General Instructions

Section references are to the Internal Revenue Code unless otherwise noted.

Purpose of Form

Use Form SS-4 to apply for an employer identification number (EIN). An EIN is a nine-digit number (for example, 12-3456789) assigned to sole proprietors, corporations, partnerships, estates, trusts, and other entities for tax filing and reporting purposes. The information you provide on this form will establish your business tax account.

Caution: *An EIN is for use in connection with your business activities only. Do NOT use your EIN in place of your social security number (SSN).*

Who Must File

You must file this form if you have not been assigned an EIN before and:

● You pay wages to one or more employees including household employees.

● You are required to have an EIN to use on any return, statement, or other document, even if you are not an employer.

● You are a withholding agent required to withhold taxes on income, other than wages, paid to a nonresident alien (individual, corporation, partnership, etc.). A withholding agent may be an agent, broker, fiduciary, manager, tenant, or spouse, and is required to file **Form 1042**, Annual Withholding Tax Return for U.S. Source Income of Foreign Persons.

● You file **Schedule C**, Profit or Loss From Business, **Schedule C-EZ**, Net Profit From Business, or **Schedule F**, Profit or Loss From Farming, of **Form 1040**, U.S. Individual Income Tax Return, **and** have a Keogh plan or are required to file excise, employment, or alcohol, tobacco, or firearms returns.

The following must use EINs even if they do not have any employees:

● State and local agencies who serve as tax reporting agents for public assistance recipients, under Rev. Proc. 80-4, 1980-1 C.B. 581, should obtain a separate EIN for this reporting. See **Household employer** on page 3.

● Trusts, except the following:

   1. Certain grantor-owned trusts. (See the **Instructions for Form 1041**.)

   2. Individual Retirement Arrangement (IRA) trusts, unless the trust has to file **Form 990-T**, Exempt Organization Business Income Tax Return. (See the **Instructions for Form 990-T**.)

● Estates

● Partnerships

● REMICs (real estate mortgage investment conduits) (See the **Instructions for Form 1066**, U.S. Real Estate Mortgage Investment Conduit Income Tax Return.)

● Corporations

● Nonprofit organizations (churches, clubs, etc.)

● Farmers' cooperatives

● Plan administrators (A plan administrator is the person or group of persons specified as the administrator by the instrument under which the plan is operated.)

When To Apply for a New EIN

New Business. If you become the new owner of an existing business, **do not** use the EIN of the former owner. IF YOU ALREADY HAVE AN EIN, USE THAT NUMBER. If you do not have an EIN, apply for one on this form. If you become the "owner" of a corporation by acquiring its stock, use the corporation's EIN.

Changes in Organization or Ownership. If you already have an EIN, you may need to get a new one if either the organization or ownership of your business changes. If you incorporate a sole proprietorship or form a partnership, you must get a new EIN. However, **do not** apply for a new EIN if:

● You change only the name of your business,

● You elected on **Form 8832**, Entity Classification Election, to change the way the entity is taxed, or

● A partnership terminates because at least 50% of the total interests in partnership capital and profits were sold or exchanged within a 12-month period. (See Regulations section 301.6109-1(d)(2)(iii).) The EIN for the terminated partnership should continue to be used. This rule applies to terminations occurring after May 8, 1997. If the termination took place after May 8, 1996, and before May 9, 1997, a new EIN must be obtained for the new partnership unless the partnership and its partners are consistent in using the old EIN.

Note: *If you are electing to be an "S corporation," be sure you file **Form 2553**, Election by a Small Business Corporation.*

File Only One Form SS-4. File only one Form SS-4, regardless of the number of businesses operated or trade names under which a business operates. However, each corporation in an affiliated group must file a separate application.

EIN Applied for, But Not Received. If you do not have an EIN by the time a return is due, write "Applied for" and the date you applied in the space shown for the number. **Do not** show your social security number (SSN) as an EIN on returns.

If you do not have an EIN by the time a tax deposit is due, send your payment to the Internal Revenue Service Center for your filing area. (See **Where To Apply** below.) Make your check or money order payable to Internal Revenue Service and show your name (as shown on Form SS-4), address, type of tax, period covered, and date you applied for an EIN. Send an explanation with the deposit.

For more information about EINs, see **Pub. 583**, Starting a Business and Keeping Records, and **Pub. 1635**, Understanding your EIN.

How To Apply

You can apply for an EIN either by mail or by telephone. You can get an EIN immediately by calling the Tele-TIN number for the service center for your state, or you can send the completed Form SS-4 directly to the service center to receive your EIN by mail.

Application by Tele-TIN. Under the Tele-TIN program, you can receive your EIN by telephone and use it immediately to file a return or make a payment. To receive an EIN by telephone, complete Form SS-4, then call the Tele-TIN number listed for your state under **Where To Apply**. The person making the call must be authorized to sign the form. (See **Signature** on page 4.)

An IRS representative will use the information from the Form SS-4 to establish your account and assign you an EIN. Write the number you are given on the upper right corner of the form and sign and date it.

*Mail or fax (facsimile) the signed SS-4 **within 24 hours** to the Tele-TIN Unit at the service center address for your state.* The IRS representative will give you the fax number. The fax numbers are also listed in Pub. 1635.

Taxpayer representatives can receive their client's EIN by telephone if they first send a fax of a completed **Form 2848**, Power of Attorney and Declaration of Representative, or **Form 8821**, Tax Information Authorization, to the Tele-TIN unit. The Form 2848 or Form 8821 will be used solely to release the EIN to the representative authorized on the form.

Application by Mail. Complete Form SS-4 at least 4 to 5 weeks before you will need an EIN. Sign and date the application and mail it to the service center address for your state. You will receive your EIN in the mail in approximately 4 weeks.

Where To Apply

The Tele-TIN numbers listed below will involve a long-distance charge to callers outside of the local calling area and can be used only to apply for an EIN. THE NUMBERS MAY CHANGE WITHOUT NOTICE. Call 1-800-829-1040 to verify a number or to ask about the status of an application by mail.

If your principal business, office or agency, or legal residence in the case of an individual, is located in: ▼	Call the Tele-TIN number shown or file with the Internal Revenue Service Center at: ▼
Florida, Georgia, South Carolina	Attn: Entity Control Atlanta, GA 39901 770-455-2360
New Jersey, New York City and counties of Nassau, Rockland, Suffolk, and Westchester	Attn: Entity Control Holtsville, NY 00501 516-447-4955
New York (all other counties), Connecticut, Maine, Massachusetts, New Hampshire, Rhode Island, Vermont	Attn: Entity Control Andover, MA 05501 978-474-9717
Illinois, Iowa, Minnesota, Missouri, Wisconsin	Attn: Entity Control Stop 6800 2306 E. Bannister Rd. Kansas City, MO 64999 816-926-5999
Delaware, District of Columbia, Maryland, Pennsylvania, Virginia	Attn: Entity Control Philadelphia, PA 19255 215-516-6999
Indiana, Kentucky, Michigan, Ohio, West Virginia	Attn: Entity Control Cincinnati, OH 45999 606-292-5467

CONFIDENTIALITY/NON-COMPETE AGREEMENT

The Confidentiality and Non-Compete Agreement is designed to protect you when you work with another party and they learn confidential and/or proprietary information about you and/or your business. For example, another party you are working with on a project you are building. A confidentiality/non-compete agreement may help to prevent that party from disclosing any information he/she may have obtained in the course of doing business with you, and it binds them from competing against you for the same or very similar products or services in the future.

However, keep in mind that unscrupulous people will steal your ideas even if they have signed an agreement. They will risk the chance of being sued if the idea is good enough. With this in mind, reveal only that information that pertains to your working relationship.

Be sure to have the other party sign the confidentiality and non-compete agreement as soon as he/she begins working with you—even when you are in the early stages of discussion about a project. It is a very common form, and nobody should be offended or feel that you don't trust them if you ask them to sign it.

SOURCE: **http://americanexpress.com/smallbusiness/resources/starting/contracts/confide.shtml**

SAMPLE

CONFIDENTIALITY AND NON-COMPETE AGREEMENT

The undersigned, representing _____ [COMPANY NAME], hereby acknowledges that the nature of the work to be performed for [YOUR COMPANY] involves his/her access to trade secrets, confidential information, files, records and forms of [YOUR COMPANY], collectively Confidential Information. Confidential Information includes, but is not limited to, any information relating to [YOUR COMPANY]'s organizational structure, marketing philosophy and objectives, project plans, data models, strategy and vision statements, business initiatives, business requirements, systems design, methodology, processes, competitive advantages and disadvantages, financial results, product features, systems, operations, technology, customer lists and other information which would give the Company an opportunity to obtain an advantage over its competitors, or which the Company is ethically obligated to protect from unauthorized sources. None of this information shall be deemed to be in the public domain. The undersigned hereby agrees that he/she will not disclose proprietary information acquired pursuant to this meeting or any other discussions he/she has had with _____, representing [YOUR COMPANY] and other [YOUR COMPANY] representative, ot any other party. This agreement shall not apply to any information which was in the undersigned's possession prior to the time of disclosure; in the public domain prior to disclosure; becomes part of the public domain not due to any unauthorized act or omission on the undersigned's part; or, is supplied to the undersigned by a third party as a matter of right. The undersigned agrees that he/she will not now, or at any future time, divulge or appropriate to his/her own use or the use of others, reproduce, transmit or provide information regarding [YOUR COMPANY] business or plans for business or any part thereof to any person or persons not connected with your organization.

The undersigned agrees that he/she will maintain information in strict confidence, and not discuss and/or provide Confidential Information to sources outside of [YOUR COMPANY], including, without limitation, at conferences, seminars, meetings of professional organizations, or by publication in a journal or granting of interviews to journalists and other members of the news media. In addition, the undersigned agrees not to use information gained in this or any other meeting or discussion, to compete with [YOUR COMPANY], or to use the information gained from this or any other meeting or discussion with [YOUR COMPANY], to create a product that is similar to the one that is being discussed.

The undersigned agrees that any work product produced or developed by him/her in the performance of his/her duties hereunder shall be Confidential Information subject to this agreement and such work product is, and shall remain, the property of the Company.

Signed,

_____

Representing: _____

Dated: _____

> *Provided only as a sample agreement. Contact your lawyer for legal advice before using.*

SOURCE: **www.americanexpress.com**

SCHEDULE C-EZ (Form 1040) Department of the Treasury Internal Revenue Service (99)	**Net Profit From Business** (Sole Proprietorship) ▶ Partnerships, joint ventures, etc., must file Form 1065. ▶ **Attach to Form 1040 or Form 1041.** ▶ **See instructions on back.**	OMB No. 1545-0074 19**97** Attachment Sequence No. **09A**

Name of proprietor	Social security number (SSN)

Part I General Information

You May Use This Schedule Only If You:
- Had business expenses of $2,500 or less.
- Use the cash method of accounting.
- Did not have an inventory at any time during the year.
- Did not have a net loss from your business.
- Had only one business as a sole proprietor.

And You:
- Had no employees during the year.
- Are not required to file **Form 4562,** Depreciation and Amortization, for this business. See the instructions for Schedule C, line 13, on page C-3 to find out if you must file.
- Do not deduct expenses for business use of your home.
- Do not have prior year unallowed passive activity losses from this business.

A Principal business or profession, including product or service

B Enter principal business code (see page C-6) ▶

C Business name. If no separate business name, leave blank.

D Employer ID number (EIN), if any

E Business address (including suite or room no.). Address not required if same as on Form 1040, page 1.

City, town or post office, state, and ZIP code

Part II Figure Your Net Profit

1 **Gross receipts. Caution:** *If this income was reported to you on Form W-2 and the "Statutory employee" box on that form was checked, see **Statutory Employees** in the instructions for Schedule C, line 1, on page C-2 and check here* . . . . ▶ ☐ | **1** |

2 **Total expenses.** If more than $2,500, you **must** use Schedule C. See instructions . . . . . | **2** |

3 **Net profit.** Subtract line 2 from line 1. If less than zero, you **must** use Schedule C. Enter on **Form 1040, line 12,** and ALSO on **Schedule SE, line 2.** (Statutory employees **do not** report this amount on Schedule SE, line 2. Estates and trusts, enter on Form 1041, line 3.) . . . . . | **3** |

Part III Information on Your Vehicle. Complete this part ONLY if you are claiming car or truck expenses on line 2.

4 When did you place your vehicle in service for business purposes? (month, day, year) ▶ ___ / ___ / ___ .

5 Of the total number of miles you drove your vehicle during 1997, enter the number of miles you used your vehicle for:

a Business _____ **b** Commuting _____ **c** Other _____

6 Do you (or your spouse) have another vehicle available for personal use? . . . . ☐ Yes ☐ No

7 Was your vehicle available for use during off-duty hours? . . . . ☐ Yes ☐ No

8a Do you have evidence to support your deduction? . . . . ☐ Yes ☐ No

b If "Yes," is the evidence written? . . . . ☐ Yes ☐ No

For Paperwork Reduction Act Notice, see Form 1040 instructions. Cat. No. 14374D Schedule C-EZ (Form 1040) 1997

Instructions

You may use Schedule C-EZ instead of Schedule C if you operated a business or practiced a profession as a sole proprietorship and you have met all the requirements listed in Part I of Schedule C-EZ.

Line A

Describe the business or professional activity that provided your principal source of income reported on line 1. Give the general field or activity and the type of product or service.

Line B

Enter the four-digit code that identifies your principal business or professional activity. See page C-6 for the list of codes.

Line D

You need an employer identification number (EIN) only if you had a Keogh plan or were required to file an employment, excise, estate, trust, or alcohol, tobacco, and firearms tax return. If you need an EIN, file **Form SS-4,** Application for Employer Identification Number. If you do not have an EIN, leave line D blank. **Do not** enter your SSN.

Line E

Enter your business address. Show a street address instead of a box number. Include the suite or room number, if any.

Line 1

Enter gross receipts from your trade or business. Include amounts you received in your trade or business that were properly shown on **Forms 1099-MISC.** If the total amounts that were reported in box 7 of Forms 1099-MISC are more than the total you are reporting on line 1, attach a statement explaining the difference. You must show all items of taxable income actually or constructively received during the year (in cash, property, or services). Income is constructively received when it is credited to your account or set aside for you to use. Do not offset this amount by any losses.

Line 2

Enter the total amount of all deductible business expenses you actually paid during the year. Examples of these expenses include advertising, car and truck expenses, commissions and fees, insurance, interest, legal and professional services, office expense, rent or lease expenses, repairs and maintenance, supplies, taxes, travel, 50% of business meals and entertainment, and utilities (including telephone). For details, see the instructions for Schedule C, Parts II and V, on pages C-2 through C-5. If you wish, you may use the optional worksheet below to record your expenses.

If you claim car or truck expenses, be sure to complete Part III of Schedule C-EZ.

Optional Worksheet for Line 2 (keep a copy for your records)

a Business meals and entertainment	**a**	
b Less: 50% of business meals and entertainment subject to limitations (see the instructions for lines 24b and 24c on page C-4)	**b**	
c Deductible business meals and entertainment. Subtract line **b** from line **a**	**c**	
d _____	**d**	
e _____	**e**	
f _____	**f**	
g _____	**g**	
h _____	**h**	
i _____	**i**	
j **Total.** Add lines **c** through **i**. Enter here and on line 2	**j**	

♲

SCHEDULE C
(Form 1040)

Department of the Treasury
Internal Revenue Service   (99)

Profit or Loss From Business
(Sole Proprietorship)

▶ **Partnerships, joint ventures, etc., must file Form 1065.**

▶ **Attach to Form 1040 or Form 1041.**   ▶ **See Instructions for Schedule C (Form 1040).**

OMB No. 1545-0074

1997

Attachment
Sequence No. **09**

Name of proprietor

Social security number (SSN)

A Principal business or profession, including product or service (see page C-1)

B Enter principal business code
(see page C-6) ▶

C Business name. If no separate business name, leave blank.

D Employer ID number (EIN), if any

E Business address (including suite or room no.) ▶
City, town or post office, state, and ZIP code

F Accounting method: **(1)** ☐ Cash   **(2)** ☐ Accrual   **(3)** ☐ Other (specify) ▶

G Did you "materially participate" in the operation of this business during 1997? If "No," see page C-2 for limit on losses.   ☐ **Yes** ☐ **No**

H If you started or acquired this business during 1997, check here . . . . ▶ ☐

Part I   Income

1	Gross receipts or sales. **Caution:** *If this income was reported to you on Form W-2 and the "Statutory employee" box on that form was checked, see page C-2 and check here* . . . . . . ▶ ☐	**1**	
2	Returns and allowances	**2**	
3	Subtract line 2 from line 1	**3**	
4	Cost of goods sold (from line 42 on page 2)	**4**	
5	**Gross profit.** Subtract line 4 from line 3	**5**	
6	Other income, including Federal and state gasoline or fuel tax credit or refund (see page C-2) . . .	**6**	
7	**Gross income.** Add lines 5 and 6 . . . . ▶	**7**	

Part II   Expenses. Enter expenses for business use of your home **only** on line 30.

8	Advertising	**8**		**19** Pension and profit-sharing plans	**19**	
9	Bad debts from sales or services (see page C-3) . .	**9**		**20** Rent or lease (see page C-4):		
10	Car and truck expenses (see page C-3)	**10**		**a** Vehicles, machinery, and equipment .	**20a**	
11	Commissions and fees . .	**11**		**b** Other business property . .	**20b**	
12	Depletion	**12**		**21** Repairs and maintenance . .	**21**	
13	Depreciation and section 179 expense deduction (not included in Part III) (see page C-3) . .	**13**		**22** Supplies (not included in Part III) .	**22**	
				23 Taxes and licenses	**23**	
14	Employee benefit programs (other than on line 19) . . .	**14**		**24** Travel, meals, and entertainment:		
15	Insurance (other than health) .	**15**		**a** Travel	**24a**	
16	Interest:			**b** Meals and entertainment .		
a	Mortgage (paid to banks, etc.) .	**16a**		**c** Enter 50% of line 24b subject to limitations (see page C-4) .		
b	Other	**16b**		**d** Subtract line 24c from line 24b .	**24d**	
17	Legal and professional services	**17**		**25** Utilities	**25**	
				26 Wages (less employment credits) .	**26**	
18	Office expense	**18**		**27** Other expenses (from line 48 on page 2)	**27**	

28	**Total expenses** before expenses for business use of home. Add lines 8 through 27 in columns . ▶	**28**	
29	Tentative profit (loss). Subtract line 28 from line 7	**29**	
30	Expenses for business use of your home. Attach **Form 8829**	**30**	
31	**Net profit or (loss).** Subtract line 30 from line 29.		
	• If a profit, enter on **Form 1040, line 12,** and ALSO on **Schedule SE, line 2** (statutory employees, see page C-5). Estates and trusts, enter on Form 1041, line 3.	**31**	
	• If a loss, you MUST go on to line 32.		

32 If you have a loss, check the box that describes your investment in this activity (see page C-5).

• If you checked 32a, enter the loss on **Form 1040, line 12,** and ALSO on **Schedule SE, line 2** (statutory employees, see page C-5). Estates and trusts, enter on Form 1041, line 3.
• If you checked 32b, you MUST attach **Form 6198.**

32a ☐ All investment is at risk.
32b ☐ Some investment is not at risk.

For Paperwork Reduction Act Notice, see Form 1040 instructions.   Cat. No. 11334P   **Schedule C (Form 1040) 1997**

Schedule C (Form 1040) 1997   Page **2**

Part III **Cost of Goods Sold** (see page C-5)

33 Method(s) used to
    value closing inventory: **a** ☐ Cost   **b** ☐ Lower of cost or market   **c** ☐ Other (attach explanation)

34 Was there any change in determining quantities, costs, or valuations between opening and closing inventory? If
    "Yes," attach explanation . . . . ☐ **Yes**   ☐ **No**

35	Inventory at beginning of year. If different from last year's closing inventory, attach explanation . .	**35**
36	Purchases less cost of items withdrawn for personal use	**36**
37	Cost of labor. Do not include salary paid to yourself	**37**
38	Materials and supplies	**38**
39	Other costs	**39**
40	Add lines 35 through 39	**40**
41	Inventory at end of year	**41**
42	**Cost of goods sold.** Subtract line 41 from line 40. Enter the result here and on page 1, line 4 . .	**42**

Part IV **Information on Your Vehicle.** Complete this part **ONLY** if you are claiming car or truck expenses on line 10 and are not required to file Form 4562 for this business. See the instructions for line 13 on page C-3 to find out if you must file.

43 When did you place your vehicle in service for business purposes? (month, day, year) ▶ _____ / _____ / _____ .

44 Of the total number of miles you drove your vehicle during 1997, enter the number of miles you used your vehicle for:

a Business _____ **b** Commuting _____ **c** Other _____

45 Do you (or your spouse) have another vehicle available for personal use? . . . . ☐ **Yes**   ☐ **No**

46 Was your vehicle available for use during off-duty hours? . . . . ☐ **Yes**   ☐ **No**

47a Do you have evidence to support your deduction? . . . . ☐ **Yes**   ☐ **No**

 b If "Yes," is the evidence written? . . . . ☐ **Yes**   ☐ **No**

Part V **Other Expenses.** List below business expenses not included on lines 8–26 or line 30.

_____	
_____	
_____	
_____	
_____	
_____	
_____	
_____	
_____	
48 **Total other expenses.** Enter here and on page 1, line 27	**48**

SBA Form 4-L (6/94)

U.S. SMALL BUSINESS ADMINISTRATION
APPLICATION FOR BUSINESS LOAN (UP TO $100,000)
Maximum amount of loan $100,000, including existing SBA loans

OMB Approval No. 3245-0016
Expiration Date: 9/30/97

Corporate Name (If any)

Trade Name & Street Address _____ Corporate Structure: Proprietorship ___ Partnership___ Corp.___ LLC___

City _____ County _____ State ____ Zip _____ Phone (___)_____ TaxID#_____

Mailing Address (if different) _____

Type of Business _____ Date Established _____ Time as Owner _____ No. of Employees:_____

MANAGEMENT (Proprietor, partners, officers, directors owning 20% or more of the company)—Must account for 100% of the business

Name	Address		City	State	Zip		
Social Security #	*Veteran		*Gender	*Race	US Citizen		Alien Reg. #
Name	Address		City	State	Zip		
Social Security #	*Veteran		*Gender	*Race	US Citizen		Alien Reg. #

*This data is collected for statistical purposes only. It has no bearing on the credit decision to approve or decline this application. Disclosure is voluntary.

Are any of the above individuals (a) presently under indictment, on parole or probationt or have they ever been (b) charged for any criminal offense other than a minor vehicle violation, or (c) convicted, placed on pretrial diversion, or placed on any form of probatio n including adjudication withheld pending probation for any criminal offense other than a minor vehicle violation? Yes __ No __ **If yes, loan request must be submitted under regular 7(a) loan program.**

Have you employed anyone to prepare this application? Yes __ No __ If yes, how much have you paid? $ _____ How much do you owe? $ _____

Have you or any officer of your company ever been involved in bankruptcy or insolvency proceedings? Yes __ No __ If yes, provide details to bank.
Are you or your business involved in any pending lawsuits? Yes __ No __ If yes, provide details to bank.

DESCRIBE YOUR BUSINESS OPERATION:

IS BUSINESS ENGAGED IN EXPORT TRADE? Yes ____ No ___ DO YOU INTEND TO BEGIN EXPORTING AS A RESULT OF THIS LOAN? Yes ____ No ___

SUMMARY OF MANAGEMENT'S BUSINESS EXPERIENCE, EDUCATION, AND TRAINING:

LOAN REQUEST: HOW MUCH, FOR WHAT, WHY IT IS NEEDED

INDEBTEDNESS: Furnish information on ALL BUSINESS debts, contracts, notes, and mortgages payable. Indicate by an (*) items to be paid with loan proceeds.

To Whom Payable	Original Amount	Original Date	Present Balance	Rate of Interest	Maturity Date	Monthly Payment	Collateral	Current or Past Due
	$		$			$		
	$		$			$		
	$		$			$		
	$		$			$		

PREVIOUS SBA OR OTHER GOVERNMENT FINANCING : If you or any principals or affiliates have ever requested Government Financing complete the following:

Name of Agency	Loan Number	Date Approved	$ Amount	Loan Balance	Status

If you knowingly make a false statement or overvalue a security to obtain a guaranteed loan from SBA you can be fined up to $10,000 or imprisoned for not more than five years or both under 18 USC 1001.

I hereby certify that all information contained in this document and any attachments is true and correct to the best of my knowledge.

If applicant is a proprietor or general partner, sign here: By:_____ Title _____ Date _____

If corporation sign below: Corporate Name _____

By: _____ Date: _____ Attested By: _____
Signature of President   Signature of Corporate Secretary

SBA Form 4-L (6/94)

FOR BANK USE ONLY

LENDER'S APPLICATION FOR GUARANTY

Name of Lender   Address   Telephone(A/C)   Fax #

Date of Guaranty Agreement (SBA Form 750) _____

Applicant's Trade Name

We request SBA to guarantee ____% of a loan in the amount of $_____ for ___ years, with monthly (P&I payments of $_____ / principal payments of $_____ plus interest) beginning _____ month(s) from date of note. **(If applicable: Interest only payment to begin ___ months from date of note).**
The interest rate is to be fixed at ____% **OR** variable with a base rate of ___%, spread ___%, and an adjustment period of _____

Lender's Experience with Applicant and Assessment of Management's Character and Capability:

CREDIT REPORTS (CR):   CR Company _____ Risk Score _____ SIC Code _____ Summary of Business Credit:

OWNERS, GUARANTORS, AND CO-SIGNERS:
Owners of 20% or more of business must guarantee the note. Lender must obtain personal credit reports on all owners, guarantors, and co-signers.
Name (Indicate co-signers with *)   Address   Individual Credit Reports Analysis

Personal F/S: Lender should obtain **signed** personal financial statements for all owners, guarantors, and co-signers.
   Do owners' personal unpledged liquid assets exceed $50,000 (not including IRA, CV Life Insurance, or savings for education)? Yes ___ No ___
   Comments on personal resources, including any supplementary or outside sources of income available for debt service or to secure loan:

P&L: Average annual gross sales, including all affiliates, for the last 3 years (if applicable) $_____
   Year end cash flow last 3 years (if applicable) FY ___, $_____, FY ___, $_____, FY ___, $_____
   One year projected cash flow after owner's compensation $_____   Total annual debt service (including interest) after the loan $_____
   Comments on repayment ability:

Pro Forma Balance Sheet: Debt/NW Ratio _____   Current Ratio (CA/CL) _____   Comments on balance sheet:

IF NEW BUSINESS OR FOR PURCHASE OF EXISTING BUSINESS, AMOUNT OF APPLICANT INJECTION - CASH $_____   OTHER $_____

Lender's Analysis of Risk (If there are affiliates, submit analysis of financial condition of affiliate and potential impact on applicant business. Affiliates include all businesses owned by applicant or spouse of applicant, even though not in a related business. Comment on bankruptcies and pending lawsuits. Include lien position on collateral.)

Collateral Market Value *		Use of Proceeds:	
Inventory	$_____	Inventory	$_____
Equipment	$_____	Fixed Assets	$_____
A/R	$_____	Real Estate	$_____
R/E **	$_____	Note Payment	$_____
_____	$_____	Working Capital	$_____
	$_____	SBA Payoff	$_____
* Value determined by:		_____	$_____
Lender __ Appraisal __		_____	$_____
		_____	$_____
Other (specify)_____			
** Furnish Legal Description or		**TOTAL** $_____	
Property Address & Lien Data			

For loans over $50,000 and up to $100,000, the following must be submitted:
   1. **Lender's internal loan report, including cash flow analysis and pro forma balance sheet**
   2. **Income tax schedule C or front page of corporate returns for past 3 years (if applicable)**
   3. **Personal F/S's for all guarantors**

IF LOAN IS TO PURCHASE AN EXISTING BUSINESS
Include copy of terms of sale and F/S on the existing business. Also, comment on any benefit to the business as a result of the change of ownership. Are buyer & seller related? Yes __ No __State relationship _____

I submit this application to SBA for approval subject to the terms and conditions outlined above. Without the participation of SBA to the extent applied for we would not be willing to make this loan, and in our opinion the financial assistance applied for is not otherwise available on reasonable terms. I certify that none of the Lender's employees, officers, director or substantial stockholders (more than 10%) have a financial interest in the applicant.

Signature of Lender Official: Title   Date

OMB Approval No. 3245-0016
Expiration Date: 10-31-98

U.S. Small Business Administration

APPLICATION FOR BUSINESS LOAN

Individual	Full Address

Name of Applicant Business	Tax I.D. No. or SSN

Full Street Address of Business	Tel. No. (inc. A/C)

City	County	State	Zip	Number of Employees (including subsidiaries and affiliates)
Type of Business		Date Business Established		At Time of Application
Bank of Business Account and Address				If Loan is Approved
				Subsidiaries or Affiliates (Separate from above)

Use of Proceeds: (Enter Gross Dollar Amounts Rounded to the Nearest Hundreds)	Loan Requested		Loan Requested
Land Acquisition		Payoff SBA Loan	
New Construction/ Expansion Repair		Payoff Bank Loan (Non SBA Associated)	
Acquisition and/or Repair of Machinery and Equipment		Other Debt Payment (Non SBA Associated	
Inventory Purchase		All Other	
Working Capital (Including Accounts Payable		Total Loan Requested	
Acquisition of Existing Business		Term of Loan - (Requested Mat.)	___ Yrs.

PREVIOUS SBA OR OTHER FEDERAL GOVERNMENT DEBT: If you or any principals or affiliates have 1) ever requested Government Financing or 2) are delinquent on the repayment of any Federal Debt complete the following:

Name of Agency	Original Amount of Loan	Date of Request	Approved or Declined	Balance	Current or Past Due
	$			$	
	$			$	

ASSISTANCE   List the names(s) and occupations of any who assisted in the preparation of this form, other than the applicant.

Name and Occupation	Address	Total Fees Paid	Fees Due
Name and Occupation	Address	Total Fees Paid	Fees Due

PLEASE NOTE: The estimated burden hours for the completion of this form is 19.8 hours per response. If you have any questions or comments concerning this estimate or any other aspect of this information collection please contact, Chief Administrative Information Branch, U.S. Small Business Administration, Washington, D.C. 20416 and Gary Waxman, Clearance Officer, Paperwork Reduction Project (3745-0016), Office of Management and Budget, Washington, D.C. 20503.

SBA Form 4 (5-92) Previous Edition is Obsolete

Page 1

ALL EXHIBITS MUST BE SIGNED AND DATED BY PERSON SIGNING THIS FORM

BUSINESS INDEBTEDNESS: Furnish the following information on all installment debts, contracts, notes, and mortgages payable. Indicate by an asterisk(*) items to be paid by loan proceeds and reason for paying same (present balance should agree with the latest balance sheet submitted).

To Whom Payable	Original Amount	Original Date	Present Balance	Rate of Interest	Maturity Date	Monthly Payment	Security	Current or Past Due
Acct. #	$		$			$		
Acct. #	$		$			$		
Acct. #	$		$			$		
Acct. #	$		$			$		

MANAGEMENT (**Proprietor, partners, officers, directors all holders of outstanding stock - <u>100% of ownership must be shown</u>**). Use separate sheet if necessary.

Name and Social Security Number and Position Title	Complete Address	% Owned	*Military Service From	To	*Race	*Sex

*This data is collected for statistical purpose only. It has no bearing on the credit decision to approve or decline this application.

THE FOLLOWING EXHIBITS MUST BE COMPLETED WHERE APPLICABLE. ALL QUESTIONS ANSWERED ARE MADE A PART OF THE APPLICATION.

For Guaranty Loans please provide an original and one copy (Photocopy is Acceptable) of the Application Form, and all Exhibits to the participating lender. For Direct Loans submit one original copy of the application and Exhibits to SBA.

1. Submit SBA Form 912 (Personal History Statement) for each person e.g. owners, partners, officers, directors, major stockholders, etc.; the instructions are on SBA Form 912.

2. If you collateral consists of (A) Land and Building, (B) Machinery and Equipment, (C) Furniture and Fixtures, (D) Accounts Receivable, (E) Inventory, (F) Other, please provide an itemized list (labeled Exhibit A) that contains serial and identification numbers for all articles that had an original value greater than $500. Include a legal description of Real Estate offered as collateral.

3. Furnish a signed current personal balance sheet (SBA Form 413 may be used for this purpose) for each stockholder (with 20% or greater ownership), partner, officer and owner. Social Security number should be included on personal financial statement. It should be as of the same date as the most recent business financial statements. Label the Exhibit B.

4. Include the statements listed below: 1,2,3 for the last three years; also 1,2,3,4 as of the same date, which are current within 90 days of filing the application; and statement 5, if applicable. This is Exhibit C (SBA has Management Aids that help in the preparation of financial statements.) All information must be **signed and dated**.

1. Balance Sheet   2. Profit and Loss Statement
3. Reconciliation of Net Worth
4. Aging of Accounts Receivable and Payable
5. Earnings projects for at least one year where financial statements for the last three years are unavailable or where requested by District Office.
  (If Profit and Loss Statement is not available, explain why and substitute Federal Income Tax Forms.)

5. Provide a brief history of your company and a paragraph describing the expected benefits it will receive from the loan. Label it Exhibit D.

6. Provide a brief description similar to a resume of the education, technical and business background for all the people listed under Management. Please mark it Exhibit E.

ALL EXHIBITS MUST BE SIGNED AND DATED BY PERSON SIGNING THIS FORM

7. Do you have any co-signers and/or guarantors for this loan? If so, please submit their names, addresses, tax id Numbers, and current personal balance sheet(s) as Exhibit F.

8. Are you buying machinery or equipment with your loan money? If so, you must include a list of equipment and cost as quoted by the seller and his name and address. This is Exhibit G.

9. Have you or any officer of your company ever been involved in bankruptcy or insolvency proceedings? If so, please provide the details as Exhibit H. If none, check here: ☐Yes ☐No

10. Are you or your business involved in any pending lawsuits? If yes, provide the details as Exhibit I. If none, check here: ☐Yes ☐No

11. Do you or your spouse or any member of your household, or anyone who owns, manages, or directs your business or their spouses or members of their households work for the Small Business Administration, Small Business Advisory Council, SCORE or ACE, any Federal Agency, or the participating lender? If so, please provide the name and address of the person and the office where employed. Label this Exhibit J. If none, check here: ☐Yes ☐No

12. Does your business, its owners or majority stockholders own or have a controlling interest in other businesses? If yes, please provide their names and the relationship with your company along with a current balance sheet and operating statement for each. This should be Exhibit K.

13. Do you buy from, sell to, or use the services of any concern in which someone in your company has a significant financial interest? If yes, provide details on a separate sheet of paper labeled Exhibit L.

14. If your business is a franchise, include a copy of the franchise agreement and a copy of the FTC disclosure statement supplied to you by the Franchisor. Please include it as Exhibit M.

CONSTRUCTION LOANS ONLY

15. Include a separate exhibit (Exhibit N) the estimated cost of the project and a statement of the source of any additional funds.

16. Provide copies of preliminary construction plans and specifications. Include them as Exhibit O. Final plans will be required prior to disbursement.

DIRECT LOANS ONLY

17. Include two bank declination letters with your application. (In cities with 200,000 people or less, one letter will be sufficient.) These letters should include the name and telephone number of the persons contacted at the banks, the amount and terms of the loan, the reason for decline and whether or not the bank will participate with SBA.

EXPORT LOANS

18. Does your business presently engage in Export Trade? Check here: ☐Yes ☐No

19. Do you have plans to begin exporting as a result of this loan? Check here: ☐Yes ☐No

20. Would you like information on Exporting? Check here: ☐Yes ☐No

AGREEMENTS AND CERTIFICATIONS

Agreements of non-employment of SBA Personnel: I agree that if SBA approves this loan application I will not, for at least two years, hire as an employee or consultant anyone that was employed by the SBA during the one year period prior to the disbursement of the loan.

Certification: I certify: (a) I have not paid anyone connected with the Federal Government for help in getting this loan. I also agree to report to the SBA office of the Inspector General, Washington, D.C. 20416 any Federal Government employee who offers, in return for any type of compensation, to help get this loan approved.

(b) All information in this application and the Exhibits are true and complete to the best of my knowledge and are submitted to SBA so SBA can decide whether to grant a loan or participate with a lending institution in a loan to me. I agree to pay for or reimburse SBA for the cost of any surveys, title or mortgage examinations, appraisals, credit reports, etc., performed by non-SBA personnel provided I have given my consent.

(c) I understand that I need not pay anybody to deal with SBA. I have read and understand SBA Form 159 which explains SBA policy on representatives and their fees.

(d) As consideration for any Management, Technical, and Business Development Assistance that may be provided, I waive all claims against SBA and its consultants.

If you make a statement that you know to be false or if you over value a security in order to help obtain a loan under the provisions of the Small Business Act, you can be fined up to $5,000 or be put in jail for up to two years, or both.

If Applicant is a proprietor or general partner, sign below.

By: _____
                                              Date

If Applicant is a Corporation, sign below:

Corporate Name and Seal   Date

By: _____
                  Signature of President

Attested by: _____
                  Signature of Corporate Secretary

APPLICANT'S CERTIFICATION

By my signature I certify that I have read and received a copy of the "STATEMENTS REQUIRED BY LAW AND EXECUTIVE ORDER" which was attached to this application. My signature represents my agreement to comply with the approval of my loan request and to comply, whenever applicable, with the hazard insurance, lead-based paint, civil rights or other limitations in this notice.

Each Proprietor, each General Partner, each Limited Partner or Stockholder owning 20% or more, and each Guarantor must sign. Each person should sign only once.

Business Name _____

_____ By _____
Date   Signature and Title

_____
Date   Signature

_____
Date   Signature

_____
Date   Signature

_____
Date   Signature

Chapter Fig. No.	Page #	Credit
Figure 1.2	p. 4	© Bil Keane. Reprinted with permission of North America Syndicate.
	p. 16	Evan C. Williams, "Top 15 Things I Learned My First Year in Business," Entrepreneurial Edge Magazine Online—service of the Edward Lowe Foundation. www.edgeonline.com.
Figure 2.1	p. 20	© *Newsweek*, "Reeling in the Years," (April 13, 1998) pg. 14. All rights reserved. Reprinted by permission.
	p. 21	Reprinted with permission of the Families and Work Institute.
Figure 2.2	p. 24	Reprinted with permission of *As We Change* catalog, 1-800-203-5585.
Figure 2.3	p. 24	© *Business Week*, March 17, 1998.
Figure 2.4	p. 25	© *Los Angeles Times*, March 25, 1998.
Figure 2.5a	p. 26	Reprinted from *American Demographics* magazine, with permission. © 1998 PRIMEDIA/Intertec, Stamford, CT.
Figure 2.5b	p. 26	Reprinted from *American Demographics* magazine, with permission. © 1998 PRIMEDIA/Intertec, Stamford, CT.
Figure 2.6	p. 30	Courtesy of NAMM–International Music Products Association.®
Figure 3.2	p. 43	Courtesy of NAMM–International Music Products Association.®
Figure 3.3	p. 46	Courtesy of NAMM–International Music Products Association.®
	pp. 58, 59	© Gina Imperato and *Fast Company*, April/May 1996, p. 83.
	p. 66	Reprinted by permission from Lloyd C. Russow, Philadelphia College of Textiles and Science. http://ib.philacol.edu/ib/russow.html.
Figure 4.1	p. 67	Reprinted with permission of SRI International.
Figure 4.2	pp. 69, 70	Reprinted courtesy of SRDS.
Figure 4.3	p. 74	Reprinted with permission of Minority Business Entrepreneur.
	pp. 83, 84	Reprinted with permission of *Inc.*, Goldhirsh Group, Inc., 38 Commercial Wharf, Boston, MA 02110 (www.inc.com). "Why the New Market Research?" Joshua Macht, July 1998. Reproduced by permission of the publisher via Copyright Clearance Center, Inc.
	pp. 88, 89	© Gina Imperato and *Fast Company*, April/May 1998, p. 274.
	p. 97	Reprinted with permission of *Inc.*, Goldhirsh Group, Inc., 38 Commercial Wharf, Boston, MA 02110 (www.inc.com). "Face to Face," Michael Treacy, April 1995. Reproduced by permission of the publisher via Copyright Clearance Center, Inc.
Figure 6.1	p. 102	Reprinted courtesy of SRDS.
	p. 106	Lesley Ronson, Lee Wayne Company, "Powerful Promotional Merchandise." Reprinted by permission.
	pp. 112, 113	Excerpted by permission, *Nation's Business*, May 1998. © 1998, U.S. Chamber of Congress.
	pp. 116, 117	© *Orange County Register*, July 12, 1998, p. 1.
	p. 122	Reprinted with permission of *Entrepreneur*, October 1997.
	pp. 130, 131	Reprinted with permission of the National Business Incubation Association.
	p. 148	Reprinted with permission of American Booksellers Association.
	p. 152	Reprinted with permission of American Booksellers Association.
	p. 152	Reprinted with permission of American Booksellers Association.
	p. 153	Reprinted with permission of American Booksellers Association.

Chapter Fig. No.	Page #	Credit
Table 8.9a	pp. 161, 162	Reprinted with permission of The Dryden Press, Harcourt Brace & Company.
	p. 164	© *Orange County Register.*
	pp. 185, 186	Reprinted with permission of *Inc.,* Goldhirsh Group, Inc., 38 Commercial Wharf, Boston, MA 02110 (www.inc.com). "Why Start-ups Fail," Norm Brodsky, December 1995. Reproduced by permission of the publisher via Copyright Clearance Center, Inc.
	pp. 192, 193	Reprinted with permission of Carol Sorgen, a freelance journalist. This material originally appeared in the *Balitmore Business Journal.*
	p. 194	© *Working Woman,* March 1998, p. 69.
	pp. 197, 198	This information is from the 'Lectric Law Library website at www.lectlaw.com.
Figure 10.1a	p. 199	Reprinted with permission of the State of California, Office of the Secretary of State, Limited Liability Company Unit.
Figure 10.1b	p. 200	Reprinted with permission of the State of California, Office of the Secretary of State, Limited Liability Company Unit.
	pp. 212-214	© 1997-1998 Intuit, Inc.
	pp. 222, 223	Excerpts from "Legal and Illegal Pre-Employment Inquiries," by Fred S. Steingold, Nolo Press, 1998 (Fourth Edition). Reprinted by permission.
	pp. 230, 231	© Joe Hadzima. This article has no relationship to any work by Stephen Covey.
	p. 235	© Gina Imperato and *Fast Company,* Issue 10, p. 192.
	pp. 237, 238	Courtesy of EntreWorld.org.
	p 246	© Gina Imperato and *Fast Company,* December 1997.
	p. 249	© *Time,* May 25, 1998.
	pp. 259, 260	© 1998 American Express Company. All Rights Reserved.
	pp. 261, 262	Reprinted with permission of the National Association of Certified Valuation Analysts.
	pp. 263, 264	Reprinted with permission of Deloitte Touche.
	pp. 271, 272	Reprinted with permission of VR Business Brokers.
	pp. 284, 285	Reprinted with permission of Geraldine M. Strozier, "Buying A Franchise? Investigate Before It's Too Late–It's Not So Elementary, Watson," *Entrepreneur* (January 1990) pp. 69-73.
	pp. 309, 310	Leo Helzel, *A Goal Is a Dream with a Deadline,* New York: McGraw Hill, 1995.
	p. 314	Reprinted with permission of Forum for International Trade Training.